MARKETING: Theory and Application

THE HARBRACE SERIES IN BUSINESS AND ECONOMICS

MARKETING
THEORY AND APPLICATION

Walter B. Wentz

Gerald I. Eyrich
Claremont Men's College

HARCOURT, BRACE & WORLD, INC.
NEW YORK · CHICAGO · SAN FRANCISCO · ATLANTA

To Our Parents

ISBN: 0-15-555110-8

Library of Congress Catalog Card Number: 74-105696

Printed in the United States of America

FOREWORD

Marketing is a field in which the interplay between analytical and synthetic thinking—that is, between the deductive and the intuitive—is all-important. At the level of the individual firm, marketing involves large-scale resource-allocation decisions that are important to both the profitability of the organization and the efficiency of the economic system as a whole. Because resource-allocation problems are inherently quantitative, an analytical-deductive approach is necessary if sound marketing decisions are to be made. But good marketing also depends critically upon "soft" factors. For example, questions about the content of promotional messages—as opposed to the number and distribution of such messages—are difficult to deal with quantitatively. The same difficulty arises in questions of designing products, motivating salesmen, working with middlemen, understanding consumer behavior, and assessing the actions of competitors. The effectiveness of a marketing program often depends on finding highly creative solutions to these and other problems, solutions that require intuitive insight as well as logical analysis.

Marketing: Theory and Application presents the beginning student with the solid theoretical underpinning necessary for conceptualizing resource-allocation problems and relating the subject of marketing to courses in economics and quantitative methods. I believe that this is sound pedagogical practice, and essential in a modern marketing textbook. But any conceptual treatment is barren unless it is continuously interpreted in terms of the realities of marketing management. The authors effectively combine theory and application by drawing on their extensive experience both in the classroom and in dealing with actual marketing management problems. The emphasis on the creative application of marketing concepts to the problem-solving process makes the book distinctly managerial in flavor; at the same time, the conceptual framework of the book enlarges its scope by permitting institutional and social considerations to be studied. The result is, I believe, an extremely relevant and teachable work that answers the needs of marketing instructors today.

WILLIAM F. MASSY

Stanford, California

PREFACE

Effective marketing decisions are based upon a wide range of disciplines. Psychology, sociology, organization theory, economics, law, and quantitative analysis are essential ingredients in any theory of marketing. The introductory marketing student, however, often has little or no background in most of these areas, and his first course in marketing is often an exercise in remembering facts rather than in developing a basis for sound decision-making. In *Marketing: Theory and Application* we have attempted to eliminate this problem by using an integrated approach to marketing that explains both *why* and *how* marketing decisions are made. No specific knowledge of other disciplines is assumed, and those aspects of other fields that are needed to explain the marketing decision process are developed within the text. Extensive use is made of simple mathematical examples to demonstrate the application of the techniques and concepts studied to specific marketing problems.

The book presents a balanced mixture of institutional, behavioral, economic, and quantitative materials, affording the instructor great flexibility in orienting the introductory course according to his objectives and the interests and background of his students. The economic and mathematical frameworks of marketing decisions are developed in Parts I, II, and III, which include a discussion of the relationship between the marketing department and the firm, the theory of the operation of the firm, the use of marketing decision values, and the various techniques of resource allocation and control. Part IV analyzes consumer behavior as a function of economic, psychological, and sociological motives. Parts V through IX discuss the four areas in which the marketing manager makes decisions—price, product, distribution, and promotion—and the marketing-research techniques used to evaluate these decisions. Finally, Part X looks at the laws that affect marketing decisions and the agencies that enforce them. The extensive lists of supplementary readings at the end of each part provide additional source material.

The book is intended for use in the introductory marketing course. A one-quarter or one-semester introductory course at the undergraduate level would normally include the following core material: Chapter 1 / Introduction; Chapter 2 / Marketing's Role in the Firm; Chapter 11 / Demand, Supply, and Equilibrium; Chapter 12 / Price and Income; Chapter 13 /

Pricing Strategies; Chapter 14 / Product Innovations and Protection; Chapter 15 / Product Mix, Line, and Marketing Strategies; Chapter 17 / Market Dimensions, Channels, and Institutions—Selection Criteria; Chapter 19 / Advertising; Chapter 20 / Personal Selling; Chapter 21 / Types of Marketing Research; and Chapter 22 / Historical Research. Such a core would still allow topics in resource allocation and control, consumer behavior, marketing research, and law and marketing to be considered in greater depth.

Although the book has benefited greatly from the efforts of a large number of people, particular thanks are due to Professors William Massy and Robert Davis of the Stanford Graduate School of Business, who reviewed the entire manuscript and whose numerous suggestions materially improved the text. Professor Paul Ecker of the United States Naval Postgraduate School and Professor Michael Uhlmann of Claremont Men's College read selected chapters and also made significant contributions. We are indebted to the Literary Executor of the late Sir Ronald Fisher, F.R.S., and to Oliver and Boyd Ltd, Edinburgh, for their permission to reprint Table IV from their book *Statistical Methods for Research Workers*. Finally, we are very grateful to Mary Gammons, Diane Dickerson, and Geraldeane Eyrich for their secretarial assistance in preparing the manuscript.

WALTER B. WENTZ
GERALD I. EYRICH

CONTENTS

MARKETING: Theory and Application

CHAPTER 1

Introduction

MARKETING DEFINED

There are probably as many definitions of marketing as there are textbooks, teachers, and practitioners dealing with the subject. The reader, as well, is likely to start with his own idea of what marketing is—a conception that will become more precise as his knowledge of the field becomes more extensive. However, some sample definitions selected from a cross-section of literature are appropriate to start him on his way.

Marketing—the performance of business activities that direct the flow of goods and services from producer to consumer or user.[1]

mar·ket·ing *n* : the act of selling or purchasing in a market.[2]

Marketing is the process in a society by which the demand structure for economic goods and services is anticipated or enlarged and satisfied through the conception, promotion, exchange, and physical distribution of such goods and services.[3]

Marketing is traditionally viewed as the business function . . . of finding customers.[4]

[1] Ralph S. Alexander and the Committee on Definitions of the American Marketing Association, *Marketing Definitions* (Chicago: American Marketing Association, 1960), p. 15.
[2] *Webster's Third New International Dictionary* (Springfield, Mass.: Merriam, 1965), p. 1383.
[3] Theodore N. Beckman, William R. Davidson, and James F. Engel, *Marketing* (New York: Ronald Press, 1967), p. 4.
[4] Philip Kotler, *Marketing Management* (Englewood Cliffs, N. J.: Prentice-Hall, 1967), p. 3.

Marketing is . . . those activities necessary and incidental to bring about exchange relationships.[5]

Marketing is the interface between supply and demand. Economists consider it part of the production function and include it in computing a firm's costs. Marketing also influences demand—and hence revenue—by manipulating consumer taste. Whereas in an authoritarian or other controlled economy goods and services are allocated by government edict, in a free or mixed economy it is the *market system* that serves as the mechanism for the distribution of resources. In a free economy the questions of what will be produced, how much will be produced, and for whom it will be produced are ultimately decided in the marketplace. Thus marketing is as significant to anyone concerned with either economics or social welfare as it is to the businessman.

Although we recognize that marketing has implications for many fields, we shall concentrate here on its applications to business economics. Marketing is essentially an applied subject, with the businessman its chief practitioner; its theoretical foundations are primarily the work of economists.

From the student's viewpoint, marketing cannot properly be called a discipline—certainly not in the sense that mathematics, psychology, physics, and biology are called disciplines. Instead, it is best viewed as a field of study that embraces parts of many disciplines—bits and pieces of economics, mathematics, sociology, psychology, and law. In practice as well as in theory, marketing stresses whatever skills and disciplines are appropriate to a particular problem and comfortable to the practitioner or teacher.

The interdisciplinary nature of marketing is both a blessing and a curse. It allows breadth and variety in both study and application and provides opportunity for a vast assortment of interests and skills, but it also encourages fragmentation into specialties that may not be directly related. Marketing lacks the formal structure and the central, commonly held body of unique theory one associates with traditional disciplines. It demands both specialists, who must allot most of their time to remaining knowledgeable and proficient in one area, and generalists, who must synthesize the specialties into a balanced whole. In this last respect it is similar to other applied sciences in an industrial society—witness, for example, engineering, medicine, and business administration.

Marketing can be reduced to more specific and manageable dimensions by examining each of its five basic components: (1) pricing, (2) product determination and mix, (3) distribution, (4) promotion (advertising and personal selling), and (5) marketing research. These are convenient units of study, as well as the basic instruments of the practicing marketer. They also serve to define the general field more precisely.

[5] Robert J. Holloway and Robert S. Hancock, *Marketing in a Changing Environment* (New York: Wiley, 1968), p. 6.

ECONOMICS' CONTRIBUTION TO MARKETING

Anyone who does not believe that a significant body of economic theory is at work in the marketplace ought simply to visit the New York Stock Exchange, Paris' Les Halles, or London's Billingsgate and see for himself the truth of the matter. "There [Billingsgate] . . . in a Victorian shed, are all the noise and drive and delight of unrefined commerce—the gray demand curves and marginal prices of plodding economists suddenly sprung all alive and colorful in the give and take of gleaming fish stalls."[6]

Economics might well be defined as the study of resource allocation—the assignment of land, capital, labor, and technology to the production and distribution of goods and services. As such, it lays the theoretical foundation for the practice of business and particularly for the management of marketing. It illuminates the mysteries of the marketplace, explains market phenomena, and provides insight to the options confronting the firm.

Microeconomics—that branch of economics dealing with the context and operation of individual enterprise—provides the basis for rational decision-making within the firm. As the reader will discover in Chapter 3, we derive from it both the theoretical rationale and the fundamental tools for marketing decisions.

The art, or science—for it is both—of management is essentially the art or science of resource allocation on the micro level. All executives, be they in industry, government, the military, or a private institution, must in some fashion deploy resources. This is especially true of marketing executives, who must ration limited resources of money, men, and materials so as to maximize the welfare of the firm.

Economics is to marketing as physics is to engineering or as biology is to the practice of medicine. If one fails to grasp the economics underlying a particular market phenomenon, one has simply learned of a symptom without understanding the cause. This is poor learning, as it will leave one bewildered when a new event fails to conform to a textbook case or to resemble a previous experience. Worse yet, it provides no sound basis for innovation. Successful marketing is not achieved by following simple rules or blindly applying past experience to new situations. The marketer must understand the "why" of things, and the "why" of much that happens in the marketplace is found in economic theory.

To take just one example, marketing management is frequently faced with pricing decisions. The marketer with an understanding of the supply and demand schedules confronting an industry and a firm can readily perceive the consequences of alternate pricing strategies. He can also gain insight into the manipulation of the other four marketing variables and can

[6] Paul Mandel, "The Most Walkable City in the World," *Holiday*, Vol. 43, No. 3 (March 1968), p. 76.

gauge more accurately the effect of decisions in these areas on his ability to manipulate price.

Economic theory is included in this text not as an end in itself but to illuminate market phenomena and to provide a conceptual understanding of marketing principles. Practical problems are seldom identical to situations previously encountered. They can be attacked intelligently only if the decision-maker has some insight into their underlying causes and their sensitivity to the five basic instruments of marketing. Economics provides much of this insight.

MATHEMATICS' CONTRIBUTION TO MARKETING

Virtues and Limitations. Sooner or later nearly every marketing decision must be quantified. No matter how inherently qualitative a problem may be, or how subjective the decision process, the final answer must usually be expressed in numbers. A given quantity of advertising must be ordered, a specific commission must be offered, a certain number of units must be released for production, a minimum inventory must be selected, a specific price must be chosen, a particular number of salesmen must be assigned, and so on. Even something as qualitative as the value of a market analyst must be expressed in numbers when the time arrives for a salary review.

Mathematics is the basic tool for the resolution of numerical problems. It is not a substitute for judgment or for an understanding of the nonnumerical aspects of marketing, yet it does allow much more rigor in the decision process and often assists the marketer in understanding the economic, social, and psychological facets of the marketplace. It is indispensable to a systems-management approach.

Most of the mathematical techniques that are applied in marketing have been around for hundreds—in some cases, thousands—of years. Why, then, the recent emergence of mathematics as a widely used tool in marketing decisions? The answer is found in two events, both of which occurred in the post–World War II era: first, the introduction on a wide scale of the high-speed computer, which could manipulate large quantities of data with a precision and speed impossible to achieve using manual methods; and second, the accumulation of large quantities of relevant data, a process aided greatly by the computer.

As their manipulative ability has improved and the quantity of data has mounted, many economists and mathematicians have begun to address themselves to the problems of marketing. Their efforts have resulted in a growing body of theory and methodology that is directly applicable to the practice of marketing. Powerful techniques have emerged that allow the marketer to define his alternatives more precisely and to make his decisions more rigorously. It is now possible to define markets, to estimate risks, to predict costs, to analyze consumer behavior, to forecast revenues, and to distribute resources with far more accuracy than was possible when the marketing manager was confined to making decisions based only on experience and intuition.

This is not to say that experience and intuition are not valuable. On the contrary, experience becomes more understandable and intuition more precise with the aid of mathematics. Nor do we wish to imply that mathematics can be substituted for imagination. Actually, the two are complementary. Mathematics—with the aid of computer technology—can relieve much of the drudgery of conventional analysis, hence freeing the marketer to concentrate on new problems and on innovation. Quantitative analysis can also provide insights that make the creative process more productive.

Mathematics serves to prove—or to formulate—assumptions, relationships, and hypotheses concerning the marketplace. For the marketer, it is a very powerful tool. Because mathematics is a universal language that lends itself to brevity and manipulation, it enables him to explain marketing phenomena in a way that is concise, descriptive, and precise.

The broad, interdisciplinary character of marketing makes it impossible for either teacher of practitioner to master every facet of the subject. However, both are well advised to develop an awareness and appreciation of all areas of marketing, in order to better relate their own specialties to the whole. This is particularly true in the case of marketing mathematics, which can be used to advantage in all specialties. Although one can hardly expect all advertising directors, consumer behaviorists, and sales managers to be competent mathematicians, they should be able to communicate with mathematicians and to recognize opportunities for the application of mathematics. There is much to be gained from simply understanding the language and a few of the basic concepts. The marketer need not be proficient in higher mathematics, but he should have a knowledge of its usefulness and limitations.

To overcome the anxiety of the reader who is fearful of having embarked on a cram course in abstract mathematics, we shall take a moment to examine those aspects of applied mathematics relevant to marketing. Only the first two—mathematical functions and mathematical notation—are used extensively in this book, although the reader should be aware of how the others are sometimes used. This will serve to remove some of the mystery frequently associated with the subject.

Mathematical Functions.   A *mathematical function* is a statement of the relationship between two or more variables. If one variable is dependent on another, we say that the first variable (the dependent variable) *is a func-*

tion of the second (the independent variable). For example, the quantity of goods a firm sells may be dependent on the number of salesmen it has; thus the quantity of goods sold is a function of the number of salesmen.

This can be expressed more concisely by using symbols to represent the variables. For instance, we can express the previous statement in the form $Q = f(S)$, where Q represents the quantity of goods sold, S represents the number of salesmen, and f is an operational symbol meaning "a function of." This is a *general function*. It states what variables are involved, but it does not specify their exact relationship. If we knew the exact relationship, we could write an *explicit function,* which would show *how* the variables were related. For example, if we knew that each salesman could sell 300 units of the product, we could write the explicit function $Q = 300S$. The quantity sold would equal the number of salesmen multiplied by 300.

A function may contain more than two variables. For example, a firm's sales (Q), might be a function of the price of its product (P), its advertising expenditure (A), and the number of salesmen it has (S). This would be expressed as $Q = f(P,A,S)$ or if the exact relationship were known, perhaps as $Q = 200S + .05A - 8P$.

Mathematical Notation. Mathematical notation is the shorthand of mathematics; it allows us to show concisely complex relationships or statements that would require much space and energy to explain verbally. For example, if we want to say that the total revenue earned by a chain of 25 retail stores selling a particular product is equal to—that is, is a function of—the sum of the quantity sold by each store multiplied by the price charged by each store we can write

$$R_T = \sum_{i=1}^{25} (P_i Q_i), \text{ where}$$

R_T = total revenue

P = price

Q = quantity

i is a subscript representing each store, from the 1st to the 25th, and

$\sum_{i=1}^{25}$ is a summation sign that tells us to add all the products $(P_i Q_i)$ for stores 1 through 25. ($\sum$ is simply the Greek letter sigma.)

This notation is considerably more convenient than the verbal explanation. It is also more manageable than the equivalent arithmetical notation,

$$R_T = P_1 Q_1 + P_2 Q_2 + P_3 Q_3 + P_4 Q_4 + P_5 Q_5 + P_6 Q_6 + \cdots P_{25} Q_{25}$$

Differential Calculus. Differential calculus gives us the *rate of change* of a function. It tells us what will happen to one variable if we manipulate another. For example, assume that the demand for a product is a function only of its price and can be expressed as $Q = 4,000 - 5P^2$, where Q is the quantity demanded (i.e., units sold) and P is the price. By the simple rules of calculus introduced in Chapter 3, it can be shown that $dQ/dP = -10P$. dQ/dP, the derivative of Q with respect to P, is the rate of change of the quantity sold as a function of a price change. For example, if the price is $5, $dQ/dP = (-10)(5)$, or -50. Thus a price increase of $1 will result in a decrease in sales of 50 units $((-50)(1) = -50)$. Conversely, a price decrease of $1 will result in an increase in sales of 50 units $((-50)(-1) = 50)$.

Calculus also serves to determine *minimum* and *maximum points* in a function. Hence the marketer can determine what quantity of output will maximize profits, what level of inventory will minimize costs, and so on.

Statistics. Statistics provides methods for presenting data and techniques for estimating variables. For example, the actual sales of a store might be expressed as an average of $800 per day. Or the potential sales of a product in a new market might be estimated at 30,000 units. By statistical inference, the market analyst might claim to be 98 percent confident that the true figure would be within plus or minus 5,000 units of his estimate of 30,000 units—that is, 98 times out of 100, actual sales would be between 25,000 and 35,000.

Probability Theory. Probability theory, which is the basis for statistical estimation, gives us techniques for computing the chance that an event will or will not happen, thus allowing the marketer to enter *uncertainty* into his calculations. For example, if 10 percent of the members of a community watch a particular television program and half of the viewers are known to ignore the commercial, then the probability of an individual in the community receiving an advertising message on that show is .05. This is expressed as $P(x) = .05$; event x will happen an average of 5 times out of 100.

This area of mathematics also allows the computation of *expected values,* which are useful in decision-making. For example, if a salesman will earn an $80 commission every time he sells a housewife a vacuum cleaner, but the probability of his making a sale during any given demonstration is .2, then the expected value of a demonstration is $16. If his cost averages $3 per demonstration, he can expect to earn, on the average, $13 per demonstration.

Linear Programming. Linear programming is a mathematical technique for solving a system of linear equations subject to constraints. The equations describe various processes—for instance, the sales that would result from certain forms of advertising—and the constraints specify maximum or minimum values or relationships between certain variables. For example, in advertising allocations, one constraint would be the budget; other constraints might be the optimum relationships between different media. Linear programming can be used to develop an *optimum solution* to such a problem—optimum in that the sales obtained are the maximum possible given the constraints imposed.

Game Theory. Game theory is a mathematical technique for determining *optimum strategies*. In many real-life problems, it is impossible to establish a probability distribution for the various actions a competitor can take. Game-theory techniques can yield the optimum strategy for an individual or firm, given such a situation.

A typical example would be a firm trying to decide whether to increase, decrease, or maintain constant its advertising budget. Since the competition would also have the same set of choices—that is, to increase, decrease, or maintain constant its advertising budget—there are nine possible outcomes. Each of the three actions of the firm would have three possible competitive actions associated with it. If the effect of each of the nine possible outcomes on the firm's profit can be quantified, game theory can then be used to determine the optimum advertising strategy for it to follow. Game theory is valuable because only the possible actions of the competing firm need be identified, not the probability of their occurrence. Obviously, the former can normally be established, while the latter is usually impossible to determine.

Simulation. Simulation is a method of making decisions and manipulating variables without going into the marketplace. By creating a synthetic environment, patterned after the real world, the marketer can change inputs in his marketing mix and observe the effects of these changes quickly and without material loss (or gain).

A simulation model is essentially a game. The player is given a limited quantity of resources—usually a budget—and the privilege of making certain plays. For example, he may increase the price of his product, he may spend some of his budget on advertising, he may reduce the number of distributors, or he may buy market information. The game's objective is usually the maximization of profit. How well the player meets the objective depends on both the plays (decisions) he himself makes and on those made by the other players, who represent competing firms.

Simulation models specify the relationships between the profit (or loss) of each player and the various decision variables. For instance, a player may increase his sales, thereby increasing revenue and perhaps profit, by increasing his advertising. However, a competing player may respond with an in-

crease in his advertising or a reduction of his price, thereby decreasing the
sales, and hence the profit, of the first player. If a model is constructed that
approximates the relationships actually existing in the marketplace, the
firm can try out its decisions and observe their consequences without any
material risk.

Virtually all simulation models are prepared for use with a computer.
In addition to handling the complex relationships associated with the more
sophisticated models, the computer can calculate the outcome of the manipulations of the players with great rapidity, providing him with a nearly instantaneous print-out. Data that might take weeks to generate and gather
in the real market can thus be obtained in minutes.

The computer can also assume the role of one or more of the players.
This is especially useful when one "player" is nature, or the aggregate of
a large number of consumers. For instance, variations in weather, consumer
preferences, and brand loyalty can be simulated using statistical histories
and Monte Carlo methods to program a *player profile,* or *response pattern.*
This allows a single player, representing the company, to play the game
alone.

The major shortcoming of simulation is its failure to portray reality
accurately. Although the method works extremely well when applied to the
physical sciences, where relationships are more precisely defined, it often
falters when applied to problems in the social sciences, where relationships
are often crudely defined. The marketer in particular is frequently faced
with a dearth of precise information. However, when the real world can be
reconstructed with some accuracy, simulation is very useful. It serves two
practical purposes: first, it allows the marketer to "test" a decision before
applying it in the marketplace; second, it is a training aid that lets the marketer practice his trade free of risk and with virtually no cost.

THE BEHAVIORAL SCIENCES' CONTRIBUTION TO MARKETING

The behavioral sciences, especially psychology and sociology, have made
a substantial contribution to the theory and practice of marketing. In fact,
they provided the theoretical foundation for the bulk of traditional marketing literature. This literature—which can be described generally as qualitative, descriptive, institutional, or behavioral—monopolized the field until
very recently. It was not until the early 1960's that economists and mathematicians began to seriously influence marketing, both academically and
practically.

Although the behavioral sciences may occasionally bow to economics
in the explanation of market phenomena, the various disciplines more often
serve to reinforce one another. Each has special qualities that are uniquely

suited to certain aspects of marketing. The forte of the behavioral sciences is that they provide explanations for the *"why"* of consumer behavior, an area that economics ignores. On the other hand, economics, reinforced by mathematics, can often identify and specify the *"what"* and *"how"* of market phenomena. For example, given the necessary data, an economist can describe precisely the relationship between sales and price, advertising, personal selling, and the distribution system. But although the economist might tell us what a change in price or an increase in advertising will do to the demand for a given product, we must turn to the behavioral scientist if we are to learn how to make people less sensitive to price or how to prepare more effective advertising. In short, we need economics and mathematics to identify and quantify the relationships between marketing variables. We need the behavioral sciences to learn how to change them.

Psychology. Psychology defines and explains the determinants of behavior that lie within the consumer, thus providing insights into how the potential buyer might be influenced by the marketer. These determinants include both biological drives, such as the avoidance of hunger and pain, and learned drives, such as fear, acquisitiveness, and the pursuit of status.

Psychology also provides insight into the processes of learning and perceiving, thus aiding the marketer in his attempts to communicate with the consumer. The marketer must be able to transmit messages to potential customers. He must also be able to get information from these people— information that may be both illusive and distorted if he relies solely on objective methods.

Sociology. Sociology defines and explains the nature and determinants of group behavior. Although groups seldom make purchasing decisions, they play a significant role in shaping the behavior of the individuals who do. In addition, certain properties of the group—such as its mores, customs, taboos, and laws—may serve as either barriers to or opportunities for a product or a promotional or distributional instrument.

Social Psychology. Social psychology defines and explains the behavior of individuals with respect to the group; thus it brings together the two behavioral sciences most relevant to marketing. It aids the marketer in identifying the social values that he needs to accommodate or change, or use to advantage to increase the efficiency of his operation.

SUMMARY

Marketing is an interdisciplinary subject with a wide range of definitions. It is made up of five elements that are both the basic instruments of the practitioner and convenient subdivisions for the student and scholar. These are: (1) pricing, (2) product determination and mix, (3) distribution, (4) promotion (advertising and personal selling), and (5) marketing research.

Economics provides the theoretical basis for marketing, although recognition is also due sociology and psychology for their contributions. Microeconomics in particular gives us the theoretical rationale and the fundamental tools for marketing decisions. The economics of marketing not only illuminates the various market phenomena but, perhaps more important, allows the student and the practitioner to generalize, and thus to solve new problems resulting from different combinations of factors.

Mathematics is a powerful tool for solving marketing problems, most of which must have quantitative answers. The emergence of the computer—which allows for the accumulation, storage, and rapid manipulation of data—has enabled marketers to be more rigorous in the solution of problems that previously were handled with intuition and a minimum of quantitative information.

Even for the marketer who does not elect to specialize in mathematics or computer applications, a limited knowledge of some basic mathematical techniques is nevertheless important. These skills will allow him to understand and explain market phenomena more quickly, as well as to communicate with mathematicians or computer programmers, who can be of considerable help in the solution of specific problems. The techniques most useful to the marketer are mathematical notation, differential calculus, statistics, probability theory, linear programming, game theory, and simulation. The first two are the most basic and will receive the most emphasis in this text.

The behavioral sciences, particularly psychology and sociology, provide insight into the "why" of consumer behavior. Economics, reinforced by mathematics, can identify variables and specify their relationships. However, only psychology and sociology offer the techniques necessary for understanding and changing these relationships.

Questions and Problems

1. Formulate a definition of marketing.
2. List the five basic instruments of marketing and suggest an application for each of the following disciplines: (a) economics, (b) mathematics, (c) sociology, and (d) psychology.
3. Suggest a marketing application for each of the following types of mathematics: (a) algebra, (b) differential calculus, and (c) statistics.
4. Using the table of contents, footnotes, and supplementary readings, name three specialized tasks of marketing—such as cost analysis, describing the consumer of a particular good, estimating demand, forecast-

ing the result of a price change, or analyzing the selection of advertising media—and cite two applicable books or journal articles.

5. The total profit earned by a chain of 5 grocery stores is expressed by the formula $\pi_T = \sum_{i=1}^{5} (R_i - C_i)$, where π_T = total profit, R_i = revenue of the ith store, and C_i = cost of the ith store. Given the following data, compute the total profit for the five-store chain.

Store (i)	Revenue (R)	Cost (C)
1	$50,000	$48,000
2	90,000	85,000
3	28,000	30,000
4	55,000	50,000
5	68,000	58,000

Supplementary Readings

BOOKS

ABBOTT, LAWRENCE, *Economics and the Modern World,* 2nd ed. (New York: Harcourt, Brace & World, 1967).

ALDERSON, WROE, and SHAPIRO, STANLEY, eds., *Marketing and the Computer* (Englewood Cliffs, N. J.: Prentice-Hall, 1962).

BARISH, NORMAN N., *Economic Analysis for Engineering and Managerial Decision Making* (New York: McGraw-Hill, 1967).

BASS, F. M., et al., eds., *Application of the Sciences in Marketing Management* (New York: Wiley, 1968).

DINWIDDY, CAROLINE, *Elementary Mathematics for Economists* (London: Oxford University Press, 1967).

FRANK, RONALD E., KUEHN, ALFRED A., and MASSY, WILLIAM F., eds., *Quantitative Techniques in Marketing Analysis* (Homewood, Ill.: Irwin, 1962).

GRAWOIG, DENNIS E., *Decision Mathematics* (New York: McGraw-Hill, 1967).

ARTICLES

DORFMAN, ROBERT, "Mathematical, or 'Linear,' Programming: A Nonmathematical Exposition," *American Economic Review,* Vol. 43 (December 1953), pp. 797–825.

KOTLER, PHILIP, "Operations Research in Marketing," *Harvard Business Review* (January–February 1967), p. 30.

———, "The Use of Mathematical Models in Marketing," *Journal of Marketing,* Vol. 27, No. 4 (October 1963), pp. 31–41.

Part I

MARKETING AND THE FIRM

Viewed as an economic organism, the firm is a production unit that consumes inputs and produces outputs. The difference in value between the inputs and the outputs is called "economic surplus." For the purpose of this discussion, economic surplus can be equated with profit.[1]

The economic inputs consumed by the firm are land, capital, and labor. Technology, in a highly industrialized society, is sometimes added to this list of basic ingredients of production. Capital is perhaps the most unfamiliar of these terms, since its technical definition varies somewhat from its popular usage. It consists of plant and equipment, as well as the money required to pay accounts receivable until revenues come in at a rate equal to or greater than that required to satisfy creditors. The task of management is to select and manipulate the economic inputs to produce an output whose value exceeds the aggregate value of the inputs. The relative importance of the inputs will vary according to the type of industry and the role played within the industry by a particular firm. A modern farm, for example, needs a large amount of land and capital but little labor. A symphony orchestra, on the other hand, would put a great deal of emphasis on the labor input, but none on land and little on capital.

---

[1] Economic surplus is also a source of funds for government, charitable organizations, and educational institutions. The Bureau of Internal Revenue is but one of many agencies ready to remind us that surplus should be shared.

The complexity of the input mix, the uncertainty of the marketplace, and the emergence of management as a science have combined to place considerable emphasis on the administrative and entrepreneurial functions of the firm. Managerial skills have become highly sophisticated in many industries, so much so that the quantity and especially the quality of its executive talent is today a key variable in the performance of the firm.

The marketing function has not been spared by the forces of change associated with the mid-twentieth century. Complexity and technical sophistication are qualities frequently associated with marketing's role in the modern firm. In order to attain an in-depth understanding of marketing, the student must first understand the role of marketing within the context of the firm. A prerequisite to this is a comprehension of how the firm is structured, its basic functions, and—most important of all—the objective which these functions collectively serve. Thus we shall turn now to a brief exposition of the theory of the firm, which provides the basis for practical decision making in the marketing sector. The discussion of theory is supported by an explanation—prepared for the nonmathematically inclined reader—of differential calculus and its application to marketing decisions.

CHAPTER 2

Marketing's Role in the Firm

BASIC FUNCTIONS OF THE FIRM

In general, the basic functions that are performed by all industries are product design and development, manufacturing, and marketing. The importance of each varies in different industries and firms, and the basic economic inputs will be apportioned differently among these functions. Some functions will not be performed at all by particular firms; many companies today are specialized to the point where they depend on other firms to do certain jobs that are necessary in the flow of goods and services from maker to ultimate consumer.

For example, a manufacturer may concentrate on product design and development and production and leave the marketing function to an independent marketing organization. The firm performing the marketing function might well represent several manufacturers and specialize entirely in marketing.[1] Prior to the twentieth century, the sales company usually branded, packaged, and priced the goods as well as performing most of the other marketing tasks. In fact, the bulk of the nation's marketing was performed by these middlemen. Today, this is not the norm. Although there are important exceptions, the manufacturer generally performs most of the marketing functions, short of retail sales.

To take a few other examples, a farmer too may concentrate on production, letting a farm cooperative handle all the marketing functions connected with the sale of the crop. Advertising agencies specialize in a subset of the marketing function. Research and development firms may specialize

[1] From another point of view, we could consider the marketing of the manufacturer's goods as the service, or the production effort, performed by the sales organization. The sale of this service to other manufacturers then becomes the marketing function of the sales company.

15

in product design and development but exclude the production and marketing functions.

Because our objective in this text is to explain the basic principles of
marketing, the organizational model we refer to most frequently is the
integrated consumer-goods manufacturer. This choice is convenient, as most
of the different marketing tasks are performed within such a company. It
does not imply any particular virtue on the part of such firms—an integrated
firm can be as mismanaged and inefficient as any other. However, it does
provide a convenient vehicle for explaining marketing functions and the context in which they must be carried out.

A glance at Figure 2.1 shows that a product is shaped by many minds
and hands between its inception and its delivery to the customer. All have
their own unique contributions to make. Many influence revenue and all
influence cost. All compete for resources. Most goods must be designed; all
must be grown, extracted, or manufactured; and all must be sold. Hence we
have the initial distribution of work between three *line organizations*—
engineering (including product research), manufacturing, and marketing.
Economies of scale suggest the combining of certain service functions such
as legal counsel, plant security, accounting, and personnel. Consequently,
we have a *staff organization,* collectively called an administration, whose
responsibility it is to provide necessary services to the line departments.

What executive or group dominates an organization depends on the
type of industry, the structure of the company, and the personalities of the
executives. In the missile industry, engineering is clearly dominant. In industries that approach the model of pure competition, such as certain segments
of agriculture and the petroleum industry, the production aspects are clearly
the most important, as price is given and the market can absorb all the possible output of the individual firm. In the field of consumer durables, such
as appliances and automobiles, marketing generally dominates the company.
In the field of convenience goods, such as soap, breakfast foods, and cigarettes, it almost invariably does so. However, in business the exceptions
can be nearly as numerous as the rule; in some cases we even have examples of staff executives—particularly lawyers and accountants—controlling a
firm.

The marketing manager is frequently faced with the necessity to suboptimize[2] his resources. Money is both finite and rationed within the firm.
Although he may believe that another $5,000 spent on a particular adver-
tising medium will be far more productive than that same amount spent on
product design, a new milling machine, a management training program, or
an employee picnic, he may be unable to convince his superiors, the chief

[2] "Suboptimizing" is decision-making in which only a few of the total variables are
controlled. Suboptimization reflects the manager's inability to manipulate all the factors
that may affect the final outcome.

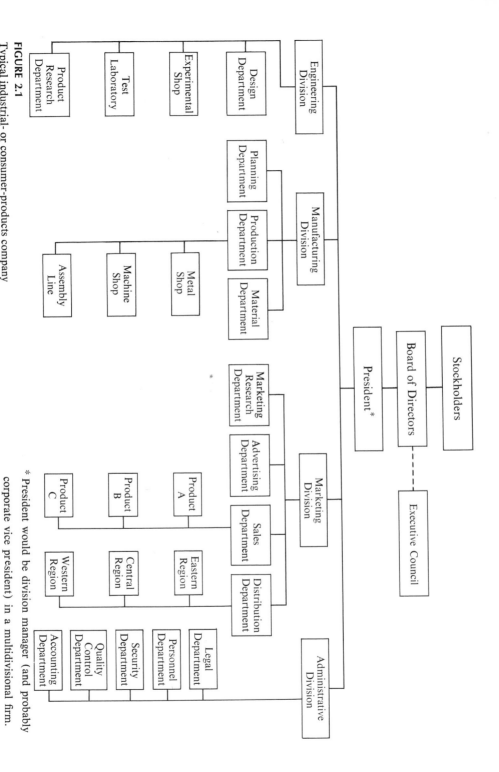

FIGURE 2.1
Typical industrial- or consumer-products company

Stockholders

Board of Directors

President*

Executive Council

Engineering Division
- Design Department
- Experimental Shop
- Test Laboratory
- Product Research Department

Manufacturing Division
- Planning Department
- Production Department
  - Material Department
  - Metal Shop
  - Machine Shop
  - Assembly Line

Marketing Division
- Marketing Research Department
- Advertising Department
- Sales Department
  - Product A
  - Product B
  - Product C
- Distribution Department
  - Eastern Region
  - Central Region
  - Western Region

Administrative Division
- Legal Department
- Personnel Department
- Security Department
- Quality Control Department
- Accounting Department

* President would be division manager (and probably corporate vice president) in a multidivisional firm.

engineer, the factory manager, or the director of personnel. What might otherwise be a beautifully optimized decision may be reduced to a sub-optimum choice by simple budgetary considerations.

An executive is also constrained by the inertia of the organization—especially in large companies—and the distribution of authority within the hierarchy. The informal organization and traditions of the company, which often have nothing to do with economic considerations, also restrict the ability of the marketing manager to manipulate certain variables that some-times must be changed to achieve an optimum solution to a marketing problem. Some organizations require a consensus before certain changes can be made. In others, all important decisions are made by a single man. Occasionally, informal coalitions emerge that usurp most of the decision-making power.

These are the realities a marketer must face. Yet the fact that the en-vironment is not ideal should not distract us from using quantitative tech-niques or applying economic theory. On the contrary, an objective approach by the marketing department may be needed to compensate for subjective thinking in other parts of the organization. Nor is lack of data necessarily justification for reverting to subjective judgments. Uncertainty is almost always a factor in executive decisions. Complete knowledge is often unavail-able or, at best, far too costly to acquire. Rational behavior is the selection of choices based on their estimated payoffs and their respective probabilities of success. The marketing manager can at least suboptimize the firm's revenue and cost functions by making the most rational choice of the real options that confront him. We stress "real" because one must clearly dis-tinguish between that which is possible and that which is ideal. No manager can afford to waste resources in attempting the clearly impossible.

Many choices confront a firm every day—the selection of a new em-ployee, the choice of an advertising medium, the setting of a price, the design of a product, the purchase of a drill press, and so forth. Some decisions—such as the price for the product of a gold mine—are obvious; others—such as the color of a cereal box—are not. Some—such as the setting of optimum inventory levels—lend themselves easily to quantitative techniques; others—such as the choice of advertising slogans—do not.

Marketing choices deal with the selection and allocation of resources used in the sale and distribution of goods and services. For convenience, they are grouped into the five basic marketing functions described in Chap-ter 1. Actually, however, few decisions are made in isolation. Price affects sales, which in turn affect production and employment. Product variations affect design, manufacturing, and sales. Distribution affects packaging and materials. Promotion has legal implications. In the short run, every dollar spent by the marketing department is generally one less dollar available for engineering, manufacturing, and staff functions.

MARKETING FUNCTIONS

The marketing functions are the core of this book. Other topics are discussed only to the extent that they illuminate these functions. For example, resource allocation is important because it is a way of manipulating the marketing variables. Law is significant because it constrains and protects the use of competitive instruments in the marketplace.

Traditionally, the four basic marketing functions have been (1) pricing, (2) product determination and mix, (3) distribution, and (4) promotion (advertising and personal selling). We shall add a fifth item—marketing research. Pricing, promotion, and marketing research are generally the province of the marketing manager, although major decisions may be reviewed by the president, an executive council, or even the board of directors. Product determination—decisions regarding the physical character, quality, and mix of the product line—is a responsibility generally shared with the engineering and manufacturing divisions. The more complex and expensive the product, the more diffused this decision process is likely to be. Distribution decisions, especially those concerning the physical aspects of distribution, are also likely to involve the marketing manager's counterparts in engineering, manufacturing, and administration.

Pricing is theoretically the single most important instrument of competition in a market economy. With some exceptions, the freedom of the firm to set its own price for its products is essential to a free-enterprise system. However, legal constraints on the price system have restricted this variable in many industries and shifted emphasis to product variation.

Product determination and mix is particularly important in industries with complex and changing technologies. It is an especially effective instrument in markets where the consumer is affluent and has an elaborate system of preferences.

Distribution—a term once synonymous with marketing—is the logistics of the market. It is the flow of purchase orders from consumer to producer via the chain of intermediaries. It is also the physical movement of goods or services from the producer to the consumer. This "physical distribution" is reflected in the cost function and lends itself to quantitative analysis more readily than many marketing processes.

Promotion includes both personal selling and advertising. Depending on how they are used, both these instruments can be powerful or ineffective weapons in the competition for customers. They are probably the most controversial topics in the field.

Marketing research is the gathering, reduction, and analysis of market data. Because it describes and evaluates demand, the behavior of buyers and intermediaries, and competition, it allows more rational and efficient deci-

Table 2.1   Distribution of output of American industries

Consumer-goods industries	33%
Industrial-goods industries	22%
Service industries	35%
Government contractors	10%
Total	100%

SOURCE: This table is an approximation based on 1968 data published in the *Survey of Current Business, Statistical Abstract of the U. S.,* and *Economic Fact Book.*

sion-making. Research is the key to an optimum allocation of marketing resources.

Before studying each of these instruments in depth, we need to expand our understanding of the context in which they are employed. This suggests an exploration of the various roles of marketing management, which vary from industry to industry and from firm to firm.

The role of the firm's marketing organization varies, but the differences tend to be more pronounced between industries than they are between companies within the same industry. Although a thorough discussion of inter-industry differences would submerge us in more detail than could be handled in an introductory or survey course, a brief look at variations among four general types of industries is appropriate. From the marketer's standpoint, industries are conveniently divided into four categories, or sets, in mathematical parlance: (1) consumer-goods industries, (2) industrial-goods industries, (3) service industries, and (4) government contractors. Their relative size is suggested by Table 2.1, which shows the distribution of output among the four categories.

The distinctions between these four groups are significant for marketing, although the division may be inappropriate from an engineering, a production, or an administrative viewpoint. For example, although there are numerous exceptions to almost all generalizations, the pricing strategies that are acceptable in the consumer-goods area are generally unacceptable in the government sector. And product variation tends to be much more flexible in the consumer-goods field than in the industrial-goods market.

CONSUMER-GOODS INDUSTRIES

Consumer goods are any products "destined for use by ultimate consumers or households and in such form that they can be used without commercial processing,"[3] such as houses, automobiles, furniture, appliances, cigarettes, ice cream, shoes, and toys. However, many consumer goods may also be sold as industrial or government goods, depending on whether the final user will be a household,[4] an industrial firm, or a government agency.

Within this set—consumer goods—are several subsets: convenience goods, shopping goods, and specialty goods.

Convenience goods are those "which the customer usually purchases frequently, immediately, and with the minimum of effort in comparison and buying,"[5] such as cigarettes, newspapers, candy, and many food products.

Shopping goods are those "which the customer in the process of selection and purchase charactistically compares on such bases as suitability, quality, price and style,"[6] such as furniture, shoes, major appliances, and women's ready-to-wear clothing.

Specialty goods are those "with unique characteristics and/or brand identification for which a significant group of buyers are habitually willing to make a special purchase effort,"[7] such as specific brands of fancy foods, cameras, men's suits, and new automobiles.

The consumer-goods industry is the most useful model for the exposition of marketing theory and is the richest in marketing experience. Marketers have more freedom to manipulate the five basic marketing instruments than in other industries. Marketing management dominates more firms and demands a greater portion of available resources. In product lines such as phonograph records, books, clothing, jewelry, and hi-fi equipment, more funds may be allocated to the marketing function than all other functions combined. Table 2.2 illustrates this point in dollar terms.

The instrument of competition most readily identified with a free market economy is price, especially when consumer goods are being sold. If we include retail establishments in this set, it is clear that considerable price flexibility is possible. In fact, price manipulation separates the consumer-goods industry from other industries more than any other marketing instrument. Even in local markets—say one as small as Pasadena, California, or Champaign, Illinois—we find a wide variation in prices for essentially identical products. One seldom pays the same price for a Polish ham at a delicatessen as at a supermarket. Nor does a women's specialty store ordinarily offer a pair of nylons at the same price as a Sears store.

[3] Ralph Alexander and the Committee on Definitions of the American Marketing Association, *Marketing Definitions* (Chicago: American Marketing Association, 1960), p. 11.
[4] We shall follow standard economic usage in generally equating the household with the ultimate consumer, or the smallest divisible purchasing unit.
[5] Alexander, *op. cit.,* p. 11.
[6] *Ibid.,* p. 21.
[7] *Ibid.,* p. 22.

Table 2.2   Marketing cost of selected consumer goods

Type of Goods	Marketing Cost (as a percentage of total retail cost)
Products of printing and publishing	22%
Food and kindred products	27%
Leather and leather products	30%
Textile products	32%
Tires and other rubber products	33%
Furniture and fixtures	37%
Fabricated metal products	40%

SOURCE: Reavis Cox, *Distribution in a High Level Economy,* © 1965. Reprinted by permission of Prentice-Hall, Inc., Englewood Cliffs, N. J.

Product variation is more common in the consumer-goods field than in other areas. The number of products and brands is the greatest here, as is the mortality rate. This phenomenon is caused by two factors associated with this product group.

First, the consumer does not define his preferences until after he is confronted with the product. If it is well received, the marketer, engineer, and manufacturer then know they have made a correct product decision. If the consumer rejects the item, they know that their decision was wrong, but the information comes too late to prevent a loss by the firm. This is a major reason for the emergence of marketing research—the attempt to identify and measure consumers' tastes before making substantial commitments to a given product or product variation—as the fifth instrument in the marketing mix.

Second, the ease of entry in many consumer-product lines, particularly where there is a mass market, encourages many marginal, and usually short-lived, producers, large numbers of whom base their hopes for success on a single product or product variation that they feel will attract a substantial number of buyers. The majority of these ventures end in disaster. Examples of quick failures abound in the electronics, trailer, boat, clothing, and retailing industries.

Distribution networks—both the channels for the flow of orders inbound from consumer to producer and the channels for the flow of physical goods outbound from producer to consumer—are generally more complex in the consumer-goods industries than in other areas. It is easier to appreciate the scope of the distribution problem if one reflects on the implications of a domestic market of up to 200 million consumers—such as that confronting the clothing, shoe, and food industries. Compare, for example, the distribution problem of the marketing manager responsible for selling men's shirts to 60 million potential customers with the distribution problem confronting his counterpart in the machine-tool business or the aerospace industry.

Promotion is common to all industries, although it varies considerably in both magnitude and form. Nowhere, however, is it practiced on such a lavish scale and with such flamboyance as in consumer-goods industries. In many fields, such as motion pictures and cosmetics, a producer may spend more on promotion than on all other functions combined, including manufacturing.

This has led some economists to condemn promotion, especially advertising, as an inefficient allocation of the nation's resources.[8] The magnitude of promotional outlays and their significance in consumer-goods industries are suggested by Table 2.3.

Extensive research is not unique to the consumer-goods field. There is, however, a special class of research associated almost exclusively with con-

Table 2.3 Advertising outlays for 1968
(*In millions of dollars*)

Agriculture, forestries, and fisheries	$ 171
Mining	34
Construction	265
Manufacturing	8,185
Public utilities	605
Wholesale trade	1,255
Retail trade	4,520
Trade not allocable	70
Finance, insurance, and real estate	1,475
Services	1,760
Business not allocable	10
Total	$18,350

SOURCE: Reprinted with permission from the March 3, 1969, issue of *Advertising Age*. Copyright © 1969 by Crain Communications, Inc.

[8] For an exploration of this subject, see O. J. Firestone, *The Economic Implications of Advertising* (Toronto, Ont.: Methuen, 1967).

sumer behavior. Motivation research—contracted to "MR" in the trade—is the application of the behavioral sciences to the analysis of consumer behavior. It is particularly prevalent in consumer-goods industries. General marketing research, however, is common to all four industrial categories. If one includes the analysis of product variation under this heading, industrial-goods producers and government contractors would probably take the lead in terms of total dollars spent.

The consumer-goods model also serves to illustrate some exceptions to the generalizations that are required in any study of marketing. Certainly the small farmer has little opportunity to use price as a marketing instrument in his sale of food to the consumer. Promotion has little significance for the local water company. Product variation offers small opportunity to the power company attempting to increase its profits. Distribution is fixed for the telephone company. Marketing research is futile for the farmer. Yet all these firms produce what are essentially consumer goods—that is, products ultimately consumed by the household unit.

INDUSTRIAL-GOODS INDUSTRIES

Industrial goods are "goods which are destined to be sold primarily for use in producing other goods or rendering services as contrasted with goods destined to be sold primarily to the ultimate consumer."[9] Raw materials, machine tools, fertilizers, buildings used for business, computers, maintenance supplies, and semifinished products (parts to be incorporated into other goods) are broad examples of industrial products. Paint, milling machines, manure, digital computers, floor cleaners, rough castings, and automobile tires are specific examples. Some of these items, of course, may also be consumer goods. Tires sold to the General Motors Corporation are, by our definition, industrial goods; tires sold to the owner of a private car are not.

Price is an important competitive instrument in the industrial-goods sector, especially where product characteristics are clearly specified by the buyer. However, price flexibility is more limited. It may be difficult, or even illegal, to discriminate between buyers, except on the basis of quantity and then only if order size carries demonstrable economies of scale. Competitive bidding is common, especially where similar products are manufactured by two or more companies. Price is not so much the "take it or leave it" amount that it often is in the consumer goods field.

Product variation is important in segments of the industrial-goods industries where technology is rapidly changing. Here maintenance of the

[9] *Ibid.,* p. 14.

status quo can lead to technological obsolescence and financial disaster. Change may be the only viable strategy, in spite of the risks—and these can be considerable. In chemicals, electronics, and drugs, the firm must not only develop new products but must also deal with the problem of *innovation diffusion* (the spread of new ideas). The product instrument is closely related to the promotion instrument in the introduction of radically different goods. This is true in both industrial- and consumer-goods industries.

Distribution methods vary in industrial-goods industries, although the actual networks are generally simpler than in the consumer-goods or service industries. The potential customers and the aggregate potential market are easier to define than in other fields, except government contracting. Also, the price per pound of many industrial goods—especially machine tools, computers, and office equipment—is often so large as to make physical distribution costs a nominal percentage of the total cost. This is not the case with raw materials. However, the bulk and other physical properties of the goods may restrict the manufacturer to only one or two modes of physical distribution. For example, the transportation of coal from West Virginia mines to Indiana blast furnaces can only be done by rail. On the other hand, the transportation of crude oil from offshore Louisiana wells to New Jersey refineries can be accomplished by pipeline, tanker, railroad, or a combination of the three. Nevertheless, the variables in such a decision are relatively few, and the tools of quantitative analysis generally render the optimum choice obvious.

Industrial goods, especially raw materials, are often differentiated not by their physical properties but by the service that accompanies them. The ability to respond quickly to customer demands is often an instrument of competition. Quick response means a distribution system where order processing and delivery are fast and inventories are complete. Thus the trade-offs between inventory costs, local warehousing, air transportation, and computerized order processing can be important in the marketing mix decision.

The extent and type of promotion vary considerably, depending primarily on the ability of the producer to differentiate his products and services from those of his competitors. Industrial buyers tend to be more knowledgeable and objective in their selection of products than householders, although this point may be debatable. Purchasing agents are less likely to be susceptible to emotional and noneconomic appeals, particularly when they must fill material requisitions that are quite specific in regard to product characteristics, quantity, and delivery. Nevertheless, they do have egos, attitudes, and biases that make them susceptible to promotional efforts. An advertisement proclaiming the reliability of Texas Instrument transistors, the service provided by IBM, the promptness of U. S. Steel's customer service, or the reliability of TWA's schedules can shade customer attitudes. A small favor or a salesman's confidence can feed a buyer's ego. A sales talk or demonstration can increase a purchasing agent's awareness of a product's characteristics.

The innovation status (newness) of the product is another determinant of the level of promotional activity. An item that has already been accepted in the marketplace is generally in less need of promotion than a new product. This is particularly true of technically complex goods such as chemicals and drugs, or a new industrial material or process. One reason behind the rapid adoption of new drugs by the medical community in this country is the aggressive promotional campaigns—particularly the heavy use of personal selling—of pharmaceutical companies.

Marketing research in the field of industrial goods is a function of—that is, is dependent on—the rate of technological change and the fixed cost of new products. Where a market is experiencing rapid technological change, research is necessary to keep abreast of the customers' present and emerging needs. For instance, a supplier selling hydraulic equipment to the aerospace industry must anticipate tomorrow's hardware requirements and develop products accordingly. For this reason, the rate of technological change in an industry may in turn be a function of marketing research. Research often identifies the need for a product, hence the potential sales—which gives impetus to technological change. Even where the rate of technological change is very low, research may still be required to estimate demand and identify prospective buyers.

If marketing research estimates of potential sales are inaccurate, the firm's error in judgment can be disastrous. This is especially true in industries like the chemical industry, where a large capital investment in plant and equipment is often necessary before the first units can be put on the market. Companies like Olin Mathieson are likely to spend a minimum of $100,000 on marketing research before committing themselves to the introduction of a new product.[10]

Yet emphasis on marketing research is not a criterion that readily separates the industrial-goods industries from other categories. Rather, marketing research is a function that must be closely tailored to the individual firm, to the rate of technological change, and to the nature of the market. Frequently the customer can define his needs more clearly than the supplier can anticipate them. This is typically the case where the customer is in a state of rapid technological change. Here the supplying firm had best allocate resources to the maintenance of a dialogue between himself and his customers, particularly the customer's engineers and planners, who will be the first to perceive future needs. Two strategies are available. The firm can respond to the needs of the market as perceived by the customers—which necessitates a dialogue

[10] This estimate was made by David Lowry, manager, Industrial Market Development, Olin Mathieson Corp., in a conversation with Walter B. Wentz, January 1967.

between the firm and the innovators; or it can itself provide the leadership, thus assuming the burden of perceiving the future needs of the market. The producer then supplies the innovations, as is typical in the pharmaceutical industry. The latter alternative places a heavy load on the product research and promotional staffs, who must identify and cultivate the innovators and the early adopters among the market population. In some areas, particularly in the field of drugs and medical technology, acceptance by the innovator group is a prerequisite to the success of a new product.[11]

SERVICE INDUSTRIES

Services are "activities, benefits, or satisfactions which are offered for sale or are provided in connection with the sale of goods."[12] Motels, television repair shops, medical centers, legal firms, advertising agencies, accounting services, car-rental agencies, and taxi companies are typical service firms. The personal nature of most of these services, the low cost of entry in most areas, and the small-scale efficiency we generally associate with this sector encourage small firms. The limited resources of these companies result in unsophisticated styles of marketing. The field abounds with small proprietorships where a particular technical competence, convenience of location, or word-of-mouth reputation compensates for the lack of aggressive marketing. In some subsets of the service field, particularly the professions, marketing instruments such as promotion and price competition are looked on with distaste and thus are seldom used. For example, in the medical profession the use of advertising borders on the unethical.

Again, there are exceptions; not surprisingly, these appear to be associated with size. Large motel chains, big auto-rental agencies, and restaurant chains employ all the basic marketing instruments, often with considerable skill and usually with large budgets. In addition, the emergence of the franchise, a post–World War II phenomenon, has allowed the small proprietor—such as the "ma and pa" owner-managers that are common in the motel business—to benefit from sophisticated marketing programs made possible by large resources. The motel, donut shop, restaurant, dance studio, or car-rental agency is owned wholly or partly by the individual. The parent firm, or franchiser, collects an initial fee and a percentage of the revenue. In return, the owner, or franchisee, is allowed to use the parent company's trademark, receives training and supervision, and is supported by nationwide promotion. Travel Lodge, Winchell's Do-Nuts, International House of

[11] James Coleman, Elihu Katz, and Herbert Menzel, "The Diffusion of an Innovation Among Physicians," in Ralph L. Day, ed., *Marketing Models* (Scranton, Pa.: International Textbook Co., 1964), p. 100.
[12] Alexander, *op. cit.*, p. 21.

Pancakes, and Arthur Murray Dance Studios are typical examples of this trend.

There are three special classes of firms whose outputs fit our definition of services but whose size and operations do not conform to the model just described. These are transportation companies, utility companies, and banks. All are closely regulated by the government, especially regarding price and product (service) variation. Tariffs and rates are set by federal and state agencies either directly (as is the case with transportation firms and utility companies), or indirectly (as is the case with banks). Equipment and operational standards are rigorously prescribed; even distribution is controlled, in the sense that routes are awarded or denied, areas are assigned, and charters are issued. Ancillary services can still be varied—airlines can offer exotic in-flight meals, and telephone companies can offer different-colored telephones. Banks have some latitude in setting interest rates. However, only the last two marketing instruments, promotion and research, are really open to manipulation by the firm. Promotion is often practiced on a grand scale, especially by the airlines. Marketing research has not been used extensively in the past, but this is changing. For example, research is often used today to support petitions to regulatory agencies. These requests are typically for increased rates or services (such as additional routes) and must be justified with elaborate economic and market data and analyses.

GOVERNMENT CONTRACTORS

Government contractors are firms that sell goods and services directly to federal, state, or local government agencies. Many firms compete in both the commercial and the government sectors. Many corporations doing substantial business with the federal establishment also market consumer goods, industrial products, or civilian services—companies like General Electric, IBM, North American Rockwell, and Pan American Airways compete in all four areas.

Corporations serving as prime contractors on major federal programs generally have separate divisions to handle their civilian and government work. Security regulations, accounting requirements, quality-control practices, and even marketing techniques differ so much between the two areas as to make this separation virtually mandatory. Where exceptions are found, the federal management practices usually dominate the firm and the marketing of the civilian products, if not their manufacture, remains the function of a separate section.

From the marketer's viewpoint, the thing that sets government-oriented firms apart from consumer- and industrial-goods producers is the monopsonist[13] character of the customer. (Occasionally foreign sales and compatible civilian product lines provide a minor exception to this rule.) Because the buyer, either a government agency or a prime contractor to an agency, generally defines his product requirements in great detail, conventional promotion (especially advertising) and distribution functions are not important. Both are relegated to very minor positions in the firm's arsenal of marketing functions.

Not too many years ago, a lengthy discussion of government contractors would have been inappropriate in a marketing textbook. The marketing functions were diffused throughout the firm, and such instruments as advertising, distribution, and marketing research were either not employed in the marketing sense or were used in subtle forms alien to conventional marketing practices. Engineers, production managers, and accountants dominated contract proposals, negotiations, and customer relations. Marketing departments, per se, did not exist, and the company payrolls showed no "salesmen." Promotion was accomplished by company executives and key technical personnel, who cultivated the decision-makers in the federal establishment.

New sales were made by qualified companies responding to invitations for bids. The cost of preparing estimates was actually paid by the customer, since it was included in the firms' overhead, which in turn was distributed over present government contracts held by the company. Where substantial contract proposals were involved, such as those for production of the B-58 bomber, the Atlas missile, and the early atomic reactors, the government would provide special funds for the surviving competitors to use in preparing final detailed proposals after less promising bids had been rejected. As long as costs were absorbed by the government, it was a viable marketing strategy to bid on every invitation mailed to the plant. Thus there was no problem of allocating marketing resources among prospective programs.

Where follow-on sales (sales that occur after the original order) were involved, the original contractor frequently found himself the sole bidder. It is hardly economical to shift the manufacture and testing of highly complex hardware, such as Apollo moon capsules, Saturn boosters, and C-5A transports, to other companies once the first units have come off the line. Under these circumstances the marketing function is assumed by the contract negotiators, who attempt to define the new order so as to maximize their profit on the follow-on production. Their "competitors" are the NASA or Defense Department negotiators, whose job is to get the material at the lowest cost commensurate with an acceptable delivery schedule and product quality.

[13] A monopsonist is a monopoly buyer—that is, it is the sole market for a particular good or class of product.

In the 1960's, Secretary of Defense Robert McNamara, a former president of the Car Division of the Ford Motor Company, changed the marketing environment of the military products industry by introducing incentive contracting and insisting that competing firms allocate some of their own resources to preparing contract proposals. His philosophy and methods were soon adopted by other federal departments, and today bidders must choose carefully between programs. They must assist the agencies in defining product mix, and they must invest their own resources. Boeing, Douglas, and Lockheed, for example, can no longer bid on every airplane contract. To do so would be to spread their marketing resources so thin as to assure that they would not be competitive on any of the contracts. For instance, it cost Boeing and Lockheed over $10 million each to prepare their proposals on the C-5A transport plane. For Douglas to have competed with a substantially smaller outlay, say $2 million, would have been a waste of marketing resources, for such a modest outlay would assure failure.

The fact that cost is now a factor forces resource allocation decisions, market analyses, pricing strategies, and product decisions that one associates with conventional marketing. This does not mean that we may expect the introduction of motivation research, trading stamps, network television commercials, or discount outlets in government contracting, but it does imply the emergence of formal marketing departments and marketing specialists, especially in firms that are interested in exploiting their federally sponsored technology in the civilian sector or in diversifying their clientele in the federal establishment.[14]

THE MARKETING ENVIRONMENT

The interindustry differences just described suggest a variety of roles for marketing personnel. These differences are magnified when one explores the specialized functions that individual firms can perform within a given industry. If a marketer fails to understand the realities of his particular environment, he will make poor—perhaps disastrous—decisions. Although departure from convention, experimentation, and innovation are frequently essential to business success, and even survival, grasp of his marketing environment must underlie the marketer's decisions. In short, he must know where he, and his firm, stand. Since it is equally important for him to know where he, and the firm, are going, we turn now to the objectives of the firm.

[14] For a more detailed exploration of the new marketing environment in government contracting, see Walter B. Wentz, "Aerospace Discovers Marketing," *Journal of Marketing*, Vol. 31, No. 2 (April 1967), pp. 27–31.

OBJECTIVES OF THE FIRM

Marketing—that body of resources allocated to the sale and distribution of goods and services—is not an end unto itself. This may be disturbing to those marketers who view their craft as the center about which all other activities of the firm orbit. Nevertheless, marketing is but a means to an end, and must compete with other means that also serve as instruments to further the objectives of the firm. Aristotle perceived the nature of such things 300 years before the birth of Christ:

Every art or applied science and every systematic investigation, and similarly every action and choice, seem to aim at some good. . . . But it is clear that there is a difference in the ends at which they aim: in some cases the activity is the end, in others the end is some product beyond the activity.[15]

This is the context within which marketing must be studied and applied. In order to understand the principles and practices of marketing, one must also understand the objectives, theory, and organization of the firm.

Economic Objective.   The primary objective of the firm is the *long-run maximization of profit,* given an initial level of investment. This fundamental premise, if it is properly constrained by the legal and moral dictates of society, is the best single criterion for management decisions.

Profit is the difference between revenue and cost, expressed notationally as $\pi = R - C$. Although this definition is both accurate and simple, the solution of the profit equation can be a difficult and controversial task. The difficulty usually lies in deciding what expenditures should be included in the cost term. The revenue value can also prove elusive, especially with respect to public institutions that receive little or no payment for their services.

These matters are explored in detail in later chapters—for now, a less rigorous and broader definition will suffice. Profit may be viewed as *economic surplus,* which is the difference between the value of the inputs of an enterprise and the value of its outputs. These values may be expressed in dollars or in some other absolute value. For example, output might be measured in terms of the number of cars manufactured, the number of college students graduated, or the number of passenger-miles flown. Expressing output in terms of physical goods precludes the computation of a value for profit. (How, for example, does one subtract dollars of cost from the number of students graduated?) However, it does allow one to compare the effi-

[15] Aristotle, *Nicomachean Ethics* (*ca.* 345 B.C.), trans. by Martin Ostwald (New York: Bobbs-Merrill, 1962).

ciency of different institutions or methods of production on the basis of *units of output per dollar cost.*

No matter how it is measured, the value of the economic surplus must be positive. The enterprise and the society must view the outputs of the institution as equal in value to, or worth more than, the inputs. This economic surplus rewards those who assume risk, provides an incentive to produce, pays for losses, and finances research. Perhaps most important, it is the means by which the enterprise can enlarge and improve its plant and equipment. This is essential if a firm is to be more efficient, proliferate jobs, and sustain a rising standard of living for its employees.

The concept of profit maximization is not alien to other economic and political systems. Although the word "profit" may not be used in socialist or communist societies, if we substitute the term "economic surplus" which is sufficiently synonymous for our purposes, the objective of the firm in these systems is the same. Stated again, economic surplus—or "profit"—is simply the difference between the value of the goods or services produced by the firm and the cost of the resources that went into their production and distribution. Measured against the investment required to establish and maintain the firm, economic surplus is a test of efficiency. For a firm, to show an excess of value produced over value consumed is to demonstrate a net positive contribution to the economy and presumably to the welfare of the people and institutions that make up the economy. To do otherwise—to consume more capital and labor in the productive process than the goods and services produced are worth—is to do violence to the commonweal. Although the terms used to describe it and the methods by which it is distributed and then assimilated back into the economy differ, economic surplus is as crucial to the welfare of the Soviet Union and the Peoples Republic of China as it is to the Federal Republic of Germany and the United States.[16] Thus the profit maximization criterion is as appropriate for the director of the Izhevsk Auto Plant as it is for the president of the General Motors Corporation.

This defense of the profit criterion at the macro level is similar to the defense of the profit criterion at the micro level—that is, at the level of the individual firm. The firm needs economic surplus just as society does. Without profit the firm will die. Although it could conceivably survive with profit equal to zero, observation suggests that no company remains for long at the break-even point (that fine line between profit and loss). Eventually, it goes one way or the other. If losses continue, it must eventually go out of business, at which time it will serve no one's interests at all. As long as it shows a profit, the firm may serve whatever ends its owners choose to serve. These ends, whether they are selfish, altruistic, illegal, stupid, or moral, can only be served in the long run with the economic surplus generated by the enterprise.

[16] See Peter F. Drucker, *The New Society* (New York: Harper & Row, 1949) for an extensive discussion of this thesis.

The greater the profit, the greater will be the firm's capacity to expand, provide jobs, assume risks, proliferate new products, aid education, pay salaries to its managers, or maintain a luxurious standard of living for its owners. Hence the maximization of profit is, in general, the appropriate criterion for management decisions.

Economic surplus, or profit, is measured over time. The period used is specified by the firm's accountants and generally conforms to a convention set by the federal government. In the United States profit is usually measured over one year and expressed as annual earnings. However, were a firm to limit its planning horizon also to one year, long-run profits would tend to be sacrificed for short-run gains—no value would be placed on investments that offered significant rewards in future years. Such an approach would not yield maximum profits in the long run, and business planning horizons normally extend well beyond twelve months. Although profit maximization is an important consideration in short-run decisions,[17] it is essentially a long-run criterion.

Noneconomic Objectives. As any behaviorist will point out, numerous noneconomic objectives influence the decisions of the firm.[18] The desire for job security, organizational longevity, avoidance of risk, hopes of personal advancement, nepotism, ego, compassion, and the drive for status all compete with the purely economic goal of profit maximization.

These forces may not always be in conflict, particularly if we stress the long-run aspect of profit. The alternative offering the maximum potential profit can also be the one that offers the greatest opportunity for disaster. The manager who selects an option offering a lesser profit but carrying a lesser penalty if it fails may not be derelict in his duty as a long-run profit maximizer. On the contrary, the avoidance of nonessential risks and the furtherance of organizational longevity are both legitimate considerations for long-run profit maximization.[19]

The art of management certainly includes balancing objectives—making rational trade-offs between conflicting goals. The trick is to exercise the economic criterion within the context of noneconomic objectives. Although the various goals perceived by the firm's stockholders, managers, and work-

---

[17] The modern concept of profit is "present value," which allows future streams of profit to be adjusted for time. Obviously, an investment paying $1000 five years hence is not as profitable as one paying $1000 this year, for the profit received this year could be invested to earn more money during the five-year wait. This concept is developed in detail in Part III.

[18] See H. A. Simon, *Administrative Behavior* (New York: Macmillan, 1957) or Mason Haire, ed., *Modern Organization Theory* (New York: Wiley, 1959) for a discussion of noneconomic goals in decision-making.

[19] These ideas are explored in Kenneth Galbraith, *The New Industrial State* (Boston: Houghton Mifflin, 1967).

ers may frequently conflict, especially in the short run, the escalation of stock values, the payment of dividends, the enlargement of salaries and bonuses, and increases in jobs and wages are all dependent on the firm's creation of an economic surplus. The profitability of the firm is the unions' dominant argument in wage disputes and one of the most important criteria in wage arbitration.[20]

Constraints.   Having made a defense of the profit criterion, we must now recognize the *constraints*—moral and legal—within which it operates. A manager does not have to be a humanist to recognize the limits that morality and law impose. To exceed these bounds invites retaliation by society. Since strikes, consumer boycotts, and punitive legislation hardly enhance the long-run profit of the industry or firm against whom such measures are directed, compliance with the moral and legal constraints is not incompatible with the economic objective.

We shall examine the legal restrictions and protections afforded in the marketplace in Part X. However, a detailed exploration of the social and philosophical aspects of the firm is outside the scope of this book. The moral aspects of the marketing environment, too, we shall leave to the conscience and curiosity of the reader, since the literature in that area is also large. For now, it is sufficient simply to recognize their existence.

[20] See John E. Maher, *Labor and the Economy* (Boston: Allyn & Bacon, 1965), p. 142.

CHAPTER 3

Theory of the Firm

To lay the theoretical foundation for what follows, we need to take a brief excursion into microeconomics. Here we examine the theory of the firm, which explains the process by which a rational firm maximizes profit, given a finite and rationed quantity of investment. Capital, like land and labor, is limited and must be allocated among competing firms, government, and private households.

FUNDAMENTAL ARGUMENT

The fundamental argument of the theory of the firm is that *profit will be maximized by increasing output until the cost of the last increment of output equals the revenues derived from the sale of the last increment of output.* Marginal revenue is the revenue derived from an additional increment of output. Conversely, *marginal cost* is the cost incurred by producing and marketing an additional increment of output. *When, at some given total output, marginal cost becomes equal to marginal revenue, profit is maximized.* In mathematical calculations, marginal revenue is symbolized by MR or $\Delta R / \Delta Q$, the change in revenue for a change in quantity (output), where the Greek letter delta, Δ, represents change. Marginal cost is conventionally labeled MC or $\Delta C / \Delta Q$, the change in cost for a change in quantity; and profit is represented as π, the Greek letter pi. Thus, in mathematical terms,

$$\pi = \text{maximum, where } MR = MC, \text{ or} \tag{3-1}$$

$$\pi = \text{maximum, where } \frac{\Delta R}{\Delta Q} = \frac{\Delta C}{\Delta Q} \tag{3-2}$$

35

PROFIT FUNCTION

We can prove that profit is greatest when marginal revenue equals marginal cost by examining the profit function and the relationship between total revenue and total cost. We mentioned in Chapter 2 that profit is defined as the difference between total revenue and total cost. This can be stated in the form of a definitional equation, or identity:

$\pi = R - C$, where   (3–3)

$\pi = $ total profit

$R = $ total revenue, and

$C = $ total cost

This suggests that the firm should not attempt to maximize revenue or minimize cost separately, but instead should select that level of output that will maximize the positive difference between the two. Selecting the value for one or more independent variables so as to maximize a dependent variable is called *optimizing*. In this case, R and C are the independent variables that determine the value of π, the dependent variable the firm desires to maximize. Expressed in general mathematical form, $\pi = f(R, C)$; in explicit form, $\pi = R - C$.

However, both revenue and cost are in turn dependent on output, Q. Hence, $R = f(Q)$ and $C = g(Q)$. (Note that f and g are used to distinguish different functions of Q; R and C do not each have the same relationship to Q.) To further complicate matters, output is dependent on the variable price, P. Hence, $Q = f(P)$. Thus, to maximize profit the firm must select an appropriate value for price. However, the process of optimizing the values for P, Q, R, and C is not as complicated as it may seem, given a few simple mathematical skills. This leads us to an analysis of the revenue and cost functions. We shall deal with the revenue function first.

REVENUE FUNCTION

Revenue is simply the product of the quantity of goods sold and the average price received for those goods. The firm is seldom able to hold price constant throughout its range of output. (The one exception is when the firm is operating under conditions of pure competition.[1]) This is due to one of the basic tenets of economics—that the demand for a particular good is a function of the price of that good and will decline as the price increases. In other

---

[1] Pure competition is discussed in Part V.

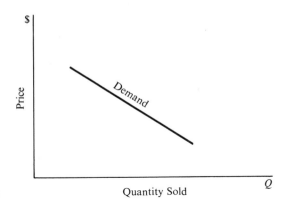

FIGURE 3.1
Demand function

words, the higher the price, the fewer units will be sold. Conversely, the lower the price, the more units will be sold. This relationship is expressed graphically in Figure 3.1.

This hypothesis is intuitively reasonable.[2] It tells the marketing manager that he must continually reduce price if he is to sell more and more units of output, assuming everything else remains constant. In this case, "everything else" includes promotion, consumer tastes, income, and the price of substitute products.

Obviously, some buyers are willing to pay more than others. However, it is usually impractical, and often illegal, to charge different prices to different buyers. The solution is to compute the total quantities that will be sold at various universal prices. The optimum price-quantity is then selected, and that price becomes the set price for all buyers. It is this set price that determines the total quantity of goods that will be sold, other things being equal.

While quantity is dependent on price, revenue is dependent on both quantity and price. The firm's revenue is determined by how many units are sold and the price received for each unit. The *general* mathematical equation for revenue is thus

$R = f(P, Q)$, where   (3–4)

R = revenue

f is an operational symbol denoting "a function of"

P = price, and

Q = quantity

[2] For a rigorous proof, see George J. Stigler, *The Theory of Price,* 3rd ed. (New York: Macmillan, 1966), Chapter 3, or A. Kooros, *Elements of Mathematical Economics* (Boston: Houghton Mifflin, 1965), pp. 51–60.

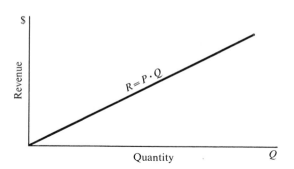

FIGURE 3.2
Linear revenue function

Equation 3–4 tells us that R is a dependent variable, the value of which depends on the independent variables P and Q. However, it does not show *how* R is determined by P and Q. For this we need an *explicit* equation,

$$R = P \cdot Q \qquad (3\text{–}5)$$

where R is revenue and is equal to the product of P, the average price, multiplied by Q, the quantity sold.[3] ("Average" is denoted by the bar over the P. However, we normally omit the bar, as P is understood to be the average price in the revenue equation.) If price remains constant—that is, if $P = k$, where k is a constant—then no matter what quantity is sold, the revenue function will be linear and will plot as a straight line (see Figure 3.2).[4]

If the price changes with different quantities of goods sold, our revenue function is no longer linear but is curved, as in Figure 3.3. Such a function is called *nonlinear* or *curvilinear*.

This concept warrants further explanation. Assume, for example, that a marketing research group has experimented with different prices in the marketplace and has determined the various quantities that can be sold—the *demand*—at each price. This information is tabulated in Table 3.1. Using the revenue equation, $R = P \cdot Q$, we can determine the revenues that will accrue at various prices. The range of prices selected varies from $5.00, which would discourage all buyers, to $.50, which we assume to be the minimum direct cost of manufacturing the item. (We could have taken price to

---

[3] There is no rigid convention in the selection of symbols representing numerical values. For example, profit could be shown as π, P, X, etc. However, the symbols representing mathematical relationships and operations are rigidly prescribed. Thus, there is no ambiguity in the use of $=$, $+$, $-$ and so on.

[4] A linear function with only one independent variable always plots as a straight line. A nonlinear function always plots as a curve. Examples of linear functions are $y = a + bx$ and $R = P \cdot Q$. Examples of nonlinear functions are $y = a + bx^2$, $R = P \cdot Q^2$, and $R = P \cdot Q^{\frac{1}{2}}$. Note that the exponent determines linearity. If the exponent of each variable is 1, the function is linear; otherwise it is nonlinear.

Table 3.1   Price, demand, and revenue

Price (P)	Quantity (Q)*	Revenue (R = P·Q)
5.00	0	0
4.50	100	450
4.00	200	800
3.50	300	1050
3.00	400	1200
2.50	500	1250
2.00	600	1200
1.50	700	1050
1.00	800	800
.50	900	450

* Note that quantity sold is dependent on price; that is, $Q = f(P)$. In this example, $Q = 1000 - 200P$, a linear equation. This expression for Q can be substituted in our revenue equation, $R = P \cdot Q$, giving us $R = P \cdot (1000 - 200P)$, or $R = 1000P - 200P^2$, which is nonlinear and would plot as the curve in Figure 3.3.

the extreme of zero, where we would discover the quantity of the product that could be disposed of if we gave it away. Figure 3.3 illustrates the change in revenue as output increases. Revenue is maximized at $Q = 500$ and declines if a greater quantity is sold. Note that revenue depends on price and quantity and that quantity is a function of price.

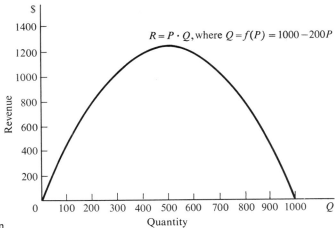

FIGURE 3.3
Nonlinear revenue function

Any marketing manager who proposes selling more than 500 units should be sent back to college for a refresher course. It hardly makes sense to sell more than 500 units when the firm can make just as much money by selling fewer units. For example, it can sell 800 units simply by setting the price at $1.00, thus earning $800 in revenue. But why bother? Setting the price at $4.00 will bring in the same amount of revenue, but the firm will only have to manufacture and market 200 units, which obviously would cost less. Hence the firm should never operate—that is, it should never set output—beyond the point that produces the maximum revenue.

However, our objective is not to maximize revenue, but to maximize profit. As profit is the positive difference between revenue and cost, we shall next examine the *total cost function,* hereafter referred to simply as the *cost function.*

COST FUNCTION

The cost of the firm's output consists of two basic elements—fixed costs and variable costs. The general equation for cost is thus

$C = f(F, V, Q)$ where   (3–6)

C = total cost

F = fixed cost

V = variable cost, and

Q = quantity

The fixed cost, F, refers to the expenses of building and maintaining the plant and facilities required to produce and distribute the product. Since it is a constant by definition, it is always a fixed value. It excludes the costs of materials and labor that go directly into the manufacture and sale of the individual goods, which are variable costs. As the adjective implies, variable cost varies directly with the quantity of units produced. The total cost is a combination of the fixed and variable costs and can be expressed in explicit mathematical form as

$C = F + VQ$, where   (3–7)

C = total cost

F = fixed cost

V = variable cost per unit, and

Q = quantity

The cost per unit, or *unit cost,* is the cost associated with the production of a single unit of output. It may be expressed as an average cost or as the cost of a particular unit. For example, if a total of $100,000 is required to build five houses, then the average unit cost is $20,000. However, if the houses were built in sequence, we might find that their individual unit costs were $26,000, $22,000, $19,000, $17,000, and $16,000. This is common, because, for reasons explained below, the cost of each succeeding unit is usually less. However, the reduction in unit cost diminishes as the firm approaches its most efficient level of output. Beyond that point, additional units will cost more than their predecessors. That point is shown as Q_p in Figure 3.4, which illustrates what economists call the *U-shaped cost curve.* It is the point where unit cost is lowest.

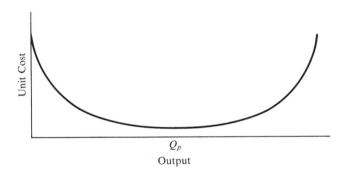

FIGURE 3.4
Unit cost function

The U-shaped cost curve is a result of economies of scale and the learning phenomenon, which we shall discuss in detail in Parts II and VI. The economy of scale is apparent in savings obtained from task specialization, large-quantity purchases, large-lot production releases, production tooling, and mass-media advertising. The per-ton cost of steel is considerably lower in car lots than in less-than-car lots. The production order and set-up time for a small-quantity run is identical to that required for a large run, and the cost of a big order can be distributed over many more units. The cost of a unit of advertising may also be less with larger orders.

Learning also causes a reduction in unit cost as the total number of units is increased. This is because human beings become more proficient at a task as it is repeated. As a result, a worker spends less time building the second unit than he took building the first one. The third will be completed quicker than the second, and so on until he reaches the peak of his efficiency. Beyond that point the unit labor cost will remain constant, or may even rise if boredom or fatigue sets in. This learning phenomenon is evident in most

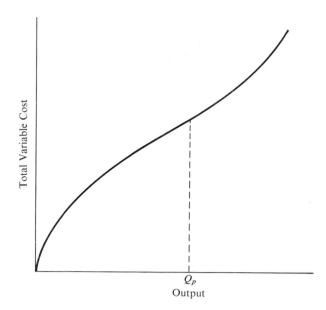

FIGURE 3.5
Total variable cost function

repetitive tasks—for example, in assembling television sets, programming computers, or selling automobiles.

As output Q_p is passed, the phenomenon reverses itself, and the output resulting from additional inputs (called *marginal product*) begins to decrease. This is because excessive output increases coordination costs, drives up prices, and overloads equipment and personnel. Advertising becomes redundant and less effective. More and more effort must be expended to achieve the same results, particularly in the marketing sector. Thus the unit cost curve bends upward.

If we plot the *total* variable cost curve, it will initially move upward at a decreasing rate, until it reaches the pivotal output. As in Figure 3.5, the curve will then continue upward but at an increasing rate. Although *unit costs* can be reduced up to the pivotal quantity Q_p, *total costs* are never reduced by increasing output.

Since $C = F + V$, we can depict the total cost function by adding the total variable cost curve to the fixed cost curve, as in Figure 3.6.

REVENUE, COST, AND PROFIT

To locate the level of output that will maximize profit, we simply impose our total cost curve over our total revenue curve, as in Figure 3.7. We can

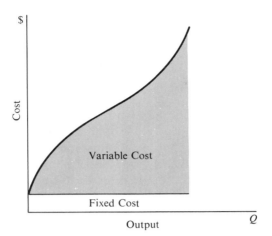

FIGURE 3.6
Total cost function

ignore that part of the revenue curve that extends beyond the maximum revenue point, since it is not relevant to the discussion. By examination, we determine our maximum profit position as output Q_2, where the positive difference between the cost and revenue functions—that is, profit—is maximum. Between zero and Q_1, the difference between revenue and cost is negative; hence the firm is operating at a loss. Q_1 is the initial break-even point. This point can be determined graphically, as shown in Figure 3.7. The initial break-even point can also be computed mathematically by the following formula:

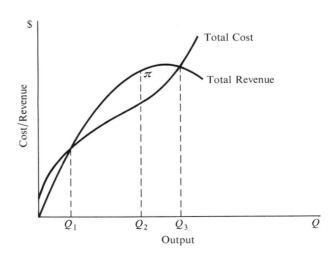

FIGURE 3.7
Total cost vs. total revenue

$$Q_B = \frac{F}{P - V}, \text{ where} \tag{3-8}$$

Q_B = the break-even quantity

F = fixed cost

P = price, and

V = variable cost

The break-even quantity is especially important to the marketing manager, since he must be reasonably confident of his department's ability to sell an output in excess of that quantity before recommending that a product or service be offered by his firm. Both the level of confidence in the market forecast and the reliability of the cost estimate become more important as the fixed cost increases. A large error in the determination of either the demand estimate—which is the basis of the revenue function—or the cost function, can be disastrous. The experience of the General Dynamics Corporation is one example. The actual break-even point for their Convair 880 jet airliner proved to be far in excess of the initial estimate. Compounding this error was the failure of the marketing personnel to deliver the sales that they had forecast. The result was an all-time record loss for American business—$425 million.[5]

Q_3 is the second break-even point. Here the cost curve again crosses the revenue curve, and their difference becomes negative. To operate to the right of Q_3, or even in the vicinity of Q_3, would be nonrational behavior, despite the marketing manager's natural zeal for setting new sales records and maximizing revenues.

Actually, there is a more precise and faster method of locating optimum output than drawing graphs and measuring vertical distances between the revenue and cost curves. To understand it, we need a more rigorous proof of the argument that profit is maximized when marginal revenue equals marginal cost.

Marginal Revenue. Marginal revenue, $\Delta R/\Delta Q$, is the change in total revenue induced by a change in total output. It is the *rate of change* of the revenue function. It is also the slope of the revenue curve, represented by the tangent of the revenue curve at each output. We can illustrate these concepts by a linear revenue function, such as that which might confront a firm in an industry characterized by pure competition.[6]

---

[5] R. A. Smith, "How a Great Corporation Got Out of Control," *Fortune*, Part I (January 1962) and Part II (February 1962). Similar errors were made by Ford and Lockheed, which lost $200 million on the Edsel automobile and $121 million on the Electra airplane respectively.

[6] In a purely competitive industry, no firm is large enough to influence price. Hence price is a constant for all levels of output.

If a firm operates under conditions of pure competition, and if the market price for its products is $2, the firm's revenue function is:

$R = 2Q$, where

R = total revenue in dollars

2 = the going price in dollars, and

Q = the quantity of output

This function, $R = 2Q$, and the marginal revenue associated with it, $\Delta R / \Delta Q$, are portrayed graphically in Figure 3.8.

A change in quantity from Q_1 to Q_2 induces a change in revenue from R_1 to R_2. These increments of change are represented by ΔQ and ΔR respectively. $\Delta R / \Delta Q$, the change in revenue for a change in quantity, is called the *difference quotient* of R and Q. Our definition of marginal revenue can now be expanded to

$$MR = \frac{\Delta R}{\Delta Q} = \frac{R_2 - R_1}{Q_2 - Q_1}, \text{ where} \tag{3-9}$$

R_2 and R_1 = the revenues after and before the change in quantity, respectively, and

Q_2 and Q_1 = the new quantity and the original quantity, respectively

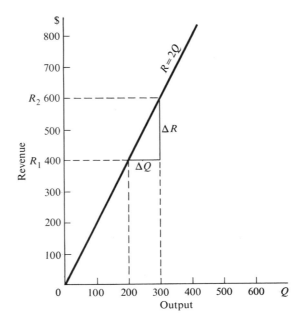

FIGURE 3.8
Linear revenue function
$(R = 2Q)$

Solving for the values in Figure 3.8,

$$MR = \frac{\Delta R}{\Delta Q} = \frac{600 - 400}{300 - 200} = \frac{200}{100} = 2$$

For the revenue function $R = 2Q$, the rate of change—that is, the ratio between a change in revenue and a change in quantity—is 2. An increase of 1 unit of quantity will cause an increase of 2 units of revenue, and a decrease of 1 unit of quantity will cause a decrease of 2 units of revenue.

Knowing the marginal revenue, we can readily compute the change in R for any change in Q. For example, if we increase output by 300 units,

$MR = \dfrac{\Delta R}{\Delta Q}$ Given

$2 = \dfrac{\Delta R}{300}$ By substitution

$\Delta R = 2 \cdot 300$ By algebraic manipulation

$\Delta R = 600$ By arithmetic

revenue increases by $600.

Because revenue is a linear function in this example, MR will be the same throughout the range of Q. This is an appropriate example within a competitive industry where the market price, perhaps "$2 a bushel," cannot be influenced by the output of the individual firm, and hence is "given."

Firms almost never operate under conditions of pure competition, however. Consequently, price will normally be a variable and will have to decrease if additional quantities of output are to be sold. This causes R to be a nonlinear function, as in Figure 3.9 on page 48. The computation of marginal revenue is more difficult for nonlinear functions than for linear functions, since there are more variables to be taken into account. We can illustrate this point by an example.

Assume that a marketing research group has analyzed the data in Table 3.1, which shows the quantities of a particular product that can be sold at various prices. The equation that expresses the exact relationship between the quantity sold and the price for this product is

$Q = 1000 - 200P$, where

Q = quantity demanded, and

P = price

Quantity demanded—that is, the output the firm can sell at a given price—is obviously dependent on price. It is an *inverse* function of price, since quantity will increase as price decreases and decrease as price increases.

Usually the dependent variable is placed on the left side of an equation and the independent variable on the right side. Thus, if x is dependent on y, we write

$$x = f(y)$$

Through algebraic manipulation, however, we can isolate P on the left side of the equation and solve for price, as follows:

$Q = 1000 - 200P$ Given

$P = \dfrac{1000 - Q}{200}$ By algebraic manipulation

$P = 5 - \dfrac{Q}{200}$ By arithmetic

Since revenue is arrived at by multiplying price and quantity, we simply substitute the equation above for price in Equation 3–5 in order to derive an explicit expression for revenue as a function of quantity.

$R = P \cdot Q$ Given

$P = 5 - \dfrac{Q}{200}$ Derived from the demand equation $Q = 1000 - 200P$

$R = \left[5 - \dfrac{Q}{200}\right] \cdot Q$ or   By substitution

$R = 5Q - \dfrac{Q^2}{200}$ By arithmetic

Note that the revenue function gives the total amount of revenue that will be received at a given price-quantity combination. Once the optimum price has been selected, thereby fixing quantity, price remains constant for all sales. In other words, the first customer is charged the same price as the last customer. This is normally the case, except where the firm can separate buyers and charge different prices to different groups. (See Chapter 13 for alternative pricing strategies.)

To return to our example, we now have an equation that gives us the revenue we will receive for any given quantity of output sold. The important property of this equation is that it takes into account the fact that quantity sold is dependent on price *and* permits us to express *revenue* directly as a function of *quantity,* by substitution.

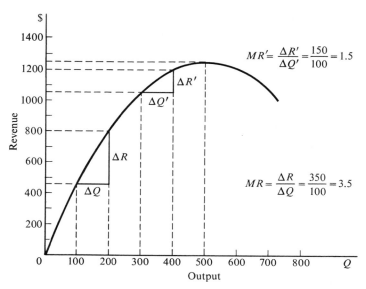

$$MR' = \frac{\Delta R'}{\Delta Q'} = \frac{150}{100} = 1.5$$

$$MR = \frac{\Delta R}{\Delta Q} = \frac{350}{100} = 3.5$$

FIGURE 3.9
Nonlinear revenue function
$(R = 5Q - \dfrac{Q^2}{200})$

The fact that one of the terms, $Q^2/200$, has an exponent different than 1 tells us that the function is nonlinear. This becomes obvious when we graph the equation, as in Figure 3.9.

In our example, a given change in output—say $\Delta Q = 100$—will result in a *different* change in revenue, ΔR, for each different initial value of output. The value for marginal revenue will vary throughout the range of Q *whenever revenue is a nonlinear function.* This is illustrated by the two marginal revenues in Figure 3.9. $MR = \$3.50$, but $MR' = \$1.50$. In mathematical notation $MR \neq MR'$.

Marginal revenue is now dependent on output, whereas when the revenue function was linear MR remained constant regardless of the value of Q. To compute marginal revenue under competitive conditions, algebra alone is not adequate. We must invoke a more powerful mathematical tool—differential calculus. An understanding of the fundamental concepts of differential calculus is essential for serious quantitative work in marketing. Fortunately, a working knowledge of at least the basic principles is not difficult to acquire.

DIFFERENTIAL CALCULUS: BASIC CONCEPTS

A brief excursion into the field of higher mathematics is appropriate at this point. For the reader without prior work in this area, the discussion will be an introduction to a powerful quantitative tool. The principles covered here are sufficient to work simple problems and, more important, will provide the mathematically unsophisticated reader with the background necessary to comprehend much that is being written today about marketing, particularly in the areas of marketing research and the theory of the firm. The more curious student will find a rigorous explanation of the subject in Appendix I, although this is not a prerequisite to understanding the balance of the book. The reader with a calculus course behind him will find this section a simple review. As for the mathematicians among our readers, we advise them to turn at once to page 59 and proceed through the remainder of the text.

Differential calculus is that portion of mathematics which deals with the problem of computing the rate of change of a function. It allows us to measure the change in one variable resulting from a change in another and is applicable to both linear and nonlinear functions. In discussing the nonlinear revenue function $R = 5Q - Q^2/200$, we said that the ratio of the change between two variables can vary according to where we take our measurements. Differential calculus enables us to find the rate of change, or *derivative*, for any particular point in the function. The *derivative* is the *rate of change of a function with respect to an independent variable*. The mathematical symbol for the derivative of a function is dy/dx, meaning the ratio between the change in the dependent variable (y) and the change in the independent variable (x). The derivative of the revenue function is thus written dR/dQ, the rate of change of the revenue function with respect to a change in output, or quantity.

The derivative, dy/dx, is essentially the same thing as the difference quotient, $\Delta y/\Delta x$. However, although they are computed in the same way, there is a technical difference. The derivative represents the rate of change at an infinitely small *point* on the curve; the difference quotient represents an *arc* on the curve. Δy and Δx are measurable, finite increments, whereas dy and dx are not. The derivative is an *instantaneous rate of change*. Hence dy/dx will not always be the same value as $\Delta y/\Delta x$. In Figure 3.10, for example, the slope of the function $y = f(x)$ at point P is different from the slope of the arc of the triangle formed by Δx and Δy.

To illustrate the applications of differential calculus, let us look at the derivative of the nonlinear revenue function $R = 5Q - Q^2/200$. By applying a rule we shall soon learn, we find that $dR/dQ = 5 - Q/100$. This tells us the ratio between a change in revenue, dR, and the change in quantity,

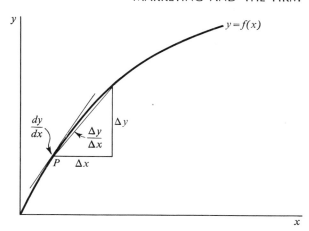

FIGURE 3.10
Derivative vs.
differential quotient

dQ, at any particular output, Q. For example, if output, Q, is 300 units, this ratio—that is, the derivative, dR/dQ—equals 2. We simply substitute the output selected, 300, for Q in the derivative equation. Thus,

$$\frac{dR}{dQ} = 5 - \frac{Q}{100}$$ Given

$$\frac{dR}{dQ} = 5 - \frac{300}{100}$$ By substitution

$$\frac{dR}{dQ} = 2$$ By arithmetic

Now that we have a value for the derivative, we can easily determine the change in revenue resulting from a change in quantity at that point. Say the firm wants to increase output by 1 unit:

$$\frac{dR}{dQ} = 2$$ Given

$$\frac{dR}{1} = 2$$ By substitution

$$dR = 2$$ By arithmetic

Revenue would increase by $2. If its cost function indicates it could produce *and* market the additional 1 unit for less than $2, it would be wise to increase output from 300 to 301 units.

The "instantaneous" nature of the derivative leads us to the key notion of differential calculus. This is the concept of a "limit," which can be readily

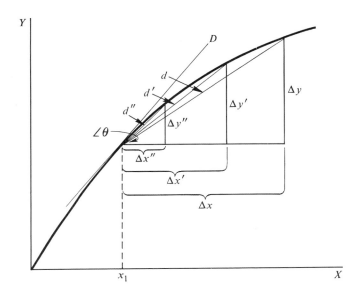

FIGURE 3.11
Approximations of the
slope of a nonlinear
function at point X_1

understood if we examine a segment of a nonlinear function, such as that
plotted in Figure 3.11.

The rate of change of a function is the slope of the curve representing
that function. (The term "curve" is used by mathematicians in referring to
the graph of a function, regardless of whether the function is linear or nonlinear.) If the function is linear, the slope is the same at all points. If it is
nonlinear, the slope is different at each point on the curve. *The slope at any
one point is equal to the slope of the tangent to the curve at that point.* In
a nonlinear function, marginal revenue will always vary with different levels
of output. For example, in Figure 3.9, $MR = 3$ when $Q = 200$, but $MR = 2$
when $Q = 300$.

The slope of a curve is defined as the ratio of the distance on the
vertical (y) axis to the distance on the horizontal (x) axis. If we think of
the slope as the hypotenuse of a right triangle, then the vertical axis distance
and the horizontal axis distance become the opposite and adjacent legs of
the angle formed by the slope and the horizontal axis ($\angle \theta$ in Figure 3.11).
Three examples of such a triangle are shown in Figure 3.11, with hypotenuses d, d', and d''. The slopes of these hypotenuses represent the average
slopes of the curve over the segments they adjoin. However, the slope of the
curve at any particular point is defined more precisely as the slope of the
tangent to the curve at that point. An example in Figure 3.11 is line D. The
slope of D is the true slope of the curve at point X_1.

If we want to measure the slope at a particular point, such as X_1 in
Figure 3.11, we can do so by crude approximation. Selecting a ΔX gives us

a corresponding ΔY, which in turn gives us the hypotenuse d. Yet the slope of d is not the same as the slope of D, the true slope of the curve at X_1 —that is, the slope of the line tangent to the curve at X_1.

If we make ΔX smaller, ΔY is also smaller, and the hypotenuse of the triangle changes. The slope of d' is a closer approximation of the slope of D. As we continue to reduce ΔX even more, we get closer and closer to the true slope. As ΔX approaches zero, d, d', and d'' approach D; each succeeding d is a closer approximation of the slope of the curve at X_1. This is clear from the series of reducing triangles, and their hypotenuses—d, d', and d''— in Figure 3.11.

Thus the derivative of a function—which is simply the slope of the curve at a given point—can be expressed notationally as:

$$\frac{dy}{dx} = \lim_{\Delta x \to 0} \frac{\Delta y}{\Delta x} \tag{3-10}$$

which says that the ratio of a change in y, dy, over a change in x, dx, equals the limit of a finite change in y, Δy, over a finite change in x, Δx, as Δx approaches zero.[7] If y is a function of x, the derivative of y with respect to x is denoted as $\frac{d}{dx}(y)$ or $\frac{dy}{dx}$.

To plot curves and draw extremely tiny triangles is a bit awkward. To measure their sides accurately is very difficult. In fact, as Q approaches zero, the chore becomes impossible. What differential calculus does is to give us a set of rules with which to calculate the slopes—that is, the rate of change of functions—directly from the functions themselves, without going near a piece of graph paper. We need only to know the functional relationship between the dependent variable and the independent variable(s) and to assure that the functional relationship is continuous.

RULES OF DIFFERENTIATION

In this discussion we will initially assume that the dependent variable y is a function only of the independent variable x. We shall use the rules of differentiation to find the derivative of y with respect to x. This will give us an equation for the slope, dy/dx, of the function $y = f(x)$.

[7] Convention dictates the use of the symbols x and y for variables when an equation or statement of universal application is made. We could use $\frac{dR}{dQ} = \lim_{\Delta Q \to 0} \frac{\Delta R}{\Delta Q}$ just as easily. In fact, we will use such symbols when computing the derivative of a revenue function.

Rule I.   The derivative of a constant is zero. Thus, if $y = f(x) = k$, where k is a constant, then:

$$y = k$$

$$\frac{dy}{dx} = \frac{d}{dx}(y) = \frac{d}{dx}(k) = 0$$

Example: $y = 12$

$$\frac{dy}{dx} = \frac{d}{dx}(12) = 0$$

Rule II.   The derivative of an independent variable raised to the power of 1 is 1.[8] Thus, if $y = f(x) = x$, where x is the independent variable, then:

$$\frac{dy}{dx} = \frac{d}{dx}(x) = \frac{dx}{dx} = 1$$

Examples: $y = x$ $y = 7x$

$$\frac{dy}{dx} = \frac{d}{dx}(x) = 1 \qquad \frac{dy}{dx} = \frac{d}{dx}(7x) = 7$$

Rule III.   The derivative of an independent variable raised to a power is equal to the exponent times the variable raised to a power of one less than the original exponent. Thus, if $y = f(x) = x^n$, where x is the independent variable and n is the exponent,[9] then:

$$\frac{dy}{dx} = \frac{d}{dx}(x^n) = nx^{n-1}$$

Examples: $y = x^3$ $y = 5x^2$

$$\frac{dy}{dx} = \frac{d}{dx}(x^3) = 3x^2 \qquad \frac{dy}{dx} = \frac{d}{dx}(5x^2) = 10x$$

Rule IV.   The derivative of the product of two functions is the first function multiplied by the derivative of the second function plus the second function multiplied by the derivative of the first function. Thus, if $y = uv$, where u is a function of x, say $f(x)$, and v is another function of x, say $g(x)$, then $y = f(x) \cdot g(x)$, and

---

[8] Where 1 is a factor or a power, it is generally not expressed. Thus, x is really $(1)x^{(1)}$.
[9] Rules I and II are actually special cases of Rule III. Since $x^{(n-1)} = x^0$ when $n = 1$, and since anything raised to the power of zero is by definition equal to one, $nx^0 = n$.

$$\frac{dy}{dx} = \frac{d}{dx}(u \cdot v) = u\frac{d}{dx}(v) + v\frac{d}{dx}(u)$$

Example: $y = f(x) \cdot g(x)$, where $f(x) = x^2$ and $g(x) = 3x$

$y = x^2(3x)$ By substitution

$\dfrac{dy}{dx} = x^2\dfrac{d}{dx}(3x) + 3x\dfrac{d}{dx}(x^2)$ By Rule IV

$\dfrac{dy}{dx} = x^2 \cdot 3 + 3x \cdot 2x$ By Rules II and III

$\dfrac{dy}{dx} = 3x^2 + 6x^2$ By arithmetic

$\dfrac{dy}{dx} = 9x^2$ By arithmetic

Rule V. The derivative of a sum (or a difference) of two functions is equal to the sum (or the difference) of their derivatives. Thus, if $y = u + v$, where u is a function of x, say $f(x)$, and v is a function of x, say $g(x)$, then:

$$y = u + v = f(x) + g(x)$$

$$\frac{dy}{dx} = \frac{d}{dx}(u) + \frac{d}{dx}(v) = \frac{d}{dx}(f(x)) + \frac{d}{dx}(g(x))$$

Example: $y = f(x) + g(x)$, where $f(x) = x$ and $g(x) = x^2$

$y = x + x^2$ By substitution

$\dfrac{dy}{dx} = \dfrac{d}{dx}(x) + \dfrac{d}{dx}(x^2)$ By Rule V

$\dfrac{dy}{dx} = 1 + 2x$ By Rules II and III

Although calculus textbooks would give a separate rule for the derivative of a quotient, we shall not do so here. The quotient rule is awkward to use and is applicable only when there is a denominator other than a constant in one or more terms of an equation. Problems of this type can be easily solved with the product rule (Rule IV) by simply rearranging the equation so that all the variables appear in the numerator.

Example: $y = \dfrac{2}{x^3}$

$y = (2)(x^{-3})$ By algebraic manipulation[10]

$\dfrac{dy}{dx} = (2)(-3x^{-4})$ By Rule III

$\dfrac{dy}{dx} = -6x^{-4}$ By arithmetic

$\dfrac{dy}{dx} = \dfrac{-6}{x^4}$ By algebraic manipulation

Partial Derivatives. So far in our discussion of differential calculus we have assumed that y, the dependent variable, is always a function of *one* independent variable—that is, that $y = f(x)$. It is clear, however, that factors such as revenue, cost, and demand will often be a function of more than one variable. For instance, if a firm produces two products, Q and Z, then total revenue, R, will be dependent on the quantity of output of both products. This can be expressed as follows:

$R = P_1 Q + P_2 Z$, where

$P_1 =$ price of Product Q

$P_2 =$ price of Product Z

$Q =$ quantity of output of Product Q, and

$Z =$ quantity of output of Product Z

The total revenue function thus contains the two independent variables Q and Z. The relationship between a change in only one of these independent variables, say Q, and the corresponding change in R can be obtained by holding all other variables constant (that is, by assuming that their values are independent of the value of Q) and finding $\Delta R / \Delta Q$, the difference quotient of R and Q. If we let ΔQ approach 0, then the limit of $\Delta R / \Delta Q$ becomes a derivative. Since the function contains more than one independent variable, such a limit is called a *partial derivative,* in order to indicate that all other independent variables were held constant in obtaining it. Partial derivatives are denoted by ∂ (the Greek letter delta) rather than d (the symbol for the ordinary derivative).

---

[10] Whenever you bring a variable into the numerator from the denominator, you must change the sign of the exponent. For example:

$\dfrac{1}{x^2} = x^{-2}$ $\dfrac{4}{x^5} = 4 \cdot x^{-5}$ $\dfrac{1}{x} = x^{-1}$

The partial derivative of $R = P_1Q + P_2Z$ with respect to Q is:

$$\frac{\partial R}{\partial Q} = \frac{\partial}{\partial Q}(P_1Q + P_2Z)$$

$$\frac{\partial R}{\partial Q} = \frac{\partial}{\partial Q}(P_1Q) + \frac{\partial}{\partial Q}(P_2Z)$$

$$\frac{\partial R}{\partial Q} = P_1\left(\frac{\partial Q}{\partial Q}\right) + P_2\left(\frac{\partial Z}{\partial Q}\right)$$

But $\partial Q/\partial Q = 1$ by Rule II, and $\partial Z/\partial Q = 0$ by Rule I, since Z is held constant. Thus:

$$\frac{\partial R}{\partial Q} = P_1$$

Rule VI.   The partial derivative of a function containing more than one independent variable with respect to one of those variables is obtained by holding all other independent variables constant and finding the ordinary derivative with respect to the variable in question.

Example: $y = 5x^2 + 3xz + 2z + pz$, where x, p, and z are all independent variables

$$\frac{\partial y}{\partial x} = \frac{\partial}{\partial x}(5x^2 + 3xz + 2z + pz)$$

$$\frac{\partial y}{\partial x} = \frac{\partial}{\partial x}(5x^2) + \frac{\partial}{\partial x}(xz) + \frac{\partial}{\partial x}(2z) + \frac{\partial}{\partial x}(pz)$$

By Rule V

$$\frac{\partial y}{\partial x} = 10x + z\left(\frac{\partial x}{\partial x}\right) + x\left(\frac{\partial z}{\partial x}\right) + 2\left(\frac{\partial z}{\partial x}\right) + p\left(\frac{\partial z}{\partial x}\right) + z\left(\frac{\partial p}{\partial x}\right)$$

By Rules II, III, and IV

$$\frac{\partial y}{\partial x} = 10x + z$$

By Rule II $\left(\dfrac{\partial x}{\partial x} = 1\right)$ and Rule I

$\left(\dfrac{\partial z}{\partial x} = 0 \text{ and } \dfrac{\partial p}{\partial x} = 0, \text{ since } z \text{ and } p \text{ are held constant}\right)$

Similarly:

$$\frac{\partial y}{\partial z} = \frac{\partial}{\partial z}(5x^2 + 3xz + 2z + pz)$$

$$\frac{\partial y}{\partial z} = \frac{\partial}{\partial z}(5x^2) + \frac{\partial}{\partial z}(3xz) + \frac{\partial}{\partial z}(2z) + \frac{\partial}{\partial z}(pz)$$

By Rule V

$$\frac{\partial y}{\partial z} = 10\left(\frac{\partial x}{\partial z}\right) + 3x\left(\frac{\partial z}{\partial z}\right) + 3z\left(\frac{\partial x}{\partial z}\right) + 2\left(\frac{\partial z}{\partial z}\right) + z\left(\frac{\partial p}{\partial z}\right) + p\left(\frac{\partial z}{\partial z}\right)$$

By Rules II and III

$$\frac{\partial y}{\partial z} = 3x + 2 + p$$
By Rule II $\left(\frac{\partial z}{\partial z} = 1\right)$ and Rule I

$\left(\frac{\partial x}{\partial z} = 0 \text{ and } \frac{\partial p}{\partial z} = 0,\right.$ since x and p are held constant$)$

We can place our rules in list form for convenient reference:

RULES OF DIFFERENTIAL CALCULUS

Given: $y = f(x), u = g(x), v = h(x)$

I. If $y = k$, then $\frac{dy}{dx} = 0$

II. If $y = x$, then $\frac{dy}{dx} = 1$

III. If $y = x^n$, then $\frac{dy}{dx} = nx^{n-1}$

IV. If $y = u \cdot v$, then $\frac{dy}{dx} = u \cdot \frac{dv}{dx} + v \cdot \frac{du}{dx}$

V. If $y = u \pm v$, then $\frac{dy}{dx} = \frac{du}{dx} \pm \frac{dy}{dx}$

Given: $y = f(x, z)$

VI. If $y = f(x, z)$, then $\frac{\partial y}{\partial x} = \frac{\partial}{\partial x}(f(x, z))$, with z held constant

Examples.   We can best illustrate the use of our rules of differentiation by taking the derivative of y with respect to x for various types of equations:

Given

$y = 3$	$\dfrac{dy}{dx} = 0$	By Rule I
$y = x$	$\dfrac{dy}{dx} = 1$	By Rule II
$y = x^3$	$\dfrac{dy}{dx} = 3x^2$	By Rule III
$y = x \cdot z$	$\dfrac{dy}{dx} = x \cdot \dfrac{dz}{dx} + z \cdot \dfrac{dx}{dx}$	By Rule IV
	$\dfrac{dy}{dx} = x \cdot \dfrac{dz}{dx} + z$	By cancellation
$y = x^4 + x$	$\dfrac{dy}{dx} = 4x^3 + \dfrac{dx}{dx}$	By Rule V
	$\dfrac{dy}{dx} = 4x^3 + 1$	By cancellation
$y = 3x^4$	$\dfrac{dy}{dx} = 12x^3$	By Rule III
$y = \dfrac{1}{x^3}$	$y = x^{-3}$	By algebraic manipulation
	$\dfrac{dy}{dx} = -3x^{-4}$	By Rule III
	$\dfrac{dy}{dx} = \dfrac{-3}{x^4}$	By algebraic manipulation
$y = \sqrt{x}$	$y = x^{\frac{1}{2}}$	By change of symbol (Note that $\sqrt[n]{x}$ may be written as $x^{1/n}$.)
	$\dfrac{dy}{dx} = \dfrac{1}{2} x^{-\frac{1}{2}}$	By Rule III
	$\dfrac{dy}{dx} = \dfrac{1}{2\sqrt{x}}$	By algebraic manipulation
$y = 400 + 2x^2$	$\dfrac{dy}{dx} = 4x$	By Rules V and III
$y = xz^2 + 5z + 3x$	$\dfrac{\partial y}{\partial x} = z^2 + 3$	By Rules II, III, IV, and VI

PRACTICAL APPLICATIONS

Let us now turn to the applications of differential calculus to the problems confronting the firm. Assume that the marketing research group of a large conglomerate corporation has analyzed its different markets and has estimated the sensitivity of sales to changes in price for its various product lines. It has used these relationships to derive equations for revenue as a function of quantities sold $(R = f(Q))$ for each product. The marketing manager wants to know how much additional revenue will result from a small change in quantity, starting at the present level of output. Stated mathematically, the question becomes, "What is the change in revenue with respect to a change in quantity at a given output?" or, more precisely, "What is the derivative of the revenue function?" Given the following revenue functions for each product, let's find out.

Product A

$$R = \$8500 \qquad \text{Given}$$

$$\frac{dR}{dQ} = 0 \qquad \text{By Rule I}$$

Here revenue is constant; it will not change with output. This situation may seem unlikely, but might occur, for example, if Product A were fresh water and the firm had agreed to provide all that a particular customer needed for a fixed price of $8500.

Product B

$$R = Q \qquad \text{Given}$$

$$\frac{dR}{dQ} = 1 \qquad \text{By Rule II}$$

Here revenue will change in direct proportion to quantity. There will be a $1 increase in revenue for each additional unit sold. The fact that price remains constant (it is always $1) suggests that Product B is sold under conditions of pure competition—that the output of the firm is such a small portion of the output of the entire industry that the firm cannot influence the market price. Product B might be corn, wheat, eggs, or livestock.

Product C

$$R = 8Q \qquad \text{Given}$$

$$\frac{dR}{dQ} = 8 \qquad \text{By Rule II}$$

Product C is in the same situation as Product B, except that the ratio of revenue change to quantity change is $8 for every unit sold. ($8 is obviously the price.) Notice that the coefficient, "8," of the variable Q is carried on into the derivative. We simply multiply it by the derivative of the variable—in this case, 1. ($8 \cdot dQ/dQ = 8 \cdot 1 = 8$)

Product D

$$R = 200Q - Q^2 \qquad \text{Given}$$

$$\frac{dR}{dQ} = \frac{d}{dQ}(200Q) - \frac{d}{dQ}(Q^2) \qquad \text{By Rule V}$$

$$\frac{dR}{dQ} = 200 - 2Q \qquad \text{By Rules II and III}$$

Here the revenue change is not proportional to changes in output but varies depending on the level of output, Q, at the time of change. For example, if Q is at 60, dR/dQ equals $80. Hence revenue will change by $80 for a 1-unit change in quantity. If Q is at 95, dR/dQ equals 10, and a change in output of 1 unit will change revenue by only $10. Obviously, the price of Product D varies with the quantity sold. It may be a special piece of electronics test equipment, with a limited market and competitively priced substitutes.

Product E

$$R = (5Q - 9000)(100 - Q^2) \qquad \text{Given}$$

$$\frac{dR}{dQ} = (5Q - 9000) \cdot \frac{d}{dQ}(100 - Q^2)$$

$$+ (100 - Q^2) \cdot \frac{d}{dQ} \cdot (5Q - 9000) \qquad \text{By Rule IV}$$

$$\frac{dR}{dQ} = (5Q - 9000)(-2Q) + (100 - Q^2)(5) \qquad \text{By Rules V, I, II, and III}$$

$$\frac{dR}{dQ} = -10Q^2 + 18{,}000Q + 500 - 5Q^2 \qquad \text{By multiplication}$$

$$\frac{dR}{dQ} = -15Q^2 + 18{,}000Q + 500 \qquad \text{By collecting terms}$$

An alternative method in this case would be first to multiply and collect terms, then to differentiate:

$$R = (5Q - 9000)(100 - Q^2) \qquad \text{Given}$$
$$R = 5000Q - 5Q^3 - 900{,}000 + 9000Q^2 \qquad \text{By multiplication}$$
$$R = -5Q^3 + 9000Q^2 + 500Q - 900{,}000 \qquad \text{By collecting terms}$$
$$\frac{dR}{dQ} = -15Q^2 + 18{,}000Q + 500 \qquad \begin{array}{l}\text{By Rules V, II, I}\\ \text{and III}\end{array}$$

Here revenue will increase sharply as we initially increase output, Q. However, as output approaches 600, the rate of change, dR/dQ, decreases. (Were we to graph the revenue function for Product E, the curve would move up steeply at first, then begin to level off as Q increased. This suggests that the market for Product E begins to saturate above 600 units, and a greater total output could be sold only at reduced prices. For example, at $Q = 600$, $dR/dQ = 5{,}400{,}500$. At $Q = 1000$, $dR/dQ = 3{,}000{,}500$.

Product E might be a jet airliner, able to operate profitably only on a limited number of routes. In order to increase sales, the manufacturer would have to reduce the price until purchase became profitable for more airlines. (Remember that price for the seller is cost for the buyer.)

Products C and D

$$R = 8Q + 200Z - Z^2 + 5QZ \qquad \text{Given}$$

$$\frac{\partial R}{\partial Q} = \frac{\partial}{\partial Q}(8Q) + \frac{\partial}{\partial Q}(200Z)$$

$$\qquad - \frac{\partial}{\partial Q}(Z^2) + \frac{\partial}{\partial Q}(5QZ) \qquad \text{By Rule V}$$

$$\frac{\partial R}{\partial Q} = 8 + 0 - 0 + 5Z$$

$$\frac{\partial R}{\partial Q} = 8 + 5Z$$

By Rules II, III, and VI (Note that $\frac{\partial}{\partial Q}(5QZ) = 5Q\left(\frac{\partial Z}{\partial Q}\right) + 5Z\left(\frac{\partial Q}{\partial Q}\right)$ from Rule IV. Since Z is held constant, $\frac{\partial Z}{\partial Q} = 0.$)

In this case, revenue is a function of the outputs of two products. The output of Product C is Q, and the output of Product D is Z. The fact that the last term in the total revenue function is positive $(+5QZ)$ indicates that the two products are *complements*. As either Q or Z increases, the value of the last term increases. Such a revenue function is appropriate to goods that create positive demands for other goods. Examples of complementary goods are shoes and shoelaces, automobiles and automobile tires, safety razors and razor blades. If the last term were negative, the two products would be *supplements*—that is, increased demand for one good would decrease the demand for the other. Examples of supplementary goods are electric shavers and razor blades, tubeless tires and tubes.

MR AND dR/dQ

When applied to a revenue function, the derivative provides a measure of the change of revenue with respect to a change in output; the derivative of the revenue function is therefore equal to marginal revenue. This can be stated in several ways notationally, as follows:

$$MR = \frac{dR}{dQ} = R' = \lim_{\Delta Q \to 0} \frac{\Delta R}{\Delta Q} = \frac{df(Q, P)}{dQ} \qquad (3\text{-}11)$$

This exposes a slight contradiction in terms. Whereas we previously defined MR as $\Delta R/\Delta Q$, we now define MR as dR/dQ, which is the instantaneous rate of change of R with respect to Q. $\Delta R/\Delta Q$ will equal dR/dQ only in linear function, as we saw by comparing Figure 3.2 with Figure 3.3.

We can escape this dilemma by recognizing that economists are more pragmatic than mathematicians and marketers are more pragmatic than either one. In short, we shall use $MR = dR/dQ$ when convenient and $MR = \Delta R/\Delta Q$ when that form suits our purpose.

For example, in solving optimization problems, which we will introduce shortly, the derivative is most convenient. However, in estimating the added revenue the firm will receive by selling additional units of output, $\Delta R/\Delta Q$ is more suitable; one can hardly deal in infinitely small changes in revenue resulting from an infinitely small change in output. We will find it practical to deal in one airplane, one ton of steel, one carload of appliances, or one case of breakfast cereal.

In making quantitative decisions, we generally think of marginal revenue as that additional increment of revenue resulting from an additional unit of output. Or, conversely, marginal revenue can be the loss of revenue resulting from the deletion of a unit of output. For all practical purposes, this ratio is accurately stated by the derivative of the revenue function.[11] In fact, at large levels of output such as we find in the automobile, appliance,

---

[11] The derivative is a ratio and hence has no unit of measurement. "Marginal" conventionally means a single unit. For example, marginal cost is the cost of producing one additional unit. "Incremental" implies more than one unit, as in the "incremental" revenue from the sale of ten cars. However, the two terms are sometimes interchanged.

and food industries, it may be practical to deal in increments of a dozen or even several hundred units. The derivative of the revenue function is still appropriate in these cases, although it becomes less precise as the size of Δx increases—a fact made obvious in Figure 3.11.

MARGINAL COST

Now that we are armed with the necessary mathematical skills, we can address ourselves to the question of marginal cost. We define marginal cost as the ratio of the change in cost to a change in revenue. It is also the additional increment of cost resulting from an additional increment of output. In more mathematical language, marginal cost is the derivative of the cost function, expressed symbolically as

$$MC = \frac{dC}{dQ} \qquad (3\text{-}12)$$

However, in dealing with applied problems, it may be convenient to consider MC as equal to $\Delta C/\Delta Q$, where ΔC and ΔQ are not infinitesimal values but manageable quantities. (ΔQ would normally be one unit of output, and ΔC the additional cost resulting from the production and sale of ΔQ.) Even large values may sometimes be appropriate. Under these circumstances, we shall consider the derivative of the cost function a sufficiently accurate estimate of $\Delta C/\Delta Q$ for all practical purposes.

Computation of MC. Let us assume that we have analyzed the production and marketing tasks involved in the manufacture and sale of a number of products, F through J. We have computed their respective cost functions and now must determine the additional costs that their producers will incur if they are to make and sell larger quantities of the different goods.

Product F

$$C = 20,000 \qquad \text{Given}$$

$$\frac{dC}{dQ} = 0 \qquad \text{By Rule I}$$

Here, marginal revenue is zero; the cost will not change with changes in output. All costs are fixed costs, and there are no variable costs. This suggests that Product F is a service, where the cost of operation remains constant regardless of the number of customers. For example, Firm A might operate a movie theater, a skating rink, a parking lot, or marina.

Product G

$$C = .05Q \qquad\qquad \text{Given}$$

$$\frac{dC}{dQ} = .05 \qquad\qquad \text{By Rule II}$$

Here cost varies directly with quantity, by a ratio of 1:20, throughout the range of output. There is no fixed cost term; hence the only cost is the variable cost of 5 cents per unit. The cost function is thus linear, and its derivative is equal to a constant, .05.

A linear cost function is very unusual; so, too, is a cost function with no fixed cost term. Thus we are limited in our examples, especially if we include marketing in the cost. Newspapers sold by an independent news vender may be the best illustration. Here the vender will pay exactly the same amount for each additional paper he buys within his range of possible outputs. His overhead—that is, his fixed cost—may be limited to a bicycle or an automobile that he would own anyway. The cost of operating his vehicle in support of his paper route will be in direct proportion to the length of his route, and hence to the number of papers he sells. This could easily be a linear function that would be included in the variable cost. Product G could be a paper costing $3\frac{1}{2}$ cents to purchase plus $1\frac{1}{2}$ cents to deliver, with no fixed expenses. The production function would be $C = F + VQ$, where $F = 0$ and $V = .035Q + .015Q$, or simply $C = .05Q$.

Product H

$$C = 8000 + .01Q \qquad\qquad \text{Given}$$

$$\frac{dC}{dQ} = .01 \qquad\qquad \text{By Rule II}$$

The cost function for Product H is essentially the same as that for Product G, except for the fixed cost of $8000. The ratio of variable cost to quantity remains the same (here, it is .01) throughout the range of possible outputs. Product H might be a $\frac{1}{2}$-inch bolt, a small piston, an oil plug, or any other item appropriate to a fixed-rate tool (one with a constant rate of output) such as an automatic screw machine. After the initial outlay of $8000, the variable cost of production remains constant. Each additional unit will cost the same as the preceding unit.

Product I

$$C = 10,000 + 4Q + .0005Q^2 \qquad \text{Given}$$

$$\frac{dC}{dQ} = 4 + .001Q \qquad\qquad \text{By Rule V, I, II, and III}$$

Here the cost of building additional units will be close to $4 each until Q becomes large, say over 1000 units. At $Q = 10,000$, an additional $14 of cost will be incurred for each additional unit of output. To determine the product's marginal cost at any point, we substitute that level of output for Q. At outputs of 200, 5000, 10,000, and 20,000, for example, marginal cost (dC/dQ) will be $4.20, $9, $14, and $24 respectively.

The increasing cost of producing Product I implies that the manufacturing process involved becomes less efficient—perhaps due to an overloading of plant and equipment—or that proportionately larger promotional efforts are needed as output increases. Product I might be a Christmas toy or an automobile accessory.

Product J

$$C = 1,000,000 + 7000Q + 2Q^2 + .001Q^3 \qquad \text{Given}$$

$$\frac{dC}{dQ} = 7000 + 4Q + .003Q^2 \qquad \text{By Rules I, II, and III}$$

Product J's cost function is similar to Product I's, except that it is a third-order equation—that is, the highest exponent is 3. Thus the cost will increase more rapidly as output approaches large values. At an output of 1000 units, marginal cost is $14,000. At $Q = 2000$, it will cost $27,000, nearly twice as much, to build and market an additional unit.

Rapidly increasing costs at high levels of output are typical of products that are nonessentials or luxury items, where the cost of manufacturing, and especially of marketing, becomes exorbitant once the initial market is satisfied. (This is particularly true if the list price is held constant and adjustments in the real price are included in the cost function as "discounts.") Product J might be a light airplane, a cabin cruiser, or a home videotape recorder.

Products H and I

$$C = 8000 + .01Q + 10,000 + 4Z$$
$$+ .0005Z^2 - .001QZ \qquad \text{Given}$$

$$\frac{\partial C}{\partial Q} = .01 - .001Z \qquad \text{By Rules I, II, III, V, and VI}$$

This function represents the cost of producing two products together. The output of Product H is Q, and the output of Product I is Z. The fact that the last term of the cost function is negative ($-.001QZ$) indicates that production of the two products together reduces costs—that is, the two products are *complements in production*. This cost reduction is attributable to economies of scale created through production efficiencies or through the use of common inputs. Examples of such products are station wagons and standard passenger cars, canned peas and frozen peas. If the last term of the cost function were positive, the two products would be *supplements in production*. With supplementary products, production costs are higher than they would be if the goods were produced separately, because of total output limitations.

THEORY OF THE FIRM CONFIRMED

At this point, let us return to the objective of the firm—namely, the maximization of profit. Since profit is the positive difference between total revenue and total cost ($\pi = R - C$ where $R > C$), it will be maximum wherever the absolute difference between the revenue and cost functions is greatest. We can determine this point graphically by measuring the distance between the two functions, as in Figure 3.12. The distance between the revenue

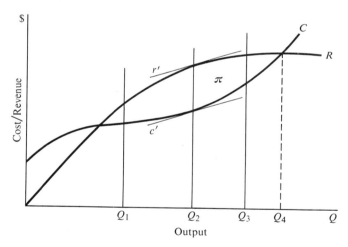

FIGURE 3.12
Cost and revenue functions

curve, R, and the cost curve, C, is greatest at output Q_2. Hence profit, π, is maximum at Q_2.

If we look closely, we can see that the slopes of the two curves, indicated by the tangential lines r' and c', are parallel at Q_2. They are by definition the derivatives of the two functions. If the slopes are parallel, then the derivatives of the two functions must be equal at that point. Hence

$dR/dQ = dC/dQ$ at the maximum-profit output. In conventional terms, we would say that profit is at a maximum when marginal revenue equals marginal cost. Or, π is maximum when $MR = MC$.

We can confirm this intuitively by examining the slopes of the curves immediately before and after the point where profit becomes maximum.[12] At Q_1 the slopes are not parallel; the slope of R is greater than the slope of C. Obviously the derivatives of the two functions will not be equal at Q_1. Profit is clearly not maximized.

As we move to the right of Q_1, the distance between R and C increases, reaching a maximum at Q_2. Beyond Q_2, the slopes are again unequal, but now the slope of C is greater than the slope of R. As we move from Q_2 toward Q_3, therefore, the distance between R and C decreases. To continue to move farther to the right will only make matters worse, as the curves come closer together. At Q_4 the curves touch; the distance between them—hence the profit—is reduced to zero. Beyond this intersection, the firm's demand for red ink increases sharply. Nowhere are the slopes of the two curves—hence the derivatives of the functions—the same, except at the maximum-profit position, Q_2.

We have now arrived once more at the fundamental argument of the theory of the firm—that the firm should increase output until the revenue derived from an additional unit of output is equaled by the cost of producing and marketing that additional unit. In short, it should set MR equal to MC for maximum profit (or minimum loss, if total revenue never exceeds total cost).

This argument refutes many of the performance criteria espoused by the business community. The objective of the firm is *not* served by maximizing revenue, setting new unit sales records, or minimizing cost. It is served by selecting a level of output that will maximize the positive difference between total revenue and total cost. This has been demonstrated again and again by corporate profit-and-loss statements showing an increase in unit sales and a decrease in profits, or a new high in revenue and a decrease in profits, or an increase in cost and an increase in profits.

PRACTICAL APPLICATION OF THE THEORY OF THE FIRM

Having become familiar with the theory of the firm, we can now proceed to the most fundamental problem of optimization—that of selecting the quantity of production, the level of marketing effort, and the price that will maximize profit.

We have said that the total cost function includes all the production and marketing costs associated with producing *and* selling a given quantity

---

[12] A more rigorous mathematical proof is found in Appendix I, p. 654.

of output. We know also that the total revenue function depends on price and the quantity sold and that generally we must decrease price in order to sell larger quantities of output. Given the demand function—that is, the relationship between the quantity sold and the price—and the total cost function, we can select the level of output that will maximize profit. Once output is known, then price, total revenue, and total cost can easily be computed by the following steps:

1. Solve the demand equation for P.
2. Substitute the right-hand side of the equation in Step 1 for P in the total revenue equation, $R = PQ$.
3. Find MR by differentiating the revenue equation obtained from Step 2.
4. Find MC by differentiating the cost equation.
5. Set MR equal to MC and solve for Q.
6. Find P, C, and then π by substituting the value found for Q in the appropriate equations.

For example, assume that a firm's market analysts estimate the demand function of a new product to be $Q = 20,000 - 1000P$, where Q is the quantity demanded—that is, the output that will be sold at any price, P. Complying with Step 1, we get the following expression for P:

$$P = 20 - \frac{Q}{1000} \qquad \text{By algebraic manipulation}$$

Following Step 2, we then substitute the right-hand side of our equation for P in the revenue equation, $R = PQ$, and get

$$R = \left(20 - \frac{Q}{1000}\right) \cdot Q \text{ or} \qquad \text{By substitution}$$

$$R = 20Q - \frac{Q^2}{1000} \qquad \text{By arithmetic}$$

Following Step 3, we find marginal revenue, MR, by taking the derivative, dR/dQ, of the revenue function from Step 2.

$$R = 20Q - \frac{Q^2}{1000} \qquad \text{Given from Step 2}$$

$$MR = \frac{dR}{dQ} = 20 - \frac{2Q}{1000} \qquad \text{By rules of calculus}$$

$$MR = 20 - \frac{Q}{500} \qquad \text{By division}$$

With the assistance of the manufacturing and marketing departments, the accounting department computes an equation for the total cost of producing and selling any output, Q. This gives us an estimated cost function of $C = 40,000 + 2Q$, where \$40,000 is the fixed cost and \$2 is the variable cost. We can now, as directed by Step 4, take the derivative, dC/dQ, of the cost equation to find marginal cost, MC:

$$C = 40,000 + 2Q \qquad \text{Given}$$

$$MC = \frac{dC}{dQ} = 2 \qquad \text{By rules of calculus}$$

$$MC = 2$$

Following Step 5, we set MR equal to MC—which is the condition that maximizes profit according to the theory of the firm—and solve for Q. This value of Q will be our optimum output for profit maximization.

$$MR = MC \qquad \text{Condition at maximum profit}$$

$$20 - \frac{Q}{500} = 2 \qquad \text{By substitution}$$

$$Q = 9000 \qquad \text{By algebraic manipulation}$$

Having determined the optimum output, Q, we can easily find the optimum price, P; the total revenue, R; the total cost, C; and the maximum profit, π. We simply comply with Step 6, and substitute 9000 for Q in the appropriate equations. Thus,

$$P = 20 - \frac{Q}{1000} \qquad \text{Price equation from Step 1}$$

$$P = 20 - \frac{9000}{1000} \qquad \text{By substitution}$$

$$P = \$11 \qquad \text{By arithmetic}$$

$$R = PQ \qquad \text{Revenue equation}$$
$$R = 11(9000) \qquad \text{By substitution}$$
$$R = 99,000 \qquad \text{By arithmetic}$$

$$C = 40,000 + 2Q \qquad \text{Given}$$
$$C = 40,000 + 2(9000) \qquad \text{By substitution}$$
$$C = 58,000 \qquad \text{By arithmetic}$$

$$\pi = R - C \qquad \text{Profit equation}$$
$$\pi = 99,000 - 58,000 \qquad \text{By substitution}$$
$$\pi = \$41,000 \qquad \text{By arithmetic}$$

Optimum output, Q, is 9000 units. To sell all these untis, the firm must set price at or below $11. The $11 price is optimum because it will produce the most revenue at the optimum output. To offer the product at a lower price would only reduce revenue when output, Q, has been set at 9000. An output of 9000 and a per-unit price of $11 yields $99,000 in revenue, at a total cost of $58,000. The firm's profit of $41,000 is the maximum profit possible.

Having determined the optimum output, we know what the total cost will be; hence we have the budget for this particular product. The distribution of this budget between manufacturing and marketing will be arrived at by reviewing the breakdown of the cost figures that the accounting department used to compile the cost function. (Presumably the marketing manager provided the accountants with the costs of the different levels of marketing effort that would be needed to successfully market the different quantities of output.)

Marginal Profit Equals Zero at Maximum Profit. Using the graph of the cost and revenue functions (Figure 3.12), we can readily plot the profit function. Since $\pi = R - C$, we can obtain the profit, π, at any output, Q, simply by measuring the distance between the revenue and cost curves at that particular point. If we plot the profit function throughout the range of Q, as in Figure 3.13, we will need the lower part of our graph, where the vertical

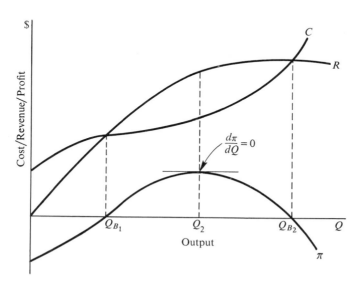

FIGURE 3.13
Revenue, cost, and profit

axis is negative. Profit will be negative—that is, the firm will be operating at a loss—anywhere outside the two break-even points, Q_{B_1} and Q_{B_2}.

Profit will continue to increase (hence its slope will be positive) until the point of maximum profit is reached, at output Q_2. Beyond Q_2, the optimum output, the slope of the profit curve will be negative, as profit will decline with increases in output.

At Q_2 the slope of the profit function is neither positive nor negative. The only value that has the characteristic of being neither positive nor negative is zero. Hence, at Q_2—the point where the profit curve has stopped climbing but is not yet descending—the slope is zero. In other words, the rate of change of profit at Q_2 is zero. Likewise, the derivative of the profit function is zero at the point of maximum profit. In notational form,

$$\frac{d\pi}{dQ} = 0, \text{ where } \pi \text{ is maximum} \tag{3–13}$$

This equation gives us a slightly different method for determining optimum output and maximum profit when price is known. This is a practical skill, as a firm is frequently confronted with a predetermined price. For example, in a purely competitive market, such as that for wheat or soybeans, no one firm can influence price. In an oligopolistic market,[13] such as that for steel or cement, the individual company cannot significantly influence price. An exception occurs where one firm is the dominant firm in an oligopoly and sets the price that must be followed by all the other producers.

To illustrate, let us assume an established market price of $450 for a particular product and a cost (supply) function as follows:

$$C = 1500 + 3Q^2$$

By substituting PQ for R, we can construct an explicit profit function and solve for optimum quantity and maximum profit:

$\pi = R - C$	Profit equation
$\pi = P \cdot Q - C = 450Q - (1500 + 3Q^2)$	By substitution $(R = P \cdot Q$ and $C = 1500 + 3Q^2)$
$\pi = -1500 + 450Q - 3Q^2$	By substitution and arithmetic
$\frac{d\pi}{dQ} = 450 - 6Q$	By differentiation

[13] An oligopolistic market is one in which only a few firms produce all the output. A restrictive case of oligopoly is duopoly, in which only two firms produce all the output.

$$\frac{d\pi}{dQ} = 450 - 6Q = 0$$ The condition of profit maximization

$$-6Q = -450$$ By algebraic manipulation

$$Q = 75$$ By arithmetic

$\pi = -1500 + 450(75) - 3(75)^2$ By substitution
$\pi = -1500 + 33,750 - 10,575$ By arithmetic
$\pi = 24,675$ By arithmetic

Thus we have an optimum output of 75 units and a maximum profit of $24,675.

Linear vs. Nonlinear Functions. In the examples given thus far, either one or both of the revenue and cost functions has been an equation with order greater than 1.[14] That is, they have had at least one term with

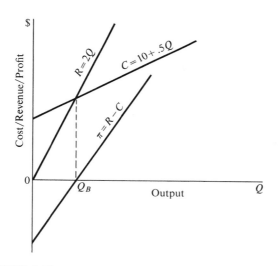

FIGURE 3.14
Linear cost vs. linear revenue functions

---

[14] A first-order equation has no term with an exponent greater than 1. For example, $y = 3x$, $y = 6x + 2$, and $R = P \cdot Q$ are all first-order equations. A second-order equation has at least one term with the exponent 2. Thus, $y = x^2$, $y = x^2 + x - 5$, and $C = 100 + Q^2$ are second-order equations. A third-order equation has at least one term with the exponent 3, and so on. The term with the largest exponent determines the order of the equation. For example, $y = x^3 + 2x^2 + 5x - k$ is a third-order equation.

an exponent greater than 1. Given this condition, a function is nonlinear. If both functions were first-order equations, both would be linear and could cross only at one point. Given this condition, we would have no optimum output. Profit would simply become greater and greater once the break-even point, Q_B, had been passed. This is shown graphically in Figure 3.14.

In this situation, the rational producer would increase output toward infinity and watch his profit grow accordingly. Unfortunately, this condition does not exist in the real world; sooner or later the firm must find itself on the ascending portion of the classical U-shaped cost curve (Figure 3.4), where production, and particularly marketing, costs begin to escalate rapidly. Theoretically, the revenue curve must eventually bend downward as lower prices become necessary in order to sell more units of output. The practical exception to this is the very small firm in a very large and competitive industry.

Occasionally, a firm is confronted with a linear revenue function because price is fixed over the range of output within which the company can operate. This would be the case in a purely competitive industry, where the firm's output is too insignificant to affect market price. It might also be the case in a regulated industry.

Mathematical manipulation, as well as graphical presentation, is easier with a linear function than with a nonlinear function. For this reason, a market analyst may find it convenient to express the revenue function as linear. To do so, he must consider price as being a fixed value. He may accommodate this problem by considering any change in price as a "discount" and including it in the cost function, which will probably be nonlinear anyway. For example, if price must be lowered from $20 to $18 to increase sales from 10,000 to 13,000 units, price—for purpose of computation—may be held at $20 if cost is increased by $2 per unit. This practice is not alien to the marketplace. Many firms, such as building-material suppliers, hold their published prices constant while adjusting their discounts to accommodate changes in supply or in the market demand.

The composition of the cost, revenue, and profit functions and their mathematical forms are explored in depth in Part III. However, the linear or nonlinear quality of these functions has no bearing on the essential nature of the profit maximization objective and its realization through marginal analysis. As long as output is extended to the point where marginal revenue equals marginal cost, the economic objective of the firm will be achieved.

Summary of Marketing and the Firm

ORGANIZATION OF THE FIRM. The firm is an economic organism, composed generally of land, capital, labor, and technology. Its basic functions are product design and development, manufacturing, and marketing, although it may specialize in only one of these. The tasks performed by marketing are pricing, product determination and mix, distribution, promotion (which includes advertising and personal selling), and marketing research. Some of these tasks are handled entirely by the marketing division, while others are shared with engineering, manufacturing, or one of the staff departments. Each division and department competes with the others for the limited resources of the firm.

VARIOUS ROLES OF MARKETING MANAGEMENT. From the marketer's viewpoint, it is convenient to categorize industries as consumer-goods producers, industrial-goods producers, service industries, and government contractors. The use of the five basic marketing instruments differs among these industries, because the opportunities for the use of marketing instruments, and the restrictions imposed on them, vary. This difference in marketing environments makes for different roles for marketing management.

OBJECTIVES OF THE FIRM. Marketing is not an end unto itself; rather, it serves the firm in the achievement of its goals. The most important goal of the firm is economic—the maximization of profit in the long run. Profit, or economic surplus, is the best criterion of performance, regardless of a society's political and economic orientation. It is also the basic criterion for management decisions. However, the profit criterion is subject to legal and moral constraints and must compete with noneconomic goals.

THEORY OF THE FIRM. The fundamental argument of the theory of the firm is that profit is maximized by increasing output until the cost of the last increment of output—called marginal cost—equals the revenue from the last increment of output—called marginal revenue. In other words, profit is at a maximum when marginal revenue equals marginal cost. This condition exists when the derivative of the cost function, dC/dQ, equals the derivative of the revenue function, dR/dQ. The technique management uses to compute the derivatives is differential calculus. Given explicit cost and revenue functions, management can invoke the simple rules of differential calculus to compute optimum output, optimum price, and maximum profit. In addition, the firm can calculate the change in profit that would result from a change in such marketing variables as advertising, price, product cost, and personal selling, as well as in demand itself.

Questions and Problems

1. Within the basic functions of the firm there are subsidiary functions that affect revenue and costs. Often their effect on revenue is difficult to measure, as is the case with plant safety and institutional advertising. Name some subsidiary functions and suggest a basis for their appraisal. How would you allocate resources to these activities?
2. What are some of the constraints and conflicting goals that hinder the maximization of profit? Which of these may reduce profit in the short run but increase it in the long run?
3. Which of the constraints and conflicting goals mentioned in question 2 are especially significant to the marketing manager? Why?
4. Why are maximization of sales, maximization of revenue, and minimization of cost generally inappropriate goals for the firm?
5. Find the first derivative of y with respect to x in each of the following equations. Cite the rule(s) of calculus required for your solution.

a. $y = 9$

b. $y = x$

c. $y = x^5$

d. $y = 3x^3$

e. $y = x^3 + 2x^3 - 5$

f. $y = f(x) \cdot g(x)$

g. $y = x^4(2x^2)$

h. $y = x^2(\sqrt{x})$

i. $y = \dfrac{1}{x^2}$

j. $y = x^3 + 100x^2 - x + 250$

k. $y = x^5 + x^{-2} + k$

l. $y = 30x^6 - \dfrac{50}{x^3} + 2x^2 - \dfrac{3}{\sqrt{x}}$

6. Find the marginal revenue for each of the following revenue functions.

a. $R = 10{,}500$

b. $R = 3 \cdot 5Q$

c. $R = 300Q - Q^2$

d. $R = 500 + 10Q - Q3$

e. $R = P \cdot Q$

f. $R = P \cdot Q$, where $Q = 100 - 2P$

7. Find the marginal cost for each of the following cost functions.

    a. $C = 200,000$ c. $C = 5000 + 10Q + Q^2$

    b. $C = 5Q$ d. $C = 10,000 + (500Q^{-1})(2Q^2)$

8. The sales manager for Product A believes he can sell an additional 2000 units, at a price of $8, if he runs a series of small ads in *Life* magazine. These ads will cost a total of $8000. The 2000 units will add $9000 to the present manufacturing and distribution expense. Should the marketing manager approve the idea?

9. Find the optimum quantity, optimum price, and maximum profit for Product B, which has the following demand and cost functions:

    a. $Q_D = 4000 - 20P$

    b. $C = 3500 + 4Q$

10. What is the break-even quantity and revenue for Product B in question 9?

11. Firm A's advertising agency believes that an increase of $1000 in the introductory advertising budget will increase the sales of Product B above by 50 units. Should the firm's marketing manager approve this increase? Why?

12. a. Product C requires $1,000,000 in plant and equipment, which will be depreciated to zero over the life of the product. Another $1,000,000 is required over the life of the product to cover overhead expense and advertising. In addition, a budget of $500,000 is necessary for introductory promotion. The per-unit variable production cost is $8. Salesmen's commission is a flat $2 per unit. A market study suggests a demand for Product C that can be expressed mathematically as $300,000 - 5000P$, where P is price. Is this a profitable item? What is the optimum quantity and price? What is the maximum profit (or minimum loss)?

    b. The sales manager assigned to Product C believes that the demand for his product can be increased by more aggressive personal selling. He feels the necessary incentive would be provided by adding $1 per unit to the salesmen's commission. In talks with the market analyst who directed the survey for Product C, the demand equation was changed to $Q_D = 300,000 - 4800P$ to reflect the increase in sales that was expected to result from the more generous commission. Should the marketing manager approve the increase in the commission? Why or why not?

  c. The market analyst suggests that the demand for Product C could be improved to $Q_D = 300,000 - 4500P$ if an additional \$90,000 were allotted to the advertising budget. (Assume that the salesmen's commission is held at \$2 per unit.) Is this a good idea? Is it a better alternative than (1) increasing sales commissions or (2) leaving everything the same?

  d. The marketing manager wants to know whether he should increase both the advertising budget, as suggested in question 12. c., and the sales commission for Product C. Has he enough information to make this decision? If not, what other data does he need?

13. Product D is a standard industrial good manufactured by hundreds of firms. None is large enough to influence price, which is \$20 per barrel. Your firm can easily enter this market with a cost function of $10,000 + 5Q + .003Q^2$, where Q is the quantity in barrels. Should the firm enter this market? If so, what will be the maximum attainable profit, and what output should the firm select?

Supplementary Readings

BOOKS

  ABBOTT, LAWRENCE, *Economics and the Modern World,* 2nd ed. (New York: Harcourt, Brace & World, 1967).

  GRUCHY, ALLAN G., *Comparative Economic Systems* (Boston: Houghton Mifflin, 1966).

  HAIRE, MASON, ed., *Modern Organization Theory* (New York: Wiley, 1959).

  SAMUELSON, PAUL A., *Economics: An Introductory Analysis,* 7th ed. (New York: McGraw-Hill, 1967).

  SIMON, HERBERT A., *Administrative Behavior,* 2nd ed. (New York: Macmillan, 1957).

  STIGLER, GEORGE J., *The Theory of Price,* 3rd ed. (New York: Macmillan, 1966).

  WILF, HERBERT S., *Calculus and Linear Algebra* (New York: Harcourt, Brace & World, 1966).

Part II

MARKETING DECISION VALUES

Having examined the relationship between profit, revenue, and cost—expressed in very general form as $\pi = R - C$—we can begin a more detailed exploration of each of these variables. Although the basic concepts are simple, their application to real-world problems can be very complex. Numerous factors, including a variety of exogenous variables such as taxes, labor unrest, and inflation, affect the way in which the firm pursues its goal of profit maximization.

The most complex and elusive term in the profit equation is cost. It warrants examination from the viewpoints of the accountant, the economist, and the businessman, for each perceives it differently at times, and these differences have important implications for the decision-maker.

Revenue is equally important but, as a rule, not so complex as cost. Profit is the most important value for marketing decisions. It is easily computed, once revenue and cost are known; however, it too may be viewed in several ways, each of which should be understood by the marketer.

The influence of the learning phenomenon and other causes of economies of scale, as well as the effect of time, on key values—this too is important to the decision-maker. The break-even point, the return on investment, and the present value of future income streams are also key values for marketing decisions.

The use of cash-flow charts and the computation of capital requirements are also important to the marketer. Each of these concepts will be explored in some depth in this section.

CHAPTER 4

Cost and Revenue

COST

The computation of costs can be viewed in two basic ways. Accountants figure costs one way (theirs is the traditional and prevalent method), and economists another way. The two methods are similar in the long run, but very different in the short run. The marketing manager will encounter both and should know when each is appropriate.

The traditional accounting position is to distribute *all* costs to each good or service produced by the firm. Economics suggests that only those costs that are directly influenced by a product—in other words, only variable costs—should be allocated to the product. This is the essential difference between the two positions. In the long run, all inputs, and therefore all costs, are variable. Thus, the accountant and the economist would be likely to agree in their analysis of costs relative to a long-run decision. This is not the case in the market period (the time in which all costs and output are fixed) and in the short run, time periods that are usually more important from a marketing standpoint.

Accounting's View of Costs. Accountants view the cost term as having two basic elements: fixed and variable costs. Fixed costs do not vary with output. Variable costs vary directly and measurably with output. Depreciation of plant and equipment, salaries of staff members such as the personnel director and the firm's legal counsel, license charges, and most local taxes are examples of fixed costs. Labor and material directly traceable to the output of a good or service sold by the company are variable costs.

Sometimes a third classification of costs, called *semifixed costs,* is established. Semifixed costs (sometimes labeled "semivariable") are expenses that are not traceable to a particular unit of production, but do vary roughly with output. Advertising, personal selling (when commissions are not used), research, and plant maintenance costs may be assigned to this category. They are similar to fixed costs in that they do not vary with small changes in output and are similar to variable costs in that they do vary with large changes in output, even in the short run.

Advertising presents a convenient example of cost classification considerations. A quantity of advertising is generally necessary to introduce a new product. Its cost may be incurred before even the first unit is sold. It will be money spent regardless of the degree of consumer acceptance of the good. Thus, it is a fixed cost. Once the product has been introduced, additional advertising will probably be purchased in discrete increments. Although these discrete increments of advertising serve to increase sales, it is usually not possible to link a particular increment of advertising to a specific increase in demand. In this case, advertising would be assigned to semivariable costs. On the other hand, if a quantity of advertising in a local market were promised as part of a contract to sell a given quantity of goods —as is the case with cooperative advertising between a producer and a retailer—then that increment of advertising would be traceable to a particular increment of output and would be classified as a variable cost.

From the standpoint of the stockholder, the bank, or the Bureau of Internal Revenue, what difference does it make how an expense is classified? All costs must eventually be paid out of revenues or the stockholders' equity. Generally speaking, it makes very little difference how an item is classified when the time arrives to close the books and compute the profit or loss for the preceding accounting period. Eventually, all costs must be included in the profit function.[1]

Cost allocation is extremely important in short-run decisions because it influences the computed profit of the alternatives. The decision process consists of arraying alternatives and then selecting among them on the basis of their respective profits, and cost allocation plays a vital role in the choice of options.

Traditional accounting holds that all costs must be allocated on some basis to every product or service. This position is enforced by government edict in many regulated industries, most notably among the railroads. The allocation of fixed costs is arbitrary, and many different methods of assigning costs are presently used. Although a firm will normally separate fixed costs into two broad classifications—overhead and general and administrative expense (G & A)—many variations of this basic system are found.[2] Many

[1] However, from the standpoint of taxes and corporate stock values, the allocation of costs to a capital or an expense account is an important decision to the firm. (Capital and expense accounts are found on the firm's balance sheet and profit-and-loss statement, respectively.) This is because taxes and corporate stock values are both determined over the short run and not over the long run.

[2] G & A normally includes executive-office salaries, the costs of the accounting department, and the costs of similar general or administrative functions. Overhead usually includes the remainder of the fixed costs—for example, factory supervision, utilities, and building maintenance.

firms have separate overhead costs for different departments, such as engineering and manufacturing. There may also be a separate category for material procurement costs. This element of overhead is normally classed as a material-handling charge and includes the costs of purchasing, receiving, inspecting, and storing input materials or services.

After fixed costs are pooled in some manner, they must then be allocated to direct costs. Again, the method of allocation is determined by the firm (assuming that it operates in an unregulated industry), and many different systems are used. Direct labor hours, floor space, number of personnel, direct costs, and the purchase price of material are common denominators for allocating fixed costs to the products or services sold by the firm. For example, a machine shop having a fixed cost of $150,000 per month and having spent 30,000 hours of direct labor on a variety of products manufactured during that period would probably allocate $5 of fixed cost for every hour of direct labor spent on a given item. If a valve required 25 man-hours, it would be allocated $125 of fixed cost. The cost of the direct labor and material going into the valve would be added to get the total cost assigned to that product. The total cost of the valve would be calculated as follows:

Fixed costs, $5 × 25 hours	$125
Direct labor, 25 hours @ $4 per hour	100
Direct material	30
Total Cost	$255

Given this seemingly logical criterion for cost allocation, any price below $255 would mean a loss for the firm. The sales manager would be foolish to quote a price below that value plus the minimum profit required to justify staying in business. This is the traditional accounting position.

Economics' View of Costs.   Economic theory states that profit is maximized when marginal cost equals marginal revenue. As long as marginal revenue exceeds marginal cost, output should be increased. This suggests that only those costs that vary—either increase or decrease—with changes in output should be included in the profit-maximization model. In the long run, all inputs, and therefore all costs, are variable and would be included in the model. The firm can buy and sell land, plants, and equipment and get into or out of business. Thus, in the long run, the cost-determination method used by the economist yields essentially the same cost figure as the method used by the accountant.

In both the market period and in the short run, the economist would reject any fixed cost in computing profit as a basis for decision-making. Using the previous example, the marginal cost of the valve would be $130 ($100 + $30), and any revenue in excess of that value would be viewed as marginal profit. Thus, a price well below the accountant's cost figure of $255 would justify the production and sale of an additional unit of output. For example, a price of $180 would mean a marginal profit of $50, although the traditional accounting method of figuring costs would show a loss of $75 on the valve.

Whether marginal profit is viewed as a direct contribution to profit or as a contribution to the payment of fixed costs—costs incurred regardless of the change in output—a positive marginal profit will always increase the firm's total profit. Hence, the economist's marginal analysis is more appropriate to short-run decisions than the traditional accounting approach. It is not unusual for a firm to have idle capacity for short periods. Since the cost of maintaining this capacity continues during slumps, any work that will defray part of this cost is worthwhile. As long as a job produces more revenue than direct cost and does not exclude more profitable work, it should be undertaken. The marginal revenue thereby produced will materially improve the company's financial situation. Profit, both long-run and short-run, will be increased.

Business' View of Costs.   Every businessman must master, to some extent, the art of rational compromise. The marketer, in particular, must amalgamate a variety of skills and disciplines in the practice of his trade. In choosing between the traditional accounting approach and the economic approach to cost analysis and profit computation, the firm must acknowledge exogeneous constraints, the nature of the decision, and the form of the data. The Securities and Exchange Commission and the Bureau of Internal Revenue, for example, demand traditional accounting methods for stockholders' reports and declarations of income. Regulatory agencies such as the Interstate Commerce Commission, the Public Utilities Commission, and the Civil Aeronautics Board also require reports conforming to the conventional accounting format. These reports are used as a basis for approval or rejection of rate changes and subsidies. The results can sometimes be detrimental to both the firm and the public, yet the company has no choice but to conform.[3]

The accountant's format, which must be maintained for the reasons just given, is useful for budgeting and control. In addition, it is almost always applicable to long-run decisions, where it conforms closely to the economist's format.

For market-period and short-run decisions, where only variable costs can be manipulated, marginal analysis should be invoked. Many firms use an accounting system that provides for both *average cost analysis* (the accounting method) and *marginal cost analysis* (the economic method).

---

[3] See Stanley Berge, "Why Kill the Passenger Train?" *Journal of Marketing,* Vol. 28, No. 1 (January 1964), pp. 1–6, for an enlightening discussion of the blind application of traditional accounting to regulatory and company decisions.

This is usually accomplished by determining marginal costs on a limited basis, since the determination of marginal costs requires a greatly expanded, and hence more expensive, accounting system. Marginal costs are typically determined for the first production lot of a new product or the introduction of a new sales area into the marketing mix. This data can then be used for future decision-making, and thus the need for a continuing marginal-cost accounting system is eliminated. Every marketer, however, should realize that accounting sytsems are normally average-cost oriented and that special procedures will be required if marginal-cost data are to be accumulated.

The marketing manager is often hampered by an accounting system that insists on a rigid allocation of all fixed and semivariable costs to each direct labor hour, product, or department. Allocation systems are necessarily arbitrary and can distort management's perception of profit and growth opportunities. The allocation problem is compounded by the difficulty of reducing overhead expense as direct labor costs decline and by the ease of increasing overhead expense as direct labor costs rise. (Social pressures make employee termination psychologically harder than employee procurement, especially when managerial personnel are involved.) The net result can be an excessive estimate of the cost of doing future work. In turn, too-high estimates can result in the rejection of work or a product alternative that could have been profitable.

Consider, for example, a company doing extensive engineering work to develop a new product line. Both the engineering overhead—supervisors' salaries, the cost of office space and equipment, and so on—and direct engineering labor costs would be high. As product development was concluded and the new line accepted in the market, emphasis would shift to production, and direct engineering labor would decline. With fewer direct engineering labor hours and fewer jobs over which to spread the department's overhead expenses, the average unit cost for engineering services would get higher and higher. If this allocation system were followed blindly, new development programs would appear excessively expensive and hence might not be undertaken. The same problem can emerge on the manufacturing side when a product phases out of production. The average unit cost will escalate because of the firm's inability to reduce its overhead costs as fast as output declines. When the marketer must quote prices equal to the current average unit cost plus a standard mark-up—a practice typical of government contracting—the result can be disastrous. The price will not be competitive; hence sales and output will decline, pushing the average unit cost even higher.

The large fixed costs invariably associated with new-product development often results in the accounting approach yielding a loss for the new product during the first several years after its introduction in the market. For example, consider Figure 4.1. Assume that the total fixed costs are determined primarily by development expenditures, all of which are in-

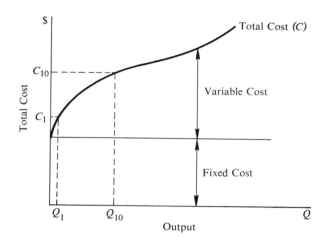

FIGURE 4.1
Total cost vs. output
(With high fixed cost)

curred during a one-year period. If at the end of one year Q_1 units have been sold, the average unit cost is C_1/Q_1. If at the end of three years Q_{10} units have been sold, the average unit cost is C_{10}/Q_{10}. Obviously, C_{10}/Q_{10} is less than C_1/Q_1, and the marketing manager would argue that the introductory price of the new product need only be greater than C_{10}/Q_{10} in order to assure a profitable product (assuming that total sales for the three-year period had been accurately forecast as Q_{10} units and that C_{10} includes any financing costs appropriate to the longer time period). The accountant would argue that the price should be greater than C_1/Q_1, since during the first year this was the average cost of the new product.

Establishing an average cost is more difficult when the introductory phase of a new product extends over a period of several years. Traditional accounting theory is oriented toward annual profit determination, and it is often hard for accountants to take an economic view of costs if the appropriate time period for analysis extends past one year.

Cost Classifications. Since we have discussed the fundamental differences between the broad categories of fixed costs and variable costs, it is appropriate to define some of the terms that will confront the marketer in his discussions with his firm's accountants and in his review of marketing reports and literature.

Outlay costs are real costs that would be, or are, incurred as a result of a particular decision. They are dollars actually spent.

Opportunity costs are the profits that the firm must forgo in selecting among mutually exclusive alternatives. For example, if products A and B would earn $100,000 and $150,000 respectively, but only one of them could be selected, then the opportunity cost of the selected product would be the profit that could have been earned by the foregone alternative. If product B were selected, its opportunity cost would be $100,000.

Historical costs, or costs incurred in the past, are widely used to estimate the cost of future goods and services. This method of estimating costs assumes that market conditions will not change significantly. This is often a naive assumption, in a period of inflation, political unrest, changing technology, fluctuating material prices, and proliferating labor unions.

Future costs are costs that will be incurred at some future time and can be estimated only from historical data or by a detailed analysis of development, manufacturing, and marketing plans. This is often a laborious and expensive job, since it may involve soliciting new bids from suppliers, estimating direct labor and material hours from product drawings, and forecasting marketing costs.

The terms *marginal cost* and *incremental cost* are generally used interchangeably, especially in marketing literature. This text is no exception. Both refer to the change in cost, ΔC, resulting from a change in output, ΔQ. However, the economist would cite a subtle distinction: technically "marginal" refers to the change of output by a single unit, whereas "incremental" denotes a change of more than one unit.[4]

Variable costs, direct costs, and *traceable costs* are synonymous terms for those costs that can be identified with a particular product and that vary with the output of that product.

Indirect costs are costs that cannot be identified with a particular good, except in a single-product plant, and that do not vary directly with output.

Common costs are costs that are traceable to two or more products and vary with their joint output. A common cost, however, cannot be divided between the common products except through an arbitrary distribution.

Accounting and Economic Periods.   Accounting periods are normally increments of a year—semi-annual, quarterly, and so on. Although the fiscal year for a particular firm may not coincide with the calendar year, the concept of a year is implicit in all accounting periods.

Economic periods are much less structured. The ability of management to manipulate variables depends on the period in which the decision will be effective. For example, the marketing director for an automobile manufacturer can manipulate many more variables in the traditional three-year model period than he can during the inventory liquidation period at the

---

[4] When a derivative of a cost function is used as the marginal cost, it is assumed that output is continuous and not discrete. In actual practice, the error encountered is small if the level of output is large. If the level of output is small, however, as in the case of ICBM's, then a large error could result from taking the derivative to calculate marginal cost. In such cases, the actual difference in cost that results from producing one more or one less unit should be calculated.

end of the first year. Only price can be varied in the latter period. Consequently, the costs that are appropriate to a decision with a long planning horizon differ from those that are significant when the planning horizon is short. Economists refer to three time periods that affect the mix of variables in the firm's decision process: the market period, the short run, and the long run. The length of each—measured in hours, days, weeks, months, or years—varies between industries. Hence they are best defined by the costs and output that can be manipulated during their span.

A *market period* is a period during which all costs and output are fixed. In agriculture, for example, after the harvest output cannot be changed and all land, labor, and capital costs have already been incurred. In this case, the length of the market period would depend on the growth cycle of the crop. The market period for fresh vegetables would be a few weeks, whereas for wheat or lumber it could be a few months or several decades.

In the *short-run period,* certain inputs and the output can be varied within limitations imposed by the firm's land, plant, and equipment. Again, the agricultural firm is a convenient example. Once it has invested in a quantity of land and equipment and the planting season is upon it, only seed, labor, and fertilizer can be changed to increase or decrease production. Nevertheless, this allows output to be varied from zero to the maximum amount that can be produced on a given number of acres. The costs of material and labor can be manipulated, and hence are variable, whereas the costs of land and capital are fixed.

In the *long-run period,* all inputs, hence all costs, and output are variable. The firm in the example above can buy more land and equipment or sell what it has. It can change location as well as crops, or it can get out of the industry and invest its wealth elsewhere. The firm's actions are limited only by the extent of its wealth and credit and the ease of entry into other fields. The period can be only minutes long, as is the case with stock speculators, whose assets are extremely liquid, or it can run for years, as is the case with large-capital-investment firms such as steel producers.

THE LEARNING FUNCTION

A major factor influencing cost, and hence the profit function and decision process, is learning. The learning function is simply an explicit statement of the reduction in unit cost that occurs as a result of an increase in output. If the Chrysler Corporation built only a dozen Plymouths, they would cost tens of thousands of dollars apiece. Similarly, if Boeing built only one 707 jet, it would cost over $100 million. However, as output reaches a high level, the learning phenomenon, combined with other economies of scale, allows the unit cost to be reduced so that Plymouths can be sold profitably for under

$3,000 and a 707 jet for only $8 million. An understanding of the practical applications of the learning function is extremely helpful in making many marketing decisions, especially in manufacturing firms. It is mandatory for major government contractors.

As either a human being or an animal repeats a task, he becomes more proficient in its execution. This is the learning phenomenon. If the reader will reflect on his own experience in mastering the multiplication tables, driving an automobile, or playing tennis, he will understand the essential nature of the learning function. If an individual is performing an economic task—such as designing electronic equipment, assembling telephones, or selling encyclopedias—his output, per unit of time, will increase with his experience. At first, the increase will be pronounced. Then, after the task has been repeated many times, improvement will decline to where it is hardly perceptible. This phenomenon is portrayed graphically in Figure 4.2.

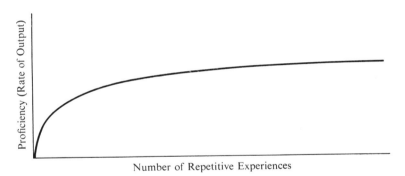

FIGURE 4.2
The learning function

The amount of task repetition may be expressed directly in terms of output, or as the total hours or weeks spent on the job. Proficiency is expressed as output per unit of time—as, the number of computer cards punched per hour, radios wired per day, or automobiles sold per week. For instance, we might observe that an average insurance salesman sells six policies per month after one year of experience and eight policies per month after two years. The actual learning curve plotted for a specific individual will be a bit erratic, because of exogenous disturbances such as physical or emotional upset, but will generally resemble the curve in Figure 4.2. The slope of the curve, indicating the individual's personal learning rate, will vary from person to person according to differences in ability and motivation and the nature of the task involved. However, curves may be drawn that will closely approximate the average performance of a group of people doing a particular task. These *average learning functions* have been found to be so universal in certain types of industries that they are published in tabular form. Such tables are very useful in estimating the costs of complex jobs, particularly if the job involves a high degree of repetition and the firm must quote prices on different quantities of output.

The learning phenomenon is observable at the team and organizational level, where proficiency, and therefore productivity, improves with experience. An increase in organizational efficiency may result from improvements in communication and planning, the earlier detection and correction of errors in engineering drawings, improvements in tooling processes, better promotional techniques, or the accumulation of technical and market data, which allow more accurate management decision models.

The application of learning theory is especially important to the marketer selling goods to the nation's largest customer—the federal government.[5] It is significant for most firms engaged in competitive bidding or offering sales contracts with fixed prices on as-yet unproduced products. An example is the aircraft industry, in which the empirical work on the industrial applications of learning theory was first accomplished.

Researchers studying the aircraft industry discovered that the cumulative average unit cost of labor was reduced by a fixed percentage every time the total output was doubled. The reduction ran approximately 20 percent—that is, every time the *total* output was doubled, the resultant average unit cost for the *entire* quantity produced was 80 percent of the previous value. For example, if the first unit took 100,000 man-hours of direct labor, the cumulative average unit cost for the first two units would be 80,000 man-hours. If the quantity of output was doubled to four units, the cumulative average unit cost would be 64,000. The relationship between output, cumulative average unit cost, and total cost is shown in Table 4.1. Note that total cost is simply the product of cumulative average unit cost times total output.

The cumulative average unit cost, the total cost, and the cost for a single unit or segment of output can easily be computed, using either mathematical or graphical techniques. Mathematical techniques obviously have the advantage of greater precision. Graphical methods are often more convenient, however, especially when a variety of values must be determined or when a visual display is desired and precise answers are not necessary. The data required to calculate these costs are the actual or estimated cost of the first unit and the learning rate. The direct cost of the first unit, hence the cumulative average unit cost (the dependent variable), can be expressed in labor

[5] See Walter B. Wentz, "Aerospace Discovers Marketing," *Journal of Marketing,* Vol. 31, No. 2 (April 1967), p. 27, for a detailed analysis of the strategy of marketing in the federal sector.

**Table 4.1   Direct labor cost at an 80-percent learning rate
(cost of first unit = 100,000 man-hours)**

Total Output (n)	Cumulative Average Unit Cost (in man-hours) (U_n)	Total Cost (in man-hours) (L_n)
1	100,000	100,000
2	80,000	160,000
4	64,000	256,000
8	51,200	409,600
16	40,960	655,360
32	32,768	1,048,576
64	26,214	1,677,696

hours or in dollars.[6] Hours can be converted into dollars simply by multiplying them by the mean average labor cost (the average hourly rate for labor) plus the cost of payroll taxes and fringe benefits (which varies directly with labor hours).

The learning rate, which is expressed as a percentage, indicates the lower quantity of labor required per average unit when total output is increased. For example, if the prevalent learning rate in a firm is 80 percent, then the average unit cost for *all* units produced will be 80 percent of the average unit cost for the previous output if that output is doubled. This is called the "cumulative average unit cost" because it includes all units, starting with the first.

The learning rate is normally estimated from past experience—which is one reason why a firm should have an accounting system that can provide marginal cost data. In order for a firm to determine its learning rate, the accounting department must be able to establish the number of man-hours expended to produce particular units or to accomplish particular functions.

If an aircraft company had an 80-percent learning rate, and if the production of 8 identical airplanes took an average of 51,200 man-hours per plane, doubling the output to 16 aircraft would cause the cumulative average unit cost to drop to 40,960 man-hours (51,200 × .80). In order to bring the average for *all* the aircraft down from 51,200 hours to 40,960 hours, the cost of units 9 through 16 must average well below 40,960 hours. That this

[6] A firm need not always estimate the labor for the first unit; it could just as easily estimate the labor for, say, the tenth or twentieth unit and then work backward to determine the labor for each unit produced.

is in fact what happens will become evident when we graph the learning function. First, however, we will develop the mathematical solution. The equation for the learning curve is

$U_n = C_1 \cdot r^p$, where

$U_n = $ *cumulative average* unit labor cost at the nth unit

$C_1 = $ labor cost of the first unit

$r = $ learning rate, and

$p = $ an exponent that is computed as $\log_2 n$, which is the logarithm[7] to the base 2 of n (the total output).

To illustrate, let us assume that the marketing director of an aircraft company has been ordered to prepare a bid on 32 military airplanes. The price will be a function of the total cost plus the mark-up prevalent at the time. In computing cost, the most variable cost element is usually direct labor hours. Assuming that company records indicate a learning rate, r, of 80 percent, the cumulative average unit cost, U_n, can be computed as follows:

$C_1 = 100,000$	Cost of unit 1, determined from manufacturing and engineering estimates
$n = 32$	Given
$r = .80$	Given
$p = \log_2 n$	Given
$p = \log_2 32$	By substitution
$p = 5$	By use of base-2 logarithms[8]
$U_n = C_1 r^p$	Given
$U_n = (100,000)(.80)$	By substitution
$U_n = 32,768$	By arithmetic

Once the cumulative average unit cost is known, it is a simple matter to compute total costs. We use the equation

$L_n = n \cdot U_n$, where

$L_n = $ total direct labor cost through the nth unit

$n = $ total number of units produced, and

$U_n = $ cumulative average unit cost at the nth unit

[7] See Appendix, p. 661, for an explanation of logarithms.
[8] See Appendix, p. 666.

The total direct labor cost, L_n, for 32 planes would equal the product of $n(32)$ and $U_n(32,768)$, or 1,048,576 hours. If we assume an average labor cost of \$5 per hour, the dollar value of the direct labor would total \$5,242,880.

If a table of logarithms to the base 2 is not available, a table of logarithms to the base 10 can be used to solve for p, by making the following substitution:

$$p = 3.322 \log_{10} n$$

If the cost for a *particular unit* is required, it can be found by the following formula:

$C_n = L_n - L_{n-1}$, where

C_n = direct labor cost of the nth unit

L_n = total direct labor cost of the first n units, and

L_{n-1} = total direct labor cost of the first $n - 1$ units

In our example, the cost of the 32nd unit would be computed as follows:

$C_n = L_n - L_{n-1}$	Given
$C_{32} = L_{32} - L_{31}$	By substitution
$C_{32} = 1{,}048{,}576$ $\quad - 31(100{,}000) \cdot (.8)3.322 \log_{10} 31$	By substitution
$C_{32} = 1{,}048{,}576 - 1{,}028{,}022$	By arithmetic and use of a base-10 logarithmic table
$C_{32} = 20{,}544$	By arithmetic

The cost of a segment of production can be computed by the equation

$L_{n_1-n_2} = L_{n_2} - L_{n_1-1}$, where $\qquad\qquad$ (4-1)

$L_{n_1-n_2}$ = total direct labor cost of units n_1 through n_2

L_{n_1-1} = total direct labor cost of the first unit through unit $n_1 - 1$ (note that unit $n_1 - 1$ is the unit immediately before unit n_1), and

L_{n_2} = total direct labor cost of the first unit through unit n_2

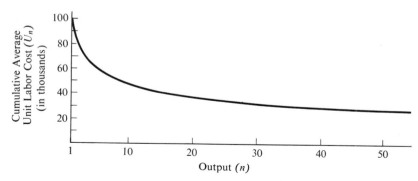

FIGURE 4.3
Arithmetic graph of cumulative average unit cost of labor (U_n)
(Learning rate = 80%, C_1 = 100,000 hours)

Again using our aircraft company as an example, we can find the direct labor cost of producing units 5 through 8 as follows: (Note that $n_1 = 5$ and $n_2 = 8$, hence $n_1 - 1 = 4$.)

$L_{n_1-n_2} = L_{n_2} - L_{n_1-1}$	Given
$L_{5-8} = L_8 - L_4$	By substitution
$L_{5-8} = 409,600 - 256,000$	By substitution
$L_{5-8} = 153,600$	By arithmetic

There are two graphical techniques for portraying or computing the values for U_n. First, we can construct a curve representing the function on arithmetic graph paper.[9] Plotting the cumulative average unit cost, U_n, of the preceding example on arithmetic paper gives us the curve in Figure 4.3. Note that the curve always starts at unit number 1, falls rapidly at first, and then continues to fall but at a constantly decreasing rate. The area under the curve represents the total direct labor cost for that segment of production. Note also that the function is asymptotic—that is, it approaches, but never reaches, the output axis.

Mathematicians call this type of curve an *exponential function*. This information would be of no significant interest to the marketer were it not for the fact that an exponential function plots as a straight line on log-log graph paper. This type of graph paper has both axes scaled as logarithms. Using it saves market analysts a good deal of work when it is necessary to

[9] The distance between lines is equal on arithmetic graph paper. This is by far the most common type of grid.

approximate values of U_n. The analyst simply computes any two values of U_n, plots these points on logarithmic graph paper, draws a straight line through them, and thus has all the U_n values for the range of n. In the example above, the value of U_1 was given as 100,000, and the value of U_8 was computed as 51,200. By plotting U_1 and U_8, as in Figure 4.4, and connecting them with a straight line extended to the 64th unit, the analyst can obtain all the values for U_n for the entire range of output $n = 1$ through $n = 64$. Additional values can be found simply by extending the line farther. The disadvantage of this method is the lack of precision that results from the inability to draw extremely accurate lines and the difficulty in reading values, with a sufficient number of significant digits, off the direct labor axis.

If actual values are available—if, say, units 1 through 5 have been completed—then two of those values can be plotted and the line drawn through them, extending to whatever n value is appropriate. This reveals the learning rate, r, connected with the job.

As cost data is usually "dirty"—that is, it contains some nonrepresentative time or omits some representative hours—it is advisable to first adjust the data by correcting the values for unique and nonrepetitive occurrences such as work stoppages, equipment failure, material shortages, and the charging of bogus time. Even after these corrections are made, there will still be random variations attributable to the fact that human beings are more attentive and energetic on some days than on others. These variations can be averaged out, or dampened, by plotting all the available points and then drawing (or computing) a line of best fit through the scatter.

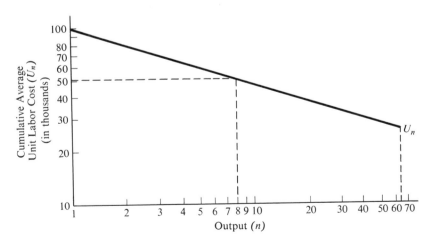

FIGURE 4.4
Logarithmic graph of cumulative average unit cost of labor (U_n)
(Learning rate $= 80\%$, $C_1 = 100,000$ hours)

In negotiating a contract, particularly one with a federal agency, the marketer will often be asked to justify both his original unit estimate and the assumed learning rate. For this he usually relies on detailed historical data provided by the accounting department or on estimates, made from drawings, provided by the company's industrial engineers. The marketer must be able to communicate with these people and to present their findings to the customer intelligently. To do this, he needs a knowledge of both cost accounting and the learning function.

The learning function is equally applicable in negotiating for inputs, especially when the inputs are made to order for the buyer—as are, for example, automobile frames, aircraft landing gears, and engine castings. By plotting the learning curve, the buyer can estimate the supplier's labor cost. By adding material costs, he can get an approximate figure for total direct costs, which he can use as a basis for evaluating the price quoted by the supplier. If his negotiating position is strong—which it presumably would be if his firm were the sole customer for that particular good or service—he can use this information to ensure that his company pays a fair price.

Finally, learning curves provide both a method of measuring performance and a technique for evaluating the effect of increased output on costs. If learning theory is used in the cost decision process, then a predetermined standard is being established against which management can measure the future performance of the firm. Such a control technique also permits a more precise determination of the cost savings that would result from increased investment in capital equipment. If the learning function is not taken into account, then the decreased labor costs that would result from repetitive operations will not be considered in deciding whether to substitute capital for labor, and the cost savings due to capital investment will be exaggerated.

Similarly, if learning theory is not considered in establishing the costs for a new product, the marketing department may be confronted with a too-high cost estimate, which may result in a price, for the first units that prohibits market penetration. In this case, the average cost of the total number of units that the marketing department feels it can sell over the life of the product is the appropriate cost. The cost of the first few units—which will be high on the learning curve—is disproportionately large and may make the product appear prohibitively expensive.

Scale.   Scale, or size of operation, is important because it has great influence on efficiency and therefore cost. Economies of scale result primarily from job specialization, the distribution of fixed costs over a large number of units, purchasing economies, and the ability of large producers to substitute machines for labor. The distribution of fixed costs over a large output allows heavy capital investment. These efficiencies, combined with the learning phenomenon, result in the economies of scale associated with mass production. They provide the low unit costs—hence generally lower prices—associated with large producers serving mass markets.

The more an employee can specialize—that is, the narrower, and thus more repetitive his job becomes—the more proficient he becomes,[10] and hence the greater is the reduction in unit labor costs. The larger the plant, the more various operations can be broken down into specialized tasks. This fragmentation not only increases specialization, hence efficiency, but also means that each employee requires less training. It is easier to learn to run a drill press or a lathe than every tool in the machine shop. A salesman can learn the intricacies of selling shoes or cosmetics long before he can learn to sell every line in the store. The engineer, production foreman, or marketer can keep better abreast of his own special area than he can of the entire field of engineering, manufacturing, or marketing operations.

Many costs remain constant no matter what the output is. It takes no longer to write a purchase order, prepare a planning ticket, or set up a machine for 100 units of production than it does for just a few. Designing an advertisement that is to appear in a single magazine costs no less than designing one that is to be used in several. Producing a television commercial for the Dallas market is no cheaper than producing the same commercial for network television. The greater the output, the smaller the proportion of fixed cost borne by each unit, hence the lower the cumulative average unit cost.

The suppliers providing inputs to the firm are also confronted with economies of scale. This results in lower unit prices as the size of purchases increase. The net effect is lower unit material costs for the firm.

As far back as history records, man has been inventing tools and machines that enable him to work faster and produce more. This has allowed producers to reduce direct labor costs, but at the expense of increasing capital investment, and hence fixed costs. If output can be increased past the point where the saving in labor exceeds the added capital cost, the average unit cost can be reduced. With the rapid advancements in manufacturing technology machines have become both sophisticated and expensive. Yet labor cost can be drastically reduced if sufficient output can be sold to justify capital investment in machines.

A stamping press and dies for an automobile fender can cost over $500,000 but can reduce the per-unit labor cost from $30 to less than $2. If 1 million auto fenders are produced over the life of the equipment, the total

[10] Other factors, such as boredom, may come into play, thus reducing efficiency once the employee has passed a certain level of experience. That social as well as psychological factors may also be involved was demonstrated clearly in the famous Western Electric Hawthorne studies. (See F. J. Roethlisberger and W. J. Dickson, *Management and the Worker* (Cambridge, Mass.: Harvard University Press, 1939).)

direct cost, less material, will be less than 10 percent of what the handmade cost would be. This illustrates the effect of machines on unit costs. However, the outlay for machinery can be justified only if there is a large output, which in turn requires a large demand for the product. *The establishment and satisfaction of demand is the role of marketing.* The stimulation of demand is essential if economies of scale are to be obtained. Hence it is the economic, as well as the social, rationale for the promotional function in marketing.

Use of Cost Data.   Cost identification and allocation is important to marketing management as an instrument of measurement and control. One cannot judge the efficiency of an instrument of marketing, the profitability of a product, the risk of a commitment, or the wisdom of a decision if its actual or anticipated cost cannot be measured. Nor, without the ability to compare actual costs with a budget, can one intelligently control the allocation of resources.

Cost information is crucial to many marketing decisions. For example, without an approximation of the cost function, the marketing manager cannot optimize output and price. In a competitive bidding situation—where output is usually set by the buyer but various prices are offered by competing suppliers—a precise knowledge of costs is a prerequisite to survival. Bidding a price below cost will cause the firm to lose money, and bidding a price too far above cost will cause it to lose contracts. Either way, the firm can go broke.

In evaluating cost data, the marketer must understand the method used for allocating costs and must identify those costs that will be influenced by a particular decision. This requires a perception of the economic period in which the decision will have its effect and a critical understanding of the allocation system used.

The marketing department is only one among several groups within the firm making demands on the same finite resources—resources that must be rationed between departments, each competing for the company's funds. To get the allocations he needs to support his various functions, the marketing manager must justify those functions in terms of their effect on revenue as opposed to their costs. Many marketers also have a keen personal interest in cost analysis. Merchandisers in retailing are usually paid, promoted, or fired on the basis of the profit-and-loss statements prepared for their operations. Buyers and store managers are often presented with a monthly tabulation of their revenues, costs, and profits. The fixed costs are distributed to each department—such as sporting goods, men's shoes, and women's ready-to-wear clothing—on the basis of floor space or some other arbitrary criterion, and the profit or loss is used to judge the performance of the manager or buyer in charge of the department.

At this point, it should be apparent that the ability to establish accurate cost data is essential to the success of the firm as well as to the success of the marketing program. The accumulation of accurate cost data requires an effort that cuts across all the departments and activities of a firm and cannot be accomplished by an accounting department alone, regardless of how thorough and complete the accounting system is. The important question is not simply what the past costs of producing a certain product are, but what factors make up these costs and what they will be in the future, given the internal and external changes that are certain to occur in any successful firm.

REVENUE

Computation. Revenue, R, is the other independent term in the profit equation. Once price has been selected, the computation of revenue is rather simple and not as ambiguous as is the determination of cost. The subtlety to remember in calculating revenue is that the published price is not always the price received by the producer; it must be adjusted for discounts and allowances. The value used in computation is the average amount actually received by the firm. Given this figure and the quantity of output sold, or expected to be sold, revenue can be computed by the following formula:

$R = P \cdot Q$, where

R = revenue

P = average price received, and

Q = quantity sold

The price-quantity combination is usually selected with the aid of the demand equation, which expresses the quantity sold (the dependent variable) as a function of the price (the independent variable). This concept was introduced in Chapter 3 and will be explored in more detail in Chapter 12.

Often the price is set by the market, as is the case in pure competition or in an undifferentiated oligopoly when the firm is not the price leader. Quantity, too, can be fixed, as is the case in government contracting where the firm is invited to bid on a specific number of units.

Allocation of Revenues. Sometimes management wishes to allocate revenues between different products or between departments. This can be difficult where goods or services are sold jointly or where several departments participate in the design, manufacture, and sale of a product. Consider, for example, a package deal offered on books, automobile accessories, or entertainment. If the Book-of-the-Month Club offers a selection of three books for ten dollars, how much of the ten dollars should be credited to each book? If there is a twin-feature bill at a movie theater, how much of the ticket revenues is each movie responsible for? These questions, like the questions regarding the distribution of common costs, must be answered. As in cost analysis, the answers must eventually be quantified, and the only way to do this is to make a distribution based on some arbitrary criterion such as product cost or an index of demand. Yet such a distribution is necessary when alternative product mixes are evaluated.

The allocation of revenues to separate departments is necessary when the firm has a management-incentive program that uses the profit of each department as a criterion for evaluating performance and hence for determining bonuses or salary increases. Here the value-added concept comes into play. The changes in the product contributed by each department, from the time it emerges from raw material until it reaches the first buyer, are each considered partially responsible for the revenue ultimately received by the firm. As the product gets nearer to completion and sale, it presumably becomes more valuable. The increment of added value is credited to each line department and is a portion of the total revenue received for that item. One criterion for distributing revenue is the prevailing price charged by outside firms for the work done by a particular department. For example, if a machine shop would charge $3 per unit for the facing and drilling of a steel casting, then $3 might be an appropriate value-added figure to credit to the producer's own machining department. Prices received for the individual parts making up the primary product—that is, spares—might also be used as a basis for distributing the revenue from the complete product. In certain types of firms, a more precise allocation of revenues may be possible. In retailing, for example, separate tallies can be made on the sales of meats, fresh produce, sporting goods, automobile accessories, men's clothing, and so on, and revenues can be credited to the departments handling each particular type of merchandise.

The allocation system is important for both costs and revenues. If it is inappropriate or the data are inaccurate, the value assigned profit will be distorted. This can lead to bad decision-making, particularly when decisions are being determined—as they should be—in terms of the profit criterion.

CHAPTER 5

Profit and Other Key Values

PROFIT

The computation of profit is straightforward, once the two independent variables in the profit equation, revenue and cost, are known. Profit, π, is the difference between revenue, R, and cost, C: $\pi = R - C$. The equation itself is simple; the difficulty is in the computation of R and C, especially C.

Obviously, since profit is the dependent variable, it will be expressed in the same terms as revenue and cost. If marginal revenue and marginal cost values are used, π will be the marginal profit. If revenue and cost are computed for a single unit or product class, the result will be the profit attributable to that unit or class.

We have said that profit is the most useful single criterion for decision-making. However, management must select the type of profit, hence the type of revenue and cost terms, appropriate to a particular decision. Generally speaking, marginal profit is more relevant to market-period and short-run decisions. Net profit, based on the distribution of all costs, is appropriate for long-run decisions. The long-run consequences of a market-period or short-run decision must also be considered, however. For example, will a price selected as optimum for a market period set a precedent or trigger a competitor response that will be detrimental to profits in the long run? Answers to such questions are often conjectural, but they must ultimately be transformed into a quantitative estimate of the total effect on profit of the available alternatives.

OTHER KEY VALUES FOR DECISION-MAKING

Having defined profit, revenue, and cost and explored alternative methods of computation, we can now turn to an examination of some important related variables. These are values that may also play a key role in marketing decisions. Three values in particular—the break-even point, the return on investment, and the present value of future income and expense streams— are often critical factors in decision-making. More sophisticated decision models will reflect additional variables, especially time. Again, it is important to remember that the input values used to compute the decision variable must be relevant to the decision. As a rule, only those variables that can be influenced by the decision should be considered. The analyst must be careful, however, not to exclude a profit, revenue, or cost item that will be affected, or one that is necessary to his calculations.

The degree of complexity of the decision model should correspond to the importance of the decision in terms of its effect on the firm. Decision models can vary from a very simple model—such as the estimation of the annual cost of adding one new salesman compared to the estimated annual profit on the increased sales he will bring in—to models that require computer simulation. Obviously, a decision to introduce a new product that would require a substantial investment—for example, General Motors deciding to enter the commercial aircraft market—would warrant the expense of a significant study. Many decisions, however, are made using simple models. Often neither the amount of investment nor the cost of failure is substantial enough to justify the expense of a complex model. The three models described below are commonly used in decision-making.

Break-Even Point.   The break-even point is the quantity of units sold where revenue equals cost. It can be expressed as units of output or as the minimum amount of revenue, in dollars, that must be received to cover cost. The break-even point is quickly identifiable graphically as the point of intersection of the cost and revenue curves, shown as Q_2 in Figure 3.7 (page 43). Before the level of output Q_1, the revenue curve is below the total cost curve and profit is negative—the firm is operating at a loss. Beyond Q_1, profit is positive. It increases until marginal revenue equals marginal cost and then begins to decline as the two curves converge. They intersect again at Q_3, the second break-even point. Beyond Q_3, a loss is again incurred.

The conventional formula for determining the break-even quantity assumes that variable cost, V, will be linear. Given this assumption,

$$Q_B = \frac{F}{P - V}, \text{ where} \tag{5-1}$$

Q_B = break-even quantity (output)

F = fixed cost

P = price, and

V = variable cost

Although the calculation involved is simple, the formula makes the naive assumption that variable cost, which is the sum of direct labor and material for a single unit, is constant.[1] This implies that the firm has a 100-percent learning rate—that is, that the nth unit will take as many direct labor hours and expenditures for material as the first unit. This would hold true only for a fully automated plant and a sales force on straight commission. A more realistic approach is to assume that the per-unit variable cost changes with output. This suggests that U_n, the cumulative average unit cost, be substituted for V. However, U_n is a variable; it changes with changes in output. The U_n needed is the U_n for $n = Q_B$. Thus we need to know Q_B to find U_n. Ironically, we also need U_n to find Q_B. This dilemma is resolved by solving the following equation by iterative or graphical techniques.

$$Q_B = \frac{F}{P - C_1 r^{\log_2 Q_B}}, \text{ where} \tag{5-2}$$

Q_B = break-even quantity (output)

F = fixed cost

P = price

C_1 = variable cost of the first unit, and

r = learning rate

A precise mathematical solution of Equation 5–2 requires a process of iteration. Various values must be selected and substituted for Q_B in the equation. The value that puts the equation in a state of equality—that makes the left side equal the right side—is the break-even quantity. Iteration is essentially a trial-and-error method; an initial value of Q_B is estimated, and then increased or decreased as necessary to bring the equation toward equality. It can be a bit laborious, although not difficult, if done manually, and can be done far more rapidly on a computer.

A graphical solution provides a less precise, but often acceptable, estimate of Q_B when the variable cost function is nonlinear. We simply add the variable cost curve to the fixed cost curve, as in Figure 5.1, to get the total cost curve. The intersection of the revenue function, $R = P \cdot Q$, and the total cost curve determines the break-even quantity.

The break-even point can be expressed in dollars if we multiply price times the quantity at the break-even point. By definition, cost and revenue

---

[1] "Variable," in the phrase "variable cost," is an adjective indicating that the cost varies with total output. If the variable cost is a constant—say $10 per unit—then total cost will change (vary) by the same amount for each unit added to the output. If it is a variable—say $20 for the first unit, $16 for the second unit, and so on—then total cost will increase by a different amount for each unit added to output.

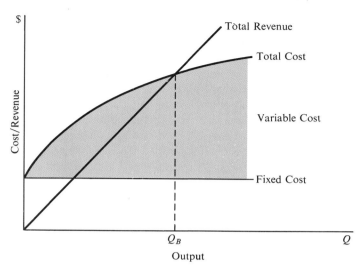

FIGURE 5.1
Break-even quantity
(Nonlinear cost function)

are equal at the break-even point; hence the computed value will represent both the cost that will have been incurred and the revenues that must be received in order to break even. This amount is generally viewed as the *total sales required to break even*. Thus,

$$Q_{B\$} = P \cdot Q_B, \text{ where} \qquad (5\text{–}3)$$

$Q_{B\$}$ = total cost and total revenue at the break-even point

P = price, and

Q_B = break-even quantity (output)

To illustrate some applications of the break-even formulas, let us assume that $5000 is required to cover the design, test, tooling, and intro-ductory advertising costs for Product A. Let us further assume that variable cost will be a constant $15 per unit for direct labor, material, and com-missions. If the optimum price for Product A is $25, what is the break-even quantity—the number of units that must be produced and sold before the company begins to make money on the item?

$$Q_B = \frac{F}{P - V} \qquad \text{Given by Equation 5–1}$$

$$Q_B = \frac{5000}{25 - 15}$$ By substitution

$Q_B = 500$ units — By arithmetic

$Q_{B\$} = P \cdot Q_B$ — Given by Equation 5–3

$Q_{B\$} = 25 \cdot 500$ — By substitution

$Q_{B\$} = 12{,}500$ — By arithmetic

A more realistic illustration would include the assumption that the variable cost of Product A will reflect the learning phenomenon. For example, if a firm's records indicate an 80-percent learning rate, and if \$15 is the variable cost for the first unit, what is the break-even quantity and revenue for Product A?

To solve this nonlinear problem (note that the variable cost—hence the total, or aggregate, cost—does not plot as a straight line), we use Equation 5–2. We begin by assuming an initial value, say 128 units, for Q_B', the break-even output.

$$Q_B = \frac{F}{P - C_1 r^{\log_2 Q_B}}$$ Given by Equation 5–2

$$128 = \frac{5000}{25 - (15)(.8)^7}$$ By substitution[2]

$$128 = \frac{5000}{25 - 3.146}$$ By arithmetic

$128 \neq 228$ — By arithmetic[3]

Obviously, 128 is a poor estimate of the break-even point. If we select a higher number, say 256, we have

$$Q_B = \frac{F}{P - C_1 r^{\log_2 Q_B}}$$ Given by Equation 5–2

$$256 = \frac{5000}{25 - (15)(.8)^8}$$ By substitution

$256 \neq 222$ — By arithmetic

The second value selected for Q_B is still wrong, but it is much better than the first number chosen. As 256 appears to have overshot the mark,

[2] The $\log_2$ of 128, rounded to the nearest integer, is 7.
[3] The equality sign, $=$, has been changed to an inequality sign, $\neq$, to show that the equation is not in balance.

we next select a somewhat lower value, say 222. This gives us the inequality $222 \neq 223.5$, which may be sufficiently close for practical purposes. If not, other values between 222 and 223.5 can be tried.

The marketing manager must be confident that sales will exceed the break-even value, or the firm would be ill advised to embark on the project. The break-even value also suggests the degree of financial liability the firm will incur. In considering a project with a low break-even point, the company can afford to be less certain about the venture's success, for the stakes will not be so high. In considering one with a large break-even value, such as that for commercial airplanes, management must be fairly sure of its ability to sell the break-even quantity of output or court financial disaster.

Return on Investment. The return on investment is the ratio between the profit obtained from an investment and the magnitude of the investment necessary to receive that profit. It is normally expressed as a percentage (the ratio being multiplied by 100), as follows:

$$E_G = \frac{\pi}{I} \cdot 100, \text{ where} \tag{5-4}$$

E_G = gross return on investment, expressed as a percentage of the investment

π = profit, and

I = investment

To illustrate how this value may affect decision-making in the firm, let us assume that the firm's marketing manager has proposed a new product. Marketing research and internal cost analysis indicate that the product will net $80,000 profit over its lifetime. However, the firm must commit $500,000 of its capital assets over the life of the product in order to successfully introduce it on the market. Applying the gross-return-on-investment formula, we can compute the return on this amount of investment.

$$E_G = \frac{\pi}{I} \cdot 100 \qquad\qquad \text{Given by Equation 5-4}$$

$$E_G = \frac{80,000}{500,000} \cdot 100 \qquad \text{By substitution}$$

$$E_G = 16\% \qquad\qquad\qquad \text{By arithmetic}$$

This appears to be generous return. However, it may be inadequate if the opportunity costs over time are taken into account. Let us assume that management knows it can get a return elsewhere of 4 percent *per year* on the same investment and that it must pay 7 percent a year if it is to borrow the money. In order to compare the product's return on investment to other alternatives and to interest rates, the return must be expressed as an annual rate. This is easily accomplished by dividing the gross return on the investment by the number of years that the capital will be committed. This annual rate can be computed directly, by the following formula:

$$E = \frac{\pi}{n \cdot I} \cdot 100, \text{ where} \tag{5-5}$$

E = annual return on investment, expressed as a percentage of that investment

π = profit

n = number of years the capital is invested, and

I = investment

If we assume that the life of the product, hence the duration of the capital investment, is 3 years and that the other values are the same as in the preceding example, the annual rate of return will be

$$E = \frac{\pi}{n \cdot I} \cdot 100 \qquad \text{Given by Equation 5-5}$$

$$E = \frac{80,000}{3 \cdot 500,000} \cdot 100 \qquad \text{By substitution}$$

$$E = 5.33\% \qquad \text{By arithmetic}$$

Thus the product would be acceptable if the firm had no alternative other than the 4-percent investment and did not have to borrow the money.

However, if the required capital is to be borrowed, then the interest paid must be included in the cost function and the borrowed capital excluded from the investment value. For instance, a project might require $150,000 in capital throughout its 3-year life span. If the firm borrowed $100,000 at a 7 percent interest rate, then $21,000 would be added to the project's cost (.07 × $100,000 × 3). This would leave $50,000 to be invested by the company itself. Thus the investment variable, I, would be $50,000.

The annual return on investment can be a good long-run decision criterion. In the short run, a substantial quantity of the firm's capital is committed to a particular mix of plants and equipment, and alternative investments are severely limited. Hence, profit is a simpler—and usually an adequate—criterion. Management seeks simply to earn the greatest profit possible given the present capital facilities.

Profit is also an adequate criterion in long-run decisions when all the capital is to be borrowed. The cost of the borrowed capital—computed by multiplying the interest rate times the quantity of capital times the period of time the capital will be borrowed—is included in the cost function. Thus profit becomes a net value and can be compared directly with the normal return on invested capital.

For example, if management had a choice of two mutually exclusive products, the first with an annual gross profit of $150,000 and the second with an annual gross profit of $90,000, it would not select the first with confidence until it knew the amount of capital both required. If the first required $400,000 in capital to be borrowed for 5 years at 5-percent annual interest, it would yield a net profit of only $50,000. If the second required only $100,000 over 5 years at 5 percent, it would yield a net profit of $75,000. Clearly, the latter is the superior alternative.

If the firm were using its own capital, the gross return on investment would be 37.5 percent and 90 percent for the respective products. The annual return on investment, assuming revenues were received equally over the life of the products, would be 7.5 percent and 18 percent, respectively. Again, the second product is obviously the better choice.

Present Value.   *Present value* is the value of future streams of income expressed in current dollars. The concept of present value is based on the assumption that a dollar received today is worth more than a dollar received in the future—not because of inflation but simply because a dollar received today can be put to work (invested) to earn more money during the time one would be waiting to receive the future dollar. For example, if the prevailing interest rate is 5 percent, a dollar received today and invested will be worth $1.05 a year hence. A dollar received one year from today, however, will be worth just $1.00 to the recipient at that time. Put another way, $1.00 received a year from now is equivalent to $.952 received today, assuming a 5-percent interest rate.

The present value of a future income stream can be readily computed using the following formula:

$$P_R = \frac{A}{(1 + i)^x}, \text{ where} \qquad\qquad (5\text{--}6)$$

P = present value of A dollars received x years in the future

A = amount received

i = prevailing discount rate,[4] and

x = time in years

To illustrate, let us assume that the marketing division's research department is forecasting sales of $600,000 for Product A. However, because of the amount of time that will be consumed in the design, development,

[4] A common form of discount rate is interest, which is the amount charged a borrower by a lending institution; it is expressed as a percentage of the amount borrowed.

testing, manufacture, and delivery of the product, this revenue will not be realized for 3 years. The marketing manager wants to discount this revenue to its present value so that it can be compared to revenue that has been forecast for other product alternatives. Given a discount rate of 5 percent, and using Equation 5–6, we have

$$P_R = \frac{A}{(1 + i)^x} \qquad \text{Given by Equation 5–6}$$

$$P_R = \frac{\$600,000}{(1 + .05)^3} \qquad \text{By substitution}$$

$$P_R = \$518,152 \qquad \text{By arithmetic}$$

The present value of the expected revenue of Product A is $518,152. The marketing manager now compares this present value to that for Product B, which would use the same plant and equipment and require the same cash outlay as A. Sales of Product B are expected to amount to only $580,000, but the money will be received in 2 years. The marketing manager would choose Product B, since the present value of its future revenue is $526,500. (The reader can confirm this by computing P_R for Product B.)

Although the income stream is often discounted at the prevailing interest rate, other discount rates may be employed in calculating P_R. For instance, the firm's current or average rate of return on investment, the cost of issuing debt securities, the ratio of dividends to market price of its stock, or the cost of borrowing money from other sources may be more appropriate in certain situations.

Until our discussion of the return on investment, we did not include the time element as a significant factor in the decision process. Our models were static, implying that output, revenue, cost, and profit all occur at once. Although eliminating the time factor simplifies the explanation of some fundamental relationships, it makes the simulation model necessarily less accurate for most real-world problems. Although a static model is generally superior to intuition or random choice, it is generally inferior to a dynamic model. A *dynamic model* explicitly includes time as one of its variables. A *static model,* on the other hand, ignores the effect of time.

By using present value—sometimes called *discounted present value* because it discounts future money flows to their equivalent in present dollars—time can be introduced explicitly into most cost-revenue-profit models. A present-value model adjusts the computed values of revenue, cost, and profit to reflect time. Future streams of income and cost can be adjusted to their present values and compared, regardless of the varying lifespans of alternative projects.

The converse of the argument that a dollar today is worth more to the recipient than one received in the future applies to a dollar spent in the future as opposed to one spent today. If the firm can delay an expenditure, the money can be used to earn interest or profit in the meantime. The present value of delayed cash outlays (future streams of expenses) can be computed as follows:

$$P_C = \frac{C}{(1 + i)^x}, \text{ where}$$ (5–7)

P_C = present value of an expenditure made x years hence

C = cost of expenditure

i = discount rate, and

x = time in years

Profit is equal to revenue minus cost. If one elects to use a present-value model and thus include time in the analysis, profit is computed by subtracting the present value of costs, P_C, from the present value of revenues, P_R. To simplify computation, the analyst can determine the profit for each year of the proposed program and then discount the resultant annual profit to obtain a present value. Alternative investments—say, mutually exclusive products A, B, and C—that have different levels of profit over time are best evaluated using a present-value model.

The aggregation of future profits, discounted to their present value, is represented symbolically as follows:

$$\pi_p = \sum_{j=0}^{n} \frac{(R_j - C_j)}{(1 + i)^j}, \text{ where}$$ (5–8)

π_p = total profit, discounted to present value

R_j = revenue for year j

C_j = cost for year j

i = discount rate, and

j = number of years from start of program

Present-value analyses are often made using cash-flow charts that present both the incomes (revenues) and outlays (costs) expected for each accounting period—usually one year—over the life of the program. In addition to providing a convenient method for arraying revenues and costs, a cash-flow chart enables the analyst to determine the minimum amount of capital that must be committed. By comparing the charts for each alternative, he can readily perceive their cost, revenue, and profit, and thus evaluate the potential return versus the potential risk for different projects.

Capital Requirements. Capital requirements are the amounts of capital, usually expressed in dollars, required for each year of a project's lifespan. They are usually an important consideration, because the capital available to the firm is limited. Even if the firm can acquire adequate capital to finance a given project, that project will reduce the amount of capital available for other projects, and perhaps cause them to be dropped. The decision-maker is interested not only in the maximum amount of capital needed, but also in the length of time for which it will be needed. Normally, future streams of profit are used to both pay off debts and finance new projects. Capital requirements are computed as follows:

$$K_j = \sum_{i=0}^{j} (R_i - C_i), \text{ where} \tag{5-9}$$

K_j = total accumulated capital outlay at year j

R_i = revenue for year i, and

C_i = cost for year i

An example of this problem, and of the use of the present-value formulas, is shown in Table 5.1, a typical cash-flow chart. Table 5.2 shows a comparison matrix for three products, A, B, and C. Both tables assume a three-year planning horizon and a discount rate of 5 percent.

If the firm's ability to increase its capital is not limited, it would be well advised to produce all three products, since each promises a substantial profit.

Table 5.1 Cash-flow chart for Product A
          (Discount rate = 5%)

Year (j)	Revenue for Year (R_j)	Cost for Year (C_j)	Profit for Year ($\pi_j = R_j - C_j$)	Discounted Present Value of Profit (π_p)	Accumulated Capital Outlay ($K_j = \sum_{i=0}^{j}(R_i - C_i)$)
0 (start)	None	$400,000	$-400,000	$-400,000	$ 400,000
1	$ 300,000	300,000	None	None	400,000
2	1,000,000	300,000	700,000	635,200	-300,000
3 (finish)	500,000	200,000	300,000	259,300	-600,000

Aggregate profit discounted to present value: $\pi_p = \sum_{j=0}^{3} \dfrac{(R_j - C_j)}{(1 + .05)^j} = \$494,500$

Table 5.2   Comparison matrix for Products A, B, and C

	Product A	Product B	Product C
Discounted Present Value of Accumulated Profit (π_p)	$ 495,000	$ 300,000	$ 500,000
Capital Outlay			
Start	400,000	500,000	600,000
1st Year	400,000	400,000	1,000,000
2nd Year	−300,000	−280,000	800,000
3rd Year	−600,000	−250,000	−700,000

If capital is limited, however, then Product A should be produced before B or C. It yields virtually the same profit as Product C but requires a capital investment less than one-half as great (a maximum investment of $400,000 versus a maximum investment of $1,000,000).

APPLICATIONS OF THE KEY VALUES

The key values we have described are not a substitute for judgment, but they do provide a basis for rational decision-making. Which values should be considered in any particular situation will depend in part on the availability and cost of data and also on which variables can be manipulated; dynamic models are normally preferable to static models. The more common key values used for optimizing decisions involving cost, revenue, and profit are summarized in Table 5.3.

Table 5.3 Key values for marketing decisions

Key Value	Formula	General Application
Profit	$\pi = R - C$	Long-run decisions involving selection, rejection, and arraying of alternatives
Marginal Profit	$\Delta\pi = R - \Delta C$	All short-run decisions
Return on Investment (Gross)	$E_G = \dfrac{\pi}{I} \cdot 100$	Selection of alternatives for capital investment when the planning horizon and expected payoff rate is the same for each alternative
Return on Investment (Annual)	$E = \dfrac{\pi}{nI} \cdot 100$	Selection of alternatives for capital investment
Break-Even Point (Quantity)	$Q_B = \dfrac{F}{P - V}$	Analysis of risk, with linear total cost function
Break-Even Point (Quantity)	$Q_B = \dfrac{F}{P - C_1 r^{\log_2 Q_B}}$	Analysis of risk, with nonlinear total cost function (learning phenomenon is considered)
Break-Even Point (Dollar Value)	$Q_{B_\$} = P \cdot Q_B$	
Present Value Revenue	$P_R = \dfrac{A}{(1 + i)^x}$	Comparison of future streams of income
Cost	$P_C = \dfrac{C}{(1 + i)^x}$	Comparison of future streams of expenses
Profit in Year j	$\pi_{p_j} = \dfrac{(R_j - C_j)}{(1 + i)^j}$	Comparison of future streams of profit
Aggregate Profit	$\pi_p = \sum \left(\dfrac{(R_j - C_j)}{(1 + i)^j} \right)$	Selection, rejection, and arraying of alternatives
Capital Requirements	$K_j = \sum\limits_{i=0}^{j} (R_i - C_i)$	Determination of capital needs and exclusivity of alternatives

Summary of Marketing Decision Values

There are two fundamental approaches to cost analysis—accounting's and economics'. The essential difference between the two methods is in the allocation of fixed costs. Classical accounting methods distribute fixed costs to each unit of output, necessarily on an arbitrary basis. Microeconomics assigns only variable cost to output for purposes of decision-making, since profit will be increased as long as the marginal cost associated with the product is less than the marginal revenue. Since all costs vary in the long run, the long-term models of an accountant and an economist would be the same.

Federal law prescribes the use of the accounting method of cost analysis by most firms for tax purposes. This method is also appropriate to budgeting and control. However, decisions involving the manipulation of the production variables—especially the marketing instruments—are generally best handled by taking an economic approach. The need for cost information in the decision process suggests that marketers are well advised to have a working knowledge of cost-analysis methods, cost classifications, the economic periods prescribed by the cost variables, and the learning function. They should also be aware of the nature of cost data and the fact that it must often be adjusted before it can safely be used in the decision model.

Once an optimum price has been selected and the output estimated, revenue is easily computed. Profit is readily determined once revenue and cost are known. Profit is one of several key values for decision-making. Other relevant values are the break-even point, the return on investment, and the present value of future income and expense streams. The break-even point is useful in evaluating capital requirements and risk. The return on investment is relevant to long-run product decisions and the selection of exclusive alternatives. Determining present value introduces a time element into the decision process; the resultant dynamic model is closer to reality than a static model would be. If several alternatives must be evaluated, each with a different time span, then future streams of costs and revenues, hence profits, should be discounted to their present values for purposes of comparison and choice.

Questions and Problems

1. Cite an example of each of the following costs: (a) variable, (b) fixed, (c) semi-fixed, (d) opportunity, and (e) marginal.
2. Define and estimate the time of the market period, short-run period, and long-run period for two industries.
3. Discuss the advantages of scale for a farm, a retail shoe store, and an automobile factory.
4. A marketer must prepare a bid involving a long-run commitment by the firm. The accounting department provides the following data:

Fixed Cost	$400,000
Variable Cost	
Material	$ 50,000 per unit (flat rate)
Labor	$ 5 per hour
Historical Learning Rate	90%

Thirty-two units are to be built. An industrial engineer estimates that the first unit will require 5,000 man-hours of direct labor. Company policy specifies a price equal to 110 percent of total cost. Using a static model, compute a recommended bid (total price).

5. A product has an initial fixed cost of $200,000, an optimum price of $30, and a linear variable cost of $26. What is the break-even quantity, or output? What must sales be, in dollars, before the firm starts to show a profit?
6. A market analyst estimates a gross profit over a 10-year period of $40,000, $60,000, and $50,000 for products A, B, and C, respectively. The investments required for these mutually exclusive alternatives are $80,000, $200,000, and $150,000. Which is the best investment under each of the following conditions? (a) The firm has no other way to use its capital resources. (b) The firm must borrow the money at 5.5–percent annual interest.
7. A marketing manager is confronted with the following cash-flow data for three mutually exclusive products. The firm requires all future project costs and revenues to be discounted at a 10 percent rate (i.e., this is the minimum annual rate of return required for the approval of new investment projects). Which product should be selected, and why?

	Product A		Product B		Product C	
Year	Cost	Revenue	Cost	Revenue	Cost	Revenue
Start	$500,000	None	$500,000	$ 100,000	$1,000,000	None
1st	500,000	None	600,000	500,000	500,000	None
2nd	800,000	$ 400,000	700,000	1,000,000	200,000	$1,000,000
3rd	900,000	1,000,000	800,000	1,500,000	200,000	1,000,000
4th	400,000	2,700,000	700,000	1,000,000	100,000	500,000

Supplementary Readings

BOOKS

FERTIG, PAUL E., ISTVAN, DONALD F., and MOTTICE, HOMER J., *Using Accounting Information: An Introduction* (New York: Harcourt, Brace & World, 1965).

LERNER, EUGENE M., and CARLETON, WILLARD T., *A Theory of Financial Analysis* (New York: Harcourt, Brace & World, 1966).

SPENCER, MILTON H., and SIEGELMAN, LOUIS, *Managerial Economics: Decision Making and Forward Planning,* rev. ed. (Homewood, Ill.: Irwin, 1964).

ARTICLES

BAUMOL, WILLIAM J., and SEVIN, CHARLES H., "Marketing Costs and Mathematical Programming," *Harvard Business Review,* Vol. 35, No. 5 (September–October 1957), pp. 52–60.

DAVIDSON, SIDNEY, "Old Wine into New Bottles," *Accounting Review,* Vol. 38, No. 2 (April 1963), pp. 278–84.

GOGGANS, TRAVIS P., "Break-Even Analysis with Curvilinear Functions," *Accounting Review,* Vol. 40, No. 4 (October 1965), pp. 867–71.

HIRSCHLEIFER, JACK, "The Firm's Cost Function: A Successful Reconstruction?" *Journal of Business,* Vol. 35, No. 3 (July 1962), pp. 235–55.

OXENFELDT, A. R., and BAXTER, W. T., "Approaches to Pricing: Economist vs. Accountant," *Business Horizons,* Vol. 4, No. 4 (Winter 1961), pp. 77–90.

MENGE, JOHN H., "Style Change Costs as a Market Weapon," *Quarterly Journal of Economics,* Vol. 76, No. 4 (November 1962), pp. 632–47.

STIGLER, GEORGE J., "The Economics of Scale," *Journal of Law and Economics,* Vol. 1 (October 1958), pp. 54–71.

STURMEY, S. G., "Cost Curves and Pricing in Aircraft Production," *Economic Journal,* Vol. 74, No. 296 (December 1964), pp. 954–82.

Part III

MARKETING RESOURCES MANAGEMENT

The foundation of rational resource allocation is microeconomics, particularly the theory of the firm given in Chapter 3. In brief, management maximizes profit by selecting those alternatives that maximize the positive difference between revenue and cost. As additional increments of revenue are gained by incurring additional increments of cost, profit continues to increase until it reaches a maximum. At that point marginal revenue equals marginal cost, and additional outlays of resources will result in a net decrease in profit. The primary objective of management should be to allocate the firm's resources in a way that will maximize profit in the long run.

The cost, revenue, and profit analyses and the key values discussed in Chapter 5 provide a basis for resource-allocation decisions. However, the applications of these ideas need to be developed further. Also, as both theory and application are expanded and made more sophisticated to conform more closely with the realities of the marketplace, we must take into account two more factors—risk and uncertainty.

If management's primary duty is resource allocation, its secondary duty is resource control. Knowledge is imperfect, errors are made in allocation, internal conditions change, and exogenous variables bring about outcomes that contradict predictions. This is true throughout the firm, but it is especially true in marketing. The best-laid plans can go astray, and marketing programs are no exception. Once resources have been assigned, they must be controlled to ensure proper performance.

Hence, resource allocation and resource control are simply opposite sides of the same coin. The techniques used in these areas are common to most fields of human endeavor involving group action. They are especially important in marketing, where they provide the foundation for rational decision-making in the manipulation of a wide assortment of resources, both human and material.

CHAPTER 6

Resource Allocation

RULE OF PROPORTIONALITY

The rule of proportionality states that *the distribution of resources between alternate instruments of production (including marketing) will be optimum when the ratio of the incremental change in revenue to the incremental change in cost is equal for each alternative.* This can be expressed mathematically as

$$\frac{\Delta R_1}{\Delta C_1} = \frac{\Delta R_2}{\Delta C_2} = \cdots \frac{\Delta R_n}{\Delta C_n}, \text{ where} \tag{6-1}$$

ΔR = incremental change in revenue

ΔC = incremental change in cost, and

$1, 2, \ldots n$ represent each of the instruments of production

For example, assume that a firm's marketing department had collected revenue and cost data from sales regions 1, 2, 3, 4, and 5, and has computed their incremental revenue–incremental cost ratios, $\Delta R/\Delta C$, as 9, 8, 4, 7, and 7, respectively. The first region is obviously the most productive at the margin; another dollar of expenditure in region 1 will produce another $9 of revenue $(\Delta R_1/\Delta C_1 = 9)$. The third region is clearly the least productive at the margin; another dollar of expenditure will produce only $4 in revenue $(\Delta R_3/\Delta C_3 = 4)$. Obviously, resources should be moved from region 3 to region 1. A dollar taken from region 3 will reduce revenue by $4, but when added to region 1 it will increase revenue by $9. Only when the ratios for all five regions are equal will there be no reason to shift resources among them.

If region 1 is the most productive, why not take all the resources allocated to regions 2, 3, 4, and 5, and assign them to region 1? This would generally not be wise, for three reasons. First, the relationship between revenue and cost is seldom fixed; normally, it varies with input. As more resources are transferred into region 1, the operation there will eventually become less efficient and $\Delta R_1/\Delta C_1$ will drop, ultimately to the level of most of the other regions. In fact, as the resources assigned to the other regions are reduced, this incremental revenue–incremental cost ratio may increase.

Second, practical considerations often make reallocation difficult, especially in the short run. Office space, salesmen, supporting personnel, and equipment are not always easy to move about. In addition, resources cannot always be moved in the increments suggested by the theoretically optimum solution. A firm can hardly transfer 13 percent of a salesman, or 5.7 automobiles.

Third, specifying the incremental revenue–incremental cost ratio at each level of cost within the possible range of expenditures is a problem. $\Delta R_1/\Delta C_1$ may be 9 at the present level of expenditure, say \$50,000, but what will it be at a higher level, say \$100,000? Often, the answer to a question such as this can be found only by a trial-and-error process. Small shifts in resources are made, the changes in revenues are observed, and another set of marginal values is computed. This process is repeated—each cycle being called an iteration—until $\Delta R/\Delta C$ is equal, or nearly equal, for each region.

Another example will help to illustrate the problems in applying the rule of proportionality. Let us assume that a firm's advertising director must decide how to distribute his advertising budget among media 1, 2, 3, 4, and 5. A survey of buyers indicates that the increment of revenue, R, contributed by each medium during the preceding advertising period was \$50,000, \$10,000, \$15,000, \$18,000, and \$30,000, respectively. The incremental costs were \$10,000, \$2,000, \$2,000, \$3,000, and \$8,000, respectively.

If we applied the rule of proportionality to the above data, we would obtain the following incremental revenue–incremental cost ratios:

$$\frac{\Delta R_1}{\Delta C_1}, \quad \frac{\Delta R_2}{\Delta C_2}, \quad \frac{\Delta R_3}{\Delta C_3}, \quad \frac{\Delta R_4}{\Delta C_4}, \quad \frac{\Delta R_5}{\Delta C_5} \qquad \text{Given}$$

$$\frac{50,000}{10,000}, \quad \frac{10,000}{2,000}, \quad \frac{15,000}{2,000}, \quad \frac{18,000}{3,000}, \quad \frac{30,000}{8,000} \qquad \text{By substitution}$$

Arranging the ratios in descending order, we have

$$\frac{15,000}{2,000} > \frac{18,000}{3,000} > \frac{50,000}{10,000} = \frac{10,000}{2,000} > \frac{30,000}{8,000} \qquad \text{By arraying[1]}$$

The most efficient medium is apparently number 3, which has the greatest incremental revenue–incremental cost ratio. This suggests a reallocation of

[1] "Arraying" means to place in a particular order; here, larger values precede smaller values.

the advertising budget: a shift of funds from the less efficient media, especially number 5, to the more efficient, especially number 3.

The incremental revenue–incremental cost ratios above are actually gross approximations of the slopes of the curves that would result if we plotted the relationship between revenue and cost for each production input—in this case, the five advertising media. If these curves, or functions, were always linear, the obvious solution would be to put all available funds into the medium with the highest ratio. However, the relationship between a production input's contribution to revenue and its cost is usually nonlinear; hence one value is seldom accurate for all levels of input. This is particularly true in marketing, where so many exogenous variables enter into the determination of revenue. In advertising, for example, saturated exposure of a relatively fixed audience—that reached by a particular medium—leads to diminishing returns, to the point where additional advertising in the medium produces no additional sales.

Let us assume, realistically, that the relationship between sales and expenditures for each of the advertising media 1, 2, 3, 4, and 5 is nonlinear. The incremental increase in sales resulting from a given incremental increase in advertising will not be constant throughout the range of advertising in any given medium. For example, medium 1 produced *total* sales of $50,000 for a *total* expenditure of $10,000 during the preceding period. Thus the *average* ratio of sales to expenditures for this medium, through the range zero to $10,000, is 5:1. However, the advertising director has no assurance that another dollar spent on medium 1 will produce $5 in revenue. On the contrary, medium 1's audience may already be saturated with the firm's advertising and may not respond to any additional advertising. In fact, the present level of revenue attributable to medium 1 might be sustained with a slightly lower outlay. From an aggregate measure (here, $R = \$50,000$ and $C = \$10,000$), there is no way to tell. What we need are the precise marginal values of the incremental revenue–incremental cost ratios at different levels of input. For example, the marginal incremental revenue–incremental cost ratio for medium 1 might be 2:1 at an aggregate expenditure of $10,000. Thus an additional expenditure of $1,000 would produce about $2,000 in additional sales. The advertising director would be wise to shift resources gradually, until the $\Delta R / \Delta C$ ratios at the margin become evident.

What we need to use for our rule of proportionality, therefore, is the marginal value of the incremental revenue–incremental cost ratio. The marginal value of incremental revenue is called the *marginal revenue product* (*MRP*). This is the product of the price of the output, or *marginal revenue* (*MR*), and the *marginal physical product* (*MPP*). Marginal physical product is the marginal relationship between output and input. (For instance, if, at the margin, 10 units of an input are required in order to obtain 1 unit of output, then the marginal physical product is $\frac{1}{10}$, or .1.) This relationship can be expressed as follows:

$$MRP_i = MR \cdot MPP_i, \text{ where} \tag{6-2}$$

MRP_i = marginal revenue product of the output with respect to input i

MR = marginal revenue of the output, and

MPP_i = marginal physical product of the output with respect to input i

The marginal value of incremental cost is called the *marginal factor cost (MFC)* and is simply the marginal price paid for one additional unit of input. Since the marginal revenue product reflects the price of the output and the marginal factor cost reflects the cost of the input, the substitution of MRP and MFC in our rule of proportionality will yield both the optimum allocation of resources between alternate instruments of production and the optimum *total* allocation of resources. This occurs because marginal revenue product and marginal factor cost are more sophisticated determinants of marginal revenue and marginal cost than an aggregate measure, for they measure the marginal revenue and marginal cost attributable to each input.

As we have previously demonstrated, profit is maximized when marginal revenue equals marginal cost; therefore, profit will be maximized when $MRP = MFC$ for each input. In order to obtain both an optimum allocation of resources between production instruments *and* an optimum allocation of total resources, the ratio of MRP to MFC must be 1 for each input. This is the *rule of perfect resource allocation,* which states that *both the level and distribution of resources will be optimum when*

$$\frac{MRP_1}{MFC_1} = \frac{MRP_2}{MFC_2} = \cdots \frac{MRP_n}{MFC_n} = 1, \text{ where} \tag{6-3}$$

MRP = marginal revenue product

MFC = marginal factor cost, and

$1, 2, \ldots n$ represent each of the instruments of production

Since the marginal revenue product for each production instrument is the product of the marginal revenue (which is constant for all factors when perfect resource allocation has been obtained) and the marginal physical product for that instrument; the perfect-resource-allocation rule may be re-expressed in a more useful form as follows:

$$\frac{MPP_1}{MFC_1} = \frac{MPP_2}{MFC_2} = \cdots \frac{MPP_n}{MFC_n} = \frac{1}{MR} = \frac{1}{MC}, \text{ where} \tag{6-4}$$

MPP = marginal physical product

MFC = marginal factor cost

MR = marginal revenue for the output when perfect resource allocation has been obtained

MC = marginal cost for the output when perfect resource allocation
has been obtained, and

1, 2, . . . n represent each of the instruments of production

Marginal physical product, MPP, is usually thought of as the ratio between a single unit of output—one automobile, one theater ticket, or one
haircut—and the units of input required to obtain it. Marginal factor cost,
MFC, is the cost (the price paid by the firm) of an additional unit of input—
one ton of steel, one salesman, or one television commercial. Marginal revenue, MR, is normally considered to be the price that the producer receives
for the product, and marginal cost, MC, is the cost of producing one additional unit of output. It should be noted that we have defined these marginal
measures in terms of delta, Δ, rather than the calculus derivative d. If we
were using calculus definitions, we would substitute the term "infinitesimal
change" for "units."

The perfect-resource-allocation model indicates how to allocate available
resources and, if resources are not limited to a below-optimum level, how to
maximize profit. Profit can be maximized by increasing or decreasing the
use of each input until Equation 6–4 is satisfied. This method provides an
optimum solution for both total and relative allocation of resources.

MARKETING RESOURCES

A firm is usually started with a quantity of money capital, either cash or a
line of credit. As the firm matures, monetary resources are converted into
other forms of capital, such as land, buildings, equipment, and inventories of
material and unsold products. Some of the original capital is also consumed
by wages, expendable material, depreciation, and similar expenses, but normally this amount will be covered by the firm as revenues start to come in.

Many resources, particularly capital assets, are not liquid—that is, they
cannot easily be converted into other forms. As a result, in the market and
short-run periods many resources cannot be reallocated. A milling machine
cannot be exchanged for more advertising; a piece of land cannot be converted to a product improvement. In the long run, however, all company
assets are convertible into money and hence are variable. Thus the firm's
total resources may be expressed as an aggregate dollar value.

In other periods, many of these resources are fixed and should be
viewed as distinct instruments of production. In marketing, these instruments, also called "resources," "factors," and "inputs," can be broadly
categorized as price, product, promotion, distribution, and marketing research. Some inputs are fixed, such as advertising already contracted for,
warehouses, and computers. Some are semifixed, such as salaried personnel

and certain employee benefits. Others are readily variable, such as uncommitted advertising budgets and cash.

The marketing manager usually has considerable discretion in the distribution of marketing resources, within the limit imposed by the department's allocation. The rule of proportionality is applicable to budgeting decisions within the department and can be used to determine the optimum allocation of available resources. However, the marketing manager often must settle for a suboptimum solution because he is unable to get sufficient additional resources to satisfy the rule of perfect resource allocation. For instance, if he cannot find more salesmen, if he cannot afford to increase his inventory, or if his budget is limited, he may be unable to approximate the optimum allocation indicated by the rule of perfect resource allocation. Conversely, he may have been over-allocated by the company and have excessive resources at his disposal. Unless he is willing to return part of his budget—thus setting a precedent for reducing future budgets—the excessive expenditures necessary to absorb the department's share of the firm's total resources may result in a failure to maximize profit. This is most likely to occur where the marketer's performance is judged by such criteria as total sales or the firm's share of the market, rather than by his department's contribution to profit.

The allocation of resources to specific marketing instruments will be explored in detail in Parts V through IX. Here, our objective is to develop a keener understanding of the basic techniques of resource allocation—techniques that can be generalized to all facets of marketing management. Quantitative allocation methods, such as the rules of proportionality and perfect resource allocation, have their limitations. Although most inputs can be evaluated in terms of their marginal factor costs, many defy a rigorous quantification of their marginal physical product or marginal revenue product. The contributions to revenue of management training, employee services, legal counsel, public relations, or institutional advertising, for example, are not easy to assess. Nevertheless, where reasonably accurate data are available, quantitative techniques can be of great help. The constraints of limited resources and hard-to-shift factor inputs often mean that only a suboptimum solution is possible. However, the rules of proportionality and perfect resource allocation, as well as other quantitative methods, are still powerful techniques for finding the best possible solutions to resource-allocation and redistribution problems.

OPTIMIZING BETWEEN TWO INPUTS

Often a variety of combinations of two inputs can produce the same output. The mix of inputs is optimized by selecting that combination which provides the desired output at the lowest cost. A typical example is the problem of allocating resources between two promotional instruments. Assume that a firm wishes to sell a fixed quantity of goods. Both advertising and personal selling serve this end. As the firm increases the quantity of advertising, less personal selling is needed, and vice versa. The relationship between the two factors is shown graphically by a series of isoquant lines,[2] each representing a fixed quantity of output (sales) that will be produced by the input combinations depicted by the curve. Figure 6.1 illustrates a two-input, single-output optimization problem.

Similarly, the cost relationship can be represented by an *isocost line* showing the input combinations that can be purchased for a given cost. Where an isocost line is tangent to an isoquant line, the cost of a given quantity of output is minimum. By connecting a series of these tangential points, we can construct an optimum-input-mix/minimum-cost line for various outputs.

Isoquant lines, like S_1, S_2, and S_3 in Figure 6.1, tend to be hyperbolic and convex to the origin. This is because the mix of variables becomes less efficient as either variable approaches an extreme. For example, an excessive

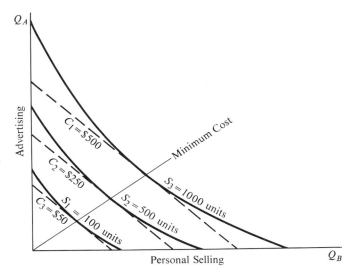

FIGURE 6.1
Isoquant and isocost curves for two inputs
(C = cost, S = sales)

---

[2] An isoquant line is a line of fixed quantity; that is, each point on the line represents a different combination of inputs, but the same output.

amount of advertising would be required to produce a given number of sales if there were little or no personal selling. Conversely, a disproportionate amount of personal selling would be needed to compensate for a near or total absence of advertising. In some cases, isoquant curves are asymptotic—that is, they approach one or both axes but never touch them. The classical example of this phenomenon is the mixing of inputs of labor and land to produce crops. One input can be increased at the expense of the other to produce the same yield, yet neither can be completely eliminated.

Note that the isocost lines in Figure 6.1 are linear. This is not an unrealistic assumption, except when the firm's purchases are large enough to influence price or when short-run conditions make marginal cost increase as an input is increased. The latter condition occurs when, for example, a firm must pay overtime rates for extra hours put in by present employees because sufficient time is not available to hire and train additional personnel, and production deadlines must be met.

The problem of optimizing between two inputs can be solved graphically by first constructing an isoquant curve for the quantity of output desired. An isocost curve is then obtained by selecting an arbitrary total cost and plotting the ordered pairs of input values that will give that cost. (If the cost relationship is linear, we can simply compute any two points, or ordered pairs, and draw a straight line through them.) A line drawn parallel to the initial isocost curve and tangent to the isoquant curve will give the point where the combination of input quantities is optimum—that is, where their combined total cost will be minimum—for the desired output and will also give the total cost of the optimum combination of inputs.

A more precise solution than that yielded by graphical methods is possible because of the mathematical properties of the relationship between the isocost and isoquant lines at the optimum condition. First, the lines are tangent, hence they must be parallel at the point of tangency.[3] If they are parallel at the point of tangency, then their slopes must be equal; that is, the derivative of the isocost function must be equal to the derivative of the isoquant function. Second, at the point of tangency, the value of Q_A (see Figure 6.1) must be the same in both the isocost and isoquant functions. The value of Q_B, too, must be the same in both functions. Consequently, if we know the desired output, the cost of the inputs, and the production function (the relationship of the output to the inputs), we can select the optimum combination of inputs for a given output.

To illustrate the mathematical approach to optimizing between two inputs, let us assume that a regional branch manager has been assigned a quota of 4000 units of Product A per week and must choose a promotional

---

[3] They are parallel only at the solution point. They converge on one side of the point and diverge on the other, as one moves from left to right on the graph.

mix that will minimize the cost of selling that output in his area. We assume two marketing inputs—advertising and personal selling. We also assume that the average cost of advertising is $5 per column inch and that salesmen can be employed for $30 a day, including expenses and fringe benefits. The production function (or the relationship between the output and the inputs) for this sales office is assumed to be $S = 2Q_A + 30Q_B - Q_B^2$, where $S =$ sales, $Q_A =$ column inches of advertising, and $Q_B =$ man-days of personal selling.

In order to determine the optimum combination of advertising and personal selling, we need to find the slopes of the isoquant and isocost lines. This can be accomplished by taking the derivatives of the production function and the cost function. When these derivatives are equated, the optimum amounts of Q_A and Q_B can be determined. The mathematical steps are presented below.

$$S = 2Q_A + 30Q_B - Q_B^2 \qquad \text{Given as the marketing production function}$$

$$4,000 = 2Q_A + 30Q_B - Q_B^2 \qquad \text{By substitution}$$

$$Q_A = \frac{Q_B^2}{2} - 15Q_B + 2000 \qquad \text{By algebraic manipulation}$$

$$\left(\frac{d}{dQ_B}(Q_A)\right)_S = Q_B - 15 \qquad \text{By calculus (slope of the production function)}$$

$$C = 5Q_A + 30Q_B \qquad \text{Given as the cost function}$$

$$Q_A = \frac{C}{5} - 6Q_B \qquad \text{By algebraic manipulation}$$

$$\left(\frac{d}{dQ_B}(Q_A)\right)_C = -6 \qquad \text{By calculus (slope of the cost function)}$$

$$\left(\frac{d}{dQ_B}(Q_A)\right)_S = \left(\frac{d}{dQ_B}(Q_A)\right)_C \qquad \text{By equating the two slopes}$$

$$Q_B - 15 = -6 \qquad \text{By substitution}$$

$$Q_B = 9 \qquad \text{By arithmetic}$$

$$Q_A = \frac{Q_B^2}{2} - 15Q_B + 2000 \qquad \text{The production function after algebraic manipulation}$$

$$Q_A = \frac{(9)^2}{2} - 15(9) + 2000 \qquad \text{By substitution}$$

$$Q_A = 1905.5 \qquad \text{By arithmetic}$$

Therefore, the optimum input mix is 1905.5 column inches of advertising and 9 man-days of personal selling. The cost, C, is computed as follows:

$$C = 5Q_A + 30Q_B \qquad \text{Given}$$
$$C = 5(1905.5) + 30(9) \qquad \text{By substitution}$$
$$C = 9554.50 \qquad \text{By arithmetic}$$

The cost of the optimum mix is thus $9554.50.

CONTINUOUS VERSUS DISCRETE FUNCTIONS

Thus far, we have assumed in our decision models that the cost and production functions are continuous within bounds. That is, we have assumed that within the plausible range of inputs and outputs, any quantity of input, and the resultant output, could occur. This has allowed us to plot the functions as continuous lines and to reach the mathematical solutions by familiar techniques. Although this is both a convenient and a useful assumption, it is not a rigorous one. The firm cannot easily order 8.7642 pages of advertising, hire 3.9 salesmen, or sell 300.65 airplanes. In the real world, the cost and production functions are actually discontinuous—that is, they are composed of a discrete series of points, as the firm increases advertising from 8 to 9 pages, enlarges its sales staff from 3 to 4 men, or increases its output from 300 to 301 units.

In defense of the continuous-function assumption, it is fair to point out that most inputs can be purchased in increments sufficiently small as to approximate continuity. Even labor can be added in quantities other than unity through the use of overtime, the sharing employees between products or departments, and the use of job shops or part-time personnel. Output can also be varied by fractional quantities, if spare parts are included. When one considers the assortment of spares produced by a typical hard-goods manufacturer, a total output lying between two whole numbers is easy to visualize. Besides, an acceptable working level of accuracy can usually be obtained by rounding off the key values to the nearest whole number. In the example given above, advertising would probably be rounded from 89.5 to 90 column inches.

OPTIMIZING BETWEEN MULTIPLE INPUTS

The marketer can acknowledge the discrete nature of inputs and at the same time accommodate complex relationships involving many variables through

the use of desert-and-oasis charts.[4] This approach to the selection of optimum marketing mixes, formulated by P. J. Verdoorn, is a formal expression of a technique frequently practiced by firms confronted with a complex
assortment of marketing variables.

Given a particular product and its price, the marketer first decides
which marketing techniques are relevant—that is, to whom the product
can be sold and what methods will induce potential customers to buy it.
Once this decision has been made, he evaluates the total cost of different
combinations of the marketing inputs required to market the product. He
includes values for each of the instruments that compose the particular mix.
He estimates the quantity of advertising and personal selling, the distribution methods, and the product characteristics necessary to sell a given
quantity of output. The cost of each of these inputs is aggregated, thus providing a point estimate—that is, a single value—for each likely input. These
point estimates (oases) are then plotted on a dollars-versus-output chart
(the desert). Each point represents the total cost (measured along the
vertical axis) of a particular marketing mix. The oases are plotted on the
horizontal axis, above the output (sales) that they are expected to produce.

Figure 6.2 shows a desert-and-oasis chart for seven marketing mixes.
The scatter of oases represents the cost function, the straight line represents
the revenue function, and M_1, M_2, . . . M_7 represent the various mixes.
The broken line, sketched through those oases providing the lowest costs for

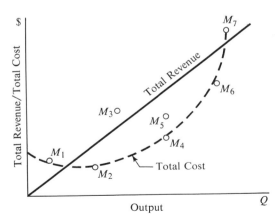

FIGURE 6.2
Desert-and-oasis map for selected marketing mixes

[4] P. J. Verdoorn, "Marketing from the Producer's Point of View," *Journal of Marketing,* Vol. 20, No. 2 (January 1956), pp. 49–56.

given outputs, Q, suggests the aggregate cost function. By identifying the oasis that is furthest below the revenue curve—M_4, in Figure 6.2—the marketer locates the maximum profit position, and hence the optimum marketing mix. Such points as M_1, M_3, and M_7, which lie above the revenue curve, are obviously very inefficient mixes.

OPTIMIZING WITH CONSTRAINTS

Often, the marketer is confronted with constraints that limit his flexibility and restrict his choice of variables. For example, fear of federal prosecution for monopolizing the market, fear of attracting new competitors because of an overly attractive profit, or fear of being sued for unfair competition on account of predatory pricing tactics may restrain the firm in its pursuit of profit.

A graphical solution to the problem of optimizing with constraints can be obtained by constructing a series of total revenue curves, based on different pricing tactics, and their companion total cost curves. The constraints are then imposed on the graph in the form of boundaries. The area between the boundaries—the shaded area in Figure 6.3—includes all the possible options.

The largest profit, π_1, is provided by Option 1. However, that alternative must be rejected because its price—as reflected by its revenue curve, TR_1—is above the maximum price constraint. Presumably the threat of entry by new firms is too great at that price. Option 2 appears to offer the next highest profit, π_2, but it is rejected because it results in too small a share of the market. Having an insufficient market share carries the risk that control or dominance may be relinquished to a competitor, that exclusivity in selected stores may be lost, that the product lines may be rejected by distributors demanding high-volume items, or that the size of the operation may be reduced to the point where the firm's ability to introduce new products is limited. Option 5 is out of bounds because of the low price, which is perhaps predatory in the eyes of the Justice Department. Alternatives 3 and 4 remain, as well as a segment of Option 2. However, alternatives 2 and 4 show a smaller profit *within* the boundaries than does Option 3. Thus Option 3 would be the rational choice; the output (hence the budget) and the marketing mix indicated at q_3 should be selected.

The mathematical technique for optimizing with constraints is similar to the graphical method. First, any alternatives involving a price beyond the price boundaries are rejected. Second, the optimum price, quantity, and profit are determined for each option. If the resultant output and total costs put the maximum profit point beyond the constraints, the maximum profit within the boundaries is computed. This would be the profit at the boundary,

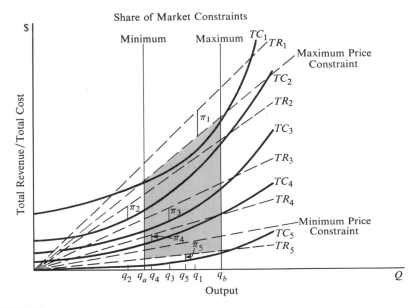

Share of Market Constraints

FIGURE 6.3
Revenue-cost functions subject to constraints
(For options 1, 2, 3, 4, and 5)

given the convex shape of the cost curve. A comparison of the within-bounds profits—along with the consideration of other key values—would identify the optimum choice.

LINEAR PROGRAMMING

Linear programming is a technique for solving linear functions that are subject to constraints. Suppose, once again, that a marketer wishes to maximize the allocation of his sales resources between advertising and personal selling. The weekly sales production function is $S = 10Q_A + 40Q_B$, where S = sales, Q_A = column inches of advertising, and Q_B = man-hours of personal selling. The marketer's total budget is $500 per week. Advertising costs $5 per column inch, salesmen cost $10 per hour, and the marketer cannot use more than one salesman (40 man-hours per week). Thus, the problem is to maximize sales in the function $S = 10Q_A + 40Q_B$, subject to the following constraints:

$$5Q_A + 10Q_B \leq 500 \qquad \text{(Budget constraint)}$$
$$Q_B \leq 40 \qquad \text{(Sales-force constraint)}$$

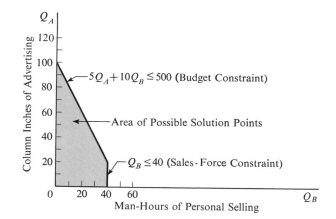

FIGURE 6.4
Acceptable combinations of two promotional inputs

By plotting the two constraints, as in Figure 6.4, we can find the area of possible solution points (given that Q_A and Q_B must be positive quantities).

A powerful theorem in linear programming states that any maximizing solution must occur at a corner of the feasible solution space. In our example, four corners exist: $Q_A = 0$, $Q_B = 0$; $Q_A = 100$, $Q_B = 0$; $Q_A = 0$, $Q_B = 40$; and $Q_A = 20$, $Q_B = 40$. Since $S = 10Q_A + 40Q_B$, the sales that would result from each of the four mixes are

$$Q_A = \quad 0, \quad Q_B = \quad 0 \qquad S = \qquad 0$$

$$Q_A = 100, \quad Q_B = \quad 0 \qquad S = 1000$$

$$Q_A = \quad 0, \quad Q_B = 40 \qquad S = 1600$$

$$Q_A = \quad 20, \quad Q_B = 40 \qquad S = 1800$$

Sales are therefore maximized when the $500 weekly budget is used to purchase 20 column inches of advertising and to employ a salesman 40 hours per week. The same result can be obtained graphically by imposing the sales equation, $S = 10Q_A + 40Q_B$, on the diagram showing the area of possible solution points, as in Figure 6.5. The point of tangency between the area of possible solution points and the sales production function is the optimum solution.

A graphical solution is appropriate for solving linear programming problems involving up to three variables. For problems involving a larger number of variables, there exist several methods of solution that involve matrix algebra. These mathematical techniques can be used to solve linear programming problems containing any number of variables.[5]

PROBABILITY AND EXPECTED VALUE

Probability is defined as *the chance that an event will occur.* It is expressed mathematically as a percentage between 0 and 100, inclusive, or as a decimal value between 0 and 1, inclusive. We shall generally use the decimal value in this text.[6]

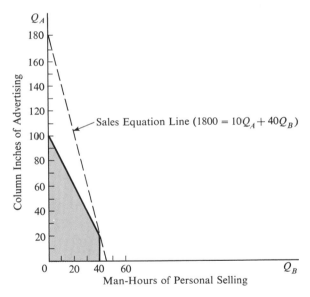

FIGURE 6.5
Graphical solution of a sales-budget allocation problem

---

[5] Any textbook on operations research will discuss linear programming. A suggested text is *Operations Research: Methods and Problems* by Maurice Sasieni et al. (New York: Wiley, 1959).
[6] A precise mathematical definition of probability is: "If an event can occur in N mutually exclusive and equally likely ways, and if n_A of these outcomes have an attribute A, then the probability of A is the fraction n_A/N." (Alexander M. Mood and F. A. Graybill, *Introduction to the Theory of Statistics,* 2nd ed. (New York: McGraw-Hill, 1963), p. 7.)

Perhaps the most familiar illustration of probability is flipping a coin. If a coin is flipped, there are two possible outcomes, heads and tails. The probability of a heads is 50 percent, or .5. The sum of the probabilities of all possible outcomes—in this case heads and tails—is always 1. Thus, the probability of getting a tails is .5 $(1 - .5 = .5)$. If a marketer has identified all the possible outcomes that could result from a particular course of action —say, an increase in advertising—the sum of their individual probabilities must equal 1.

The extremes of probability, 0 and 1, are seldom reached, although they are often approached. Zero probability means that the outcome is impossible—it will never occur as a result of the course of action. A probability of 1 means that the outcome will always occur, given a particular action. A probability of 1 is one way of defining a certainty model. If the probability of outcome A occurring is 1, then no other outcome can occur. Outcome A is therefore certain to occur.

The marketer can estimate the probabilities of occurrence of different outcomes by numerous techniques. He can base his estimate on his own experience in a particular field, on the judgment of knowledgeable people, on marketing research, or on any other data sources available to him. For example, if in the past a product's price was increased in 25 local markets and the outcome was a corresponding price increase for competing goods in 5 of those markets, he might estimate the probability of this outcome (a price increase by competitors resulting from a price increase by the firm) as .2, or 20 percent, based on this experience. However, this is a historical probability and carries no assurance that future outcomes will be the same. Exogenous factors do change, and competitors may respond differently in the future than they have in the past. This is particularly true if the consequences of their past behavior proved unfavorable to them.

Probability estimates are often based on the judgment of experienced personnel. Often, a number of knowledgeable people are canvassed and asked to estimate the probability of an outcome, given a particular course of action. For example, the marketing manager might ask his advertising director, his research analyst, his product manager, and the account executive assigned to the firm by its advertising agency to each estimate the probability that the competition would increase its advertising outlay if the firm escalated its advertising budget. The consensus arrived at by these men would then determine the probabilities to be used in decision-making.

To introduce probabilities into the decision process, we need to know something about the concept of "expected values," which allows us to incorporate risk explicitly into the decision model. *Expected value* is defined as the probability of a payoff times the value of that payoff. It is expressed mathematically as

$E = p \cdot V$, where   (6-5)

E = expected value of the payoff

p = probability of the payoff, and

V = value of the payoff

Again, flipping a coin is a good example. If you were to be paid $1 for flipping a heads, and nothing for a tails, the expected value of the game would be 50 cents ($E = .5(\$1.00)$). Although the expected value for each flip is 50 cents, you would obviously never receive that amount. If the outcome were a tails, you would get nothing; if it were a heads you would get $1. However, if you flipped again and again, you would average 50 cents.[7]

If you were offered a chance to play this game at a charge of less than 50 cents per flip—say, 49 cents—you would make a profit in the long run. Although you would lose 49 cents on half the flips, you would earn 51 cents ($\$1.00 - \$.49$) on the other half. With an expected value of $.50 and a cost of $.49 per flip, you would average a penny profit per flip. If you were asked to play the game for over 50 cents per flip, you would be foolish to accept. Although you would make money on half the flips, you would lose more money on the other half. It is the expected value of 50 cents, not the payoff of $1, that you would compare against your cost in deciding whether or not to play. The same reasoning applies to marketing decisions.

The expected value of a course of action involving several possible independent outcomes is the sum of the expected values of each possible outcome. Expressed mathematically,

$$E_T = \sum_{i=1}^{n} E_i, \text{ where}$$ (6-6)

E_T = total expected value of the course of action

E_i = expected value of the outcome i, and

i = each possible outcome, from 1 through n

In the coin flip example, the course of action (flipping a coin) has two independent outcomes—heads and tails. Each has a probability of .5, which gives us a total probability of 1 (it is certain that either heads or tails will show). If one is rewarded with $1 for a heads and nothing for a tails, the value of each outcome is $1 or zero, respectively. The probability of each

---

[7] As a practical matter, you would come very close to a 50-cent average. As the number of trials—that is, flips—increased, you would come closer and closer to the average, or expected, value. However, it is unlikely that you would get exactly 50 heads from 100 flips or 500 heads from 1000 flips, and so on.

outcome times its value is the expected value of the outcome. Thus the
expected value of a heads, E_1, is 50 cents (.5 · $1.00), and the expected
value of a tails, E_2, is zero (.5 · 0). The expected value, E_T, for the course
of action (coin-flipping), equals the sum of the expected values for each
possible outcome (E_1 and E_2), or 50 cents:

$E_T = \sum_{i=1}^{n} E_i$ Given

$E_T = E_1 + E_2$ Long form of $E_T = \sum_{i=1}^{n} E_i$

$E_T = p_1 V_1 + p_2 V_2$ From Equation 6–5

$E_T = .5(1) + .5(0)$ By substitution

$E_T = .50$ By arithmetic

Thus the course of action will be profitable if it costs less than 50 cents per
flip to play the game.

Profit can be substituted for the payoff, or gross revenue, used in the
illustration, to give us an alternative statement of value for each outcome.
For example, the value of the outcome "heads" could be 51 cents, which is
the profit resulting from a revenue of $1 less a cost of 49 cents. The value
of the outcome "tails" is −49 cents, which is the loss resulting from a cost
of 49 cents and no revenue. Using formulas 6–5 and 6–6, we can obtain
the expected-value profit of the coin flip:

$E_T = \sum_{i=1}^{n} E_i$ Given as Equation 6–6

$E_i = p \cdot V$ Given as Equation 6–5

$E_T = E_1 + E_2$ By substitution

$E_T = p_1 V_1 + p_2 V_2$ By substitution

$E_T = .5(.51) + .5(-.49)$ By substitution

$E_T = .255 - .245$ By substitution

$E_T = .01$ By arithmetic

This seemingly trivial example illustrates the fundamental technique
for introducing explicitly the element of chance into the marketing decision
process. Probability formulas allow the marketer to construct decision
models that are closer to reality.

CERTAINTY, RISK, UNCERTAINTY, AND IGNORANCE MODELS

So far, all our decision models have assumed that the marketer has a perfect knowledge of the relationship between variables and the nature of the determinants of cost and revenue. Both endogenous and exogenous variables have been viewed as either constant or predictable. Although the models can be moved closer to reality by introducing time as a variable, the use of a decision model where all things are "certain" is often inadequate for major or complex decisions. In reality, we seldom know the precise relationship between variables—and sometimes do not even know a relationship exists. Nor does the firm know with certainty what value each variable will assume in the future. *Exactly* how much will revenue increase for a given increase in personal selling? *Precisely* how will consumer tastes be influenced by an alternative advertising campaign? *Will* a new product be accepted by the consumer? *What* will be a competitor's response to a price change? *How* will the Justice Department react to a substantial increase in the firm's share of the market? *Will* the union go on strike? *Exactly* how high will interest rates be next year? *Will* the recommended price attract new competitors into the industry? *What* price will the leading competitor charge next season? *Precisely* what will the inputs cost next year?

These dilemmas are not unique to the marketing department, although such problems are probably more acute there than anywhere else in the company. The success of the marketing department—and hence the ultimate success of the firm—is dependent on many variables that are difficult even to identify, let alone evaluate or forecast. Market conditions can change quickly; tastes are volatile and competitors often unpredictable.

The instrument that serves to moderate this problem is marketing research. Research is used to identify, quantify, and predict variables, specify their relationships, and appraise the level of risk or uncertainty associated with alternative strategies. The methodology of marketing research—the gathering, reduction, analysis, and evaluation of data—is explored in Part IX. For now, it is important only to expand the theoretical bases of the marketing decision models that enable the marketer to use this research data intelligently. This necessitates the introduction of risk and uncertainty, two conditions that are prevalent in the real world. First, we need to define the four possible decision conditions, one of which will always confront the marketer.

Certainty exists when the exact outcome of each alternative course of action is known. For example, a firm may know that if it increases its advertising the competition will react a certain way and profit (the outcome) will be changed by an exact amount. This perfect state of knowledge is the condition assumed by both the static and dynamic models we have used thus far in this text. Unfortunately, nothing is ever known with complete certainty. However, it is often both convenient and practical to *assume* certainty in calculating approximate values.

Risk exists when each possible outcome can be identified and the probability of the occurrence of each can be determined. A firm may know that if it increases its advertising the competition will react with either a price cut, no price change, or an increase in advertising. If the decision-makers can agree that the probability of each outcome occurring is .4, .1, and .5, respectively, then an expected-value model can be used to determine the effect on profit of increasing advertising.

Uncertainty exists when each possible outcome can be identified but the probability of the occurrence of each can be neither determined nor assessed. For example, if we again assume that the competition can react only with a price cut, no price change, or an increase in advertising, we have specified each possible outcome. If the firm cannot determine, or satisfactorily estimate, the probability of each of the three actions the competitor could take, it will have to make a decision involving uncertainty. In this case, the firm knows only that one of the three outcomes will occur. It can determine how much profit (or loss) would result from each competitive action, but it cannot determine the expected value of its decision to increase advertising.

Ignorance exists when the outcomes, and therefore their probabilities, cannot be identified. The decision-maker does not know what outcomes are possible given a particular course of action. Ignorance is the fourth—and clearly the worst—condition under which the firm can make decisions. It is virtually a theoretical condition, for in almost every case the decision-maker has some idea of one or more of the possible outcomes. If he is operating in or near a condition of ignorance, he must either gather more information until he can construct an uncertainty or a risk model or simply choose at random among his alternatives and trust to luck.

The first three conditions, certainty, risk, and uncertainty, can be illustrated by a set of 1×3 matrices, like those in Figure 6.6. Again, for our example we can use the decision to increase advertising. Each cell, or box, represents the profit or loss that will result from a particular course of action—here, an increase in advertising. At the bottom of each cell is the probability of the outcome, when known. If all possible outcomes are known, their probabilities must total 1.

The objective of marketing research is to provide data that will allow the marketer to move from an uncertainty model toward a certainty model. A certainty model is rarely possible, but a risk model can be shifted closer to a certainty model as additional research is conducted.

The uncertainty model is the point where marketing research usually begins. This model serves to identify the outcomes that could result from

GENERAL FORM
Possible Outcomes

	Outcome 1	Outcome 2	Outcome 3	
Course of Action	Value of Outcome 1 (Probability)	Value of Outcome 2 (Probability)	Value of Outcome 3 (Probability)	Expected Value $X

CERTAINTY MODEL
Competitors' Response
Make No Change

Increase Advertising		$100,000 (1.0)		Expected Value $100,000

RISK MODEL
Competitors' Response

	Cut Price	Make No Change	Increase Advertising	
Increase Advertising	−$20,000 (0.4)	$100,000 (0.1)	$60,000 (0.5)	Expected Value $32,000

UNCERTAINTY MODEL
Competitors' Response

	Cut Price	Make No Change	Increase Advertising	
Increase Advertising	−$20,000 (?)	$100,000 (?)	$60,000 (?)	Expected Value Unknown

FIGURE 6.6
Certainty, risk, and uncertainty models

alternative courses of action. The effect of each of these outcomes can then be quantified in terms of its effect on unit sales and/or price, and the profit or loss to the firm can be calculated. The estimated outcomes of alternative courses of action, and the resulting effects on the firm's success, would then suggest the degree of marketing research required. The decision to introduce the Mustang, for instance, had certain estimated outcomes with such serious effects on the Ford Motor Company's profit and growth that considerable marketing research was performed. On the other hand, a decision to make a small change in body style from the preceding year would require minimal marketing research, if any.

The uncertainty model has little value as a decision tool until some assumptions are made about the probabilities of its outcomes. As soon as this is done, it becomes a risk model. Uncertainty models are used mainly to identify, hence exclude, alternatives with unacceptable outcomes. For example, one option might be to lower price. However, one outcome of this decision might be a disastrous price war with a resultant loss so great that the firm could not risk its happening. Yet even this judgment implies some assumption of probability—hence transformation of the decision model into a risk model—since the price-war outcome has a probability in excess of zero. Thus one might claim that the uncertainty model, in its pure form, serves only as a steppingstone—although often a very important one—to a true decision model.

APPLICATIONS OF THE RISK MODEL

"Philosophers and social scientists have suggested that a person's behavior might be called rational if in situations involving . . . risks he always chooses the alternative which has the highest mathematical expectation [present value]."[8] The risk model—which shows the possible outcomes for each alternative, their payoffs, and their probabilities—provides a mechanism for making rational decisions when the marketer does not know with certainty which outcome will occur, given a particular course of action.

To illustrate, assume that three alternative marketing strategies are under consideration: (1) to increase advertising, (2) to lower price, and (3) to make no changes in present strategy. Experience indicates that the competition will respond in one of four ways: (a) by increasing its advertising, (b) by lowering price, (c) by increasing its sales force, and (d) by making no change. The outcomes of these various combinations of events can be shown as profits and losses. Prior experience and the judgment of key marketing executives allow the analyst to assign probabilities to each outcome. If one assumes a single competitor, or all competitors responding in unison, the data can be conveniently displayed in a 3 × 4 matrix as in Figure 6.7. This matrix constitutes the risk model for this strategy decision.

Given the specified conditions, the best strategy is to increase advertising. However, if this option were denied—say, by capital limitations precluding an increase in the advertising budget—the best choice would then be to make no change in the present strategy. However, this last alternative carries the threat of a substantial loss. If the competitors lower their price, the firm will experience a loss of $40,000. Management may not be willing to risk so large a loss, even though the probability of its occurrence is only .1. Thus the no-change strategy might be rejected in favor of lowering price, even though that strategy offers a lesser expected value.

[8] John E. Freund and Frank J. Williams, *Elementary Business Statistics: The Modern Approach* (Englewood Cliffs, N. J.: Prentice-Hall, 1964), p. 155.

COMPETITORS' RESPONSE

Firm's Alternatives	Increase Advertising (a)	Lower Price (b)	Increase Sales Force (c)	Make No Change (d)	Expected Value
(1) Increase Advertising	$40,000 (0.4)	$10,000 (0.1)	$20,000 (0.2)	$60,000 (0.3)	$39,000
(2) Lower Price	$30,000 (0.2)	−$10,000 (0.6)	$50,000 (0.1)	$100,000 (0.1)	$15,000
(3) Make No Change	$10,000 (0.1)	−$40,000 (0.1)	$15,000 (0.1)	$30,000 (0.7)	$19,500

FIGURE 6.7
Sample 3 × 4 risk model

As in the coin-flipping example, the expected value is not the amount that will be gained from a single action; it is the *average value* that will result from numerous repetitions. If the increase-advertising strategy is selected, the actual payoff will be either $40,000, $10,000, $20,000, or $60,000—not the expected value $39,000—depending on which course of action the competitor takes.

The marketer must recognize that, if a strategy is to be repeated only once or a few times, the actual payoff may be quite different from the expected value used to make the decision. For this reason, the cells containing all the outcomes and their probabilities should be examined. Often, good judgment will lead the marketer to select a tactic that does not yield the maximum expected value, as would be the case if the firm could not chance the $40,000 loss. Although the total expected values might favor a particular alternative, the firm must be prepared to assume the risk of each possible outcome identified with that course of action. Often, one or more of these outcomes would have disastrous consequences that might even mean bankruptcy for the firm.

The values in the cells must be comparable, although they may be any dimension (unit of measurement) appropriate to the decision. Profit is the most universal and often the most convenient choice. If other dimensions are selected, they must usually be converted to profit or to a useful proxy of profit. For example, revenues, expressed as expected values, must be contrasted with the costs of the alternatives before the alternatives themselves can be compared and a selection made.

If profits are discounted to their present values prior to posting in the cells, then the time element has been explicitly introduced into the model. A model that is both dynamic and probabilistic—that takes into consideration both time and chance—is very close to the real-world situation. In theory, its predictions should be quite good. However, in practice the decision model is often compromised by the inability of the decision-maker to obtain adequate data or reliably estimate probabilities. Yet this does not justify discarding the model. Decisions must still be made; alternatives must be defined, appraised, and selected. A decision model, even one based on imperfect knowledge of the market situation, still serves to structure the problem, thus providing a frame of reference that allows a more rigorous approach to the solution. If nothing else, it will at least highlight the need for specific information, thus aiding in the allocation of marketing research resources.

CHAPTER 7

Resource Control

Control is achieved by *monitoring expenditures and performance* and *re-allocating resources*. Monitoring requires a feedback system that can provide timely, accurate, and sufficient information on the expenditures for, and the results of, a given program. This data is used to identify mistakes, recognize opportunities, and refine decision models. The ultimate goal of this process is the reallocation of resources to reduce costs and/or increase revenues—hence to improve profit. Monitoring techniques vary, depending on the size of the firm. In very small firms, management may be personally aware of each facet of the company's operation. Very large companies, especially those in the aerospace industry, generally have complex computerized systems for program evaluation and control.

The feedback system and the resource reallocation process are themselves subjects for the assignment of resources. As such, they must be evaluated and controlled. Information costs money. Its contribution to profit, by enhancing revenues or lowering costs through the medium of better decision-making, must be measured against its marginal cost. Thus yet another variable is added to the already complex mix of inputs affecting the cost, revenue, and profit functions of the firm.

Information flows to a marketing manager from many sources and through numerous channels. The accounting department advises him of his costs. His research director provides data—gathered from publications, surveys, and experiments—and estimates of elasticities, growth functions, and consumption. His salesmen contribute intelligence on activities in the marketplace and customer attitudes. Suppliers suggest new inputs and provide biased appraisals of the effectiveness of their own goods and services. Trade publications indicate trends in the industry. Supervisors report on the performance of their subordinates and on problems and successes emerging in their areas of responsibility. The manager must filter, analyze, and apply this information and adjust the distribution of resources to correct initial

143

allocation errors and accommodate changes that have occurred in the market. He must define the realities facing the firm and compare the estimates on which resources were previously allocated to the actual market situation. He must make adjustments in budgets, personnel, advertising copy, promotion media, prices, the distribution network, and the product. He must evaluate new opportunities and reject or exploit them. He must deal with problems as they arise. The job of controlling the distribution of resources is continuous; the only truly predictable element is the reality of change.

STANDARDS FOR RESOURCE CONTROL

Before the marketing manager can effectively use the information provided by his feedback system—or, for that matter, design an efficient monitoring system for acquiring that information—quantitative standards of performance must be established. Feedback is of little value if it cannot be judged against a standard of performance. Either absolute values or ratios can be used in setting these standards. Actual expenditures may be compared with budget estimates. Sales may be compared with quotas. Actual delivery dates may be compared with scheduled delivery dates. The actual ratio of sales to advertising expenditures may be compared to a historical or standard ratio. The firm's present market share may be compared to its previous market share, or to an established goal. Some typical performance standards are shown in Table 7.1.

When actual performance in any area is poorer than the projected or standard performance, management should direct its attention to that particular instrument of marketing. Either resources should be reallocated—by changing the personnel, adjusting the budget, selecting new media, or some other action—or the standard should be revised to conform more closely to reality.

If performance exceeds the standard, an investigation is also in order. If the standard is unrealistically low, it should be revised upward. If the instrument is especially productive, two courses of action should be considered. If the objective is fixed (as it is when the firm wishes to sell a given number of units), then a portion of the resources should either be withdrawn to reduce total cost or reassigned to other areas. For example, if output is fixed (as it is in the market period) and sales are occurring so fast that the firm will run out of merchandise before demand is fully satisfied, advertising should be stopped or curtailed, thus reducing both demand and cost, or the discount should be reduced, thus increasing price and revenue.

If output is not fixed, a redetermination of the optimum price-output combination is suggested when performance exceeds the forecast. Under this condition, revenue will be greater than anticipated for a given outlay of

Table 7.1   Typical performance standards

Sales (Revenues)	*Profit (or Contribution to Profit)*
Total	Total
By product	By product
By market	By market
By salesman	By customer
By customer	By function
By geographical area	By geographical area
By distribution medium	
	Ratios
Costs	
	Sales: cost
Total	Market share
By product	Percentage of sales change
By market	
By customer	*Performance Proxies*
By department	Number of new accounts opened
By function	Number of repeat orders
By geographical area	Number of inquiries
By advertising medium	

resources. Above-standard performance indicates an error in the original (estimated) production function. Provided the below-standard performance of another instrument does not cancel the effect of the superior-performance instrument, *MR* and *MC* will intersect farther to the right than originally estimated, and the firm should increase output in order to maximize profit.

If the aggregate cost and revenue curves have not changed, then one instrument's poor performance may be canceling another instrument's excellent performance. This suggests a shift of resources from the inefficient instrument to the efficient instrument—a task in which the rule of proportionality would be invoked. Another possibility is that the poor performance of one instrument is a result of inadequate funding. For example, a distribution point—perhaps a regional warehouse—may be losing sales because of delays in delivery that result from inadequate staffing.

The administrative philosophy we have just described is known as "management by exception." The manager monitors his department by constantly comparing actual data with performance standards. When the disparity between the two exceeds a prescribed limit, he immediately investigates, determines the cause, and takes corrective action. Although it is seldom stated as a formal company policy, this is the way executives generally handle the day-to-day running of a department. Management by exception is a pragmatic approach, and it does an excellent short-run job of allocating the executive resource to where it will do the most good—that is, to where its marginal output will be the greatest. (Marginal input, the executive's time, is relatively fixed.) However, long-run optimization requires the allocation of a portion of the executive resource to long-range plans. This is often accomplished by putting together a specialized staff—perhaps establishing a long-range planning department—exclusively for that purpose.

Performance standards also have socio-psychological aspects. They represent an idealized model of performance, and most performance can ultimately be traced to human beings, who seldom behave "ideally." When a discrepancy between a standard and an actual performance is detected, the superior or inferior behavior of an individual or group is often the cause. Thus the establishment, monitoring, and control of standards has flesh-and-blood implications. For example, an unrealistically high sales quota can so discourage a salesman that his productivity may actually decline. Standards can provide an incentive *if* they are realistic in the eyes of the performer. This is especially true if success is identified with some form of recognition.

Fear of a reduction in resources, such as the lowering of a budget or the discharge of employees, can encourage a group to restrict its output to the level prescribed by the standard. Fear of corrective, or disciplinary, action in the event of failure to meet a standard can encourage the manipulation of data as it passes through the feedback system. For example, man-hours that are actually spent on Product A may be charged to Product B if the budget for A is about to be exceeded and the allocation for B is excessive. The consequence would be a distorted estimate of the production function for each product.

Although a detailed analysis of these problems is outside the scope of this text, their existence should be recognized. In general, these problems can be avoided by establishing realistic standards, by involving those who must measure up to the standards in their determination, by auditing the input data, by reevaluating standards frequently, by penalizing poor performance and rewarding outstanding performance, and by using judgment when analyzing actual performance versus standards.

CONTROL TECHNOLOGY

Control technology is that body of techniques dealing with the control of resources. It involves the collection, storage, reduction, presentation, and analysis of data, both numerical and verbal. Control technology has progressed rapidly in the past two decades, thanks to the development and mass production of high-speed computers, which allow data to be manipulated in great quantities and with a speed and an economy impossible with manual methods. Thus the marketer today is able to handle a vast input of information. However, expertise in instructing the computer how to collect, reduce, and display information is essential. Computer programming is a job for a specialist, but the marketer still must know what information he needs and the form in which it is needed, and he must be able to communicate this knowledge to the computer programmer.

A number of commonly used control techniques are readily adaptable to marketing. Generally, they involve the displaying of two forms of information—standard and actual performance—for each instrument or project under control. The larger or more general instruments or projects are normally subdivided into their smallest manageable elements. Each element, as well as the whole, is monitored. In this way, the information is at a level of detail and coverage appropriate to the level of management at which it is being presented. The director of advertising is interested in a level of information that the marketing manager would find too detailed. The company president needs a broader picture than does the marketing manager. Only when an acute problem or a significant opportunity emerges is the more senior executive interested in the level of detail the junior man requires in the daily management of his special function. Information should match the level of control; thus the hierarchy of information will approximate the hierarchy of the organization. Figure 7.1 presents a typical hierarchy of information appropriate to the cost of a particular product.

MANAGEMENT CONTROL SYSTEMS

A management control system consists of performance standards, an information-feedback network, data-presentation techniques, and a mechanism for reallocating resources. The standards provide a basis for judgment, the feedback network provides empirical data, the data presentation compares the standard to the performance, and the reallocation mechanism provides procedures for change. In the center of the system is the decision-maker.

To illustrate the use of a control system, let us consider the problem of controlling personal selling. First, sales quotas (standards) are established, using marketing-research projections. Second, arrangements are made with the regional sales offices or the accounting department to get monthly reports of actual sales (the feedback system). Third, the standards and the actual sales over time are plotted on a sequence chart (the data presentation). Fourth, procedures are established whereby the sales manager (the decision-maker) can add, discharge, train, and transfer personnel.

This simple model can be sophisticated to allow more precise control. For example, the feedback network can be expanded to allow the standard to be adjusted for significant changes in exogenous variables by including

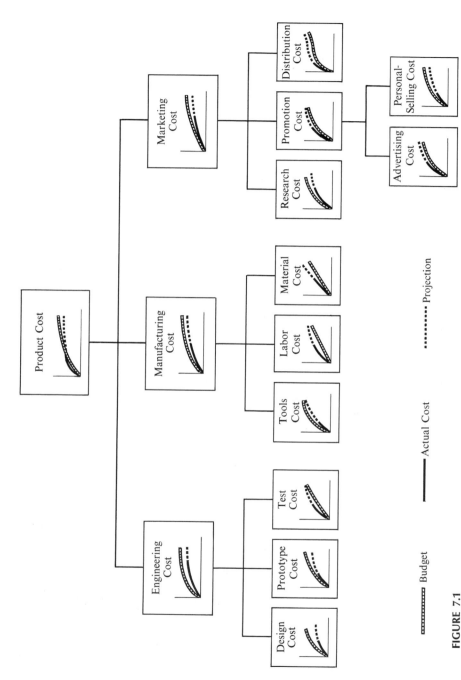

FIGURE 7.1
Hierarchy of cost information   (Cumulative total costs vs. time)

data on the market and on competitors. Data presentation may be broken down by regional office or by salesman. The district sales manager may be encouraged to vary such factors as training, cooperative advertising, discounting, and incentives in order to meet the standard, as long as he does not exceed his overall budget.

The more variables that the executive can manipulate, the greater will be his need for more detailed information and presentations. This, in turn, means that he must devote a greater percentage of his time to evaluating data prior to making decisions. One solution to this dilemma is to provide the executive with staff assistants, or to allow him to delegate some of the lesser decisions to subordinate managers who are more intimately involved with specific problems. Unfortunately, these recourses involve either the expansion of the staff—thus adding another increment to semifixed costs—or the diffusion of control. The respective merits of these alternatives are the subject of considerable discussion in the literature of administration. There is little agreement even in the general sense, and any specific question can be answered only within the context of a particular problem. Economists, sociologists, psychologists, and advocates of scientific management all view the problem differently.

The focal point of a control system is the data-collection, analysis, and presentation functions. These serve as the basis for decision-making, prescribe the information-input requirements, and generally determine the form of the control system. Since presentations are the ultimate output of a data system, we shall examine a number of the more common presentations and the systems they represent.

Sequence Charts.   A sequence chart displays a standard—actually, a forecast—usually plotted over time, and a series of actual values, plotted against the same time variables as the standard. By comparing the two curves and examining the magnitude and the location of their differences, the manager can readily detect discrepancies between the firm's plans and reality, thus identifying any areas that warrant attention.

A sequence chart is the simplest formal control technique. This kind of data presentation is common in cost control and market monitoring. For example, expected cumulative sales may be plotted over time. If the product is new to the company, an allowance should be made for the market-penetration rate. If the product is new to the market, consideration must be given to the expected rate of diffusion. The possible forms of such curves, and their mathematical computation, are explored in Chapter 26. Generally, new-product-sales curves (and revenue curves) have the "S" shape shown in Figure 7.2.

Having plotted the expected total sales over time for the product's planning horizon, the marketer responsible—perhaps the product manager,

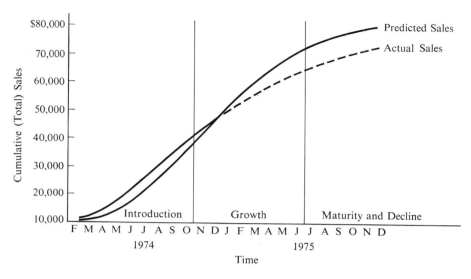

FIGURE 7.2
Sequence chart
(Predicted vs. actual sales)

the sales manager, or the vice president for marketing—can begin comparing actual sales with those forecast. In Figure 7.2, both the predicted- and actual-sales curves are shown. The broken portion of the actual-sales curve represents a revised forecast indicating the sales that will accumulate if current conditions remain constant and the trend is not modified through reallocation of the marketing resources assigned to the product. Sales may be measured in dollars or in units.

Figure 7.2 suggests a number of possibilities worthy of investigation by the marketer. It appears that in April 1970 the market was being penetrated faster than expected. Several possibilities might account for this. The aggregate potential market might be greater than anticipated—indicating the need for a consumer survey to determine if buyers other than those expected to use the product were purchasing it. The rate of brand-switching or new-product adoption might be greater than anticipated—indicating that a re-evaluation of consumer tastes or a reappraisal of the effectiveness of the introductory advertising is in order or possibly that a reduction in marketing activity by competitors has occurred.

By January of the second year, actual sales had fallen below the prediction line; that is, the target, or quota, values were not being reached. At this point the marketer might look for a change in strategy by competitors; a change in buyer attitudes toward the product; a lower level of potential demand; a slackening of effort by salesmen, distributors, or retailers; or a decrease in the effectiveness of the advertising program. An analysis of competitors' current marketing practices, a consumer survey, an evaluation of the product in the field, a reappraisal of the potential market, or an audit of the distribution system might be in order to explain the deviation of actual from predicted sales. Once a problem or opportunity is discovered—and this is the function of the sequence chart—it must be defined, explained, and remedied. Often the solution is an indirect one, as is the case when the cause of the difficulty—say, an increase in the competitors' advertising—is outside the control of the firm. In this case, the marketer would seek to nullify the change in this exogenous variable by a change in his own marketing strategy—possibly an increase in advertising or a decrease in price.

Loading Charts. The four product phases—introduction, growth, maturity, and decline—suggest the need for a data-presentation technique that will show the amount of effort, in dollars or in labor, that each area of the firm will have to contribute in order to sustain the product during its life cycle. Figure 7.3 illustrates a method for presenting such time-phased data. This form of presentation, often called a loading chart, can be used to show performance as well as planning and budgetary data.

The new-product marketing plan shown in Figure 7.3 provided for an increasing personal-selling effort during the introductory and growth stages

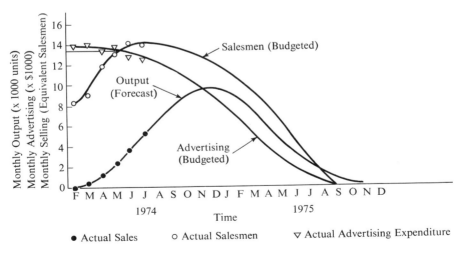

FIGURE 7.3
Loading chart
(Output, advertising, and selling vs. time)

followed by a decrease in personal-selling effort. The plan also provided for heavy advertising early in the product's life cycle, in order to introduce the product to potential buyers. The advertising budget was to be gradually reduced as the product entered the maturity stage.

By plotting actual advertising expenditures and the equivalent[1] number of salesmen promoting the product, the marketer can readily see whether he is staying within his budget allocation. A sequence chart, showing the cumulative expenditures and budgets over time for both advertising and personal selling, would also help. However, the loading chart shows clearly how much advertising should be bought and how many equivalent salesmen need to be assigned for each time period. For example, in Figure 7.3 it is obvious that advertising orders must be reduced and salesmen reassigned or laid off after May and July 1974, respectively.

The total requirement for any particular input can be obtained by combining all the requirements for that input on one loading chart. This allows a sales manager, for instance, to anticipate his future staff requirements. Figure 7.4 shows the loading curves for three products, A, B, and C, with respect to personal selling for a two-year planning horizon. The sum of the individual product curves indicates the size of the total sales staff that must be hired, trained, and supervised over the period.

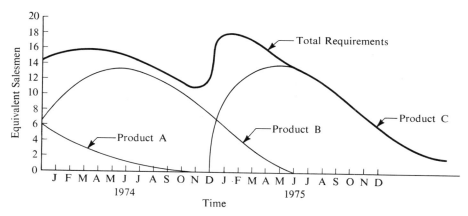

FIGURE 7.4
Loading chart
(Personal-selling requirement)

---

[1] A salesman may be spending only a fraction of his time selling a particular product. Hence the term "equivalent salesman" is used in planning and control. An equivalent salesman may be one salesman working 40 hours per week on a particular product, or four salesmen each working 10 hours per week, and so on.

The curves in Figure 7.4 are typical of the theoretically correct loadings that often confront marketing management. The total requirement for salesmen is relatively steady until July 1974; then it drops abruptly until November. Between November and December it increases radically from approximately 11 to 18. In practice, it is generally difficult to hire and discharge personnel in quantity over short periods of time. If the job demands much training or experience, the staffing process is expensive and lengthy, and radical adjustments in total personnel are uneconomical. Also, it may be impractical to maintain the optimum level of manpower indicated by the loading chart when the sales of the firm are subject to peaks during less busy periods.

A number of alternative solutions are available. First, the marketing department can rely on the sales force of middlemen, such as manufacturers' representatives, sales agents, and wholesalers. Second, the firm can diversify its product line so as to include goods whose sales peak in the off-season period of the present line. Third, new markets can be opened, in order to fill slumps or extend the life cycle of the product. Fourth, the firm can develop new products to be introduced when the demand for the present product dies. (Product C in Figure 7.4 is an example of this type of product timing.) Fifth, the firm can maintain an average level of input whereby the sales department is slightly understaffed during peak periods and slightly overstaffed during lulls. (This latter situation can be partially accommodated by using the extra man-hours available in the off-season for training personnel.) Sixth, overtime can be used to provide additional man-hours during peak seasons. Seventh, the staff can be kept at a level that is only high enough to handle the minimum expected load. Additional personal selling would then be provided by part-time help (which is not always available) or by the sales force of middlemen.

The loading problem illustrated here is not unique. The personnel, facilities, and plant requirements of the entire firm tend to fluctuate with the firm's aggregate sales. The loading curves for engineering and manufacturing inputs, for example, will also vary radically with changes in demand. In the more volatile industries, the desirability of a smooth revenue function is a major incentive for diversification.

Performance-Ratio Charts. A performance-ratio chart compares an actual-performance ratio with a standard-performance ratio. A performance ratio is simply the output of a given factor divided by the input—for example, the number of sales per dollar of advertising in medium X. It may also indicate boundaries that represent the tolerable limits of deviation between the actual and planned values. Whenever an actual value exceeds the upper limit, or falls below the lower limit, the marketer knows it is time for action.

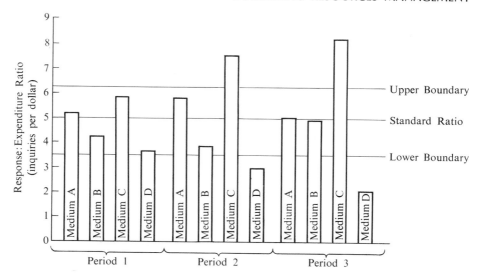

FIGURE 7.5
Performance-ratio chart
(Advertising media A, B, C, and D)

The application of performance-ratio charts to the monitoring and control of resources is illustrated in Figure 7.5, using advertising media as an example. The number of inquiries in response to each advertisement in a given medium—obtained by coding reader-response coupons—is compared with the cost of the ad. This ratio (inquiries per dollar of expenditure) is then plotted for each advertising period (perhaps one month, in the case of periodicals).

In Figure 7.5, the actual ratio for the four media indicates that the performance standard is realistic. However, medium C is performing beyond the upper limit, which suggests a shift of present resources, or the assignment of additional resources, to this medium to exploit its exceptional efficiency. Medium D, on the other hand, is performing poorly, which suggests the withdrawal of that portion of the budget remaining for use in medium D. However, if medium D has performed well during previous campaigns, it might be appropriate to experiment with the advertising copy for an issue or two prior to making a final decision to drop the publication.

Boundaries can be developed in a number of ways. Subjective boundaries can be used, or boundaries can be developed from previous statistical data. A commonly used statistical technique is to assume that the distribution of responses about their average follows a "normal" distribution such as that shown in Figure 7.6.

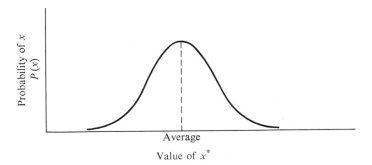

Average

Value of x^*

* x may be an absolute value, such as units sold, or a ratio, such as responses per dollar of advertising. Obviously it would be the latter when the curve is being used to establish the boundaries of a performance-ratio chart.

FIGURE 7.6
Normal distribution curve

The exact shape of the normal distribution of a particular variable can be determined from the values of two parameters—its arithmetic mean and its standard deviation. The arithmetic mean measures the location, or central tendency, of the distribution, and the standard deviation measures the variability, or dispersion, of the distribution. Figure 7.7 shows two normal distributions, both with the same mean but one having a standard deviation twice as great as the other. The mean is usually identified by the Greek letter μ (mu), and the standard deviation by the Greek letter σ (sigma).

The mean and the standard deviation can be computed for any set of data by the following formulas:

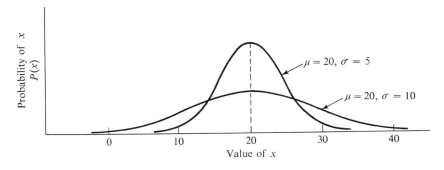

FIGURE 7.7
Comparison of two normal distributions

$$\mu = \frac{\sum\limits_{i=1}^{n} X_i}{N} \qquad\qquad (7\text{--}1)$$

$$\sigma = \sqrt{\frac{\sum\limits_{i=1}^{n} (X_i - \mu)^2}{N}} \qquad\qquad (7\text{--}2)$$

where N observations of the variable X exist.

The percentage of a population contained within the mean, plus or minus a specified number of standard deviations, is readily determined by reference to an appropriate normal distribution table.[2] For now, it is sufficient to note that in a normal distribution $\mu \pm 3\sigma$ contains 99.74 percent of the population, $\mu \pm 2\sigma$ contains 95.44 percent of the population, and $\mu \pm 1\sigma$ contains 68.26 percent of the population. Figure 7.8 illustrates this

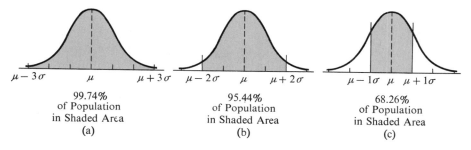

99.74% of Population in Shaded Area (a) 95.44% of Population in Shaded Area (b) 68.26% of Population in Shaded Area (c)

FIGURE 7.8
Illustration of population percentages of a normal distribution.

concept—that a given portion of a normally distributed population will be contained within a range specified by the standard deviation. For example, if the average sales, μ, for a team of salesmen is 200 units (per salesman) and the standard deviation is 30 units, then 95.44 percent of the salesmen will have sales within the range 140 to 260, which is $\mu \pm 2\sigma$, as shown in Figure 7.8(b). Men whose sales are outside this range will be very rare, because such salesmen represent only 4.56 percent of this salesman population. A performance chart can be constructed using the value of the mean, μ, as the standard and making the boundaries a function of the standard deviation, σ.

[2] See Appendix II, p. 657, for an explanation of normal distribution tables.

To take another example, if we assume that an advertising director has records of the number of inquiries received in response to advertisements in each of 30 different media, a performance ratio, X, can be computed for each medium by dividing the number of inquiries by the cost of running the ad. The data for each medium is contained in Table 7.2.[3]

Table 7.2   Advertising media performance calculations

Medium (i)	Performance Ratio (X_i)	Deviation $(X_i - \mu)$	Deviation Squared $(X_i - \mu)^2$
1	5.3	.3	.9
2	6.8	1.8	3.2
3	3.0	−2.0	4.0
.	.	.	.
.	.	.	.
.	.	.	.
30	4.9	−1.1	1.2
	$\sum X_i^* = 150.0$		$\sum(X_i - \mu)^2 = 67.5$

$$\mu = \frac{\sum X_i}{N} \qquad\qquad \sigma = \sqrt{\frac{\sum(X_i - \mu)^2}{N}}$$

$$\mu = \frac{150.00}{30} \qquad\qquad \sigma = \sqrt{\frac{67.5}{30}}$$

$$\mu = 5.0 \qquad\qquad \sigma = 1.5$$

* By convention, $\sum_{i=1}^{n} X_i$ may also be written as $\sum X_i$ or $\sum X$, as long as the index range—that is, the range of i—is obvious.

Since the arithmetic mean, μ, is 5.0, a ratio of 5 inquiries per dollar of advertising expenditure would be selected as the standard. If the advertising manager wished to identify the media that produced results in the top 16 percent or the bottom 16 percent of the media population, he would establish $\mu - 1\sigma$ and $\mu + 1\sigma$ as his lower and upper boundaries. $\mu \pm 1\sigma$ contains 68 percent of the population; hence 32 percent of the population must lie outside this area (16 percent above and 16 percent below). These two boundaries correspond to performance ratios of 3.5 and 6.5, respectively.

[3] Those with a background in statistics will recognize that large-sample statistics have been employed and that the 30 observations are assumed to constitute a population.

Scheduling Charts. A scheduling chart displays the key events associated with task accomplishment over time. It serves to alert management as to when resources should be available, when jobs should be finished, and what functions are in operation at a given time. When actual start and completion times are posted, the manager can readily see where deadlines have been, or are likely to be, missed. Since many tasks are dependent on the prior completion of other tasks, an entire marketing program can be compromised by a slip in one critical event. Thus, the timing of tasks and the *rate* of resource expenditure must often be controlled as rigidly as the assignment of resources. If the tasks are kept on schedule, costs, too, tend to stay within bounds.

Figure 7.9 shows a typical scheduling chart for the marketing of a moderately priced consumer durable. The shaded bars indicate the period of time over which a particular task is to be performed. Tasks that are dependent on one another are connected with solid lines, meaning that a particular task must be completed before the following task can begin. For instance, the firm must recruit and select salesmen before it can begin to train salesmen. The deadlines for major events, such as "Approve product" and "Start deliveries," are shown by heavy vertical lines, appropriately labeled. The individuals to be held responsible for each task are also indicated. Although some activities are continuous, none extend beyond the reevaluation date (as shown by the broken bars). At this time, market conditions and the profitability of Product A will be reappraised, and it may possibly be deleted from the firm's product mix.

PERT

"PERT"[4] is a contraction of the phrase "Program Evaluation and Review Technique." It is a sophisticated application of several of the control methods previously discussed and is similar to several other schedule-cost management systems now in use, such as the "Critical Path Method" (CPM) and the "Program Evaluation Procedure" (PEP). It is especially useful when a large number of different inputs must be integrated into a complex product. For this reason, it is generally used in the management of major space and weapons programs. Although the system was developed for the management of federal programs, it is equally applicable to commercial projects.

---

[4] An excellent abbreviated explanation of PERT, which includes a list of terms and definitions, is found in Leonard J. Garrett and Milton Silver, *Production Management Analysis* (New York: Harcourt, Brace & World, 1966). The definitive guide to PERT, as it is required to be applied in industries engaged in government contracting, is the National Aeronautics and Space Administration's *PERT Time and Cost Guide* (Washington, D. C.: U. S. Government Printing Office, 1962).

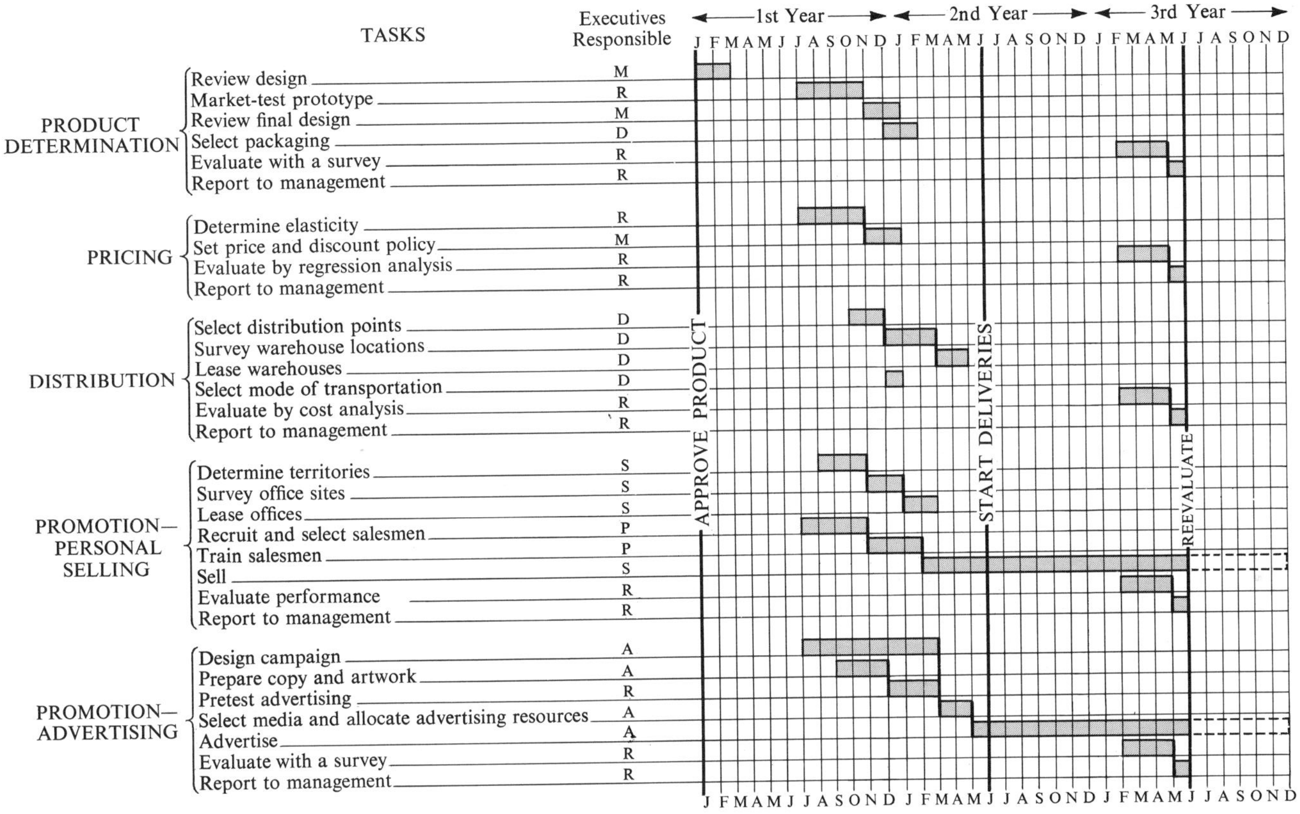

TASKS — Executives Responsible

PRODUCT DETERMINATION
- Review design — M
- Market-test prototype — R
- Review final design — M
- Select packaging — D
- Evaluate with a survey — R
- Report to management — R

PRICING
- Determine elasticity — R
- Set price and discount policy — M
- Evaluate by regression analysis — R
- Report to management — R

DISTRIBUTION
- Select distribution points — D
- Survey warehouse locations — D
- Lease warehouses — D
- Select mode of transportation — D
- Evaluate by cost analysis — R
- Report to management — R

PROMOTION—PERSONAL SELLING
- Determine territories — S
- Survey office sites — S
- Lease offices — S
- Recruit and select salesmen — P
- Train salesmen — P
- Sell — S
- Evaluate performance — R
- Report to management — R

PROMOTION—ADVERTISING
- Design campaign — A
- Prepare copy and artwork — A
- Pretest advertising — R
- Select media and allocate advertising resources — A
- Advertise — A
- Evaluate with a survey — R
- Report to management — R

Timeline headers: —1st Year— —2nd Year— —3rd Year— (months J F M A M J J A S O N D)

Milestones: APPROVE PRODUCT, START DELIVERIES, REEVALUATE

A = Advertising   S = Sales   R = Marketing research   D = Distribution   M = All marketing executives   P = Personnel

FIGURE 7.9

Scheduling plan for marketing Product A

The objective of PERT is to provide all levels of management with performance data on schedules and costs—that is, to indicate when tasks are behind schedule, or are likely to slip behind schedule, and when costs exceed, or are likely to exceed, budget allocations. It identifies and monitors critical tasks, a delay in which can prevent the entire program from being completed on schedule. PERT is a goal-oriented system; it relates the schedule and cost of each input to the schedule and cost of the final output.

The PERT *network*, which is the framework of the PERT system, is a schematic representation of the events and activities that go into the program. The network is constructed by linking together the tasks—called "events"—that must be accomplished to achieve the final goal. The events are viewed as "milestones" and are linked together by "activities." The activities are the expenditures of resources necessary to reach the milestones. Events are conventionally depicted by numbered circles; activities are shown as straight lines.

To illustrate, assume that six events—① program initiation, ② design of campaign strategy, ③ completion of copy and artwork, ④ completion of pretest, ⑤ media selection, and ⑥ start of advertising—are linked by six activities, which are (a) design campaign strategy, (b) prepare copy and artwork, (c) pretest advertising, (d) select media, (e) revise and deliver ads, and (f) order advertising. Each event is essential to the objective, which in this case is to advertise the product. *Flow time,* how long resources must be expended to reach a particular milestone, as well as resource requirements, can be displayed. The network can be represented diagrammatically, as in Figure 7.10, or the relationships it delineates can be fed into a com-

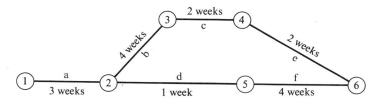

FIGURE 7.10
PERT network for advertising program

puter, which will provide a tabulation of the events, activities, and resource allocations and the expected completion dates of the milestones (events).

The *critical path* is the series of sequential activities and events that places the greatest time constraint on the program. In the example, it is the path ①-②-③-④-⑥, which totals 11 weeks. The critical path is the one that consumes the most time; hence, it is the pacesetter. Events in this path must be monitored closely, for if any one event slips behind schedule, the entire program will slip behind the target date, unless the lost time can be made up in subsequent tasks. For example, it will take 11 weeks to prepare the advertising program and get it going. If activities (d) or (f) should take up to 3 weeks longer than planned, event ⑥, the goal of the network, will not be delayed. However, if activity (a), (b), (c), or (e) should take longer than planned, thus delaying ②, ③, ④, and ⑥, the critical-path events, the program will not be completed on schedule. In this case, the advertising would not be ready when needed.

By constructing PERT networks for each marketing function associated with a particular good or product line, the entire marketing program can be displayed schematically and the critical path for the whole program can be identified. By constructing networks for engineering and manufacturing as well as marketing and tying together all three networks to form a master system, the firm can establish a basis for planning and controlling all the resources associated with a particular good, service, or product line. By providing a feedback system that frequently posts the status of each activity and event, PERT enables management to immediately recognize where trouble is beginning to develop and take appropriate action. In the example above, a week's delay in media selection, ⑤, would require no action. However, a delay in copy and artwork completion, ③, would warrant immediate action should it be imperative that the advertising program start on schedule. Overtime might be authorized in order to hurry the preparation of copy and artwork (b), the pretesting plan might be shortened (c), or less time might be allowed for revision of ads (e). If the critical path for the marketing program as a whole did not include this portion of the advertising program, the marketing manager might be petitioned to approve a delay in the start of advertising, ⑥, as this would not affect the schedule for the product itself.

By attaching the values of the allocated resources to each activity, management can integrate its cost control with its schedule control. Actual expenditures can be fed back (reported) and compared with budget allocations. Where there is an *overrun*—that is, where expenditures exceed the amount allocated—the budget may need revision or corrective action may be indicated to increase the efficiency of the activity. Where there are *underruns,* funds are available to be used elsewhere or to be added to profit. Inputs of the same type—for example, warehouse space, salesmen, artists, machinists, and engineers—can be aggregated at different points in the program to produce loading curves. Thus, the requirements for resources can be displayed.

Obviously, a large quantity of data—both estimates and actual figures —must be collected, manipulated, and displayed if the PERT system is to be employed. Although a PERT network containing as many as 200 events can supposedly be managed manually with the aid of a desk calculator, large networks become unwieldy with manual techniques. However, most computing services contain standard PERT programs in their program library that can be adapted to the firm's needs.[5] The use of a computer is a virtual prerequisite to the management of a complex variety of production inputs. A computer is even more necessary if chance is explicitly introduced into the calculations, or if the estimates of time and costs are updated frequently.

Having examined the general concept of the PERT system, we can now digress to an explanation of some of its more important elements. These are (1) the computation of PERT times, (2) slack analysis, and (3) chance.

Elapsed and Expected Time. In PERT systems, "elapsed time" and "expected time" are the terms used to describe the time required for each activity and each event, respectively. *Elapsed time* for an activity, t_e, is measured from the start of the activity to its completion. The t_e is the time between two consecutive milestones. The *expected time* of an event, T_E, is measured cumulatively from event ①, the start, through the completion of the activity that preceded the event. Diagrammatically, T_E is measured along the longest activity path from event ① to the particular milestone.

The value assigned to t_e may be estimated, or the t_e for a similar task performed previously may be used. Often, three separate times are estimated and combined into a single value, using a weighted distribution that favors the most likely time. For instance, a weighted function might be created as follows:

$$t_e = \frac{a + 4m + b}{6}, \text{ where}$$

t_e = elapsed time (forecast)

a = optimistic time

m = most likely time, and

b = pessimistic time

The denominator in the equation is simply the sum of the coefficients in the numerator.

For example, if the advertising group's creative people estimate 3.5 weeks as the most likely time required for preparing copy and artwork and estimate 3 weeks and 7 weeks, respectively, as the optimistic and pessimistic times, a t_e of 4 weeks would result, as follows:

[5] Garrett and Silver, *op. cit.,* p. 377.

$$t_e = \frac{a + 4m + b}{6} \qquad \text{Given}$$

$$t_e = \frac{3 + 4(3.5) + 7}{6} \qquad \text{By substitution}$$

$$t_e = 4 \qquad \text{By arithmetic}$$

The expected time for an event, T_E, is computed by adding the elapsed times of all the activities leading up to that event via the longest activity path between it and event ①. In the example presented in Figure 7.10, T_{E3}, the expected time of event ③—the completion of copy and artwork—would be 7 weeks (3 weeks + 4 weeks). This can be converted to a due date, as soon as the start date is established, by simply adding T_{E3} to the start date. The T_E for the last event, program completion, is the total flow time along the critical path of the PERT network. In the example, it would be $T_E = 11$ weeks.

Slack Analysis. *Slack analysis* is the evaluation of the differences between the expected time of each milestone and the latest time by which it must be reached in order to complete the program on schedule. Latest time, T_L, is computed by working backward from the target event—completion of the program (event ⑥ in Figure 7.10). In that respect, it is the opposite of the estimated time, T_E, which is computed from the starting point.

The time selected for the completion event, written T_T, often differs from the estimated time for that event. This is because the target time, T_T, is selected semi-independently of T_E in order to conform to objectives outside the PERT network. For example, customer requirements, the delivery date of another product that is dependent on the completion of the product being scheduled, the availability of personnel and equipment, and capital repayment obligations can all establish or influence target dates. These dates —translated into times by subtracting the go-ahead dates from the target dates—cannot be intelligently specified without reference to the total flow time of a program. Obviously, it would be foolish to promise to reach the final milestone in two months if the total flow time for the program were 90 days. Thus the last event's T_E, derived from PERT analysis, serves as both a guide and a constraint in establishing T_T. Although the target time specified may be slightly less than the total flow time (the T_E of the last milestone), it is more likely to exceed it, with the final T_E as a minimum alternative value. The former choice might be made with an eye to compressing the original estimate of the elapsed times, t_e, along the critical path. This can often be accomplished by concentrating resources—that is, by having employees work overtime or by assigning extra personnel to the critical-path activities. (Such a decision might get the project back on schedule, but increase total expenditures.)

Slack time, T_S, is computed by subtraction, as follows:

$$T_S = T_L - T_E, \text{ where} \tag{7-4}$$

T_S = slack time

T_L = latest time, and

T_E = expected time

The completion date set for the initial advertising program in the example above might involve a target time, T_T, of say 12 weeks, as opposed to the program's flow time—determined by the critical path—of 11 weeks. The expected time, T_E, for event ④, found by tracing the most time-consuming path from event ① to event ④ and summing the values of its activities, is 9 weeks. The latest time, T_L, that milestone ④ can be reached, and still allow the program to be finished on the target date, is 10 weeks. This figure was arrived at by tracing the most time-consuming path *backward* from the completion event, ⑥, to event ④, summing the values of its activities, and subtracting that sum from the target time, T_T. In this case, there is only one activity between event ④ and event ⑥, and it carries an elapsed-time value, t_e, of 2 weeks. Hence, T_L for event ④ is 10 weeks (12 weeks − 2 weeks). Thus, the slack time, T_S, for event ④ is 1 week (10 weeks − 9 weeks). T_S was computed by subtracting T_E from T_L (Equation 7–4). T_S is positive, which means that there is a one-week margin of safety for that event—that is, event ④ has one week more time than it needs, so long as its expected time, T_E, remains 9 weeks and the target date is not moved up. However, if any of the preceding events in the longest path leading to event ④ should be behind schedule, T_E would be increased and the slack time would narrow.

Slack analysis can identify problems as well as opportunities. If $T_S = 0$, an event is on schedule; if $T_S < 0$, the event is behind schedule; and if $T_S > 0$, the event is ahead of schedule. If the firm's feedback system regularly provides actual-cost and schedule data, if adjustments are frequently made in the estimates of elapsed times, and if this information is properly displayed to management, then resources can be allocated optimally.

By monitoring the slack times and the budget overruns and underruns for every event of every program throughout the firm, management can keep reassigning—or, for that matter, adding or deleting—resources in conformity with both its goals and changing market conditions. PERT provides a formal mechanism for doing this, and also for introducing explicitly the element of chance into the evaluation of the program.

Risk is a perennial problem for the firm. Even in the direction of those activities that are mostly within its control, chance still enters the picture. (The existence of chance is implicit in the fact that three time estimates are used in the computation of a weighted-elapsed-time PERT network.) The relationship between output and man-hours is very imprecise in the short run, errors are made in accounting, jobs are incorrectly planned, equipment breaks down, employees get sick, errors are made in judgment, and so on. Suppliers, too, cause complications and delays, by providing faulty materials or making late deliveries. (Many prime government contractors now require suppliers of critical inputs to maintain PERT systems for managing their supporting programs.)

PERT and similar integrated systems are powerful tools for controlling complex programs. Such control systems become increasingly valuable as the number of events and activities in a program increases. Where many milestones must be reached before a product is successfully established in the marketplace, PERT is useful at all managerial levels. Although a computer is needed to support complex networks, a manual system is adequate for handling uncomplicated programs. Today, most products are so complex that the selection, design, manufacturing, and marketing processes they involve require some type of formal control.

Summary of Marketing Resources Management

Rational resource allocation is based on the theory of the firm. However, the theoretically ideal decision model is not always practical. Suboptimum solutions are often necessary, due to the inability of the decision-maker to judge and to manipulate every variable that ultimately affects the firm's total profit. This is normally the case in the use of marketing resources.

Optimizing between two inputs that are to some extent substitutes for each other can be done by selecting the point at which their isoquant and isocost lines are tangent. Problems involving multiple inputs can often be handled by such techniques as the Verdoorn desert-and-oasis map. Linear programming also serves this purpose. Decision models can be made more realistic by explicitly including risk and uncertainty. This is done by introducing probability and dealing in expected values.

Resource control is the other side of the resource-management coin. Control systems are necessary to correct for errors in resource allocation, changes in the marketing environment, and deficiencies in performance, as well as to identify and exploit the more efficient marketing instruments. A control system requires performance standards, an information feedback system, data presentation, and a mechanism for reallocating resources. The sequence chart, loading chart, performance ratio chart, and scheduling chart are examples of control devices.

PERT (Program Evaluation and Review Technique) is one of the most sophisticated and powerful control systems. It integrates the management of both schedules and costs and identifies the events that are most critical to the successful completion of a program. Such a system is necessary for the manufacture and marketing of complex products, or of simple products being sold in large and complex markets.

Questions and Problems

1. List four resources that could be reallocated during each of the following periods: (a) market period, (b) short run, and (c) long run.
2. Assuming ten different mixes of marketing inputs and a revenue function of $R = 2Q$, where R = revenue and Q = output (sales in units of output), construct a desert-and-oasis chart using assumed values for each mix, $M_1, M_2, \ldots M_{10}$. Select the optimum mix and defend your choice.

3. Discuss five constraints that might be imposed on a resource-allocation model.

4. Cite a marketing decision that might be made under conditions of (a) certainty, (b) risk, (c) uncertainty, and (d) ignorance.

5. Analysis reveals that the marginal factor cost for advertising in each of two magazines, five newspapers, and one mailing list is $3.00, $4.00, $2.50, $5.00, $4.50, $8.00, $7.00, and $2.00, respectively, given the firm's present marketing mix. The marginal physical product for each of the eight advertising media is 0.5, 0.6, 0.2, 1.0, 1.1, 1.0, 0.8, and 0.3 respectively. Marginal revenue is $7.00. (a) Suggest a reallocation of the advertising budget holding total expenditures constant. (b) Suggest an allocation plan if the total advertising budget could be increased.

6. A company's marketing function, the independent variables of which are personal selling and mail-order selling, is expressed as $S = 2000y + 4000x - 100x^2$, where S is weekly sales expressed in dollars, y is the number of door-to-door salesmen, and x is the number of mail-order offices. Determine the optimum allocation of marketing resources if salesmen can be maintained for $400 per week, it costs $800 per week to operate a mail-order office, and the chief salesman has given a regional manager a quota of $60,000 per week in gross sales.

7. A marketing manager is considering offering a premium in order to induce people to buy his company's breakfast cereal. If the idea is a success, the additional increment of profit will be $200,000. If it is unsuccessful, sales will not increase, but costs will go up (to cover the premium), and profit will decline by $200,000. The probability of success is .6. Do you recommend this promotional tactic? Why?

8. Firm A is dissatisfied with its performance in a local market. The marketing manager has been directed to prepare a new strategy and has selected four promising alternatives: (1) an expanded advertising campaign, (2) a price cut, (3) an increase in the sales staff, and (4) a buyer-incentive program involving a contest with prizes for the winners. One major competitor, Firm B, dominates this market, as well as a number of other local markets that it shares with Firm A. Experience in these other markets indicates that Firm B reacts to an increase in its competitors' marketing activity in one of three ways: (a) it does not change its present program, (b) it cuts its price, or (c) it increases its advertising. Experience also indicates that the probabilities of these reactions are .2, .5, and .3, respectively, for each of the strategy alternatives under consideration by Firm A. The profits estimated for Firm A for each combination of Firm A's strategies and Firm B's responses are indicated in the following matrix:

	(a)	(b)	(c)
(1)	$200,000	$ 60,000	$120,000
(2)	300,000	−50,000	150,000
(3)	250,000	−10,000	110,000
(4)	200,000	50,000	20,000

Recommend a strategy alternative for Firm A, based on expected values.

9. The quantity of warehouse space required to support the distribution of a firm's product line is found to be proportional to the firm's sales. One square yard of floor area is required for each 5 units of Product A, each 10 units of Product B, and each 2 units of Product C. Given the sales forecasts shown in the table below, construct a loading chart for warehouse requirements for 1972 through 1974.

		EXPECTED SALES		
		Product A	Product B	Product C
1972	1st quarter	500	1000	0
	2nd quarter	400	1100	0
	3rd quarter	300	1100	0
	4th quarter	250	1000	0
1973	1st quarter	200	900	0
	2nd quarter	150	800	40
	3rd quarter	100	700	80
	4th quarter	50	600	110
1974	1st quarter	0	500	140
	2nd quarter	0	450	160
	3rd quarter	0	400	180
	4th quarter	0	300	200

10. In the preceding problem, what alternatives might be best for (a) leveling the peaks (accommodating an overload) and (b) filling the valleys (using idle warehouse capacity)?

11. A sales office maintains a staff of 10 salesmen. Records kept on each of 20 salesmen who worked at one time or another for the company show the average monthly sales booked by these men to be 100, 120, 200, 90, 145, 130, 140, 165, 170, 190, 105, 120, 140, 145, 165, 170, 160, 155, 155, and 135, respectively. Construct a performance-ratio chart, showing a standard and an acceptable minimum level of performance to be used for monitoring the staff in the future. Suggest a way—to be indicated on the chart—to identify outstanding salesmen.

12. A firm's sales have increased to the level where it is now more economical for the company itself to perform the sales function that was previously handled by middlemen—in this case, a group of independent sales representatives. The vice president for marketing has hired a sales manager who is given the responsibility for the personal-selling function. The manager must set up a network of regional offices, manned by competent salesmen, in time to meet a target date, for switching the firm from using middlemen to using its own sales force, that is 24 weeks away.

To set up the offices, the manager must select the cities where they will be necessary, survey the available facilities, negotiate leases, and move his men in. These tasks appear to have optimistic times of 4, 5, 4, and 2 weeks, respectively. Pessimistic times are estimated as 6, 8, 6, and 3 weeks, and the most likely times as 4, 7, 5, and 2 weeks. After the cities are selected, local salesmen must be hired and trained. The recruiting, selection, and training of the sales personnel is most likely to take 10, 4, and 5 weeks, respectively. Optimistic estimates are 6, 3, and 5 weeks. Pessimistic estimates are 12, 5, and 5 weeks. Design a PERT network for this problem, representing each event (milestone) and activity by a number or letter.

Supplementary Readings

BOOKS

ALEXIS, MARCUS, and WILSON, CHARLES Z., *Organizational Decision Making* (Englewood Cliffs, N. J.: Prentice-Hall, 1967).

CLARK, WALLACE, *The Gantt Chart: A Working Tool of Management* (London: Pitman & Sons, 1947).

FREUND, JOHN E., and WILLIAMS, FRANK J., *Elementary Business Statistics: The Modern Approach* (Englewood Cliffs, N. J.: Prentice-Hall, 1964).

GARRETT, LEONARD J., and SILVER, MILTON, *Production Management Analysis* (New York: Harcourt, Brace & World, 1966).

MODER, J. J., and PHILLIPS, C. R., *Project Management with CPM and PERT* (New York: Reinhold, 1964).

MOORE, FRANKLIN G., *Production Control* (New York: McGraw-Hill, 1959).

NATIONAL AERONAUTICS AND SPACE ADMINISTRATION, *PERT Time and Cost Guide* (Washington, D. C.: U. S. Government Printing Office, 1962).

ARTICLES

DOOLEY, ARCH R., "Interpretations of PERT," *Harvard Business Review* (March–April 1964), p. 160.

GREENE, M. R., "Market Risk: An Analytical Framework," *Journal of Marketing,* Vol. 32, No. 2 (April 1968), pp. 49–56.

RITER, CHARLES B., "The Merchandising Decision Under Uncertainty," *Journal of Marketing,* Vol. 31, No. 1 (January 1967), pp. 44–47.

UDELL, JON G., "The Perceived Importance of the Elements of Strategy," *Journal of Marketing,* Vol. 32, No. 1 (January 1968), pp. 34–40.

VERDOORN, P. J., "Marketing from the Producer's Point of View," *Journal of Marketing,* Vol. 20, No. 3 (January 1956), pp. 221–35.

Part IV

CONSUMER BEHAVIOR

The economist, aided by the mathematician, offers the marketer many powerful tools for understanding and analyzing the marketplace. For instance, the relationships between important variables, such as sales and advertising, can often be specified with considerable precision. An efficient allocation of resources can be achieved, or at least approached with confidence. Hypotheses can be rigorously tested—given, of course, adequate time and data. In short, the "what" of marketing can be defined and explained relying chiefly on these disciplines.

In a free economy the ultimate judge of the firm's performance is the consumer. Consumer behavior will determine the fate of the enterprise. This behavior can be described by the economist, who can also tell us how it will be influenced by marketing variables such as price, promotion, product variation, and distribution. The economist's view of the consumer is part of the "what" of the marketplace.

The economist, however, makes little attempt to explain the "why" of the marketplace, especially with respect to consumer behavior. For insight into this behavior, which is vital to the firm, we must turn to the behavioral sciences. There are several distinct schools of psychology and sociology applicable to the interpretation, hence manipulation, of purchasing behavior. In this section, each will be examined and phenomena of special interest to the marketer explored. In the concluding chapter, we shall construct a model of consumer behavior. Such models are commonly used to integrate and make more manageable the various psychological and social factors that may play a part in the behavior of the firm's potential customers.

CHAPTER 8

Economic and Behavioral Aspects of the Consumer

ECONOMICS' VIEW OF THE CONSUMER

Economists have traditionally viewed consumer behavior as simply a matter of making rational choices between alternative goods. The consumer, acting on his set of preferences, called "tastes," for the products confronting him, will select that combination which yields the greatest satisfaction. This satisfaction is called "utility" and represents the degree to which the buyer's biological and psychogenic needs are satisfied. Presumably, these needs can never be completely satisfied, if for no other reason than that the consumer's acquisition of goods and services is limited by budget constraints.

Utility cannot be measured in absolute terms. (How many units of utility are derived from eating a steak dinner?) However, consumer preferences may often be revealed, and some useful generalizations made, by invoking utility theory. This is a descriptive, not an analytical, tool. Although economists may describe consumer behavior in terms of preferences and responses to changes in the marketing variables, they make no attempt to explain the underlying causes of this behavior.

Ordinalist Theory of Choice. The ordinalist theory of choice assumes that an individual's preferences for goods and services may be ranked (ordered) but cannot be measured in absolute (cardinal) terms.[1] The theory is based on the law of diminishing marginal utility, explained by economist Paul Samuelson as follows:

As you consume more of the same good, your total (psychological) utility increases. However, let us use the term marginal utility to refer to "the extra utility added by one extra last unit of a good." Then, with successive new units of the

---

[1] John A. Howard, *Marketing Theory* (Boston: Allyn & Bacon, 1965), p. 78.

good, your total utility will grow at a slower and slower rate because of a fundamental tendency for your psychological ability to appreciate more of the good
to become less keen. . . .

As the amount consumed of a good increases, the marginal utility of the
good (or the extra utility added by its last unit) tends to decrease.[2]

Most readers should find this argument intuitively acceptable. As a
person acquires more and more of a good, he is likely to find that additional
units become less and less desirable. Consequently, he will be less willing to
sacrifice units of other goods in order to increase his consumption of the
first good. A man may prefer T-bone steaks to lobsters, but if he already
has a freezer full of steaks, he may prefer to acquire a few lobsters rather
than another steak. As the marginal utility of steak declines, the value of
other goods relative to it increases. Hence the consumer will be willing to
pay more for other goods and less for steak. This phenomenon is illustrated
graphically by an indifference curve, U, showing the combinations of Product A and the aggregate of all other goods and services that provide the
same overall level of satisfaction (utility). An indifference curve is also
called an "iso-utility curve," since every point on the curve yields the same
level of utility.

In Figure 8.1, for example, the consumer is indifferent to whether he
is at (q_a, q_1), (q_b, q_2), (q_c, q_3), (q_d, q_4), or any other point on the indifference
curve. He would be willing to sacrifice relatively little of his consumption of
all other goods and services to increase his consumption of Product A from,
say, q_3 to q_4.

Since the value of other goods and services competing with Product A
is represented by their price, their aggregate quantity can be represented
by a total money value. Thus, we can say that the consumer with q_3 units
of Product A would be willing to sacrifice relatively little money (enough to
purchase only $q_c - q_d$) to acquire an additional increment $(q_4 - q_3)$ of that
product. This is the same as saying he would pay a relatively low price for
the additional units of A. Conversely, if he had only q_1 units of A, he would
sacrifice considerably more money—that is, he would pay a higher price—to
acquire more units of A.

Within limits, it is logical to assume that if an individual derives utility
from a particular product he would rather have more of the product than
less. Although he may be indifferent to whether he has, say 2 steaks and 8
lobsters, 3 steaks and 4 lobsters, or 4 steaks and no lobsters, he would surely
prefer 6 steaks and 12 lobsters to any of the other combinations. Thus consumers are assumed to have many indifference curves, each yielding a dif-

[2] Paul A. Samuelson, *Economics: An Introductory Analysis,* 7th ed. (New York:
McGraw-Hill, 1967), p. 417.

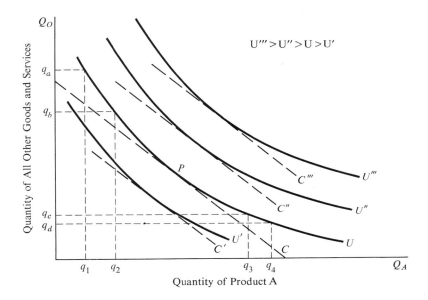

FIGURE 8.1
Indifference curves

ferent level of utility, as shown by the lighter curves U', U'', and U''' in Figure 8.1. Since each succeedingly higher indifference curve yields a higher degree of utility, the consumer will tend to operate on the furthest curve, or to maintain the highest standard of living that his budget allows.

The consumer's ability to buy different combinations of Product A and other goods along a selected indifference curve is a function of the goods' relative prices and his income. If an isocost curve showing the various combinations of A and other goods, Q_o, that can be purchased for a fixed total cost is constructed tangent to the indifference curve, the combination of goods at the point of tangency will provide the utility represented by the curve at the lowest possible cost. In Figure 8.1, the optimum combination of Product A and all other goods is located at P, the point where C, the isocost curve, touches U.

The isocost curve may be viewed as representing either the consumer's income or his budget. Assuming that the relative prices of goods remain the same, the proportions of different goods that can be purchased at any level of income will be the same. Hence the isocost curves will be parallel, as are C, C', C'', and C''' in Figure 8.1. If the buyer's income increases, he will be able to operate along an isocost line further to the right, which intersects a higher indifference curve, and his level of satisfaction will increase. A less rigorous way to put this would be to say that the consumer derives greater material and psychological satisfaction as his income, and hence his expenditures, increases.

This reasoning, which serves as the basis for some important theoretical concepts in economics and marketing, is analogous to the reasoning behind the method of selecting inputs required for a given level of output developed in Chapter 6. The consumer's indifference curve is comparable to the producer's isocost curve. The consumer attempts to maximize his utility given a total level of expenditure (his income); the producer, on the other hand, attempts to minimize his total cost given a desired level of output. Thus, some economists[3] treat the consumer—defined as an individual or a household—as similar to a production unit (or firm) in explaining consumer behavior.

The ordinalist theory is based on the premise that a buyer has an ordered system of preferences—that he prefers Product A to B, B to C, C to D, and so on—and that he will act rationally in making choices between goods. A buyer acting rationally would select one unit of Product A in preference to one unit of B or C, if the prices of the three items were the same. If their prices were unequal, the rational buyer would select the combination of goods indicated by the intersection of his isocost and indifference curves. It would be nonrational to accept a less desirable item, say C, if a more desirable one, A, were available, all other considerations being equal. Many buyers do behave nonrationally, but, say the ordinalists, the bad decisions tend to cancel each other out when large numbers of people are involved. For every time A was purchased when B was the rational choice, B will be purchased when A is the rational choice. Assuming that these mistakes are symmetrically distributed, their net effect will sum to zero and they can be safely ignored.

Demand Curves.   Demand curves, which are graphical. representations of demand functions, are the economist's method of describing consumer behavior as it relates to a particular independent variable. For instance, a demand curve may be constructed that shows how many units of a good will be purchased at each price within a given range of prices. Demand curves are both a descriptive tool for the exploration of consumer behavior and the theoretical basis of many pricing considerations.

The demand curve for a good is derived by observing the shift in the point of tangency, P, of the iso-utility curve, U, and isocost curve, C, as the isocost curve rotates due to a change in the price of the good. The prices of all other goods are held constant. For instance, if the price of Product A is increased, the quantity of A, Q_A, that may be purchased at a given level of

---

[3] Paul Samuelson, Milton Friedman, Paul Douglas, and others.

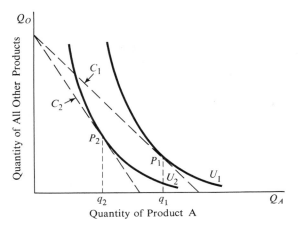

FIGURE 8.2
A shift in demand induced by a shift in price

income (represented by the isocost curve) is reduced. This is illustrated in Figure 8.2, which shows the isocost curve rotating from C_1 to C_2 and thereby reducing the quantity, Q_A, that may be purchased from q_1 to q_2. This movement must not be confused with the *shift* rightward of the isocost curves in Figure 8.1 resulting from a change in income. In Figure 8.2, income remains fixed; hence the total number of dollars available to be spent is unchanged. However, the change in the price of Product A changes the relationship between the quantity of A, $Q_{A'}$ that may be purchased and the quantity of all other goods, $Q_{o'}$ that may be bought. Here the *slope* of the isocost curve changes, while the total amount of money spent does not.

As the isocost curve pivots from C_1 to C_2, it leaves utility curve U_1 and becomes tangent to a new utility curve, U_2. Faced with this situation, the rational buyer will operate at point P_2; he can no longer operate at P_1, which is now beyond his budget (income). To shift from P_1 to P_2, he must reduce the quantity of A he buys from q_1 to q_2. The effect of the price is thus to reduce the consumption of A. Conversely, had the price been reduced, the isocost curve would have rotated upward, and the quantity of A purchased by rational buyers would have increased.

Plotting the quantities of A—q_1, q_2, . . . q_n—against the possible prices of A in the example above will give us a demand curve for Product A. This curve—and the mathematical function it represents—expresses the relationship between the quantity of A that will be purchased and price. It is the economist's way of describing how a consumer will respond to price changes for a particular product class or brand.

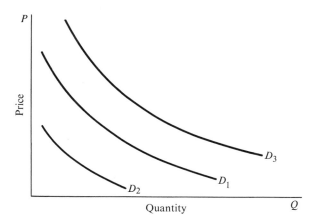

FIGURE 8.3
Demand curves*

* By labeling the vertical axis "price" and the horizontal axis "quantity," we have
conformed with economic convention but not with mathematical convention. Mathematicians place the dependent variable (in this case, quantity) on the vertical axis and
the independent variable (in this case, price) on the horizontal axis.

The economist, as well as the marketer, is primarily interested in the
behavior of the market population as a whole, not the behavior of one or
two individuals. Hence practitioners of both sciences find it convenient to
aggregate the demand curves of individual consumers into a total-demand
curve. In practice, this aggregate, or "market," demand curve is estimated
directly, usually from historical or survey data drawn from the market
population.

In Figure 8.3, the demand curve D_1 expresses the quantity, Q, that will
be consumed at a given price, P. D_2 and D_3 are other possible demand curves.
At D_3, the firm could sell the same quantity at a higher price or a greater
quantity at the same price. At D_2, the converse would be true. Knowing the
demand curve for a product allows the marketer to compute the various
revenues $(P \cdot Q)$ that will accrue at any given output within the range of Q.
By comparing this information with the firm's cost function, he can select
the optimum output/price combination for maximum profit, as demonstrated
in Chapter 3.

A shift to the left or right—from D_1 to D_2 or D_3 in Figure 8.3—can be
caused by a shift in either consumer income or taste. The firm can do little
to influence consumer income, but it can often manipulate taste. The instruments used to change consumer tastes are product variation, advertising, and
personal selling. The role of the economist is to describe the general relationship between price and consumption—that is, demand—and the effects that
changes in product, advertising, and personal selling have on the demand
curve. Economics enables the marketer to describe consumer reactions to

the changes in the instruments of marketing. Obviously, demand theory is a very powerful tool, particularly when data can be obtained to quantify the relationships between variables fairly precisely. Using the techniques of mathematical economics and econometrics, supported by marketing research, the marketer can aggregate the behavior of the consumer and express it as a function of the consumer's response to variations in the marketing mix. The act of buying (expressed as sales) is a dependent variable that can be expressed as a function of the endogenous variables of the firm. Some typical behavior patterns are shown in Figure 8.4.

The general mathematical equations for each of these relationships are shown under the graphs. These curves, or functions, describe the relationship between sales, Q, and each of the independent variables that might be manipulated by the marketer.

Such statements as $Q = f(A)$ (quantity sold is a function of advertising) imply that all other variables remain constant. Although this is seldom true, it is usually a workable assumption so far as the manipulation of the one variable is concerned. The equation still describes consumer behavior in respect to that variable. For instance, if an increase in advertising, ΔA, will increase sales by ΔQ, ceteris paribus, it will probably have a comparable effect even when changes in other variables tend to decrease sales. If changes

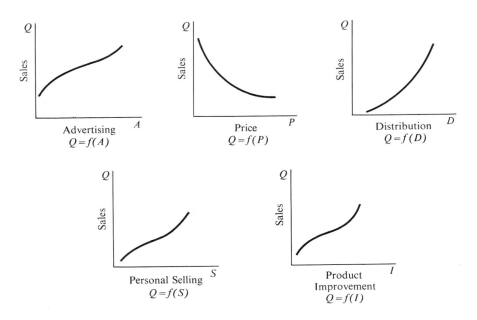

FIGURE 8.4
Consumer behavior as a function of marketing variables

in price, product characteristics, competitors' strategies, or the state of nature dominate and drive down total sales, the new level of sales still will not be as low as it would have been without the added advertising, ΔA.

In reality, sales are a function of many variables, only a few of which can be identified by the firm and even fewer of which can be controlled. Total sales, Q, will depend on the firm's price, advertising, personal selling, product characteristics, and distribution system, as well as such exogenous variables as its competitors' prices, advertising, and so on, and a number of unknown determinants. We can express this in notational form as $Q = f(P,A,S,C,D,P_c,A_c, \ldots X_n)$.

In the practical application of his craft the economist seeks to specify the explicit form of these relationships in particular circumstances. To say that $Q = f(A)$—that how much consumers purchase will be influenced by advertising—is to verbalize the obvious. It is much more difficult to determine an explicit relationship, such as $Q = 10,000 + 20A$, $Q = 20,000 + 100A - A^2$, or $Q = 8,000 + 3\log_2 A$. To do this requires market data, the acquisition of which is the object of marketing research. Once sufficient data is acquired and an explicit equation arrived at, the economist, or marketer, has a very precise description of consumer behavior in respect to a particular variable. He will know exactly how the market population will behave in response to various levels of advertising. This information is extremely useful when the time comes to make a marketing decision. Nevertheless, to describe is not to explain. Economists tell us what the nature of the marketplace is, not why it is that way.

"What" versus "Why."   The ultimate judge of the correctness of the marketer's analyses and decisions is the buyer; the final choice belongs to him. Economics aggregates the decisions of many buyers and expresses the relationship between the consumption of a particular good or service and the economic determinants of that consumption—usually the price of the product, the price of substitute products, the price of complementary goods, consumer income, and consumer taste. Change one of these determinants and the dependent variable—consumption—will respond. The instruments of change that are available to the marketer—product variation, pricing, promotion, and distribution—thus serve to manipulate consumption, hence to change the revenues and profits of the firm.

Microeconomics attempts to define the sensitivity of consumption to variations in these instruments. If the firm can define the relationship between sales and the determinants of sales, and determine the cost of manipulating those determinants, it can allocate the resources at its disposal perfectly. Perfection in allocation demands perfect knowledge, which is seldom attainable. However, the techniques of approximation and the explicit inclusion of risk in decision models permit sufficient precision for consistently rational choices.

Economics, supported by mathematics, does much to define market phenomena—to count and measure variables and quantify their relationships—but it provides little insight into why those relationships exist. Economists can estimate closely the ratio of convertibles to sedans that will be sold, the quantity of beer that will be consumed, the number of potential college students, and the ratio of Coca-Cola to 7-Up drinkers. However, they seldom attempt to explain why the demand curves and responses are what they are.

Many would argue that the marketer needs to know only the size of the economic variables and their relationships in order to optimize his choice of alternatives. If he knows that a local market contains 453,290 potential customers, that medium A will produce twice the sales of medium B, that a 10-percent increase in price will result in a 5-percent reduction in sales, that a 5-model product line will produce twice the sales of a 2-model line, that a $10 increase in commission will increase sales by 2 percent, or that one-third of the buyers prefer blue finish, what else does he need to know? Does it make any difference to the marketer *why* buyers are more sensitive to medium A, *why* 5 percent of the consumers will prefer not to buy the item if price increases, *why* having 3 more variations of the good will attract twice as many buyers, *why* salesmen will sell 2-percent more merchandise for a 10-percent greater commission, or *why* one-third of the customers prefer blue to any other color? In terms of profit maximization, the reasons "why" a thing is so are often useless information; the decision-maker need only know the probable results of each alternative choice.

On the other hand, if the marketer understood the intellectual or emotional process that leads a potential customer to accept or reject a particular good or service, he might conceive marketing strategies that would make one or more of his instruments more productive. If he perceived the nature of the drive or appetite that resulted in a given pattern of purchasing behavior, and if this drive or appetite was sufficiently prevalent among potential buyers, the marketer might design his product mix, advertising, and sales tactics more efficiently. In short, a knowledge of the "why" of consumer behavior offers an opportunity to influence that behavior. In the final analysis, the influencing of buyer behavior is the primary task of marketing, except in those few cases, such as agriculture, where the firm is a member of a purely competitive industry.[4]

Whether a marketing strategy is designed to conform to buyer behavior or to influence its determinants, the formulator of that strategy can benefit from a knowledge of those determinants. This is especially true when the marketer is dissatisfied with established techniques and is seeking to make innovations in his product or promotional instruments. Even if its current

[4] In a competitive industry the market price of the product is unaffected by the quantity each individual firm sells. Economists typically refer to a competitive industry as one in which the firm makes decisions as though changes in its output will not affect prices.

marketing practices are proving quite successful, the firm is confronted by the high probability that the future will be different. Tastes, attitudes, and behavioral patterns change, making particular marketing methods less or more efficient. By understanding the "why" of consumer behavior, the marketer can often detect trends that in effect allow him to peer into the future. This foreknowledge will enable him to tailor future strategies to tomorrow's realities rather than today's.

Although a firm could experiment blindly with new ideas, testing each idea's usefulness in the laboratory or the marketplace, such a process would be inefficient, expensive, and possibly hazardous to its long-term welfare. The alternative is to discover the intellectual or emotional process associated with the selection or rejection of a product and to innovate or choose alternatives within this context.

In the quest for insight into the behavior of the consumer, economists and marketers must defer to the behavioral sciences, especially psychology and sociology. In making an excursion into these fields, the marketer must leave behind much of the rigor and quantitative methods associated with the economic analysis of marketing. He must also be prepared to confront radically divergent theories and interpretations, since there is no single, general theory of human behavior. Nevertheless, psychology and sociology are undeniably useful in the interpretation of certain marketing phenomena. Because these fields often suggest answers to very practical problems, we turn now from the economic explanation of the marketplace and the quantitative tools of decision-making to the qualitative realm of the behavioral scientist. A convenient starting point is the examination of consumer motivation, as seen through the eyes of psychologists and sociologists.

BEHAVIORAL SCIENCES AND THE CONSUMER

Behavioral science consists of three major fields, anthropology, psychology, and sociology. Each has been applied to the explanation of phenomena of the marketplace. However, psychology and sociology, which we shall examine here, have been used the most widely. It is appropriate from the viewpoint of the marketer—as well as pedagogically convenient for our purposes—to concentrate on the major subdivisions of these fields. These are (1) experimental psychology, (2) clinical psychology, which in turn can be roughly divided into the Freudian and the Gestalt schools, (3) sociology, and (4) social psychology.

Experimental Psychology. Experimental psychology, which is sometimes referred to as "laboratory psychology," deals with the relationships between variables observed under controlled (laboratory) conditions: "The distinguishing characteristics are those of the laboratory, not of the subjects used or the topics covered."[5] The experimental psychologist seeks to determine the relationships, if any, between dependent and independent variables. The dependent variable is some form of human behavior, such as learning, and each independent variable is either an identifiable, measurable human characteristic, such as age, or a stimulus introduced by the experimenter, such as heat. The independent variable is controlled—subjects of a particular age are selected, or temperature is set at a selected level—and the dependent variable is observed and measured. Relying primarily on statistical techniques, the experimenter attempts to evaluate the degree of correlation between the two variables.

Experimental psychology places primary emphasis on drives that stem from basic biological needs—hunger, thirst, sex, and the avoidance of pain. These are referred to as "innate drives." Since human beings share these characteristics with lower animal forms, much of the theory attributable to laboratory psychology is derived from experimentation with animals such as hamsters, mice, rats, and monkeys.

An intellectually higher order of drives can be acquired, or learned. Many acquired drives are derived from innate drives. Fear, which is learned in avoiding pain, is an example. Once learned, fear may cause a particular form of behavior regardless of whether an actual threat of pain exists. In this respect, learned drives may become autonomous, functioning either with or without the presence of the basic need that they were originally acquired to accommodate. The existence of learned and autonomous drives in animals was confirmed by Ivan Pavlov, a Russian experimental psychologist.

Pavlov was the first to demonstrate the conditioned-response phenomenon. He showed how an animal, and by implication a human, could be taught, or "conditioned," to respond to a given stimulus by teaching dogs to associate the ringing of a bell with the presence of food. The results of Pavlov's famous dog experiments were published in 1906. Subsequent experimentation with both animals and humans has reinforced these findings and generalized them to man. If the reader will reflect on his own behavior, he will probably discover that he, too, has been conditioned to respond to such stimuli. For instance, the sight of a soft drink advertisement may induce the same physiological reaction as the presence of the beverage itself. Conversely, if the biological need thirst emerges, he may have been conditioned to respond with a quest for a certain brand of liquid refreshment.

Behaviorism, founded by an American, John B. Watson (1878–1958), is an outgrowth of experimental psychology. Watson believed psychology could become an objective science if it were confined to the recording and analysis of "objective," or public, data to the exclusion of introspection.

[5] Ernest R. Hilgard and Richard C. Atkinson, *Introduction to Psychology,* 4th ed. (New York: Harcourt, Brace & World, 1967), p. 9.

Behaviorism is the study of what a person *does* when subjected to particular stimuli. Behavior is public in that it can be observed and recorded; hence it is independent of the subjective information provided by introspection. Behaviorists observe, measure, and record, then correlate and generalize. They are primarily concerned with the learning of habit patterns that occurs after repeated pairings of drives with exogenous stimuli.

Contemporary behaviorism is known as *stimulus-response psychology,* contracted to "S-R psychology" in the modern vernacular. S-R psychologists view a psychological event as beginning with a stimulus and ending with a response. S-R theory holds that all behavior is in response to stimuli, whether they are overt (such as running) or covert (such as thinking).[6]

If consumer behavior is interpreted in this context, the prospective customer appears childlike, entering the world with basic drives and with the ability to receive impressions, respond, and learn behavior patterns, much like Pavlov's dogs. The role of the marketer then becomes one of *conditioning* responses. The chief instrument for achieving this is direct and repetitive advertising.

Examples of this strategy abound. It is very common in the promotion of convenience goods such as beverages and cigarettes. The Coca-Cola Company, for example, has been a consistent and successful practitioner of S-R psychology, with its persistent and heavy use of the slogan "Drink Coca-Cola" and the image of its unique bottle. The objective of Coca-Cola's advertising tactics is to teach the consumer to associate its beverage with fulfillment of the basic drive thirst. The result is a conditioned response whereby the individual automatically seeks a bottle of Coca-Cola when confronted with a thirst stimulus. The advertising is repetitious and plentiful—characteristics associated with practically all S-R promotion. Hundreds of spot announcements on radio and television, repetitious ads in periodicals, and tens of thousands of point-of-purchase signs all carrying the single, Pavlovian message: "Drink Coca-Cola."

Although one might question the validity of generalizing laboratory experience with rats, dogs, and monkeys to the consumer, such firms as Coca-Cola and the American Tobacco Company have had frequent and sometimes spectacular success with this approach to influencing buyer behavior. It is certainly useful in the establishment and reinforcement of brand recognition, which is especially important for homogeneous products (products whose physical properties are not significantly different). If all else is equal, a buyer is more apt to buy a particular brand when confronted with a choice if he has heard its name again and again in association with the satisfaction of a physical or emotional need.

However, confronted with an excessive quantity of advertising—and

---

[6] Hilgard and Atkinson, *op. cit.,* p. 18.

the urban consumer has probably long ago reached the saturation level in terms of his ability to absorb more advertising—the individual may develop a defense mechanism that filters out the repetitive, hence monotonous, S-R message. Also, the quantity of advertising necessary to bring a significant number of potential buyers across the conditioned-response threshold may be too expensive to be practical or efficient. For this reason, other strategies are often used independently of or in concert with the S-R approach.

Clinical Psychology.   Clinical psychology deals primarily with learned drives, as opposed to the primary (innate) drives that are the chief concern of experimental psychology. The former are often referred to as "psychological" factors, while the latter are called "biological" drives. Of special concern to clinical psychologists is the conflict between human biological drives and the norms of society. The resolution of this conflict can produce complex behavior patterns that are not explainable by the objective tools of laboratory psychology. The conflict between biological drives and social values frequently results in abnormal behavior. Hence the techniques of clinical psychology are often invoked in the treatment of mental disorders.

Although there is general agreement on the definition and nature of the biological drives, considerable controversy exists over the learned drives. Even clinical psychologists cannot agree on the nature or the hierarchy of the psychological factors that influence behavior. The result is an alienation between experimental and clinical psychology, and between the primary schools of clinical psychology itself. Compounding the problem is the lack of rigor in theory and application. Reports and theories are based largely on interviews, which are basically subjective. A considerable amount of inference is employed in the interpretation of the data obtained from interviews. Questions and answers are generally qualitative, and hence vulnerable to the biases of both the interviewer and the interviewee. Since absolute measurements of the psychological variables are rarely possible, quantitative analysis is extremely difficult.

A further problem is that the sources of raw data are often unreliable. The objective answers provided by the respondents, regardless of their desire to be truthful, may be divorced from the real motives for their behavior. Social pressures, according to the clinicians, suppress biological drives to lower levels of consciousness. In order to reduce conflict, the individual finds substitute expressions for his subdued needs. Hence his behavior may be an expression of a conflict recognized only in his subconscious. The conflict cannot be verbalized because he himself does not understand the real reason for his behavior. The objective of psychoanalysis, a subdivision of clinical psychology, is to penetrate beyond the respondent's conscious mind and reveal his subconscious thinking. This is often a difficult and uncertain process at the present state of the art.

Freudians form perhaps the most extreme school of clinical psychology. They perceive behavior as almost solely a function of suppressed drives, particularly the sexual appetite. Subconscious desires, which are out of the realm of the actor's awareness, motivate the actor and explain his behavior. For example, a man may or may not smoke a cigarette because of a suppressed desire for oral gratification through nursing or thumb-sucking. Freud believed that desires associated with the childhood stages of psychosexual development—oral, anal, phallic, and Oedipal—are often submerged into the subconscious rather than outgrown. Since actual satisfaction of these desires may conflict with the norms of adult society, they are usually satisfied by behavior that serves as a substitute for the desired, but unacceptable, behavior. If the cause of behavior is truly in the subconscious of the doer, then little can be learned by asking direct questions and taking the answers at face value.

If behavior is a result of suppressed desires, the product becomes an instrument for the partial fulfillment of these desires. Hence purchasing behavior, especially brand choice, may well be influenced by the symbolic as well as the functional characteristics of the product. To say that this interpretation of the consumer is not given considerable credence in the field of marketing is to ignore thousands of advertisements conspicuously identifying brands and products with sex.

In his attempt to explain personality and therefore behavior, Freud introduced the concepts of the id, ego, and superego. The *id* is the repository of the innate drives, which demand immediate satisfaction when aroused. If left unbridled by the ego, the id would cause the individual always to seek immediate gratification of biological drives and impulses. The id manifests itself at an early stage of development and is always active within the individual. If it remains unchecked, the result will be socially unacceptable behavior.[7] The *ego* exists to control the id and reflects the learning of social norms. The conflict between the ego and the id tends to be resolved by the desire for immediate pleasure being channeled into socially acceptable behavior. The success of the ego in controlling the id is the measure of a mature individual.[8] The *superego* develops out of the ego's experience with social reality, especially its encounters with parental prohibitions. The superego is nearly synonymous with *conscience* and influences the individual to strive toward an ideal self, an image of which is normally prescribed for him in early childhood.[9] The id, ego, and superego are in continual conflict with one another. Behavioral patterns will depend on which one is dominant, and this varies among individuals and over time.

[7] Hilgard and Atkinson, *op. cit.,* p. 478.
[8] *Ibid.*
[9] *Ibid.*

From a Freudian standpoint, the firm stands to gain from identifying the buyer's subconscious as well as conscious motives for purchasing a particular product or discriminating between brands. If the subconscious motives underlying purchasing behavior can be identified and generalized to a substantial number of prospective buyers, this knowledge can be exploited. Product characteristics and promotion can be manipulated to appeal to these motives. It is usually practical, as well as legally necessary, to satisfy the suppressed drives in a socially acceptable manner, hence in a way that coincides with the dictates of the consumer's ego and superego. For example, vicarious sexual satisfaction is provided if an advertisement associates masculinity with the functional properties of an automobile, a shaving lotion, or a sport shirt. Thus the sexual drive that lies in the consumer's id is partially satisfied by the product, which conforms to the constraints imposed by the ego and the superego. The product itself has no actual sexual properties but does have symbolic sexual connotations that are imparted by advertising or product design aimed at associating the item with the suppressed sexual drive.

Given the fact of subconscious responses to nonfunctional qualities of the product, the marketer is confronted with a need to identify a particular subconscious drive and the corresponding symbolic properties that will gratify it. These properties must then be incorporated into the consumer's image of the product. Neither task is easy; pinpointing both the drive that underlies a particular type of nonrational behavior and the symbols that will gratify it can be extremely difficult.

The use of Freudian psychology in marketing is very controversial. Its critics argue that it is only appropriate to the analysis of individuals, each of whom represents a unique mix of psychological characteristics; that it costs too much in time and money; and that the results are unreliable. Much of this is true. Psychoanalysis, which derives mainly from Freudian psychology, frequently employs complicated projective techniques,[10] such as the Rorschach inkblot test, that must be administered and interpreted by highly trained personnel. Psychoanalysis is a highly personal process, oriented solely toward the individual being studied. A heavily Freudian approach to marketing can result in an attempt to relate promotion and product design to socially abnormal suppressed desires. In addition, economists and many marketers view the household, which cannot be psychoanalyzed, rather than the individual, as the basic consumption unit for many product classes (automobiles, houses, and groceries, for example).

On the other hand, the supporters of Freudian psychology argue that some psychological traits are so common that a relatively small sample—

---

[10] See Chapter 25 for a discussion of projective techniques.

say, fewer than 30—is often a sufficient basis for generalization. There are countless examples of the consumption of particular goods and discrimination between certain brands that cannot be explained using any rational criteria. How do the functional or economic properties of fad items explain their sudden burst of popularity or rapid decline? Why is one brand of toilet soap, one make of sedan, one toy, or one style of dress preferred to others? A popular product often has physical properties that are essentially the same as, or even inferior to, those of competitors' products—and a higher price as well. Why were ready-made cake mixes widely rejected until the recipe was changed to make the housewife add a fresh egg to the batter? No other schools of disciplines attempt to answer such questions; yet the questions are very relevant to the art of marketing.

Gestalt Psychology.   *Gestalt* is the German word for "form," or "configuration."[11] Originated by a group of German psychologists early in the twentieth century, Gestalt psychology was initially concerned with the perception of form and the organization of the mental processes. Those most closely identified with this school of clinical psychology are Max Wertheimer and his colleagues Kurt Koffka and Wolfgang Köhler, all of whom migrated to the United States. Their work was later expanded into an influential variation by Kurt Lewin. Lewin's version of Gestalt psychology, known as *field theory,* emphasizes motivation and social psychology.[12]

Gestalt psychology contends that our perceptions depend on patterns formed by various stimuli and on the order of our experiences. We see an object in relation to its background, or environment. What we see is relative to the whole; the whole consists of parts in relationship yet it is different from the sum of the parts.[13]

The emphasis on perception, which started with color and object experiments, led Gestalt psychologists to a perceptional interpretation of learning, memory, and problem-solving. The body of thought derived from this work, known as *cognitive theory,* draws on the stimulus-response analysis of the experimental psychologists but does not consider it adequate to explain complex human behavior. A knowledge of both an individual's motives, or goals, and his cognitive perception of the environment is considered essential for the explanation of human action. Thus the cognitive theorists, like the Freudian psychologists, are dependent on introspection—the subject must provide the essential data.

Unlike the clinical psychologists of the Freudian school, however, the modern Gestalt psychologists view behavior as a function of rational motives

[11] This translation is convenient but narrow, as "gestalt" has a much broader meaning in German. However, it is not inaccurate and is sufficient for our purposes.
[12] Hilgard and Atkinson, *op. cit.,* p. 19.
[13] *Ibid.*

serving conscious drives. The individual is considered capable of verbalizing his motives, although convincing him to do so may prove difficult. For example, a man may purchase a particular style of clothing to conform to the standard prescribed by his social peers, thus satisfying a learned desire for acceptance by the group. Yet although he may be aware of this need for social acceptance and its effect on his purchasing behavior, he may be unwilling to admit it to an interviewer, giving instead a reason he thinks conforms more closely with his preferred image as an individualist or a discriminating shopper. This forces the analyst to employ projective techniques similar to those used by the Freudians, but far less complicated in their administration and interpretation.

The marketer influenced by the Gestalt school will tend to design his promotional program and product to satisfy rational, but unspoken, drives. He may stress safety to quiet fear and accommodate the desire for pain avoidance. He may emphasize speed and power to appeal to the desire for superiority and dominance. Or he may stress fun in recognition of the need for relaxation and amusement. However, he may frequently link these product characteristics to more Puritan goals, such as care of family and productive labor, in order to give the customer an opportunity to rationalize his behavior as socially admirable. For example, a supermarket may stress the low prices and high quality of its food, thus supporting the buyer in her role as mother and housewife, while at the same time offering trading stamps that can be saved to buy luxury items designed to satisfy her rational, but less Puritan, desires. The emphasis in advertising campaigns on the comfort and prestige, as well as the economy and reliability, of a new automobile is also illustrative. The marketer sees his product as an instrument for the satisfaction of rational and conscious desires, but he realizes that these needs, like subconscious motivations, are not always the most socially acceptable, nor the ones verbalized by the buyer.

Sociology and Social Psychology. *Sociology* is the study of group behavior. Although groups seldom make purchasing decisions, the individual's role as a group member is relevant to consumer behavior. *Social psychology* is the study of the individual as part of the group. It explains behavior as a function of psychological drives conditioned by environment. The social psychologist assumes that the individual is conditioned by his surroundings, especially his social environment, and that he is anxious to conform to the standards of the group.

The group is singular only for an isolated individual or one living in a primitive society. In a complex environment, a person is subject to the influence—and often the conflicting values—of a number of groups. The family, the PTA, other members of one's profession, the company for which one works, or the church one attends, for example, can all impose dislikes and preferences through their informal subcultures. Priorities among a variety of reinforcing and contradictory values are generally dictated by the hierarchy of importance of the groups as perceived by the individual.

In addition to establishing a system of preferences, groups serve as a primary medium of communication. In terms of setting tastes, information communicated within the group is much more influential than information received from impersonal sources. Under conditions of ignorance or uncertainty, and lacking clear and objective information, an individual will normally turn to other persons he knows (that is, to members of a common group) for information and guidance. Both the imposition of values by the group and its communication system are of interest to the marketer, especially in dealing with problems of product variation and promotion.

The two basic processes of social psychology are motivation and cognition. *Motivation* is the impetus of behavior.[14] A motive is a particular biological or psychogenic need (for example, hunger), coupled with the intention to attain an appropriate goal (for example, to eat a steak). The attainment of a particular goal may be an automatic, or conditioned, response, or it may involve a learning process in which the consumer searches for and examines alternatives. To infer a specific motive, such as why a particular item is purchased, it is necessary to identify the person's needs and related goals.[15] The methods used are observation and direct questioning of the consumer. Both have serious limitations, which are discussed in detail in Chapter 22.

The social psychologist views motivation as determined by an individual's *psychological field,* which consists of his physical and social environment and his internal condition. His internal condition is his state of psychological needs, both biological and learned. The goals that are appropriate to the satisfaction of these needs are prescribed by the physical environment. For example, two people could share the same biological need, say thirst, but react differently to it. If one was a German Lutheran, he might seek a glass of beer as an immediate goal, while the other, if a devout Mormon, might seek a glass of water. Thus the specific goal of the first is to seek and drink a bottle of beer, while the specific goal of the second is to seek and drink a glass of water. The general goal of both would be to quench thirst and their motive, thirst.

Given either of these acts, a knowledge of the key environmental factors, and an awareness of the common biological need, one could easily identify the drinker's motives. If either actor were queried as to why he purchased a beer or drank a glass of water, he would probably respond with an honest answer—that he was thirsty or that he likes beer or water. If asked why he

[14] Howard, *op. cit.,* p. 138.
[15] David Krech and Richard S. Crutchfield, *Elements of Psychology* (New York: Knopf, 1962), p. 272.

rejected various alternatives—a glass of milk, a bottle of soft drink, and so on—he would probably provide an equally objective answer, such as that he does not like milk or prefers plain water to soft drinks.

However, if the beer drinker insisted on a specific brand of beer, his motives might be more obscure. This is especially so if another need, such as status or affiliation (group acceptance), is coupled with thirst. If the beer drinker values his association with or aspires to membership in a group that has prescribed a particular brand as the preferred goal in satisfying thirst, he may be motivated to seek and consume brand X in order to satisfy two needs, thirst and affiliation. The identification of this second need, hence the complete explanation of his motives, may be very difficult. The actor may be unwilling to divulge secondary needs; in fact, he may not fully recognize them himself. Yet a secondary motive may be the most critical determinant of consumer behavior in discriminating between competing brands.

Cognition is the process by which we make sense of the things we perceive. It is the intellectual process by which we explain and order our observations and experiences. Perception and structure are the two main elements of cognition. *Perception* is a person's conception of the objects in his environment; it may or may not conform with reality. An individual's perception is determined by his sensitivity to stimuli and his bias. Bias in turn is determined by his experience and his values, which are largely acquired through his environment. Bias is analogous to a filter; it admits certain information and stops other data. A person is bombarded by countless stimuli—far more than he can assimilate. The degree to which a stimulus, such as a radio commercial or a billboard ad, will "register" with an individual is a function of its relative intensity, the respondent's sensitivity, and his bias. Thus the perception of an object—say the firm's product—will be determined not only by the physical properties of the objective, but also by the nature of the stimuli, the individual's sensitivity, and his bias.

Structure pertains to the organization of one's perceptions. Cognitive structure is the individual's system of memories, values, fantasies, and insights. It is the frame of reference that allows him to make sense out of his perceptions. Cognitive structure is continuously changing—a process called "cognitive reorganization"—through learning, forgetting, problem-solving, and the input of new information.

Social psychologists view environment—especially the social environment—as the chief determinant of cognitive structure, as well as of perceptual bias. In applying social psychology to the analysis of consumer behavior, the marketer looks to the environment for insights into the thought process that is behind consumer acceptance or rejection of his product. It is the individual who ultimately makes the purchase decision, and the cognitive process is the method by which the product is initially chosen. If the purchase is made repeatedly, learning may reinforce the buyer's perception and understanding of the product to the point where the purchase act becomes a matter of habit, with cognition being replaced by a conditioned response.

Perceptual bias and cognitive structure can be generalized to a large class, or segment, of buyers by making a statistical analysis, based on samples, of the beliefs and attitudes of consumers. These attitudes—the orientation toward and readiness to respond to given objectives—and beliefs represent a particular cognitive structure that, if understood, can perhaps be manipulated or appealed to by the marketer.

Social psychology also concerns itself with the influence of groups on the behavior of individuals. Human beings, who are by nature social creatures, tend to conform to roles prescribed by the groups to which they belong. *Roles* are expected behavior patterns; they may be loosely or rigorously defined, depending on the nature of the group. For example, the role of a student is rather casually prescribed compared to the role of a naval officer, which is very precisely defined, both formally and informally. The *reference group* is the group that the individual looks to for the approved behavioral pattern assigned to his role. The student looks to his college, especially his fellow students, and the naval officer looks to the military establishment. *Status* is the position, or rank, the individual holds in the group. It can be dichotomous, because the status assigned by the informal organization may be different from that assigned by the formal organization. The individual is most often a member of numerous groups and plays a different role in each one. A doctor may be a chief surgeon, a head of a household, and a member of the school board. Each role carries a different expected behavior pattern and reference group.

These sociological phenomena are important to the marketer, especially in the introduction of new brands and products and the opening of new markets. First, the firm's product or service will not be widely accepted if it conflicts with the behavioral pattern prescribed by the reference group. This is especially true of fashion items, certain foods, and alcoholic beverages. Second, the members of the reference group are an important medium of communication in the diffusion of knowledge. Role-players are generally receptive to information provided by their reference group, and they usually rely on the value judgments of its members. The significance of reference groups in the purchase of certain consumer goods is suggested in Table 8.1.

The reader should notice the distinction made between brands and products. In some cases, the reference group is significant in both the choice of a product and the selection of a brand. For example, it may substantially influence an individual's decision to smoke or not to smoke cigarettes, as well as influencing the brand he will select if he chooses to buy the product. Some products, such as clothing and radios, are widely accepted, and the reference group has little influence on whether the good will be purchased but strongly influences the choice of brands. The implications for

Table 8.1   Reference-group significance in buying selected items

	WEAK INFLUENCE	Product	STRONG INFLUENCE
Brand — STRONG INFLUENCE	Clothing Furniture Magazines Refrigerator (type) Toilet soap		Cars* Cigarettes* Beer (premium vs. regular)* Drugs*
Brand — WEAK INFLUENCE	Soap Canned peaches Laundry soap Refrigerators (brand) Radios		Air conditioners* Instant coffee* TV (black and white)

* The classification of all products marked with an asterisk is based on actual experimental data.

SOURCE: Adapted from Rensis Likert and Samuel P. Hayes, Jr., eds., *Some Applications of Behavioural Research* (Paris: UNESCO, 1961), p. 218.

marketing are obvious: The marketer's evaluation or accommodation of the reference group may be important, depending largely on the type of product sold. For instance, reference groups are much more important in the marketing of Salem cigarettes than the selling of Del Monte peaches. This is evident from the different degrees of promotional activities supporting the two items.

Social psychology is most frequently applied in the marketing of goods and services intended for the mass market. One has only to glance through the advertisements for soap, automobiles, clothes, and beverages to see the efforts to link particular products with prevalent tastes and values. The objective is to accommodate perceptual bias and to conform to the cognitive structure that has been shaped by the social environment. This approach to product variation and promotion uses to advantage the fact that a substantial portion of human behavior can only be characterized as rigid conformity to the popular dictates of society.

CHAPTER 9

Psychological and Sociological Factors in Purchasing Phenomena

The identification and measurement of the predominant psychological and sociological characteristics of a firm's market population can be extremely useful. Knowledge about these factors allows the marketing manager to prepare his strategy to exploit, modify, or accommodate the underlying causes of the acceptance or rejection of his product. It may also allow him to divide his market into "segments," which often makes the marketing function more efficient. If the market population can be segmented into groups having unique sets of psychological and sociological properties, the product and promotional resources directed toward those segments can be tailored to their particular characteristics. Depending on the economies of scale involved, this may make the various marketing instruments much more productive even when the total marketing budget is held constant.

SOCIOLOGICAL CLASSIFICATION OF CONSUMERS

Personality is "the entire psychological structure of the individual."[1] The personality classifications of psychology and sociology vary considerably. Whereas psychologists classify people by their individual psychological traits, sociologists categorize them on the basis of their group membership, which in a materialistic society is heavily influenced by income. Members of different income classifications, called "social strata," are perceived as having many characteristics in common.[2] These commonly held traits make for

[1] David Krech and Richard S. Crutchfield, *Elements of Psychology* (New York: Knopf, 1962), p. 228.
[2] For a detailed development of this hypothesis, see Ernest R. Hilgard and Richard C. Atkinson, *Introduction to Psychology,* 4th ed. (New York: Harcourt, Brace & World, 1967), and Pierre Martineau, "Social Classes and Spending Behavior," *Journal of Marketing,* Vol. 23, No. 2 (April 1959), pp. 121–30.

homogeneity within the classifications and establish the uniqueness, hence distinguishability, of each classification. A typical income-based classification of consumer-goods buyers is shown in Table 9.1.

Behavior based on class membership has important implications for the manipulation of all the marketing variables, especially promotion. Individuals tend to live in the same neighborhoods with, work with, and socialize with the people in their own social strata. Thus their area of awareness, their attitudes, their beliefs, and their psychogenic needs are largely defined by their social class. This results in a high degree of uniformity within a given class. For example, various upper-class housewives will prefer different stores, but few will be found shopping in the same stores as lower-class housewives. An upper-middle-class man may be responsive to status symbols that an upper-lower-class man would perceive as sheer snobbery. An advertisement in the *Wall Street Journal* might be read by a substantial number of upper-middle-class men but never even be seen by males in either the upper-lower or lower-lower class. Bowling is a popular sport among the lower classes, but it is seldom played by members of the upper-middle class, where golf is widely accepted.

PSYCHOGENIC NEEDS

Along with human biological needs, psychogenic, or learned, needs make up the personality of the consumer. There are probably as many different lists of psychogenic needs as there are psychology texts. Most of the lists are similar, although the terms used may differ.

Hilgard and Atkinson offer a list of psychogenic needs, given in Table 9.2, that is an adaptation of the classical work done by H. A. Murray in that area. It suggests 28 desires that may make consumers responsive to an appeal to buy a particular product. Most are rational needs that conform closely to the Gestalt model. Virtually no attention is paid to the irrational drives associated with Freudian psychology, although the inclusion of "exhibition" and "abasement" does have Freudian implications. Drives taught or shaped by environment are also included, thus giving recognition to social psychology.

A review of psychogenic needs is appropriate to the marketer examining his product variables and designing a promotional strategy. Unless an industry is one of pure competition—where all brands are perceived as perfect substitutes for one another—the firm will attempt to distinguish its brand as the superior instrument for satisfying the needs associated with its product class. These needs are usually both basic (biological) and psychogenic (learned), and seldom only one or the other.

Table 9.1 Sociological classification of consumers*

Classification	Percentage of Population†	General Properties	Examples	Marketing Significance
Upper class	1%	Prominent old families and socially important "new rich." Are traditional leaders in American society, business, and government. Hold most of nation's economic power. Are well educated with high degree of awareness and sophistication.	Rockefellers, Kennedys, Fords, executives of major firms, important government figures, and most celebrities.	Constitute "quality goods" market. Are generally unaffected by tastes and styles of others. Have conservative tastes and stress quality and service over price.
Upper-middle class	7%	Successful business and professional men. Well educated with broad horizons. Are mobile, self-confident, and willing to take risks.	Doctors, successful attorneys, managers of medium-sized firms, and successful entrepreneurs.	Tend to set styles, especially in fashion. Tend toward conspicuous consumption. Are open to innovation.
Lower-middle class	28%	White-collar workers. Are most conforming, church-going, and morally rigorous segment of society. Have some college education. Urban-oriented. Stress striving.	Technicians, tradesmen, shop owners, and junior managers.	Top half of mass "middle market." Read popular slick magazines.
. . . . Pronounced demarcation in goals, interests, and norms.				
Upper-lower class	44%	Blue-collar workers. Family-oriented. Have limited horizons and nondiscriminating tastes. Limited sense of choice.	Skilled factory workers, service workers, and local politicians.	Bottom half of mass "middle market." Read popular pulp literature and watch considerable television. Prefer to shop in discount houses and cheaper stores. Often buy on credit.
Lower-lower class	20%	Minority groups and those in unrespectable occupations. Give little thought to the future.	Immigrants, unskilled laborers, and welfare recipients.	Poor market, except for government-sponsored services and basic necessities.

* Based on the basic list of W. Lloyd Warner and Paul Lunt, *The Social Life of a Modern Community* (New Haven, Conn.: Yale University Press, 1950), as adapted by W. Lloyd Warner in his studies for the *Chicago Tribune*. See Rollie Tillman and C. A. Kirkpatrick, *Promotion* (Homewood, Ill.: Irwin, 1968), p. 67, and E. Jerome McCarthy, *Basic Marketing*, 3rd ed. (Homewood, Ill.: Irwin, 1968), for details.

† All values are approximate.

Table 9.2 Psychogenic needs

A. *Needs associated chiefly with inanimate objects*
 1. Acquisition: the need to gain possessions and property.
 2. Conservation: the need to collect, repair, clean, and preserve things.
 3. Orderliness: the need to arrange, organize, put away objects, to be tidy and clean; to be precise.
 4. Retention: the need to retain possession of things; to hoard; to be frugal, economical, and miserly.
 5. Construction: the need to organize and build.

B. *Needs expressing ambition, will power, desire for accomplishment, and prestige*
 6. Superiority: the need to excel, a composite of achievement and recognition.
 7. Achievement: the need to overcome obstacles, to exercise power, to strive to do something difficult as well and as quickly as possible.
 8. Recognition: the need to excite praise and commendation; to demand respect.
 9. Exhibition: the need for self-dramatization; to excite, amuse, stir, shock, thrill others.
 10. Inviolacy: the need to remain inviolate, to prevent a depreciation of self-respect, to preserve one's "good name."
 11. Avoidance of inferiority: the need to avoid failure, shame, humiliation, ridicule.
 12. Defensiveness: the need to defend oneself against blame or belittlement; to justify one's actions.
 13. Counteraction: the need to overcome defeat by restriving and retaliating.

C. *Needs having to do with human power exerted, resisted, or yielded to*
 14. Dominance: the need to influence or control others.
 15. Deference: the need to admire and willingly follow a superior; to serve gladly.
 16. Similance: the need to imitate or emulate others; to agree and believe.
 17. Autonomy: the need to resist influence, to strive for independence.
 18. Contrariness: the need to act differently from others, to be unique, to take the opposite side.

D. *Needs having to do with injuring others or oneself*
 19. Aggression: the need to assault or injure another; to belittle, harm, or maliciously ridicule a person.
 20. Abasement: the need to comply and accept punishment; self-depreciation.
 21. Avoidance of blame: the need to avoid blame, ostracism, or punishment by inhibiting unconventional impulses; to be well behaved and obey the law.

E. *Needs having to do with affection between people*
 22. Affiliation: the need to form friendships and associations.
 23. Rejection: the need to be discriminating, to snub, ignore, or exclude another.
 24. Nurturance: the need to nourish, aid, or protect another.
 25. Succorance: the need to seek aid, protection, or sympathy; to be dependent.

(Table 9.2   Continued)

F. *Additional socially relevant needs*

    26. Play: the need to relax, amuse oneself, seek diversion and entertainment.

    27. Cognizance: the need to explore, to ask questions, to satisfy curiosity.

    28. Exposition: the need to point and demonstrate; to give information, explain, interpret, lecture.

SOURCE: From *Introduction to Psychology*, 4th ed., by Ernest R. Hilgard and Richard C. Atkinson, copyright 1953, © 1957, 1962, 1967, by Harcourt, Brace & World, Inc., and reprinted with their permission.

PSYCHOLOGICAL CLASSIFICATION OF GOODS

Categorizing products and services according to their psychological characteristics will aid the marketer in his manipulation of the product and promotional variables, since he will know what psychogenic needs, if any, he can appeal to in order to increase sales. In addition, it may aid him in matching his product to a particular market segment.

In classifying a product, one must beware of the hazards inherent in stereotyping. Too general a stereotype is useless, yet a narrowly defined and very specific stereotype will have so many exceptions that it will be virtually useless for decision-making. Also, as soon as psychological or sociological labels are attached to an object, a vast array of values and characteristics are implied, many of which have little to do with the good in reality. Another problem is that a given product can share several psychological and sociological labels, depending on the cognition of the viewer and the circumstances of the purchase. For example, an expensive automobile can be both functional and prestigious, thus providing the purchaser with both transportation and ego gratification. The amount of ego gratification derived from a good will depend on the economic and social position of the buyer. Both clinical and social psychology are involved in the psychological classification of goods.

Goods are classified according to their psychological characteristics as (1) functional, (2) hedonic or (3) ego-involved. Ego-involved products are further subdivided into prestige, status, anxiety, and maturity goods.

Functional products are those that are purchased primarily because of their physical properties or performance characteristics. They are the antithesis of those products acquired primarily because of their ability to satisfy psychogenic needs. Tools, raw materials, prescription drugs, and electricity are examples.

In marketing functional products, the strategy most often used is simply to stress their physical attributes and performance characteristics. However, if these properties are quite similar to those of competing brands—as is the case with cutting tools, steel, penicillin, and electric power—alternative strategies are worth investigating. One alternative is to stress the services, such as delivery and availability, associated with the brand. Another is to stress product consistency (quality control), installation, or warranties. (Some marketers contend that these are product characteristics.) Or the firm might promote a complementary product, the sale of which directly influences the consumption of the primary product. The latter strategy often allows the marketer to appeal to psychogenic needs that are not directly served by the functional product. For example, a company that produces only electricity can promote the use of electrical appliances, many of which serve to satisfy psychological or social needs. The attempt, sponsored by a certain gas company, to identify natural-gas-powered products with fashionably dressed, sophisticated women in billboard, magazine, and television advertisements is another example of this strategy.

Hedonic products are those that appeal to aesthetic values, particularly the buyer's desire for pleasure. Pleasure can be provided by aesthetic properties incorporated into the product (such as the color of an automobile or the texture of a suit), by the performance characteristics of the good (such as comfort or sound), and by the image or symbolic character imputed to the item through promotion or the environment in which it is consumed. For example, lush surroundings make a dinner more satisfying than an equivalent meal served in an equally comfortable but less plush environment.[3] Examples of hedonic goods are perfumes, paintings, decorative items, and motion pictures or theatricals.

The importance of hedonic goods to a buyer varies directly with his income; thus they are more salable in an affluent society than in a poor one. This is significant to marketers of hedonic goods who are considering opening new markets, especially abroad. The marketer of hedonic products or services is also well advised to identify the predominant preferences for taste, smell, form, color, and sound as they apply to his product class before attempting to manipulate product variables. Such information often lends itself to objective measurement; color preferences, for example, can be determined by questionnaires or, where the consumer has an adequate range of choices, by observing buyer behavior.

Another relevant variable is packaging. Although the package is functional—providing a means of protection and making the good easier to carry—it can also impart an aesthetic property to the product. The signifi-

[3] For a more detailed discussion of this phenomenon, see R. M. Cunningham, "Brand Loyalty: What, Where, How Much?" *Harvard Business Review,* Vol. 34, No. 1 (January–February 1956), pp. 116–28, and M. E. John, "Classification of Values That Serve As Motivations to Consumer Purchases," *Journal of Farm Economics,* Vol. 38, No. 4 (November 1956), pp. 956–63.

cance of this phenomenon is demonstrated by the cosmetics and recording industries, where the direct-labor and material cost of the containers usually exceeds that of the products themselves.

Ego-involved products are those goods whose symbolic properties are as significant, or more significant than, their functional and hedonic qualities. These symbolic properties serve to satisfy the psychogenic needs of ambition, will power, desire for accomplishment, prestige, and affection.

Ego-gratification strategies place great emphasis on brands. A Cadillac, for example, symbolizes wealth and success far more than does merely owning a "car." The importance of the brand, or label, is a function of the buyer's perception of the prestige of the manufacturer or retailer and the degree to which this image is transferred to the product itself. It can be very significant. Certainly a dress bearing a Dior or a Neiman-Marcus label is more ego-gratifying to many people than a comparable garment—perhaps an exact copy—offered by Ohrbach's or Sears.

The evaluation and control of the effect of the company image can be a much more elusive affair than the evaluation and control of a product image. What ego-satisfying properties are imparted by the producer and the retailer is largely conjectural, although clinical psychology does offer methods of attitude measurement utilizing the consumer-survey and projective-interviewing techniques discussed in Chapter 25. However, the marketer can usually intuitively select retail outlets and prepare institutional advertising commensurate with the desired character of the product and his perception of the symbolic priorities of the potential market.

As was mentioned earlier, ego-involved products may be subdivided into four categories:[4] (1) prestige products, (2) maturity products, (3) status products, and (4) anxiety products. *Prestige products* are those whose possession imparts to their owners certain desirable attributes. They serve the possessor by reinforcing his self-image, his idealized view of himself. For example, an expensive sports car symbolizes to many people virility, power, and wealth—an image that is presumably transferred to its owner, who may begin to envision himself as a dashing, seductive, and influential man about town. Neither the symbolic implications of the product nor the owner's self-image need have anything to do with reality.

A prestige good may, of course, be evidence of an actual characteristic of its owner, rather than an imaginary quality. Conspicuous consumption of expensive nonessentials—ownership of a luxurious home, rare jewelry, an expensive airplane, or a yacht—is evidence of real wealth. Similarly, the possession of important titles and honors is evidence of—it does not just suggest—prestigious rank and accomplishment.

Marketers frequently try to give a product symbolic properties that will

[4] In the exposition of this material the authors are indebted to T. W. Wolf of Claremont Men's College.

aid the buyer in gratifying his desire for prestige. A popular technique is the association, real or implied, of his product with people who are perceived as models of the buyer's self-image. Successful people, especially those in the more glamorous fields, are paid to identify themselves with branded goods. A baseball star is hired to shave publicly with Gillette razor blades, an athlete to eat Wheaties breakfast cereal, and an actress to use Dove soap.

Class membership is an important psycho-sociological variable and one of the most influential factors in the formation of attitude. *Status products* are goods that indicate class membership, real or imagined. In this respect, they are different from prestige goods, which symbolize a unique characteristic of their owner, frequently dominance or independence. The urge to identify with a particular class (affiliation need) can dictate a narrow pattern of behavior that includes, of course, purchase activity. For example, dress is the most conspicuous badge of class membership with certain groups. Accepted dress for teenagers or businessmen is often so rigid that approved attire borders on being a uniform. Clothing, automobile accessories, haircuts, jewelry, entertainment, recreational activities, and club memberships can all be status symbols, selected in whole or in part to identify the buyer with a group that he is a member of or a class that he admires or aspires to join.

Status is exploited in the marketplace by identifying goods and services with popular classes. Even functional products such as shoes, foods, and men's shirts can have status implications. If the status symbol is not already prescribed by the group, it may come to be identified with the group through promotion. Witness the effort to identify various brands of men's clothing with the executive class or the use of dietetic foods with chic, attractive, and obviously upper-class women.

Defensiveness and avoidance of inferiority and blame underlie the demand for *anxiety products,* which satisfy these needs by minimizing various threats to the buyer's ego. These threats are often social—the loss of one's reputation, the alienation of one's friends, or failure in romance. Many products designed to increase a person's physical attractiveness—deodorants, soaps, dancing lessons, toothpastes, toupees, and health foods—fall into the category of anxiety products.

Anxiety products may also serve as rational instruments for gratifying needs arising from the biological drives. For example, fear, which is an outgrowth of the pain-avoidance drive, may be partially relieved by certain goods and services. Blow-out-proof tires, insurance, and patent medicines are anxiety products as well as functional products. In such cases, it is often difficult to judge which of the two aspects should be stressed in designing promotional strategies. Generally, the marketer is well advised to experiment with both approaches, taking measurements of consumer response in order to determine which one is more effective. Often the two approaches will reinforce each other and should be used simultaneously.

In selling a product that is both functional and anxiety-relieving, a common tactic is to stress the dire consequences of failure to use the product. This is coupled with an exposition of the functional properties that supposedly provide the necessary protection. The application of this technique is so common in magazine advertisements and television commercials that it is hardly necessary to elaborate further.

Maturity products are defined as those goods and services that young people are restricted from purchasing. The restrictions may be legal or simply a matter of custom. Liquor, tobacco, coffee, makeup, and some forms of entertainment are examples of this product class. Maturity products have several implications for marketing. Rather obviously, underage consumers must be excluded from the count of prospective buyers in defining or measuring the market for such goods. However, it may be possible, and profitable, for the firm to offer a substitute product to those who are denied the original item by law or custom. The consumption of such a product symbolizes maturity, which can be very important to a young person. An acceptable symbolic substitute can give the firm an opportunity to enlarge its original market.

The symbolic nature of the maturity product suggests its ready sale to consumers who have recently reached the critical age and are anxious to display their new status. Newcomers are encouraged to adopt a product, usually branded, previously denied them because of their age. This can be done in a number of ways. Automobiles, for example, are provided to teenagers through driver-training programs, cigarettes are given free to college students, and cosmetic samples are provided to high-school girls.

MEASUREMENT AND APPLICATION

In view of the present emphasis on the consumer's psychogenic needs and the classification of goods in terms of their psychological qualities, it has rapidly become essential for the marketer to be able to apply psychological and sociological principles in marketing programs. Motivation research, which deals expressly with the application of the behavioral sciences to marketing, is explored in some detail in Chapter 24. For now, a general description of the field is sufficient.

The objective of motivation research, or "MR," is to explain why consumers behave as they do, usually with respect to a particular product or brand. This involves the description of the consumer in psychological terms and the analysis of prevalent beliefs and attitudes concerning a specific object. By estimating the intensities of these beliefs and attitudes and their dispersion in a market population, the marketer can exploit, accommodate, or attempt to modify them in accordance with the objectives of the firm.

For example, if the prevalent belief is that prunes are essentially a laxative food eaten only by old people, the producers must either assign their promotional resources to the task of identifying their product with younger consumers or be content with a market composed only of senior citizens.

Attitude evaluation is relevant not only to the product itself but to the words and objects associated with the product. This fact is very important in the selection of brand names and the preparation of advertising copy. The connotations of a word can be critical to the perception of the firm's product. If the sale of the product is largely dependent on its gratification of psychogenic needs, it must invoke favorable beliefs and conform to or change prevailing attitudes. How successful the firm is in doing this depends largely on the psychological properties of the words and objects associated with the product.

No one individual can generalize his own psychological traits to the market population with any surety. In fact, if the clinical psychologists, especially the Freudians, are correct, a person cannot even identify his own psychogenic needs. If the marketer is to identify the psychological characteristics of his present or prospective customers, he has little choice but to defer to the analyst skilled in motivation research.

Assuming that the pertinent psychological traits of a market population can be measured with an acceptable degree of accuracy and at a reasonable cost, one question remains to be answered: Is this information really relevant to the firm's marketing decisions? There is no concise and general answer. A quest for behavioral data should be undertaken only after an appraisal of the data's application to a specific product or marketing variable.

First, the structure of the industry must be considered. If pure competition prevails, then the firm cannot influence the demand for its product, and the psychological determinants of demand are irrelevant. A wheat farmer, for example, must sell his undifferentiated product at the going price and cannot influence the behavior of the buyer. Moreover, since wheat is a functional product, the psychological properties of the buyer would have little relation to wheat sales in any event.

Where the firm's product reaches the consumer in an unaltered form, or when the good is ego-gratifying or hedonic, then psychological variables become significant. However, again the structure of the industry is important, since the firm must be either a differentiated oligopolist or a monopolist if it is to exploit these properties. If the industry is competitive, then the firm can unite with other producers and differentiate their common product from similar goods. This is frequently done in the food industry, through cooperative (jointly owned) packing houses and distributors and through trade associations. The promotion of California oranges by Sunkist and the advertising of avocados by Calavo (both growers' cooperatives) are illustrative.

Next, the good itself must be examined to see if it has—or can be given

—qualities that will satisfy psychogenic needs. Biological needs are satisfied by the functional properties of the product, which are usually obvious. Often, a survey of consumer attitudes is needed to identify the psychological characteristics of the good as they are perceived in the marketplace. A product's "image" can be described in terms of the associations the product has for most consumers. Associations can be expressed in terms of emotional responses evoked by the product or stereotypic personality classifications (which may be either social or psychological) of what consumers consider to be the typical buyers of the product.

DISCRIMINATION VERSUS GENERALIZATION

Within the marketing context, *discrimination* is the acceptance or rejection of goods based on their properties. These properties may include such product characteristics as price, performance, appearance, size, durability, reliability, warranty, operating cost, symbolic connotations, and brand reputation. The relative significance of various product characteristics is suggested by the findings of Katona and Mueller, given in Table 9.3, concerning selection of consumer durables.

These findings may at first appear startling. For example, it is difficult to believe that 39 percent of consumers are disinterested in a product's features and only 6 percent are concerned with price. On the contrary, most buyers are quite interested in both product features and price. What the figures in Table 9.3 do suggest is that many classes of consumer durables are so homogeneous in regard to various product features, especially price, that these features are not consciously used by the consumer in his selection process. For instance, price is hardly a basis for discriminating between a Ford, a Chevrolet, and a Plymouth, since they have virtually identical prices. However, where marked differences in product features do exist—either in reality or in the mind of the buyer—they clearly play a role in the consumer's decision.

Generalization, or the willingness to substitute one product for another, is the converse of discrimination. It is especially important in the choice of brands within a product class. The willingness of the buyer to generalize is a function of the similarity between brands as perceived by the consumer, the availability of preferred brands, and the drive level of the buyer. The prevalence of generalization is verified by the figures in Table 9.3, which show that product features were unimportant in 39 percent of the buying decisions.

For example, if a customer perceives cigarette B as very similar to his preferred brand, A, and finds that his usual store is out of A but has B in stock, he will probably purchase a pack of brand B. However, if the buyer believes that brand A is unique—that is, has important properties not found

Table 9.3 Product characteristics relevant in the selection of consumer durables

Product Feature	Percentage of Buyers Influenced*
No Specific Features	39
Brand	21
Mechanical Features	21
Size and Capacity	19
Appearance	13
Performance	9
Price	6
Other Characteristics	3
Not Ascertained	3
Durability, Reliability, Warranty, and Service	2
Operating Costs	1

* Column does not sum to 100%, as many buyers reported examining multiple product features.

SOURCE: Adapted from George Katona and Eva Mueller, "A Study of Purchase Decisions." Reprinted by permission of the publisher, New York University Press, from *The Dynamics of Consumer Reactions*, edited by Lincoln H. Clark, © 1954 by New York University.

in alternative choices—and thus that other brands of cigarettes are poor substitutes, he is less likely to purchase an alternative brand. Should he find that other local stores also have depleted their stock of A, he may decide to forgo smoking altogether until brand A is again available. (To use a slogan employed successfully in the promotion of Tareyton cigarettes, he would "rather fight than switch.") He is simply unwilling to generalize his desire for brand A to the product class "cigarettes." However, if brand A remains unavailable, his abstention is likely to elevate his drive level to the point where he will eventually substitute another brand for his favorite cigarette.

This phenomenon can be displayed graphically, as in Figure 9.1. The gradient of generalization is the scale of perceived similarity between products. It is represented by the horizontal axis, and the probability of a good being purchased (the behavioral act) by the vertical axis. The diagonal lines represent various drive levels, which can be estimated for purposes of illustration or determined experimentally. Often, absolute values are employed. For example, the drive levels for thirst—hence the desire, or motivation, for a class of beverage—might be expressed in hours of deprivation. The drive levels for pain avoidance, as it applies to the desire for air conditioning, might be calibrated in degrees Fahrenheit. Thus temperature would serve as a proxy measurement of the pain-avoidance drive.

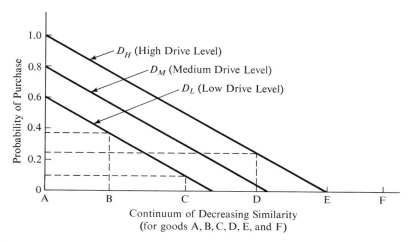

FIGURE 9.1
Gradient of generalization

SOURCE: Adapted from John A. Howard, *Marketing Management, Analysis and Planning,* rev. ed. (Homewood, Ill.: Irwin, 1963), p. 83.

Given a low drive level, D_L, the probability is .6 that the consumer will be motivated to act and purchase brand A, his favorite. If brand A is not available, the probability that B—which is similar to A in the eyes of the buyer—will be substituted is .38. If neither A nor B is available, there is a slight chance (.1) that the less similar brand C will be accepted. Given the lack of options A, B, and C, the buyer would abstain, at least until his drive level reached D_M or D_H, where goods D and E would have a chance of being selected.

This confrontation between consumer preference and product availability is typical of the market for convenience goods such as gasoline, beer, and candy. It is also detectable in the field of consumer durables. When one make of car is unavailable, perhaps because of a strike by workers at a particular plant, buyers may substitute other makes rather than delay their purchase. As the unavailability continues, the growing inconvenience of doing without a car, and hence the increasing drive to obtain one, makes substitutes more acceptable to buyers who would have preferred the first make.

The discrimination-generalization phenomenon can create a dilemma for the marketer, especially in regard to his manipulation of product and promotional variables. Should he differentiate the product so consumers will perceive it as something special, for which there is no suitable substitute? This strategy would tend to isolate the product from competing brands, reinforce brand loyalty, and allow greater flexibility in pricing. Or should he generalize the product so consumers will perceive it as an excellent substitute for competing brands? Presumably, the latter approach would make the good a greater threat to competing lines, allow more rapid market penetration by making easier the proselytizing of other firms' customers, and broaden the potential market. It would also make sales more sensitive to price, however.

Computing the firm's market share may serve to resolve this dilemma. If the firm already controls a substantial share of the market—say, over 50 percent—then product differentiation will serve to retain a large market share by convincing customers that there is no satisfactory substitute for its goods. This reinforcement of brand loyalty will discourage buyers from switching to competing products. It will also serve to discourage buyers of other brands from adopting the firm's brand, because of the lack of clear substitutability. However, the loss of its present customers is far more important to the dominant company than is the acquisition of new buyers, particularly if the threat of government intervention exists due to monopolistic trends in the industry.

If the firm's market share is low—say, under 20 percent—generalization is suggested. A company with a small market share is usually interested in expanding sales, and this means that buyers must be persuaded to switch from competing brands to the one offered by the firm. Consumers are more likely to switch brands if they consider the firm's brand as a satisfactory substitute for the one they are presently using or contemplating buying. Particularly, if the company is prepared to engage in price competition, product generalization is appropriate. If the consumer perceives the firm's brand as a good substitute for other brands, a lower price will give him an incentive to switch brands.

An alternative strategy is to stress the substitutability of the product while simultaneously emphasizing unique features that make it superior to other brands. For example, several aircraft manufacturers advertise certain models as having performance characteristics comparable to a model offered by another—and in this case more prestigious—brand, but as having the added attractions of a cheaper price and lower operating costs. Thus their products are offered as substitutes (generalization) having unique features (discrimination). This combination strategy is common in the design and sale of patent medicines. Witness the advertising for various aspirin compounds, in which not only the pain-relieving quality of the basic ingredient is stressed, but also the effect of various additives unique to a particular brand. Patents and trademarks are common legal devices for differentiating products.

The discrimination-generalization phenomenon also has implications for the other marketing variables. If the firm's strategy is to exploit the discrimination principle, a selective distribution policy is sometimes appropriate. Items that are sufficiently unique in the minds of consumers to be clearly distinguishable from competing products may be sold only through an exclusive group of stores. A system of franchises or exclusive retail territories is often useful in controlling distribution and limiting retail selling to a certain class of stores. Higher prices and markups are also common with such goods and distribution policies. Vertical price-fixing (the manufacturer sets the retail price), in states where "fair trade" laws make such a practice enforceable, serves to reinforce the price and markup policies of the manufacturer at the retail level.

Conversely, if the company's strategy is to exploit the generalization principle, a much different marketing mix is called for. A product that is represented as a substitute for competing brands should be widely distributed, especially in those markets largely controlled by competitors. When the emphasis is on brand similarity, a higher price is inappropriate, since a rational buyer would not pay a premium for a brand perceived as nearly identical to alternative products.

In dealing with the discrimination-generalization phenomenon, the marketer must remember that the willingness of a buyer to discriminate or generalize is entirely a function of his perception of a product. What the buyer perceives is in turn dependent on many factors, to be explored shortly in the consumer model in Chapter 10. Only some of these factors are product characteristics; the marketer must recognize the existence of various psychological phenomena when interpreting or predicting consumer behavior. One of the most important of these phenomena is cognitive dissonance.

COGNITIVE DISSONANCE

Cognitive dissonance is perceived incongruity between an individual's attitude and his behavior.[5] People generally attempt to reduce discrepancies between their attitudes and their behavior in one of two ways: They try either to modify their attitudes or to change their behavior. For example, a heavy smoker who fears damage to his health from continued smoking may try to stop (thereby changing his behavior) or he may convince himself that the medical findings pertaining to the relationship between health and smoking are inconclusive or untrue (thus changing his attitude). If he fails to make one of these adjustments, and the discrepancy between his attitude and his behavior becomes too great, he may, in extreme cases, suffer an emotional breakdown.

An individual's response to cognitive dissonance is part of the system of self-defense by which we all rationalize our failures and prejudices. Self-

[5] Krech and Crutchfield, *op. cit.,* p. 674.

justification is a need inherent in everyone. When a person's behavior, or the consequences of that behavior, fails to conform to his attitudes, then the attitude must be adjusted or the behavior changed. Either course may be unpleasant, difficult, or impossible. However, if the individual is to relieve his guilt feeling or anxiety—which is the normal inclination—he must somehow close the gap between attitude and behavior.

Stanley Kaish explains the cognitive dissonance theory as it applies to purchasing behavior:

According to the theory, decision making is an anxiety-inducing activity. A person forced to commit himself to one of several alternatives is faced with mental conflict that comes with having to reject all other possibilities. Both desirable and undesirable quantities are usually inherent in each alternative. Supposedly, the consumer's evaluation of the relative positive and negative strengths of these qualities in any one product precedes his decision to select one item and reject all alternatives.

Psychologists speak of "postdecision cognitive dissonance" referring to a condition approximating regret. This condition occurs when there is awareness of one or more reasons why a decision should not have been made. Anticipation of postdecision cognitive dissonance produces behavior designed to avoid or minimize it.[6]

Since a consumer can seldom customize a product (most items being designed and manufactured by the seller), he is frequently confronted with the problem of selecting among alternatives that each have one or more undesirable features. At worst, this may produce sufficient anxiety to make him reject all the available brands and purchase nothing. At best, it will make him uneasy. If he is aware of the possibility of post-decision cognitive dissonance—that is, if he suspects that he may regret his choice—the potential customer will often seek reinforcement of his decision. He may seek social approval from his peer group prior to committing himself to a purchase, or he may seek more information from salesmen, literature, friends, or experts. He may delay making a purchase or decline it entirely. Invariably, he will expend more effort in shopping for the product if cognitive dissonance exists.

If the seller perceives this problem, he has several alternatives. First, he can offer greater variety in his product line. Second, he can provide a large variety of customer options, a practice that has become prevalent in the automobile industry. Third, he can offer trials, demonstrations, warranties, or refunds. Or, finally, he can provide testimonials and extensive product information.

[6] Stanley Kaish, "Cognitive Dissonance and the Classification of Consumer Goods," *Journal of Marketing*, Vol. 31, No. 4 (October 1967), pp. 28–31.

Cognitive dissonance is a function of two variables, attitude and behavior. However, once a purchase is made, only the first variable can be manipulated by the buyer in his effort to reduce the buyer's anxiety and frustration. Typically, a buyer who has doubts about his purchase will read advertisements for the brand he selected, tending to ignore ads for competing goods. He may become defensive about his choice and look for reasons to criticize those who have selected alternatives that he rejected. Or he may generalize faults found in his own choice to all brands in that product class.

The need to rationalize behavior declines with time. The longer they own the products, the more objective buyers generally become in their evaluation of their purchases. A car buyer who was very defensive about his choice during the first six months may become an outspoken critic of the brand two years later. If his dissatisfaction continues, it may heavily influence his behavior when the time comes to replace the item. This fact has important implications in markets where goods are differentiated, word-of-mouth advertising is common, and post-decision evaluation is easy. It is especially important when the goods are periodically replaced and the seller depends on repeat purchases to sustain his sales. The positive effect of a considerable promotional outlay can be destroyed if post-decision dissonance becomes common and unresolved.

Preventive measures are the best way for a firm to deal with the problem. By designing products that conform to the tastes of the customers and maintaining a good quality-control program that prevents faulty merchandise from reaching the market, a firm can keep post-decision dissonance to a minimum. The marketer should also realize that attitude is influenced by the claims of the seller. If these claims are unrealistic, the product's performance will conflict with the buyer's expectations, and dissatisfaction is sure to result. Thus the marketer is well advised to inform the customer of the salient characteristics of his product and not to promise performance or other qualities that will not be realized. Proper instruction of the customer in the operation of the product is also important.

If preventive measures cannot be used or prove inadequate, corrective steps should be taken. Automobile and appliance dealers have long realized that good warranties and adequate and efficient service centers are prerequisites for maintaining brand loyalty. Marketing departments often include a customer-relations section that deals directly with dissatisfied buyers. Its role may include the sampling of customers to determine prevailing attitudes and identify product or service deficiencies. A customer-relations section may also reinforce the customer's purchase decision through the distribution of special literature—a practice common with automobile and private-airplane manufacturers. An active customer-relations program is almost mandatory at the manufacturer's level when independent middlemen are between the firm and the ultimate buyer. In such cases, this kind of program serves to feed information directly back to the producer—information that would otherwise be filtered through the middlemen, and perhaps distorted.

INNOVATION DIFFUSION

The technological revolution of the twentieth century has brought with it the introduction of new products on a scale undreamed of a few generations ago. More new products, as well as brands, have been introduced in the last 75 years than in all previous recorded history. Most have failed in the marketplace. The introduction of new products and new brands is an uncertain and difficult task—probably the single most precarious function of the firm's marketing department.

A wealth of theory exists on innovation diffusion, which can be defined as the spread of new ideas. A convenient starting point is to examine this phenomenon, also termed "technology transfer," with respect to time—an area in which there is sufficient empirical data to permit generalizing with some confidence.

New products, new services, and new brands—in fact, new knowledge and technology in general—tend to be assimilated slowly at first, then relatively fast as the majority of eventual adopters acquire them, then slowly again as the market approaches saturation, or the ultimate level of a product's acceptance. This phenomenon can be expressed mathematically, as a modified exponential function, or graphically, as an S-shaped curve like that in Figure 9.2, which shows the total number of adoptions of a typical new product or idea as a function of time. An "adoption" may be defined as the acceptance and continuous use of a product or an idea by a single buyer. This may involve a single sale, as in the case of a new book, or a series of sales, as in the case of a new brand of cigarettes or an industrial good. Of course, once the item is adopted, it is always subject to displacement by a superior innovation.

The term "innovation" has a variety of definitions. From a marketing viewpoint, it is appropriate to define an innovation as any new good or service having a property not previously associated with that particular product class. Some conspicuous examples would be the telephone, the diesel locomotive, television, and the airplane. Less obvious ones are the automatic transmission, the IBM 360 computer, the transistor radio, and the jet airplane—each of which is a highly improved and innovative modification of a previously existing product. Less substantive changes—such as new body styles in automobiles and new brands of cigarettes—may or may not qualify as innovations, depending on how narrowly the term is defined. When either an established product or a new brand is introduced into a

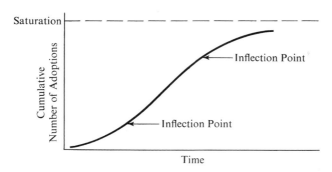

FIGURE 9.2
Adoption of a successful innovation

new market, its diffusion in that market will frequently follow the pattern of a true innovation. An illustration is the introduction of the Volkswagen—then a fourteen-year-old product—into the American automotive market in the mid-1950's.

Although the S-curve in Figure 9.2 is typical of what happens when a new product is put on the market, the curve may or may not reach the saturation level. If the curve represents a particular industry's sales, it may closely approach saturation but will probably never reach it. This is because there are usually some potential buyers—people who could afford and could justify the use of the product—who simply will not accept the new item. There are still farmers who refuse to use hybrid corn and Mennonites who will not give up their horse-and-buggy rigs in favor of automobiles.

The firm's sales will follow the industry's curve if the firm enjoys a monopoly. Otherwise, the consumption of a particular brand will tend toward a level that represents the firm's share of the industry's total market and will increase only as the total market increases. However, an individual firm's sales tend to be more variable than the industry's, because the firm can engage in practices that woo customers away from competitors.

Occasionally, a product will totally saturate a market. The diesel locomotive, for example, was ultimately adopted by every domestic railroad. In rare cases, the theoretical saturation level will be exceeded. The household radio is a case in point; many more radios have been sold than there are people to listen to them.

Not surprisingly, those who are usually first to purchase a new item tend to have certain traits in common, as do those who follow and those who are the last to accept—or never accept—the new product. In fact, the behavioral scientists argue that there are specific psychological and sociological traits that identify early, middle, and late adopters. Everett Rogers categorized adopters into five groups, with distinct properties assigned to each.

These classes, and the percentages of the population they represent, are (1) innovators (2.5%), (2) the early adopters (13.5%), (3) the early majority (34%), (4) the late majority (34%), and (5) the laggards (16%). Like many human phenomena, innovation adoption appears to follow a normal distribution curve (which explains the S-form of the cumulative adoption curve). Rogers distributed his adopter categories as in Figure 9.3.

The rate of adoption, which is the first derivative of the adoption function, increases at an increasing rate until the first inflection point; it continues to increase after that point, but at a decreasing rate, until the curve reaches its peak. There the adoption curve—that is, the rate of sales—begins to decline at an increasing rate until the second inflection point, after which the rate of decline decreases. The rate of change of the adoption rate (which is the rate of change of the S-curve in Figure 9.2) is simply the derivative of the derivative of the adoption function, or the second derivative of the adoption function.[7] The inflection points are the same as those in Figure 9.2. Differential calculus, by permitting us to compute the derivatives of the basic adoption function, allows us to specify the rate of adoption at different times in the product's life cycle.

The fact that the rate of adoption, and therefore sales, varies considerably over time is one cause of the loading problem discussed in Chapter 7.

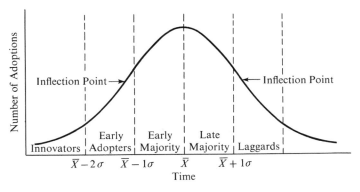

FIGURE 9.3
Innovation adopters over time

SOURCE: Reprinted with permission of The Macmillan Company from *Diffusion of Innovations* by Everett M. Rogers, © 1962 by The Free Press of Glencoe, A Division of the Macmillan Company.

---

[7] To compute a 2nd, 3rd, . . . *n*th derivative, one simply takes the derivative of the preceding derivative. For example, if the original function is $y = x^4 + 2x^2 + 5$, then the first derivative, $dy/dx, = 4x^3 + 4x$; the second derivative, $dy'/dx', = 12x^2 + 4$; and the third derivative, $dy''/dx'', = 24x$.

The implications of this are also important for product decisions, a topic that is explored in depth in Part VI. For now, we shall use the adoption function simply as a basis for categorizing adopters. These adopters are identified by common psychological and sociological traits that can be generalized to both individuals and firms.

Innovators are the initial adopters—those venturesome people who try things first. As a class, they tend to be young (young people and young firms), of a high social status, successful, members of multiple reference groups, and willing to take risks.[8] The innovators rely extensively on impersonal and scientific information sources and communicate with other innovators. They are usually cosmopolitan and are often opinion leaders. Companies that are innovative tend to have contact with universities and research centers and are usually the larger and more specialized firms.[9] Innovators are generally open and gregarious and participate actively in formal and informal groups. They attend trade shows, seminars, and conventions and have considerable social contact both in and outside of their professional circles. Of particular importance is the fact that they are an important medium of communication. They communicate among themselves as well as with the early-adopter group. Thus they are the logical target for the promotional efforts associated with the introduction of a new product.

Early adopters are similar to the innovators, but they are more cautious. They usually enjoy a high social status and are respected as the opinion leaders within a social group. Like the innovators, they are well educated and more creative than people in other adopter categories. They are widely involved in both the activities of their professional community and extracurricular activities. As a result of their conservativeness—relative to the innovators—they are the most trusted opinion-makers. They are the group to whom the majority looks for guidance.

Early adopters of consumer goods appear to have considerable mobility. They move more between institutions, jobs, economic levels, and geographical areas than members of other categories. They read and travel more and are more likely to be influenced by intellectual sources, such as technical journals or special-interest magazines.[10] Members of this group also appear to have the greatest amount of contact with salesmen, to be open to new

[8] In the context of this chapter, it is unnecessary to make the precise distinction between risk and uncertainty that is needed in the construction of the probabilistic decision models developed in Chapter 4. Here, "risk" means simply that an element of chance is involved.

[9] Gerald Zaltman, *Marketing: Contributions from the Behavioral Sciences* (New York: Harcourt, Brace & World, 1965), p. 45.

[10] These conclusions are the result of a pilot study by the Opinion Research Corporation, as cited by Zaltman, *op. cit.,* p. 46. See also Reuben Cohen, "A Theoretical Model for Consumer Market Prediction," *Sociological Inquiry,* Vol. 32 (1962), pp. 43–50.

experiences, and to have a wide variety of interests. They serve as a standard for the early majority and are an index of the ultimate success of an innovation.[11] An awareness of both these properties is obviously important to the firm in the marketing of new goods or services.

The *early majority* is the most deliberative group. Its members observe the experience of the early adopters, waiting until a substantial number have accepted the innovation before they acquire it themselves. They are genrally above-average in education and social position, are members of several reference groups, and have considerable contact with both salesmen and early adopters, the latter being frequently cited as neighbors or friends. In the commercial sector, the early majority seems to consist largely of average-sized firms.[12]

The *late majority* are below average in nearly all characteristics such as social status and income. They display little leadership and require a good deal of pressure before they will try a new product. They communicate primarily with others in the same class. Businesses in this class are usually small, relatively unspecialized, and oriented toward the maintenance of the status quo.[13] Members of the late majority are skeptical and generally reject a change until its virtues are proven by the majority of other consumers or firms.

The *laggards* are generally tradition-bound and socially isolated. They tend to belong to only one or two reference groups and are usually at the bottom of the income and social ladders. They are suspicious of change, associate primarily with other laggards, and accept an innovation only after it has become so widely accepted as to be traditional. By then the innovation is often obsolete and is being replaced with newer developments by the other groups.

Obviously, promotional efforts designed to launch a new good or service should focus on the innovator and early-adopter categories. The problem is to identify and communicate with these groups. Identification is largely a matter of knowing the market. One must deal with the individual market to isolate those doctors, farmers, businessmen, housewives, and so on, whose behavior patterns conform to those of the first two groups. The communication of innovations to and between categories, on the other hand, has been the subject of considerable study.

The form of communication network varies with both the adopter category and the stage of acceptance. The process by which a new good is accepted may be divided into five stages: (1) awareness, (2) interest, (3) evaluation, (4) trial, and (5) adoption. The first four are self-explanatory. The adoption stage begins when the individual or firm elects to use the new

[11] Zaltman, *op. cit.,* p. 48.
[12] *Ibid.*
[13] *Ibid.*

product, service, or idea on a continuing basis. Other stages are often compressed or combined, and the trial stage may be eliminated. Often, innovations do not lend themselves to sample testing, although the speed and extent of the diffusion process is enhanced by the divisibility of the item. A product is much more likely to reach the adoption stage if it can first be tried on a small scale.

The extent to which adopters are influenced by different media depends on their category and the stage in the adoption process. Impersonal communications—that is, literature and advertising media—are important in the awareness and interest stages, especially for innovators and early adopters, who are generally receptive to and can be reached by mass media. However, as adopters progress through the evaluation, trial, and adoption stages, they rely more and more on personal media. Here friends, associates, neighbors, and salesmen play an important role. The characteristics of the innovator and early adopter, however, often deny reliance on personal sources. This is especially so with the innovator, who, lacking access to people who have had experience with the product, must rely on his own judgment. Thus, for the innovators and early adopters it is venturesomeness, contrariness, cognizance, exposition, and curiosity that provide the motivating force. These are the personality traits that must often be exploited in the initial stages of the introduction of a new good.

There is some indication that the diffusion of ideas, as opposed to physical goods, requires personal communication during the early introductory phase. Federal programs for the diffusion of government-sponsored technology illustrate this fact. The federal establishment spends over $200 million per year to diffuse new technology. Where it has used highly personal sources to introduce new ideas into the civilian sector, it has been highly successful. The U. S. Department of Agriculture, for example, successfully introduced hybrid corn to the agricultural community via the land-grant colleges and county agents.[14] Conversely, agencies that have relied on "a bridge of paper work" as a medium for the transfer of technology from inventor to users have been disappointed in the results.[15]

[14] Zvi Griliches, "Hybrid Corn: An Exploration in the Economics of Technological Change," *Econometrica,* Vol. 25, No. 4 (October 1957), pp. 501–22.
[15] For detailed discussions of the experience of the federal programs, see Hyman Olken, "Spin-Offs: A Business Pay-Off," *California Management Review,* Vol. 9, No. 2 (Winter 1966), p. 17; Earl O. Heady, "Public Purpose in Agricultural Research and Education," *Journal of Farm Economics,* Vol. 43, No. 3 (August 1961), pp. 566–81; John C. Welles and Robert H. Waterman, Jr., "Space Technology: Pay-Off From Spin-Off," *Harvard Business Review,* Vol. 42, No. 4 (July–August 1964), pp. 106–18; John G.Neitner, "The Utilization of Space Derived Technology in Non-Space Applications," SRI Project 440-2 (Menlo Park, Calif.: Stanford Research Institute, 1964); and Zvi Griliches, "Research Expenditures, Education, and the Aggregate Agricultural Production Function," *The American Economic Review* (December 1964), pp. 961–74.

As the innovator and early-adopter markets are saturated and the early-majority market begins to emerge, personal communication becomes even more important to the diffusion of new products. The deterioration of reading habits as one progresses from the innovator to the laggard category, combined with increased product use, makes face-to-face communication increasingly significant. Each group is instrumental in introducing the innovation to the following group; laggards look to the late majority, the late majority looks to the early majority, and so on. The most important opinion-makers in the system appear to be the early adopters, who prove the viability of the new good and establish a precedent for the early majority, which is the first substantial market.

The importance of opinion leaders and person-to-person contact in the successful introduction of new goods has been established by numerous empirical studies. For example, Coleman, Menzel, and Katz demonstrated that the rate and extent of acceptance of new drugs by the medical community depended on the social integration of the innovative doctors. This was especially true of new drugs. When risk was involved, doctors were anxious to get the opinions of the innovators and early adopters before prescribing the drug for their own patients. Thus face-to-face contact—as occurred when a number of doctors shared an office that included an innovator—accelerated the assimilation of the new drugs. Isolated doctors tended to be late adopters.[16] A similar situation exists in the agricultural community, where the county agents have long since learned to identify the socially integrated and innovative farmers and to use them as the instrument for the diffusion of new technology throughout the balance of the farming community.

Personal influence is helpful in overcoming three barriers that often prevent successful communication through impersonal sources. The first is *selective exposure,* which is the tendency of individuals to see and hear only that material which conforms to their present beliefs and attitudes. This is similar to the cognitive dissonance phenomenon (p. 208). This barrier is particularly effective in the case of mass-media material. For example, smokers generally refuse to read literature on lung cancer, and Democrats seldom watch Republican campaign speakers. The second barrier is *selective perception,* which is the tendency to interpret new information within the framework of attitudes established by past experience. For example, a man who has had considerable misfortune with a particular brand in the past will discount—or simply reject—the claims made for that brand today, even if the product is considerably different and improved. The third barrier is

---

[16] James Coleman, Elihu Katz, and Herbert Menzel, "The Diffusion of an Innovation Among Physicians," reprinted in Ralph L. Day, ed., *Marketing Models* (Scranton, Pa.: International Textbook Co., 1964), p. 100. This article originally appeared in *Sociometry,* Vol. 20 (December 1957).

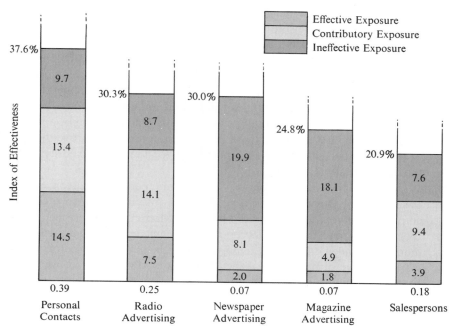

FIGURE 9.4

Influence of personal contact and other media in brand shifting
(Total number of brand shifters = 386 or 100%)*

* TYPES OF MARKETING SHIFTS MADE

Small food items	49%
Soaps and cleansing agents	37
Household goods (pots, irons, etc.)	11
Miscellaneous	3
Total (= 100%)	(386)

NOTE: The first bar, for example, reads as follows: 37.6% of all those who made a recent change in a brand or product reported some manner of exposure to personal contacts. This percentage (appearing at the upper left of the bar) may be broken down as follows (reading now from the bottom up): 14.5% of the shifters were "effectively exposed" to personal contacts; 13.4% experienced "contributory exposure" to personal contacts; and 9.7% were "ineffectively exposed" to personal contacts. The difference between 37.6% and 100% (62.4%) represents those brand shifters who were not exposed to personal contacts at all.

The second bar then means that 30.3% of all brand or product shifters reported some manner of exposure to radio advertising, of which 7.5% was "effective exposure," etc. *Note that each bar is based on the same total*—that is, the 386 people who reported some recent change in a brand or product.

That the "exposure" totals of all the bars add to more than 100% results from the fact that respondents reported more than one source of influence in connection with their shifts of brand or product.

SOURCE: Reprinted with permission of The Macmillan Company from *Personal Influence* by Elihu Katz and Paul Lazarsfeld. Copyright 1955 by The Free Press, a Corporation.

selective retention, which is the tendency to retain only that information which reinforces present beliefs and attitudes. Selective retention is also associated with cognitive dissonance, where a buyer tends to remember those things that justify his selection and ignore those that contradict it.

Person-to-person contact is generally more effective than exposure to mass media, since people are not as easily ignored or put aside as billboards, magazines, TV commercials, or third-class mail. In addition, a dialogue is possible with personal contact; hence misconceptions can be exposed and corrected. Information can be presented in a way that conforms to the individual's attitudes. Personal communication also usually leaves a stronger impression than mass-media messages, thus increasing the probability of retention. Such contact can be critical during the evaluation stage, especially for the later categories of adopters, who are poor risk-takers and rely on others for guidance and reinforcement of their judgment.

The communication aspects of diffusion theory have important implications for marketing. They are especially relevant to the promotion program. The distribution of resources between advertising and personal selling, as well as the media mix, should be different at different times in the product's life cycle. For example, the receptiveness of innovators to impersonal sources indicates that advertising in special-interest media will be most effective in the early introductory phase of a product. Since the majority of prospective buyers will wait to observe the experience of the innovators and early adopters, advertising in popular media, aimed at the mass middle-income market, should be delayed until the new item has been accepted by the innovators and most of the early adopters.

As the innovation is diffused in the early acceptor categories, a shift from specialized media to general media is in order. As acceptance of the product approaches the midpoint, the emphasis should shift toward personal selling. Neither advertising nor personal selling should be excluded at any point in the life cycle, except possibly toward the end when the marginal costs of promotional activities start to exceed the marginal revenues.

The relative effectiveness of personal influence in the diffusion of brands and products is suggested by an empirical study by Katz and Lazarsfeld of consumer shifting of brands and products. The results, shown in Figure 9.4, indicate the superior effect of personal contact as opposed to advertising, at least as far as brand and product shifting are concerned.

Innovation diffusion is illustrative of the complexity of human behavior in the marketplace. The marketer must often deal with it and the other phenomena discussed in this chapter simultaneously, or in close sequence. The construction of a model of consumer behavior, as in Chapter 10, makes this task a bit more manageable.

Models of Consumer Behavior

A SCHEMATIC MODEL

In dealing with the consumer, either as an individual or as a stereotype, the marketer is confronted with a variety of response possibilities and countless environmental variables. A schematic model of consumer behavior is useful for several reasons. First, it permits the marketer to integrate the psychological and sociological factors motivating consumers into a general explanation of the purchasing cycle. Second, it helps him to identify the variables that play key roles in the acceptance or rejection of the firm's products. And third, it provides him with a checklist of items that should be considered in preparing his marketing strategy.

In order to develop a schematic model that will be applicable to a specific problem, one must first identify the potential customers and the specific factors associated with the general variables in the model. Quantitative techniques are needed because the company must not only identify the variables but measure their relative intensity and their distribution within its prospective market. For example, if a firm is going to introduce a new product or service for senior citizens, it should know not only the number of potential customers in each of its market areas but their financial status and their position in the family cycle (senior citizen, retired, and so on) as well. These latter factors will influence both the perceptual bias of the prospect and his objective and subjective selection criteria.

By exploring each variable within the context of the market for a particular good, one can begin to isolate the significant elements. These are the elements that must be dealt with in the formulation of the general marketing strategy, as well as in the preparation of tactical plans involving advertising copy, sales presentations, and product variation. The isolation of these elements is also important to the resource-allocation process. Resources should be concentrated where they will do the most good. Although a consumer-behavior model is essentially qualitative, it serves to point the way and lay the basis for more rigorous measurement and analysis.

No perfect model of human behavior, or even of the subset consumer behavior, has yet been developed.[1] Figure 10.1 contains the essential variables that are common to most consumer-behavior models. No effort has been made to show varying intensities in the variables, since these differ radically between markets, products, brands, and phases of a good's life cycle. For example, a mature brand of convenience goods such as Coca-Cola or Lucky Strike cigarettes will enjoy an abbreviated behavior sequence. The typical buyer of these goods will respond to stimuli by automatically purchasing his usual brand, without considering the alternatives. On the other hand, when a teenager purchases his first automobile or an industrial buyer selects a new plant site, all the variables shown will probably be involved.

The Behavioral Sequence. The sequence of acts leading to the eventual purchase or rejection of a product starts with an initial response to a stimulus. The stimulus may be an advertisement, a verbal sales pitch, a comment of a friend, or a symbol. Since the average consumer is bombarded daily with hundreds of promotional messages, conversations, and symbols, most stimuli do not trigger a positive response; hence the purchase option is rejected. However, if the consumer's drive level is sufficiently high and the stimulus is strong enough, he will respond either by immediately purchasing the good or by clarifying the alternatives to the purchase. The consumer's initial response is also affected by his perceptual bias. The latter serves as a filter that may block the stimulus and thus prevent the purchase cycle from progressing further.

The speed and directness with which the consumer proceeds from the initial response to purchase or rejection depend on the strength of the stimulus, the intensity of the drive, and the extent of previous learning. If the stimulus—or accumulation of stimuli—is strong, the drive level is high, and if the consumer knows precisely what product best satisfies his need, the purchase will be made immediately. For example, an individual may be thirsty (drive), encounter a beverage advertisement (stimulus), and respond by immediately purchasing a particular brand of beer (learned response). This example is representative of the experimental psychologist's view of the consumer; ultimately, the buyer is perceived as a bundle of drives and conditioned responses that result in a readily predictable behavior when he is confronted by a sufficiently intense drive and an appropriate stimulus.

The high degree of learning illustrated by the example implies that

[1] For variations of the consumer-behavior model, see John A. Howard, *Marketing Management, Analysis and Planning*, rev. ed. (Homewood, Ill.: Irwin, 1963), p. 41; and J. F. Engel, D. T. Kollat, and R. D. Blackwell, *Consumer Behavior* (New York: Holt, Rinehart & Winston, 1968), p. 34.

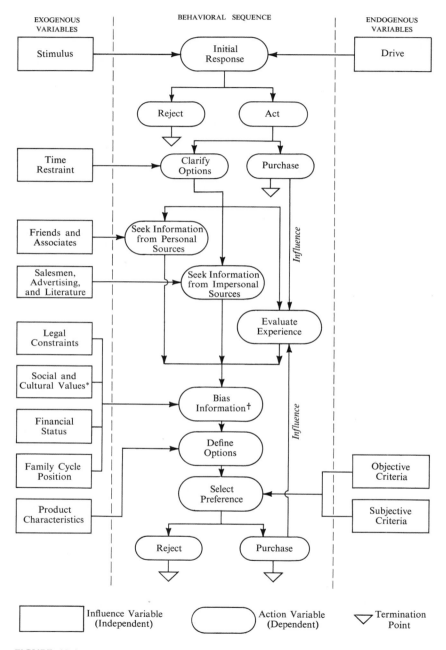

FIGURE 10.1
Consumer-behavior model

* Also influences drive level, objective criteria, and subjective criteria.
† Influences initial response.

previous purchase experience has clarified the alternative choices of goods for the individual and conditioned him to make a virtually automatic response to a given stimulus. Such a short purchase cycle is common in the market for convenience goods, where a given item is likely to be inexpensive, readily available, and repeatedly purchased. If the firm is offering a good within a product class that is associated with this kind of behavioral pattern, its promotional strategy will probably be aimed at teaching consumers a conditioned response. This strategy should be coupled with a distribution plan that will make the firm's product as readily accessible as competing brands. Behavior will tend to conform to a learned response only when the response is convenient as well as physically possible. Otherwise, the buyer may generalize a competitor's product as being sufficiently similar to his preferred brand to be substituted for it. It is doubtful that a smoker will "walk a mile for a Camel" if a Chesterfield, Old Gold, or Winston is available in the store around the corner, even though promotion and experience may have conditioned him to ask for Camels when his nerves or appetite demand a cigarette.

If uncertainty exists regarding the nature of the alternatives—and thus there is the possibility of post-decision cognitive dissonance—the prospect will attempt to clarify his options, subject to the constraints of time and his drive level. This segment of the behavioral pattern can follow one of three paths, or any combination of the three. First, the prospect may seek information from personal sources; second, he may seek information from impersonal sources; and third, he may evaluate his past experiences as they relate to the purchase options.

The prospect is generally most sensitive to advice from personal contacts. Friends and associates can be extremely influential sources of information since the individual tends to perceive them as being more objective and truthful than advertisements or salesmen representing the interests of a manufacturer or middleman would be. This hypothesis has been supported empirically by a number of studies. An example is the findings of the Bureau of Applied Social Research of Columbia University, which are the bases of Figure 9.4 (p. 218).

The feasibility of providing product information to the prospective buyer through personal sources varies considerably with the type of market, and is one reason for the importance of market definition. If the market is limited and can be precisely defined, as is often the case with luxury items or specialized industrial goods, then the personal sources of buyer information can probably be identified. If the market is broad, as is the case with most consumer goods, then it may be impossible to identify and exploit personal sources at anything close to a reasonable cost.

To illustrate, assume that a firm has developed an expensive bonding material uniquely suited to high-temperature, high-stress, lightweight structures, the logical market for which is the aerospace industry. The firms that would build structures of the type described would number only a few dozen. The prospective buyers would be the purchasing agents in the material departments of these corporations. However, the agents themselves would be a poor choice as the target of the manufacturer's initial promotional efforts. The producer would be far wiser to identify the engineers actually working on high-performance structures and inform them of the properties of its product. In filling a requisition for bonding material, the purchasing agent will probably defer to the judgment of these technical people. Although the manufacturer should also make sure that the agent is aware of the product—that is, it should establish itself in the mind of the purchasing agent as a qualified supplier of this class of products—the key to the purchase decision is clearly the engineers' evaluation of the product.

On the other hand, if the firm were serving a large consumer market— if it were selling encyclopedias, securities, or life insurance—the identification and assessment of personal information sources would be far more difficult. Often little effort is made in such cases, beyond requesting referrals from previous customers. Thus an individual may provide entrée to a friend, but he could not be depended on to spread the firm's promotional message very far.[2] However, the fact that personal sources of information may elude manipulation by the firm does not necessarily mean that they play an unimportant role in the buyer's behavioral processes. On the contrary, word-of-mouth communication can be very effective in encouraging or discouraging a purchase, especially with respect to brand choice.

Information from impersonal sources is communicated through a variety of media, often as part of the message that provides the original stimulus. Practically all promotional effort involves impersonal stimuli, the effectiveness of which is obviously compromised by the biases and ulterior motives of the originators and sponsors. (There are exceptions, such as the technical specification sheets often provided by manufacturers, especially in the introductory phase of a new brand or product.) Under these conditions of impersonal communication, the selection of advertising media can determine the success or failure of the program.

Although the consumer may be exposed to considerable information from impersonal sources, in the course of clarifying his options, this information is subject to perceptual bias. Perceptual bias is a result of environmental influences as well as personal psychological traits. Because selective exposure, selective perception, and selective retention are involved, most of

---

[2] The request for referrals, and especially the use of an individual's name in a testimonial, is often used as a come-on by unscrupulous salesmen to justify a phony discount. This practice is common in the sale of encyclopedias and in other forms of door-to-door selling, where in reality the prospect is offered a price available to any other buyer.

the information messages do not survive in their original form. The residual information that survives the filtration process—and is biased by it—is used to define the options. This process consists of weighing the costs (material, psychological, and social) of the alternative against its utility, which is determined primarily by the product characteristics (one of which is availability) perceived by the buyer. Consciously or subconsciously, the buyer arrays the options in order of preference. If the most desirable alternative has a cost that exceeds its utility value, the product will be rejected and the purchase cycle for that good will be terminated. If the cost is less than the utility value, then the good will be purchased and the cycle completed. However, if the product or service is one that will be purchased repeatedly, then the purchase act will have further effects. Information about the buyer's satisfaction or lack of satisfaction will be fed back into the system, thus influencing future behavioral sequences.

Obviously, the marketer is interested in influencing the various acts in the behavior sequence that affect the purchase or rejection of his firm's product. He does this by manipulating the exogenous variables—that is, those outside the immediate control of the consumer.

Stimuli are provided primarily by advertising. The cue, or trigger, that initiates the purchase cycle may be verbal—as in the case of radio commercials—or symbolic—as in the case of the Coca-Cola bottle. Sometimes the cue has no direct relationship to the brand or product. For example, a beer advertisement may remind a thirsty motorist that it would be nice to stop for a bottle of his favorite soft drink. The importance of the time constraint varies considerably with individuals and with the class of goods. For example, one characteristic of convenience goods is that the consumer does not spend a lot of time shopping for them. Hence, the firm's brand should be readily available, which means a wide distribution system.

The use of friends, and particularly associates, is very important in influencing buyers of industrial products. One example has already been cited. Another is the marketing of corporate jet airplanes. Although the product decision and purchase authorization invariably comes from a senior executive officer or the board of directors, the choice of a brand will be based on the recommendation of the firm's chief pilot. Thus the promotional effort must be two-pronged, one strategy directed at corporation executives and the other at their aviation departments. The two strategies demand different advertising media and copy and different personal selling techniques.

Salesmen and advertising are the traditional instruments for influencing buyer behavior. In addition to their role as stimuli, they also provide information—sometimes general and a bit exaggerated (when consumer products are involved) and sometimes specific and accurate (when industrial goods are involved). Independent literature, especially special-interest magazines, can often be used by the firm to publicize new products. Newspaper and magazine articles on new goods and services are popular and are often written by the producer. Firms also provide editors with their products or services without charge, so that they can be reviewed by the publication. This practice is typical in the automobile, aircraft, recreational vehicle, and resort businesses.

Various legal constraints establish boundaries for the promotional, product, and pricing activities of the firm.[3] They may also segment the market, as in the case of alcoholic beverages. Although legitimate enterprises think almost exclusively in terms of conformity to the law, some manipulation of legal constraints may be possible through appeals to regulatory agencies, legislative bodies, and the courts. Utilities and public transportation companies are almost continuously involved in petitioning the Interstate Commerce Commission and the Civil Aeronautics Board, as well as state regulatory agencies. Lobbyists for industry, retailers, and farmers are notoriously active in both Washington and many state capitals.

Laws are sometimes changed in the courts by marketers who elect to use civil disobedience as an instrument of change. The Anglo-American legal system rests on case law. Matters of constitutionality cannot be decided in the abstract; the law must first be broken. Thus the firm producing books, magazines, motion pictures or plays that do not conform to local obscenity laws must break the laws to determine their constitutionality. This has been done with a good deal of success during the past decade.

However, social and cultural values tend to be inert in the short run. The firm offering a good that does not conform to the mores and tastes of a society had best look for a market elsewhere or prepare for a long and expensive promotional effort. An example is the general disapproval of the use of cigarettes by women that existed prior to the mid-twenties. It took the domestic tobacco industry many years and a great deal of money to overcome this barrier, which excluded half its potential customers from the market. One device used was paying movie producers to have popular actresses smoke in motion pictures. At that time, the cinema had a powerful influence on the social values of the nation.

Financial status, classified as exogenous because it is difficult for the individual to influence in the short run, is extremely important. It not only provides a budget constraint but has considerable influence in establishing the household's social class. Social class, in turn, has considerable influence in shaping the attitudes and beliefs of the individual. There is little that the firm can do to change a prospective customer's financial status. However, it can often set price and credit policies to accommodate the financial status of a large share of its potential market population. Hence the marketing de-

---

[3] See Chapters 27 through 29.

partment should analyze this variable before making price and credit decisions.

The individual's position in the family cycle—whether he is a child, unmarried adult, a childless married person, a married person with children at home, an older married person, or a retiree—is a critical determinant of both his material needs and his tastes. Although this variable, too, is not subject to manipulation by the firm, it is important in the analysis of consumer markets.

Product characteristics—including price, availability, and service—both of the firm's goods and those of its competitors, are obviously important. They are often the most significant and variable inputs in the system. However, they may also be totally ineffective, due to consumer ignorance—especially if the prospective buyer is faced with a high cost in time or money of gathering information.

The endogenous variables—those that are internal determinants of the buyer's behavior, and at least partially controlled by him—have been discussed in Chapter 9. They include drives, objective criteria, and subjective criteria. The objective criteria have to do with rational needs and the functional properties of the alternatives. The subjective criteria are related to psychogenic needs, which may be conscious and rational or subconscious and irrational, depending on whether one interprets the consumer in terms of experimental, Freudian, Gestalt, or social psychology.

OTHER MODELS

Two other behavioral models are often used in the explanation of consumer actions. One is the Hobbesian Organizational Factors Model, and the other is the Marshallian Economic Model. Both warrant explanation.

The *Hobbesian Organizational Factors Model* attempts to show the various ways in which conflicting relationships between the goals of the individual and those of the organization are resolved. It recognizes that man will attempt to serve both his own interests and those of the group, for to serve only the former is to encourage "a war of every man, against every man."[4] The ultimate consequence of caring only about one's own interests is a life that is "solitary, poor, nasty, brutish, and short."[5] The industrial buyer, to take an example, is paid to serve the interests of his employer, yet to some extent he remains motivated by his own aspirations. This suggests that the marketer of industrial goods should prepare his appeal on two planes, designing one strategy to conform to the needs of the purchasing firm and the

[4] Thomas Hobbes, *Leviathan,* originally published in 1651 (Oxford: Basil Blackwell, 1957), p. 82.
[5] *Ibid.,* p. 83.

other to appeal to the private interests of the purchasing agent. The former should be biased toward the functional and objective, while the latter should be slanted toward the psychogenic. For example, a salesman might stress his product's virtues—quality, price, and service—on the one hand, while appealing to the buyer's ego on the other.

The *Marshallian Economic Model* was explored in Chapter 8. It presumes that man will act both rationally and in conformity with his own best interests.[6] For example, if products A and B provide equal satisfaction, but A is priced lower than B, then A will be chosen in preference to B. This is one of the fundamental tenets of microeconomic theory.

The Marshallian model suggests the following behavior processes of interest to marketing: (1) The lower the price of a product, the greater the sales. (2) The lower the price of substitute products, the lower the sales of the product. (3) The lower the price of complementary products, the higher the sales of the product. (4) The higher the real income of potential consumers, the higher the sales of the product. (5) The more is spent on promotion, the higher the sales of the product.[7]

Although not all consumers will respond rationally to a change in the price or income variable, or respond emotionally to a change in the level of promotion, those who underreact will be balanced out by those who overreact. Both types of behavior are common, and the assumption that the two will average out to an aggregate zero error is supported by both statistical theory and empirical research.

[6] Alfred Marshall, *Principles of Economics,* 9th variorum ed. (New York: Macmillan, 1961).

[7] Adapted from Philip Kotler, *Marketing Management: Analysis, Planning and Control* (Englewood Cliffs, N. J.: Prentice-Hall, 1967), p. 84. Note that if the product is an inferior good (that is, one for which total demand decreases as income increases), tenet 4 may not be true.

Summary of Consumer Behavior

Economics provides techniques for measuring consumer behavior and for estimating the relationship between consumption (sales) and such independent variables as population, income, price, and demographic characteristics. It also provides the concept of the indifference curve (based on the ordinal theory of choice), which serves as a graphical representation of taste. However, economics makes no effort to explain the "why" of consumer behavior.

For an explanation of consumer preferences, we must turn to the behavioral sciences, particularly psychology and sociology. Within these fields, there are several schools of theory and methodology, each with a different view of human, hence consumer, behavior. One of the earliest schools is experimental, or laboratory, psychology, which perceives human behavior as a pattern of conditioned responses based mainly on biological needs.

Clinical psychology, a later development, deals mainly with learned drives. It encompasses both Freudian and Gestalt psychology. The Freudian school perceives behavior as primarily a function of suppressed drives and the resolution of conflict between the id, ego, and superego. It assumes that the consumer is unaware of the real reasons for his purchase behavior, which is dictated by subconscious drives.

The Gestalt school, on the other hand, perceives human behavior as a function of complex, but conscious and rational, drives. It emphasizes the psychogenic drives and the thought processes by which individuals perceive and interpret stimuli. The consumer is seen as having desires that, although they are not satisfied by, and in fact are often unrelated to, the functional properties of a product, may nevertheless be satisfied by a product's psychogenic qualities, such as its image. Hence, consumers will frequently respond to promotional appeals having little to do with the physical and performance characteristics of a good.

Sociology and social psychology see human behavior as primarily a function of social, or group, influences. Thus, they tend to explain the consumer in terms of his role in the group, and to stress group values and group-prescribed behavior as the key to successful product and promotional appeals.

Many psychological and sociological factors influence purchase behavior. Those considered to have the most influence are personality (classified either by sociological or psychological criteria); psychogenic needs, psychological classification of goods, discrimination-generalization, cognitive dissonance, and innovation diffusion. Depending on the nature of the product or service and the market population, each can serve as an explanation of consumer behavior. Insight into these factors is often essential in order for the firm to manipulate the marketing instruments successfully.

A consumer-behavior model serves to integrate the psychological and sociological factors that determine the eventual purchase or rejection of a product. It also provides a checklist for the preparation of promotional strategies. However, for such a model to be truly useful in the decision process, the model variables must be defined in terms of the factors relevant to a particular product and market. This is the role of marketing research, which we shall discuss in Part IX.

Questions and Problems

1. Discuss how economists view consumer behavior.
2. How might each of the following acts be explained by an experimental psychologist: (a) the purchase of a bottle of Coca-Cola, (b) the selection of an automobile, and (c) the selection of a brand of cigarettes.
3. Suggest an advertising strategy for a new brand of beer that conforms to the levels of the S-R school of psychology.
4. Explain the purchase of cigarettes in terms of both Freudian and Gestalt psychology.
5. Define the id, ego, and superego, and discuss their implications for consumer behavior.
6. Suggest an advertising strategy for automobile tires that conforms to the Gestalt interpretation of human behavior.
7. What approach might a social psychologist stress in the design and promotion of a new line of inexpensive women's ready-to-wear dresses?
8. Suggest some promotional appeals that might be made to specific pychological and sociological personality types by a manufacturer of a broad line of home furniture.
9. List the psychogenic needs to which the firm might appeal in the promotion of each of the following goods: (a) toilet soap, (b) men's shoes, (c) perfume, and (d) resorts.
10. Classify the following products according to their psychological traits: (a) Chevrolet sedans, (b) Dior dresses, (c) Sherwin-Williams house paint, and (d) *Holiday* magazine.
11. A brand of cola-flavored soft drink has only 5 percent of a regional market, in spite of its wide distribution, low price, and satisfying flavor (determined by a consumer survey). Suggest an advertising theme that employs the discrimination-generalization principle, and explain why that theme should help to enlarge the brand's market share.

12. Explain the theory of cognitive dissonance. How might this theory be applied to the marketing of electrical appliances?

13. Explain, in terms of innovation-diffusion theory, how a firm might handle the marketing of a new type of commercial fertilizer throughout different phases of its life cycle.

14. Explain, with reference to a schematic model, how a firm might influence consumer behavior in the marketing of (a) a patent medicine, (b) teenage girls' dresses, and (c) aluminum.

15. Select a full-page advertisement from a popular slick magazine, such as *Life, Time,* or *Look,* and explain it in terms of the psychological and sociological factors discussed in this part.

16. Select a display advertisement in a special-interest magazine, such as *Field and Stream, Boating, Good Housekeeping,* or *Aviation Week,* and explain it in terms of the material covered in the last three chapters.

17. Select a television commercial, and explain it in terms of the material in the last three chapters.

18. Discuss the schematic model of consumer behavior as it might apply to the purchase of (a) a color television set, (b) a box of breakfast cereal, and (c) a family vacation in Europe. In each case, suggest ways in which the TV manufacturer, cereal producer, or travel agency might influence the consumer's behavioral pattern.

19. Discuss the selling of office equipment within the framework of the Hobbesian Organizational Factors Model.

20. Discuss the purchase of a newly built home in a typical suburban development within the framework of the Marshallian Economic Model.

Supplementary Readings

BOOKS

ENGEL, JAMES F., KOLLAT, DAVID T., and BLACKWELL, ROGER D., *Consumer Behavior* (New York: Holt, Rinehart & Winston, 1968).

FERBER, ROBERT and WALES, HUGH G., ed., *Motivation and Market Behavior* (Homewood, Ill.: Irwin, 1958).

FESTINGER, LEON, *A Theory of Cognitive Dissonance* (Evanston, Ill.: Row Peterson, 1957).

FRIEDMAN, MILTON, *A Theory of the Consumption Function* (Princeton, N. J.: Princeton University Press, 1957).

HILGARD, ERNEST R., and ATKINSON, RICHARD C., *Introduction to Psychology,* 4th ed. (New York: Harcourt, Brace & World, 1967).

HOWARD, JOHN A., Marketing Management, *Analysis and Planning,* rev. ed. (Homewood, Ill.: Irwin, 1963).

KATZ, ELIHU, *Gestalt Psychology* (New York: Ronald Press, 1950).

KATZ, ELIHU, and LAZARSFELD, PAUL F., *Personal Influence: The Part Played by People in the Flow of Mass Communications* (Glencoe, Ill.: Free Press, 1955).

KRECH, DAVID, and CRUTCHFIELD, RICHARD S., *Elements of Psychology* (New York: Knopf, 1962).

ROGERS, EVERETT M., *The Diffusion of Innovations* (New York: Free Press, 1962).

ZALTMAN, GERALD, *Marketing: Contributions from the Behavioral Sciences* (New York: Harcourt, Brace & World, 1965).

ARTICLES

BAYTON, J. A., "Motivation, Cognition, Learning: Basic Factors in Consumer Behavior," *Journal of Marketing,* Vol. 22, No. 3 (January 1958), pp. 282–89.

EVANS, FRANKLIN B., "Psychological and Objective Factors in the Prediction of Brand Choices," *Journal of Business,* Vol. 32, No. 4 (October 1959), pp. 340–67.

————, "Correlates of Automobile Shopping Behavior," *Journal of Marketing,* Vol. 26, No. 4 (October 1962), pp. 74–77.

KAISH, STANLEY, "Cognitive Dissonance and the Classification of Consumer Goods," *Journal of Marketing,* Vol. 31, No. 4, Part I (October 1967), pp. 28–31.

KOLLAT, DAVID T., and WILLETT, RONALD P., "Customer Impulse Purchasing Behavior," *Journal of Marketing Research,* Vol. 4, No. 1 (February 1967), pp. 21–31.

KRUGMAN, H. E., "The Learning of Consumer Preference," *Journal of Marketing,* Vol. 26, No. 2 (April 1962), pp. 31–33.

LEVY, S. J., "Symbols for Sale," *Harvard Business Review,* Vol. 37, No. 4 (July–August 1959), pp. 117–24.

MUNN, H. L., "Brand Perception as Related to Age, Income, and Education," *Journal of Marketing,* Vol. 24, No. 3 (January 1960), pp. 29–34.

MURPHY, J. R., "Questionable Correlates for Automobile Shopping Behavior," *Journal of Marketing,* Vol. 27, No. 4 (October 1963), pp. 71–72.

NELSON, B. H., "Seven Principles in Image Formation," *Journal of Marketing,* Vol. 26, No. 1 (January 1962), pp. 67–71.

POLLAY, RICHARD W., "Customer Impulse Purchasing Behavior: A Reexamination," *Journal of Marketing Research,* Vol. 5, No. 3 (August 1968), pp. 323–25.

RHODES, V. J., "The Measurement of Consumer Preferences," *Journal of Farm Economics,* Vol. 37, No. 4 (November 1955), pp. 638–51.

ROBERTSON, THOMAS S., and MYERS, JAMES H., "Personality Correlates of Opinion Leadership and Innovative Buying Behavior," *Journal of Marketing Research,* Vol. 6, No. 2 (May 1969), pp. 164–68.

SHAFFER, J. D., "The Influence of 'Impulse Buying' or In-the-Store Decisions on Consumers' Food Purchases," *Journal of Farm Economics,* Vol. 42, No. 2 (May 1960), pp. 317–24.

Steiner, G. A., "Notes on Franklin B. Evans' 'Psychological and Objective Factors in the Prediction of Brand Choice,' " *Journal of Business,* Vol. 34, No. 1 (January 1961), pp. 57–60.

Wasson, Chester R., "Is it Time to Quit Thinking of Income Classes?" *Journal of Marketing,* Vol. 33, No. 2 (April 1969), pp. 54–57.

Wells, W. D., "Measuring Readiness to Buy," *Harvard Business Review,* Vol. 39, No. 4 (July–August 1961), pp. 81–87.

Woods, W. A., "Psychological Dimensions of Consumer Decisions," *Journal of Marketing,* Vol. 24. No. 3 (January 1960), pp. 15–19.

Part V

PRICE DECISIONS

Price is the instrument most generally identified with a market economy. A free-enterprise system could not flourish without price competition. Price is the universal index of value. It is the best measure of demand. Price serves to bring the supply of goods and services produced into equilibrium with the quantity demanded. Although it serves as the primary mechanism for the allocation of economic resources only in a free society, it is also effective as an instrument of control in a managed economy.

Few countries lack a national economic policy. Such policies invariably carry provisions regarding price—who will set it, what limits will be imposed on its manipulation, and what efforts will be made to control it. Policy may be very restrictive, as it is in a controlled economy, or very permissive, as it was in the laissez-faire economies of the eighteenth and nineteenth centuries. In mixed economies, such as those of Western Europe and North America, there is a combination of control and freedom designed to protect the consumer and preserve competition. Typical examples of government control are price-setting by government agencies in regulated industries—such as communication, transportation, and power—and antitrust laws to prevent price-fixing between competitors.

The formal statement of the economic policy of the United States is found in the annual *Economic Report of the President.* Relative to the question of price, a recent report states

The immediate task in 1969 is to make a decisive step toward price stability. This will be only the beginning of the journey. We cannot hope to reach in a single year the goal that has eluded every industrial country for generations—that of providing high employment with stable prices.

There is no simple or single formula for success. But this combination can and must be achieved.[1]

The effectiveness of price as a marketing instrument is conceded even by the Soviet Union, which uses price to adjust the level of consumption. Product prices are fixed so that the level of national output allocated to the consumer sector will be matched by the total amount of personal disposable income available for consumption. Both the total quantity and the mix of consumer goods are determined by government edict. However, the only way to bring demand into equilibrium with supply, as the Russians are quite aware, is to manipulate price.[2]

Thus price decisions may well be the most important decisions made by the marketer. To make them wisely, he must understand the theoretical concepts of demand, supply, and equilibrium—in short, the sensitivity of his sales, revenue, and profit to changes in price. He must also understand the properties of price and the effect of consumer income on his sales. He should certainly know the alternative pricing strategies at his disposal and their limitations and virtues.

[1] *Economic Report of the President* (Washington, D. C.: U. S. Government Printing Office, 1969), p. 9.
[2] For an exploration of the use of price in different economies, see Allan G. Gruchy, *Comparative Economic Systems* (New York: Houghton Mifflin, 1966).

CHAPTER 11

Demand, Supply, and Equilibrium

DEMAND ANALYSIS

Determinants of Demand. The determinants of demand for a particular product in a given market are (1) the price of the product, (2) the price of substitute products, (3) consumers' income, and (4) consumers' tastes.

Of these variables, taste is by far the most ambiguous and elusive. It is difficult to define and impossible to quantify, except by some proxy measurement. Taste is determined by the countless variables that influence human behavior, only a few of which can be manipulated by the firm. Yet the problem of measurement is not so unmanageable as to restrict the market analyst to estimating only the first three variables' effects on sales. On the contrary, there are marketing research and econometric techniques that permit acceptably precise solutions of problems involving all four demand determinants. Even the endogenous variables such as advertising, personal selling, and product variation that influence taste—and ultimately aggregate demand—can be evaluated with some accuracy. In many industries, the sensitivity of the firm's sales to changes in such variables as price can be foretold simply by invoking some simple theorems of microeconomics. Expensive research and mathematical techniques are unnecessary.

Demand exists when potential buyers have both the desire for a product and the ability to purchase it. Consumer desire is awakened by promotion. Ability to purchase is a function of consumer income, product price, and credit terms. The latter two variables are controlled by the firm, within the limits imposed by government regulations and financial institutions.

The relationship between demand and its determinants can be expressed in general form as follows:

$$D = f(P, P_s, I, T), \text{ where} \qquad (11\text{--}1)$$

D = demand (sales)

P = price of good or service

P_s = price of substitute goods or services

I = consumer income, and

T = consumer taste

Econometric analysis of many products indicates that the explicit relationship between sales and its chief determinants is commonly

$$D = \alpha + \beta_1 X_1 + \beta_2 X_2 + \beta_3 X_3, \text{ where} \qquad (11\text{--}2)$$

D = demand (sales)

α = a constant

X_1 = price of the product (P in Equation 11–1)

X_2 = price of substitute products (P_s in Equation 11–1)

X_3 = consumer income (I in Equation 11–1), and

$\beta_1 \ldots _3$ = coefficients (parameters) of variables 1, 2, and 3

The symbols used subscribe to econometric convention, which uses X to symbolize all independent variables and subscripts 1, 2, . . . n to identify each variable. This system of notation is convenient when there are a large number of variables and the selection of representative letters for each could become confusing.

The econometric model represented by Equation 11–2 assumes that tastes remain unchanged; and thus the constant α reflects the effect of taste on the demand for the product. Such an assumption is realistic only for the market and short-run periods. Obviously, in the long run tastes do not remain constant, and the effects of taste would be represented by an independent variable.

The formula for demand given in Equation 11–2 is both linear and additive.[1] Although this model has been used successfully to solve practical marketing problems, it applies only to short-run demand analysis, where significant variations in the independent variables are unusual. Normally, the coefficient of X_1 (product price) would be negative, and the coefficients of X_2 (substitute-product prices) and X_3 (consumer income) would be positive.

Obviously, this equation would be a poor indicator of demand if the values of the variables were to change significantly. For instance, if consumer

---

[1] "Additive" means simply that the terms in the equation are added together.

income (X_3) were to be reduced to zero, the equation would still predict a positive value for demand—obviously incorrectly. Therefore, a multiplicative form of Equation 11–2 is often used for long-run demand analysis, where large variations in the variables could occur. The equation is

$$D = \alpha X_1^{\beta_1} X_2^{\beta_2} X_3^{\beta_3} \tag{11-3}$$

Each symbol represents the same parameter or variable as in Equation 11–2. In this model, however, if income were to be reduced to zero, demand too would drop to zero.

Demand Functions.   The single most important variable in the demand function is product price. While two of the other three variables—the price of substitutes and the level of consumer income—are outside the control of the firm, and the third variable—consumer tastes—is only partially within its control, product price can be directly and rapidly manipulated. Because of the importance of price as a demand determinant, economists generally start with a two-variable demand model, with product price, P, as the dependent variable. In the short run, this model may often be adequate for practical purposes.

To construct a demand function with respect to price, we simply make a schedule of the quantity of units that will be sold at different prices. For example, assume that by observation or experimentation in the marketplace it is estimated that the numbers of units of Product A indicated in Table 11.1 will be sold in a particular market at the prices shown.

Table 11.1   Demand schedule for Product A

Quantity Demanded (Q_D)	Price (P)
0	$100
200	90
400	80
600	70
800	60
1000	50
1200	40
1400	30
1600	20
1800	10
2000	0

The two-variable demand function can easily be portrayed graphically,[2] as in Figure 11.1, which shows the demand for Product A. (Note that the economist's convention of putting price on the vertical axis is again followed, contrary to mathematical convention, which prescribes the Y-axis for the dependent variable.)

As Figure 11.1 readily shows, the relationship between quantity and price is linear. This is a convenient assumption for explanatory purposes and is representative of relationships occasionally found in the marketplace. However, a slightly more realistic model would have a demand function that was curvilinear, and convex to the origin.

The demand schedule illustrates two important marketing phenomena. First, it shows the *threshold*, the price above which no quantity will be demanded.

Second, it illustrates that even at a price of zero, demand is not infinite. From the consumer's point of view, there is no such thing as a truly "free" product. Even the greediest of consumers would eventually discover that the marginal value he would derive from obtaining one more unit of a good would be less than the sacrifice of time and energy required to visit the store.

The demand function just described can be represented mathematically, in general form, as

$Q_D = \alpha - \beta P$, where   (11–4)

Q_D = quantity demanded at price P

α = a constant—that is, the quantity that will be demanded at $P = 0$

β = parameter of demand with respect to price, and

P = price

The explicit form of this equation representing the demand-price relationship shown in Table 11.1 and Figure 11.1 is

$$Q_D = 2000 - 20P$$

This formula, which might have been derived by any of several possible research techniques, tells the marketer how many units of Product A he can expect to sell for each alternative price, if all other marketing variables remain fixed. Obviously, if all other marketing variables are assumed fixed, the constant (α) in Equation 11–4 represents the combined effect of all variables other than price on the demand for the product.

A change in the quantity demanded induced by a change in price is

[2] A two-variable model requires two dimensions and can be portrayed on a single plane. A three-variable model requires three dimensions; hence it requires a three-dimensional drawing. Models containing four or more variables cannot be displayed graphically, only mathematically.

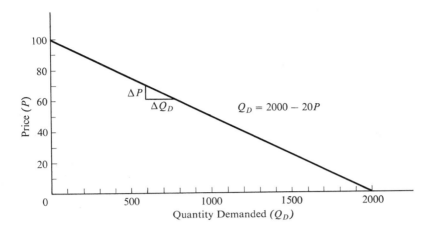

FIGURE 11.1
Demand function for Product A

simply the first derivative, dQ_D/dP, of the demand function. If an interval estimate is being made (that is, if a segment or arc along the curve is being measured), rather than a point estimate, then the change in quantity, Q_D, with respect to price, P, will be the difference quotient, $\Delta Q_D/\Delta P$, of the demand function. This is the reciprocal of the slope of the curve shown in Figure 11.1. It would be identical to the slope if it were not for the economists' insistence on placing the dependent variable, Q_D, on the horizontal axis. (Later we shall see where this practice serves a useful purpose.)

The difference quotient, $\Delta Q_D/\Delta P$, of $Q_D = 2000 - 20P$ is -20. Thus a price increase of \$10 would induce a decline in sales of 200 units. (Although similar, $\Delta Q_D/\Delta P$ is *not* the same as price elasticity, a point that will be discussed shortly.)

The general form of the demand function—that is, the negative slope of the demand curve—is based on utility theory. *Utility* is the ability of a good to satisfy human needs, either biological or psychological. The degree of utility of a good—that is, the extent to which it will satisfy needs—determines its value. The *value* of a good is the quantity of other products and services that people will be willing to exchange for it. In primitive societies, for example, a cow might be valued as equivalent to seven goats, four sheep, one large mud hut, or one wife. However, where money exists as a medium of exchange, the common denominator is the dollar—or its logical equivalent—and values are expressed accordingly. Thus value becomes equal to money price.

The theory of marginal utility contends that the utility value of additional units of the same good decreases as the quantity possessed increases.

In other words, a consumer will be willing to sacrifice less for his nth unit of a particular product than he would be willing to sacrifice for his $(n-1)$th unit. This argument, developed more fully in Chapter 8, is intuitively plausible. If generalized to the market population as a whole, it implies that the quantity of a good demanded will decrease as its price increases and increase as its price decreases.

This inverse relationship means that the slope of the demand curve—that is, the first derivative of the demand function—will always be negative, which is one of the fundamental tenets of microeconomics. Empirical evidence suggests that this is true. No one has yet found an example of demand increasing as a result of an increase in price—at least not an example that satisfies economists.[3] Although there are many time-series examples of sales having gone up during the same period that prices increased, economists reject the implied positive demand curve by invoking their unimpeachable argument that *ceteris paribus* was invariably violated. Logic suggests that they are right. An increase in consumer income, an escalation of a competitor's price, a shift in tastes, or inflation could each cause a net increase in sales despite a simultaneous price increase.

Price Elasticity.   The sensitivity of demand to changes in price is measured by an index called "price elasticity." Short of the negative slope of the demand curve, it is the most important theoretical concept so far as pricing strategy is concerned. In fact, the product's price elasticity is the basis for most price decisions.

Price elasticity is the ratio of the relative change in quantity induced by a relative change in price. The key word here is "relative"; relativity (proportionality) is what makes elasticities comparable, regardless of the quantities and prices involved. Thus the price elasticities of different products, or even of the same goods in different markets, can be compared.

The general equation for price elasticity is

$$\eta_P = \frac{dQ}{dP} \cdot \frac{P}{Q}, \text{ where} \tag{11-5}$$

η_P = price elasticity (the elasticity of demand with respect to price)

Q = quantity demanded, and

P = price

Since quantity demanded is a function of price, a different value of price elasticity will usually result for any given price or quantity. Equation 11–5

[3] If price can be used as an instrument for changing the image of a product, then a price increase can increase sales. This is a change in the product variable, however, not the price variable.

yields a point elasticity—the elasticity at a given price or quantity. Although this is the correct mathematical formulation, a more common method of computing price elasticity is to use an arc elasticity—that is, to make an interval estimate rather than a point estimate. In this form, price elasticity is

$$\eta_P = \frac{\dfrac{\Delta Q}{Q}}{\dfrac{\Delta P}{P}}, \text{ where} \tag{11-6}$$

η_P = price elasticity (the elasticity of demand with respect to price)

ΔQ = change in quantity demanded

Q = quantity demanded

ΔP = change in price, and

P = price

This equation is often seen in the alternate forms $\eta_P = \dfrac{\Delta Q}{Q} \cdot \dfrac{P}{\Delta P}$ and $\eta_P = \dfrac{\Delta Q}{\Delta P} \cdot \dfrac{P}{Q}$, which are arrived at by simple algebraic manipulation.

The values for Q and P can be the quantity and price before a change, the quantity and price after a change, or the mean average of the two.[4] The latter is the most precise and is therefore recommended. Hence, the preferred ways to define Q and P are

$$Q = \frac{Q_0 + Q_1}{2}, \text{ where} \tag{11-7}$$

Q = quantity to be used as base value

Q_0 = quantity demanded before the change in price, and

Q_1 = quantity demanded after the change in price

and

$$P = \frac{P_0 + P_1}{2}, \text{ where} \tag{11-8}$$

P = price to be used as base value

P_0 = price before the change, and

P_1 = price after the change

---

[4] Obviously, in a two-variable demand model every price change must result in a demand change, and vice versa. The only exception would be if the parameter of price were zero. In this case, the quantity demanded would be constant and independent of price. The air we breathe is a good that would have such a demand function.

By substitution, algebraic manipulation, and a bit of cancellation, equations 11–6, 11–7, and 11–8 can be combined to render equations 11–9 and 11–10, which some marketers may find more convenient. Note that ΔQ and ΔP are defined as $Q_1 - Q_0$ and $P_1 - P_0$, respectively.

$$\eta_P = \frac{\Delta Q}{Q_0 + Q_1} \cdot \frac{P_0 + P_1}{\Delta P}, \text{ or} \tag{11-9}$$

$$\eta_P = \frac{Q_1 - Q_0}{Q_0 + Q_1} \cdot \frac{P_0 + P_1}{P_1 - P_0}, \text{ where} \tag{11-10}$$

η_P = price elasticity

Q_0 = quantity demanded before the change in price

Q_1 = quantity demanded after the change in price

P_0 = price before the change, and

P_1 = price after the change

To illustrate, let us assume that in order to determine his national pricing strategy for the coming year a marketing manager needs an estimate of how sensitive his firm's sales are to price. In other words, he needs to know the price elasticity of demand. He elects to experiment in a regional market where sales, Q_0, have kept fairly consistently at a level of 550 units per week, at a price, P_0, of \$200. A new price, P_1, of \$220 is put into effect for two months in the region. At the end of the experiment, with no change having been observed in any other endogenous or exogenous marketing variables, new sales, Q_1, have fallen to 500 units per week.[5] What is the product's price elasticity, η_P?

$$\eta_P = \frac{Q_1 - Q_0}{Q_0 + Q_1} \cdot \frac{P_0 + P_1}{P_1 - P_0} \qquad \text{Given as Equation 11–10}$$

$$\eta_P = \frac{500 - 550}{550 - 500} \cdot \frac{200 + 220}{220 - 200} \qquad \text{By substitution}$$

$$\eta_P = -1 \qquad \text{By arithmetic}$$

When there is a price elasticity of -1—which is called *unitary elasticity* —the quantity demanded will change by the same proportion that price is changed, but in the opposite direction. Thus, if price is increased 10 percent,

[5] If changes in any other endogenous or exogenous marketing variables *had* occurred, the effect of the changes would need to be compensated for before a correct estimate of price elasticity could be made. Market analyses are often thwarted by a competitor who will deliberately change a price or the amount of promotion expenditure when he discovers that a market analysis is in process.

the quantity demanded, hence unit sales, will decrease 10 percent. Since elasticity is a point concept, any empirically determined value of elasticity is accurate only for reasonably small variations in price. If the manager is contemplating a large change in price, the value calculated for the price elasticity of demand must be used with caution.

The difference between a demand curve with constant elasticity and one with varying elasticity can be seen by comparing figures 11.2a and 11.2b.

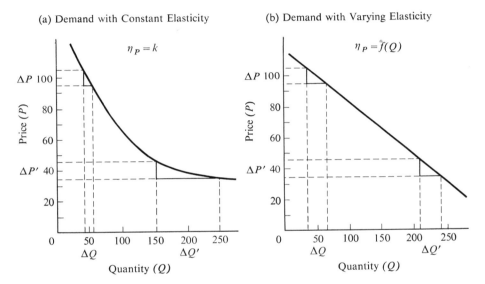

FIGURE 11.2
Demand curves and elasticities

With constant elasticity, $\eta_P = k$, a given percentage change in price will induce a particular percentage change in quantity throughout the range of quantity. In Figure 11.2a, $\eta_P = -2$; hence the proportional change in quantity will always be twice a proportional change in price. A 10-percent change in price, $\Delta P/P$, induces a 20-percent change in quantity, $\Delta Q/Q$, and a 25-percent change in price, $\Delta P'/P$, induces a 50-percent change in quantity, $\Delta Q'/Q'$. This will not be true when the demand function is like that in Figure 11.2b, where elasticity varies with quantity.

Since a line can be constructed by connecting two points, the demand function can be approximated by connecting two points, each representing a price/quantity combination. The marketer can get these points by observing either the quantity demanded for each of two prices over time or the prices in two different markets. The first type of data is called *time-series data,* and the second, *cross-sectional data.* To ensure reliability, both types of data must be corrected for any variations in other independent variables, such as buyer income or the price of substitutes. Normally, however, the marketer will choose a short enough time period or a similar enough market so that exogenous variables will not significantly change and corrections will not be required.

Connecting two points yields a straight line—that is, a linear demand function. Using the two pairs of price/quantity data and Equation 11–9, we can compute its elasticity. This will be an average value, since a linear demand function has a different elasticity for each different quantity. However, within a small range of P, this average value of η_P will generally be acceptable for practical purposes. Given more observations—that is, a larger number of price/quantity pairs—the marketer can construct a more realistic demand curve, which will probably be nonlinear. Arc elasticities can then be computed for selected values of P. If elasticity is constant, then arc elasticity will be the same as point elasticity. If elasticity varies with quantity, then arc elasticity will be the average elasticity between Q_0 and Q_1. If the value for ΔQ $(Q_1 - Q_0)$ is small, the resultant elasticity will be sufficiently precise for most market analyses.[6]

If the demand function is known, point elasticity can be used rather than arc elasticity. For example, suppose that marketing research has revealed a product's demand function as $Q_0 = 22,000 - 100P$. The product is priced at \$18.50; annual sales at this price are 35,000 units. Price elasticity can be found quickly by Equation 11–5, as follows:

$$\eta_P = \frac{dQ}{dP} \cdot \frac{P}{Q} \qquad \text{Given as Equation 11–5}$$

$$\frac{dQ}{dP} = -100 \qquad \begin{array}{l}\text{The derivative of the demand function} \\ Q = 22,000 - 100P.\end{array}$$

$$\eta_P = -100 \cdot \frac{18.50}{35,000} \qquad \text{By substitution}$$

$$\eta_P = -5.3 \qquad \text{By arithmetic}$$

With a price elasticity of -5.3, sales are very sensitive to price. A 10-percent increase in price would reduce sales by 53 percent. This *elastic* demand suggests that the product is being sold in a very competitive market. That is, there are apparently a number of other products that are readily available, comparably priced, and easily substituted for the product.

Once the marketer determines price elasticity, he has acquired con-

[6] Although the slope of the demand curve is not the price elasticity of demand, the price elasticity of demand can be easily found by multiplying the slope of the demand curve by the average value of P divided by the average value of Q.

siderable insight into the nature of his product and the consequences of manipulating its price. For example, if the absolute value[7] of the product's price elasticity is greater than 1, an increase in price will cause a loss of revenue. Conversely, if the absolute value of the product's price elasticity is less than 1, the net result of a price increase will be an increase in revenue, despite the reduction in sales. The latter condition, inelastic demand, suggests that the firm should raise its price, since marginal revenue is positive if price is increased. A price increase would also decrease sales, thereby reducing total costs. Total revenue would increase due to a positive marginal revenue, total costs would decrease, and profit would increase. Hence a price increase would increase profit.

The consequences associated with price decisions under the three conditions of elasticity are summarized in Figure 11.3.

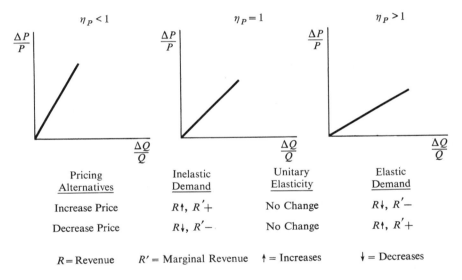

	$\eta_P < 1$ Pricing Alternatives	$\eta_P = 1$ Inelastic Demand	Unitary Elasticity	$\eta_P > 1$ Elastic Demand
Increase Price		$R\uparrow, R'+$	No Change	$R\downarrow, R'-$
Decrease Price		$R\downarrow, R'-$	No Change	$R\uparrow, R'+$

$R =$ Revenue $\quad R' =$ Marginal Revenue $\quad \uparrow =$ Increases $\quad \downarrow =$ Decreases

FIGURE 11.3
Price elasticity: categories and consequences

Cross Elasticity. *Cross elasticity* is the ratio between a relative change in the quantity demanded of a product and a relative change in the price of another good. Like all elasticity formulas, its equation takes the general form of the equation for a product's elasticity of demand with respect to its own price. Specifically,

---

[7] Absolute value is the value of a number without its sign and is depicted in mathematical notation as $|x|$. For example, the absolute values of -5, 2, -44, and 18 are depicted as $|5|$, $|2|$, $|44|$, and $|18|$ and are equal to 5, 2, 44, and 18, respectively.

$$\eta_{A,B} = \frac{\Delta Q_A}{Q_A} \bigg/ \frac{\Delta P_B}{P_B}, \text{ or}$$

$$\eta_{A,B} = \frac{\Delta Q_A}{\Delta P_B} \cdot \frac{P_B}{Q_A}, \text{ where} \qquad\qquad (11\text{--}11)$$

$\eta_{A,B}$ = elasticity of demand of Product A with respect to the price of Product B

ΔQ_A = change in quantity of Product A

Q_A = quantity of Product A

ΔP_B = change in price of Product B, and

P_B = price of Product B

If the cross elasticity is positive, then Product B is a substitute for Product A. Conversely, if the cross elasticity is negative, Product B is a complement of Product A. If the price of Product B is increased and Product A is a substitute for Product B, the demand for Product A will increase. This results directly from the definition of a positive cross elasticity. If the cross elasticity of demand is positive, then an increase in the price of Product B will increase the demand for Product A. Different brands within a product class are illustrative of substitute products. For example, Ford sales would be increased by an increase in the price of Chevrolets. Even different products can have an elastic demand with respect to each other's price, and hence be considered cross-elastic. Aluminum and steel are substitutes for each other in many industries. Manufacturers of containers, such as beverage cans, and producers of automobile parts, such as trim and grillwork, will switch from one material to the other as prices change. Prices do not always have to be made lower or matched to the substitute good's price to induce a shift between products. Often the product's physical properties—such as workability, weight, and appearance, in the case of metals—are sufficiently superior to warrant a change once a certain price threshold is crossed.

A *complementary good* is a product whose increase in sales induces an increase in sales of the primary good. Here the cross elasticity is negative. An increase in the price of the complementary good will decrease the consumption of the primary good. Examples are bread and butter, electricity and electrical appliances, and film and film-processing materials.

The degree of cross elasticity between product pairs varies considerably, depending on the type of good or service. Between grocery products, cross elasticities can be very high. Between consumer durables, they vary from moderate to low. Between goods of unrelated product classes, they can approach zero. Many economists theorize that there is cross elasticity between all goods and services—that every dollar spent on one product is one less dollar available to be spent on another product. For practical purposes, however, a product's sales is considered sensitive only to the prices of other goods or services that are clearly its substitutes or complements.

Often there is a lag in elasticities. That is, a change in the price of a good will not immediately affect the demand for the good or the demand for its substitutes or complements. This delay is caused by the time consumed in communicating the new price to prospective buyers and by the unwillingness of consumers to discard their present possessions until they are worn out or used up. For example, while a reduction in the price of electricity would encourage the purchase of electrical appliances, few households would immediately replace their gas stoves, gas heaters, and gas air conditioners. Although there would be some acceleration in the replacement market (a major factor in appliance sales), there would not be a sudden boom in appliance sales. In the meantime, the sales of electricity would increase slowly as electrical appliances replaced gas appliances.

SUPPLY ANALYSIS

Determinants of Supply. "Everything has its price" may be a philosophy of cynics, but it is also the basis for the operation of a market economy. "What things will be produced is determined by the votes of consumers—not every two years at the polls, but every day in their decisions to purchase this item and not that."[8] The greater their desire for a good, the more consumers are willing to pay for it. When their willingness to pay results in a price that assures the producer(s) an adequate profit, the good will be forthcoming. The higher the price is, the greater will be the quantity of the product that is produced.

A product is initially brought to the marketplace by an entrepreneur who perceives the demand for it, believes that the price will permit an attractive profit, and can either raise the necessary capital in the money market or divert the necessary production and marketing assets from less profitable goods. Once the market is being served, and the existence of a demand for a product has been demonstrated, others will be attracted into the industry, depending on their perception of the profit opportunities, their fear of the established or emerging competition, their ability to command the necessary resources, and the ease of entry as determined by existing patents or government protection.

Ideally, those firms that survive in the market for a good will be those that are most efficient. Competition for customers will tend to drive down prices, hence revenues; and as profit becomes lower, resources will be transferred to more promising industries. The least efficient companies will be the

[8] Paul A. Samuelson, *Economics: An Introductory Analysis,* 7th ed. (New York: McGraw-Hill, 1967), p. 42.

first to see their profits drop below an acceptable level or turn into losses. The latter condition leads eventually to bankruptcy, which is the private sector's instrument for terminating poor management or the production of goods or services no longer desired.

EQUILIBRIUM ANALYSIS

Where the demand curve for a product intersects the supply curve, the market for the good will be in equilibrium. To the left of that point, the price offered by consumers will yield an excessive return to sellers, equal to the positive difference between the demand price and the supply price. As the sellers increase their output to exploit this excessive profit, price will tend to fall toward the equilibrium value. To the right of the equilibrium point, no additional output will be forthcoming. Sellers will be unwilling to offer their products at the prices consumers are willing to pay for the additional units. These conditions are illustrated in Figure 11.4, where Q_E, P_E represents the equilibrium point for a hypothetical good.

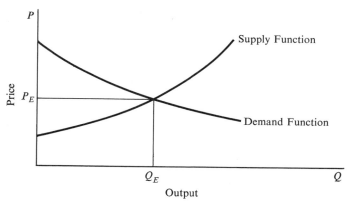

FIGURE 11.4
Supply versus demand

Ideal Versus Real Models. Thus far our discussion has been confined to the ideal pricing model, which assumes an essentially free and competitive economy in which managers make rational decisions and enjoy a clear understanding of the demand function confronting their industry, the competitive situation, and their own production function. This is seldom the way things are in reality, although economic models do serve to explain certain phenomena experienced in the real world.

Marketers do make mistakes—sometimes very bad ones—in estimating the demand for their product. Two classical examples mentioned earlier are Ford's Edsel automobile and General Dynamics' jet airliners. When this happens, the market must be "cleared" by adjusting the sellers' price to match the price prescribed by the demand function for that particular output. This is a painful and often expensive chore, as both Ford Motors and General Dynamics discovered. However, the alternative is to inventory the good, which would result in an even more depressing profit-and-loss statement.

The firm can also err by incorrectly estimating its production function, thus understating or overstating the cost associated with a given level of output. This could result in the selection of a suboptimum price/output combination. The consequence of that mistake would be a loss in the form of either absolute dollars (if profit was negative) or unrealized profits.

An exogenous event that can throw the system temporarily out of equilibrium is the shifting of the demand curve. The public's disenchantment with a fashion or style, its sudden preference for another product—perhaps an unforeseeable innovation—or a change in cultural values can each induce a disastrous or favorable movement in the demand curve. Of course, the objective of the two promotional instruments, advertising and personal selling, is to cause such a shift in favor of the firm.

Although a substantial body of economic theory argues that the competitive model is the one most suited to the perfect allocation of resources, few firms actually operate in such an environment. Price flexibility, an ingredient essential to a competitive economy, is often hampered by private and public restraints—by monopolies, government regulation, business conspiracies (generally illegal), and enforced price leadership. These restraints may decay in the long run, when substitute products may be developed or new competitors may enter the industry. Some barriers to entry, however, such as the government-authorized monopolies found in the utilities field, continue to protect the seller from price competition. A government-regulated price, or fear of attracting competitors, often serves to prevent the monopolistic firm from setting its price as high as it otherwise might.

Market equilibrium results when the quantity supplied equals the quantity demanded. In notational form, this condition is known as the *market-clearing equation*, because it states the condition at which demand will be satisfied and all output will be sold. Equilibrium exists when

$$Q_S = Q_P, \text{ where} \tag{11–12}$$

Q_S = quantity supplied, and

Q_P = quantity demanded

By substituting the demand function for Q_D and the supply function for Q_S, we can determine the price and output at the equilibrium point. Thus, if

$Q_S = 30P - 500$, and $Q_D = 2000 - 20P$,

$$Q_S = Q_D$$ Given as the equilibrium condition
$$30P - 500 = 2000 - 20P$$ By substitution
$$50P = 2500$$ By algebraic manipulation
$$P = 50$$ By arithmetic

Having solved for price, P, we can compute the equilibrium quantity by substituting the equilibrium value of P in either the demand or the supply function. Since Q_S equals Q_D at equilibrium, one solution will provide the answers for both supply and demand:

$$Q_D = 2000 - 20P$$ Given
$$Q_D = 2000 - 20(50)$$ By substitution
$$Q_D = 1000$$ By arithmetic
$$Q_S = Q_D$$ Given
$$Q_S = 1000$$ By substitution

The problem we have just solved mathematically can be solved graphically by imposing the supply curve on the demand curve, as in Figure 11.5.

Data Analysis. In observing data in the marketplace, the analyst must remember that what he sees is a point (a price-quantity combination) that lies on either or both the demand and supply curves. If the market is cleared —that is, if all the output is purchased and there is no residual demand at

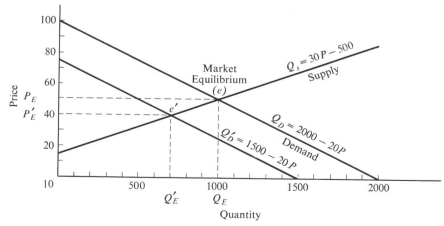

FIGURE 11.5
Demand versus supply

the market price—then the analyst is observing the intersection of the two curves. This intersection is the market equilibrium point (see Figure 11.5). If both the demand and supply functions remain constant, then this point will remain fixed and the analyst will have no way of determining the slope of either curve from the observable data.

For example, if the producers are happy to provide 1000 units at a price of $50 and the consumers are content to buy 1000 units at a price of $50 (but will not pay a higher price to get any more units), then the price-quantity point will remain fixed. Under these conditions, the market analyst would not have enough data to estimate the quantity that producers would supply at a price of $80, or the price consumers would pay if the quantity produced were limited to 500 units. In short, neither the supply equation nor the demand equation could be written.

However, if one of the curves should shift, it will inscribe a series of two or more points along the other curve, and that function, which has remained unchanged, can then be plotted (at least within the range of observable intersections). For instance, let us assume that the demand function for a particular product changes to $Q'_D = 1500 - 20P$, thus shifting the demand curve downward and to the left. In Figure 11.5, this would be represented by Q_D changing to Q'_D, due to buyers no longer being willing to pay the previous prices for the quantities shown along Q_D. The supply function has remained unchanged and a new equilibrium point, e', has been established. As both e and e' are on the same supply curve, Q_s, the equation for Q_s can be specified, for if two points on a straight line are known, the line itself can easily be constructed. Obviously, this solution assumes linearity. Linearity is usually a safe and practical assumption—though not always a precise one—within the range of the two intersections. Conversely, if the demand function is not disturbed but the supply curve shifts—perhaps new technology changes the industry's cost function—then the demand curve can be specified. Once the demand curve—that is, the equation for Q_D—is known, price elasticity, η_P, can be computed. The analyst simply takes the first derivative of the demand function. This is extremely valuable to the marketer, as it tells him how sensitive sales are to changes in price.

If the analyst is not sure which curve has shifted—or worse yet, if both curves shift—then the observed data will not permit a ready computation of either the supply or the demand function. We shall deal further with this dilemma in Chapter 26. For now, it is only necessary to warn the reader that he cannot simply observe some price/quantity pairs in the market and then plot a demand or supply curve unless he knows something of the conditions under which the prices and sales were determined.

CHAPTER 12

Price and Income

PROPERTIES OF PRICE

Who Controls Price.   The American economy—which is representative of those found in most Western nations—normally leaves pricing decisions to the managers of firms in the private sector, except in government-regulated industries. Both federal and state governments may regulate price. However, even companies that compete in regulated industries enjoy some price flexibility, since they may petition the regulatory agencies for a specific price change. In many cases, firms may sell at a price below that established by the government. In a few cases, such as California barber shops, regulated firms may charge any price they desire as long as it is equal to or greater than the price established by the government.

In some industries—notably industrial goods, securities, and residential construction—the buyer may have a significant effect on price by bidding for the good, directly or indirectly. The more common practice, however, is for the buyer to accept or reject the product on the basis of the price set by the supplier. If the price has been fixed too high for the quantity of goods manufactured, the producer will have to either lower the price in order to attract more buyers or else accumulate inventory, a practice that is extremely unprofitable.

If the pricing problems were confined to selecting a price that would bring sales into balance with output—or, stated differently, if it were a matter of setting the level of output to match consumption at a fixed price—the solution would be straightforward. Unfortunately, the problem is often more subtle. Changes in price do not only affect sales; they may also attract unwanted competition, precipitate government intervention, trigger retaliatory acts by competitors, encourage higher wage demands, alienate customers, and, occasionally, incur the wrath of the President of the United States.[1]

Although price changes do not always cause social or political reactions, they invariably have economic consequences. Price theory is the sole subject of numerous textbooks, and the serious student of marketing is well advised to address himself to a good one, such as any of those cited in the supplementary readings following this section. We shall review the basic concepts of price theory here, to lay a foundation for understanding the pricing strategies covered in Chapter 13.

Real Versus Published Price.   To define price may seem superfluous. However, the construction of a real price is often complex, and tagged, or published, "prices" may have little to do with the prices actually paid by the buyer or expected by the seller. *Price* is defined as the net amount of money, or its equivalent in goods or services, accepted in exchange for a product. If no exchange transpires, then price would be the net amount asked by the seller or offered by the buyer. Obviously, if the two prices do not coincide, there will be no transaction.

The real, or true, price may be thought of as the quoted or billed price adjusted for any discounts or special considerations not integral to the product itself. The following is a fairly inclusive list of items that must be deducted from the published price in order to determine the true price.

1. Cash discounts
2. Trade discounts
3. Quantity discounts
4. Seasonal discounts
5. Price premiums
6. Credit terms
7. Merchandise bonuses
8. Advertising allowances
9. Freight allowances
10. Price guarantees
11. Free services
12. Rebates

Discounts are a convenient means of adjusting price in a market or short-run period. They are frequently used in industries where demand is volatile and producers engage actively in price competition. For example, in

[1] The office of the President frequently brings pressure to bear on major producers to discourage "unjustified"—that is, inflationary—price hikes. The classical example is the network-television appearance of President John F. Kennedy in 1961, in which he castigated Roger Blough, president of the U. S. Steel Corporation, for the firm's increase in steel prices. Following the President's address, the steel price increases were rescinded.

the market for construction supplies—such as lumber, plumbing fixtures, shingles, and nails—the price lists may remain fixed, but the discounts granted to contractors vary frequently, sometimes changing from week to week.

Cash discounts, or reductions in price when the buyer pays in cash, are often used as an incentive to encourage customers to pay their bills promptly. They are also commonly used by middlemen in their dealings with manufacturers and other commercial buyers.

Trade discounts, sometimes called *functional discounts,* are associated with the buyer's function within the distribution system. For example, a manufacturer may prepare a retail list price for its goods and then offer a series of graduated discounts for retailers and wholesalers. The size of the trade discount is proportional to the costs incurred in reselling the product.

Retailers have the highest operating cost per unit of sales; hence they enjoy the largest trade discounts on the product's retail price. A typical discount to a retailer is 20 to 40 percent of the retail list price. Wholesalers typically receive a 25- to 55-percent discount, but since they must in turn offer a 20- to 40-percent discount to the retailer, their "real" discount is 5 to 15 percent. Thus the price *received* by the manufacturer would be 60 to 80 percent of the retail list price when it sells directly to a retailer and 45 to 75 percent of the retail list price when it sells to a wholesaler.

Margins earned by agent middlemen—who do not take title to, and usually do not take physical possession of, the goods—are usually viewed as commissions rather than price discounts. Such commissions are incorporated into the marketing-cost function. This is legitimate, since the agent middlemen perform a sales job that normally would be performed, hence paid for, by the manufacturer.

Quantity discounts are reductions in price based on the size of the purchase. The quantity discount is one of the few legally acceptable methods for discriminating between buyers at the same level of distribution. Such discounts are justified on the basis of economies of scale associated with output and order handling. As discussed in Chapter 4, the cumulative average unit cost of labor tends to decline with increases in the volume of output. These economies of scale are especially noticeable in the mechanics of order processing and shipping; hence they justify the discounts associated with the size of the purchase. Quantity discounts are almost universally used at the wholesale level and in the pricing of industrial goods. They are also common in the retail selling of consumer goods.

Seasonal discounts are price adjustments made to accommodate changes in output or demand that vary with the time of year. Their use is illustrative of the basic functions of price, namely the balancing of supply and demand. For example, the demand for the services of winter resorts is much greater in January than in July, yet the output of these services remains essentially constant throughout the year. Given high fixed costs and the inability of the firm to reallocate its resources during the summer months, it is often profitable to sustain consumption by lowering price during the off-season. Here again, marginal analysis—the economist's method of accounting—is the correct basis for pricing decisions.

Seasonal discounts are not limited to service industries. They are often offered by manufacturers to employ idle (unused) production capacity resulting from a seasonal slump in the firm's basic product line. Retailers also employ seasonal discounts, in order to clear residual inventories of seasonal merchandise. This frees both shelf space and capital for use with in-season goods. Prices for clothes, particularly women's fashions, and sporting goods are adjusted this way. Seasonal discounts are also offered on automobiles, in order to eliminate stocks of outgoing models.

Price premiums are the converse of discounts and are often required by the seller when demand exceeds supply at the established price. This practice is typical of the money market, where interest rates may be held constant but a bonus payment—expressed as a percentage of the loan amount—is required for the issuance of a loan. This extra fee, or price premium, is very flexible and may be varied daily.

Credit terms can also serve as an instrument of price manipulation. Credit concessions can be very important when large sums of money are involved. A delay in payment is an authentic reduction in price. (The reader will recognize the truth of this statement from the discussion of present-value analysis in Chapter 5). The obligation to pay a sum of money 90 days hence is clearly a lesser obligation than having to pay the same sum today. Not only is there the matter of the interest that could be earned—or paid—during the interim period, but there is also the question of the availability of capital. This is particularly important in retailing, where many firms are undercapitalized and must pay a high interest rate on borrowed money or factor their accounts.[2] If credit terms are particularly generous and the inventory-turnover period very short (as it is with Christmas trees, perishable foods, and newspapers), the retailer can virtually operate with the manufacturer's or wholesaler's capital.

The negotiation of credit is often difficult or impossible. Cash-on-delivery payments are imperative in markets where marginal firms are common; they are traditional in certain industries where oligopolistic producers can ensure that such practices are maintained. In the automobile and general-aviation industries, both oligopolistic in structure, deferred-payment plans must be arranged independently by the dealer, since the manufacturers provide no such service. Lending institutions play a vital role in these markets,

---

[2] An account is "factored" when it is sold to a lending institution at a discount. For instance, a firm that is owed $5000 by another firm might sell this account receivable to a bank or factoring house for $4500 in cash.

where they both floor the merchandise[3] for the retailer and provide financing for the ultimate consumer.

Merchandise bonuses take several forms. One is oversupply—the delivery of units in excess of the number ordered and paid for at the agreed-on price. Oversupply, usually a fixed percentage of the quantity of goods ordered, is common in foreign trade. It is used both as a price discount and as a method of compensating the buyer for damage to goods suffered in transit or for the delivery of occasional units that do not meet its specifications. This device is also used at the retail level, particularly with convenience goods, where an extra unit or quantity may be included at no additional cost when the consumer purchases a minimum number of units. A slight variation of this method of price adjustment is to offer an additional unit at a dramatically reduced price when the buyer purchases the first unit, or several units, at the regular price. This practice is frequent in the sale of toothpaste, soft drinks, and automobile tires.

Another form of merchandise bonus is the offering of a complementary good at no additional cost when the original item is purchased at the regular price. This tactic works both ways—especially at the middleman level. A retailer may be required to accept a quantity of a less desirable or unwanted product in order to get delivery of a desired, but scarce, good. It is common in the automobile industry for manufacturers to require dealers to accept a number of unwanted models in order to receive the quantity desired of a very popular one. Manufacturers use this technique, rather than increasing the price of the popular model or decreasing the price of the unwanted type, in order to ensure that their inventory of all models will be cleared. The retailer, in turn, will be unlikely to give discounts on the popular model but will discount the less desirable car. By making an acceptable average profit, he ensures a satisfactory total profit.

A third form of merchandise bonus, found at the retail level, is the trading stamp. Although this device was used prior to World War II, it did not become really popular until the mid-1960's, when many retailers, especially those selling convenience goods, began subscribing to one of the several major trading-stamp services. The stamps are purchased by the retailers, who distribute them to their customers according to the cash value of the customers' purchases. The stamps are accumulated by the consumer, who may receive the same brand of stamps from numerous retail outlets. Eventually the stamps are redeemed for either cash or merchandise, usually consumer durables, at outlets provided by the stamp producer. A similar device is the use of coupons, which are normally enclosed with the product. They are usually associated with a single branded item—often a convenience good such as

---

[3] A retailer is said to "floor merchandise" when it uses cash provided by a lending institution to place merchandise on its showroom floor. When this practice is used, the lending institution takes title to the goods until they are resold to the consumer.

cigarettes—and are redeemed for merchandise selected from a mail-order catalogue.

Coupons and trading stamps may be considered a form of price adjustment, especially when they are redeemed for cash. However, they may also be viewed as promotional instruments. Such classification is primarily a matter of convenience or accounting practice and makes little difference in the computation of optimum price and output.

Advertising allowances serve to adjust middlemen's prices and provide an incentive to promote the manufacturer's goods, especially at the retail level. Whether advertising allowances are primarily used as an instrument of price adjustment is open to dispute. How much of an advertising allowance should be viewed as a price reduction and how much should be charged to the promotional budget as an advertising expense? Or, if the product and promotional assistance are viewed as a total package by the middleman, should advertising allowances be considered an aspect of the product? There is no universal answer. However, the Department of Justice, in dealing with price-discrimination cases under the Robinson-Patman Act, considers advertising allowances as adjustments in price and insists that discrimination in the granting of these allowances is equivalent to discriminatory pricing. Advertising allowances are common among branded goods; manufacturers frequently absorb a portion of the advertising costs incurred by the store in promoting the manufacturer's goods.

Freight allowances serve to adjust the delivered price of goods. Although the f.o.b. price[4] remains the same, the cost ultimately incurred by the buyer in getting the product into his home or factory is reduced by the amount of the freight allowance. These allowances are significant in the purchase of goods with a large size-to-cost ratio, especially if they are processed or manufactured a long distance from the delivery point. Freight allowances are commonly used by retail mail-order houses in order to make their delivered prices competitive with those of local dealers. They are also favored by sellers of industrial goods, particularly raw materials. However, federal antitrust laws have diminished the use of this form of price adjustment. Freight allowances were once notorious devices for the willful destruction of competition through price discrimination.

Price guarantees manipulate price to the extent that they ensure the seller a minimum price—or, in some cases, a minimum gross profit margin. The most conspicuous example of price guarantees occurs in agriculture, where the federal government guarantees farmers a minimum price on certain commodities. However, the practice is not confined to the public sector. In the petroleum industry, for example, wholesalers usually guarantee gas-station operators a minimum markup on their gasoline regardless of the retail

[4] The freight-on-board price, which is the price of the good delivered at the seller's factory or warehouse.

price. This protects the retailer and also assures the wholesaler a market for its products in the event of a local price war—a common phenomenon in the sale of motor fuel.

Free services are special services provided at no extra charge to the buyer in return for the purchase of a quantity of goods. They are generally services, such as training, maintenance, warranty service, and promotional assistance, that the buyer would have to obtain at his own expense if they were not provided free by the seller. Sellers of aircraft and industrial equipment, for example, often provide training programs for the buyer's operating personnel. Producers of complicated consumer goods, such as television sets and automatic washing machines, usually provide service centers or pay for corrective maintenance of their products after they have been resold by retailers. Convenience-good producers and distributors often provide advertising displays, train retailers' salesmen, and do on-site personal selling and demonstrations, all at no cost to the retailer.

These services, especially if necessary to the buyer, are an effective form of price reduction and they are viewed as such by the federal authorities charged with the enforcement of price-discrimination statutes. The firm providing the services, of course, may view them as part of the product package or as instruments of promotion. Again, this is a matter of individual judgment and will depend on the circumstances of the particular firm, its accounting system, and the decision at hand. Regardless of the classification used for accounting or decision purposes, however, the marketer must remember that a free service may be construed by both the government and the competition as a manipulation of price. Unless the firm is very careful not to discriminate between its customers in the performing of such services, restraint-of-trade laws may severely constrain the offering of services on a no-cost basis.

Rebates are a retroactive form of price adjustment. They are often paid by manufacturers or middlemen at the end of an accounting period if the buyer has purchased a predetermined quantity of goods during that period. Rebates are commonly used as an incentive to encourage dealers to meet a certain sales quota. They are seldom employed at the retail level, except by consumer cooperatives, which return a portion of their annual earnings to the buyers on the basis of the volume of their purchases during the preceding year.

INCOME

Although income and price are often regarded as independent determinants of demand, an understanding of how income affects demand is essential to an understanding of the relationship between price and demand. Income is one of the classical determinants of demand. It is a highly significant variable, but one that is generally exogenous to the firm and its industry. Even the few exceptions whose expenditures perceptibly influence national income —such as the General Motors Corporation, the steel industry, and the railroad industry—cannot consider income as a marketing variable open to manipulation. Nevertheless, it should be taken into account in estimating and forecasting demand.

The sensitivity of demand to income is expressed as *income elasticity*— the ratio between a relative change in quantity demanded and a relative change in income. The general equation for income elasticity is essentially the same as the general equation for other elasticities.[5] Thus,

$$\eta_I = \frac{\frac{\Delta Q}{Q}}{\frac{\Delta I}{I}}, \text{ where} \tag{12-1}$$

η_I = income elasticity

ΔQ = change in quantity demanded

Q = quantity demanded

ΔI = change in income, and

I = income

To illustrate, assume that disposable personal income, I, in one local market was originally \$800,000,000 and that this market produced sales of \$20,000 per year, Q_0, of a particular product. When income increased to \$850,000,000, I_1, sales increased to \$20,700, Q_1. If other variables remained constant (or if the data were adjusted to compensate for changes in these variables), the sensitivity of sales to income could be computed as follows:

$$\eta_I = \frac{\frac{\Delta Q}{Q}}{\frac{\Delta I}{I}} \qquad \text{Given as Equation 12-1}$$

$$\eta_I = \frac{\frac{700}{20,350}}{\frac{50,000,000}{825,000,000}} \qquad \text{By substitution}[6]$$

$$\eta_I = .56 \qquad \text{By arithmetic}$$

[5] Again we shall deal with arc elasticities, although the same reasoning would apply if we used point elasticities.

[6] The values used for both Q and I, here and in the following examples, are average values similar to those used for the price elasticity equation (11-10).

This is an income elasticity typical of essential goods such as food and housing. It simply means that the demand for the good will increase 56 percent as much as income increases, or will decline with income by the same proportion. As a rule, luxury goods tend to be income-elastic, whereas essential goods tend to be income-inelastic, once an income threshold has been crossed. For example, food purchases are relatively inelastic once the household's income is adequate to provide satisfying meals. However, food purchases would be very elastic for a poverty-level household with hungry children.

Income elasticity for most products varies as income varies. The only major product classes that come anywhere close to being exceptions are housing and clothing, whose income elasticities remain fairly constant through a moderate range of incomes.

Income elasticities were generalized by product class as far back as 1857, when a British theologian and economist named Ernst Engel stated his "first law of consumption." His four "laws," which postulate the relationship between changes in consumption and changes in income, are worth reviewing, since they are as applicable to today's marketplace as they were to that of the mid-nineteenth century. Apparently the essential nature of consumers has not drastically altered during the last one hundred years. The consumer's basic needs have remained relatively constant, and only the variety of goods and services designed to satisfy those needs has been increased or modified.

Engel's "laws"[7] may be stated as:

1. The greater the income, the smaller the relative percentage of outlay for subsistence.
2. The percentage of outlay for clothing is approximately the same whatever the income.
3. The percentage of outlay for housing is invariably the same whatever the income.
4. The percentage of outlay for "sundries" becomes greater as income increases.

In a recent study, Richard Millican tested the validity of these laws by computing the coefficients of income elasticity for various types of consumption expenditures at a series of income levels. He used data supplied by the Bureau of Labor Statistics of the Department of Labor. The results are shown in Table 12.1.

[7] Adapted from Carroll D. Wright, *Sixth Annual Report of the Bureau of Statistics of Labor* (Boston: State Printers, 1875), p. 441, as quoted by Richard D. Millican, "A Re-examination of Engel's Laws Using BLS Data (1960–61)," Part I, *Journal of Marketing,* Vol. 31, No. 4 (October 1967), pp. 18–21.

Table 12.1   Income elasticities of various expenditure categories

	Income Level (in dollars)						
Expenditure Category	1513 to 2508	2508 to 3516	3516 to 4506	4506 to 5495	5495 to 6710	6710 to 8573	8573 to 11724
Food eaten at home	1.20	0.62	0.70	0.82	0.55	0.51	0.35
Food eaten away from home	1.60	0.90	0.32	—*	1.50	1.32	1.11
Tobacco	1.25	1.00	0.59	0.55	0.55	0.32	—*
Alcoholic beverages	1.08	1.82	1.05	1.40	1.23	0.90	0.86
Housing	0.53	0.67	0.56	0.54	0.47	0.51	0.70
Clothing	1.70	1.35	1.00	0.82	1.10	1.10	1.03
Personal care	1.15	0.82	0.44	0.50	0.55	0.76	0.60
Medical care	0.90	0.62	0.20	0.90	0.86	0.64	0.67
Recreation	1.60	0.78	1.15	0.55	1.64	1.05	1.19
Reading	0.73	2.08	0.70	0.55	1.08	0.64	0.83
Education	1.70	2.07	0.66	2.30	2.30	1.57	3.54
Transportation	1.90	2.75	1.50	0.80	0.82	0.95	0.86

*No change in level of expenditure.

SOURCE: Adapted from *Contrast in Spending by Urban Families,* Bureau of Labor Statistics, U. S. Department of Labor, Report No. 238–8, February 1965, p. 1409; and Richard D. Millican, "A Re-examination of Engel's Laws Using BLS Data (1960–61)," Part I, *Journal of Marketing,* Vol. 31, No. 4 (October 1967), p. 19 (reprinted from the *Journal of Marketing,* published by the American Marketing Association).

The first law is confirmed by the inelasticity ($\eta_I < 1$) of purchases of food eaten at home, at all but the acute poverty level. Poor urban families may be undernourished and thus disposed to put a large portion of any additional increment of income into food. Food eaten away from home is excluded from Millican's analysis of Engel's first law, since a considerable portion of this expenditure is for convenience, service, and recreation, none of which are essentials. In addition, food consumed away from home was considerably less significant when Engel's first law was formulated.

The percentage of income spent for clothing remains relatively constant, as a function of income, although there is slightly more elasticity ($\eta_I > 1$) at the poverty and subsistence levels. This tends to confirm Engel's second law of consumption, if the high elasticities identified with the lowest income groups are rationalized as reflecting the underclothed state of the poverty class. The slightly elastic values above the $5495 family-income level may be indicative of middle-class women's eagerness to participate in the fashion cycle—a point not overlooked by clothing manufacturers and retailers in this market.

The demand for housing is clearly inelastic, and the income elasticity of this category remains essentially constant at all levels of income in the range of the study. A 10-percent increase in household income will result in an increase of about 6 percent in the family's expenditures on housing, whether the family's income level is $2000 or $10,000.

Engel's fourth law states that expenditures for "sundry" items are income-elastic. (This class included personal care, medical care, recreation, reading, education, and transportation.) However, the elasticity coefficients in Table 12.1 do not support this contention with any consistency. The proportional increases in expenditures are not always higher than the proportional increases in income that induce them. In fact, 25 of the 42 observations in these categories show an inelastic demand with respect to income ($\eta_I < 1$). Millican suggests that this partial confirmation (27 observations are elastic) can be explained by the high proportion of discretionary income that is now left after the family has provided for food, clothing, and housing. When the laws were formulated in the nineteenth century, the typical household spent most of its income for these three essentials. At the present average level of income, a family can spend about 35 percent of its after-taxes income on sundry goods and services.[8] Hence, immediate desires for nonessentials are easily gratified, and additional increments of income are often diverted into savings, investments, insurance, charity, and so on.

Threshold and Perception.   In analyzing the influence of income on sales, the marketer must recognize that the income elasticity for most goods and services is fairly constant only within a certain range of income. The points at which there are abrupt changes in elasticity are called thresholds. For example, food purchases are very elastic until an income threshold of $2500 per year is reached. At this level of income, the family is no longer going hungry and begins to divert a larger portion of its marginal income to other goods and services. The income elasticity of tobacco is similar to that of food, which suggests that it, too, is perceived as an essential. The demand for tobacco is income-elastic until an income threshold of $3500 per year is crossed, an income level that presumably allows satiation of the consumer's desire for tobacco.

These inelasticities indicate that the firm selling groceries or cigarettes may expect little difference in sales between a market area of middle-class households and one of affluent families, assuming their populations are comparable. In fact, the retailer, confronted with the higher cost of property in more affluent neighborhoods, might find it less profitable to locate in such

---

[8] Millican, *op. cit.,* p. 20.

areas, unless it could increase prices. If the demand for the retailer's goods is elastic with respect to price, a price increase may simply reduce profit further. Here, an alternative might be to differentiate the product sold in wealthy neighborhoods by including services not offered in lower-income districts, such as home delivery and charge accounts. These services would impart an added quality to the goods, thereby shifting the demand curve (sales vs. price) upward and allowing the retailer to charge a higher price.

The identification of threshold points, and the estimation of the elasticities on both sides of these points, are important to the marketer in evaluating markets in terms of their present potential and their growth possibilities. The example just given of the two retail markets is illustrative of the first task. The evaluation of growth potential also involves income elasticities, because the sensitivity of sales to future rises in income is estimated by calculating the product's income elasticity in the past.

The consumer's perception of future income appears more relevant than his present money income with respect to present purchases. This is apparently true for both the household and the enterprise. Income often fluctuates in the short run, especially for the firm. The household also can experience deviations from its normal income stream. Thus consumption will depend largely on the decision-maker's perception of future income.[9] In evaluating the effects of income changes, the income of the household as a whole should be used. This recommendation is supported by many economists who believe that the family, not the individual, is the basic consumer unit outside the industrial market.[10] Consumption is much more sensitive to changes in income that are perceived as permanent—such as an increase in salary resulting from a promotion—than to changes that are viewed as unique deviations from the norm, such as overtime pay or an inheritance. The perception of future income streams as a basis for present consumption explains the willingness of millions of buyers to finance current purchases by borrowing or through installment plans. This is also why credit is often an important variable in the marketing mix. Credit plans allow the seller to exploit a demand based on future—and presumably higher—consumer or company incomes.

The subject of perception leads us back to the realm of psychology. The individual's environment greatly influences his perception of his future welfare, including income. The introduction of uncertainty by such events as war, recession, labor unrest, and political strife encourages people to discount

[9] Permanent income, not transitory income, appears to dominate purchase decisions. For a fuller development of this thesis, the student may refer to the discussions of the "permanent income hypothesis" in George J. Stigler, *The Theory of Price*, 3rd ed. (New York: Macmillan, 1966), p. 35, and in Milton Friedman, *A Theory of the Consumption Function* (Princeton, N. J.: Princeton University Press, 1957).

[10] Stigler, *op. cit.*, p. 21.

future revenues and to place greater emphasis on savings. Both effects serve to reduce present expenditures, which in turn can accelerate negative trends in an economy, such as downward movements in the business cycle. The net result can be a leftward movement of the demand curve, with output being sustained only by a reduction in price.

Income and Product Class.   The great influence of income level and income elasticity on the consumption of different goods suggests the examination of certain product classes. Such an approach provides insight into both the sensitivity of sales to income for important product classes and the problems confronting the market analyst in the gathering and analysis of data.[11]

Food is the most important product class throughout the world. This is especially true in underdeveloped areas, where the vast majority of the earth's population lives. In markets such as India, China, Africa, and Latin America, food is very income-elastic. Even a slight improvement in per capita income has an immediate effect on the demand for foodstuffs. In the industrialized nations, most households still spend more on food than on any other product class, but the majority of families are above the subsistence level and have crossed the threshold to where food sales are inelastic with respect to income. This explains why many U. S. corporations dealing primarily in agricultural products are diversifying into markets that are income-elastic. Their present market can expand only to the extent that population itself expands. Increasing affluence is of little benefit to the firm when its products' income elasticity is low.

Tobacco and alcoholic beverages are relatively insensitive to changes in income once the relevant income thresholds—$3500 and $6700, respectively—are crossed. They then become income-elastic. This fact is intuitively acceptable, since most people will agree that once a person has satisfied his desire for tobacco and liquor there is little purpose in his buying more out of additional increments of income. A man can smoke only so many cigarettes, drink only so much beer, and serve his friends only so many martinis, regardless of how appealing these products might be.

Housing is very inelastic with respect to income. Families appear to spend a relatively fixed percentage of their income on this product class, regardless of their financial position. Presumably, lumber, shingles, nails, and plumbing fixtures are also income-inelastic, since the demand for these goods is a derived demand, depending primarily on the consumption of housing. A subcategory of housing, household furnishings, appears to be more elastic, with one study indicating an income elasticity of 1.27.[12]

Clothing has a nearly unitary income elasticity ($\eta_I = 1$), once the

[11] The following discussion draws generously on the work of Richard D. Millican.
[12] See Richard Stone, *The Role of Measurement in Economics* (New York: Cambridge University Press, 1951).

$3500 threshold is crossed. Thus the size of a clothing market should be directly proportional to the income of the population. Similarly, the market's growth rate should be nearly identical to the rate of increase anticipated for income. This is one reason why clothing marketers pay considerable attention to the teenage market, where both aggregate income and per capita disposable income are increasing more rapidly than they are for other market populations.

Cosmetics, haircuts, beautician services, and other personal-care goods and services have an inelastic demand, except among households in the poverty class. Since most consumers have enough money to satisfy such needs, a rise in income does not induce a proportionately higher level of expenditure.

Medical care illustrates a problem in data analysis. Information on personal medical-care expenditures is available, but its usefulness in computing consumption and elasticity is questionable. Insurance programs—which are often paid for in whole or in part by employers or the government—and charity account for a substantial portion of medical-care expenditures. Thus individuals may consume large amounts of medical care but show little or no expenditures for such services on their income-tax statements, in consumer diaries, or on survey questionnaires.

Education is another area where a data problem often confronts marketers. Consumer expenditures do not match consumption, even with respect to private institutions. Tax-supported schools, contributions by individuals and institutions, and grant-in-aid programs often relieve consumers of most or all of the direct outlays for education. The fact that costs, hence prices, for education have escalated faster than income compounds the problem, especially in time-series analyses. Political changes—particularly the increased assistance of the federal government and certain states in financing higher education—complicates the situation even further.

The demand for recreation is generally elastic, as one might expect with a luxury good. Thus the increasing affluence experienced since World War II by the populations of the industrialized nations has provided booming markets for the producers and distributors of such items as sporting goods, toys, games, and pleasure boats and for the operators of resorts and related enterprises. Firms dissatisfied with the growth in their primary field—often due to its income-inelastic demand—have frequently chosen to exploit the postwar boom in the recreational market. An example is the Beatrice Food Corporation. With annual sales of a billion dollars in agricultural products, the company in 1967 began diversifying into the field of recreational vehicles and skis.

The demand for transportation is elastic at lower levels of income but becomes inelastic once a threshold of $4500 is crossed. This suggests real growth potential in markets where the average income is below $4500 but is increasing. Just such a potential for growth was apparently perceived by the

American automobile industry in both the youth market and the Western European markets. This judgment has resulted in extensive attention being given to teenagers in promotion and product variation, as well as the establishment, acquisition, and expansion of manufacturing and marketing operations in England and on the Continent. The populations of these markets are growing in size, and the level of per capita income, although increasing steadily, is still within an income range where the demand for automobiles is elastic.

Industrial products, particularly capital goods, are an index of a country's economic health. Sales of these products, especially of machine tools, indicate the degree of confidence that manufacturers have in the future market growth. Thus industrial goods tend to be elastic with respect to expectations of future income. Anticipation of a sharp increase in demand for the firm's output—hence an increase in its revenues—almost invariably precipitates heavy capital spending. On the other hand, an expectation of a decline in demand encourages managers to curtail or cancel capital investment.

Measurement of Income. Income is measured by several yardsticks. The correct one for a particular analysis is the one most closely identified with the market being studied. For example, either total disposable personal income or per capita disposable personal income would be an appropriate choice for an analysis of the consumer-goods market. Corporate profits would be a reasonable yardstick in measuring the market for industrial goods, whereas governmental appropriations would be the relevant indicator of market size in the field of government contracting.

A wealth of income data for the United States is readily available. The federal government, for instance, publishes this information in a variety of forms relevant to marketing. One of the most useful publications is *Facts for Marketers,*[13] which breaks down income data by standard metropolitan statistical areas (SMSA). Unfortunately, neither this quantity nor quality of information is generally available for foreign countries, particularly in the underdeveloped areas. Often, gross national product is the only income figure available, except in highly developed areas such as Western Europe.

The importance of income measurements warrants a brief definition of the more commonly used values. The following measurements of income are relevant to marketing:

Gross National Product (GNP) is the total money value of all goods and services produced within a country.

Net National Product (NNP) is gross national product less capital consumption—that is, the estimated money value of capital assets that have been used up.

[13] U. S. Department of Commerce, *Facts for Marketers* (Washington, D. C.: U. S. Government Printing Office, 1966).

National Income (NI) is net national product less indirect business taxes.

Personal Income (PI) is national income less corporate savings, taxes on corporate profits, and social insurance payments; plus interest payments and transfer payments made to private individuals by the government. Interest paid on government bonds and checks sent to veterans are examples of the two positive adjustments.

Disposable Personal Income (DPI) is personal income less personal taxes.

Discretionary Personal Income (not included in Figure 12.1) is disposable personal income less expenditures for necessities such as food, clothing, and housing, assuming that such expenditures are not drawn from savings or borrowed against future income. Although the value of discre-

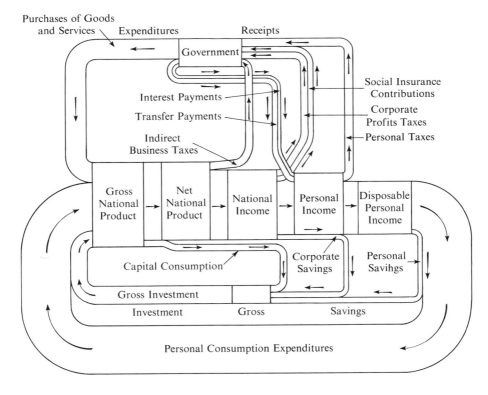

FIGURE 12.1
National income and product flows

SOURCE: Reprinted with permission of The Macmillan Company from *Marketing: The Firm's Viewpoint* by Schuyler F. Otteson, W. G. Panschar, and J. M. Patterson. Copyright © The Macmillan Company, 1964.

tionary income will vary with the level of personal income and the definition of "necessities," it appears to average approximately 35 to 40 percent of disposable personal income in the United States.

All the values defined above are measured over a one-year period unless otherwise noted. A graphical macroeconomic model of national income and product flows, like that shown in Figure 12.1, is helpful in visualizing the relationships between income types.

In the long run, the money available for the purchase of consumer goods must equal disposable personal income plus any funds allocated by federal and state governments for the purchase of such goods for institutional purposes. In the short run, however, the amount of funds available for consumer goods is different from disposable personal income, since people use personal savings and credit to finance current purchases. The expenditure of savings and the use of credit will vary with the consumers' perception of future income, with lending institutions' views of impending economic conditions, and with government monetary policy. Since all these factors affect the demand for goods and services, the marketing manager is well advised to keep abreast of economic conditions and forecasts.

CHAPTER 13

Pricing Strategies

INDUSTRY VERSUS FIRM DEMAND FUNCTIONS

Before we embark on an exposition of specific pricing strategies, it is essential to explain the difference between the demand for a product class, which is analogous to the industry's demand function, and the demand for the firm's product. (Industry here is defined by product—the automobile industry, the television industry, and so on—rather than by the broad categories established in Chapter 2.) For instance, the demand curve for automobiles is different from the demand curve for Fords, and the demand function for cigarettes is far different from the demand function for Lucky Strikes. In manipulating price, to confuse the two is to court disaster.

An industry will be confronted with a demand for its product that is either elastic ($\eta_P > 1$), inelastic ($\eta_P < 1$), or reflects a unitary elasticity ($\eta_P = 1$), depending on the product characteristics perceived by buyers and on the substitutability of other goods. For example, the demand for essentials tends to be inelastic with respect to price, especially when there is no suitable substitute. Food is an example, and so is tobacco. With an elasticity less than one, total revenue will increase as price increases. This economic truism has not escaped the politicians, who have made the federal and state governments the recipients of the lion's share of the receipts from cigarette sales.[1]

If a good borders on being a necessity, but can be replaced by another product, it will tend to be price-elastic. For instance, electricity and gas—products with quite different physical properties—will infringe on each other's markets when the price of one gets a bit high.

The industry's (or product's) demand function is significant to the firm

---

[1] The authors imply no moral judgment. The social cost of smoking as well as the economic properties of cigarettes may well justify the heavy tax burden that now accounts for most of the product's retail price.

because it indicates the aggregate demand for the product. The firm's sales depend on the aggregate demand and on the company's ability to capture its share of the market. The latter determinant is greatly influenced by the number of competing firms and the way in which they manipulate the marketing variables. Thus the shape of the firm's demand curve depends heavily on the structure of the industry in which the firm is competing—whether it is monopolistic, oligopolistic, or competitive. A comparison of the demand curves for an industry, a monopolistic firm, an oligopolistic firm, and a competitive firm is presented in Figure 13.1.

A *monopoly* is by definition a single-firm industry. Hence the industry's demand function and the firm's demand function are one and the same. Like any enterprise, the monopolist will maximize profit by setting marginal revenue equal to marginal cost and solving for the optimum price and output. If the monopolistic position can be maintained, the firm will probably enjoy a greater profit than would be possible if it were confronted by competitors. The monopolist can set output and hold price at the point where the industry's profit—hence the firm's profit—is maximum. However, excessive profit tends to attract competitors. As the number of firms in the industry increases,

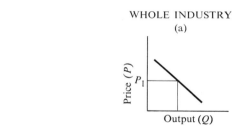

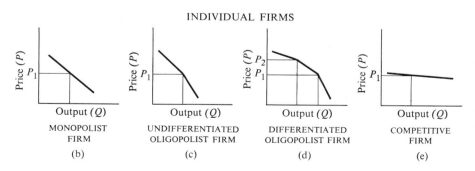

FIGURE 13.1
Common demand curves
(Price vs. output)

each firm must share the total industry's demand. If the monopolistic price is maintained, the initial firm will experience a decreased demand for its product and the profit-maximization condition (marginal revenue equals marginal profit) will be violated. In order to reobtain this condition, the firm must decrease price and/or operate at a reduced level of output. Each of the three courses of action reduces profits; thus each will eventually lead to a reduction in the number of firms desiring to enter the market.

An *oligopoly* is an industry dominated by a few firms. It may consist of only a few companies, like the automobile industry, or it may consist of a few major firms and numerous small firms. The steel and general-aviation industries are representative of the latter type of oligopoly. The essential feature of any kind of oligopoly is that a small number of firms, but more than one, control the majority of the industry's output. As a result, the price offered by any single firm must conform closely to that offered by the leading firm or firms. The precise degree of price conformity will depend on the substitutability of the products of the different companies, the willingness and ability of the price leader to discipline competitors, and the degree of government control.

An *undifferentiated oligopoly* is an oligopolistic industry in which all firms produce essentially identical products. Again, the steel industry is an example. A sheet of ½-inch 1040 stainless steel sold by the Bethlehem Steel Company is indistinguishable—except for the label or stamp—from one offered by either the Kaiser Steel Company, the United States Steel Corporation, or any other domestic or foreign producer. Under these circumstances, the marketer has little choice but to match the price offered by the price leader. This is usually the largest firm, or one of the largest that the other large firms have tacitly agreed will set the price for the industry.

The resultant demand curve for the individual firms, *except the price leader,* will then be similar to (c) in Figure 13.1. The established price is P_1, the point at which the curve kinks. If any seller increases his price above P_1, its sales will rapidly decline as buyers go elsewhere to purchase identical products. If the firm elects to lower its price in a naive attempt to attract more customers, the price leader—and hence the other competitors—will immediately match the lower price. If the firm had initially been maximizing profit by supplying a market share such that marginal revenue equaled marginal cost, then a price reduction can only decrease profit. Thus profit must be reduced whether price is increased or decreased. In an extreme case, the industry's price leader may even temporarily reduce its price below that offered by the rebellious firm in order to discipline the price breaker.

Although normally only the leading firm can manipulate price, its competitors can use the production function and the other marketing variables to maximize profit. For instance, they may be able to reduce costs by improving their manufacturing and marketing techniques. Or they may be able to increase their market share, hence revenue, by better distribution, more advertising, or an enlarged sales force. Even the product variable may be manipulated, within limits. An improvement in delivery, technical services, warranties, or an expansion of the product line can serve this end, even when the physical properties of the product itself are identical to those of the competitors' goods.

Price, too, may be open to some manipulation, depending on the tolerance of the price leader. Competitors may have some latitude in this area if they are able to perform certain services or to assure continuous product availability, either of which might induce the buyer to accept a slightly higher price. Again, the steel industry serves as an example. Importers of foreign steel cannot always guarantee quick delivery, a large selection of stock, or the quality level associated with the big domestic producers. Consequently, the slightly lower price of foreign steel is tolerated by the American oligopolists. Also, the financial strength of some foreign mills, such as August Thyssen-Hütte of Germany and Yawata Iron and Steel of Japan, makes them immune to the effects of a disciplinary price cut that could seriously injure the smaller domestic competitors. The large foreign firms simply match the retaliatory cuts, since their staying power is equal to or greater than that of the big United States mills.

A *differentiated oligopoly* (sometimes called a *competitive monopoly*) is an oligopolistic industry whose members produce slightly dissimilar products.[2] This type of oligopoly is frequent in the field of consumer durables. Product differences in such items as automobiles, appliances, television receivers, and boats encourage consumer preferences, which in turn induce brand loyalty. Brand loyalty allows some price flexibility. For example, most car buyers prefer a particular brand of automobile. This preference makes them willing to pay a higher price than they would pay for a comparable brand. The stronger the preference, the larger the price differential that will be tolerated by the customer before he shifts to a less desirable brand.

As a result, the demand curve for the firm takes the general shape of (d) in Figure 13.1. The firm can maneuver price between a certain range, P_1 and P_2 in Figure 13.1, with relative impunity. The more dissimilar its product is in the minds of potential buyers, the greater this area of manipulation will be. However, if price is raised above a certain point, customers will desert the brand in droves and sales will drop rapidly. In short, sales are

---

[2] The physical differentiation of products that is associated with a differentiated oligopoly should not be confused with the marketing strategy of "product differentiation." The latter involves not physical changes in the product, but an effort to differentiate it in the minds of different consumer groups through various promotional tactics. A less confusing term for "product differentiation" is "market aggregation," as the objective is to satisfy all market segments with a single product. A more extensive discussion of this topic occurs in Part VIII.

highly price-elastic above a certain level. On the other hand, if the firm lowers its price below a certain point, other firms in the industry will have little choice but to reduce their prices to avoid losing a large number of customers to the low-price brand. The net result would be a slight increase in sales for the firm, but at a substantial reduction in price. This inelasticity would mean a lower total revenue for the firm and an increase in output, hence cost. Since the consequence of such a move would not be pleasing to the stock-holders, the marketing manager is well advised to stay within the bounds of P_1 and P_2, and concentrate on manipulating the other marketing variables in order to shift the demand curve outward or increase the length of segment P_1-P_2.

The leading firm in a differentiated oligopoly cannot set the industry price quite so easily as its counterpart in an undifferentiated oligopoly can. This is due to the flexibility imparted to competitors by the dissimilarity of their products. The leading firm can change the length of its own P_1-P_2 segment by the same means as its competitors—that is, by product variation. It can influence the anchor end of the segment, P_1, for each firm in the in-dustry by selecting the price that will bring forth retaliation. Since size im-plies financial strength, the largest firm is usually in the best position to match or undercut a substantial price reduction. For example, the automobile industry might be indifferent to a $25 price cut on Ford convertibles, but it takes little imagination to forecast what General Motors' reaction would be in the event of a $300 price cut by Ford.

A *competitive industry* is one in which each member produces an identi-cal product, no member is large enough to influence market price, and the market is large enough so that any individual competitor can sell all its out-put at the going market price. This makes the marketer's pricing decision a very simple one. He simply sets the price of his product equal to the going market price. His demand function is extremely elastic, similar to (e) in Figure 13.1. There is no advantage in lowering price below the prevailing price, P_1, because the firm can sell its entire output at that price. To increase the firm's price above P_1, would be totally irrational, for sales would immedi-ately drop to zero.

Agriculture is perhaps the best example of a competitive industry. No ra-tional buyer will purchase a particular grade of wheat from a farmer charging a high price when he can have an identical product delivered from another farmer at the prevailing market price. Conversely, a farmer would be foolish to sell wheat at a lower price when the market offers him the prevailing price. In agriculture, low prices have encouraged farmers to unite in order to con-front buyers with a single seller, thereby changing the industry—from the marketing viewpoint—into a monopoly. The unhappy plight of American agriculture since World War I and the political power of the agricultural community have induced Congress to tolerate, and at times encourage, such monopolistic practices as price-setting and output control. Marketers in other sectors of the economy who have entertained similar ideas have not been treated so kindly by the federal establishment.

MARKET SHARE

Market share is defined as the ratio of the sales of the firm to the total sales of the industry. It is normally shown as a percentage and is expressed mathematically as

$$M = \frac{S_F}{S_I} \cdot 100, \text{ where} \tag{13-1}$$

M = market share of the firm, expressed as a percentage

S_F = sales of the firm, in units or dollars, and

S_I = sales of the entire industry, in units or dollars, including those of the firm

Market share is an important measure of the success of the firm in competing in a given market. Since it is a relative measure, it excludes the influence of exogenous variables, such as the business cycle, that may cause large fluctuations in absolute sales. Market share is also a crude indicator of the probability of government intervention. An excessively large share ("excessively large" is not clearly defined by either the courts or the Department of Justice) is often cited as evidence of restraint of trade. The size of competitors' market shares, and the trends in those shares, serve to indicate the strength of competition and help to identify those firms whose marketing tactics should be closely observed.

Professor Stewart has shown that the optimum market share for an innovating firm is 10 to 25 percent.[3] Companies with very small market shares and companies with very large market shares do not allocate resources to developing and introducing product changes when such changes cannot be protected. For them, a more appropriate strategy may be to follow the innovators, copying those product changes that attract enough of the market population to shift the laggard firm's demand curve significantly. This is precisely the policy followed by many companies, according to the empirical findings on innovation diffusion.

Small firms, especially those competing in an established industry, cannot afford large outlays for research and development. Very large firms find such expenditures unnecessary, since their market share is so large that expansion is not warranted. Thus the intermediate-sized firm has been the most

[3] George Schwartz, ed., *Science in Marketing* (New York: Wiley, 1965), p. 209.

frequent source of innovations. Obviously, there are many exceptions, particularly where innovation is dependent on large resources, where technology is changing rapidly, or where innovation serves as a barrier to the entry of competitors. IBM is an example. When the large firms—those with the resources needed for significant innovation—fail to change their product, the industry may become obsolete should a new and innovative group of firms emerge in a competing industry. The failure of the American railroads to improve and expand their passenger service, for example, led to an industry-wide decline. On the other hand, the airlines, which have continuously improved their service and equipment and have gambled on such radical innovations as the jet airplane, have grown rapidly.

TIME AND PRICE

Time has an important effect on pricing strategies. For example, all demand curves tend to become more elastic with the passage of time. This is because other firms may enter the market and substitute goods or services may be developed. Even patents expire in seventeen years. As a result, an industry moves closer to the competitive model as time passes. Like most rules-of-thumb, this one has its exceptions. Economies of scale; manufacturing, product, and distribution innovations; competitive pressures; a leftward shift of the industry's demand curve; and government intervention can all serve to destroy or exclude marginal producers. A net reduction in the number of competitors moves the industry away from the competitive model and closer to an oligopoly or monopoly.

Economic periods also affect the number and type of viable pricing options. A price well below average unit cost might be appropriate in the market period. In fact, it may be necessary in order to clear the market and avoid excessive inventories. This is especially true when merchandise is perishable or will become obsolete if stored for long. However, if storage is physically practical and the marketer foresees an eventual increase in the market price (a rightward shift in the demand curve), accumulating a large inventory might be preferable to selling at a below-cost price. A price above average unit cost is necessary in the long run if the firm is to show a profit. The only sensible alternative is to reallocate the company's resources to another field of business.

COMMON PRICING STRATEGIES

Approximately a dozen specific pricing strategies are encountered in the marketplace. None are universally applicable. Their suitability for a particular firm will depend on various factors, especially the way the industry is organized and the laws that affect it. Not even the price indicated by the rule of profit maximization—the price where marginal revenue equals marginal cost—is the best in all cases. Thus, each of the alternative pricing policies described here can be ideal for one firm and inferior, or totally irrational, for another.

Set price equal to the value indicated by marginal analysis. This is the ideal long-run pricing strategy. Although many firms are unable to use this method, due to market-period and short-run considerations, the complexities of analysis where a large number of products are involved, legal constraints, supplier restrictions, or government restrictions, marginal analysis is a practical basis for pricing for unregulated monopolists and differentiated oligopolists, particularly those with a limited product line. However, because it assures maximum profits in the short run, this strategy may attract competitors into the industry if the barrier to entry is not sufficiently great.

A long-run estimate of the demand function should reflect the possible entry of competition, hence reduced sales, that may occur at high prices. If market and short-run profit are maximized by using a demand function that excludes the possibility of competition, the result can be a price that attracts competition, thus reducing profits in the long run. One way around this problem is to estimate the profit that would attract competitors, given the degree of difficulty of entry, and then to compute the price that would yield this profit. The resultant value can be used as a constraint—that is, it can specify a price ceiling. The optimum price would still be selected by marginal analysis, but if it were higher than the maximum "safe" price, it would be reduced to the value immediately below that specified by the constraint. (The application of constraints was illustrated graphically in Chapter 6, p. 130).

Set price equal to cost plus a fixed markup. The simplicity of this method has made it the most common technique in the distribution field. It is used almost universally by retailers, although they may use other pricing strategies when necessary to clear out perishable goods, obsolete inventories, or shopworn merchandise. Markups will vary according to product class and the type of store. They may also be subject to bargaining between the retailer and the buyer. The retailer will usually have a number of different markups— expressed as a percentage of direct cost—for subcategories of his goods. For example, automobile accessories installed by the dealer will carry a larger markup than the basic automobiles. Gourmet food and liquor will carry higher markups than meat or produce, which in turn will be priced differently than canned goods.

The federal government often demands that contractors negotiate price on the basis of their estimated total cost plus a percentage markup. This necessitates a detailed audit of the supplier's cost estimate by the contracting agency. The price that is ultimately negotiated may be fixed or may vary according to a system of awards and penalties that are a function of the contractor's performance.

Many economists have been critical of this method of pricing, claiming that it serves as a crutch for those marketers who do not want to bother with marginal analysis. Since only by chance will the prices match those that would maximize profit, the firm can pay a substantial opportunity cost for the ease of "cost-plus" pricing.

Actually, this criticism may be too harsh. Government contractors have no choice but to use this method. Wholesalers and retailers with hundreds or thousands of separate items to price could not possibly manage a marginal analysis on each one, or, for that matter, use one of the other pricing systems. The problem is simply too complex.

Set price equal to the prevailing market price. This is the only viable strategy for a firm in a competitive industry. When the product class is homogeneous and no firm is large enough to noticeably influence the industry's total output, the "invisible hand"[4] will set the price. Any seller setting his price above the going market price will find his goods rejected in favor of the lower-priced identical substitutes. On the other hand, undercutting the going price will only reduce the firm's revenues, since it can sell its entire output at the market price. The alternative to accepting the prevailing market price is to inventory the goods and hope for an increase in their market value. However, the firm runs the risk of losing money should the market price decline.

Set price below the going market price. This method is known as "penetration pricing." It is appropriate for oligopolists, especially those whose products are not substantially different from their competitors' goods. The lower price is used as a wedge to get into markets that were previously served adequately by established companies. In these markets, the industrial or middleman buyer, or the ultimate consumer, may have no reason to change to an untried brand unless offered a price incentive. If the product is an innovation whose use is prerequisite to an appreciation of its functional characteristics, a low price may be helpful in inducing its acceptance by the innovator and early-adopter groups.

Once the firm has established itself, a pricing change may be in order. The difference between the prevailing market price and the penetration price might be classified as a discount and charged to the promotional ac-

---

[4] The "invisible hand" is an expression coined by the founder of classical economics, Adam Smith (*Wealth of Nations,* 1776). It refers to the operation of the price mechanism in a purely competitive economy, where numerous sellers and numerous buyers, each pursuing their own selfish interest, collectively arrive at a market price.

count. Regardless of the accounting system employed, the marketer should give thought to eliminating the price differential once his product has been accepted. The below-market price may no longer be necessary. It may also precipitate retaliatory moves by competitors, particularly the price leader, if the industry approaches the undifferentiated-oligopoly model.

Set price equal to a percentage of the price offered by competitors. This strategy is appropriate where there is a good deal of competition between many firms but the product class is not homogeneous. The difference in brands prevents the industry from conforming entirely to the competitive model, thus allowing some price flexibility. This usually takes the form of a small price differential based on the difference in the good, service, or establishment. This policy is common in retailing, where firms recognize the necessity to be competitive pricewise but also recognize the opportunity to maintain a price differential where product dissimilarities exist.

Automobile gasoline prices reflect this strategy. Producers of standard brands, with their heavily advertised products, more elaborate stations, and better service, normally charge 3 to 5 cents per gallon over the price of their less prestigious competitors. Invariably they match the price of their counterparts. However, when a price war occurs—usually triggered by an independent producer who has made a low-cost purchase of surplus gasoline being dumped by an overloaded refinery—the individual brands will respond with proportional cuts. The price differentials that prevailed during the period of stability, however, will be maintained.

Set price equal to the price offered by the price leader. This practice is typical of undifferentiated oligopolies. When one firm is large enough to control the market and there is little or no dissimilarity between brands, the price demanded by the other members of the industry must match that set by the price leader. A higher price will drive away customers, and a lower price will encourage retaliation, with the same eventual result. Thus, prices in the steel industry are set by U. S. Steel, and those in the aluminum industry by Alcoa.

Set price in collusion with competitors. This strategy enables the industry to operate as a monopoly. It will work only in an oligopoly consisting of a few trustworthy members, with no competitive fringe that could disrupt the conspiracy by undercutting the monopolistic price. This method of pricing may or may not be beneficial to the participating firms, since it may allow the survival of marginal competitors who would otherwise succumb to more competitive pricing. Except where explicitly permitted by law, as in agriculture and the maritime industry, collusion is illegal. In industries where it is permissible, the government often serves as an enforcement agency, thereby eliminating the problem of too many, or too-independent, firms.

Illegality, however, has not prevented collusion, even by major and presumably reputable corporations. The electrical-conspiracy scandal a decade ago demonstrated this.[5] In addition to overt conspiracies to fix prices, there are often casual tacit agreements that accomplish the same thing. These can be difficult to prove in court, especially in support of a criminal charge. Fortunately, such conspiracies are also difficult to enforce, as the conspirators have no legal recourse and, as a rule, are notoriously willing to break the agreement when in hot pursuit of short-run profits.[6]

Set price equal to the price prescribed by the manufacturer. Manufacturers may prescribe a "suggested retail price" that retailers adhere to voluntarily, such as the price shown on the windows of new automobiles. In states with enforceable fair-trade laws, manufacturers may prescribe a mandatory retail price—usually a minimum price below which the good cannot be sold. This practice, once common, has recently declined in popularity. The difficulty of enforcement and the questionable economic advantage of mandatory prices have diminished their usefulness. However, they are still used by manufacturers of certain consumer durables. Supposedly a fair-trade price benefits retailers by assuring them a minimum gross-profit margin (since the retailer can usually charge more than the mandatory retail price). This presumably gets the manufacturer preferential treatment, since the retailer would rather sell a good with an assured minimum price than one that can be undercut by a competitor, with the consequent reduction in profit.

In many instances, a "suggested retail price" proves to be fictitious. It may serve as a convenient starting point for bargaining, as in the case of new automobiles. But with less costly products—where higgling over price is less common—the suggested price may be a crutch used to avoid the analysis and mathematical calculation needed in other pricing strategies. However, it is likely to be discarded if the marketer discovers that the item is getting old sitting on his shelf or showroom floor.

Set price differently for different market segments. This policy is appropriate when a market can be segmented, when the parts can be kept separate, and when each market segment has a different demand function. By estimating the different demand functions, price can be optimized by segment, thus maximizing the profit in each area. Total profit will be greatest when it is equal to the sum of the maximum profits of each market segment. If a single price is used for the entire market, it will probably not be the optimum price for one or more segments.

Age, time, quantity, and patronage are common bases for market segmentation. For example, age is used to segment the market for theater tickets and airline service. Time is used to segment the market for the indus-

---

[5] See Richard Austin Smith, "The Incredible Electrical Conspiracy," *Fortune,* Part I (April 1961) and Part II (May 1961).
[6] For an enlightening and humorous exposition of the subject, see "How to Conspire to Fix Prices," *Harvard Business Review,* Vol. 41, No. 2 (March–April 1963), pp. 95–103. The author wisely chose to remain anonymous.

trial consumption of electricity and for the use of transportation facilities. Quantity is used for raw-material markets and patronage for tie-in goods. The special deals and services often offered magazine subscribers and club members are examples of tie-in products. These goods are offered to both subscribers and nonsubscribers (or members and nonmembers), but at different prices.

Setting different prices for different market segments is a profitable way to increase revenues by encouraging the use of idle capacity. The technique can be very rewarding in industries with high fixed costs. It is a good illustration of the need for marginal cost information. For example, it costs an airline virtually the same amount to fly an empty seat between two points as it does to fly the seat with a passenger in it. Hence the marginal cost of carrying an additional passenger in the otherwise empty seat is very low. If the population can be segmented by age or time, and the non-flying members attracted by youth fares or special mid-week rates, then this idle capacity can be used to produce revenues that would otherwise go to other modes of transportation. Even at the special fare rates, this marginal revenue well exceeds the marginal cost of carrying the additional passengers. Of course, the trick is to keep the segments separated, so that customers who would normally pay the full fare do not take advantage of the reduced prices.

Set price differently for different phases of the product's life cycle. This strategy, known as *step pricing* or *skimming*, is appropriate when the firm is introducing a new product, particularly when the item has some characteristics that protect it from competition from substitutes. The method is best explained using a graphical representation of the market, as in Figure 13.2.

If the optimum price, P_5, is selected for the product, a quantity of sales, Q_5, will result, with the market being cleared at the equilibrium point, E. No additional output will be forthcoming, since the firm (or industry) is un-

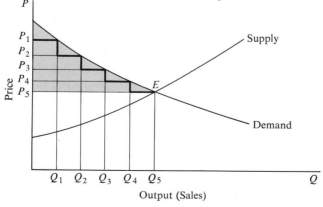

FIGURE 13.2
Step pricing

willing to produce more units at a price below P_5. However, every consumer willing to pay price P_5 or *a higher price* has been satisfied. The shaded area under line P_5–E represents total revenue.

Figure 13.2 may be pleasing to economists—price is optimum, supply and demand are satisfied, and the market is cleared and in equilibrium. However, it would have been viewed with something more akin to pain by the great "robber barons" of the nineteenth century. What would disturb them is the shaded area, P–P_5–E.[7] This area, known as "consumer surplus," represents unrealized revenue.

Consumer surplus is defined as the amount of money that consumers are willing to pay for a product above the market price. Since the area of consumer surplus is above P_5 (the optimum single price), and is to the left of Q_5 (the output that will be sold at P_5), it represents pure profit. No additional output would be required (hence no additional cost would be incurred) if this surplus could be captured by the firm.

The technique for "skimming" this potential profit is to use a series of decreasing prices, rather than the single price, P_5. The firm enters the market with a high price, P_1, and satisfies the demand to point Q_1. At that point, price is reduced to P_2, and output is increased to Q_2. At Q_2 the price must again be reduced in order to increase sales. Thus the marketer lowers price to P_3 to sell quantity Q_3, but only after all possible sales at the higher price have been made. This process is continued until price P_5 is reached. As the firm (or industry) is unwilling to increase output beyond Q_5 (since a price below P_5 would be required to clear the market), no further sales are forthcoming. The demand is satisfied, the market is cleared, and total revenue has been increased from the area under P_5–E to the area under the heavy, step-shaped line, P_1–E.

Although theoretically attractive, step pricing has some practical limitations. First, the industry must be—or act as—a monopoly. It does little good for one firm to offer a product at price P_1 if competitors are asking price P_4 or P_5. Second, the consumer willing to pay the higher price must be convinced that the price will not be lowered shortly after he makes his purchase. This is why the number of price reductions, or steps, between P_1 and P_5 is limited. If price cuts are too frequent, demand may drop drastically as potential buyers, expecting the trend to continue, await further reductions. Third, the initial high, highly profitable price might be construed as the permanent price and attract competitors who otherwise would have abstained from entering the market.

Set price equal to, or less than, cost. This technique is known as the "loss leader" method of pricing, since it means the firm must take a loss on

---

[7] For an exploration of the period of the robber barons, a time of unbridled enterprise and swashbuckling marketing, see Matthew Josephson, *The Robber Barons* (1934; reprinted, New York: Harcourt, Brace & World, 1962).

its "lead" item. To the uninitiated, it may appear to be fiscal insanity and a sure road to financial disaster. This is what it will be, if not properly executed. However, it can be a way to substantial increases in profits.

The loss leader strategy is useful in several ways. First, it serves as an instrument of promotion by attracting customers into a store, where they are induced to buy more profitable goods. Second, it is helpful in introducing new products. Thus, grocery stores run "specials" on certain items, and cosmetic manufacturers give away free samples of a new makeup product. The loss leader technique is widely practiced at the middleman level in such industries as publishing and drugs. College professors obtain a considerable number of books as free "examination" copies. Doctors get free—and usually unsolicited—samples of drugs. Third, loss leaders can be used—usually illegally—to destroy competitors that lack the financial resources necessary to survive a predatory price war.

A slight variation of this technique is the use of the loss leader as a tie-in product. An item is sometimes offered below cost in conjunction with a complementary good, whose price has not been lowered. For example, phonograph records may be given away "free" in conjunction with the sale of a hi-fi set. A second tube of toothpaste may be offered for one cent if the first tube is purchased at the regular price. The retailer is interested in the total revenue that will result from the customer's aggregate purchase, which is the basic premise for market-basket pricing.

Market-basket pricing is the determination of the optimum total price for all the items purchased by a consumer during a single visit to the store. Since profit is the difference between *total* revenue and *total* cost, it is of little consequence in market-basket pricing whether a particular item is priced above or below cost. The objective is to provide an optimum mix of both low and high prices. The low prices serve to attract customers, thus increasing Q in the revenue equation. The high prices increase the average P and provide the marginal profit. The difficulty with this system is in the selection of the price mix. Proper selection requires some feeling for the price elasticity of the various goods in the seller's line.

Market-basket pricing can be complex. Its most sophisticated application is perhaps in the large supermarkets, with whom the strategy was originally identified.[8] However, it is commonly used in industries with much simpler product mixes, often to assure a full product line. A full product line—that is, a wide assortment of models, sizes, and prices—is frequently necessary to attract customers. Many buyers will be attracted by low-priced models but will eventually be induced to trade up to the more expensive—

[8] For a further discussion of this topic, see Lee E. Preston, "Mark-ups, Leaders and Discrimination in Retail Pricing," *Journal of Farm Economics*, Vol. 44, No. 2 (May 1962), pp. 291–306.

and invariably more profitable—models. Also, a manufacturer frequently finds it necessary to offer its dealers a complete line in order to exclude competing brands.

At- or below-cost pricing was once the chief weapon of predatory firms. The original Standard Oil Company was notorious for such tactics. The firm would enter a local market and reduce price to the point where the smaller firms could not afford to be competitive. Ultimately they would be driven out of business or be forced to sell out, taking a considerable loss in the process. Once competition was destroyed, Standard Oil would be a local monopolist and would price its products accordingly. Once one local monopoly was established, the firm could use its increased profit there to destroy competition in another local market.

This abusive use of pricing in the nineteenth and early twentieth century was not limited to the petroleum industry. In fact, the practice became so common throughout the business community that the federal government, under the leadership of President Theodore Roosevelt, finally took restrictive, and in some cases punitive, action. Although price competition still performs important economic functions, including the elimination of inefficient enterprises, it is seldom used for purely predatory purposes.

Set price by government edict. In many regulated industries, such as the transportation and utilities fields, price is set by a regulatory agency or by legislation. It may be fixed, as it is in the airline industry; it may be a minimum, as it is for haircuts in the state of California; or it may be a maximum, as it is for milk in most areas.

This may appear to relieve the marketer of pricing decisions, limiting his role to the manipulation of the other marketing variables. Often this is true, especially when he represents a firm that is too small to influence the regulatory agencies or legislators or that allocates the task to a trade association or lobbying service. Yet the converse can also be true. Firms can, and frequently do, petition regulatory bodies for changes in their price schedules. Under these conditions, the marketer must not only analyze price from the viewpoint of maximizing profit but must carry the added burden of preparing economic and social justifications for the changes he requests.

Set price equal to an odd value. This practice is common in retailing. Instead of appropriate whole values such as $1.00, $5.00, or $40.00, the retailer will use odd, slightly lower prices, such as $.99, $4.98, and $39.50. The theory behind this practice is psychological. Supposedly the prospect will perceive the odd price as considerably lower than the few pennies that are removed in the reduction, and hence be more apt to buy the good. According to the theory, $4.98 seems like considerably less than $5.00, although it is virtually the same amount. At present, there is little empirical work to statistically support this claim, or to deny it.

ALTERNATIVES TO PRICE MANIPULATION

Generally speaking, each of the other marketing instruments offers an alternative to price manipulation as a method of increasing profit. However, the two options most closely related to price are (1) to shift the industry's demand curve upward and (2) to move the firm toward a monopolistic position.

The demand curve can be shifted by promotion or by changes in exogenous variables. Promotion is used by the firm to change consumer tastes in favor of its products. By enhancing the desire for a good or service, the marketer makes buyers willing to pay a higher price for the same quantity or to buy a larger quantity at the same price. This is reflected graphically by a shift to the right of the demand curve and mathematically by an increase in the constant term in the demand function.

A movement of the firm toward a monopolistic position can be accomplished by the exclusion or destruction of competition. This shifts the firm's demand function closer to the industry's demand function, thus increasing the demand for the firm's product and giving the firm much more flexibility in the manipulation of price.

The move toward monopoly can be made by legal or other means. "Other means" include such strategies as predatory pricing and collusion. Collusion enables a number of firms to fix prices or to divide the market into segments. In the latter case, the segments are divided among the colluding firms, and each then enjoys a monopoly in its particular segment. Acquisition and merger are legal means of reducing the number of competitors, thus moving the firm toward the monopolistic model. This is precisely why the Antitrust Division of the Justice Department looks critically into such matters, often filing a civil complaint to prohibit or nullify the actions of the participating corporations.

Product variation also affords the marketer the chance to move his firm closer to the monopolistic model. If the company's product can be made sufficiently dissimilar from the products offered by other members of the industry, and if the dissimilarity can be maintained, the effect is to create a new product class with the firm the sole producer. Thus a new, monopolistic industry may emerge from within a competitive or oligopolistic industry.

Product variation can be real or imagined. If the good or service is perceived as unique by the buyer, then the firm is in a monopolistic position. The difference may be sufficiently minor or ambiguous that the firm acts as a differentiated oligopolist, rather than a monopolist. However, such a position is still preferable to competing in a competitive market.

One final pricing alternative bears mentioning—namely, the clandestine, or disguised, price adjustment. This is really a form of price manipulation, but it is done covertly, with there being no outward appearance of a price change. The objective is to engage in price competition without acknowledging the fact to competitors or regulatory agencies. This method requires the complete cooperation of buyers, which makes it unreliable even with a small number of customers and impossible with a large number. Also, experience indicates that it is usually not successful, although this may be a naive assumption—a truly successful seller-buyer conspiracy would be kept secret.

The technique is to adjust price by making a concession of some kind to the buyer, with the understanding that it will be kept quiet. This is not always easy to accomplish. Word tends to get around of such concessions as cash discounts, merchandise bonuses, advertising allowances, freight allowances, and rebates. Often the concessions are revealed by the benefactors themselves, who use such offers to enhance their bargaining position with other sellers or cannot resist an opportunity to brag about their shrewdness. When this happens, competitors may retaliate, other customers may demand the same preferential treatment, or the government may intervene with charges of price discrimination.

The alternatives to price manipulation must be used judiciously; the same is true of price manipulation itself. The marketer must select and apply pricing strategies with an awareness of the constraints of his marketplace. The public, the legislators, the executive branch of the federal government, and the courts have become very unsympathetic in recent years. For instance, the number of antitrust cases brought to the courts has tripled during the past decade, and few have been decided in favor of the defendant. This does not imply that the marketer should refrain from manipulating the price variable—his firm's survival may depend on which strategy he selects and how he employs it. But he should use the price variable wisely and with a thorough understanding of its limitations as well as his alternatives.

Summary of Price Decisions

DEMAND. The demand function expresses the relationship between the quantity of goods that will be sold and their price. This relationship is determined by the price of the product, the price of substitute products, consumer income, and consumer tastes.

Price elasticity is an index of the sensitivity of demand to changes in price. It is the ratio between a relative change in quantity demanded and the relative change in price that induced the change in quantity. It is always negative, since an increase in price never induces an increase in unit sales. (If it does have such an effect, the price increase has actually served as an instrument for product change.)

Cross elasticities are indices of the sensitivity of the sales of one product to changes in the price of another. If the goods are complementary—such as bread and jam—the increase in price of one will decrease the sales of the other; hence their cross-elasticity will be negative. If the goods are substitutes —as steel and aluminum are for many buyers—an increase in the price of one will increase the sales of the other. Both price elasticity and cross elasticity can be estimated and specified mathematically for most products. Both are critical to the pricing decision.

SUPPLY AND EQUILIBRIUM. A product is originally introduced in the marketplace by an entrepreneur who perceives a demand—or the opportunity to create a demand—that will absorb an output at a price adequate to yield an acceptable profit. If the product is successful and the profit is large enough, other firms will be drawn into the market and the initial firm's market share will be reduced. The decrease in market share will require the firm to change its price and/or output in order to maximize profit under competition. Profits will be reduced and will eventually decline to the level where additional competitors and additional production will no longer be forthcoming. This is the point where the supply and demand curves intersect and is called "equilibrium." Here, the supply and demand functions are in balance; if no shift in either curve occurs, output will remain constant.

In an ideal economy, events would take this path. However, errors in marketing decisions, especially pricing, and changes in exogenous variables can throw the system out of equilibrium. Barriers to market entry, such as patents, can keep product price at a level that will continue to yield high profit levels. Even in a non-monopolistic market, price flexibility, which is essential to the smooth working of the system, is often hampered by private or public constraints.

PRICE. Price is the primary instrument of competition in a market economy. Even in controlled economies, it is the variable most often used to allocate supply. In the American market, price is normally set by the firm, with the consumer purchasing or rejecting the good at that figure. However, bargaining is common in many areas, notably the retail market for consumer durables. The sales price of an industrial good is often reached through negotiation or competitive bidding. In regulated industries, such as the transportation and utilities fields, it is set by a government agency.

If the seller's price is too high to allow the firm to dispose of all its output, it must eventually be lowered. The alternative—to inventory the unsold units—is generally untenable. If price is too low for the selected output, output must be increased or price escalated to achieve market equilibrium and maximum profit. These options are, of course, subject to the constraints of government regulation, law, fear of attracting competitors into the market, the resources of the firm, and inadequate or erroneous market information.

The real price is the value that must be used for analysis and decisions. Frequently, it is different from the published price, which may be altered by discounts, price premiums, credit terms, merchandise bonuses, advertising allowances, freight allowances, price guarantees, free services, and rebates.

INCOME. Although income and price are separate and independent determinants of demand, income plays a critical role in shaping the quantity-price relationship. The higher the level of income, the higher will be the level of sales at any given price. The sensitivity of sales to income is expressed as income elasticity. Income elasticity has been measured and specified for various product classes; it is important in analyzing the potential market growth for a product.

PRICING STRATEGIES. The basis of pricing decisions must be the demand function confronting the firm. The most important property of this demand function is its elasticity. This in turn is determined by the structure of the industry in which the firm operates. Monopolies, undifferentiated oligopolies, differentiated oligopolies, and competitive industries all have distinctive demand curves for member companies. Only in a monopoly is the demand curve for the firm the same as the demand curve for the industry.

For each type of industry, the marketer is confronted with a demand curve warranting a different pricing strategy, each of which has its own advantages and limitations. The range of pricing strategies varies considerably between the unrestricted competitive industry, with its single viable strategy, and the unregulated monopoly, with its multiple strategies.

The common pricing strategies are

(1) Set price equal to the value indicated by marginal analysis.
(2) Set price equal to cost plus a fixed markup.
(3) Set price equal to the prevailing market price.
(4) Set price below the going market price.
(5) Set price equal to a percentage of the price offered by competitors.
(6) Set price equal to the price offered by the price leader.
(7) Set price in collusion with competitors.
(8) Set price equal to the price prescribed by the manufacturer.
(9) Set price differently for different market segments.
(10) Set price differently for different phases of the product's life cycle.
(11) Set price equal to, or less than, cost.
(12) Set price by government edict.
(13) Set price equal to an odd value.

If the firm's demand function restricts its pricing flexibility, it must depend on manipulation of the other marketing variables to maximize profit.

Questions and Problems

1. What variables are likely to determine the demand for each of the following goods and services? (a) Cadillacs, (b) IBM computers, (c) Pepsi-Cola, (d) car washes, (e) bread, (f) F-111 aircraft. Which can be manipulated by the firm?
2. Identify and explain the type of demand function (elastic or inelastic) you would expect for each of the following product classes: (a) rice, (b) iron ore, (c) motion-picture tickets, (d) natural gas, and (e) milk.
3. If a 10-percent increase occurred in the price of the first product in each of the following pairs, what would probably happen to the sales of the second good or service? (a) coffee and tea, (b) bus tickets and airline travel, (c) women's shoes and matching handbags, (d) electricity and gas air conditioners, (e) automobiles and steel, (f) automobile tires and gasoline.
4. How might the published price be adjusted to a true price in each of the following transactions? (a) the sale of nationally advertised shoes to a chain of retail stores, (b) the sale of an automobile to the ultimate consumer, (c) the sale of sulphur to a chemical plant.

5. What effect, if any, would a 5-percent increase in per capita personal income have on the sales of the following goods and services, given the indicated circumstances? (a) Volkswagens, if income previously averaged $3,000 per household, (b) houses, if income previously averaged $10,000 per household, (c) medicine, in an American slum area, (d) pipe tobacco, if income previously averaged $7,000 per household, (e) canned meat, in Mexico.

6. What type of income measurement would be appropriate for an analysis of the income elasticity of each of the following goods and services? (a) ice cream, (b) milling machines, (c) stocks and bonds, (d) house painting, (e) economic research.

7. What are the possible outcomes if the true demand for new houses at a price of $20,000 is 535 units, and three general contractors build only 50, 300, and 100 units respectively, each at an asking price of $20,000? If one of the builders foresaw the disequilibrium between the total supply and the demand in this particular market, what might he do?

8. Suggest and defend a pricing policy for each of the following firms: (a) General Motors Corp., (b) Volkswagen of America, Inc., (c) a small wheat farm, (d) a large wheat farm, (e) Columbia Records, and (f) Polaroid-Land Corp.

9. Suggest and defend a pricing policy for each of the following retailing organizations: (a) a Plymouth agency, (b) a Safeway store, (c) a record store located in a large shopping center, (d) Sears, Roebuck and Co., (e) an exclusive restaurant, and (f) the retail sales division of Shell Oil Co.

10. State your answers to question 9 in mathematical form. (Greek or Arabic symbols may be substituted for the coefficients.)

11. A series of observations were taken in three markets, all homogeneous except for their populations. Given the following data, derive a demand function for the product, showing sales with respect to price.

Market	Population	Price	Sales
A	1,000,000	10	1,000
B	500,000	12	400
C	2,000,000	20	500

12. The marketing manager for a statewide chain of ice-cream stores wishes to know the sensitivity of his brand's sales to changes in price. To get the necessary data, he orders the firm's Los Angeles stores to charge 40 cents per pint for one month and 50 cents per pint for the following month, recording sales for each period. Their reports showed sales of 100,000 pints and 90,000 pints, respectively, for the two months, July and August. What is the price elasticity of the ice cream? What price

should the firm select for September, and why? What exogenous variables, if any, may have distorted the data?

13. A distributor of alcoholic beverages expects sales of $2,500,000 for the present year. By checking *Facts for Marketers,* he discovers that the median annual income in his local market is $6,200 per family. The *Survey of Current Business* discloses that family income has been increasing an average of 4 percent per year. Using the information in Table 12.1 (p. 263), forecast the firm's sales for the following year.

14. A trade association wants to provide its members with a forecast of the prevailing market price and the industry's total sales for the coming year. By conducting a market survey and making adjustments for the anticipated changes in population and income, its market analyst constructs the following demand function for consumption, Q_D, as a function of price, P: $Q_D = 4,000 - 200P$. By querying the association's members, the analyst estimates that the output, Q_S, supplied by the industry will be $Q_S = 800P - 2,000$. What will be the market price, and how many units will be produced and sold during the coming year?

Supplementary Readings

BOOKS

GRUCHY, ALAN G., *Comparative Economic Systems* (New York: Houghton Mifflin, 1966).

HARPER, DONALD V., *Price Policy and Procedure* (New York: Harcourt, Brace & World, 1966).

SAMUELSON, PAUL A., *Economics: An Introductory Analysis,* 7th ed. (New York: McGraw-Hill, 1967).

STIGLER, GEORGE J., *The Theory of Price,* 3rd ed. (New York: Macmillan, 1966).

STONE, RICHARD, *The Role of Measurement in Economics* (London: Cambridge University Press, 1951).

ARTICLES

ABRAMS, JACK, "A New Method for Testing Pricing Decisions," *Journal of Marketing,* Vol. 28, No. 3 (July 1964), pp. 6–9.

BROWN, F. E., "Price Image Versus Price Reality," *Journal of Marketing Research,* Vol. 6, No. 2 (May 1969), pp. 185–91.

GABOR, ANDRE, and GRANGER, C. W. J., "On the Price Consciousness of Consumers," *Applied Statistics,* Vol. 10, No. 3 (November 1961), pp. 170–88.

GOULD, J. R., and PRESTON, L. E., "Resale Price Maintenance and Retail Outlets," *Economica,* Vol. 32, No. 127 (August 1965), pp. 302–12.

GREEN, PAUL E., "Bayesian Decision Theory in Pricing Strategy," *Journal of Marketing,* Vol. 27, No. 1 (January 1963), pp. 5–14.

NELSEN, J. R., "Practical Application of Marginal Cost Pricing in the Public Utilities Field," *American Economic Review,* Vol. 53, No. 2 (May 1963), pp. 474–89.

OXENFELDT, A. R., and BAXTER, W. T., "Approaches to Pricing: Economist vs. Accountant," *Business Horizons,* Vol. 4, No. 4 (Winter 1961), pp. 77–90.

PEARCE, I. F., "A Method of Consumer Demand Analysis Illustrated," *Economica,* Vol. 28, No. 112 (November 1961), pp. 371–94.

UDELL, J. G., "How Important Is Pricing in Competitive Strategy?" *Journal of Marketing,* Vol. 28, No. 1 (January 1964), pp. 44–48.

Part VI

PRODUCT DECISIONS

The product instrument has many dimensions—more than any other variable in the marketing mix. The product variable consists of a number of elements that may lend themselves to manipulation by the firm, depending on the nature of the industry and the market, the extent of government involvement, the size of the firm and its position in the distribution system, and the product itself. Today, with the rising level of technology and the complexity of products, especially industrial goods and services, the product variable is becoming increasingly important in the competition for markets and the quest for profits. More new products have been introduced in the past thirty years than in the previous three thousand. With few exceptions, a greater variety of brands and models exists within each product class, and customers are offered a much larger selection of options, than ever before. Not only is the number and variety of products large and getting larger, but the obsolescence and mortality rates are the greatest ever.

Another reason for the increased importance of the product variable is the vigorous enforcement of antitrust laws during the past decade, which has placed more constraints on the use of price as a market weapon. In many major industries, notably the automobile industry, product variation has become the chief instrument of competition. Decisions involving the firm's products can be the most important ones the marketer makes. They can also be the ones most taxing of his knowledge and imagination, since they are complex and seldom lend themselves to any simple rules of thumb. Alterations in the product mix often involve uncertainty and a heavy outlay of resources; mistakes in product decisions may cost millions of dollars. Yet the rewards can be tremendous, as the Model-T Ford, the Boeing jet airliner, and the Xerox machine have demonstrated.

Few firms can avoid making product decisions, as hazardous as the risks may be. Change is the most pervasive single quality of the twentieth century, and the firm must either adapt to rapidly changing market conditions—and hopefully exploit them—or be left at the mercy of competitors that have made more successful product decisions. Thus the product variable is both the most treacherous and the most promising instrument in the marketer's bag of tools.

CHAPTER 14

Product Innovations and Protection

INNOVATION

The product instrument is frequently the hardest marketing variable to manipulate. Although standard research techniques can evaluate the effect of changes in the product variable on the firm's growth and profit, the process by which new products are created, or established ones are modified, is essentially one of human creativity and ingenuity. The creation of new products is not a controlled process. Often millions of dollars of formal research and development fail to yield a successful new product (witness the Edsel), while an idea from a single inventor can create an extremely successful one (witness the Xerox machine). Our study of the product as a marketing instrument will accordingly begin with an analysis of how innovations occur, since innovation is the key to manipulation of the product variable.

Since a modified product is essentially a new product—at least new with respect to specific properties—the term "new product" is used inclusively in this part. Even so minor a change as a new label may create a new product as perceived by the consumer. Even price has been used as a means of manipulating the product variable, although this practice is very rare. (The technique is to enhance the product's image as a quality good—a property imparted, at least by implication, by a high price.)

The creation of new products, or important modifications of existing items, has emerged as one of the most vital functions of management. There are few industries where this is not so. Even firms operating under conditions that approach pure competition must be receptive to technological changes in production and distribution. To survive competitive prices, the firm must keep its product costs at or below the average of the industry. As labor rates go up, workers must be replaced or made more efficient by the introduction of new equipment, new materials, and new methods. This is especially so when the going market price does not inflate as fast as wages.

297

Although a monopolist can afford the inefficiency of obsolescent technology, he is perennially confronted by the possibility of a technological breakthrough by potential competitors. The railroad industry, for example, enjoyed a monopoly until well into the twentieth century. Its belief that most inland freight and all people would have to employ its services resulted in a failure to attempt innovations, especially in the quality of its services. The industry remained indifferent to change even after the emergence of the truck, the Model-T Ford, and commercial airline service. The motion picture industry made the same error when television was introduced, although its awakening took only ten years, not fifty.[1]

The management of innovation is a difficult and often unrewarding job. This was apparent even before the Industrial Revolution. A look at the mortality rate of products and enterprises today is sufficient to convince one that things have changed little in the past four and a half centuries. Certainly few new-product managers would argue that innovation has become easier. The difficulty of successfully introducing new-product ideas is supported empirically by a number of studies. The results of one study, made by Booz Allen & Hamilton, Inc., the world's largest management consultant firm, are shown in Table 14.1. Booz drew on its experience with over 200 companies and 800 client assignments, each involving new products. Note that the success

Table 14.1   Rate of commercial success

	New Product Ideas	Product Development Projects	New Products Introduced
	SUCCESS PERCENTAGES		
All Industry Groups	1.7%	14.5%	62.5%
Chemical	2	18	59
Consumer packaged goods	2	11	63
Electrical machinery	1	13	63
Metal fabricators	3	11	71
Non-electrical machinery	2	21	59
Raw material processors	5	14	59

SOURCE: Booz Allen & Hamilton, Inc., *Management of New Products* (New York: Booz Allen & Hamilton, Inc., 1968), p. 12.

[1] For a further development of this thesis, see Theodore Levitt, "Marketing Myopia," *Harvard Business Review,* Vol. 38, No. 4 (July–August 1960), pp. 45–56.

rate varies little between industries. It does vary considerably between firms, however, suggesting a difference in management skill. The high mortality between the birth of an idea and its successful commercialization, combined with the high cost usually associated with the introduction and development of new products, makes manipulation of the product variable a hazardous task.

The exploitation of innovation involves imagination, time, resources, and risk. Imagination is the most difficult factor to define and the one that lends itself most poorly to manipulation by the firm. It cannot be manufactured, measured, estimated, or ordered out. However, creativity can be given an opportunity to flourish, and it can be rewarded. Both these acts are within the power of the firm. The characteristics of the firm that tend to create technical progressiveness and growth are suggested in Table 14.2.

Table 14.2   Characteristics of a technically progressive firm

---

1. High status of science and technology in the company.
2. Use of scientists and engineers on the board of directors and in executive positions.
3. Good technical service to customers.
4. Readiness to look outside the firm for ideas.
5. Willingness to share knowledge.
6. Willingness to acquire new knowledge by taking licenses for the use of patented ideas.
7. Willingness to engage in joint ventures.
8. Maintenance of a research and development department.
9. Willingness to experiment.
10. Willingness to assume risk.
11. Evaluation of the outcome of investment decisions.
12. Use of scientific management techniques.
13. Ability to attract talented people.
14. Use of training programs.
15. Use of long-range planning.
16. Participation in professional and trade associations.
17. Provisions for the recruitment, evaluation, and rewarding of superior managers.
18. Effective internal communications.
19. Deliberate survey and evaluation of new ideas.
20. Rapid replacement of machines.

SOURCE: Adapted from C. F. Carter and B. R. Williams, "The Characteristics of Technically Progressive Firms," *Journal of Industrial Economics,* Vol. 7, No. 2 (March 1959), p. 90.

The first, and most important, step in developing new products is to obtain the formal support of the board of directors and the active participation of senior executives in a new-product development program. An organized program for the conception, acquisition, screening, evaluation, selection, development, market testing, and commercialization of new products is usually necessary. Such a program, however, will be a futile exercise in bureaucracy if it does not have broad objectives, specific criteria, and the endorsement of senior management.

Time is a significant variable in new-product development. Although patience is a poor substitute for aggressiveness in the adoption of new technology and the exploitation of new ideas, the marketer should appreciate the time that it may take for an innovation to be accepted in the marketplace, the need for long-range planning, and the likelihood of substantial resistance to the product. Table 14.3 (pp. 301–06), which shows how several twentieth-century innovations have fared, illustrates this.

In addition to competing for the resources of the firm, any new-product program is inherently risky. Although both the level of resources required and the risk can be reduced substantially if the firm is a laggard—if it watches the performance of innovations in the hands of other firms before adopting them—such a policy also means forgoing profitable opportunities and leaving market leadership to be retained or captured by competitors. There are, of course, exceptions. For instance, Hills Brothers invented instant coffee, but Maxwell House dominates the market. (This suggests the need for aggressive marketing during the introductory phase of a new product, in order to exploit the initial—but often short-lived—monopoly and establish a dominant position.) Also, popular-price clothing manufacturers and retailers have successfully executed a follow-the-leader strategy with respect to women's styles. Exclusive high fashion houses introduce the style changes, which are later copied and exploited in the mass market.

PRODUCT VARIABLES

Any action taken by the firm that changes the consumer's attitude toward the firm's product in a sense creates a new product. This definition of product creation encompasses both changes in the product itself and changes in any aspect of the marketing program that will induce a change in the buyer's perception of the product. We shall begin our discussion of new-product creation by analyzing the means by which the product itself can be changed, or be made to appear changed, in the eyes of the consumer. Six primary areas for change are (1) the product's physical properties, (2) the brand and label, (3) packaging, (4) quality, (5) image, and (6) location.

Table 14.3   New-product development time

I. CONSUMER PACKAGED GOODS

Product	Company	Date Development Started or Idea Born	Test or Initial Markets	Large-Scale or National	Elapsed Time	Reference	Remarks
Birds Eye frozen foods	Birds Eye Division, General Foods	1908	1923		15 years	Printers' Ink 5/29/64	
Ban (roll-on deodorant)	Bristol-Myers	About 1948	1954	March 1955	6 years	Printers' Ink, 6/5/59 Sponsor, 4/16/56	Roll-on idea came from an outside inventor, hence presumably predates 1948. Bristol-Myers developed product that failed in test markets in 1951. Company researchers worked on plastics, finally assigned outside company job of making plastic marbles. Consumer-panel studies favorable in fall 1953. Final test markets, summer 1954. National advertising, March 1955.
Calm powder deodorant in aerosol can	Alberto-Culver	1959		February 1964	5 years	Printers' Ink 1/24/64	Non-spray powder deodorants were tried about 1948–50; did not "get off the ground" then.
Chlorodent (toothpaste)	Lever Brothers	1930's	March 1951	Early 1952	Between 11 and 21 years	Tide, 3/28/52	Idea developed in 1930's; two J. Walter Thompson vice presidents formed a company, Rystan, with a patent for chlorophyll products. Idea subsequently presented to Lever, and Lever licensed to produce toothpaste.
Citroid (cold compound)	Grove Laboratories	1954–55		1956	1 to 2 years	Advertising Agency, 10/26/56	
Coldene (cold-remedy liquid)	Pharma-Craft	1954	1955	1956	1 year	Printers' Ink, 2/7/58	
Crest (fluoride toothpaste)	Procter & Gamble	1945	January 1955	January 1956	10 years	Advertising Age, 8/1/60	Discovery that stannous fluoride is a preventive against tooth decay first made by Dr. Joseph C. Muhler in 1945, when he was a sophomore at School of Dentistry, University of Indiana. Since P&G had a parallel interest, Dr. Muhler continued to work on the project.

Table 14.3 Continued

Product	Company	Date Development Started or Idea Born	Test or Initial Markets	Large-Scale or National	Elapsed Time	Reference	Remarks
Decaffeinated instant coffee)	Nestlé	1947	1953		10 years	*Tide*, 1/25/57 Nestlé Company	
Flav-R-Straws	Frontier Foods Corp. and others	1953	April 1956	Early 1957	3 years	*Food Business*, 4/57	Inventor sold idea to Frontier in 1955. By January 1956, Frontier was in trouble, and product taken over by others.
Gerber (strained baby foods)	Gerber	1927	1928		1 year	*Business Decisions That Changed Our Lives*, Sidney Furst, Milton Sherman (Random House, 1964), p. 167.	
Hills Brothers (instant coffee)	Hills Brothers Coffee	1934	1956		22 years	*New York Times*, 11/16/56	
Johnson liquid shoe polish containers that are also applicators	S. C. Johnson	1957	February 1960	Early 1961	3 years	*Printers' Ink*, 7/14/61	
Lustre Creme (liquid shampoo)	Colgate-Palmolive	1950		June 1958	8 years	*Drug Trade News*, 5/19/58	Five years of product tests, three years of consumer research.
Marlboro (filter cigarettes)	Philip Morris	May 1953	March 1955		2 years	*Advertising Age*, 2/28/55	Marlboro had previously existed as a premium non-filter cigarette; development of filter, hard package, flip-top were new; red ("beauty") tip derived from earlier non-filter product.
Maxim (concentrated instant coffee)	General Foods	1954	May 1964		10 years	*Printers' Ink*, 5/1/64	Preserves flavor and aroma of freshly brewed coffee. Process involves freezing of freshly percolated coffee. To use, crystals are dropped into cup of boiling (or iced) water.

Product	Company				Source	Description
Minute Maid (frozen orange juice)	Minute Maid	1944	1946	2 years	*Sales Management,* 4/1/49; *Advertising Age,* 3/14/49	Introduced in 1946 under private label; and in 1947 under Minute Maid name.
Minute Rice	General Foods	1931	First quarter 1949	18 years	*Food Field Reporter,* 12/13/54; *Advertising Agency,* 11/49	Idea originally came from member of Afghanistan royal family. GF had plant ready in 1941. World War II interrupted; army used plant. Consumer-tested in spring, 1946. Began national distribution in late 1948.
Purina Dog Chow	Ralston-Purina	1951	February 1955	4 years	*Wall Street Journal,* 1/2/58	Began search for a dry dog-food in 1951; developed light aerated feed using new formula in 1953; began testing February 1955; in four additional test markets in 1955–56; achieved national distribution by April 1957.
Red Kettle (dry-soup mixes)	Campbell Soup	Before 1943	August 1962	19 years plus	*Advertising Age,* 9/24/62; *Food Field Reporter,* 8/28/61	Campbell first tested dry noodle soup in 1943–44; withdrew product because "we were dissatisfied with the processes and packages available." Resumed testing in 1959.
Stripe (toothpaste)	Lever Brothers	1952	Early 1958	5½ to 6 years	*New York Times,* 1/15/58	Inventor spent four years developing the striping device. Took Lever engineers six months to design a production machine. Product then in test markets for 14 months.
Wisk (liquid detergent)	Lever Brothers	1955	January 1956	1 year	*Fortune,* 6/59	
Wrinkle-removing creams	(Many)		1963–64			Protein used in these creams, developed during World War II.

II. OTHER CONSUMER GOODS

Product	Company				Source	Description
Bendix (washer/dryer)	Bendix	Prior to World War II	March 1953	12 years plus	*Fortune,* 3/53	
Eversharp ("Fountain Ball" ball pen)	Eversharp	January 1958	September 1958	8 months	*Sales Management,* 1/2/59	Eight months in product development; one year in product and market testing.

Table 14.3 Continued

Product	Company	Date Development Started or Idea Born	Test or Initial Markets	Large-Scale or National	Elapsed Time	Reference	Remarks
Fairchild (Mark IV 8mm. sound projector)	Fairchild Camera & Instrument	Late 1961	August 1963		2 years	New Products, New Profits, American Management Association, 1964	Fairchild describes as "better than average effort," due to technical advances in dealing with the complexities involved.
Floron (plastic floor tile)	Pabco Products	1947–48		October 1953	5 to 6 years	Sales Management, 1/1/55	
GE (electric toothbrush)	General Electric	1958–59	October 1961	April 1962	3 to 4 years	Printers' Ink 7/20/62	Electric toothbrushes available for 30 years; wall-socket recharging, new.
Polaroid Land Camera	Polaroid Corp.	1945–46	1947–48		2 years	Business Week, 9/3/49 and 1/19/63 Printers' Ink, 5/29/64 Standard & Poor's Corporate Records, 1965, p. 9745.	
Polaroid Color-pack Camera	Polaroid Corp.	1948	January 1963	May 1963	15 years plus	Business Week, 1/19/63	
Scripto Tilt Tip (ball pen)	Scripto	1959	April 1961	Mid-1961	2 years	Advertising Age, 1/30/61	
Sinclair (Power X gasoline; Extra Duty Motor Oil)	Sinclair Oil	Late 1952		April 1953	6 months	Printers' Ink 6/18/54	
Smith Corona (portable electric typewriter)	Smith Corona	1952	Early 1957		5 years	New York Times, 11/17/57	
Sunbeam (electric toothbrush)	Sunbeam Corp.				5 years	Sales Management, 9/4/64	

Product	Originator / Company				Development time	Reference	Description
Talon (zippers)	Corporate predecessor of Talon, Inc.	1883	1913	1918	30 years	*Business Decisions That Changed Our Lives*, Sidney Furst, Milton Sherman (Random House, 1964), p. 115.	Zippers first thought of as shoe-fastening device in 1883. In 1894, product first developed for use in shoes. First modern zipper concept emerged in 1908. First successful mass production, 1913; and first applications to clothing in 1913-18. In 1918, an ex-GI suggested use of zippers for money belts, and this was really the first commercial success.
Television	(Many)	1884	1939	1946-47	55 years	Federal Communications Commission, "Broadcast Primer," Bulletin 2-B, 1961.	In 1884, Nipkow, a German, patented a scanning disk for transmitting pictures by wireless. This is credited with being the first development that led ultimately to what is now known as television. In 1890 Jenkins began his studies

in the U. S. In the 1900's, Rignoux and Fournier conducted "television" experiments in France. In 1915, Marconi predicted a "visible telephone." In 1923, Zworykin applied for a patent on the iconoscope, a TV camera-tube. In 1925, Jenkins demonstrated a mechanical television apparatus. In 1927 the first experimental television was made by Bell Laboratories. In 1928 the first station, WGY, was established in Schenectady. In 1930 RCA demonstrated large-screen TV in New York. In 1936 RCA tested outdoor TV pickup in Camden. By 1937, 17 experimental stations were in existence. The first commercial program from New York to Washington. In 1939 RCA demonstrated program was authorized on July 1, 1941 by WNBT—New York, but the first TV sets were shown to consumers at the New York World's Fair in 1939, and available to consumers in 1939-40.

III. INDUSTRIAL GOODS

Product	Originator / Company				Development time	Reference	Description
Dictet (portable recording machine)	Dictaphone Corp.	1954	Early		20 months	*A Critical Look At The Purchasing Function*, Robert F. Logler, American Management Association Bulletin No. 13, 1961, pp. 113–21.	
Isothalic (chemical component to improve house paints)	Oronite Corp. (subsidiary of Standard Oil of California)	1951	Late 1957 to early 1958		6 to 7 years plus	*Sales Management*, 9/19/58	Specific development of superior house paint begun in 1951. Oronite began work on Isothalic during World War II. Isothalic reported to be ten years in development.
Krilium (soil conditioner)	Monsanto	1939	May 1952		12½ years	*Fortune*, 12/52	10 years in laboratory; 2½ years in field test.
Page Master (selective pocket-paging system)	Stromberg Carlson	1955	March 1957		2 years	American Management Association Bulletin No. 13, 1961, pp. 122–41.	

Table 14.3 Continued

Product	Company	Date Development Started or Idea Born	Test or Initial Markets	Large-Scale or National	Elapsed Time	Reference	Remarks
Penicillin	(Many)	1928	1943		15 years	*Business Week,* 3/3/45	Discovered by Sir Alexander Fleming.
Transistors	Bell Laboratories	1940	1955–56		15 to 16 years	*Business Week,* 3/26/60	First discovery accidental, in 1940. First laboratory transistor, debut in 1948. Prototype qualities available, 1954. First consumer applications in hearing aids and radios, 1955–56.
Xerox (electrostatic copying machines)	Xerox Corp.	1935	1950		15 years	*Forbes,* 9/15/62 *Fortune,* 7/62 *New York Times,* 12/10/61 *Standard & Poor's Corporate Records,* 1965, p. 4472.	[Idea from a single employee.]

SOURCE: Adapted from Lee Adler, "Time Lag in New Product Development," *Journal of Marketing,* Vol. 30, No. 1 (January 1966), pp. 18–21. Reprinted from the *Journal of Marketing,* published by the American Marketing Association.

PHYSICAL PROPERTIES

Physical properties relate to the function and form of the product. Although physical properties can often be measured numerically, only occasionally can an explicit statement of demand as a function of a product's physical properties be calculated. However, there are exceptions, such as in the markets for raw materials and industrial goods. For instance, the total demand for a given type of aviation fuel can quickly be estimated once its octane rating, volatility, and additive content are known. The market and sales volume for steel can be determined as a function of thickness, tensile strength, and finish. Both the market and the price of raw petroleum and ore are calculated on the basis of measurable physical properties.

More frequently, however, the effect of physical properties on demand must be estimated by judgment, sampling, or observations in the marketplace. By increasing the number of variations in physical properties offered to the consumer, the marketer is more apt to include the most popular ones. As marketing data accumulates, the less popular options (for example, particular sizes, colors, and accessories for which the demand is low) can be eliminated from the product line. Marginal analysis will indicate whether such a change would increase profits.

The manipulation of physical properties can be one of the most effective means of reducing or destroying competition.[2] In some markets, consumer preferences are very sensitive to style changes. Women's clothing is the most conspicuous example of this, although the same phenomenon is observable in the housing, furniture, and automobile markets. Where there are large economies of scale and heavy capital-investment requirements, the major producer can exclude or destroy competitors by instituting product changes faster or more economically than can the competing firms. The practice is not illegal in itself.

The use of product features as a predatory marketing instrument is illustrated by Figure 14.1.

If the firm can reach output Q_2 along the average unit cost curve C_{A_1}, it will realize an average profit per unit of $R_A - C_2$ (profit equals revenue, R_A, minus cost, C_2). If it can produce Q_3 units along curve C_{A_1}, then average unit profit—hence total profit—will be even greater. However, if competition forces a major product change—say a completely new body style—at Q_1, average unit profit becomes negative and the firm operates at a loss until it is beyond output Q_2, as shown by cost curve C_{A_2}.

The firm with the largest market share will reach points $Q_1, Q_2, Q_3 \ldots$ Q_n first, due to its higher rate of sales. If the firm's lead is sufficiently great—

2 See J. A. Menge, "Style Change Costs as a Market Weapon," *Quarterly Journal of Economics,* Vol. 76, No. 4 (November 1962), pp. 632–47.

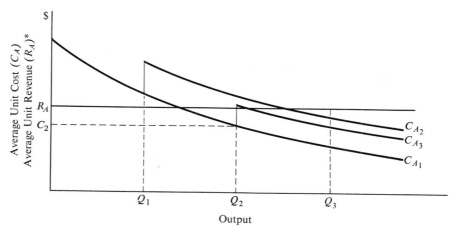

FIGURE 14.1
Effect of product change on cost

* R_A is also average price.

SOURCE: Adapted from John A. Menge, "Style Change Cost as a Market Weapon," *Quarterly Journal of Economics* (November 1962), published by Harvard University Press.

if, say, it reaches Q_3 when its competitors are still at Q_1 or Q_2—it can opt for a major product change and still make a profit. In fact, the normal wear on tooling may force its replacement at output Q_3 anyway. If this is the case, the cost of the tooling for the new model may not be much more than the cost of replacing the worn-out tooling for the present model.

The smaller competitors are not so fortunate. At the time the major firm introduces the new model, the competitors still have relatively low time on their tooling. Hence they are faced with three unpleasant options. First, they can match the leader and introduce a new model at the same time, thus moving to cost curve C_{A2} or C_{A3}, depending on their output at that date. Second, they could reduce price, a move that would lower the average revenue curve, R_A. Either of these two choices might sustain their sales, but would make average unit profit negative, causing them to operate at a loss. Third, they could choose neither of the preceding options. However, they would presumably forfeit more of their market share, hence sales, to the firm with the new models. Inaction would be disastrous in the long run, since their output might never reach Q_3. Meanwhile, the leading firm would be increasing its market share, wearing out the new-model tooling, and rapidly approaching the point where yet another major change will be introduced.

This latter event will make matters still worse for the competitors by making their products even more obsolete.

Another alternative for the smaller firms is to increase their market share, thereby increasing their production rate at the expense of the leader. This would put a competitor's output closer to the output of the leader. If the gap could be narrowed sufficiently, the product variable would no longer serve as an instrument for destroying competition. Unfortunately, the junior members of the industry may not have this option. Enlargement of a firm's market share requires more promotion, a greater network of retailers, and possibly expensive product innovations. These require an expenditure of people and money and an assumption of risk that may well be beyond the resources of the firm. The problem is illustrated by the automobile industry, where the tri-annual model change has become institutionalized. Only three firms out of the hundred or more companies initially in the industry have successfully withstood the competition—competition whose most effective instrument has been the product variable.

In addition to the high cost of retooling—which allows product variation based on style changes alone to eliminate competition—a high level of research and development can also enable the firm to introduce product changes that destroy competition. Research and development is properly viewed as a fixed cost. If fixed costs are large, average unit costs will change rapidly as a function of output. Hence the firm with the largest market share can sustain the highest level of research and development, which in turn should provide it with the greatest number of product improvements and additions, and enlarge its market share. As the leader increases its outlay in this area, the break-even quantity for firms desiring to be product-competitive becomes larger and larger. The logical conclusion to this cycle is the expulsion from the market of firms without sufficient competitive resources and, eventually, an industry dominated by two or three—or even one—giant companies. The automobile and computer industries are in this position. Presumably, only the threat of federal intervention prevents both industries from becoming duopolistic or monopolistic.

This is not an indictment either of large firms or of the heavy use of the product variable as an instrument of competition. On the contrary, this kind of competition has created great improvements in virtually every product class, provided an assortment of new products that even Jules Verne did not envision, and made American goods extremely competitive in foreign markets.[3]

Even if a company has a product that is sufficiently unique and functionally superior to penetrate a market, it may not be able to sustain its

---

[3] The reader interested in less admirable applications of the product variable is directed to Vance Packard's *The Waste Makers* (New York: McKay, 1960).

position unless it has an enforceable patent or the resources to match its competitors' innovations. North American Aviation (now North American Rockwell Corporation) demonstrated this axiom when it attempted to exploit some of its unique technology (gained from designing computers for guided missiles) in the commercial computer market. Its product was so good that it received offers from other computer manufacturers to acquire its product line. However, it failed to support its new line with adequate product variations and sufficient research and development on new and improved models. As a result, it not only lost the market share it had originally captured, but was eventually forced to withdraw from the commercial computer industry, consuming in the interim a good deal of red ink.

The experience of the American Motors Corporation with product variation was somewhat different. American Motors was falling victim to the repeated style changes of the U. S. automobile industry, when its president, George Romney, conceived the introduction of a small, austere, economical passenger car. At the time, no such vehicle was being offered by a domestic manufacturer. The result was the Rambler, which captured a noticeable segment of the U. S. market and made its producer a profitable corporation again. Instead of fighting the big three with style changes on standard-sized automobiles, American Motors opted for a unique product, but one that would keep it in the same industry, thus allowing it to utilize its present manufacturing and marketing capabilities. Unfortunately for American Motors, the competition, observing the success of the compact car, which was making inroads into the standard-sized car market, introduced their own economy-size automobile. Within a few years, American Motors was confronted with the same problem that had led it to add the compact to its line. Sales and profit again dropped, and today there is some doubt as to the firm's ability to survive in the industry.

By definition, pure competition means no product variation. However, the product variable can be very effectively manipulated in differentiated oligopolies, which are the most common form of industry in America. As long as the technological revolution of the twentieth century continues, the importance of product variation as an instrument of competition will not diminish.

BRAND AND LABEL

Brands and labels serve to identify and explain a product. Of the two, brand is normally the more significant variable. The label is essentially expository, containing ingredients, weights and measures, warnings, disclaimers, and, frequently, instructions for the good's operation, use, or servicing. It may also contain the make, model, and serial number of the product, or possibly a brief advertising message. Invariably it will identify the manufacturer or distributor, or both. From a marketing viewpoint, the preparation of the label is a relatively trivial task. However, recent federal legislation has prescribed stricter standards, and for this reason the subject is explored in some detail in Chapter 27.

The brand, on the other hand, not only identifies the product but also transfers whatever image the firm or its product family may have to the branded good. This can be a service or a disservice to the product (or its sister goods), depending on several factors. If the firm has been a producer of low-priced, austere goods and elects to add a line of expensive, prestigious goods, there may be no merit in identifying the new products with the established line. On the contrary, a brand commonly associated with a low-priced product line could easily detract from the new product's market potential.

Conversely, a firm that has established a brand image of prestige, luxury, or high quality may damage its premium line by using the same brand on a less expensive product. Buyers may select the lower-priced item in lieu of the premium good, or switch brands. In addition, identification with the low-priced line may downgrade the image of the premium line. On the other hand, commonality of brands allows the firm to exploit its reputation and reduces the need for introductory promotion. The transfer of the prestigious image to the less prestigious product may well increase aggregate demand for the firm's products. The effect of branding decisions will vary with particular markets. Analyses of historical data, the observation of competitors' experience, and consumer surveys are possible methods for determining the optimum use of branding by a firm.

A compromise branding strategy is to brand each line differently, but identify them all with the same producer. The General Motors Corporation and Chris-Craft Industries, Inc., have adopted this strategy. Each manufactures several lines that are distinctly different in price, quality, and image. Each line carries its own brand, but is clearly identified with General Motors or Chris-Craft. This practice is typical of consumer-durable and industrial-goods producers.

Convenience goods present a different problem, due to the novelty phenomenon and the need to induce repeated purchases. Even if the customer has no objection to the physical properties of the product, he will often shift brands out of curiosity or boredom. The producer accommodates this behavior by offering a number of different brands. This strategy allows the buyer to engage in brand switching yet still remain with the same producer—often unknowingly, unless he examines carefully the fine print on the label. One has only to look at an assortment of cigarettes, breakfast cereals, or canned beer to see how frequently this tactic is used.

Another common practice is the use of multiple brands for an identical product. This strategy is frequently used at the manufacturing or processing level in order to simultaneously sell in both separate and competing markets. For example, independent retailers prefer to carry brands not handled by discount houses or chain stores, especially when they are unwilling to match the lower prices associated with the other stores. Large supermarkets, particularly chains, like to carry a line of goods bearing their own brand. (These products are usually sold at prices slightly lower than regular brands.) To accommodate a conglomerate market, the producer simply attaches different brands to the same product. In the canned-foods industry, the processor just changes labels. In the case of consumer durables—clothes and automobile tires, for example—the manufacturer often changes the packaging as well as the label attached to or stamped on the product. The cost of such changes is usually negligible.

The preceding examples of brand manipulation are an application of market segmentation—an important marketing principle that will be explored again shortly. Branding also has other implications for the marketer, especially in the area of product innovation.

Branding encourages innovation, for it gives the firm the opportunity to identify itself and its products with the new product development. To some extent, this also imparts the idea that the firm has a proprietary claim on the innovation, which is especially important if other means of protection are denied. If an idea can be copied by a competitor, at least the brand name originally associated with it cannot be copied too.

Without branding, differentiated oligopolies—so frequent in American industry—would not be so common. One has only to look at the cigarette industry, where the most trivial of innovations are used to differentiate an essentially standard product, to see this.

An innovation that will do little to expand the industry's market, but will encourage brand shifting within the product class, is not important to a firm with the lion's share of market, unless it expects to be confronted with an innovation in competing brands. If so, it may have to innovate simply to maintain its market position. This suggests that there is an optimum-size market share in terms of the benefits to be reaped by innovation.

PACKAGING

Packaging includes the wrapping, boxing, crating, and preserving of the product. In addition to its obvious role as a protector and carrier, the package also serves to identify and advertise the product. In some instances, it may become part of the good itself, like the decorative bottles used to contain perfume or liquor. The package may even cost more than the product. An elaborate jacket costs more than the record it protects. Cosmetic containers often exceed the cost of their contents. A labeled catsup bottle costs just as much to produce as the food it holds.

Packaging can also influence the functional properties of the product. From the viewpoint of the middleman as well as the consumer, many considerations are involved: Does the packaging allow large quantities to be easily broken down for reassortment, distribution, sale, and consumption? Does it provide for incremental dispersion and for preservation of the residual quantity? Does it allow the product be placed directly on the table, or must it first be transferred to a more presentable container? Does it give the consumer ready access to the contents for pre-purchase inspection? Does it enhance the safety of the product?

Market observation and testing will answer many of these questions. Where image, opinion, or promotional questions arise, a consumer survey may help. The answers may not be precise, but their nature and distribution should be adequate bases for qualitative decisions.

Unfortunately, the problem is not so straightforward when questions of profit maximization and the sensitivity of sales to variations in packaging come up. Again, the impact of alternative packaging plans on the cost function is usually easy to determine. The influence of packaging on the revenue function is not as easily or cheaply established; however, a consumer survey—or, if practical, market experimentation—may be of value. There are experimental designs that lend themselves to the isolation and observation of the packaging variable as it is manipulated in the marketplace. These techniques, discussed in Chapter 24, are used frequently in the selection of package color and design, especially in the convenience-good industries.

Another question that may arise with regard to packaging is the allocation of costs. If the package becomes part of the product or is a method of advertising, how much of the expense—over and above the cost of the minimum protective container—should be debited to the product, and how much to the promotional budget? The answer is not clearcut, but one possibility is to assign that portion of the packaging cost identifiable with the functional or aesthetic properties of the product itself to the product, and that portion associated with promotion to advertising. As a practical matter, the question is generally left to the judgment and negotiating ability of the departmental managers.

QUALITY

Product *quality* has two dimensions, reliability and durability. *Reliability* is the measure of assurance one has that a product is exactly what it is represented to be and will perform as it is intended to perform. It is expressed as a probability: Only 3 bottles out of 1,000 will contain less than 1 quart of milk. The engine will start 99 times out of 100. Every production lot of 500 television sets delivered to retailers will contain 4 or fewer improperly wired sets. The chance of a transmission failure during the first 50,000 miles of driving is .008.

High reliability is a function of good design, good craftsmanship, and stringent quality control. Traditionally, quality control meant the inspection of the product and the parts that went into it. This operation started at the receiving end, where inputs from the suppliers were counted, measured, and tested to make sure that they conformed to orders and specifications. Components fabricated within the firm were also subject to inspection, as were the final products, in order to identify and reject faulty materials, parts, and finished products. The rejected items were then returned for reworking or scrapped.

Although these practices are still part of the quality-control function, the concept of reliability, or quality assurance, has been broadened to include the participation of quality-control specialists in the design, planning, and manufacturing stages of product development, and in the after-sales service program. Most of the sophisticated quality-assurance techniques in use today were developed in the aerospace industry, where the failure of a one-dollar part could cause the destruction of a multimillion-dollar missile, spacecraft, or airplane. These techniques are now being applied in civilian industries, especially where complex and expensive products are involved. Fail-safe design, employing redundant circuitry or structures and in-service checkout equipment, is also becoming common.

Durability is the measure of a product's expected lifespan. It is stated in calendar time or in terms of the amount of use the product can endure and still be reliable: The house paint will last eight years. The engine will run 1,500 hours. The light bulb will last 2,000 hours. The tire will last 25,000 miles.

Both reliability and durability can be varied by the firm within the limits imposed by the current state of technology. However, an improvement in either usually means higher costs. In addition, the more durable the product is, the longer the time before it must be replaced. This means fewer replacement sales, with a resultant reduction in revenue and profit.

The importance of the replacement market has suggested to some firms the intentional design and manufacture of less durable goods and planned obsolescence. In the 1960's, this opened a Pandora's box of controversy on the intent and morality of American manufacturing and marketing practices, which reached a zenith in popular literature with the publication in 1960 of Vance Packard's *The Waste Makers*. This best seller was a tirade on the alleged practices of U. S. industry, which Packard claimed intentionally produced goods that would wear out or break down after a relatively short lifespan, thus requiring replacement. Packard also attacked industry for changing products solely for the sake of change, in order to make owners dissatisfied with what they presently have. One has only to look at the numerous, frequent, and nonfunctional changes in automobiles to realize Packard's charges are not entirely imagined.

The defenders of industry argue that change is healthy; that it stimulates demand, thereby increasing sales and employment, that it improves products, relieves monotony, and provides a greater variety of products to the consumer. They point to the improvements made in warranties and performance characteristics of modern products. Furthermore, they suggest that the benefits of a further improvement in quality, given the present state of the industrial arts, would be more than offset by the increase in cost, hence price. Thus the battle goes on.

The firm's dilemma is to decide what trade-offs should be made between product quality and other product characteristics and marketing variables. Frequently, the expenditure of resources on quality improvement means a heavy sacrifice in other areas, such as appearance and delivery. Statisticians say that perfect quality is unobtainable. Nothing can be made 100-percent reliable or be built to last forever, regardless of the amount of resources the firm is willing to allocate to the task. This makes the quality decision a relative one.

Although the relationship between level of quality and cost can usually be reflected in the firm's cost function, the explicit relationship between demand and reliability is far more elusive. Particularly in the field of consumer goods, many questions are difficult to answer. What is the elasticity of demand with respect to reliability? What will a 10-percent increase in durability do to total revenue? Will the loss of replacement sales be made up by the enlargement of original sales resulting from a superior—that is, more durable—good?

In some cases—as in the manufacturing of drugs, aircraft, and guided missiles—the government sets quality standards, or at least minimum values for product reliability and durability. Sometimes trade associations will recommend minimum standards for an industry. If the firm is left to its own devices, it might look to the prevailing practice in its industry as a guide. This is not uncommon. In fact, many companies regularly purchase competitors' products and subject them to critical tests. Occasionally these tests are useful in promotion, as when the Ford Motor Company discovered the sound level in its sedans to be lower than that found in other brands, including Rolls Royce. Ford wasted little time in exploiting the test results in its advertising.

Another possibility is to manipulate the image of quality and measure the effect on sales. This can be done most directly by varying the length and conditions of the warranty. The prospect's perception of the product's quality may be influenced by the manufacturer's guarantee, although no change has been made in the product itself. In fact, the buyer may not be too concerned about whether the good is actually improved, as long as the seller will repair or replace the item if it does break down or wear out.

The quality decision, especially with respect to warranties, also impinges on the distribution problem. The marketer can look forward to a large number of alienated consumers and middlemen (the latter usually receive the initial brunt of user complaints) if quality claims or warranties are not enforced. This means that service centers must be established, or steps taken to ensure that retailers or wholesalers are staffed, equipped, and willing to correct problems. The second alternative generally involves cost sharing, with the manufacturer providing replacement parts and absorbing part of the labor cost. Depending on circumstances, either training programs, field representatives, or additional customer-service personnel may be in order. All of these devices are used by the automobile, computer, and aircraft industries.

IMAGE

Image refers to the characteristics of the product as they are perceived by the consumer. It can be solely a function of the physical properties of the good, or it may also be influenced by branding, packaging, and promotion. The buyer of a Cadillac, a Dior original, or Beefeater gin surely perceives qualities not immediately detectable by observation of the good itself.

Advertising is the most obvious means of imparting an image to a product. It serves to educate the prospect on the actual appearance and function of the good or service and also imparts psychogenic properties. On a less ethical plane, it may convey a form or function that is not truly part of the product. Advertising is especially important for consumer goods, whose symbolic properties may exceed their physical properties in importance. Perfume, luxury automobiles, high-fashion apparel, and membership in ostentatious clubs are examples.

Image may often be manipulated more readily and less expensively by promotion than by physical variations in the product itself. Frequently, manipulating the product's image is the firm's only option, as the physical properties of the good do not lend themselves to much change. First-class air travel, premium beer, and cigarettes are such products.

LOCATION

Location is an important product variable for service industries such as the hotel industry, gasoline distributors, apartment or home builders, and theater chains. It is often related to other product variables and marketing instruments. For example, the closer the goods are to the consumers, the larger the number of warehouses or stores that are required and the smaller the size of the local inventories that can be maintained. Location may influence the type and cost of construction, the style and size of the buildings, and pricing strategy. It may also determine the size and characteristics of the potential market.

PROTECTION OF NEW PRODUCTS

Truly radical innovations are rare and often expensive. If they can be protected, they may also be extremely effective weapons in the marketplace. Secrecy is one way of protecting an innovation. It is widely practiced in regard to industrial processes as well as in the preparation of new products. Witness, for instance, the secrecy surrounding the chemical and automobile industries. However, if the innovation is conspicuous in the good itself, secrecy ceases to exist once the item is exposed in the marketplace. At that point, only the time and cost of copying the idea will constrain competitors, unless another barrier is placed in their way. Thus firms rely heavily on patents, copyrights, and trademarks to protect their product innovations.

Patents and Copyrights.[5] A *patent* is actually a federally granted monopoly for the exclusive use of an innovation, usually for 17 years. A *copyright* is a special form of patent applying to printed material. Without this protection, management may be unwilling to commit funds to the design and development of new or improved products. Such expenditures must ultimately be included in the product's cost function, thus forcing a higher price, at least until the firm can recoup the research-and-development costs. If other firms can copy the innovation, without incurring these costs, the higher price may suddenly become noncompetitive. However, if the market can be exploited and the product well entrenched before the entry of competition, then step pricing may allow the firm to make a considerable profit from its innovation, despite the research-and-development costs.

If a firm cannot obtain a patent on a new product, the longevity of innovation monopoly will be a function of five factors: (1) the profitability of the innovation, (2) the design and tooling costs, (3) the exclusivity of the technical know-how and the manufacturing process, (4) the lead time required for preparation and introduction of the copy, and (5) the originator's ability to establish a strong image identifying the innovation with its brand. An obviously profitable item will attract competitors and speed their entry

[5] See Chapter 28 for a detailed exploration of this topic.

into the market, thus reducing the time the innovative firm can operate as a monopoly. Conversely, if the new product requires either a large design and tooling outlay or a long manufacturing lead time, this factor will increase the length of the innovator's monopoly.

One of the hindrances faced by the government in marketing federally sponsored technology has been the lack of patent protection. Federally sponsored innovations, especially product ideas that result from military and space programs, must often be modified for adaptation to the civilian market. Commercial firms are generally unwilling to spend the money for these adaptations if they can be immediately copied by competitors. The result has been a restricted program of licensing, which appears to have encouraged the acceptance of federally developed technology.

Trademarks. A *trademark* is a brand that has been given protection under the law. Both statutory law and common law protect trademarks that serve to identify a product's origin and distinguish it from other brands. If a brand can meet the requirements of originality, first use, distinction, and out-of-context use, as well as several other minor requirements, it can be registered under the Lanham Act (1947). This provides the firm with exclusive use of the brand and with recourse in the federal courts in case of infringement. Without protection, either by legislation or common law, the manufacturer would have no assurance that it would not spend considerable resources introducing and promoting a brand name and then have it usurped by an unscrupulous competitor.

CHAPTER 15

Product Mix, Line, and Marketing Strategies

PRODUCT MIX

Product mix is "the composite of products offered for sale by a firm or business unit."[1] It is the collection of products manufactured or distributed by a given company. The product decision can involve many variables and be extremely complex. A change in product mix implies effects on the price, promotion, distribution, manufacturing, and possibly the product characteristics of each item offered or being considered by the firm. In many cases, the optimum solution to a product-mix problem would require the marketer to interpret or manipulate an unmanageable quantity of information, most likely under conditions of uncertainty. Fortunately, suboptimum techniques are often available that will provide near-optimum answers and involve only the significant variables, whose number is more manageable. Essentially, the important variables that will be affected must be isolated, their effects in terms of the changes in costs and revenues that will occur estimated, and a marginal analysis made of the subsequent profit.

Product-mix changes are frequently made for purposes of diversification. They may involve use of the firm's present plant and facilities, including the marketing organization, or they may require the divestiture or acquisition of independent operations. The acquisition of going enterprises—whose products are often far removed from all the firm's present product lines—has been a major postwar phenomenon in American business. This broadening of the product mix by many firms has served two ends—growth and diver-

[1] Ralph S. Alexander and the Committee on Definitions of the American Marketing Association, *Marketing Definitions* (Chicago: American Marketing Association, 1960), p. 19.

sification. Through acquisition and merger,[2] the conglomerate corporations use their capital resources to enter industries with promising growth possibilities. By acquiring an established product line, they are relieved of the pioneering work and much of the uncertainty associated with the penetration of a new market. In fact, two of the common criteria for choosing which firms to absorb have been successful management and a history of increasing profits.

Having a broad product mix also spreads the risk of failure over a greater number of product lines. This is an application of the "don't put all your eggs in one basket" philosophy that makes considerable sense when one views the rapidity with which a single product line can become outmoded or obsolescent, and hence unprofitable. Witness the horse and buggy, the passenger train, the bamboo fishing rod, and fox-trot music.

In any case, the fates of the blacksmiths, the railroads, the coal industry, and the vaudeville theater have not gone unnoticed. The Ford Motor Company, which has entered the astronautics and home-appliance fields, and the Columbia Broadcasting System, which has acquired a publishing house and a major-league baseball club, are but a few of the firms that have opted for diversification as a method of expansion.

PRODUCT LINE

A *product line* is "a group of products that are closely related either because they satisfy a class of need, are used together, are sold to the same customer groups, are marketed through the same type of outlets or fall within given price ranges."[3] Sporting goods, carpentry tools, restaurant supplies, groceries, and dime-store products are examples of product lines. Sub-lines within a product line may be distinguished. Hammers, saws, and levels are sub-lines of carpentry tools. Meat, produce, canned goods, and sundries are sub-lines of grocery products.

The same terms that are used to describe product lines may be used to describe industries and define markets, although this can sometimes be misleading. For example, "paper towels" accurately defines a product line, but serves poorly to define an industry (paper products) or a market (grocery, industrial supply, restaurant supply, and so on). Worse yet, the appropriate term for a product class is often a poor indicator of competitive and complementary goods. It can also lead to too narrow and restrictive a definition of

---

[2] Although often used interchangeably, the terms are technically different. An "acquisition" is the purchase of another firm, which then becomes part of the acquiring company. A "merger" is the combining of two or more firms into what then becomes a new company. The Justice Department, the chief enforcement agency for antitrust laws, uses "merger" in the inclusive sense; that is, the combining of two or more previously separate companies is called a "merger."

[3] Alexander, *op. cit.*, p. 18.

the firm's business. If railroad management had perceived itself as being in the transportation industry instead of in the railroading industry, perhaps railroads would still be transporting the majority of fare-paying passengers (although probably not with trains) and would also have retained their share of the freight market.

There are two variables to consider in product-line decisions—width and length. *Width* refers to the number of types, or models, in a given price-quality class. *Length* pertains to the range and density of the price-quality spectrum—whether there are a few closely priced products, a few widely priced products, a number of products priced closely together, or a number of products spread over a broad range of prices. The General Motors Corporation, with automobiles priced at close intervals ranging from below $2,000 to over $6,000, is an example of the latter combination. Within each price-quality stratum there is a variety of models—convertibles, coupes, two-door sedans, four-door sedans, and station wagons.

Sales and revenues tend to increase with increases in either the width or the length of the product line. An increase in width satisfies a greater variety of tastes within a given income group. An increase in length satisfies a greater number of income groups. This is not to imply that income groups do not occasionally buy goods that are generally associated with other income classes. On the contrary, a poor family may buy a Cadillac, and a wealthy one may own a Chevrolet. However, the greater the range of price and quality in the product line, the greater will be the number of different income classes buying the firm's products.

An expansion of the product line in either dimension may benefit the manufacturer or middleman by excluding competitors from the establishments that carry their goods. In fact, a complete product line is frequently necessary at the retail level as well as the wholesale level. Since it is often more convenient as well as economical for the buyer to deal with a smaller number of suppliers, a seller generally improves its competitive position by expanding its offerings. This has been the trend over the past two decades.

Unfortunately, an increase in the firm's product line is usually accomplished at some cost. As the number of different tasks, the inventory requirement, and the need for more capital equipment (especially tooling) increase, the resulting diseconomies of scale cause an escalation in both total and unit costs. The engineering, manufacturing, and marketing functions become more complicated as the product line is expanded. Possibly the most discouraging result of an expanded product line is that the introduction of new products often detracts from the sales of the firm's established line.

Competition within the product line is a perennial problem. Although the inclusion of another model with a different price and quality is designed to increase the total quantity of sales by attracting buyers who would otherwise have spent their money elsewhere, unfortunately the new product often captures sales that would have gone to a sister product. Sometimes the introduction of a new item will attract customers who ultimately purchase one of the original products. This is one rationale for an economy model, which may offer little or no profit in itself but may attract prospects who then "trade up" to a more expensive item.

Improvements in manufacturing technology have given manufacturers greater flexibility in the size and diversity of their product lines. Modern tooling is considerably more adaptable than that used a decade ago. Also, design engineers have developed techniques for using many of the same parts for different products. Commonality of design is especially prevalent in automobile manufacturing (where it is cleverly disguised) and airplane production. Even the marketer has done his share, by creating demands large enough to make product diversification economically feasible. When sales reach the level where additional manufacturing capacity is needed, the added capacity can often be in plants and tooling for different products. The cost of this may be little higher than the cost of duplicating the production facilities of the present products.

Analyses of product-line problems obviously must be tailored to the circumstances. In general, the alternatives must first be defined (usually by qualitative analysis) and then quantified. If each alternative represents an aggregate of all the items that would be included in a particular product line, then an analysis of all long-run costs and revenues is in order, with profits being discounted to their present value. If the alternatives consist only of products to be dropped from or added to the line, then marginal analysis, giving due regard to the opportunity costs involved for each option, is appropriate. Since the arraying and comparison of alternatives normally produce discrete values, rather than a continuous function that one could differentiate (that is, take the derivative of) to determine the maximum profit and the optimum selection of inputs, a desert-and-oasis map may be the most suitable tool of analysis.

Marketing Properties. *Marketing properties* pertain to the effect that a product has, or would have, on the firm's overall marketing program—whether it reinforces or displaces the demand for the firm's other goods competing in the same markets, and whether the product is compatible with the present distribution system and promotional instruments. For example, a company may introduce a new item simply for reasons of prestige—for the effect it will have on the prospective buyer's perception of the quality and status of the regular line. Or, the firm may select a design to be added to its line because of its outstanding marketability, while recognizing the negative effect the item will have on the demand for its other products. This opportunity cost is accepted in anticipation of a substantial profit on the added item. Thus the Ford Mustang was introduced with full knowledge that it would detract from the sales of other Ford cars. The product may also serve as an instrument of exclusion. By offering a full line, the firm discourages middlemen from dealing with competitors and consumers from shopping elsewhere.

A new product's compatibility with the present distribution system will be reflected in the product's break-even point and the projected marginal profit of the expanded product line. If the present distribution system has idle capacity, the marginal distribution cost of the new product may be nominal. If considerable money must be allocated to the expansion of the system, then both the marginal cost and the break-even quantity will increase accordingly.

The same considerations hold for the promotional instrument. If there is no need—at least in the introductory or trial stages—for additional salesmen or a substantial increase in advertising, the marginal cost of promotion will be low and the break-even point will be reached more quickly. However, there may be an opportunity cost, if the diversion of personal selling effort or a shift in advertising emphasis causes sales of items in the established product line to fall.

The idle capacity of the distribution system or the promotional instrument may be continuous or seasonal. If it is seasonal, the new product may help defray fixed cost (again marginal analysis is appropriate) or enable the firm to maintain more facilities and personnel on a year-round basis.

Manufacturing Properties. A new product's *manufacturing properties,* especially its compatibility with the company's present manufacturing capacity and technical know-how, are an important consideration for the firm. Although these properties have significant implications for the marketing department, the evaluation of product compatibility is usually in the hands of the firm's engineers and manufacturing experts. In fact, the product may originate there as a by-product of a going process, as was the case with barbecue charcoal. This backyard-cooking fuel was originally the "useless" by-product of the coke ovens used in the manufacture of steel.

We have said that a new product, by enabling the firm to utilize idle plant capacity, may sustain employment of trained personnel during slumps or off-season periods. However, if a product is introduced for this reason, the marketing manager may find himself unable to fill orders if the new product is subordinated to established items and the output of those products is suddenly increased, displacing the new item. This has been one of the hazards of utilizing plants and equipment operated primarily for government contracting to manufacture civilian products.

A new product may also possess "leader qualities." That is, it may attract to the firm buyers who are likely to purchase other goods in the seller's product line. Leaders are usually either low-priced items carrying the same brand as higher-priced ones, or unique goods.

Low-priced leaders attract shoppers by offering them a price incentive.

Often the low-priced unit is an austere (stripped-down) model, and the prospect is switched to a more luxurious (hence more expensive and profitable) item. Unique items, on the other hand, attract shoppers by appealing to their curiosity or by offering them a vicarious experience (as for instance, the shopper who looks at a Ford dealer's special race cars before buying a sedan). They are frequently expensive and impractical products whose main virtue is their sensational nature. Their purpose is often limited to attracting customers and imparting a bit of glamour to the regular product line or the store that carries it. A colorful example of this tactic is the Neiman-Marcus Christmas gift promotion. This elegant Dallas department store features such items as his-and-hers airplanes and diamond-studded toothpicks during the Yuletide season. The intent is not only to obtain publicity but to impart an air of luxury and aristocracy to the firm and its merchandise.[4]

PRODUCT MARKETING STRATEGIES

Most firms attempt to make their products appear different from those of their competitors. This process, known as *product differentiation,* can involve manipulation of either the product, promotion, or pricing variables. Product marketing strategies can also be based on the exploitation of individual markets. The firm will often plan product, promotion, or price changes for a particular submarket in order to fully exploit the different preferences of various consumer groups. There are a number of criteria for such a division of markets. The more common are (1) demographic characteristics (age, sex, and family status), (2) income, (3) time, (4) geographical area, and (5) function. These criteria can be used singly or in combination.

Market Segmentation.   The term *market segmentation* is often used to refer to any division of the firm's total market for the purpose of differentiating prices, promotion strategies, or products between buyers. With respect to the product variable, it means the division of the aggregate market into parts and the production of a different good or service for each part. The parts (segments) must be identifiable, separable, and relatively homogeneous, and must have significantly different demand functions. The products are tailored to conform to the preference systems (demand functions) of the individual segments.

There are many examples of market segmentation: Shoe manufacturers segment their market by age and sex. Theaters segment their customers by time and age. Hotel chains split up their markets by geographic area. Air-

---

[4] The Neiman-Marcus "Christmas special" has become a national news item. Also, to the admitted surprise of the store's management, a few of these exotic offerings, such as his-and-her airplanes and diamond-studded toothpicks, are even sold.

lines divide their market by age, time, geographic area, military/nonmilitary status, and group/individual purchases. Appliance manufacturers offer prices and services to wholesalers that are different from those they offer factory-direct retailers.

In some industries, different products, services, or prices are offered to each segment of the market population. For example, most movie theaters offer lower-priced tickets to patrons under 18 and to those willing to attend matinee performances. The major airlines offer no-reservation, economy-class services and reduced-price tickets to minors and military personnel. Gasoline refiners blend a different product for Denver than they do for Palm Beach.

Segmentation recognizes the existence of multiple demand curves in a market and tailors a product to each one. It presumes that the sum of the individual demand curves is greater than a single demand curve generalized to the entire market, since the more a product is tailored to the tastes of a particular buyer or buyer class, the higher is the probability of a sale. If the market is properly segmented, if the buyers' respective preference systems are accurately defined, and if all segments are properly served, the sales volume should be larger than if the same product were offered to all buyers.

Another advantage of segmentation is that marketing can be more specialized, and promotion better suited to the characteristics of the buyers. More specialized, hence presumably more efficient, media can be used, advertising copy can be less general, and personal selling can be focused on a smaller buyer population. This specialization may increase marketing efficiency, provided that it does not bring about large diseconomies of scale.

Segmentation also has certain disadvantages. If not all the submarkets are served, then the total market population is less. Highly specialized products can be difficult to sell outside their own market segments. Too, a greater variety of goods means more designs, more tests, a larger variety and usually a greater number of tools, and a more complicated marketing program. Logistics become more complex, with a greater variety of distribution channels and higher inventory requirements. Segmentation seldom results in economies of scale; thus average unit costs tend to increase.

In spite of these drawbacks, the trend in marketing is toward market segmentation. Several factors encourage this. First, in many industries the aggregate market is so large that output exceeds that of the optimum-size plant. Hence, additional plants are constructed, usually in different areas. Since the cost of building a plant to produce a moderately different product is not much greater than the cost of reproducing the original plant, economies of scale are retained.

Second, technology in manufacturing and communications has improved to the point where flexibility in both product and advertising is practical. For example, continuous-flow production lines can be designed to allow model variations to be made without interrupting production. Most nationally distributed, large-circulation magazines, for example, print regional editions. Some even offer editions that are specialized by subscriber.

Third, affluence is both increasing and diffusing. Segments of the population that historically have had a low level of purchasing power now have significant incomes. They represent important submarkets with tastes different from those of the larger market. Examples are minority ethnic groups and teenagers.

Market Aggregation. *Market aggregation,* as opposed to market segmentation, is the production of a single product that is offered to the entire market. Submarkets are appealed to only through changes in promotion variables or price. No change is made in the product itself; identical units are offered to each segment.

With a market-aggregation strategy, promotion, especially advertising, is used to shift the segments' demand curves by making the product attractive to the various submarkets. In the marketing of soft drinks, resort services, certain automobiles, milk, and branded oranges, for example, the objective frequently is to generalize a single product or a limited product line to all consumers of the product class.

Perhaps the ultimate form of market aggregation is the political campaign—often directed by individuals or firms who also specialize in the promotion of consumer goods. The party can offer only one candidate for the job, who must be made to appeal to a majority of the voters. It is irrelevant, other than ethically, whether his "voter appeal" is based on real or imagined qualities. Voters usually have a wide range of interests and values, many of which are conflicting. Since the campaigner must appeal to a plurality of the voters, he will generally try to project qualities appropriate for several different voter groups.

The chief advantage of market aggregation is the economies of scale associated with a large output of a given product, although this advantage diminishes as the firm comes closer to full utilization of an optimum-sized plant. Another advantage is that logistics are usually simpler and less costly, due to the lower inventories and standardization of packaging and shipping that result from the use of a single, or very limited, product line. Promotion may or may not be less expensive than it is with a market-segmentation strategy. This will depend on the difficulty of generalizing the product to a variety of tastes and how widely the tastes differ.

Composite Strategies. A combination strategy involving both market segmentation and market aggregation is common. The aggregate market is first divided into segments, usually by some single criterion, such as income. The segments are large enough to permit the output of each different product to approach an optimum level, or at least to ensure reasonable economies of scale. The individual products are then generalized, through promotional or pricing strategies, to the various submarkets within each segment.

Again, the automobile industry provides an example. The General Motors Corporation, for instance, builds five distinctively different brands of cars, each at a different average price that can be generally associated with a particular consumer-income level (market segmentation).

These major segments are again divided, and different models of each brand are produced to satisfy the subsets of the population segments. The division here is largely demographic. The coupes, sedans, convertibles, and station wagons that result are clearly another exercise in segmentation.

Next, the individual brands and models are each generalized through advertising to appeal to a broad range of personality and vocational types (market aggregation). A given brand-model is publicized as satisfying a variety of transportation needs, depending on the copywriter's perception of the values and interests of the segment's population.

Virtually all large firms and most small ones use a composite marketing strategy. As we have noted, market segmentation is used to increase total demand, while market aggregation is used to reduce total costs. The choice of an appropriate composite strategy can often mean the difference between profit and loss for the firm.

CHAPTER 16

New-Product Development and Commercialization

The creation of new products—including substantial modifications of existing products—is a prerequisite to survival in many industries. Appliances, automobiles, women's apparel, airplanes, and computers, for example, begin their journey toward obsolescence as soon as they are introduced. In fact, their replacements are being designed as they go on the market.

Sometimes the evolution of a product class consists primarily of style changes, as in the case of dresses and furniture; other times it reflects the continuous stream of new technology, as in the case of aircraft and computers. Often a combination of both stylistic and technological innovations is involved, as in the case of the automobile. In infrequent and often exciting cases, a totally new product is invented, resulting in the emergence of a new industry and the development of a previously unexploited market. The telephone, the airplane, and television were such products.

Product changes can also be important for non-manufacturing firms. Innovation, or the lack of innovation, has meant success or failure to countless service firms. Retail distribution, banking, medical care, and appliance repair companies—to name only a few examples—have all been drastically changed by the introduction of innovations in the past few decades.

SOURCES OF NEW-PRODUCT IDEAS

No institution or individual has a monopoly on new-product ideas. As Table 16.1 shows, housewives, band leaders, backyard inventors, and industrial laboratories have all contributed new product ideas, each worth many millions of dollars. (The toilet cleaner, the food blender, the electrostatic copier, and the transistor, respectively, are inventions of the sources above.) Table 16.2 indicates the most likely sources of new-product ideas. This list can easily be adapted by the firm to suit its industry and markets.

Table 16.1   Sources for new products—Selected examples

Company	New Product	Source of Idea
Meat packer	Onion soup	Executive's wife
Meat packer	Canned chicken product	Salesman
Manufacturer of industrial equipment	Steam-producing unit	Advertisement for the sale of manufacturing rights
Tin-plate converter	Bread box	Marketing research agency assigned to study new product possibilities
Electrical-appliance manufacturer	Foot warmer	Customer inquiries
Manufacturer of golf equipment	Golf bag "toter"	President of company
Manufacturer of service equipment for garages	Hoist for garage	Garage mechanic contacted during survey of product users
Chemical company	Deodorant for garbage	Advertising agency, which learned of local use
Chemical and film company	Detergent	Laboratory
Die-casting company	Line of dejuicers	Company executives
Manufacturer of plastic products	Film-viewing device	Inventor
Manufacturer of kitchen utensils	Kitchen gadget	Register of patents for licensing or sale (U. S. Patent Office)
Chemical products company	Insecticide	List of government-owned patents available for licensing
Manufacturer of office equipment and machinery	Index device, envelope-opening device, pencil gripper	Office managers, also jobber and wholesaler catalogues
Canner	Apple juice	Food broker
Appliance manufacturer	Electric bottle-warmer	Customers

Table 16.1   Continued

Company	New Product	Source of Idea
Film company	Film	Engineer
Landscape supply and equipment company	Fiberglass blanket to place around trees to keep down weeds and retain moisture in soil	Register of patents available for licensing or sale
Container manufacturer	Reusable container	President of company, who noticed waste of materials
Manufacturer of plumbing equipment and supplies	New washer	Sales report
Manufacturer of hardware	Bedroom door-knockers. Also, miniature jewelry door-knockers	Executive considering idea of reducing size of regular door-knockers
Pottery manufacturer	New vase	Museum exhibit
Plastic products company	Plastic shield for wall light switch	Inventor
Plastic products company	Film-slide viewer	List of needed inventions published by a bank

SOURCE: U. S. Department of Commerce, *Developing and Selling New Products* (Washington, D. C.: U. S. Government Printing Office, 1950).

Serendipity—the happy faculty of discovering by accident something worthwhile—also plays a role in the creation of new products. Floating soap (Procter & Gamble's Ivory soap), a non-stick coating for cookware (Du Pont's Teflon), and the vulcanizing process that makes rubber suitable for automobile tires (Charles Goodyear's discovery) were all invented by accident while the innovator was manufacturing or doing research on other products. Some companies, like IBM and Monsanto, file patent claims on all discoveries to ensure exclusive rights if the item later proves to have market potential.

A survey of 70 major U. S. industrial corporations and several research institutes engaged in the study of technology diffusion reveals that innovations used by the firm generally come from sources closely associated with the company.[1] The most frequent originators of untried ideas are employees.

[1] Unpublished study by Walter B. Wentz.

Table 16.2   Checklist of major sources for new-product ideas

1. Company staff, records, experience

Research and engineering staffs
Sales staff
Market research department
Sales reports and other records

Employee suggestions
Customer suggestions,
   inquiries, and complaints

2. Distributors

Brokers
Factory distributors
   (Manufacturers' agents)

Wholesalers or jobbers
Retailers

3. Competitors

Customers of competitors
Competitors' products
Mail-order catalogues

Exhibits and trade shows
Foreign products

4. Miscellaneous

Inventors
Patent attorneys and brokers
Firms going out of business
Manufacturers of parts and accessories
Suggestions from the public
   or industry) as a result of
   advertising
University and institute
   laboratories
Commercial laboratories

Industrial consultants
Management engineers
Product engineers
Marketing research agencies
Advertising agencies
Trade associations of
   executives and
   laboratory personnel
Trade-magazine writers
   and editors

SOURCE: U. S. Department of Commerce, *Developing and Selling New Products* (Washington, D. C.: U. S. Government Printing Office, 1950).

Other prolific sources are customers, salesmen, and technical personnel sent by suppliers to aid in machinery installation or material use. New-product ideas that result from correspondence, magazine advertisements, and mailings are seldom assimilated. Surprisingly, the independent inventor is also a poor source and usually receives rather cool treatment when he approaches a large corporation.

The indifference to private inventors is not simply attributable to shortsightedness on the part of management or the inertia associated with bigness. Those firms that have maintained an open-door policy toward the independent inventor have had little to show for it. IBM, which acquired several useful product ideas from this source, is an exception. Most of the survey respondents reported a history of petty lawsuits and humorous experiences with crackpot inventors. Yet, when one contemplates the fact that the inventor of the Xerox electrostatic copying machine called on 20 companies before he found a sponsor (IBM, for one, turned him down), the general indifference toward backyard inventors may seem a bit imprudent.

Those associated with a large organization have a terrific advantage over outsiders in the competition for the acceptance of innovations. An employee or a supplier will have access to the channels of communication and be knowledgeable about the capabilities, limitations, and needs of the firm. His understanding of the company's manufacturing and marketing capabilities and his access to the decision-makers can prove invaluable in gaining acceptance of a new idea.

The companies contacted in the study above were all among the 500 largest industrial firms in the United States. Each had an enviable record of profit and growth. All were engaged in commercial operations, and some in government contracting. Practically all reported some type of formal program for the acquisition of new product ideas. Although the practice of these companies are sufficiently consistent to be representative of the attitude of most major industrial firms, they may not be typical of the small company. Small firms generally go through an entrepreneurial phase during which innovation, change, and risk are the distinguishing characteristics of the enterprise.

MANAGEMENT'S ROLE IN NEW-PRODUCT DEVELOPMENT

A new-product program cannot be intelligently managed without a statement of objectives and the concurrence of senior managers on the criteria for product selection. Although judgment will necessarily play a large role in the new-product decision process, goals and standards must be defined or the program will be useless.

New-product goals will vary with the firm's size, capital, product line, growth phase, and management philosophy, as well as with the characteristics of the industry in which the firm competes, and should be determined within that context. Some of the more common objectives of new-product programs are (1) growth, (2) the replacement of obsolete products, (3) diversification, (4) improved utilization of plant and equipment, (5) the exclusion of competitors from a market, and (6) improved profits. The last is a long-run objective that should be common to all programs.

A list of selection criteria should contain the elements to be included in the decision model, the bases for their measurement, their limit values, and their relative weights. For example, profitability should be one criterion. It can be measured in absolute dollars, in dollars discounted to their present value, or in terms of the return on investment. Limit values (such as a minimum profit or a minimum return on investment) should be selected to eliminate alternatives with inadequate earning potential. Since criteria will vary in importance, weights may be assigned in order to aggregate the criteria.

Management's list of objectives and selection criteria should include a statement of the company's attitude toward methods of exploiting innovations. A broad policy statement is important, for each new-product idea has unique properties, and no product-development, manufacturing, or marketing alternative should be rejected out of hand. However, management too will have a unique body of experience, and unique capabilities and prejudices, which should be reflected in the choices made between the internal development of new products, joint ventures, and other methods of exploitation. Both preferences and objectives should be taken into account. The choice of procedures is important because it establishes the frame of reference for both the screening and evaluation phases of new-product analysis.

EXPLOITATION OF NEW-PRODUCT IDEAS

Having acquired a new-product idea, management must next address itself to possible methods of exploitation. The options are (1) internal development, (2) joint venture, (3) licensing, (4) sale, and (5) a combination of these alternatives. Each option has its own profit-risk values, with the profit potential usually increasing as risk increases.

Internal development offers the greatest rewards and carries the heaviest burden of risk. It is the most exciting and usually the most complex of the alternatives, involving as it does the acquisition, screening, evaluation, development (which includes design completion, prototype manufacture and testing, and production), test marketing, and commercialization of the innovation.

The *joint venture* enables the firm to share the risk of undertaking a new product, but at the cost of sharing the rewards. It is appropriate when the firm lacks adequate capital, sufficient manufacturing or marketing capabilities, or the technical knowledge needed to develop the product, and a partner is available with the requisite input. Joint ventures are common in large-scale government contracting, heavy construction, and petroleum exploration, and in the chemical, motion-picture, and aircraft industries.[2] A joint venture may mean a sharing of development, production, and marketing responsibilities; it may involve the establishment of a jointly operated facility; or it may mean the incorporation of a jointly owned subsidiary.

---

[2] Often, such joint ventures are formed solely to meet capital requirements, diffuse risk, or take advantage of technical provisions in the tax laws and are not associated with innovation.

A variation, or adaptation, of the joint-venture method is the acquisition of an established company that has the capability the firm lacks for a new product's development, manufacture, and eventual commercialization. This frequently results in further vertical integration, as is the case when middlemen are acquired to ensure a distribution channel for the new product, or suppliers are acquired to provide necessary parts or material inputs.

Licensing involves the leasing of patentable technology to other firms, frequently competitors. It is normally confined to manufacturing processes that have already been tested in the factory or products that have been accepted in the marketplace. Licensing is a low-cost device for the further exploitation of demand. As it can increase competition in the firm's own markets, licenses are often granted to avoid claims of restraint of trade and subsequent government intervention. This practice is typical in the automotive, computer, and electronics industries. Where the technology is a consequence of federally sponsored research, licensing—if not outright sharing —is usually required by the government.

The *sale* of new-product ideas has a relatively poor record. Although fortunes have been made from the sale of untried ideas, they are certainly the exception. Generally, neither the individual nor the firm can enter the marketplace with its ideas as easily as it can enter with goods and services. The demand for unproven products is simply too low to justify the cost of marketing them. IBM, whose inventive capability is hardly open to question, files patent claims for all worthwhile inventions. However, it has given up trying to sell those innovations which do not fit into the firm's present or proposed product lines. When these patented ideas were marketed, the revenues failed to cover the selling costs. Now "surplus" ideas are published in IBM literature and are free to anyone who wishes to exploit them. IBM can cite numerous examples of profitable adoptions of their free inventions.

North American Aviation, Inc. (now the North American Rockwell Corporation) established its Navan subsidiary to license and sell patentable ideas that emerged in the company's aerospace divisions but had no applications in those areas. Later, Navan also solicited proprietary innovations from outsiders. Although the revenue and cost data are private, indications are that the venture has been only financially marginal over its 20 years of existence.

The federal government, which spends over $200 million annually on the diffusion of technology, has had only moderate success in transferring commercially unproven ideas to the civilian sector. The exception is the U. S. Department of Agriculture's Agricultural Extension Service, which has used the land grant colleges and the county agent program to *personally* demonstrate and gain acceptance of new technology and new products.

The problem was well summarized by a senior executive of the General Electric Company, as follows:

We know from experience that technology is intimately related to people and usually cannot be successfully transferred as an impersonal commodity of value in its own right. Best results are obtained when a person who is expert in a particular technology is given an opportunity to work on the new application himself.[3]

A *combination of alternatives* is sometimes practical, although domestic examples are scarce. A firm may develop a product through a prototype model and then sell or license its design to another company for production and marketing. Foreign markets are often exploited this way. Also, a firm may internally develop an innovation and maintain exclusive rights in the domestic market, but license it to a foreign corporation for manufacture and sale abroad. This practice is common in the aircraft, appliance, and chemical industries.

SCREENING OF NEW-PRODUCT IDEAS

A firm's statement of objectives and criteria serves as the basis of a screening model against which the company can test or make a preliminary evaluation of new-product ideas. Ideally, the model should be developed and applied by representatives of the engineering, manufacturing, and marketing departments and whatever staff groups (such as company lawyers) are appropriate. It should include each selection criterion and their relevant weights, scales of measurement, and limit values.

Although contribution to total profit is the ultimate criterion for undertaking development of a new product, other considerations should also be included in the preliminary evaluation. These considerations, called *resource utilization factors,* pertain to the compatibility between the new product and the present engineering, manufacturing, and marketing resources of the firm. Most of these factors cannot be evaluated on a monetary scale. In fact, their measurements, although usually quantitative, are not comparable.

In order to aggregate the separate factors into a single value that will point to the selection or rejection of an innovation or method of exploitation, one must convert them to a *utility-value scale.* This can be done by assigning utility-value points to each of the following judgments: excellent, good, satisfactory, poor, and very poor. The relative importance of each factor is indicated by the weights assigned. A factor's rating value is multiplied by its weight to yield its utility value.

An example of a new-product screening model, showing selected factors and their rating criteria, is given in Table 16.3. An application of the model to a hypothetical innovation is shown in Table 16.4. The purpose of the

[3] J. S. Parker, vice president and group executive, General Electric Co., in letter to Walter B. Wentz, dated June 13, 1966.

Table 16.3 New-product screening model
(With selection criteria)

RESOURCES UTILIZATION	WEIGHT	Excellent 50	Good 40	Satisfactory 30	Poor 20	Very Poor 10	Expected Utility Value‡
ENGINEERING							
Professional personnel	3	Requirements available	Increase <10%	Increase 11–40%	Increase 41–70%	Increase >70%	
Technicians	2	Same	Same	Same	Same	Same	
Equipment	1	Same	Same	Same	Same	Same	
Space	1	Same	Same	Same	Same	Same	
Technical capability	2	No deficiencies	Few deficiencies	Moderate deficiencies	Many deficiencies	Totally deficient†	
Probability of technical success	3	100%	90–99%	80–89%	60–79%	60%†	
Utilization of idle capacity	3	100%	80–99%	60–79%	40–59%	40%	
MANUFACTURING							
Skilled personnel	2	Requirements available	Increase <10%	Increase 11–40%	Increase 41–70%	Increase >70%	
Semiskilled and unskilled personnel	1	Same	Same	Same	Same	Same	
Equipment	2	Same	Same	Same	Same	Same	
Space	2	Same	Same	Same	Same	Same	
Manufacturing capability	2	No deficiencies	Few deficiencies	Moderate deficiencies	Totally deficient		
Utilization of idle capacity	3	100%	80–99%	60–79%	40–59%	<40%	
Raw materials and suppliers	1	100%	80–99%	60–79%	40–59%	<40%	
MARKETING							
Distribution channels	3	Present ones adequate	<10% new	10–59% new	60–99% new	100% new	
Price	2	$\eta_p < |2|$	$\eta_p < |1|$	$\eta_p = |1|$	$\eta_p > |1|$	$\eta_p > |2|$	

RATINGS

LIMIT LINE *

	Criterion	Weight	Total Expected Utility Values				
RESOURCES UTILIZATION	Sales personnel	1	Requirements available	Increase < 10%	Increase 11–40%	Increase 41–70%	Increase 70%
	Advertising	1					
	Life cycle	1	> 6.9 years	5–6.9 years	3–4.9 years	1–2.9 years	< 1 year
	Patent protection	2	Allows no competition	Allows little competition	Allows moderate competition	Few barriers to competition	None
	Effect of present products	3	Increases sales	Increases sales < 30%	None	Reduces sales < 29%	Reduces sales > 30% †
	Market share	1	Increase > 30%	Increase 10–29.9%	Increase 5–9.9%	Increase < 5%	Remains constant
	Seasonality	1	Monthly output is constant	Fluctuation from maximum < 10%	Fluctuation from maximum 10–20%	Fluctuation from maximum 20–40%	Fluctuation from maximum > 40%
	Sensitivity to business cycle	1	Not sensitive	Slightly sensitive	Moderately sensitive	Very sensitive	Extremely sensitive
FINANCIAL EVALUATION	**PROFIT**						
	Absolute value (in thousands)	15	> $700	$400–$699	$200–$399	$100–$199	< $100
	Return on investment (annual)	15	> 16.9%	13–16.9%	9–12.9%	5–8.9%	< 5%
	CAPITAL REQUIREMENTS (in millions)	10	< $.3	$.3–$.9	$1–$1.9	$2–$3.9	> $4

* Reject product if most probable outcome falls to right of line.

† Acceptable only if total expected utility value of financial evaluation is greater than 1200.

‡ Consider alternative method (joint venture, etc.) if expected utility value of profit is greater than 900.

§
Total Expected Utility Value	Action
> 3360	Commit product to production.
2521–3360	Commit product through prototype and market test.
1681–2520	Execute further research and analysis, especially on marginal items.
< 1681	Reject product.

Table 16.4 New-product screening model
(With sample product evaluation)

LIMIT LINE*

	WEIGHT	RATINGS Excellent 50	Good 40	Satisfactory 30	Poor 20	Very Poor 10	Expected Utility Value‡
ENGINEERING							
Professional personnel	3	150 (0)	120 (.2)	90 (.7)	60 (.1)	30 (0)	93
Technicians	2	100 (0)	80 (.1)	60 (.8)	40 (.1)	20 (0)	60
Equipment	1	50 (.1)	40 (.8)	30 (.1)	20 (0)	10 (0)	40
Space	1	50 (.1)	40 (.8)	30 (.1)	20 (0)	10 (0)	40
Technical capability	2	100 (0)	80 (.9)	60 (.1)	40 (0)	20† (0)	78
Probability of technical success	3	–	120 (1.0)	–	–	–†	120
Utilization of idle capacity	3	150 (0)	120 (0)	90 (0)	60 (1)	30 (0)	60
MANUFACTURING							
Skilled personnel	2	100 (0)	80 (.9)	60 (.1)	40 (0)	20 (0)	78
Semiskilled and unskilled personnel	1	50 (0)	50 (.4)	30 (.6)	20 (0)	10 (0)	38
Equipment	2	100 (.1)	80 (.8)	60 (.1)	40 (0)	20 (0)	80
Space	2	100 (.1)	80 (.8)	60 (.1)	40 (0)	20 (0)	80
Manufacturing capability	2	100 (0)	80 (.8)	60 (.2)	40 (0)	20 (0)	76
Utilization of idle capacity	3	150 (0)	120 (0)	90 (0)	60 (.9)	30 (.1)	57
Raw materials and suppliers	1	50 (.1)	40 (.8)	30 (.1)	20 (0)	10 (0)	40
MARKETING							
Distribution channels	3	150 (.2)	120 (.8)	90 (0)	60 (0)	30 (0)	126

RESOURCES UTILIZATION

338

	Weight						Expected Utility Value
RESOURCES UTILIZATION							
Price	2	100 (0)	80 (.8)	60 (.2)	40 (0)	20 (0)	76
Sales personnel	1	50 (.5)	40 (.5)	30 (0)	20 (0)	10 (0)	45
Advertising	1	50 (.5)	40 (.5)	30 (0)	20 (0)	10 (0)	45
Life cycle	1	50 (.2)	40 (.6)	30 (.2)	20 (0)	10 (0)	40
Patent protection	2	100 (.1)	80 (.8)	60 (.1)	40 (0)	20 (0)	80
Effect of present products	3	150 (0)	120 (1)	90 (0)	60 (0)	30† (0)	120
Market share	1	50 (.1)	40 (.8)	30 (.1)	20 (0)	10 (0)	40
Seasonality	1	50 (1)	40 (0)	30 (0)	20 (0)	10 (0)	50
Sensitivity to business cycle	1	50 (.2)	40 (.8)	30 (0)	20 (0)	10 (0)	42
FINANCIAL EVALUATION — PROFIT							
Absolute value (in thousands)	15	750 (0)	600 (.1)	450 (.8)	300 (.1)	150 (0)	450
Return on investment (annual)	15	750 (0)	600 (.2)	450 (.7)	300 (.1)	150 (0)	465
CAPITAL REQUIREMENTS (in millions)	10	500 (0)	400 (.5)	300 (.5)	200 (0)	100 (0)	350

LIMIT LINE*

TOTAL EXPECTED UTILITY VALUE§   2869

* Reject product if most probable outcome falls to right of line.

† Acceptable only if total expected utility value of financial evaluation is greater than 1200.

‡ Consider alternative method (joint venture, etc.) if expected utility value of profit is greater than 900.

§ Total Expected Utility Value

Total Expected Utility Value	Action
> 3360	Commit product to production
2521–3360	Commit product through prototype and market test.
1681–2520	Execute further research and analysis, especially on marginal items.
< 1681	Reject product.

model is to identify and discriminate between (1) new-product ideas that are so obviously superior as to warrant immediate commitment to production, (2) new-product ideas that are sufficiently good to warrant immediate commitment to production of a prototype and market testing, (3) new-product ideas that warrant additional analysis, and (4) new-product ideas that should be rejected without further expenditure of company resources. Thus the model serves as a filter, whose coarseness is a function of the degree of depth and precision of the analysis.

Obviously, such a model can also help in deciding the appropriate method of exploitation. For instance, if a new idea had screening ratings of "excellent" in every category except manufacturing, then a joint venture or licensing arrangement might be indicated as the best exploitation technique.

In order to provide consistency in the screening of new-product ideas, the rating system used for resource evaluation must remain constant for the evaluation of all new-product ideas. Otherwise the ratings will not provide a legitimate ranking of alternatives. The determinants of the screening model are normally selected subsequent to management's preparation of a policy statement on new-product goals and objectives.

The applications of the screening model are easily illustrated. For example, using the model in Table 16.3, a product requiring 15 percent more professional people to be added to the engineering staff would cause the "professional personnel" factor to be rated "satisfactory" and awarded 30 points. The scarcity and cost of scientists and engineers make this an important factor with a weight of 3. Thus, the total utility value assigned to this factor would be 90.

Like most marketing decisions, new product judgments are subject to error. A decision model that takes this into account is more useful than one that fails to do so. If the inherent uncertainty of the problem is recognized, probabilities can be estimated and assigned to each possible outcome. In Table 16.4, these probabilities are shown in parentheses at the bottom of each cell. (Note that the probability distribution for each factor must total 1.)

Multiplying the probability times the utility value (which is the product of the rating value and the weight) gives us the expected value of the outcome. Summing the unexpected values of each outcome then yields the factor's total expected utility value. Thus, for the "professional personnel" factor in Table 16.4, the expected values for the five outcomes are 0, 24, 63, 6, and 0, respectively. (Expected value, as explained earlier, is the product of an outcome's value times its probability. Hence $150 \times 0 = 0$, $120 \times .2 = 24$, and so on.) Adding these yields a total expected utility value of 93 for that factor. A simpler method is to multiply the rating values (50, 40, 30, 20, and 10) by their probabilities, add their products, and multiply the total by the factor's weight. The answer will be the same. *If the probabilities are* equally distributed about the most likely rating, then the total expected utility value may be computed simply by multiplying that rating value by the factor's weight.

The rating a factor is assigned is determined by reference to an appropriate criterion—preferably one that can be expressed quantitatively, although a qualitative criterion may be necessary. The probability distribution used for a given factor can be based on appropriate historical data (rarely available for new products) or estimated intuitively. Probability estimates are best made by managers or specialists who have some expertise in an area relevant to the factor. Often, several estimates for a factor are made and the analyst must decide which is the best, or take an average. These estimates are known as "prior probabilities." Later, when program data becomes available, they could be modified to "posterior" probabilities by invoking statistical theorems and formulas. These posterior probabilities can then be used in evaluating similar new-product possibilities.

The factors and weights used in screening programs will vary considerably between industries and firms. For example, a retailer would have no interest in an innovation's engineering and manufacturing costs (unless it involved a capital alteration to his store) but would be vitally concerned with inventory requirements, customer compatibility, credit characteristics, demonstrability, reorder speed, space requirements, and brand image. A computer manufacturer would put more emphasis on engineering than would a toy company.

A new-product screening model like that in Table 16.4 can reliably identify product ideas that are so meritorious as to warrant an immediate—and possibly substantial—commitment of company resources, provided it is based on a moderately thorough analysis, which itself costs money. Sometimes a hierarchy of models is more economical: A primary screening model to reject the obvious misfits; a secondary model to screen the survivors, narrowing the number to a more manageable quantity and selecting those few promising ideas that justify expensive, detailed analyses; and a final model to evaluate the remaining ideas and provide the basis for the final management decision.

A model of any kind is no substitute for executive judgment. On the contrary, it is to a great extent a codification of judgment, particularly in regard to the weighting of factors and the statement of rating criteria. Thus, constructing a decision model without the approval of the same people who will decide whether the innovation actually will be allocated company resources and ultimately join the product mix is a waste of resources.

The virtue of a decision model is that it organizes the decision process and provides a standard for judgment. It is not a substitute for imagination, insight, and an environment that encourages both exploration and the questioning of present products and practices. For example, one of the Cessna Aircraft Company's most successful products—the first commercially manufactured tandem-powered twin-engine airplane—was developed almost solely on the basis of the insight and insistence of one vice president, supported by the confidence of his fellow executives in his foresight and skill.

TEST MARKETING

Test marketing consists of producing a limited number of units, usually on a small pilot production line, and entering them in a local market, supported by an appropriate level of promotion. Sales are then measured and generalized to the total potential market. In addition, consumer reaction is evaluated and product performance is observed. This gives the firm empirical data on the basis of which it can revise its sales, revenue, and cost estimates and make needed changes in both the product and the marketing plan. If the results of the test marketing program are disastrous, management has an opportunity to discontinue the product before even greater losses are sustained. King-size Coca-Cola was put to such a test before the final commitment was made to spend the millions of dollars necessary for new bottling equipment, new glassware, and the introductory advertising campaign required to launch the product on a national scale. The experience of the pilot plant and the results of the local market experiment confirmed the existence of a profitable market and consumer acceptance of large-bottle Cokes. The new product was then put on the national market.

Often, test marketing is carried out solely to aid the manufacturer in the analysis and manipulation of the product variable, with no attempt being made to estimate the demand function. Motion-picture producers often preview their films in commercial theaters prior to the announced release date. The audience reaction to various scenes and dialogue is sampled, by questionnaire or by observation, and the objectionable portions cut from the final version.

Testing by commercial laboratories or consumer juries is useful in analyzing the product variable, as an alternative to testing in the marketplace. Although this kind of testing is of little value in specifying the demand function, it does have the advantage of security, in that competitors are far less likely to become aware of the company's product plans if the innovation can be kept completely off the market until its formal introduction.

Tests made by commercial laboratories are similar to those that would be made by the firm's own engineering department during prototype testing or by its quality-control department during the production phase. The product's operation (how well it performs its functions), durability, and reliability are evaluated and compared with that of similar products. By having an outside group do this, however, the company will hopefully get an objective, detached, and fresh view of the product. These services are offered by such firms as the United States Testing Company and Underwriters Laboratories, Inc., which also certifies certain goods as meeting prescribed safety standards. Outside testing is common in the electrical-appliance field, and many appliances even carry the label of the testing company.

Some manufacturers maintain their own panel of consumers, such as the consumer jury operated by the Research Center of the General Foods Corporation. The jury members—in this case, a cross-section of housewives —use the new product under conditions simulating those under which it would be used by prospective buyers. They report their experiences and impressions to the manufacturer, which makes appropriate alterations in the product before it is committed to full production and entered in the marketplace.

The decision to test a product outside the firm is essentially a safeguard to hedge against the possibility of bad judgment in the selection, design, and marketing of a new product. Hopefully it will forestall any major mistakes in these areas, and may also identify any more subtle problems that may exist. There is occasionally an economic advantage resulting from the efficiencies associated with specialization. In fact, the use of an outside testing agency may be required due to a lack of special equipment or skills within the firm.

The final decision to reject or accept a market test plan should be made on the basis of a marginal analysis of costs and risk. Four values are necessary: (1) the cost of the test, (2) the cost of failure of the product after it is launched, (3) the probability of failure without testing, and (4) the probability of failure with testing, assuming the test is "positive." The difference in the expected values of failures with and without testing is the maximum amount that should be spent for testing. This difference can be viewed as the expected savings that would result from testing. The mathematical calculation of expected values was shown in Chapter 5.

FINAL EVALUATION

Even products that the firm commits to production as a result of the preliminary screening must be further evaluated to determine more precisely the extent of their market and to estimate their market penetration rates. This is necessary in order to determine how large the initial production order should be and to prepare the marketing programs. Often, innovations that survive the initial screening process must subsequently be analyzed in depth to provide a basis for their final acceptance or rejection.

Acceptance may mean the commitment of extensive resources to production. This would necessarily be the case with a new resort, a new store, or any other new good or service that is not divisible, hence does not lend itself to trial on a small scale. Acceptance may also mean a limited commitment of resources, to produce only a prototype, or a pilot production line that would provide units for testing in the market. This is usually the case when the product is a convenience good. In some industries, such as defense and commercial aircraft, management acceptance will mean the expenditure of considerable resources for engineering studies and designs and for marketing, but production will not be initiated until a minimum number of units have been ordered by customers who have signed purchase contracts. (These contracts generally specify the price and delivery date and guarantee certain performance minimums.)

Ideally, the acceptance/rejection decision—often called the "go/no-go decision" in computer and engineering parlance—should focus on the expected value of the discounted present value of profit.[4] However, the resource utilization factors cited in the screening model should not be ignored in making the final decision. For firms with idle capacity and high fixed costs, they will probably be crucial. If necessary, these factors can be integrated into the final decision, just as they were in the screening process, by converting profit into a utility value.

In view of the uncertainty associated with new ventures, the final evaluation of a new-product proposal should include a precise statement of the break-even point. By this time the price should be set (hence the revenue function can be precisely stated) and costs should have been accurately estimated, at least for the early part of the product's life cycle. Since this will probably include the break-even output, the break-even point can easily be computed with a high degree of precision. Multiplying the break-even quantity by the price yields the break-even revenue; as revenue equals cost at the break-even point, the break-even cost is automatically revealed.

COMMERCIALIZATION OF A NEW PRODUCT

The commercialization of a new product—especially one representing a radical innovation or the entry of a new brand into a particular market—requires skillful manipulation of the promotional instrument. The promotion, in turn, must be supported with an adequate distribution system and a production release that will satisfy demand. Risk is obviously involved.

In preparing the promotional strategy and setting the initial quantity of output, certain product qualities must be taken into account. Protectability is very important. The ability of the firm to protect its product from infringement—through a patent or unique technical or manufacturing know-how—will determine the duration of the producer's monopoly. If it is short,

---

[4] See Chapter 5, p. 108.

the firm must move into the market quickly, be able to satisfy demand readily, and exploit its innovation before the competition can offer a good substitute.

Another relevant factor is the new product's price elasticity and the ease and rapidity with which it can be copied. The demand for a particular good tends to become more elastic (that is, more sensitive to changes in price) the longer it is on the market. The reason is that, normally, competitors can develop substitutes, given enough time to work on the problem. They do this through product innovation, the breaking or expiration of patents, or the redesigning of a product to avoid direct patent infringement. It is difficult to name a branded product that has been on the market more than a couple of years for which there is no suitable substitute. The Polaroid-Land camera is one of the few exceptions.

The prevalent relationship between short- and long-run demand suggests several ideas for the commercialization of a new product. First, patent protection is helpful in maintaining the initial price inelasticity over a longer period of time. Second, in lieu of a barrier to entry, secrecy is important in order to delay the start of competitors' reactions, at least until the innovation is on the market (this is one argument against pretesting). Third, the firm should prepare to exploit quickly its initial success if the new product is well received in the marketplace. Implementing this last rule-of-thumb can be very risky, for the manufacturing and distribution state-of-readiness it implies may require a heavy capital investment in plant, equipment, inventory, and marketing capability. A compromise may be to have long-lead-time items, such as special tooling, and alternative sources of supply ready to go at the time of market entry. Agent middlemen may be temporarily employed if demand exceeds the forecast by an amount that cannot be handled by the regular sales force. Finally, the firm may be able to immediately adjust supply to demand by increasing price until output can be increased (step pricing). However, this method has several disadvantages, and may well speed the entry of competitors into the market.

Summary of Product Decisions

The product instrument has many dimensions. These can be catalogued under several broad headings: physical properties, image, quality, package, brand and label, and location. The effect of a change in the product variable can often be measured, hence specified in relation to sales, by marketing research including quantitative analyses of consumer response. However, product ideas are dependent on the imagination and creativity—the "innovativeness"—of people. This is not a controllable process, although management can stimulate and exploit innovation in many ways.

From the marketing viewpoint, a product is what it is perceived to be in the minds of the consumers. Thus "new" products can be created by manipulating any dimension of the product variable, although many of these manipulations may be so trivial as not really to warrant calling the product "new."

New products can be given some protection from infringement by competitors through the use of patents and trademarks. These devices seldom assure a monopoly, although they usually exclude exact copies from the marketplace.

Product mix and product line are important variables. An alteration in either mix or line can have significant implications for each of the basic marketing instruments. For instance, the addition of a new item can displace a portion of the market for an established item, or it may complement, hence reinforce, the original line. Expansion of a line may be necessary to satisfy distributors or exclude competitors. A change in mix may be needed to more evenly load plant and equipment as well as to better utilize the sales force. Excessive costs may call for the elimination of a product.

Market segmentation and market aggregation (product differentiation) are the two general strategy alternatives with respect to the product variable. Market segmentation means the division of the total market into submarkets and the offering of a different product to each one. Market aggregation means offering the same product to every part of the total market, but attempting to differentiate the product by different promotional appeals in order to adapt it to the tastes of the various submarkets. Occasionally both strategies are used concurrently.

New-product development—although largely dependent on innovativeness—can be encouraged and exploited. Management can identify and communicate with new-product sources, actively involve itself in the search for and evaluation of ideas, establish criteria for the selection of new products, engage in test marketing, and be willing to experiment and to assume risk. Confronted by the ongoing technological revolution of the twentieth century, no industry can afford to remain static. The continual analysis and manipulation of the product variable is usually essential to the exploitation or accommodation of change.

Questions and Problems

1. How might the physical properties, image, quality, package, brand or label, or location of each of the following products be changed? (a) Ford two-door sedans, (b) Coty perfume, (c) Duz soap, (d) a slightly modified model of a G.E. computer.
2. Where might each of the following find new product ideas? (a) a small machine shop, (b) Boeing Aircraft Co., (c) General Mills, (d) Bullocks Department Stores.
3. Would a high learning rate—say 85 percent—encourage or discourage frequent alterations in a product's physical properties? Why?
4. How would you rate the performance of the marketing department if the firm's sales have declined from $4 million to $1.9 million while the industry's sales have gone from $20 million to $18 million? Suggest a possible cause and a solution for the firm's difficulties.
5. How might you protect each of the following products from infringement by competitors? (a) a new synthetic fiber, (b) a new perfume, (c) a new dress style, (d) a new toy.
6. What would be the possible advantages and disadvantages of (a) a toy manufacturer with a single product line enlarging its product mix, and (b) a wholesaler of hardware supplies enlarging its product line.
7. Would you recommend a strategy of market segmentation or market aggregation for each of the following products? (a) a household appliance with a very high fixed cost, and (b) the services of a marketing consultant. State the reasons for your answers.
8. Design a model for screening innovations for a firm in *one* of the following fields: (a) sporting goods, (b) machine tools, (c) motion pictures, or (d) pharmaceuticals.
9. Evaluate a hypothetical product, using the screening model in question 8.

Supplementary Readings

BOOKS

Booz Allen & Hamilton, *Management of New Products* (New York: Booz Allen & Hamilton, 1968).

Burns, Tom, and Stalker, G. M., *The Management of Innovation* (Chicago: Quadrangle Books, 1962).

Meitner, John G., *The Utilization of Space-Derived Technology in Non-Space Applications*, SRI Project 1440–2 (Menlo Park, Calif.: Stanford Research Institute, 1964).

PACKARD, VANCE, *The Waste Makers* (New York: McKay, 1960).

ROGERS, EVERETT M., *Diffusion of Innovations* (New York: Free Press, 1962).

ROSENBLOOM, RICHARD S., *Technology Transfer: Process and Policy* (Washington, D. C.: National Planning Association, July 1965).

ARTICLES

ADLER, LEE, "Time Lag in New Product Development," *Journal of Marketing,* Vol. 30, No. 1 (January 1966), pp. 18–21.

AMES, B. CHARLES, "Keys to Successful Product Planning," *Marketing Horizons,* Jack R. Wentworth, ed. (Bloomington, Ind.: Indiana University, 1965), pp. 78–85.

BASS, FRANK M., "A New Product Growth Model for Consumer Durables," *Management Science,* Vol. 15, No. 5 (January 1969), pp. 215–27.

BERENSON, CONRAD, "Pruning the Product Line," *Marketing Horizons,* Jack R. Wentworth, ed. (Bloomington, Ind.: Indiana University, 1965), pp. 78–85.

BERGLAS, EITAN, "Investment and Technological Change," *Journal of Political Economy,* Vol. 73, No. 2 (April 1965), pp. 173–80.

CARTER, C. F., and WILLIAMS, B. R., "The Characteristics of Technically Progressive Firms," *Journal of Industrial Economics,* Vol. 7, No. 2 (March 1959), pp. 87–104.

CLAYCAMP, H. J., and MASSY, W. F., "A Theory of Market Segmentation," *Journal of Marketing Research,* Vol. 5, No. 4 (November 1968), pp. 388–95.

NELSON, RALPH L., "Market Growth, Company Diversification and Product Concentration, 1947–1950," *American Statistical Association Journal,* Vol. 55, No. 292 (December 1960), pp. 640–49.

OLKEN, HYMAN, "Spin-Offs: A Business Pay-Off," *California Management Review,* Vol. 9, No. 2 (Winter 1966), pp. 17–24.

OLSEN, ROBERT M., "The Strategy of Market Segmentation," *Kansas Business Review,* Vol. 21, No. 9 (September 1968), pp. 3–6.

O'MEARA, JOHN T., JR., "Selecting Profitable Products," *Harvard Business Review,* Vol. 39, No. 1 (January–February 1961), pp. 83–89.

SAMLI, A. COSKUN, "Segmentation and Carving a Nitch in the Market Place," *Journal of Retailing,* Vol. 44 (Summer 1968), pp. 35–49.

UDELL, JON G., and ADERSON, EVAN E., "The Product Warranty as an Element of Competitive Strategy," *Journal of Marketing,* Vol. 32, No. 4, Part I (October 1968), pp. 1–8.

URBAN, GLEN L., "A Mathematical Modeling Approach to Product Line Decisions," *Journal of Marketing Research,* Vol. 6, No. 1 (February 1969), pp. 40–47.

WASSON, CHESTER R., "How Predictable Are Fashion and Other Product Life Cycles?" *Journal of Marketing,* Vol. 32, No. 3 (July 1968), pp. 36–43.

"Why Diversity? It Means Growth to Giants, Strength for Beginners," *Printers' Ink,* Vol. 270, No. 12 (March 18, 1960), pp. 27–29.

WONG, YUNG, "Critical Path Analysis for New Product Planning," *Journal of Marketing,* Vol. 28, No. 4 (October 1964), pp. 53–59.

Part VII

DISTRIBUTION DECISIONS

Distribution, defined in the broadest sense, encompasses all the marketing functions. In many instances, the terms distribution and marketing are used interchangeably. This was once appropriate, since the institutions between the producer and the ultimate consumer—the intermediaries who constitute the channels of distribution—did at one time perform all the classical marketing functions. From the beginning of the industrial revolution until the end of the nineteenth century, these middlemen priced, promoted, determined the product characteristics of, and physically distributed virtually all consumer goods. The producer simply responded to demand as it was interpreted for him by the intermediary and concentrated exclusively on the product function. He did little to influence conditions in the marketplace, except in cases of monopoly. (The Standard Oil Company, for example, engaged in marketing to the extent of restraining trade and fixing prices.)

The continuing technological revolution during the twentieth century disrupted this institutional arrangement. Manufacturing became far more sophisticated and efficient, but at a large scale that required heavy capital investment. Radical changes in communications technology allowed producers to appeal directly to consumers. The power to manipulate the marketing variables shifted to the manufacturers.

The great economic gains that resulted from the industrial revolution were due in many cases to the increased efficiency that resulted from a divisibility of labor.[1] As an economic body—whether it is a firm, an industry, or a nation—grows in size, labor can become specialized, machinery can begin to replace labor, and increasing returns to scale can be obtained. Consider the bootmaker at the beginning of the twentieth century. He purchased tanned hides, and then, in a one-man shop, performed all the operations required to produce and *market* a pair of boots. When his sales increased, the bootmaker added an apprentice who cut the leather to the proper size, but he still performed all the sewing operations himself and waited on the customers. As his sales increased further, he added more apprentices and began to be a business manager rather than a bootmaker. Eventually the size of his business justified purchasing a sewing machine. As its growth continued, he introduced more and more labor specialization and increasingly substituted machinery (capital) for labor. Eventually he added salesmen, accountants, and production managers, all because specialization of labor resulted in increased productivity per employee—or increased returns to scale.

Eventually the bootmaker, now the president of a successful manufacturing and retail business, decides to concentrate further on production and sell his output to other shoe stores for subsequent resale to the consumer. He is now confronted with a different problem—how to provide adequate sales coverage of the many stores that could sell his shoes in the retail market. He analyzes the cost of performing this function within his own organization and realizes that selling his product through a wholesaler who deals in shoes and boots would cost him much less than hiring his own sales force. Thus, greater specialization of labor again increases his profit.

When his sales become large enough, his cost and revenue functions may indicate that greater profits could be earned if he performed the intermediary functions himself. He may then move closer to his ultimate consumers by establishing his own sales force to sell directly to the retail stores, by-passing the wholesalers. If his product line becomes sufficiently broad, with a wide variety of styles and prices, he may even establish his own chain of retail outlets.

In this example, which is typical, the firm grows through a process

[1] For an excellent discussion of the divisibility of labor, see George J. Stigler, "The Division of Labor Is Limited by the Extent of the Market," *Journal of Political Economy* (June 1951), pp. 185–93.

involving increasing returns to scale—that is, it gets more efficient as it gets larger. At every stage, however, the optimum degree of labor specialization depends on the level of production. In turn, the level of production depends on the size of the firm's market. The fact that the producer's ability to develop his market influences his production efficiency is one of the economic and social justifications of the marketing function.

As changing manufacturing technology encouraged the formation of large-scale production units, a technological revolution occurred in communications. The advent of the high-speed printing press, the wide distribution of periodical literature, and radio and television allowed producers to communicate directly with their ultimate consumers, by-passing the middleman. This encouraged the branding of merchandise to retain the identification of the product with the manufacturer as it flowed through the channels of distribution.

By branding their goods, and by communicating directly with consumers, producers became less dependent on the intermediaries. In many cases, the role of the middleman has diminished to mere order-taking and physical distribution in local markets. Mass media for a television program (the audience frequently numbers as high as 60 million) have also given the producer an instrument for the development of mass markets. Telephone systems, teletype and computer networks, closed-circuit television, long-range radio, and improvements in transportation enable manufacturers to control far-flung organizations. This has reinforced the trend toward integration—by both internal expansion and merger—that has characterized American business since World War I. The trend has accelerated in the past decade, in spite of interference by the courts and federal agencies.

Not only have producers expanded forward in the direction of the consumer, but retailers have frequently moved backward in the direction of the producer and even to the sources of the raw material. Two major examples are Sears, Roebuck and Company and the Atlantic & Pacific Tea Company. Over the years, Sears has acquired many of its sources of supply. A & P has acquired food brokers in the course of its ambitious—and sometimes illegal—efforts to control the entire channel of distribution between the farm and the housewife.

Those independent middlemen who survived the onslaught of technology and acquisition—and there are many who did—have frequently been relieved of many of their traditional functions. A large number of

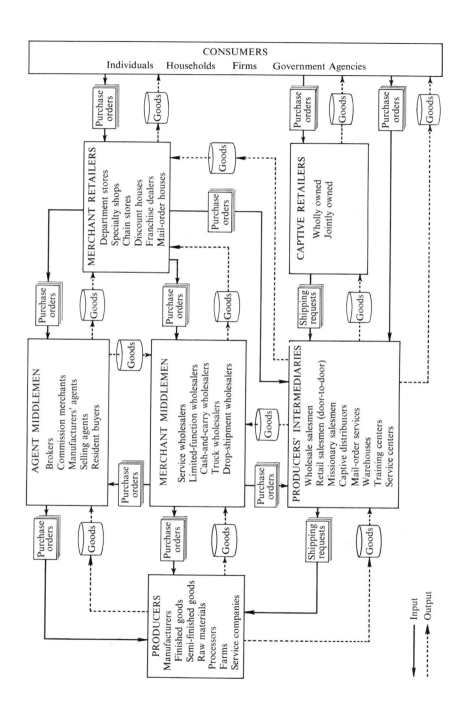

general-line wholesalers still remain. However, many middlemen have evolved into specialists who perform a limited number of functions and whose services are tailored to the needs of the markets they serve.

The economic concept of divisibility of labor, whether applied to a firm, an industry, or a nation, explains both the growth and decline as well as the relative importance of the many marketing intermediaries found in a distribution system. Although the basic structure of the distribution system is essentially fixed, at least in a developed economy, the number of ways in which the firm can organize its marketing channels is almost unlimited.

The basic channels of distribution are presented in the figure opposite. Over 200 networks can be constructed from different combinations of these distribution institutions. If we consider the five basic modes of transportation—air, rail, truck, ship, and pipeline—we have over a thousand possibilities. If we consider all the variations or subsets of the basic institutions and modes, the number of theoretical combinations becomes staggering. Of course, the number of alternatives diminishes, and thus becomes manageable, when one eliminates those alternatives that are inappropriate to a particular market. We will, therefore, begin our analysis of distribution by discussing the means by which a firm can determine, describe, and measure the market it serves, from the viewpoint of its distribution needs.

CHAPTER 17

Market Dimensions, Channels, and Institutions—Selection Criteria

MARKET DEFINITION

In order to select channels and allocate resources properly, the producer must define its market. Market definition may precede or follow the conception of a new product or product variation, depending on the philosophy of the firm. Some companies continually search for new markets and, when one is discovered, design a product to satisfy it. Other firms develop new products—sometimes as by-products of established lines—and then search for markets. Frequently both methods are used by a company.

A market can be defined in many ways—geographically, demographically, institutionally, politically, and so on. Marketers refer to "the New York market," "the teenage market," "the college market," "the English market," or a combination market such as "the automobile market," "the women's ready-to-wear market," or "the beer market." Often the distribution level defines a market—"the wholesale market" or "the retail market," as does the type of retailer—"the drugstore market," "the department-store market," or "the restaurant market."

The purpose of market definition is to divide potential buyers into groups that are homogenous with respect to some characteristic. The characteristic selected should be appropriate to the instrument that the definition serves. For example, defining a market according to its level in the distribution system is appropriate for some pricing decisions. Defining a market geographically is important for physical distribution decisions. Defining a market demographically or institutionally may be appropriate for some promotional decisions.

Units of Measurement. By defining the market, the firm can often estimate its size and location. This is why characteristics should be selected that offer some possibility of measurement. For example, if the product

354

serves the needs—and hopefully conforms to the tastes—of female teen-agers, the firm might define its market in accordance with census data. From the population figures for the female teenage population, management could quickly estimate the number of potential customers. This general category (female teenagers) could then be broken down geographically to allow for a more detailed analysis of channel requirements. Figures for regions, states, and standard metropolitan statistical areas are easily obtainable.

When possible, the marketer should adhere to standard classifications of a given characteristic. This is especially important in the collection of data. The richest source of data relevant to marketing decisions, especially forecasting and channel selection, is the federal government. Population data, demographic data, income data, trade data, and selected production data are amassed in quantity. This information is reduced, analyzed, and arrayed in a variety of statistical forms, then published in government documents that are readily available from the U. S. Government Printing Office, federal agencies, regional depositories, and local libraries. Government statisticians are fairly consistent in their use of terminology, geographical divisions, and distribution ranges. The firm should use comparable terms and categories if it wishes to relate the data it acquires to the corresponding government statistics.

Once the market and submarkets have been defined, the problem of channel selection becomes much more manageable. If the market for the good can be estimated as a function of measurable (and preferably fore-castable) variables, the marketing manager is close to a solution of his firm's demand function. The key to market measurement is the proper selection of the units of measurement. The potential customers must be defined in terms that can be quantified—preferably terms that have already been quantified by a government agency, trade association, chamber-of-commerce, or research organization, or by the company itself.

For example, population figures are readily available for customers defined by age, sex, income, race, and marital status. Data on the number of firms and their sizes are available for industrial consumers in selected fields, such as the automobile, steel, aluminum, aircraft, liquor, railroad, and airline industries. Where the industry is regulated, as is the case with the airline, railroad, alcohol, and utility industries, data are almost always available. If the marketing manager can define his potential buyers in common terms, he can usually determine their aggregate number and their geographical distribution.

If future values for any of these variables—such as population by age—can be predicted, then the future market, as well as the present market, can be estimated. For example, the demand for college educations in 1980 will depend primarily on the number of people between 18 and 22 years of age. This figure is predictable within one percentage point, and can be found in several Bureau of the Census *Population Reports.* To take another example, the demand for construction materials at a certain time can be estimated from the number of building permits issued 90 days earlier. Various techniques of prediction are explored in detail in Chapter 26. For now, it is important only to appreciate the need for selecting appropriate dimensions in defining a market.

As the marketing manager subdivides his original market into manageable segments, it may be appropriate to change the descriptive terms. The dimensions of the total market—which reflect the properties of the potential consumers of a particular good—may be altered in defining the segments. Thus the total market for fiber boxes might be defined as "all manufacturing firms producing packaged goods," for which data are available in the *Annual Survey of Manufacturers: General Statistics for Industry Groups and Industries,* published by the federal government. The market might then be subdivided on the basis of industry or geographical area. Since the aggregate data can be broken down both ways, the criterion for selecting one or the other, or both, would depend on the marketing manager's preference regarding the organization of his sales staff. If the market is essentially determined by location, geographical segmentation would be preferable. On the other hand, if the market is determined by the application of the product in a particular industry, then a subdivision by industry is appropriate. If the buyer population is geographically distributed, but industry oriented, then a geographical-industrial description of the market segments may be best.

Some useful dimensions for market definition and measurement are suggested by Tables 17.1 and 17.2, which show statistical cells[1] frequently used by government and private agencies to array data and define markets.[2] Table 17.1, "Geographical Statistical Cells," shows the geographical divisions and subdivisions generally used by federal agencies in arraying and displaying data. For instance, population, income, employment, and school-enrollment data are available in this form.

Table 17.2, "Standard Metropolitan Statistical Areas," lists statistical cells of special interest to marketers. These SMSA's consist of one or more local political subdivisions; each is defined to allow a convenient division of business data. Divided between 35 states, they represent definable local markets, especially for consumer goods, and include over 75 percent of all consumers and over 85 percent of all retail businesses. Population, housing, income, employment, retail sales, wholesale sales, selected trades, and consumer expenditure data are all gathered and reported for these cells. The SMSA's often conform to the natural trading areas of the firm.

---

[1] A "cell" is a unit of statistical data. For example, if sales were aggregated for each of three states—say California, Washington, and Oregon—each of those states would be a statistical cell.

[2] See Chapter 22 for a list of data sources.

Table 17.1   Geographical statistical cells

<table>
<tr><td colspan="6" align="center">UNITED STATES</td></tr>
<tr><td colspan="2" align="center">*North Central*</td><td colspan="2" align="center">*Northeast*</td><td></td><td></td></tr>
<tr><td>East
North Central</td><td>West
North Central</td><td>New England</td><td>Middle
Atlantic</td><td></td><td></td></tr>
<tr><td>Illinois
Indiana
Michigan
Ohio
Wisconsin</td><td>Iowa
Kansas
Minnesota
Missouri
Nebraska
North Dakota
South Dakota</td><td>Connecticut
Maine
Massachusetts
New Hampshire
Rhode Island
Vermont</td><td>New Jersey
New York
Pennsylvania</td><td></td><td></td></tr>
<tr><td colspan="2" align="center">*South*</td><td></td><td colspan="2" align="center">*West*</td><td></td></tr>
<tr><td>East
South Central</td><td>West
South Central</td><td>South Atlantic</td><td>Pacific</td><td>Mountain</td><td></td></tr>
<tr><td>Alabama
Kentucky
Tennessee</td><td>Arkansas
Louisiana
Oklahoma
Texas</td><td>Delaware
Florida
Georgia
Maryland
North Carolina
South Carolina
Virginia
West Virginia</td><td>Alaska
California
Hawaii
Oregon
Washington</td><td>Arizona
Colorado
Idaho
Montana
Nevada
New Mexico
Utah
Wyoming</td><td></td></tr>
</table>

SOURCE: U. S. Department of Commerce, *Statistical Abstracts of the United States* (Washington, D. C.: U. S. Government Printing Office, 1969).

Another system of statistical subdivision that is of particular interest to the marketer is the *standard industrial classification*. The SIC divides U. S. economic units—including commercial firms, government services, and private households—into 78 major groups. These are further divided into about 160 subgroups, which in turn are subdivided into about 500 sub-subgroups. The major classifications and their subdivisions are numerically coded with a four-digit numbering system.[3] For example, Major Group 36 is "Electrical Machinery, Equipment, and Supplies"; Subgroup 363 is "Household Appliances"; and Sub-subgroup 3635 is "Household Vacuum Cleaners."

The federal government, which developed the SIC system, accumulates considerable data classified on this basis. The system and data provide a means of identifying and evaluating both industrial and consumer-goods markets.

[3] For a complete listing of the classifications and codes and a thorough explanation of their application, see Bureau of the Budget, *Standard Industrial Classification Manual* (Washington, D. C.: U. S. Government Printing Office, 1967).

Table 17.2   Standard metropolitan statistical areas

New England	Indianapolis	*West South Central*
Boston	Columbus	Houston
Providence, Pawtucket	Dayton	Dallas
Warwick	Toledo	New Orleans
Hartford	Akron	San Antonio
Springfield, Chicopee,	Gary, Hammond,	Oklahoma City
Holyoke	East Chicago	Tulsa
Bridgeport	Youngstown, Warren	El Paso
Worcester	Grand Rapids	Beaumont, Port Arthur
New Haven	Flint	Shreveport
	Canton	
Middle Atlantic	Peoria	*Mountain*
	Lansing	
New York City	South Bend	Denver
Philadelphia		Phoenix
Pittsburgh	*East South Central*	Salt Lake City
Newark		Tucson
Buffalo	Louisville	
Paterson, Clifton, Passaic	Memphis	*West North Central*
Rochester	Birmingham	
Albany, Schenectady, Troy	Nashville	St. Louis
Jersey City	Knoxville	Kansas City
Syracuse	Mobile	Minneapolis, St. Paul
Allentown, Bethlehem,	Chattanooga	Omaha
Easton		Wichita
Harrisburg	*Pacific*	Davenport, Rock Island,
Wilkes-Barre, Hazleton		Moline
Utica, Rome	Los Angeles, Long Beach	Duluth, Superior
York	San Francisco, Oakland	Des Moines
Binghampton	Seattle, Everett	
Johnstown	San Diego	*South Atlantic*
Lancaster	Portland	
Reading	San Bernadino, Riverside	Washington, D. C.
Trenton	Ontario	Baltimore
	Anaheim, Santa Ana,	Atlanta
	Garden Grove	Miami
East North Central	San Jose	Tampa, St. Petersburg
	Sacramento	Norfolk, Portsmouth
Chicago	Honolulu	Jacksonville
Detroit	Fresno	Richmond
Cleveland	Tacoma	Wilmington
Cincinnati	Bakersfield	Fort Lauderdale, Hollywood
Milwaukee	Spokane	Orlando
		Charlotte

SOURCE: U. S. Department of Commerce, *Facts for Marketers* (Washington, D. C.: U. S. Government Printing Office, 1966).

TRADING AREA

Trading areas are an important concept in market determination. A *trading area* is "a district whose size is usually determined by the boundaries within which it is economical in terms of volume and cost for a marketing unit or group to sell and/or deliver a good or service."[4] A trading area may be established naturally, as is the case with a restaurant, a gas station, or an independent grocery store. Or it may be set by the firm itself during a period of expansion or subdivision.

The determination of the firm's trading area will vary greatly between firms on different levels in the channels of distribution. A manufacturer's area may cover several nations, a wholesaler's, several states, and a retailer's, a single town or a few city blocks. Consider, for example, the trading areas for firms, from the producer down to the retailer, in the petroleum industry. A description of the firm's trading area is an important aspect of market definition. It is essential both to the selection of distribution channels and to the allocation of promotional resources, especially advertising.

The structure of the industry, the physical properties of the product, the density and location of the market(s), and the willingness and ability of customers to travel are the rational determinants of the firm's trading area. The nonrational determinants—at least in the economic sense—are the firm's desire for power, growth, size, prestige, and other instruments of ego satisfaction, which are only of passing interest here.[5]

Transportation Costs.   If the industry approaches the purely competitive model, then the trading area will be a function of the transportation costs. This is the case, for instance, in the marketing of agricultural products, coal, or cement. The geographical outreach of the firm from its production facilities is determined by the transportation cost of the product. Since the products of each firm are homogeneous in a competitive industry and any firm must include transportation in its cost function, a company must take a reduction in profit as it expands its geographical market. This implies a natural market roughly circular in shape, with the producer at the center. As the natural trading areas of different firms expand and come into contact with one another, a series of hexagons will be formed, each representing the semi-exclusive market area of an individual producer.[6] (This ideal model assumes that all firms have an identical cost function and demand the same rate of profit, thus precluding price cutting.)

The firm in a competitive industry will be sensitive to transportation costs, especially if it produces items that have a low value-to-weight ratio.

---

[4] Ralph S. Alexander and the Committee on Definitions of the American Marketing Association, *Marketing Definitions* (Chicago: American Marketing Association, 1960), p. 22.

[5] For an exploration of these determinants, see William G. Scott, *Human Relations in Management: A Behavioral Science Approach* (Homewood, Ill.: Irwin, 1962).

[6] August Lösch, *The Economics of Location,* tr. from 2nd rev. ed. (New Haven, Conn.: Yale University Press, 1954), pp. 105–08, as cited by George Schwartz, ed., *Science In Marketing* (New York: Wiley, 1965), p. 286.

To expand its trading area, the firm must either build plants nearer the prospective buyers or differentiate its product. With the product-differentiation strategy, the buyer may be convinced to discriminate between brands and pay a slightly higher price (for what he perceives to be a superior good or service), which would absorb the extra delivery or freight costs.

Price and Trading Areas.   Price is not a long-run marketing instrument in a competitive industry. However, it is often employed in the short run or market period. A price cut may enable a firm to penetrate a market served by an established seller, who may be protected by a transportation-cost advantage.

Price was once used extensively as a predatory instrument for the destruction of local competition through the capture and monopolization of a trading area. A large firm would penetrate a local market and clear it of competitors by offering a price—usually one below cost—that would bankrupt the established firms. Once the trading area was monopolized, price would be raised to exploit the monopoly, with buyers usually being forced to pay more than if competition had prevailed. The high profits could then be used to cover the temporary losses incurred in monopolizing still other areas. This practice became so common and so abusive that it is now illegal.

A price cut designed to eliminate surplus inventory may be confined to a market outside the firm's normal trading area to avoid disturbing the price equilibrium of the primary trading area. This practice, called "dumping," was once used extensively in foreign trade. Dumping, often in the dumper's own trading area, is a common occurrence in the automobile fuel business. Refineries offer surpluses to independent jobbers and retailers, who exploit their reduced cost by engaging in a price war that temporarily redistributes the retail market. The effect is normally short lived, and as the major-brand dealers retaliate, the proselyted customers revert to their former loyalties.

If the sellers or the buyers are clustered together, transportation costs will have little influence on the distribution of the market between firms. With transportation costs equal for those producers capable of serving a given set of buyers, factors other than the natural trading area will determine the division of markets among sellers.

Retail Areas.   Retail areas are a special class of trading areas and are generally less susceptible to change by a firm than are the trading areas associated with industrial and institutional goods. The reason is that the buyer usually comes to the seller, except for the relatively small amount of selling done by mail-order houses and door-to-door salesmen.

The retail-trading area is especially sensitive to the shopping habits of the community, the convenience of public transportation, the highway system, the distribution of households between the metropolitan area and the suburbs, and the nature of the retailers' prices, goods, and services. Only the last three items—prices, goods, and services—can be manipulated by the seller.

A significant postwar phenomenon in retail merchandising is the diffusion of metropolitan shopping centers into the suburbs. This trend, which started in the late 1940's, has accelerated with the population migration to the suburbs, the decay of the cities, and the growing inadequacy of public transportation. It has been mitigated only by the expansion of the highway system, which makes downtown areas more accessible but which may also make shopping in the outlying suburbs more convenient. The retail merchant has two alternatives. He can either follow the migration to the suburbs, which has been the prevailing reaction; or he can differentiate his goods and services (specialty shops still do this to some extent) or engage in price competition to draw customers back to the central store. Price cutting has generally failed as a method of drawing shoppers back to the central cities. The stores that have grown have done so by establishing themselves in new trading areas as these arose on the outskirts of the old communities.[7]

Manufacturers' Areas. Manufacturers' trading areas tend to be much broader than those of retailers. This is especially true for industries in which there are substantial economies of scale, fixed costs are a large percentage of total costs, or the value-to-weight ratio of the product is high. Except for the last item, these factors tend to concentrate resources. Thus the firm may prefer to absorb the higher distribution costs rather than pay for the inefficiencies that result from dispersing production facilities. For example, aluminum can be manufactured economically only near large sources of cheap electrical power and with massive equipment. Petroleum products require large refineries with high fixed costs. Hence both aluminum and petroleum production are concentrated, although their customers are widely dispersed. The ability to differentiate products also encourages a manufacturer to absorb distribution costs, for it relieves the pressure of price competition and allows a sufficient profit margin for the firm to be insensitive to small differences in transportation costs. Cameras and certain sporting goods—especially those fair-traded or advertised nationally at a fixed price—are sufficiently differentiated that the profit margin allows the producer to absorb differences in shipping costs.

Unlike the retailer, the manufacturer does not have to draw buyers to his place of business. With modern transportation and communication methods, he can solicit sales over a wide area. Twentieth-century technology in transportation and communication also encourages centralized warehousing, which in turn decreases the need for decentralized production facilities.

[7] Techniques for measuring and defining a firm's retail-trading area are given in Chapter 18.

The chief incentives for the construction of widely separated plants are usually the availability of labor, taxes, tariffs, declining efficiencies of scale beyond an optimum plant size, cheap and abundant power, or raw materials. Most new plants are built in previously established trading areas and are a result of manufacturing, not marketing, decisions. The availability of cheap labor was admittedly a factor in the decision of many domestic textile firms to move from the New England area to the South. Similarly, the establishment of light manufacturing in the Commonwealth of Puerto Rico occurred primarily because of the quest for both cheap labor and tax refuge.

CHANNEL FUNCTIONS

The channels of distribution are best defined in terms of their functions. Distribution is the mechanism that accommodates the inflow of purchase orders from the consumer to the producer and the outflow of goods or services from the producer to the consumer. This implies two channels. One channel provides for the solicitation and processing of orders, the other for the physical transfer of goods and services. Although frequently both channels flow through the same institutions, they may be partially or fully separate.

The order for a sporting rifle, for example, flows from the consumer, through the retailer, through the wholesaler, to the arms manufacturer. The gun itself then proceeds from the producer to the sportsman backward along the same route. On the other hand, the order for a magazine subscription may flow from the consumer, through the retailer (possibly a bookstore or door-to-door salesman), through a local distributor or independent publisher's representative, and then back to the publisher, while the magazine itself goes directly from the publisher to the subscriber via the postal service.

The magazine example illustrates the use of different channels for orders and goods. The publisher's revenues may flow in via distributors, retailers, its own door-to-door salesmen, or direct customer orders solicited through mail, newspaper, or magazine advertising. The periodicals may be delivered directly from publisher to reader, via the post office, or through a network of distributors and retailers. As a rule, all these channels will be operating simultaneously.

Input Functions. Input functions include all tasks performed in the solicitation and processing of orders, exclusive of institutional or product advertising prepared by the producer and directed at the market in general. The inflow of orders is the reverse of the process of the outflow of goods and services. Purchase orders—oral or written—are initiated by many buyers in consumer-goods markets, by fewer in industrial-goods markets, and by just a handful in government contracting. These orders are collected, sorted, and combined by the intermediaries, who reissue fewer, but much larger, orders for the producers. The paperwork involved is usually simple and clerical, but massive.

The timing and the size of reorders, as well as the clerical cost, can influence the profit function of the producer, intermediary, or retailer. Both revenue and cost may be affected. Too-frequent reordering excludes the advantage of large-quantity discounts and lower freight rates and increases processing costs. Too-infrequent reordering can mean high inventory costs if large stocks are maintained; it can mean lost revenues if low stocks are maintained and the depletion of inventory results in lost sales. Consequently, inventory decision models are used to optimize both reorder time and size.

When a producer depends on independent intermediaries to process orders, it is sometimes advisable to support their system. For example, a manufacturer may send representatives, called "detail men," to call on wholesalers or retailers to check the stocks of its products. If inventories are low, the detail men will prepare orders to replenish depleted stocks. These orders are normally processed through the regular middlemen, who receive full credit for the sales.

As has been pointed out, the input channel may or may not coincide with the output channel. The producer may find it more efficient to operate its own sales and order-processing network, while leaving physical distribution in the hands of independent middlemen. Or, the producer may reinforce the regular input channel with its own field staff, which concentrates on missionary work (making an initial sale to a new customer), point-of-purchase promotions, trouble-shooting, and monitoring the work of the intermediaries.

With long-lead-time goods such as boats, appliances, trailers, and automobiles, it is important for distributors and retailers to anticipate future demand and process orders in sufficient time to allow delivery before the demand materializes. This is especially true with seasonal items such as recreational vehicles and toys. The alternative—for the manufacturer to build and inventory large quantities of its product—is both expensive and risky. Consequently, manufacturers use a variety of promotional and pricing techniques to encourage early ordering by both distributors and retailers. These include elaborate sales conventions, discounts, and merchandise bonuses.

Although promotion—advertising and personal selling—is usually essential to support the input function, the mechanics of order flow should not be neglected. It does little good to spend money on promotion if prospective customers are frustrated by a cumbersome, slow, or unreliable order system. It does no good to stimulate desire for a product if the satisfaction of that desire is prevented at the first step by depleted inventories or an order system unresponsive to the demands of the potential buyer.

Output Functions. The output functions include all tasks related to the transportation and storage of finished goods, as well as the operations involved in any further processing of the goods (assembly, packaging, installation, and servicing) that may be required to make them acceptable to the ultimate consumer.

Collection. Frequently, a large variety of goods from a number of producers are brought together by middlemen. This operation is appropriate for specialized items, especially where economies of scale can be achieved only with high-quantity—hence concentrated—production, yet the individual buyer has a low level of consumption. In the retail food industry, for example, the grocery wholesaler collects the outputs of a wide variety of specialized producers, thus enabling the retail-store buyer to satisfy a group of related, yet separate, low-quantity needs at a single location.

Sorting. The sorting function is the complement of the collection function and is generally performed by the same intermediary. Large lots are broken into smaller quantities appropriate to the consumer or the next intermediary. Complementary goods are often combined during this process. In the food industry, large quantities of a particular product are broken down and repacked by grocery wholesalers, who obtain economies of scale by packaging different goods with similar processes.

Storage. Intermediaries generally must provide physical protection, and sometimes insurance coverage, for goods awaiting further transfer en route to the consumer. The storage operation can be performed in conjunction with other middlemen tasks or separately, as is the case with a public warehouse. (A public warehouse, which is available to anyone, is useful for the small middleman who cannot justify the cost of maintaining a private warehouse.)

Inventory. The inventory function is closely related to the storage function, but it implies managerial skills in order to maintain an appropriate assortment of goods that are readily available to the consumer or the next intermediary. This operation offers perhaps the greatest opportunity for cost reduction, release of capital for other purposes, and improved customer service. It also lends itself to the application of quantitative techniques—particularly waiting-line theory, probabilistic analysis, statistics, and linear programming.

Transportation. The transportation function is generally performed by public carriers during the intercity legs of the trip from producer to consumer. However, there are notable exceptions. In the petroleum industry, for example, producers frequently operate their own tanker and truck fleets. Local transportation is handled by both public carriers and middlemen, with either the seller or the buyer providing transportation to the next intermediary or consumer.

Transportation decisions have traditionally been made on the basis of simple cost analysis involving little more than the comparison of rates for different classes of goods in different modes of transportation and differences in insurance charges and packaging costs. The systems approach to management suggests more complex decision models, with the effects of inventory and storage costs, delivery-response time, en-route handling, and customer service requirements included in the revenue and cost functions. Transportation decisions directly affect the cost function and indirectly affect the revenue function by influencing service and product availability.

Service. The service function, which includes the installation and maintenance of goods, has become increasingly important with the emergence of complex consumer products. In the appliance and electronics fields, the retailer is often incapable of servicing a broad assortment of fairly technical items. Even the wholesaler often deals in too great a variety of products to maintain a staff technically proficient enough to service all of them. Specialized distributors, such as air-conditioning equipment and executive-aircraft distributors, however, often have a high degree of technical ability and will provide complete installation and maintenance services.

A common alternative is for the producer to establish local repair stations to service his products in the local market. This is now customary for manufacturers of television sets, photographic equipment, and appliances. For example, General Electric operates several dozen service centers in the United States. Another alternative, appropriate to smaller producers, is to contract with local repair shops for the fulfillment of warranties and other after-sales services.

Support Functions. Support functions are those tasks performed by the producer in direct support of its middlemen. They give the producer a degree of control over the distribution process that it would not have if it relied solely on the middlemen. Some typical support functions are missionary selling, cooperative advertising, sales incentives, and training.

Missionary salesmen are employed by a manufacturer to call on customers of its distributors and promote the sales of the manufacturer's goods.[8] Missionary selling is appropriate with branded, low-priced goods having a low volume-to-retailer ratio, such as gourmet foods, hardware items, and cosmetics. The producer of such goods cannot economically service the hundreds, or perhaps thousands, of retailers that sell them. Hence it relies on distributors for order-taking and physical distribution. Since the distributors, in turn, are handling hundreds of individual items supplied by dozens of manufacturers, they cannot be expected to devote much time to the promotion of a particular item. The missionary salesman complements the dis-

---

[8] Alexander, *op. cit.,* p. 17.

tributor's salesmen by locating new customers, booking initial orders (which are usually credited to the distributor), setting up point-of-purchase displays, giving demonstrations, or providing free samples of the product. The demonstrations or samples are provided to both the retailer and the ultimate consumer on the premises of the retailer. The missionary's objective is to pull his firm's goods through the channels of distribution by stimulating demand at the retail level. It is analogous to priming a pump, in that the flow of goods can be maintained by the distributor once the initial demand is created at the retail level.

Cooperative advertising is used to encourage the retailer to allocate more of its own resources to the sale of a manufacturer's product. The advertisements promote both the store and the product. They serve the producer by directly stimulating consumer demand and by increasing point-of-purchase promotion by the retailer. Cooperative advertising is widely used, especially in the markets for grocery products, cosmetics, women's ready-to-wear clothing, and automobiles. Although it is also a form of price reduction, as the manufacturer absorbs some of the promotional costs normally borne by the retailer, it cannot be used as a discriminatory pricing technique. This abuse is specifically prohibited by federal laws.

Sales incentives and training are used to motivate the distributor's salesmen and to make them more proficient in the sale and servicing of the manufacturer's goods. Incentives are effective when the salesmen must put forth special effort to sell a particular item, as they must when a new product is being introduced. They are also useful when the producer must compete with other manufacturers for the attention of its distributor's salesmen. Training can involve both sales and service, the latter being significant when after-sales service influences brand reputation and therefore future demand. Training is important with complex goods, such as automobiles, machine tools, and office equipment. It is especially appropriate when the product must be carefully selected to match the needs of the customer. The General Motors Corporation, the Cessna Aircraft Company, and the Hughes Tool Company, for instance, all operate training programs for middlemen. Cessna and Hughes also offer training to their customers, who must acquire certain skills in order to successfully operate and maintain their products. Customer training is often provided as part of the sales contract, and therefore becomes part of the product mix. This is a common practice in military and industrial sales.

CHANNEL INSTITUTIONS

Merchants Versus Agents.   The two major types of middlemen, for purposes of definition, are merchants and agents. A *merchant* is "a business unit that buys, takes title to, and resells merchandise."[9] Wholesalers and retailers are the most common types of merchants. An *agent* is "a business unit which negotiates purchases or sales or both but does not take title to the goods in which it deals."[10] The agent receives its revenues from commissions or fees, which may be paid by the buyer or the seller of the good, but seldom both, since the agent is usually prohibited from representing both in the same transaction. However, an agent may represent sellers and buyers in different transactions. Stockbrokers, real-estate agents, resident buyers, and manufacturers' agents are common examples of agent middlemen.

Service Wholesalers.[11]   Prior to the twentieth century, the service wholesaler dominated the field of marketing, performing practically all the marketing functions. Historically, it performed such functions as branding goods, financing producers, and extending credit to retailers. Today, the service wholesaler is a merchant, usually organized according to the type of retailer or industry that it services. Like the limited-function wholesaler, a service wholesaler buys and resells merchandise to retailers and other merchants or to industrial or other commercial users. It carries a full line of products appropriate to its clientele and makes these items readily available in appropriate assortments at the local level. It does not sell to the ultimate consumer.

Limited-Function Wholesalers.   The limited-function wholesaler is a merchant that performs some but not all of the services associated with wholesaling. Cash-and-carry wholesalers, who do not extend credit or provide delivery service; drop-shipment wholesalers, who rely on the producer to inventory the product and to ship directly to the buyer; and truck wholesalers, who combine selling, delivery, and collection into one operation, are common examples of limited-function wholesalers.[12]

Brokers.   The term "broker" is loosely used in a generic sense to include such business units as freelance brokers, manufacturer's agents, selling agents, and independent purchasing agents. The broker is an agent middleman "who does not have direct physical control of the goods in which he deals but represents the buyer or seller in negotiating purchases or sales for his principal."[13] Examples are real-estate agents, stockbrokers, yacht brokers,

---

[9] *Ibid.*
[10] *Ibid.*, p. 9.
[11] The service wholesaler is sometimes called a "full-service wholesaler," "jobber," or "distributor"—the latter terms being more inclusive, since they cover all types of wholesalers.
[12] *Ibid.*, p. 23.
[13] *Ibid.*, p. 10.

and business brokers. Although the broker's powers are limited by the principal, who contracts with the broker to buy or sell for him under specific conditions and at certain prices, its role as a middleman is not always narrow. A firm doing business as a broker may also perform functions associated with other intermediaries. A real-estate agent may buy and sell property for himself. A stockbroker may own shares of a particular security or serve as an underwriter for a new issue. A yacht broker may take title to a used sailboat or may be a retailer for a line of new cabin cruisers. Brokers frequently handle competing goods.

Commission Merchants. The commission merchant (sometimes called a commission house) is "an agent who usually exercises physical control over and negotiates the sale of the goods he handles."[14] The commission merchant usually has more latitude than the broker in establishing the price and conditions of sales. Although the operations of commission merchants vary, they generally arrange for delivery, extend credit, and collect payment. The principal receives his money from the commission house, after the agent's fee has been deducted.

Manufacturer's Agent. The manufacturer's agent is an intermediary "who generally operates on an extended contractual basis; often sells within an exclusive territory; handles non-competing but related lines of goods; and possesses limited authority with regard to prices and terms of sale. . . . He may be authorized to sell a definite portion of his principal's output.[15]

The manufacturer's agent is common in industries with small producers and many widely dispersed buyers. Manufacturers of electronics components, toys, and low-value industrial goods frequently use these agents to sell their output to wholesalers, retailers, or ultimate consumers. The manufacturer's agent usually serves a specific market, defined either by clientele or geography. Thus a producer may contract with several agents to assure complete coverage of his total market.

The term *manufacturer's representative* is sometimes used synonymously with "manufacturer's agent," especially in the electronics industry. However, salesmen employed by the manufacturer sometimes represent themselves as "manufacturer's representatives." Such a salesman is not an independent business unit. Thus the term "manufacturer's agent" is less ambiguous and is the better choice when referring to an independent middleman of the type just described.

Selling Agents. The selling agent—sometimes called a "sales agent"— is an intermediary "who operates on an extended contractual basis; sells all

[14] *Ibid.,* p. 10.
[15] *Ibid.,* p. 15.

of a specified line of merchandise or the entire output of his principal, and usually has full authority with regard to prices, terms, and other conditions of sale. He occasionally renders financial aid to his principal."[16]

The selling agent is common in the agricultural field, often in the form of a cooperative that is jointly owned by the producers. The cooperative is separately incorporated—that is, it is a legal entity apart from its owners—and functions as an independent business unit in its day-to-day operations. Hence, it is properly called an agent. A typical example is Sunkist, a citrus-growers' cooperative with a virtual monopoly over certain types of oranges. Examples are also found in nonagricultural fields, such as the garment industry.

Resident Buyers. The resident buyer is "an agent who specializes in buying, on a fee or commission basis, chiefly for retailers."[17] This type of agent normally lives or maintains offices in a market city. Resident-buyer offices may be retained either cooperatively by a group of retailers or privately by a single retailer. The former are called *associate offices,* and the latter *private offices.* Private offices are not independent, hence are not, strictly speaking, properly called agent middlemen. However, the term "resident buyer" is frequently used both in this case and in referring to an employee residing in a market city and serving as a buyer for the home store.

Resident buyers are particularly useful for retailers handling a specialized good requiring expert selection and sold in a market far removed from the retailer's place of business. For example, high-fashion garments are sold primarily in New York and Paris; a resident buyer in one of these cities might represent department stores and women's specialty shops throughout the world.

Resident buyers are also used by manufacturing firms which need inputs that require careful point-of-purchase inspection or stringent quality control. Firms in the tobacco industry, the meat industry, and the aerospace industry, as well as federal government agencies, frequently depend on independent resident buyers or on their own personnel living in the market city or stationed at the seller's factory.

The technology of communication has reduced the need for resident buyers for many firms. In addition, the supersonic jet may soon make all centers of industry and commerce sufficiently convenient to be served by buyers working out of retailers' or manufacturers' home offices.

Relative Importance of Channel Institutions. The relative importance of the various channel institutions will vary between industries, with the structure, sociology, and tradition of the industry determining the most ap-

[16] *Ibid.,* p. 21.
[17] *Ibid.,* p. 19.

propriate mix.[18] In the theatrical industry, talent is sold almost exclusively by selling agents. In the electronics industry, components are sold both directly and through manufacturers' agents. Securities of publicly held corporations are sold exclusively through brokers. Groceries normally move from producer to consumer via wholesalers and retailers, although both are occasionally by-passed. Table 17.3 shows the share of sales[19] handled by various institutions in the distribution field.

Table 17.3 Distribution institutions
(Exclusive of retailers)

Rank	Institution	Share of Sales
1	Merchant middlemen	42%
2	Manufacturers' sales branches	33
3	Agent middlemen	15
4	Petroleum bulk stations	7
5	Assembler (farm products)	3
	Total	100%

SOURCE: Values estimated from tables in Reavis Cox, *Distribution In A High Level Economy,* © 1965. Reprinted by permission of Prentice-Hall, Inc., Englewood Cliffs, N. J.

SELECTION CRITERIA

Quantitative Considerations. The ultimate criterion for the selection of the distribution channel is profit. Annual profit is the most relevant factor in short-run decisions; however, future costs, revenues, and profits must be discounted to their present value before comparing alternatives involving long-run streams of costs, revenues, and profits.

A distribution decision will normally affect profit. The selection, switching, deletion, and addition of middlemen, as well as changes in transportation, warehousing, the use of detail men, and inventory maintenance, will affect

[18] For a discussion of the noneconomic aspects of channel selection and operation, see Almarin Phillips, *Market Structure, Organization, and Performance* (Cambridge, Mass.: Harvard University Press, 1962); Joseph Cornwall Palamountain, *The Politics of Distribution* (Cambridge, Mass.: Harvard University Press, 1955); Bert C. McAmmon, Jr., and Robert W. Little, "Marketing Channels: Analytical Systems and Approaches," in *Science in Marketing,* George Schwartz, ed. (New York: Wiley, 1965).
[19] A share is an institution's portion of the total dollar sales of all distributors, exclusive of retailers.

revenue or costs—and often both. Marginal analysis is usually appropriate, with the incremental change in profit, $\Delta\pi$, the likely decision criterion. If this value can be calculated for each of the options facing the decision-maker, the optimum channel is usually obvious.

When the marketer cannot measure the ultimate effect on profit of each of his alternatives, other bases for choice may be invoked. For instance, when faced with multiple channel options—that is, when allocating resources between two or more channels operating simultaneously—he can apply the rule of proportionality, shifting resources to the channel with the highest net revenue-to-cost ratio. This process should be continued until the ratio of marginal net revenue to marginal channel cost is equal for all channels, or intermediaries. Additional resources, if available, should be allocated to distribution until the marginal net revenue is equal to the marginal channel cost for each intermediary. According to the theory of the firm, the contribution to profit of the distribution function will be maximized under that condition. Expressed mathematically,

$$\frac{MNR_1}{MCC_1} = \frac{MNR_2}{MCC_2} = \cdots \frac{MNR_n}{MCC_n},^{[20]} \text{ where} \tag{17-1}$$

MNR = marginal net revenue (total marginal revenue after considering all costs except the channel cost)

MCC = marginal channel cost, and

$1, 2, \ldots n$ indicates each of the different channels or intermediaries

To illustrate, assume that the firm is operating through two channels, direct-mail orders and wholesalers. The mail-order service is owned by the manufacturer, and the wholesalers are independent. (This model conforms quite closely to the marketing of phonograph records by the major producers.) A wholesaler is employed for each of the four geographical regions that comprise the national market—Northeast, North-Central, South, and West. The net revenues—which vary because of different trade discounts—and the costs per 100 records sold are shown below. The subscripts 1, 2, 3, 4, and 5 indicate mail-order service and the Northeastern, North-Central, Southern, and Western wholesalers, respectively.

	Mail-Order Service (1)	Wholesalers NE (2)	NC (3)	S (4)	W (5)
Marginal net revenue	$35	20	22	15	16
Marginal channel cost	10	12	11	10	20

[20] This is merely an alternative form for expressing the MPR:MFC resource-allocation rule (Equation 6-3).

The rule of proportionality shows that the ratios are unbalanced:

$$\frac{MNR_1}{MCC_1} = \frac{\$35}{\$10} = 3.50$$

$$\frac{MNR_2}{MCC_2} = \frac{20}{12} = 1.67$$

$$\frac{MNR_3}{MCC_3} = \frac{22}{11} = 2.00$$

$$\frac{MNR_4}{MCC_4} = \frac{15}{10} = 1.50$$

$$\frac{MNR_5}{MCC_5} = \frac{16}{20} = .80$$

Obviously, additional funds allocated to the mail-order service will produce more revenue than additional funds spent on the other channels. Also, the allocation to the Western distributor should be reduced, since marginal resources in that region are producing less revenue than they cost. Thus the firm should shift resources from the Western distributor to the mail-order service. To perfectly allocate its resources, it should shift them among the intermediaries until the ratio of marginal net revenue to marginal channel cost is equal for each intermediary.

Although determining the total distribution budget and the allocation of the budget among the various channel intermediaries in this manner will maximize short-run profit, long-run profit may not necessarily be maximized. For instance, the Western wholesaler may have just recently acquired the firm as an account and not yet had sufficient time to develop the potential market. Thus, if the firm had an operational criterion of short-run profit maximization, subject to the constraint that it desired to retain the Western wholesaler because of the potential market, the amount of the distribution budget allocated to the Western wholesaler might not be reduced.

If alternative channels are open to the firm, these should be included in the equilibrium equation. Those that are relatively inefficient will be discarded if their $MNR : MCC$ ratios are lower than those of the other channels at the optimum output. As an example, the firm might consider changing to a new Western wholesaler if after a period of time the $MNR : MCC$ ratio of the Western wholesaler had not improved.

The simplified model we have just described illustrates the principle of channel selection and suggests a framework for the analysis of practical problems. However, it has several shortcomings and does not give us a simple mechanical procedure that eliminates the need for marketing judgment.

First, it is difficult to identify all distribution costs with respect to specific intermediaries. In our example, promotional aids provided to the wholesalers (and thus charged against them) may influence the revenues received by the mail-order service. Conversely, mail-order advertising may stimulate demand that is satisfied through purchases made at the retail stores served by the wholesalers.

Second, it is not always possible to shift small increments of resources. If the firm maintains regional sales managers, working in support of the wholesalers, a fraction of their services cannot be transferred to another region. Nor can advertising in national media always be apportioned by region.

Third, it may be necessary to maintain a channel at a minimum level of activity to exclude competition. The entry of a competitor into the market via that channel might prove far more damaging to profits than the disproportionate allocation of resources to a less efficient channel.

Fourth, capital limitations may preclude increasing the distribution budget to the level where marginal cost equals marginal revenue for the firm as a whole.

Fifth, the element of uncertainty associated with an untried channel may discourage management from shifting resources, especially if the calculated efficiency of the new channel is not significantly greater than that of the present channels, or if there is considerable difficulty involved in dismantling a portion of the current system.

Finally, the number of variables the marketing manager can manipulate may be highly restricted. Maneuverability diminishes as one moves down the organizational hierarchy. Consequently, an optimum solution to the problem, in terms of total company profit, may not be possible. This means the decision must be suboptimized—that is, profit will be maximized to the extent permitted by the real alternatives. The criterion that is used—short-run profit, long-run profit discounted to present value, or wealth maximization—may be suggested by logic, managerial edict, or the availability of data.

The optimizing and suboptimizing of channel decisions by quantitative techniques is dealt with more extensively in Chapter 18. First, however, we shall examine the qualitative aspects of distribution decisions, particularly those variables that influence the long-run performance of the firm but do not lend themselves to quantification.

Qualitative Considerations. Managers are most comfortable when costs are predictable, overhead expense is minimum, control is maximum, risk is limited, and resources are allocated to produce maximum profit. Unfortunately, this delightful situation occurs rarely. More often a manager must make the same sort of compromises in business that he makes in his personal life. The benefits of one alternative must often be gained at the sacrifice of the advantages of another. In dealing with channel options, the costs of various alternatives are expressed in numbers. However, qualitative judgment often plays a role, as when channel decisions involve different ratios of fixed to variable costs. For example, if the total costs of two or more mutually exclusive channels differ appreciably and the revenues generated by each are essentially identical, then the lowest-cost option is probably the superior choice. However, when the efficiencies of the channels are comparable, the fixed-cost-to-variable-cost ratio is critical. For example, most of the cost of distributing through a service wholesaler is variable—that is, it is proportional to sales. The manufacturer is paid for his goods within thirty days after delivery, and the middleman assumes all further distribution costs and risks. The manufacturer's distribution cost is limited to the discount taken by the wholesaler, which varies directly with the quantity of goods sold. The producer has no fixed distribution costs, except for factory inventory and his shipping-department costs. Overhead expense is minimum. If sales drop, distribution costs drop proportionately.

This has decided advantages. First, if a product line does not perform as forecasted or fails completely, the producer is not confronted with a continuing high distribution cost resulting from fixed expenses. Neither does the manufacturer face the possibility of having substantial capital tied up in idle facilities, such as local warehouses, sales offices, and service centers—all of which may be difficult to liquidate. Second, the manufacturer is not required to make a large capital investment in its distribution program, either in facilities or in recruiting and training personnel. The wholesaler or agent middleman offers a complete distribution system.

Predictability is another virtue of a low fixed-cost-to-variable-cost ratio. Unit costs must ultimately reflect the fixed costs that are amortized over the life of the product or a set time period. The greater the output, the lower the portion of fixed costs assigned to each unit. Thus, unit costs are especially sensitive to quantity when fixed costs are high. If the distribution costs are primarily variable, the total unit cost will vary less with variations in output. Hence, total unit cost is more predictable.

For example, assume that Product A can be sold through a selling agent who charges a flat commission of $10 on each unit sold. Thus the distribution cost of Product A is $10 per unit (plus whatever inventory and shipping are incurred by the manufacturer), regardless of the quantity sold. An alternative way of distributing Product A might be through a network of producer-operated sales offices whose facilities and staff cost $500,000 per year. If 100,000 units were sold annually, the unit cost would be $5 for distribution. If only 25,000 units were sold, however, the unit cost for distribution would be $20.

Obviously, the more costs can be shifted from fixed to variable, the less risk the firm assumes. Also, the cash flow of the firm is improved. Since variable costs are not incurred until the good is produced and sold, there is less time between outlay and income. This in turn relieves the need for working capital. Tax considerations are also involved, since variable costs are generally treated as current expenses and deducted for the year they were incurred. On the other hand, some forms of fixed cost—such as those for warehouse construction and the purchase of office furniture—are depreciated over a number of years.[21]

An intermediary is not always the optimum choice, of course. If the producer's output is sufficiently large, it may enjoy economies of scale in distribution equal to or better than those of an independent middleman. The intermediary must also make a profit, which must be reflected in its price. Hence, the producer's ownership of that segment of the distribution channel may offer economies that justify the high fixed cost.

A firm gives up some of its control of the market if it chooses to reduce fixed costs by delegating the distribution function to independent intermediaries. Distribution is one of the basic marketing instruments. It cannot be fully controlled by the producer when critical functions are performed by middlemen. The intermediary may be more skilled than the producer, more knowledgeable about the market, and better equipped to perform the distribution task, but his goal is the maximization of his own profit, not the producer's.

The intermediary's cost and revenue functions are different from those of the manufacturer; hence its optimum output will seldom coincide with the optimum required to maximize the producer's profit. Yet the manufacturer's actual output must match the aggregate output of the middlemen handling his goods. The only alternatives are for the manufacturer or middlemen to accumulate unsold inventory (hardly an acceptable condition in the long run) or for the middlemen to book orders that cannot be filled, an equally ridiculous choice.

If the intermediary controls sales, as it does in the case of the selling agent, the manufacturer is clearly at the mercy of the middlemen. Even where the service is more limited and the contract less exclusive, the intermediary still makes many decisions that are crucial to the acceptance of the manufacturer's products. It can manipulate the channel variables—such as the sales force, warehousing, customer service, and local promotion—to serve its own goals, and only assumes risks proportionate to its capital investment in the product, not the investment of the manufacturer, which is many times greater.

The middleman's allocation of resources between the product lines he represents may conflict with the best interests of the manufacturer. Sometimes these goods are in direct competition, as are houses listed by real-estate

---

[21] This problem may be accommodated by leasing facilities and equipment. The lease payments are generally recognized as a current expense for tax purposes.

agents and securities handled by stockbrokers. Other times they are not substitutes for one another, but still compete for the attention of the middleman, who must ration his resources between the different lines.

The knowledge that the intermediary will put his own goals first and those of the producer second complicates the problem of channel selection for the manufacturer. Maintaining a private distribution system will mean high fixed costs and possible inefficiencies of scale, but also complete control of the operation. Using wholesalers and merchant middlemen will mean low fixed costs, economies of scale, and a ready-made distribution system, but less control. A third alternative is to use a wholesaler or agent, but support this system by a parallel channel maintained by the manufacturer. This offers the best of the first two alternatives, but at the cost of redundancy, since the producer duplicates certain functions expected of the middlemen.

The dollars-and-cents consequences of conflicting goals, diffused loyalties, and the fragmentation of control between producers and middlemen are seldom predictable prior to actual operation with a selected distribution-channel mix. Once the channels are established, however, certain distribution variables can be manipulated and their effects measured. For example, missionary salesmen can be employed, incentive programs tried, cooperative advertising attempted, and customers surveyed to test the efficiency of the channel instruments. If data are properly accumulated, it will be possible to relate expenditures in these areas to revenues and make readjustments in resource allocation. At this point the effects of the variables—the channels and instruments—can be quantified and their use or rejection decided on a more rational basis. Also, since the performance of the product itself will be more clear by that point, the entire marketing program can be reviewed against a more quantified set of criteria.

This last point—the need for product performance data in order to fully evaluate the marketing program—suggests the use of middlemen until an item has proven itself in the marketplace. By starting with a low fixed cost for distribution, the producer reduces its break-even point and thus, at least presumably, reduces the risk in introducing a new product. However, this kind of policy can be dangerous if the channels selected prove inadequate in meeting or stimulating demand.

Another problem implicit in the distribution decision is the acquisition of market intelligence. Middlemen are a frequent source of data for researchers. They are sometimes essential in measuring local and short-run sales. If the producer engages in market experimentation—if, for example, it manipulates advertising in one of the standard metropolitan statistical areas—it will want to measure the resultant change in sales. The only practical way to get this data may be to query the local wholesaler, as the manufacturer may be too far removed from the retailers to sense fluctuations in sales during the time the experiment is conducted.

The willingness and ability of the middlemen to provide intelligence service is another qualitative variable. It seldom dictates the channel selection, but is often cause for modification of the system. For example, manufacturers frequently own and operate a few intermediaries, particularly retail stores, in order to gather market information. These establishments may also serve collateral functions by providing a place to experiment with sales aids and different merchandising tactics.

Exogenous Determinants.   There are certain determinants of channel selection over which the producer has little control and which limit his choice.

First, if the industry or the market is highly institutionalized—as is, for example, the stock market—the seller will have little or no choice. The channel decision is fixed.

Second, if the product is highly seasonal, as are most agricultural products, it may be economically unfeasible for the producer to maintain its own wholesale or retail outlets. The firm may have to rely on middlemen who have product lines that can support them in the producer's off-season.

Third, if the product must be assembled with other products that are not made by the same firm before it is sold to the retailer or ultimate consumer, it must be handled by an intermediary with adequate facilities and sources of supply. Construction supplies are an example.

Fourth, if the product has a low price and low volume of sales per store at the retail level—as is the case with certain hardware items—it is impractical for the producer with a limited product line to serve a large number of retailers. The small per-store sales would not justify the cost. Such a manufacturer must rely on wholesalers to service the retail outlets.

Fifth, if the product is complex, requires elaborate installation or service, or is custom tailored to the unique needs of the ultimate consumer, the manufacturer cannot delegate the distribution function to intermediaries. It must work directly with the consumer. The computer industry is a typical example.

Sixth, if the producer's financial resources are limited, it may have no choice but to hire the services of an established channel.

Often these exogenous determinants limit the manufacturer's distribution options to only one or two logical alternatives, at least so far as the primary distribution channels are concerned. What can be manipulated in such cases are the supporting variables, primarily promotion, which can be used to reinforce the established channels.

CHAPTER 18

Optimizing Distribution Resources

OPTIMIZATION VERSUS SUBOPTIMIZATION

According to the profit-maximization criterion, the firm should allocate whatever funds are necessary to bring output to the level where marginal revenue equals marginal cost. Additional increments of funds should be added to each element in the design-production-marketing-administration system until marginal cost and marginal revenue are equal for each area. If the budget for each element within the firm is drawn up on the basis of its contribution to profit compared to its cost, and allocations for each are brought to the point where the marginal values are equal, the rule of perfect resource allocation will be satisfied. The firm's resources will be optimally allocated, and since marginal revenue will equal marginal cost for each input, the firm will also be operating at the maximum profit level.

Unfortunately, in practice, imperfect knowledge and noneconomic constraints prevent a firm from functioning in this theoretically ideal fashion. However, this fact does not preclude the use of economic theory in selecting between alternatives and allocating funds. When management perfectly optimizes its resource allocation, it manipulates all the endogenous variables. It does not spend more money on one element of the firm's production function without considering what revenues that same expenditure would generate if it were allocated to one of the other elements instead. For example, management would spend $100,000 more on advertising in medium X only if it were sure that the money would not produce more profit if allocated to product improvement, new machine tools, or another sales office. Nor would it spend the money at all if the net increase in revenue (total revenue less the cost incurred in manufacturing and distributing the units sold by the added advertising) did not exceed or equal the outlay.

Total optimization is seldom practical. Although some attempt at total optimization is made in the budgeting process, most management decisions are made well down in the organizational hierarchy. Here, the budgets are already established; the options that are open and the variables that can be manipulated are limited. The decision-maker is knowledgeable in a specialized area, and is generally oriented only toward the performance and welfare of his own department. The advertising manager, for example, is concerned with the productivity of the company's advertising; the sales manager is concerned with the quantity of sales booked by his subordinates. Neither worries about—or is able to judge—the sensitivity of profit to the operation of, say, the machine shop.

Thus the decision-maker must choose between alternatives without considering the many other options that face the firm as a whole and must allocate resources within the limits of a relatively rigid budget established by his superiors. The process of selecting among limited alternatives and manipulating variables within preset limits is called *suboptimization*. It may disturb the economist, but it makes the processes of analysis more manageable.

The following discussion presents techniques for suboptimization of the distribution channels. However, it must be remembered that the suboptimization of each individual element will not necessarily lead to optimization for the firm as a whole.

SELLING CHANNELS — SELECTION AND BUDGET

The selection of selling channels is generally determined by the size and function of the firm and the degree of institutionalization of both the industry and the market. Some variation is possible, but usually the firm finds it impractical to deviate widely from the standard channels. This is especially true if the firm is small. If the firm is large, it is probably well established in the market and will be confronted with a good deal of inertia—in the form of both vested capital and personal interests—when it considers making a radical change in its basic system of selling channels. The growing firm is the most likely candidate for change, since the economies of scale that will emerge as the company gets larger will encourage it to assume a more active role in the entire distribution process.

The allocation of resources, once the proper channels have been identified, is approached differently before market penetration and after. Once experience in the marketplace can be evaluated, the rule of proportionality is an appropriate guide. However, before the product is established in the marketplace, precise revenue data are unavailable (although estimated sales figures may be). Thus the marketer must look for another technique for channel selection. Usually the size of the potential market is the best criterion for determining the initial budget.

The first task in selecting selling channels is to estimate the aggregate market for the product. Assuming that revenue will be a function of price and a given level of marketing effort, a total revenue curve can be plotted against the total cost curve, thus suggesting an optimum price-output combination. This optimum output establishes the firm's position on its total cost curve, hence sets the total budget for the design, manufacturing, and marketing of its product. This budget, which is determined by the firm's production function, includes the amount estimated as necessary for the marketing effort.

The sales budget is generally estimated from past experience with comparable products and is a gross value based on the aggregation of the firm's entire market—perhaps the United States, Western Europe, or the automobile industry. The problem confronting the marketing director or sales manager is how to distribute this budget between the various segments that make up the total market. His objective is to maximize total sales. This means that a dollar spent in market A should produce the same number of sales as a dollar spent in markets B through n. Lacking revenue data on the product, he can only allocate the sales budget in proportion to the estimates of the potential sales in markets A . . . n. The initial allocation can be refined as experience (sales data) is accumulated.

Assuming that the market itself has been defined and the submarkets identified, management must estimate the potential demand within each segment. For the purpose of distributing the sales budget, these estimates can be absolute, relative, or in terms of an appropriate indicator. For example, the sales manager might describe market n as having $50,000 in potential sales, being 8 percent of the total market, or having 125,000 households. By using an indicator, such as households, he assumes that the actual sales will be approximately proportional to the indicator.

Sophisticated methods of estimating the potential market will be explored in Part IX, "Marketing Research." We shall examine some of the simpler techniques here in order to clarify the allocation of selling resources.

INDICES OF MARKET POTENTIAL

Market estimates for industrial goods are usually based on the number and size of the firms using, or capable of using, the product. Estimates can be adjusted for differences between types of firms by using consumption figures for the different classes of industry. For individual firms, such figures are often provided by trade associations. At the industry level, they are compiled by such institutions as Scientific American, Inc. Thus, if there are ten electrical machinery firms with a total of 6,500 employees in the Phoenix standard metropolitan statistical area, and they consume an average of $390 worth of fiber boxes per employee annually, then the potential market for fiber box sales in the Phoenix SMA is $553,600 per year. If Phoenix was defined as a market segment by a firm introducing a line of fiber boxes especially designed for packaging electrical machinery, $553,600 would represent the segment's potential sales. If that value was 7 percent of the total potential market, the rule of proportionality would call for 7 percent of the selling channel resources to be allocated to the Phoenix area.

Market estimates for consumer goods, on the other hand, are usually based on the classical economic determinants of consumption: the price of the product, the price of substitute products, population, and income. Theoretically, all these factors should be taken into account in estimating the aggregate market. However, since both the price of the product and the price of substitutes will generally be similar between market segments, population and income may be more relevant to selling-channel decisions.

Population. Population is the most general indicator of the size of a potential market. It is a convenient basis for market estimates because of its predictability and the availability of data. Population data can usually be found in such federal sources as the *Statistical Abstract of the United States, Current Population Reports (P-20 Series), Population Estimates (P-25 Series)*, and the *United States Census of Housing,* as well as in various state publications available from departments of economics, planning, or vital statistics.[1]

For some product classes, such as beer and soft drinks, population is an extremely accurate basis for estimating consumption. Either total population figures or statistics for selected age groups may be used, depending on the nature of the product. For example, the market potential for alcoholic beverages would be better estimated by using the values for the population segment 21 years of age and older than by using total population figures.

Income. People alone do not form a market. They must have sufficient income to buy the firm's class of goods. Hence income also serves as an indicator of market potential. The commonly used indices of income are gross national product (GNP), personal income, disposable personal income (personal income less taxes), and discretionary personal income (disposable personal income less expenditures for essentials). GNP is useful only in estimating the total national market. Figures are available for personal income and disposable personal income at the national, regional, state, and local levels and are valuable in estimating market segments.[2] Statistics for discretionary personal income are appropriate to market estimates for nonessential goods, but are usually not directly available and must be estimated from other income and household data.

[1] See Chapter 22 for additional sources.
[2] See p. 485 for a list of data sources.

Buying-Power Index. The influence of both population and income on the demand for consumer goods suggests the usefulness of an index number that would be a relative measurement of the effective buying power of a market segment. Marketing Statistics, Inc., a marketing research firm, computes such an index under the sponsorship of *Sales Management* magazine, which publishes the data annually. This statistic is called the *buying-power index,* or BPI. It is a *relative* measurement of consumer purchasing power, based on the population, income, and retail sales figures for a given geographical market. Retail sales figures are included to weight the index number for the propensity to consume (which is obviously biased by the propensity to supply) of the local market. The formula for the computation of this index is

$$BPI = \frac{5D + 3S + 2P}{10}, \text{ where} \tag{18-1}$$

BPI = buying-power index (percentage of potential U.S. buying power)

D = net effective buying income (disposable personal income), expressed as a percentage of total national disposable personal income

S = retail sales, expressed as a percentage of total national retail sales, and

P = population, expressed as a percentage of total national population

The buying-power index is not an absolute measure of how much a particular market may consume, although it may be used in a predictive equation once actual sales data are accumulated. Rather, it is an approximate measurement of the relative ability of an area to purchase consumer goods. Hence, if area A has a BPI of .1550, its market potential is twice that of an area—say, market B—with a BPI of .0775.

The BPI is useful in allocating selling-channel resources such as distributors, salesmen, missionary salesmen, cooperative advertising, and point-of-purchase displays. For example, assume that a budget of $200,000 has been allocated to the selling channels in a particular area. This budget must be distributed between the five counties that make up the area. The solution —using BPI data—is found by preparing the matrix in Table 18.1. We shall assume, for simplicity, that all other variables influencing the purchasing decision remain constant or cancel one another out between market segments. This is seldom true, of course. The demand for snow tires, for example, would not be the same in Florida as it would be in a northern state with the same BPI. Weather, taste, and law all vary between markets and can have a

Table 18.1   Distribution of selling-channel resources by BPI

County*		BPI†	Percentage of Territory BPI‡	Budget§
A		.0460	5.77	11,540
B		.5420	68.00	136,000
C		.1220	15.31	30,620
D		.0200	2.51	5,020
E		.0670	8.41	16,820
	Totals	.7970	100.00	$200,000

* Geographical market segments selected by the firm
† Buying Power Index, from *Sales Management*
‡ Distribution of total market territory, computed by the ratio

$$\frac{\text{BPI for County}}{\text{BPI for Territory}} = \frac{\text{BPI for County}}{.7970}$$

§ Computed by multiplying column 3 by $200,000 (total budget)

considerable influence on the consumption of certain products. Such factors must be considered when using BPI data as a decision variable.

Quality Index and Index of Sales Activity.   Per capita expenditures are another criterion for allocating selling resources. It is particularly useful in identifying markets for quality goods and determining areas that might be especially sensitive to promotion—such as areas with high discretionary income. The *quality index* (QI), also published in *Sales Management,* is a relative measure of the per capita purchasing power of a geographical market. It can be determined by the following equation:

$$QI = \frac{BPI}{P}(100), \text{ where} \tag{18-2}$$

QI = quality index

BPI = buying-power index, and

P = population, expressed as a percentage of the total national population

Since $QI = 100$ for the nation as a whole, a quality index greater than 100—for example, $QI = 120$—would indicate a high-quality market. Conversely, a QI equal to 80 would indicate a low-quality market. This index is significant, however, only if used in conjunction with some indicator of market size, such as population or retail sales. For example, a *QI* of 150 would not indicate an important market if the area consisted only of 200 households.

Another measure of sales potential, also compiled by Marketing Statistics, Inc., under the sponsorship of *Sales Management,* is the *index of sales activity*. ISA is a *relative* measure of retail sales activity that is relevant to products sold through retail stores. It is computed as

$$ISA = \frac{S}{P}(100), \text{ where} \tag{18-3}$$

ISA = index of retail sales activity

S = retail sales, expressed as a percentage of total national retail sales, and

P = population, expressed as a percentage of total national population

The ISA is used in much the same manner as the quality index. $ISA = 100$ is the national average, with $ISA < 100$ and $ISA > 100$ indicating below-average and above-average retail sales per unit of population, respectively. Like the QI, the index of retail sales activity must be used in conjunction with an appropriate measure of market size. It could be misleading for any market, such as a purely residential community, where household needs are often satisfied at retail shopping areas outside the community limits.

RETAIL OUTLETS — SELECTION AND LOCATION

Perhaps the characteristic that most clearly distinguishes the retailer from other channel intermediaries is its direct relationship with the market. There is generally much less flexibility in selecting locations for retail outlets than in choosing sites for warehouses or production facilities. Once a retail market is defined and selected for penetration, the means of satisfying consumer demand must be located in that market. Even a mail-order house must deliver catalogues to prospects where they live. With the present high level of competition in the retail trades, the prospective urban buyer does not need to go far to satisfy most of his material wants.

The choice of local markets is based on potential sales, which are estimated from population or income data or an appropriate index. Once the geographical market is selected, management must choose the type, size, number, and location of retail outlets. The type of retailer selected—a discount house, a specialty shop, mail-order office, a prestigious store, and so forth—will depend on the characteristics of the product, the institutional nature of the market, and the profile of the potential buyer. In a mature market the retail outlet is usually dictated by the structure of the established channels. However, some of marketing's greatest successes have been attributable to innovations that ran contrary to entrenched practices. Witness the discount house, the mail-order record club, and the drive-in theater.

The number and size of outlets are determined by estimates of potential sales and the optimum ratio of floor space, sales personnel, or stock to sales. These ratios can be determined from company records or estimated from industrial-engineering studies. Once the outlet size is established in terms of a particular standard, such as floor space per dollar of sales, then equipment requirements, personnel needs, and other factors can be readily estimated.

After the total capacity required to serve the selected market is known, the optimum number and location of outlets must be determined. Should the capacity be concentrated in one location or diffused throughout the market? Where should outlets be located? Obviously, the number of outlets needed to penetrate an area will vary with the product. Specialty goods, especially those which have few substitutes, have larger trading areas than convenience goods, for which there are many substitutes. A convenience good will require many more stores than a shopping good (that is, a good for which buyers have a strong brand preference). The Gulf Oil Company, for instance, requires many more outlets than does the General Motors Corporation in order to service a given region properly.

The number of stores required to serve a market is determined by the size of the natural retail trading area of an outlet for the product class being sold. If the area of the market—for example, Los Angeles County or the San Francisco SMSA—is divided by the trading area, the dividend becomes an approximation of the number of stores needed to cover the market. For example, if the market area measured 100 square miles and the trading area was estimated at 25 square miles, 4 stores would be needed for complete coverage. This figure is useful as a first approximation but would have to be adjusted for geographical characteristics, transportation facilities, local purchasing habits, and the amount of competition in a specific marketing area.

There are a number of simple numerical and mathematical techniques for estimating the size and sales potential of a retail trading area. One method is to count the number of cars in a given shopping center and record a sample of their license plates. By using vehicle-registration data—usually available from the state's department of motor vehicles—the market analyst can determine the addresses of the owners. These are plotted on a map, thus providing a rough picture of the trading area of the shopping center. By comparing the number of automobiles observed with the total number of cars registered in the area, a crude approximation can be made of the portion of the population attracted to that particular location.

Food sales in a given area can be estimated by multiplying the population by the amount the average family spends on food. This figure can be combined with the figure for the extent of grocery-store facilities—measured in square feet—in the area to produce a market-saturation index. Expressed algebraically,[3]

$$I = \frac{C \cdot E}{F}, \text{ where} \qquad\qquad (18\text{-}4)$$

I = index of market saturation

C = number of consumers (obtained from population statistics)

E = average food expenditure per consumer, and

F = retail food outlets (in square feet)

For example, a supermarket chain might define a geographical market that has a population, C, of 100,000. Assuming that the Department of Agriculture has estimated a per capita food expenditure of $12 per person per week, E, and that a survey of retail food markets in the designated area has indicated an optimum total floor space, F, of 300,000 square feet, we can compute the probable weekly revenue per square foot of facilities in this particular market:

$$I = \frac{C \cdot E}{F} \qquad \text{Given}$$

$$I = \frac{100,000(\$12)}{300,000} \qquad \text{By substitution}$$

$$I = \$4 \qquad \text{By arithmetic}$$

Once I is known, the analyst can determine how attractive the market is by referring to the firm's cost and revenue figures. For example, if weekly sales of $3 per square foot provide sufficient revenue to justify the risk and the cost of building a store, then one should be established. Since building the new store will decrease I by increasing the total floor space, the firm should build the quantity of floor space necessary to maximize profit.

I can also be viewed as the revenue, R, produced by one square foot of floor space. If cost, C, is expressed in terms of floor space, then the profit equation, $\pi = R - C$, will yield the profit per unit of floor space. Since profit, π, is maximized when its derivative is equal to zero (see Chapter 3, p. 70), differential calculus can be invoked to determine the optimum quantity of floor space, F. F is the decision variable—that is, F is the quantity management must determine in deciding the optimum store size.

[3] B. J. la Londe, "New Frontiers in Store Location," *Super Market Merchandising* (February 1963), as cited in Delbert J. Duncan and Charles F. Phillips, *Retailing: Principles and Methods* (Homewood, Ill.: Irwin, 1967), p. 101.

Through algebraic manipulation and an application of calculus that is slightly beyond the scope of this text, one can demonstrate that profit will be maximized when the floor area established by the supermarket equals the area computed by solving the equation

$$F_N = -F \pm \sqrt{\frac{C \cdot E \cdot F}{S}} \text{, where} \qquad (18\text{–}5)$$

F_N = optimum size of the retail market (in square feet)

C, E, and F are the same as in Equation 18–4, and

S = the cost per square foot of building and operating the new outlet[4]

Since this is a solution of a quadratic equation, it will have two roots, and thus two answers. However, the negative answer may be ignored.

Given the values contained in the previous example, the optimum floor space for the supermarket chain preparing to penetrate this particular market is computed as

$F_N = -F \pm \sqrt{\dfrac{C \cdot E \cdot F}{S}}$	Given
$F_N = -300,000 \pm \sqrt{\dfrac{100,000(\$12)(300,000)}{\$3}}$	By substitution (Assume $S = \$3$)
$F_N = -300,000 \pm \sqrt{120,000,000,000}$	By arithmetic
$F_N = -300,000 \pm 347,000$	By arithmetic
$F_N = 47,000 \text{ or } -647,000$	By arithmetic
$F_N = 47,000$	By rejecting negative value

Having computed the optimum size of the facilities justified by the geographical market, the firm must then decide if they should be concentrated in a single unit or diffused through several stores. The actual number of outlets will depend on two things. The first consideration is the natural trading area of a store. In the case of the supermarket, the analyst will probably rely on previous experience and on studies of how far housewives are willing to travel to patronize a particular store. The second consideration is the most efficient size of a single retail outlet. Once this limit is exceeded—as it may well be by the total facility size justified by the market—it becomes more economical to build multiple units.

One way to measure the size of the natural trading area is to use a for-

[4] The cost of building the supermarket must be changed to an annual, or period, cost before it can be used in the equation. This can easily be accomplished by considering the cost of the building as a rental cost.

mula known as Reilly's *law of retail gravitation*.[5] Reilly hypothesized that the ability of a shopping center to attract customers was directly proportional to the population of the trading area and inversely proportional to the square of the distance between the shopping center and the prospective buyer. His conclusions have been supported by empirical findings establishing the boundaries—that is defining trading areas—between competing shopping centers. Reilly's formula is as follows:

$$\frac{T_1}{T_2} = \frac{P_1}{P_2}\left(\frac{D_2}{D_1}\right)^2 \text{, where} \tag{18–6}$$

$\dfrac{T_1}{T_2}$ = ratio of the shoppers from an intermediate location who will patronize shopping center 1 (T_1) to those who will patronize shopping center 2 (T_2)

P_1 = population of trading area 1

P_2 = population of trading area 2

D_1 = distance between shopping center 1 and the intermediate location and

D_2 = distance between shopping center 2 and the intermediate location

The relationship expressed in the equation can be shown clearly with the aid of a diagram. Figure 18.1 shows the shopping centers as circular areas and the intermediate location, perhaps a small town, as X. Using the values given in the figure, and applying Reilly's formula, we have

$$\frac{T_1}{T_2} = \frac{P_1}{P_2}\left(\frac{D_2}{D_1}\right)^2 \qquad \text{Given}$$

$$\frac{T_1}{T_2} = \frac{600,000}{200,000}\left(\frac{10}{30}\right)^2 \qquad \text{By substitution}$$

$$\frac{T_1}{T_2} = \frac{1}{3} \qquad \text{By arithmetic}$$

Thus, for every shopper from location X who patronized shopping center T_1, three shoppers would patronize shopping center T_2. That is, T_2 would get 3 times as many shoppers from X as would T_1.

A further adaptation of Reilly's law was worked out by P. D. Converse,[6] who showed that the boundary between two shopping centers can be estimated by the formula

[5] William J. Reilly, *The Law of Retail Gravitation* (New York: William J. Reilly, 1931).
[6] P. D. Converse, "New Laws of Retail Gravitation," *Journal of Marketing*, Vol. 14, No. 3 (October 1949), pp. 379–84.

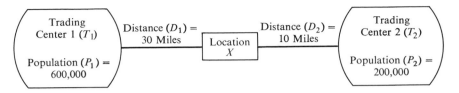

FIGURE 18.1
Retail trade gravitation diagram

$$D_{B_2} = \frac{D_T}{1 + \left(\dfrac{P_1}{P_2}\right)}, \text{ where} \tag{18-7}$$

D_{B_2} = distance of the boundary from shopping center T_2

D_T = total distance between shopping centers

P_1 = population of trading T_1, and

P_2 = population of trading area T_2

In the preceding example, the boundary between T_1 and T_2—the point beyond which a majority of shoppers will patronize the other trading center—is 14.6 miles from T_2.

$$D_{B_2} = \frac{D_T}{1 + \left(\dfrac{P_1}{P_2}\right)} \qquad \text{Given}$$

$$D_{B_2} = \frac{40}{1 + \left(\dfrac{600,000}{200,000}\right)} \qquad \text{By substitution}$$

$$D_{B_2} = \frac{40}{1 + 1.73} = 14.6 \qquad \text{By arithmetic}$$

The distance of the boundary from T_1, D_{B_1}, equals the total distance less the distance D_{B_2}, or 25.4 miles in the example. Consumers living beyond the boundary would tend to shop in the competing shopping area, as was the case with the inhabitants of X, three-fourths of whom preferred shopping center T_2. To serve the market represented by X, the firm should establish an outlet in shopping center T_2, and perhaps another in T_1, if the potential market is large enough to justify two stores. The producer should allocate marketing resources between shopping centers T_1 and T_2 proportionally, on a 1:3 basis. This assumes that other variables—transportation, parking facilities, sales taxes, costs, and so on—are equal, or average out, between the two centers. If not, adjustments will be necessary.

Converse also developed an equation to predict the division of sales between two shopping centers, one located in the downtown area of a large city and the other in a satellite town. This is another adaptation of Reilly's law. Converse estimates that the most effective area for a trading center normally has a radius of 4 miles. An urban trading center and satellite town would therefore divide the trade of the town approximately in direct proportion to their population but inversely as the square of the distance between them (when the distance is measured in terms of the trading center's most effective area of 4 miles). Mathematically, this relation becomes

$$\alpha = \frac{P_2}{P_1} \left(\frac{4}{d}\right)^2 \times 100, \text{ where} \qquad\qquad (18\text{-}8)$$

α = the percentage of the satellite town's trade that is captured by the trading center T_1

P_1 = population of T_1

P_2 = population of T_2, and

d = distance between T_1 and T_2 in miles

For example, assume that a central city, T_1, and an outlying suburb, T_2, have populations of 500,000 and 100,000, respectively. The distance between them is 20 miles. Thus 20 percent of the satellite town's trade will be captured by the trading center T_1, as shown below:

$$\alpha = \frac{P_1}{P_2} \left(\frac{4}{d}\right)^2 \times 100 \qquad\qquad \text{Given}$$

$$\alpha = \frac{500,000}{100,000} \left(\frac{4}{20}\right)^2 \times 100 \qquad\qquad \text{By substitution}$$

$$\alpha = (5)\left(\frac{1}{25}\right) \times 100 = .20 \times 100 \qquad\qquad \text{By arithmetic}$$

$$\alpha = 20\% \qquad\qquad \text{By arithmetic}$$

Again, the results given by the formula must be modified to reflect the differences in transportation, parking facilities, commuting patterns, sales tax, and so on, between the two centers.

The choice and location of retail outlets is often a complicated problem. A considerable amount of data may be needed, and sophisticated mathematical tools are often invoked. An exception is when the present institutional arrangements in the marketplace limit the choice to only one or two options.

The marketer need not be proficient in the use of complex quantitative skills, but he should be sufficiently aware of their applications to know when to call on the services of a mathematician or operations research specialist.

WAREHOUSES — NUMBER AND LOCATION

Economies of scale make it profitable for a manufacturer to produce large quantities of a good, while the limited needs (and income) of the average buyer tend to make consumers purchase small quantities of a given good. Thus, as products flow from manufacturer to ultimate consumer, they are handled in smaller and smaller quantities and are usually mixed with a greater and greater variety of other goods. To satisfy the wants of buyers, supplies of a particular product must be made available before a prospect's tastes change or he finds a substitute. For cigarettes or soft drinks, this time can be measured in seconds—hence the retailer must have the merchandise on the shelf. For new fighter planes or spacecraft, the time is measured in years, and the seller maintains no inventory.

The warehouse serves as a link in the physical distribution process whereby the retailer, or occasionally the ultimate consumer, can be readily supplied with goods. In order to ensure that no sales will be lost, stocks of products would need to be maintained in such quantities and at such locations that the demands of local buyers can be satisfied immediately. This would also simplify the merchant's reordering problems. Although the cost of such a system is prohibitive for most firms at the present time, the computerization of retailer inventory control and the improvement in transportation technology are moving the producer in the direction of near-instantaneous response.

Decisions as to the number and location of a firm's warehouses are based on (1) warehouse operating costs, (2) plant-to-warehouse transportation costs, (3) warehouse-to-buyer transportation costs, and (4) the costs of delivery delays. Inventory costs and optimum production release quantities are assumed to be independent of the number of warehouses and their location, and are therefore ignored in this discussion. Obviously, suboptimization is involved.

Warehouse Operating Costs. Total warehouse cost is generally a function of floor space, measured in square feet. The relationship is fairly linear when the firm is renting public warehouse space but becomes curvilinear (the unit cost curve has the typical U shape) when the warehouses are company-owned. The linear cost of renting space is due to the tariff schedule common to public warehouses. Company-run warehouses, on the other hand, involve economies of scale that allow fixed and semifixed expenses to be apportioned over a greater number of units as size increases. Management, labor, insurance, depreciation of buildings and equipment, utilities, and security are typical elements of the total cost. Total warehouse operating costs, for a given level of sales, tend to decrease as the number of warehouses decreases.

Plant-to-Warehouse Transportation Costs. Plant-to-warehouse transportation costs are generally a linear function of the distance between the plant and the warehouse. In computing these costs, the distance must sometimes be weighted—that is, adjusted higher or lower—to compensate for differences in the difficulty of transportation over particular routes. Yet, given a constant volume of sales, plant-to-warehouse transportation costs will usually decrease as the number of warehouses decreases due to economies of scale in shipping. Similarly, plant-to-warehouse transportation costs will increase as the number of warehouses increases.

The net effect of increasing the number of warehouses can be either an increase *or* a decrease in *total* plant-to-warehouse costs. In general, however, the nearly linear relationship between transportation costs and the distance between the plant and warehouses will outweigh the effects of economies of scale in shipping. Thus if additional warehouses will reduce the average weighted plant-to-warehouse shipping distance, plant-to-warehouse transportation costs will be reduced. Obviously, plant-to-warehouse transportation costs will increase if the average weighted shipping distance is increased.

Warehouse-to-Buyer Transportation Costs. Costs associated with the transportation of goods from the warehouse to the buyer are called *delivery costs*. They are generally a linear function of the distance between the warehouse and the customer and include vehicle operating expenses, drivers' wages, insurance, licenses, and dispatchers' pay. The total delivery cost tends to decrease as the number of warehouses increases and the average warehouse-to-customer distance decreases. Although the customer may take delivery at the warehouse,[7] transportation is still an element of the buyer's cost and hence part of the effective price.

Costs of Delivery Delays. *Delay time* is the time between the receipt of an order by the seller and the delivery of the merchandise to the buyer.[8] It is often dictated by industry practice. Delivery delays always carry the threat of order cancellation, especially if the competition can respond more

---

[7] This is called f.o.b. (freight-on-board) delivery.

[8] This would be computed as the minimum time needed to respond to a purchase order. Often, goods will be ordered months in advance of a specified delivery date. This assures availability of the merchandise, and the buyer does not have to stock or pay for the goods until they are needed. The practice is typical where the products are seasonal goods such as Christmas merchandise.

quickly. Sales lost because of delay times—an opportunity cost—should be considered in deciding the number of warehouses. Delay time will obviously decrease as the number of warehouses increases.

As a practical matter, the firm will probably select a maximum acceptable delay time—such as 24 hours for 90 percent of its customers—and use this constraint in determining the minimum number of warehouses necessary to serve the market. The 90-percent figure is usually considered to be distributed among customers—that is, a given customer is disappointed only 10 percent of the time. However, a delay time that causes 10 percent of the customers to be disappointed 100 percent of the time is a different matter, and might result in a complete loss of the outlying market if competition can do better. Delay time is a function of distance. The relationship is not precise (due to variations in road, traffic, and schedule conditions), but it can be used to define *approximately* the number and size of warehouses needed.

Since the maximum distance between warehouse and customer is set by the maximum acceptable delay time, the maximum area that one warehouse can serve can be determined by solving the equation:

$$D = S \cdot T, \text{ where} \tag{18-9}$$

D = maximum warehouse-to-customer distance

S = average delivery speed, and

T = maximum allowable time in transit, which is equal to the maximum acceptable delay time less the warehouse order-processing and loading time

For example, assume that the firm's sales department must guarantee buyers a maximum of one day's delivery time in order to match the service offered by competitors and that the firm has only one eight-hour work shift per weekday. If it takes three hours to process an order and load the merchandise, then the maximum transit time, T, would be five hours if the firm did not want to incur overtime costs. If the average delivery speed is forty miles per hour, then

$$D = S \cdot T$$
$$D = 40(5)$$
$$D = 200$$

Thus there must be a warehouse within 200 miles of each customer. Knowing the market area it wished to cover, the firm could determine from the equation above how many warehouse areas it includes, hence how many warehouses are needed.

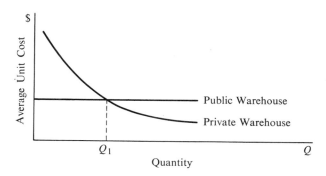

FIGURE 18.2
Comparative warehouse costs

When entering a new market, especially with a new product, the producer may choose to ship directly from the factory or from a warehouse in an adjacent market or to use a public warehouse. In this way the firm avoids the substantial capital outlay, high fixed costs, and long-term commitment associated with leasing or owning the warehouse. Once the penetration phase is complete and the producer is sure of an adequate level of sales, it may then open its own warehouse to exploit the cost advantages associated with large-scale operations. The threshold for shifting to a privately owned warehouse is determined simply by locating the crossover point of the public warehouse and private warehouse cost curves. This is illustrated in Figure 18.2. Decreasing unit costs indicate the desirability of a private warehouse beyond quantity Q_1. At Q_1, the fixed costs are spread over enough units to make the average unit cost equal to the flat rate charged by the public warehouse. Beyond Q_1, the average cost declines to below the flat rate, and the private warehouse offers a cost advantage.

INVENTORY CONTROL

Inventory control is critical to both manufacturing and marketing. Excessive stocks imply excessive real costs (not just opportunity costs), while inadequate stocks can mean, at worst, a shutdown and, at best, unsatisfied customers. The shutdown of an atuomobile assembly plant due to the lack of steel or a particular part and the loss of customers due to stock shortages are common examples of what happens when a firm runs out of inventory. Although we shall deal with inventory control from the marketing viewpoint in this book, the ideas and techniques discussed here are equally applicable to manufacturing—or, for that matter, to any operation that is dependent on the availability of material inputs.

Inventory control involves two decisions: when to order, and how much to order. On the one hand, a small inventory is attractive because of lower insurance, damage, depreciation, storage, and interest costs. There is also less chance that the product will become obsolete before the stock of it is sold out. Large inventories, on the other hand, mean lower processing and transportation costs, less risk of shortages, and quantity discounts. The virtues of a low-inventory philosophy becomes the vices of a high-inventory philosophy, and vice versa. This dilemma is portrayed graphically in Figure 18.3.

Inventory control is reflected in the firm's revenue function as well as in the cost function. Although it does nothing positive to influence the revenue function, a low-inventory policy can reduce sales if stocks run out and the

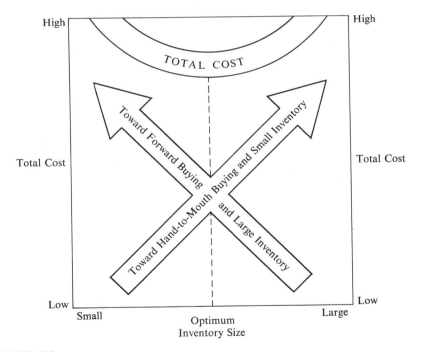

FIGURE 18.3
Axis of inventory size

SOURCE: Adapted from Robert J. Holloway and Robert S. Hancock, *Marketing in a Changing Environment* (New York: Wiley, 1968), p. 350.

buyer can turn to a substitute brand before they can be replaced. Thus poor inventory control can cause a loss of revenue, which may or may not be preferable to the increased costs that would be incurred by maintaining a higher level of goods on hand.

The firm can make inventory-control decisions based solely on the cost function if lost sales are viewed as a cost rather than a loss of revenue. This simplifies the decision model by reducing it to a single equation. Treating lost sales as a cost is most satisfactory for tactical decisions about minimum inventory levels and order quantities. However, it is inappropriate for the computation of actual profit. In computing actual profit, only real costs may be included.

The real, money costs of inventory are processing costs and carrying costs. These are the elements ultimately reflected in the firm's profit-and-loss statement. Adding these costs to the opportunity cost gives us the following inventory cost function for purposes of decision-making:

$C_I = P + K + L$, where   (18–10)

C_I = total inventory cost

P = order-processing cost (including discounts for large-quantity orders)

K = carrying cost, and

L = opportunity cost (lost sales)

The inventory-replenishment decision—when to order—depends on the order lead time and the usage rate (the rate at which inventory is depleted). These are mathematically related as follows:

$R = L \cdot U$, where

R = reorder point, expressed as the minimum inventory level

L = lead time, and

U = usage rate

For example, if the lead time is 5 days, the usage rate is 10 units per day, and the firm elects never to run out of inventory, then the reorder point is an inventory level of 50 units.

$R = R \cdot U$ Given

$R = 5(10)$ By substitution

$R = 50$ By arithmetic

The optimum order quantity is determined by three variables—the annual carrying cost per unit, the cost of placing an order, and the annual demand, in units. These variables are related as follows:

$$Q = \sqrt{\frac{2DS}{C}} \text{, where} \qquad\qquad (18\text{--}11)$$

Q = optimum order quantity

D = annual demand in units (sales)

S = cost of placing one order, and

C = cost of carrying one unit in inventory for a year

Thus if the cost of carrying one unit in inventory for a year is $10, the cost of processing an order is $20, and the annual demand is for 2500 units, then the firm's optimum order quantity for a particular distribution point is 100 units.

$$Q = \sqrt{\frac{2DS}{C}} \qquad\qquad \text{Given}$$

$$Q = \sqrt{\frac{2 \cdot 2500 \cdot 20}{10}} \qquad\qquad \text{By substitution}$$

$$Q = \sqrt{10,000} \qquad\qquad \text{By arithmetic}$$

$$Q = 100 \qquad\qquad \text{By arithmetic}$$

Thus, in the previous example, when the inventory level reached 50 units an order would be placed for 100 additional units.

CHOOSING THE TRANSPORTATION MODE

The most common criterion used for transportation decisions is still the rate. The mode selected is generally the one that costs the least, as long as the goods are delivered within the maximum allowable time. The decision may be sophisticated to the extent that orders are combined to take advantage of reduced rates, yet the process is still essentially clerical. Often, with low value-to-weight goods such as heavy bulk items, there is only one reasonable mode. For example, the inland transportation of coal is entirely by rail, except for small-quantity local deliveries, and the transoceanic shipment of petroleum products is strictly via tankers.

However, both the supply and demand functions of transportation are changing. New technology, especially in air transportation, the increasing importance of delivery time, and the increasing value-to-weight ratio of many goods are changing the nature of the transportation decision. A systems approach is beginning to emerge, whereby all the variables affected by the mode of transportation are taken into account. These include, but are not limited to, insurance, warehousing, opportunity costs, inventory, product perishability, and packaging. Decision models are becoming more complex, sometimes requiring sophisticated linear programming and computer techniques for their solution.

The five basic modes of transportation are highway, rail, air, water, and pipeline. Their relative merits, in terms of speed, frequency of service, dependability of service, capability (the ability to handle large and/or heavy goods), availability, and cost, are indicated in Table 18.2. For example,

Table 18.2   Relative characteristics of transportation modes

Characteristic	(Best)			*Relative Merit*					(Poorest)
Speed	Air	>	Pipeline	>	Highway	>	Rail	>	Water
Frequency*	Pipeline	>	Highway	>	Air	>	Rail	>	Water
Dependability	Pipeline	>	Highway	>	Rail	>	Water	>	Air
Capacity	Water	>	Rail	>	Highway	>	Air	>	Pipeline
Availability	Highway	>	Rail	>	Air	>	Water	>	Pipeline
Cost	Pipeline	>	Water	>	Rail	>	Highway	>	Air

* "Frequency" means the number of times the service is available during a given time period. For example, there are more truck trips per day from Los Angeles to San Diego than there are freight-train runs.

SOURCE: Adapted from John L. Heskett, Robert M. Ivie, and Nicholas A. Glaskowsky, Jr., *Business Logistics: Management of Physical Supply and Distribution,* © 1964, The Ronald Press Company, New York.

shipping by air is faster than shipping by water, but much more expensive. Transporting suitable products by pipeline is cheaper than transporting them by truck, but only a relatively small number of pipeline terminals are in operation.

SUPPORTING FUNCTIONS — SELECTION AND BUDGET

Supporting functions are provided to move goods through one or more links in the distribution system. They are provided both by producers and by intermediaries further up the line seeking to reinforce the marketing activities of a middleman. Examples are cooperative advertising, product service, missionary selling, training, and promotional pricing.

Supporting functions may be performed on a continuous basis, as is the case with product service, or only during the early phases of a product's life cycle, as is the case with missionary selling and local introductory advertising. They are distinguished from other promotional activities by their being in direct support of an intermediary, usually with its cooperation and participation. Supporting functions are performed by a firm that would otherwise be dependent solely on middlemen, in order to control certain aspects of the distribution process.

Decisions about the type of supporting functions that should be undertaken and the budget for these functions should be based on the rule of proportionality, using the ratio of marginal net revenue to marginal factor cost as a measure of the efficiency of a particular supporting activity. The actual selection and resource allocation may of course be subject to exogenous constraints outside the firm's control. Often, the need for a particular supporting function is dictated by the nature of the product or the institutional character of the industry or market. This narrows the decision process to the budgeting of resources to prescribed supporting functions. For example, it is very difficult to successfully introduce an inexpensive specialty good such as a toy or hardware item without missionary selling or local promotion directed at the retailer or ultimate consumer. The jobbers handle too many products to be able to spend adequate time introducing a new item.

Because supporting functions are essentially local, their marginal values can usually be determined through past experience or experimentation. If the local test market is defined as a standard metropolitan statistical area, the results of selected supporting activities can easily be projected to obtain regional or national estimates. The sensitivity of revenue to supporting functions is the most difficult parameter to determine. Middlemen costs are predictable because they usually represent a predetermined variable cost—frequently a set percentage of the unit price. The following example illustrates one approach to determining the effect of supporting functions on revenue.

Suppose that a small toy manufacturer has produced a new game that is being sold through four manufacturer's agents, each covering a large area. Samples have been delivered to the agents, who have booked small orders with jobbers and a few of the large retail stores. As usual, the manufacturer has to engage in supporting functions to prime the market—that is, to start goods flowing downstream through the distribution channel. He is interested in considering only two options, missionary salesmen and local advertising.

Past experience indicates that sales of a new item will equal .01 percent of the 1,000,000 households that constitute the potential market, if the firm relies on the middlemen and engages in no supporting activity. Missionary selling will bring in additional sales equal to .2 percent of the households, at a marginal cost of $20 per retail store. The firm's product is sold through 150 retail stores. Cooperative advertising will increase demand by .3 percent at a marginal cost of $10 per 1000 households, $5 of which will be paid by the local jobber. The firm's total cost (including distribution but not supporting functions) of manufacturing the toy is $1 per unit, and its revenue is $3 per unit. Thus marginal net revenue is $2 per unit. The firm can readily compute the marginal cost of each alternative, their marginal net revenues, and the contribution to profit offered by the two alternatives, as in Table 18.3.

Table 18.3   Example of the selection of supporting functions
(Market consists of 1,000,000 households and 150 retail stores)

Alternative	Marginal Net Revenue*	Marginal Cost	Contribution to Profit	$\dfrac{MNR}{MC}$
Missionary Selling	$4000(2000 · $2)	$3000(150 · $20)	$1000	1.3
Cooperative Advertising	$6000(3000 · $2)	$5000(1000 · $5)	$1000	1.2

* Marginal unit sales attributable to missionary selling would be (1,000,000)(.002) = 2,000 units, and marginal unit sales attributable to cooperative advertising would be (1,000,-000)(.003) = 3,000 units.

The MNR : MC ratio indicates that missionary selling is the more efficient instrument. The contribution to profit of each is coincidentally the same. In view of the smaller cash flow involved ($3,000 vs. $5,000), missionary selling is the appropriate choice. However, the reach of missionary selling may be limited, and its MNR : MC ratio may decline sharply beyond an outlay of $3,000. If the alternatives are not mutually exclusive, both might be employed, with resources going first to missionary selling. In some cases, where options are mutually exclusive, the less efficient instrument may be appropriate if it yields a greater contribution to profit.

The next step is to actually use missionary salesmen on a sample basis, say in 20 stores, in order to determine whether the effect is as estimated. The resulting data will allow a more accurate estimate of the contribution to profit and the marginal revenue–marginal cost ratio of missionary selling. If the sample verifies the results of the preliminary analysis, more resources should be allocated to missionary selling in this market. Since the MNR : MC ratio has not reached unity, added increments of missionary selling will cost less than the revenues they generate. The MNR : MC ratio must be constantly reevaluated as the level of missionary selling is increased, since obviously a point of diminishing returns will ultimately be reached.

When missionary selling has been increased to the level where MNR : MC is below 1.2, any additional resources available for supporting functions should be allotted to cooperative advertising, which will be more efficient than additional missionary selling. If the total marketing budget allows it, both supporting instruments should be used and expanded until their respective MNR : MC ratios reach unity.

The same technique is applicable in distributing the available funds among other local markets. The system model would then be:

$$\frac{MNR_{M,1}}{MC_{M,1}} = \frac{MNR_{C,1}}{MC_{C,1}} = \cdots \frac{MNR_{M,j}}{MC_{M,j}} = \frac{MNR_{C,j}}{MC_{C,j}} = 1, \text{ where}$$

$MNR_{M,1}$ = the marginal net revenue of missionary selling in the 1st market

$MC_{M,1}$ = the marginal cost of missionary selling in the 1st market

$MNR_{C,1}$ = the marginal net revenue of cooperative advertising in the 1st market

$MC_{C,1}$ = the marginal cost of cooperative advertising in the 1st market

$MNR_{M,j}$ = the marginal net revenue of missionary selling in the jth market

$MC_{M,j}$ = the marginal cost of missionary selling in the jth market

$MNR_{C,j}$ = the marginal net revenue of cooperative advertising in the jth market, and

$MC_{C,j}$ = the marginal cost of cooperative advertising in the jth market

This model is called a "system model" because it incorporates all the alternatives of the supporting function system. It illustrates the use of simple mathematical skills to rigorously structure a decision model.

Summary of Distribution Decisions

Distribution has changed considerably with changes in manufacturing and communications technology. The middleman no longer dominates this marketing function as he did before the turn of the century. Economies of scale have encouraged the development of large manufacturing firms; mass media have given these firms the ability to directly influence the ultimate consumers of their products.

Market definition is the first step in the selection of distribution channels and the allocation of resources to them. A variety of dimensions—geographical, demographic, institutional, political, and so on—may be used, often in combination, to describe markets. The firm's trading area will vary with transportation costs, price, and the buying habits of its customers. Obviously, the trading area for a retailer will be much different from that of a manufacturer.

Distribution functions are categorized as input or output functions. Input functions relate to the mechanical flow of orders from the ultimate consumer to the producer. Output functions involve the physical movement of goods from the producer to the ultimate consumer. They include the collection, sorting, storage, inventory, transportation, installation, and maintenance of goods, as well as supporting activities such as cooperative advertising and missionary selling. The input and output functions may or may not occupy the same distribution channel.

Channel institutions vary between industries and change in both form and importance over time. There are three basic types: those owned by producers, and merchants and agents, who are independent. Merchants take title to, and usually physical possession of, the goods. Agents do not take title to goods but may take physical possession of them. They act as intermediaries between buyers and sellers, receiving a fee or commission for their services. Wholesalers are merchant middlemen. Brokers, commission merchants, manufacturers' agents, manufacturers' representatives, selling agents, and resident buyers are agent middlemen.

Selection criteria for distribution channels involve both quantitative and qualitative considerations and are subject to exogenous constraints. The effect of a particular channel on the firm's total profit is the ideal criterion. However, budget constraints or the lack of complete information may preclude its use and force the firm to use a suboptimum criterion such as proportionality between marginal net revenues and marginal channel costs. Even suboptimum models are often restricted by the inability of the decision-maker to identify all revenues and costs associated with a particular channel, to shift small increments of resources, or to alter the system in the short run. Such exogenous variables as the institutional structure of the industry, capital availability, and the threat of competition, as well as uncertainty, limit his options.

Optimizing distribution resources involves a decision model that maximizes the total company profit. Since this is seldom practical, suboptimum models are employed in selecting and budgeting selling channels, trading areas, retail outlets, warehousing, inventory, transportation modes, and supporting functions.

Questions and Problems

1. Name two postwar innovations in communication or transportation and discuss their effects on the distribution of goods and services.
2. Define the markets for automobile accessories among industrial users, wholesalers, retailers, and consumers.
3. Describe the role of each of the following middlemen: (a) service wholesalers, (b) brokers, (c) commission merchants, (d) selling agents, and (e) resident buyers.
4. Diagram a hypothetical distribution system for frozen vegetables, showing intermediaries and the input and output flows.
5. Name and discuss two qualitative considerations that sometimes influence channel decisions.
6. The marginal net revenues being produced by a firm's four regional wholesalers, NE, NC, S, and W, are $17, $20, $12, and $13, respectively. Their marginal costs are $15, $10, $8, and $14. Suggest a redistribution of channel resources.
7. A standard metropolitan statistical area is being evaluated as a potential market for a consumer durable. According to the *Statistical Abstract of the United States* and *Facts for Marketers,* the area is shown to have a population of 200,000 a disposable personal income of $700,000,000, and retail sales of $300,000,000 per year. Assuming that the national figures are 200,000,000, $600,000,000,000, and $400,000,000,000, respectively, compute the BPI, the QI, and the ISA for this market.
8. a. A supermarket chain is interested in locating a new store in Sheffield, a town with a population of 50,000 and an average per capita food expenditure of $10 per week. A survey reveals that 13 grocery stores already serve the community, and their combined floor space is estimated to be 150,000 square feet. The food chain believes it needs a revenue of at least $3.95 per square foot per week to justify building a store. Should management approve the new store? Why or why not?

b. Several stores in Sheffield have gone out of business, thus reducing the total floor space to 100,000 square feet. If the other values remain the same, should the food chain enter the local market? If it does, how large a store should it build?

Supplementary Readings

BOOKS

COX, REAVIS, *Distribution in a High Level Economy* (Englewood Cliffs, N. J.: Prentice-Hall, 1965).

HESKETT, JOHN L., IVIE, ROBERT M., and GLASKOWSKY, NICHOLAS A., JR., *Business Logistics: Management of Physical Distribution and Supply* (New York: Ronald Press, 1964).

LÖSCH, AUGUST, *The Economics of Location,* tr. from 2nd ed. (New Haven, Conn.: Yale University Press, 1954).

PALAMOUNTAIN, JOSEPH CORNWALL, JR., *The Politics of Distribution* (Cambridge, Mass.: Harvard University Press, 1955).

PHILLIPS, ALMARIN, *Market Structure, Organization, and Performance* (Cambridge, Mass.: Harvard University Press, 1962).

SCHWARTZ, GEORGE, ed., *Science in Marketing* (New York: Wiley, 1965).

U. S. DEPARTMENT OF COMMERCE, *Facts About Major Appliance Wholesaling* (Washington, D. C.: U. S. Government Printing Office, 1969).

ARTICLES

BALLOU, R. H., "Dynamic Warehouse Location Analysis," *Journal of Marketing Research,* Vol. 5, No. 3 (August 1968), pp. 271–76.

BRUCE, GRADY D., "The Ecological Structure of Retail Institutions," *Journal of Marketing Research,* Vol. 6, No. 1 (February 1969), pp. 48–53.

GOULD, JOHN P., and SEGALL, JOEL, "The Substitution Effects of Transportation Costs," *Journal of Political Economy,* Vol. 77, No. 1 (January–February 1969), pp. 130–37.

HERRMANN, R. O., and BEIK, L. L., "Shoppers' Movements Outside Their Local Retail Area," Part I, *Journal of Marketing,* Vol. 32, No. 4 (October 1968), pp. 45–51.

HOLLANDER, S. C., "The Wheel of Retailing," *Journal of Marketing,* Vol. 25, No. 1 (July 1960), pp. 37–42.

HUFF, DAVID L., "Defining and Estimating a Trading Area," *Journal of Marketing,* Vol. 28, No. 3 (July 1964), pp. 34–38.

MALLEN, BRUCE, "Introducing the Marketing Channel to Price Theory," *Journal of Marketing,* Vol. 28, No. 3 (July 1964), pp. 29–33.

STERN, LOUIS W., "The Concept of Channel Control," *Journal of Retailing,* Vol. 93, No. 2 (Summer 1967), pp. 14–20.

STIGLER, GEORGE J., "The Division of Labor Is Limited by the Extent of the Market," *Journal of Political Economy,* Vol. 54, No. 3 (June 1951), pp. 185–93.

Part VIII

PROMOTION DECISIONS

Promotion, consisting of advertising and personal selling, attempts to shift the demand curve through direct persuasion of prospective buyers. It is the most nebulous of the five basic marketing instruments, and it is not surprising that it lends itself more readily to contradiction, controversy, conformity, imagination, subjective judgment, and bizarre management decisions than do the other marketing variables. Promotional efforts often rely as much on the philosophy of P. T. Barnum[1] as on management science.

The essence of promotion is the influencing of buyer tastes in favor of the goods or services of the firm—or the industry as a whole in the case of a joint promotional effort. Its objective is to displace the demand curve to the right, thus allowing more units to be sold at the present price, or the same number of units to be sold at a higher price.

The scope and form of promotional programs depend primarily on the knowledge and imagination of the marketer. He can blindly follow the prevalent practices in his industry—or he can innovate and experiment, limited only by the law, his ingenuity, his budget, and his willingness to assume risk. One need not search far to find both extremely successful and utterly disastrous examples of either approach.

[1] P. T. Barnum, of Barnum & Bailey Circus fame, was one of the most successful promoters of the twentieth century. He operated on the principle that "a sucker is born every minute," and made millions of dollars in the process.

The techniques discussed in Parts I and III for selecting the optimum marketing programs can easily be adapted to promotion decisions. The distribution of resources between elements of the promotional mix offers an opportunity to apply the rule of proportionality. Marginal analysis is the appropriate tool in deciding what the total budget should be. Risk models are applicable to the selection of alternative promotional strategies. In addition, there are a number of specialized techniques designed, or adapted, to handle specific elements of the promotional mix. These are generally sub-optimization methods for dealing with a single variable, such as the quantity of advertising to be placed in a particular medium or the number of salesmen to be assigned to a given territory.

Before describing the methods appropriate to promotion decisions, we shall discuss the several sequential tasks promotion performs in order to lead the market population from a state of ignorance about the firm's product to the act of purchasing it. Certain functions can often be combined, or, in the case of mature products, ignored. The establishment of promotional tasks, however, serves to organize the promotional decision process and to make the selection of alternatives more manageable.

When a firm enters a new market, the market population is generally in a state of ignorance regarding its products. Even if a product has been previously offered by another company, the firm's brand name will be unknown. Thus the first task of promotion is to move potential buyers from a state of ignorance to a state of awareness.

The second promotional task is to raise the prospects from a state of awareness to one of interest. This is the stage where potential customers are sufficiently motivated to seek additional information, perhaps by writing to the manufacturer for literature or visiting a store for a personal inspection of the product.

Given prospect interest, the third promotional task is to create in the potential buyer a desire to possess the firm's good.

The fourth, often the last, and usually the toughest task is to raise desire to the point where the prospect crosses the decision threshold and purchases the good or service.

A fifth task—which is not always appropriate—is to reinforce the buyer's confidence in his purchase decision and prevent the development of post-decision cognitive dissonance, so that he will continue to purchase the product.

The elements of the promotional mix will vary in efficiency as the prospects pass from stage to stage. Advertising may be the best way to bring the market population from ignorance to awareness and then to interest, but personal selling may be necessary to induce desire and to bring the prospects over the critical threshold to a purchase decision. The relative importance of each instrument will also vary with the firm's position in the distribution channel. For instance, a retail-goods manufacturer who depends on middlemen for distribution is limited primarily to advertising as a method of persuading the ultimate consumer and pulling its products through the distribution system.

There is evidence that the optimum promotional mix can vary between firms in the same industry and at the same level in the distribution system. Electrolux, Hershey,[2] and Avon have done very well selling vacuum cleaners, candy bars, and cosmetics with little or no advertising and the bulk of their promotional resources allocated to personal selling. Hoover, Peter Paul, and Revlon have also made impressive profits manufacturing and marketing vacuum cleaners, candy, and cosmetics, but with the aid of heavy advertising budgets and considerably less personal selling than the first three firms. This suggests that there are not only market segments for different products, but market segments that respond differently to various promotional mixes. For example, housewives whose children, location, or lack of transportation make it difficult to visit a store in response to advertising-induced interest and desire may be excellent prospects for door-to-door salesmen.

Creativity plays an important role in advertising and personal selling. The scientific method and quantitative techniques lend themselves nicely to allocating resources to *known* alternatives and measuring the results. They can be neatly explained in textbooks, and it is difficult to overrate their usefulness as a basis for management decision-making. However, they are no substitute for imagination. One brilliant product or promotional idea can compensate for a complete lack of scientific decision-making, as well as for previous errors in judgment. The experiences of Ford, Hearst, Watson, and Barnum illustrate this.[3] The optimum way to manage the firm, however,

---

[2] Prior to 1969, Hershey spent no money on advertising, yet grew to be one of the largest firms in the industry.

[3] For insight into the days of unrestrained promotional activity, see Harry Bennett, *We Never Called Him Henry* (New York: Fawcett, 1951); W. A. Swanberg, *Citizen Hearst* (New York: Scribner's, 1961); and M. R. Werner, *Barnum* (New York: Harcourt, Brace & World, 1923).

is to use quantitative decision models where they are applicable but maintain an environment that stimulates innovation and imagination.

The limitations—and, at times, total impotency—of promotion should also be recognized. In the short run, it has succeeded in selling such useless products as sites for underwater homes, hair restorers, and stock in nonexistent companies; but it has seldom sustained the output of grossly inferior merchandise. The sales of goods and services whose properties are not commensurate with prevailing tastes or are obviously inferior to those of readily available and comparably priced substitutes can rarely be profitably sustained with promotion. In other instances—for example, when the firm is in a purely competitive industry—advertising and personal selling may be useless; the firm's market share is too small and its products too similar to its competitors' for it to influence demand.

Before a promotional strategy can be developed, the promotional goal must be defined. It may be an increase in sales, the establishment or maintenance of a market share, the expansion of a territory, the destruction of competition, the introduction of a new product, or an increase in retail outlets. The promotional goal serves the firm's ultimate goal, the long-run maximization of profit.

The promotional strategy is part of the overall marketing plan and is normally executed in conjunction with other strategies. A price reduction, for example, would probably be supported with advertising. A new product would be introduced by a promotional campaign. An expansion of the distribution system would be supported with personal selling.

The promotional strategy may be an intensification of personal selling, a nation-wide advertising campaign, a contest, a coupon-redemption program (this alternative is often considered part of the product variable), a dealer-incentive program, trade show participation, an increase in public relations activity, a sales training program for dealers (this may also be considered part of the distribution variable), or a combination of these or other options.

The implementation of any of these strategies involves numerous tactical decisions, many of which lend themselves to quantitative suboptimization techniques. Examples are the setting of budgets, the selection of advertising media, the computation of the number of salesmen, the sizing of territories, and the allocation of salesmen's time. Choosing between strategies affords an opportunity to apply the certainty, risk, and uncertainty models developed previously (see Chapter 6).

Although advertising and personal selling are both elements of the promotional variable, in most instances they serve different purposes. Advertising can seldom be substituted for personal selling, and vice versa. For this reason, and because they are generally handled through suboptimum decision models, we shall analyze each separately.

CHAPTER 19

Advertising

From the marketer's viewpoint, advertising serves only one end—increased sales.[1] Advertising expenditures are justified by comparing the marginal revenues they produce with the marginal costs they incur. "Image," "awareness," "readership," "attitude," "motivation," "response," and the rest of the advertising community's rhetoric are of little importance, except as crude proxies of sales.

Unfortunately, measuring advertising's contribution to sales can be extremely difficult, especially at the level where many advertising decisions are made. How many additional Chevrolets will be sold by placing a particular advertisement in *Life* magazine? Will the added cost of a color advertisement be justified by the increase in sales? Would more sales be created if the same amount of money were spent on television spot announcments?

These questions are easy to ask but difficult to answer. The aggregate demand for a product is affected by the other marketing variables, the actions of competitors, and economic and cultural changes. Also, advertising has a cumulative effect. Repeated exposure to small amounts of advertising can often induce more sales than a single concentrated exposure. Similarly, advertising can often cause sales long after an advertising program has been discontinued or significantly changed.

When large advertising outlays are involved, there are many possible options, and the marketing manager or his advertising director must develop some method by which to evaluate the sales effectiveness of different copy and media. More often than not, the marketer will use measurements of proxy variables in determining the optimum advertising program for his firm.

---

[1] Some forms of institutional advertising serve other purposes, such as the influencing of legislators, government agencies, or investors. An example is the use of advertising by utility companies to influence public opinion and thereby make utility commissions more receptive to petitions for rate changes or legislators more sympathetic to tax relief proposals.

A proxy variable serves as an indirect measure of sales. Changes in the proxy variable are assumed to be closely related to sales. Moreover, they are usually much cheaper to measure than changes in sales. For example, magazine and newspaper advertisements often contain reader-inquiry coupons. These coupons may be coded so that each one is associated with a particular advertisement. Tabulating the number of coupons returned yields a proxy measurement of the effectiveness of different ads and media. Although the coupons only suggest the degree of reader interest and do not establish the advertisement's influence on sales, the two variables (reader interest and sales) are probably related in some positive way. However, a simple count of reply cards cannot indicate the extent to which the readers' behavior was influenced by other promotional activities. The ad credited with causing the response may have played a very small part in awakening interest in the prospect.

Problems of proxy measurements are explored further in Part IX. However, it is important here to recognize their limitations and their relationship to the different effects of advertising.

EFFECTS OF ADVERTISING

Successful advertising has a number of effects on consumers. Each effect can be matched with the promotional task it serves to accomplish and the method by which it can be measured, as in Table 19.1. Many of these effects can be measured directly or estimated with an acceptable degree of precision at a reasonable cost.

If the promotional mix relies on personal selling to escalate desire and move the buyer across the purchase threshold, then the advertising director has a strong argument for measuring and evaluating the effectiveness of his advertising program at a level below that of sales. Although this is a sub-optimization approach and relies on proxy data that may or may not correlate with advertising's influence on revenue, it is often appropriate.

For example, an introductory advertising campaign executed early in the life cycle of an industrial good or an expensive consumer durable cannot be expected to sell the product, although it will play a vital role in moving the prospect toward the purchase threshold. In this case, the purpose of the advertising is to make the market population aware of the product and to raise interest to the level where prospects will solicit additional information, thus identifying themselves as potential buyers. Ideally, they will be sufficiently motivated to visit showrooms or stores. At that point the introductory advertising has served its purpose, and personal selling and the product variables are invoked to escalate desire and induce a purchase. If each of the marketing instruments has been properly manipulated, sales will occur. How-

Table 19.1 Hierarchy of advertising effects

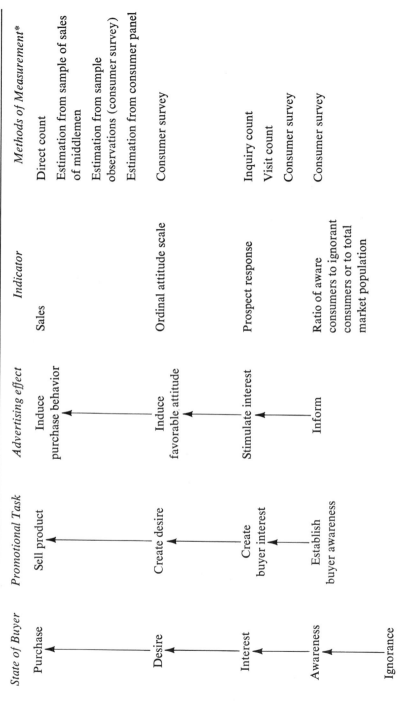

State of Buyer	Promotional Task	Advertising effect	Indicator	Methods of Measurement*
Purchase	Sell product	Induce purchase behavior	Sales	Direct count
				Estimation from sample of sales of middlemen
				Estimation from sample observations (consumer survey)
				Estimation from consumer panel
Desire	Create desire	Induce favorable attitude	Ordinal attitude scale	Consumer survey
Interest	Create buyer interest	Stimulate interest	Prospect response	Inquiry count
				Visit count
				Consumer survey
Awareness	Establish buyer awareness	Inform	Ratio of aware consumers to ignorant consumers or to total market population	Consumer survey
Ignorance				

* See Chapter 25 for a detailed explanation of methods for measuring customer response.

ever, if a gross error has been made in pricing, product, distribution, or marketing research, advertising or personal selling can seldom compensate for the deficiency.

The Edsel disaster is illustrative. The advertising and public relations job done in support of the Edsel was outstanding. The introductory campaign brought the public's level of awareness and interest to an intensity sufficient to bring millions of prospects into the showrooms during the first few days after the car's introduction. However, neither advertising nor personal selling could make up for the mistakes made in the design of the product. The public's interest faded upon exposure to the poorly styled automobile, and the supporting advertising that followed was of no avail. Within a year the Ford Motor Company abandoned the product, having sustained a loss of over $200 million.

BUDGETING FOR ADVERTISING

Only the world's religions can top advertising in the number of decisions made on the basis of blind faith. Advertising is generally accepted as an essential ingredient of any marketing mix, yet it is seldom rationally correlated with sales. Advertising expenditures are frequently reduced as sales decline and increased as sales climb. Over 2 percent of the nation's gross national product is allocated to advertising, yet arguments often rage about both its effectiveness and its economic justification. The American public has long ago passed the point where it can absorb more than a minute fraction of the advertisements that confront it.

Every day 4.2 billion advertising messages pour forth from 1,754 daily newspapers, millions of others from 8,151 weeklies, and 1.36 billion more each day from 4,147 magazines and periodicals. There are 3,895 AM and 1,136 FM radio stations broadcasting an average of 730,000 commercials a day; and 770 television stations broadcast 100,000 commercials a day. Every day millions of people are confronted with 330,000 outdoor billboards, with 2.5 million car cards and posters in buses, subways, and commuter trains, with 51.3 million direct mail pieces and leaflets, and with billions of display and promotional items.[2]

How is this tremendous effort budgeted? In a free-enterprise system the total amount that is spent on advertising is reached by the summation of hundreds of thousands of individual decisions, each representing the perception, analysis, and philosophy of individual marketers. However, there are

[2] Leo Bogart, *Strategy in Advertising* (New York: Harcourt, Brace & World, 1967), p. 2.

a number of allocation systems that are sufficiently common to warrant exploration.

Theoretically, advertising expenditures should be at a level where the marginal cost of the advertising is equal to the marginal revenue that results from it. Since this criterion presupposes a degree of knowledge the firm seldom possesses, it is not surprising that few of the common advertising allocation systems satisfy this microeconomic ideal.

Percentage of sales is an allocation method in which the advertising budget is computed as a percentage of sales, or revenue. This makes advertising a function of sales, which is a curious assumption in view of the fact that advertising is supposedly used to increase sales. The firm advertises in order to sell. Making advertising the dependent variable results in reduced advertising as sales decline—the very time when more advertising is often needed to support output. Conversely, advertising is generally increased as sales climb.

This does not mean the firm should blindly increase its advertising as sales plummet. Again, marginal analysis is appropriate. If the increase in revenue would not equal or exceed the added outlay for more advertising (plus the other sales and production costs of a greater output), then an increase in the advertising budget is not in order. Conversely, an unexpected increase in sales may suggest an opportunity that can be exploited by increasing the advertising budget. In short, there is no rational rule of thumb for relating advertising to sales. On the contrary, sales are only partially a function of advertising. Changes in the level of sales can help to estimate the effectiveness of advertising, and thus assist the marketer in allocating resources to this instrument. However, setting the advertising budget equal to a percentage of sales confuses the dependent with the independent variable, and often leads to irrational advertising decisions.

Spend all you can—sometimes called the "affordable method" of budgeting—is an allocation philosophy even less defensible than the percentage-of-sales method. First, "affordable" cannot be precisely defined. Second, it makes no economic sense to spend money simply because it is there. The only time this method would be valid is when the constraints on the company's liquid assets and line of credit place the level of available funds below the advertising budget indicated by marginal analysis. An advertising director who simply, without investigation, recommends a budget equal to the funds the controller says are available shows that he does not have the foggiest idea of the relationship between sales and advertising.

Spend nothing is a philosophy appropriate for those who believe advertising is not a necessary ingredient in their marketing mix and that its tasks can be more efficiently performed by other marketing instruments. The rice grower, the tobacco farmer, the gold miner, and the cattle rancher follow this rule, and properly so. Those engaged in pure competition have little to gain from advertising.

However, there are a number of major companies in differentiated oligopolies which have also demonstrated that a firm can be very successful yet spend little or no resources on advertising. The classical example is Hershey, whose success in the domestic candy market did not involve a nickel of expenditure on advertising before 1969. Avon, which ranked 178th in *Fortune*'s list of the nation's 500 largest industrial firms in 1968, also does very little advertising. Yet it earns a profit that has yielded a return on invested capital of over 35 percent—the highest rate of return among companies on *Fortune*'s list.[3] Avon relies almost entirely on personal selling to sustain its output of cosmetics.[4]

Task-alternative-cost budgeting is a four-step method. The advertising goal is defined, alternative methods of achieving it are specified, their costs are computed, and the cheapest option is selected. This method is especially useful when the available sales data are insufficient to specify the relationship between revenue and advertising outlay, as may be the case with a new product.

Although the ultimate objective and sole justification of advertising is to increase sales, when sales data are lacking the marketer may have to rely on some other yardstick to measure its effectiveness. For example, if a new product or brand is being introduced, the initial advertising task will be to inform the market population. Then the alternative choices of copy and media can be described. Once this is done, costs can be computed and the optimum choice made.

To illustrate the task-alternative-cost method, let us assume that the advertising task is to introduce a new brand of detergent to housewives in the Western region of the United States. The specific advertising objective might be to expose the product to 50 percent of all the housewives in that area. The most feasible media are daytime television, daytime radio, newspapers, women's special-interest magazines, direct mail, and point-of-purchase advertisements (posters or other supermarket displays). By reference to media performance data,[5] the advertising director of the firm can select different combinations of media that will ensure the product's exposure to an acceptable number of housewives. He can then select the lowest cost option, thereby revealing the budget requirement.

Buyer awareness is a function of exposure and retention; hence the re-

[3] "The Fortune Directory of the 500 Largest U. S. Industrial Corporations," *Fortune*, May 15, 1969.

[4] Avon products are sold exclusively by door-to-door saleswomen.

[5] Most media managers maintain quite thorough statistics on both the degree of exposure their media provide and the demographic composition of their audiences.

lationship between the size and copy of advertisements and the rate of retention must be estimated, sometimes through the use of special research techniques for obtaining data. By multiplying the retention rate times the number of exposures for the most promising combinations of advertisements and media, the marketer can estimate the number of consumers that will be made aware of the new product. Once the cost of each advertisement-media combination has been computed, the alternatives can be arrayed and a selection made that will assure the necessary number of informed prospects at the lowest cost.

Normally, the use of several media will be indicated in order to reach a sufficiently large portion of the market. This introduces the problem of redundancy, since the audiences and readership of various media will probably overlap. This overlap should be taken into account in estimating total exposures. Later, as sales data accumulate and as other marketing research techniques are invoked, a more precise evaluation of the efficiency of the advertisements and media can be made. Better yet, the effect of advertising on sales can be measured more directly. Once the relationship between sales and advertising is known, marignal analysis can be used to bring the marketer closer to the optimum solution in terms of the ultimate criterion, profit.

Competitive parity is a method of resource allocation based on the follow-the-leader principle. The quantity of advertising purchased by one or more competitors is estimated, and the firm's budget is set as a percentage of that value. This technique is often used to determine the advertising budget for mature products, when the overall marketing objective is to maintain a fixed share of the market. However, it is a naive approach, since the marketer has no assurance that the same result could not be obtained by a less costly combination of promotional variables.

The competitive-parity method has been defended on two counts: first, because it relies on the collective wisdom of the industry (when the aggregate outlay for the industry is used as the basis for the computations) and second, because it prevents an advertising war from developing as competitors leapfrog one another's advertising budgets. Both assumptions are shaky, however.[6]

Peckham's formula offers a rule of thumb for setting the advertising budget according to the size of the market share the firm wishes to capture and maintain. It is an adaptation of the competitive-parity method in that it uses the amount of competitors' advertising as a basis for computation.

Peckham analyzed the relationship between advertising and sales for a number of consumer-product classes, notably new grocery, toiletry, and drug items. Using store-audit data for a four-year period, supplied by the A. C. Nielsen Company, he noted that successful new products were sup-

[6] Philip Kotler, *Marketing Management: Analysis, Planning and Control* (New York: Prentice-Hall, 1967), p. 462.

ported with a relative advertising expenditure about 60 percent higher than their market share. That is, a new brand that captured 10 percent of the market would be promoted with an advertising outlay equal to 16 percent of the total advertising done by the industry for that particular product. This led him to develop Peckham's formula, which states that the relative advertising budget for the first 24 months of the product's life cycle should be 1.5 times as large as the desired market share.[7] Stated notationally,

$$A_I = 1.5M, \text{ where} \tag{19-1}$$

A_I = introductory advertising, expressed as a percentage of the industry's total advertising expenditure, and

M = desired market share, expressed as a percentage of the industry's total market

Once A_I is determined, it is multiplied by the total dollar value of the industry's advertising to get the advertising budget needed for the new item.

Peckham also observed that the brands with the highest shares of sales had the highest shares of advertising. During the maturity phase, the larger market shares were usually sustained by advertising outlays that exceeded slightly the size of the market shares. This suggests that once the desired market share is achieved, advertising may be reduced to a level slightly above the market share.

Although this relatively simple approach to the budgeting of advertising may be quite practical on occasion, several properties of Peckham's data limit its applicability. First, his study was confined to convenience goods. Second, the leading products were nationally advertised brands. (Marketing these items is a bit different from marketing house brands or local brands.) Third, Peckham's case studies indicated that there is considerable variation in the relationship between advertising and market share in the short run. Furthermore, the distribution of expenditures over the 24-month introductory period significantly affects the results of advertising.

There are several other general methods of budgeting advertising that vary slightly from the models described above, but they do not warrant elaboration. A number of analytic methods that have the advantage of being theoretically rigorous are also available. These provide a sound basis for the allocation of resources to advertising when sufficient data are available. Even when data are inadequate, they serve to structure the problem and to direct the marketer's attention to the information he must gather in order to optimize his use of the advertising resources. From a pedagogic viewpoint, the analytic techniques are an excellent vehicle for explaining several important

[7] Bogart, *op. cit.*, p. 22.

advertising phenomena. Thus, for the remainder of this section we shall concentrate on these techniques.

A STATIC MODEL OF ADVERTISING BUDGETING[8]

The *basic static model of advertising budgeting* is a sound basis for determining advertising budgets both in theory and, when data are obtainable, in practice. It also provides insight into the nature of the advertising function.

The relationship of sales, or revenue, to advertising is invariably nonlinear, except for very short periods, and shows decreasing returns to scale as advertising is increased. Two typical forms of the relationship between revenue and advertising are shown in Figure 19.1. The solid curve, $R = f(A)$,

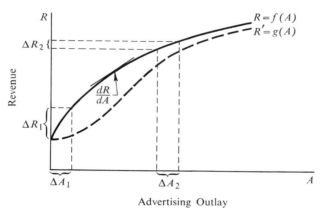

FIGURE 19.1
Revenue vs. advertising

indicates that as initial increments of advertising are purchased, the resultant increases in revenue (sales) are large. As the total advertising expenditure is increased, however, additional increments of advertising result in smaller increases in revenue. For instance, an initial amount of advertising, ΔA_1, results in an increase in revenue of ΔR_1; but an equal increase in advertising, ΔA_2, at a higher total level of advertising results in a smaller increase in revenue, ΔR_2. If $R = f(A)$ is a continuous function, then the slope of the curve at any point indicates the derivative of revenue with respect to advertising,

[8] The authors draw on the work of William R. King, *Quantitative Analysis for Marketing Management* (New York: McGraw-Hill, 1967), for several of the terms and equations in the remainder of this chapter.

dR/dA. This derivative gives us the change in revenue that will be induced by a change in advertising.

The decreased effect of additional increments of advertising on revenue is intuitively reasonable. As more advertising is purchased and the number of individual exposures increases, the market population becomes more indifferent and each additional exposure becomes less effective. (This does not necessarily mean that the added exposure is always unimportant. The next exposure may be the one that pushes the prospect over the purchase threshold and results in a sale.)

The function may sometimes resemble R'. The initial segment of this S-curve indicates a situation in which the first few increments of advertising produce few sales; but as their effect accumulates, prospects begin to cross the purchase threshold. Both curves intercept the revenue axis well above zero, indicating that some sales will occur with no advertising. This is an assumption that has been proven by such firms as Hershey, Kirby, and Electrolux. Actually, all these conditions—the non-zero intercept and the shapes of the two curves—have been supported with empirical findings.

As we have seen, profit can only be maximized when its first derivative, π', is zero with respect to any decision variable, such as advertising expenditure, price, sales commissions, or warehouse space. Using certain formulas developed previously and adapting them to the variables in the advertising problem, we can arrive at an explicit statement for the optimization of the advertising budget, as follows:

$C = C_1 + A$, where   (19–2)

C = total cost

C_1 = total cost, exclusive of advertising, and

A = advertising cost

$C_1 = f + VQ$, where

C_1 = total cost, exclusive of advertising

f = fixed cost, exclusive of advertising

V = variable unit costs, exclusive of advertising, and

Q = output (sales)

$R = PQ$ Equation 3–5, p. 38

$Q = \dfrac{R}{P}$ By algebraic manipulation

$C_1 = f + V\left(\dfrac{R}{P}\right)$ By substitution

$$\pi = R - C \qquad\qquad\qquad \text{Equation 3–3, p. 36}$$

$$\pi = R - \left[f + V\left(\frac{R}{P}\right) + A \right] \qquad \text{By substitution}$$

$$\pi = R\left(1 - \frac{V}{P}\right) - f - A \qquad \text{By algebraic manipulation (19–3)}$$

$$\frac{d\pi}{dA} = \left(1 - \frac{V}{P}\right)\frac{dR}{dA} - 0 - 1 \qquad \text{By rules of calculus (Note that since } R = f(A), A \text{ is a variable.)}$$

$$\frac{d\pi}{dA} = \left(1 - \frac{V}{P}\right)\frac{dR}{dA} - 1 = 0 \qquad \text{By rule of profit maximization}$$

$$\frac{dR}{dA} = \frac{1}{1 - \dfrac{V}{P}} \qquad\qquad \text{By algebraic manipulation (19–4)}$$

The derivative dR/dA is the slope of R in Figure 19.1. Hence Equation 19–4 reveals the point at which advertising outlay is optimized. The firm should increase its advertising expenditure until the slope of R reaches the value revealed by Equation 19–4.

For example, assume that a consumer product has a price, P, of $6 and a variable cost, V, of $4 per unit. Thus,

$$\frac{dR}{dA} = \frac{1}{1 - \dfrac{V}{P}} \qquad \text{Given}$$

$$\frac{dR}{dA} = \frac{1}{1 - \dfrac{4}{6}} \qquad \text{By substitution}$$

$$\frac{dR}{dA} = 3 \qquad \text{By arithmetic}$$

The slope of R at the optimum point is 3. Thus the firm should continue to purchase additional increments of advertising until it reaches the point where an additional dollar of advertising will produce only 3 additional dollars of revenue.

Rather than continuing to buy additional increments of advertising and observing the resultant sales—a rather awkward, trial-and-error method— the marketer can compute the total optimum advertising budget directly. However, there is one precondition—he must know the explicit form of the revenue-vs.-advertising equation, $R = f(A)$. This can often be estimated from marketing research data. Once the explicit form of $R = f(A)$ is known, its first derivative, dR/dA, may be computed and set equal to the value indicated by Equation 19–4. The optimum advertising budget can then be obtained simply by solving for A.

For example, a common form of $R = f(A)$ is $R = a + b(\log_{10}A)$. This is a curve similar to R in Figure 19.1. Revenue increases sharply at first, then begins to level off as the marginal productivity of advertising decreases because additional increments of advertising become less efficient. This occurs with virtually all promotional media.

Assume that experience or marketing research has revealed the relationship between annual sales of the consumer product in the previous example and advertising as $R = 100,000 + 60,000(\log_{10}A)$. (The firm may have estimated this relationship from proxy measurements of sale response.) The optimum annual advertising budget may then be found as follows:

$$R = 100,000 + 60,000 \ (\log_{10} A) \qquad \text{Given}$$

$$\frac{dR}{dA} = 60,000 \left(\frac{.4343}{A}\right) = \frac{26,058}{A} \qquad \text{By rules of calculus}^{9}$$

$$\frac{dR}{dA} = \frac{26,058}{A} = \frac{1}{1 - \dfrac{V}{P}} \qquad \begin{array}{l}\text{The condition for profit} \\ \text{maximization (Equation 19–4)}\end{array}$$

$$A = 26,058 - 26,058 \left(\frac{V}{P}\right) \qquad \text{By algebraic manipulation}$$

$$A = 26,058 - 26,058 \left(\frac{4}{6}\right) \qquad \begin{array}{l}\text{By substitution (using the} \\ \text{values } V = 4 \text{ and } P = 6 \text{ from} \\ \text{the previous example)}\end{array}$$

$$A = 8,686$$

Thus the optimum advertising budget would be $8,686.

A DYNAMIC MODEL OF ADVERTISING BUDGETING

The model above is a static model and does not reflect the effect of time on the revenue-advertising relationship. Thus it ignores such important advertising phenomena as sales decay, market saturation, and sales response. The basic dynamic model of advertising budgeting includes these three parameters through the use of (1) a sales-decay constant, λ; (2) a market-saturation level, M; and (3) a sales-response constant, s. Although the dynamic model is more complex than the static model, its accuracy in depicting the actual relationship between revenue and advertising more than compensates for this disadvantage.

---

[9] The mathematically inclined reader can verify this by recalling that $d/dx \ \log_e u = (1/u) \ du/dx$ and $\log_{10}u = .4343 \ \log_e u$. Therefore, $d/dx \ \log_{10}u = d/dx \ (.4343 \ \log_e u) = .4343 \ d/dx \ \log_e u = .4343 \ (1/u) \ du/dx$. Since $u = A$ and we are taking the derivative with respect to A, $du/dA = 1$ and $d/dA \ \log_{10}A = .4343\left(\frac{1}{A}\right)$.

Sales Decay.   The sales-decay constant, λ, measures the reduction in the effectiveness of an advertisement with the passage of time. Empirical studies show that while all buyers will not react immediately to an advertisement, fewer and fewer will respond as time goes on. M. L. Vidale and H. B. Wolfe concluded that the revenue (sales) rate,[10] R, declines with time, t, in accordance with the following formula.[11]

$$R_t = R_0 e^{-\lambda t}, \text{ where} \tag{19–5}$$

R_t = revenue rate at time t

R_0 = revenue rate at the time advertising was stopped

e = Napierian number[12]—that is, 2.718

λ = sales-decay constant, and

t = time, measured in appropriate units, from the date advertising was stopped

Equation 19–5 states that the total effect of an advertisement will not be felt immediately. The total impact will be spread over time and will gradually decline. This phenomenon holds true for a single ad or an entire advertising campaign. Once the ad has been placed or the campaign terminated, the effect on sales will decline. Figure 19.2 shows this graphically.

Suppose, for example, that a product is being promoted in the Oakland Standard Metropolitan Statistical Area with an advertising outlay of $300

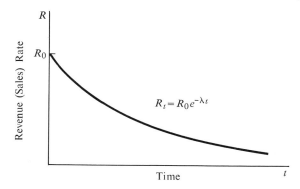

FIGURE 19.2
Sales decay

---

[10] The revenue rate is the amount of revenue received per unit of time—for example, $10,000 per month, $8,000 per day, etc.; t indicates the point in time at which the rate was observed—for example, $400 per week at the 10th week ($t = 10$).

[11] Adapted from M. L. Vidale and H. B. Wolfe, "An Operations Research Study of Sales Response to Advertising," *Operations Research,* Vol. 5, No. 3 (June 1957), p. 380.

[12] The number 2.718—the "Napierian number"—is a constant with some unique mathematical properties, hence is frequently incorporated into formulas.

per week for spot announcements on a local radio station. This produces a sales rate, R_t, of \$1,400 per week. Previous experience with spot announcements in this type of market and with this class of product has revealed the weekly sales-decay constant, λ, as .5. Using this data and Equation 19–5, we can estimate the weekly sales, R, at any given time, t, after termination of the advertising. To illustrate, assume that the product manager wishes to estimate his revenue rate in the Oakland SMSA market four weeks after the spot announcements have stopped.

$R_t = R_0 e^{-\lambda t}$ Given

$R_4 = 1400(2.718^{-.5(4)})$ By substitution

$R_4 = 1400(2.718^{-2})$ By arithmetic

$R_4 = 1400 \cdot \dfrac{1}{2.718^2}$ By algebraic manipulation

$R_4 = 189$ By arithmetic

Therefore, four weeks after the spot announcements are terminated weekly sales will have dropped from \$1,400 to \$189.

Market Saturation.   The *market-saturation level, M,* is the maximum number of sales that could conceivably be generated, given the audience limits of the media mix. For example, if the media mix reached 80,000 housewives, each of whom consumed an average of one pound of detergent per week, the market-saturation level for detergent, given that particular media mix, would be 80,000 pounds per week. Unless all prospective users can eventually be induced to buy the product, the saturation level will never be reached.

Advertising becomes less effective as sales move closer to the saturation level, since the number of prospects remaining decreases as more buyers adopt the firm's brand. The detergent example is illustrative. When the firm first enters the market, its advertising outlay buys exposure to 80,000 prospective buyers. When the firm has established a market position—say a 25-percent market share—then the same advertising outlay will reach only 60,000 prospects (80,000 − 20,000).[13] If the firm should capture half the market, then the media mix (whose cost remains constant) will provide exposure to only 40,000 prospects. Assuming that the advertising has approximately the same effect on all non-customers, the total effect of the constant advertising outlay will be reduced to half of what it was when the firm entered the market. (This assumes, of course, that the customers who have accepted the product

[13] Market share in this example refers only to the market that the advertising-media mix can affect (the 80,000 housewives) and not to the total market confronting the firm.

require no additional exposure to advertising in order to continue their purchase behavior.)

The saturation level can be increased by adding media to the mix that will expand the number of qualified prospects exposed to the firm's advertising message. If the firm has captured a significant portion of the prospects reached by its present media mix and if the audiences of other media are potential buyers, then the most efficient allocation of marginal advertising funds might well be the purchase of space in the unused media. The cost per prospective buyer could be one basis for the decision. However, with repeatedly purchased goods, the advertiser should not overlook the need to reinforce the brand loyalty of customers captured by the original medium.

Sales Response and Advertising Efficiency. The *sales-response constant, s,* is the ratio between revenue and advertising. It is used to measure the efficiency of particular advertising media in producing sales. Since the efficiency of advertising will decline as sales move toward the market-saturation level, the sales-response constant is defined as the ratio between revenue and the *initial* advertising outlay. For example, if experience in comparable markets indicates that an initial outlay of $1,000 in a particular advertising medium will produce $20,000 in sales, then $s = 20$.

The *coefficient of advertising efficiency* at any given level of revenue, R, is designated as s_R. It is less than the original sales-response constant by an amount determined by the difference between the market-saturation level, M, and the revenue level, R. Stated mathematically,

$$s_R = s\left(\frac{M - R}{M}\right), \text{ where} \tag{19-6}$$

s_R = coefficient of advertising efficiency at revenue level R

s = sales-response constant

M = market-saturation level, and

R = current level of revenue (sales)

Since s_R represents the efficiency of advertising, it can be used to estimate the change in revenue, ΔR, that will result from a change in advertising, ΔA. The following formula applies:

$$\Delta R = s_R \, \Delta A, \text{ where} \tag{19-7}$$

ΔR, s_R, and ΔA are as previously defined

Unfortunately, s_R changes as total revenue, R, changes, since M is a constant. Hence the equation yields only an approximate answer—a problem we shall deal with shortly.

To illustrate the use of s_R in a decision situation, let us assume that the market-saturation level, M, of a product is sales of \$80,000 per week and that the firm currently has 40 percent of the market (thus $R = \$32,000$ per week). When the brand was introduced in various local markets, the initial advertising, in a particular medium, produced \$4 in sales for each dollar of advertising ($s = 4$). The advertising director is considering increasing the firm's advertising, using the same medium. The first question that must be answered is, what is the efficiency of the advertising medium at the present level of revenue? This is readily computed:

$$s_R = s\left(\frac{M - R}{M}\right) \qquad \text{Given}$$

$$s_{32,000} = 4\left(\frac{80,000 - 32,000}{80,000}\right) \qquad \text{By substitution}$$

$$s_{32,000} = 2.4$$

Advertising efficiency has dropped from 4 to 2.4 due to the capture of 40 percent of the potential customers. Hence another dollar of advertising will produce only \$2.40 in additional revenue. If the total marginal cost, including advertising, is less than 2.4 times the cost of the additional advertising, the advertising budget should be increased.

Although the example above is a valid one, a marketer might have some qualms about the application of Equation 19–6. This is because s_R is a point value and declines steadily as the market share increases. In the example, advertising efficiency is 2.4 with a market share of 40 percent. However, as soon as additional advertising is purchased, sales will increase, and the coefficient of advertising efficiency, s_R, will decline. Hence the additional revenue resulting from added advertising will steadily decrease as the amount of advertising is increased.

If the value of s_R computed from Equation 19–6 is used in computing the increase in revenue that will result from an increase in advertising, the effect of the advertising will always be overestimated. If the change in market share that would result from an increase in advertising is reasonably small (say, less than 10 percent), then the error resulting from the use of the previous formula will be negligible. However, a precise estimate of the increase in sales, ΔR, that will result from an increase in advertising is possible with the more complex formula

$$\Delta R = \left\{ \frac{s\left(\frac{M - R}{M}\right) + s \cdot \left[\dfrac{M - R - s\left(\dfrac{M - R}{M}\right)\Delta A}{M}\right]}{2} \right\} \cdot \Delta A \qquad (19\text{–}8)$$

where s, M, R, and A are as previously defined.

Let us assume that an additional $5,000 per week is spent on advertising. The simple efficiency formula would indicate an increase in revenue of $12,000, as shown below.

$$s_R = s\left(\frac{M - R}{M}\right) \qquad\qquad \text{Given}$$

$$s_{32,000} = 4\left(\frac{80,000 - 32,000}{80,000}\right) \qquad\qquad \text{By substitution}$$

$$s_{32,000} = 2.4$$

$$\Delta R = s_R \cdot \Delta A \qquad\qquad \text{Given}$$

$$\Delta R = (2.4)(5,000) \qquad\qquad \text{By substitution}$$

$$\Delta R = 12,000 \qquad\qquad \text{By arithmetic}$$

The actual increase in revenue will be $10,500, as shown below by using Equation 19–8.

$$\Delta R = \left\{ \frac{s\left(\frac{M-R}{M}\right) + s\left[\frac{M - R - s\left(\frac{M-R}{M}\right)\Delta A}{M}\right]}{2} \right\} \cdot \Delta A \quad \text{Given}$$

$$\Delta R = \left\{ \frac{4\left(\frac{80,000 - 32,000}{80,000}\right) + 4\left[\frac{80,000 - 32,000 - 4\left(\frac{80,000-32,000}{80,000}\right)(5,000)}{80,000}\right]}{2} \right\} \cdot (5,000)$$

By substitution

$$\Delta R = \left[\frac{2.4 + 4\left(\frac{48,000 - 12,000}{80,000}\right)}{2}\right] \cdot (5,000) \qquad\qquad \text{By arithmetic}$$

$$\Delta R = \left(\frac{2.4 + 1.8}{2}\right)(5,000) \qquad\qquad \text{By arithmetic}$$

$$\Delta R = (2.1)(5,000) \qquad\qquad \text{By arithmetic}$$

$$\Delta R = 10,500 \qquad\qquad \text{By arithmetic}$$

Applications of the Dynamic Model. All three parameters just discussed—the sales-decay constant, λ; the market-saturation level, M; and the sales-response constant, s—can be incorporated into a dynamic model that yields considerable insight into the advertising budgeting problem. The increase in revenue, ΔR, as a function of advertising has previously been shown to be $\Delta R = s_R \cdot \Delta A$. By substituting the right-hand side of Equation 19–6 for s_R, we get

$$\Delta R = s\left(\frac{M - R}{M}\right)\Delta A$$

Thus ΔR is clearly dependent on s, the sales-response constant, on $\dfrac{M - R}{M}$, which measures the degree to which the firm has captured the total market, and on ΔA, the change in advertising expenditure.

The effects of advertising decrease, however, as time passes, and this effect can be estimated by Equation 19–5, $R_t = R_0 e^{-\lambda t}$. At the end of one period of time, the decrease in advertising effectiveness would be:

$$R_0 - R_{t-1} = R_0 - R_0 e^{-\lambda},$$

or

$$\Delta R = R(1 - e^{-\lambda}) \tag{19–9}$$

If the firm wishes to maintain a certain level of sales, then, for each time period, the positive change in revenue due to advertising must be equal to the negative change in revenue due to the sales-decay effect. Thus, $s\left(\dfrac{M - R}{M}\right)$ $\cdot \Delta A$ must equal $R(1 - e^{-\lambda})$. If

$$s\left(\frac{M - R}{M}\right) \cdot \Delta A = R(1 - e^{-\lambda})$$

then, by rearranging the terms,

$$\Delta A = \frac{R(1 - e^{-\lambda})}{s\left(\dfrac{M - R}{M}\right)} \tag{19–10}$$

Suppose, for example, that the firm has captured 20 percent of its total market and has a monthly revenue of \$40,000. The sales-decay constant, λ, is .3, and the sales-response constant, s, is 4. In order to maintain the present level of sales, the amount of monthly advertising required is:

$$\Delta A = \frac{R(1 - e^{-\lambda})}{s\left(\dfrac{M - R}{M}\right)} \qquad \text{Given}$$

$$\Delta A = \frac{40{,}000(1 - e^{-.3})}{4(.8)} \qquad \text{By substitution}[14]$$

$$\Delta A = \frac{40{,}000(1 - .741)}{3.2} \qquad \text{By arithmetic}$$

$$\Delta A = 3{,}240 \qquad \text{By arithmetic}$$

Thus the firm must spend $3,240 per month on advertising to maintain sales of $40,000 per month.

This simple dynamic model illustrates some basic relationships between advertising and the other variables. If the firm's share of the market increases but all other factors, including the market-saturation level, remain constant, then an increase in the amount of advertising will be required in order to maintain sales at the new, higher level.

This can easily be shown:

$$\Delta A = \frac{R(1 - e^{-\lambda})}{s\left(\dfrac{M - R}{M}\right)}$$

but

$$\Delta A = \frac{R}{M - R}\left(\frac{1 - e^{-\lambda}}{\dfrac{s}{M}}\right) = \frac{R}{M - R} \cdot k, \text{ where}$$

k is a constant equal to $\dfrac{1 - e^{-\lambda}}{\dfrac{s}{M}}$

If R increases by a given amount, ΔR, then

$$\Delta A = \frac{R + \Delta R}{M - (R + \Delta R)} \cdot k, \text{ and}$$

$$\frac{R + \Delta R}{M - (R + \Delta R)} > \frac{R}{M - R}$$

[14] If the firm has captured 20 percent of the market, $\dfrac{R}{M} = .2$. Since $\dfrac{M - R}{M} = 1 - \dfrac{R}{M}$, then $\dfrac{M - R}{M} = 1 - .2 = .8$.

Thus advertising must be increased if sales are to remain constant. If, on the other hand, the market-saturation level increases and the firm's share of the market remains constant, then

$$\Delta A = \frac{R(1 - e^{-\lambda})}{s\left(\dfrac{M - R}{M}\right)} = R \cdot k, \text{ where}$$

k is a constant equal to $\dfrac{1 - e^{-\lambda}}{s\left(\dfrac{M - R}{M}\right)}$

Thus the amount of advertising needed would again increase. If the firm's revenue remains constant as the market-saturation level increases, the firm's market share will decrease, $M - R$ will increase, and the firm will need less advertising to maintain its present sales level. The change in advertising needed will equal

$$\Delta A = \frac{R(1 - e^{-\lambda})}{s\left(\dfrac{M - R}{M}\right)} = \frac{1}{\left(\dfrac{M - R}{M}\right)} \, k, \text{ where}$$

k is a constant equal to $\dfrac{R(1 - e^{-\lambda})}{s}$

As the market-saturation level increases, $\dfrac{M - R}{M}$ approaches 1 and the amount of advertising needed is reduced.

The amount of advertising required to maintain a constant sales level becomes less as λ approaches zero or s is increased. In particular, if $\lambda = 0$, then the sales-decay effect is zero, and a constant sales level can be maintained with no further advertising. This can easily be verified in Equation 19–10 by recalling that any number raised to the zero power equals 1.

Finally, if a firm stops advertising, a constant decrease in sales can normally be expected, due to the sales-decay effect. Sales could be maintained or increased only if enough personal selling were used to compensate for the sales-decay effect.

Although the dynamic advertising model we have discussed is extremely simple, it can still illustrate how changes in the advertising elements that affect s, M, or λ can vary the advertising budget.

If the advertising expenditure rate is held constant, the revenue rate can be increased by increasing the sales-response constant, s, or the market-saturation level, M; or by decreasing the sales-decay constant, λ. Given no increase in the advertising budget, s can be changed by changes in the advertising copy and artwork, changes in the media mix, or changes in the placement of ads in the present media, aimed at improving the appeal or the impact of the advertising message. There is no rule of thumb for accomplishing this. The most the firm can do is to hire imaginative and technically competent people to handle its advertising. However, research techniques are available that allow the marketer to estimate the degree to which such changes are successful.

The market-saturation level, M, is increased by changing the media mix to a combination that reaches a larger number of qualified prospects. If M is already maximized for the geographical area served by the firm, the only alternative—as far as increasing M is concerned—is to enter other geographical markets. This option may seriously affect the other marketing variables, especially personal selling and distribution. Even the product variable may be involved; motor fuels and houses, for example, must be adapted to the climatic conditions of various geographical markets. Hence, what starts out as an advertising decision may ultimately involve the entire marketing department, as well as other areas within the company.

The sales-decay constant, λ, may lend itself to manipulation through either the advertising message or the product variable when the product is purchased repeatedly, especially when the firm has captured what it considers to be an acceptable share of the market. The trick is to establish and maintain brand loyalty by differentiating the product in the minds of the buyers. This can be done by advertising (witness automobile fuel, cigarettes, and beer) or by manipulating the product variable (witness automobiles, houses, and candy). If strong brand loyalty can be instilled, once the buyer has been induced to purchase the firm's brand he is likely to repeat the purchase without additional advertising. Thus brand loyalty serves to sustain sales. If brand loyalty is strong, revenues will not decay as fast as when advertising is stopped or curtailed. If advertising is held fixed and brand loyalty is high, then the increase in sales resulting from the attraction of new buyers will not be canceled out by the loss of old customers, and there will be a net increase in sales.

MEDIA-SELECTION PROBLEMS

Decisions about which media to use and how to allocate the advertising budget among those selected may seem unmanageable in the face of the tens of thousands of alternatives available today. The media-mix problem is indeed difficult when the marketer is promoting a product that is sold to a nation-wide market with a large and diverse buyer population. Give thought for a moment to the task of allocating the advertising budget of the Ford Motor Company, General Electric, or American Airlines.

The complexity of this task suggests a random selection of media, with funds being allocated in proportion to the size of the audience. Although this approach is not totally without merit, a considerably more precise selection-and-allocation procedure is usually possible. In many cases, the nature of the product narrows the selection to a handful of options. In addition, geography, demography, promotional objectives, time, audience identification, technical requirements, and cost normally limit the number of alternatives.

In some cases the product may dictate the media. The number of potential customers for many highly specialized goods and services is limited, and they can be reached through one or two special-interest media. For example, a producer of office equipment would probably advertise in *Fortune, Forbes,* or the *Wall Street Journal* but would not advertise in *Good Housekeeping.* Similarly, a toy manufacturer would probably buy television time during programs that appeal to children.

The capability of computers for data storage and access and the flexibility of modern printing equipment now allow periodicals to publish multiple editions. Advertisers can often buy space confined to copies destined for a particular geographical area or a specialized audience. For example, *Time* magazine offers regional editions. Products uniquely suited to one region but of little interest to the remainder of *Time's* readership would dictate selection of the restricted-circulation edition, in which advertising is available at a reduced cost.

A variety of mailing lists are now available that provide the names and addresses of purchasers of major durables such as automobiles, trailers, and private aircraft, together with the brand owned. Many states sell their computerized lists of residents, as well as registrations of particular goods. An ingenious marketer can often use such a list to isolate a potential market. A manufacturer of camping equipment, for example, might use a mailing list comprised of holders of gun permits or hunting and fishing licenses. A person need only scan the direct-mail advertising he receives for a week or so to appreciate the use of mailing lists as a promotional tool.

Social custom or law may also restrict the media choice. For example, birth-control devices cannot be advertised in general-circulation media in most states.

The firm's geographical market helps define the media alternatives. Advertising a product sold only in the western states in a nation-wide periodical or on a network television show would be pointless. The firm would have to pay for coast-to-coast exposure, most of which would be of no value. However, the emergence of regional editions of many national publications and the availability of spot announcements on local television stations that broadcast network programs have expanded the number of media options open to the local marketer.

The demographic characteristics—age, sex, family status, income, and ethnic grouping—of the market and media audiences can also help define media alternatives when these characteristics can be specified.

Promotional objectives, too, may indicate the use of particular media. If the marketer is seeking to nullify the advertising of a competitor, for example, one tactic is to match the competitor's advertising in the same media. If the purpose is to establish an image or identify the brand with a particular social or ethnic group, a medium that itself has the desired image or that caters to a particular social or ethnic group may be an obvious choice. Bogart cites an example of a firm marketing to Afro-Americans. Advertisements in mass media would reach far more of these people than advertisements in *Ebony, Jet,* or a newspaper catering exclusively to the black community. However, advertisements in the ethnic publications identified the brand with the colored consumer; hence media of this type were valuable in making the good acceptable to the black market population.[15]

Time can play an important role in media selection. If a good or service must be publicized on short notice—say, within a week or two—many media must be excluded. The lead time for nationally distributed slick magazines may be as long as two months; network television prime time is sold six months to a year in advance. Often newspapers and radio are the only media that can respond quickly. The only way to avoid this predicament—other than by anticipating advertising needs well in advance—is to purchase magazine space or television time on a long-term basis. This assures the firm of space and time and often means a reduction in unit advertising cost. Many manufacturers purchase time and space well in advance, to assure themselves a favorable position or time and to exclude competition. This is why the same brand is often seen month after month in the same choice position in a particular medium.

Effect time—the length of time during which an ad can create a response—varies between classes of media. An ad in yesterday's newspaper has probably had its last exposure, whereas an ad in last week's magazine or on a billboard may be seen for weeks to come. The instantaneous impact of newspaper ads, TV and radio commercials, and handbills make these media appropriate to the promotion of short-time specials associated with the retailing of goods such as food products or theater tickets. The prolonged effect of other media would be of little value in these cases.

The manufacturer or retailer of expensive consumer durables is faced with an arduous task in moving prospects from a state of ignorance to pur-

---

[15] Bogart, *op. cit.,* p. 212.

chase behavior. Since this sort of selling must be sustained by continuous promotion, the slower effect of the other media is appropriate. However, they can be supplemented, or replaced, with newspaper, television, or radio advertising if such advertising is continuous.

In selecting advertising media, the marketer should attempt to match the media audiences to his firm's market population. The nature of the product and the size of the geographical market serve to define the market population. Once the market population is defined, the next step is to select media that will reach the right audiences. In some cases, this can easily be done using restricted-distribution magazines.[16] The marketer of specialized production equipment or services, for example, would be assured of access to a substantial portion of his firm's prospective buyers if he advertised in periodicals such as *Industrial Engineering.*

Other special-interest publications, such as *Good Housekeeping, Field and Stream*, and *Flying*, appeal to a select readership but do not control their distribution. Hence advertisers can buy exposure to a more intensified and presumably more receptive audience than would be afforded by a general-interest medium such as *Life, Look,* or the *New York Times;* however, the composition of the audience cannot be defined with the precision that a controlled-distribution magazine or a mailing list provides.

As his market population broadens, the marketer finds himself in an increasingly ambiguous position regarding media selection. For instance, consider the seller of a consumer durable such as a watch, a camera, or a portable radio. His market population has a wide variety of characteristics that seldom coincide precisely with those of the audience of any single medium. However, once the product is on the market, research techniques are available for estimating the efficiency of the various media.

Technical requirements may also limit the media options. For example, television is the obvious choice for a new product whose virtues must be demonstrated to be adequately appreciated by the consumer. Of course, two other alternatives would be to emphasize personal selling and provide free samples. Obviously, the latter policy is feasible only with very inexpensive convenience goods, such as toothpaste and hairdressings, which can be packaged in small quantities. Exceptions sometimes occur in the industrial goods field, where a manufacturer may give or loan a unit or two to a customer in hopes of having his product adopted. This is a common practice in cases where the potential customer is experimenting with a new product of its own and, once the item is in production, could have a large

---

[16] Some special-interest magazines control their distribution, restricting subscriptions to people actively engaged in their special field. These periodicals are often delivered without charge to qualified subscribers, and advertisers are offered audited subscription lists, which contain detailed information on subscribers.

demand for the firm's good. In this instance, the potential supplier will normally provide free samples during the customer's preliminary development stage in the hope that the successful performance of the sample will result in a substantial order when the customer releases his product for quantity production.

Cost is another variable that may serve to eliminate a number of media. Yet with the availability of restricted-distribution editions, local spot announcements, and mailing lists that can be varied in size, there are few media, including national magazines and major metropolitan newspapers, that cannot be afforded even by the firm with a small budget.

Cost is also used—or misused—as a criterion for selecting between competing media. The basis for such selection is often cost per thousand readers, viewers, or listeners.[17] If the audiences of various media were comparable, this would be the way to array media in terms of efficiency. However, is reaching a thousand readers of *Good Housekeeping* as valuable as reaching the same number of readers of *Sports Illustrated* (and vice versa)? The answer may be "yes" for an automobile manufacturer (assuming that the wife's role in the new-car purchase decision is as important as her husband's). It is obviously "no" for a producer of pipe tobacco or a distributor of baby powder.

The value of the cost-per-thousand criterion becomes even more dubious when variations in audience buying power and tastes, in methods of audience measurement, and in media reach and impact are considered. The crux of the issue is, as one advertising specialist has pointed out, "cost per thousand what?"[18]

Ideally, the answer should be "sales." Unfortunately, cost-per-thousand sales can seldom be specified, and the marketer must usually search for a measurable proxy. In other words, he seeks a variable that will lend itself to measurement and that will correlate with sales. For purposes of distributing the advertising budget among media, the correlation need not be specified, although hopefully the accumulation of data would eventually allow the correlation to be estimated. Until sales can be equated to advertising—either directly or through a precise correlation with some measurable proxy—the advertising budget cannot be optimized.

A hierarchy of some common proxies was suggested by Seymour Banks, a well-known media theorist who headed a committee of the Advertising Research Foundation. In descending order of desirability, but in ascending order of availability, they are:

[17] The units of measurements in common use are not consistent. Circulation (number of subscribers plus newsstand sales), readership, audience, sets in use per commercial minute, cumulative reach, and so on, are all quoted. See Bogart, *op. cit.*, p. 256, for a more detailed analysis.

[18] *Ibid.*, p. 248.

1. *Sales response:* number of units sold (not a proxy).
2. *Advertising communication:* number of prospects who move toward the purchase threshold.
3. *Advertising perception:* number of people who view and understand the advertisement.
4. *Advertising exposure:* number of people who view the advertisement.
5. *Vehicle exposure:* number of people who are exposed to the advertising vehicle—for example, a magazine, a radio program, a television show, or a billboard.
6. *Vehicle distribution:* number of households receiving the vehicle.[19]

Audited figures on vehicle distribution are normally available. Data are published on the circulation of periodicals, as well as on the number of households viewing a particular television show or listening to a particular radio station. Even the number of cars that pass a given billboard on a given day is often counted. However, as one moves up the hierarchy toward the ultimate yardstick, "sales response," measurement gets progressively more difficult and expensive. As the marketer reaches "advertising perception," the advertisement itself begins to play an important role. A bland ad in a good vehicle may produce a far poorer audience reaction than an attention-getting, high-impact ad in a less popular medium.

There are a number of research techniques for estimating both the higher-order proxies and sales response. Some can be used prior to the general use of the ad or vehicle. Unfortunately, the techniques become more complicated, more expensive, and less reliable as one moves up the ladder of proxies toward sales response.

MEDIA-SELECTION METHODS

The proxy or sales-response values of alternative media or media combinations can be used to array options in terms of their efficiency. The advertiser then selects the number 1 medium, the number 2 medium, and so on until the budget constraint is encountered or the efficiency of the nth choice drops below an acceptable level. This process can be made more precise by adjusting subsequent media for audience redundancy, or overlap. For example, if 20 percent of medium number 3's audience is duplicated in media numbers 1 and 2, then an adjustment should be made in medium number 3's value before deciding whether to add it to the advertising mix.

If sales response can be estimated directly or derived from a proxy, a media-allocation model of the type developed by King[20] can be applied to

---

[19] Adapted from Bogart, *op. cit.,* pp. 257–58.
[20] King, *op. cit.,* p. 374.

the problem. King's model is an extension of the basic static model, used in Equation 19–3, for optimizing the total advertising budget. The only difference is that the advertising cost, A, is expressed as the summation of the advertising costs, $A_1, A_2, \ldots A_n$, for each medium. The reasoning is analogous, as King showed in the following formula:

$$\pi = R\left(1 - \frac{V}{P}\right) - f - \sum_{i=1}^{n} A_i, \text{ where} \qquad (19\text{--}11)$$

π = profit

R = revenue

V = variable unit costs, exclusive of advertising

P = price

f = fixed costs, exclusive of advertising, and

A = advertising costs for media 1 through n

To maximize profit, King set the partial derivative of π with respect to advertising, A, equal to zero for each medium, i.[21] Expressed notationally,

$$\frac{\partial \pi}{\partial A_i} = 0 \text{ at maximum profit}$$

By the same process we used in arriving at Equation 19–4, it can be shown that the preceding expression is equivalent to

$$\frac{\partial R}{\partial A_i} = \frac{1}{1 - \dfrac{V}{P}} \qquad (19\text{--}12)$$

If the variable cost, V, is \$4, and the price, P, is \$6, then by substitution and arithmetic $\partial R / \partial A$ would equal 3 for each medium, i. Thus if the sales-response function had been estimated for each medium, the optimum allocation would be revealed by solving for A_i in the expression for $\partial R / \partial A$, with $\partial R / \partial A$ set equal to 3.

For example, using the values for V and P just given (hence, $\partial R / \partial A = 3$ at maximum profit), assume that the aggregate revenue function for the three media selected for a hypothetical advertising mix is

$$R = 100{,}000 + 80{,}000 \log_{10} A_1 + 70{,}000 \log_{10} A_2 + 30{,}000 \log_{10} A_3$$

---

[21] Partial derivatives were discussed in Chapter 3, page 55.

The revenue equation normally will have an element of time specified; here, we will assume the relevant time period to be one month. Thus revenue will be $100,000 per month if no advertising is purchased. Since each of the three advertising vehicles is assumed to have mutually exclusive audiences, their contributions to revenue are independent and additive. Finally, as the logarithmic form of the equation indicates, marginal revenue product, $\partial R/\partial A$, decreases as additional amounts of each advertising medium are purchased. Figure 19.3 demonstrates this characteristic.

We already know that profit will be maximized when the marginal revenue produced by each advertising medium is equal to 3. The optimum advertising budget for each of the three media can easily be determined:

$$\frac{\partial R}{\partial A_1} = (.4343)\left(\frac{80,000}{A_1}\right) \qquad \text{By rules of calculus}$$

$$\frac{\partial R}{\partial A_2} = (.4343)\left(\frac{70,000}{A_2}\right) \qquad \text{By rules of calculus}$$

$$\frac{\partial R}{\partial A_3} = (.4343)\left(\frac{30,000}{A_3}\right) \qquad \text{By rules of calculus}$$

$$3 = \frac{34,744}{A_1} \qquad \text{By substitution}$$

$$3 = \frac{30,401}{A_2} \qquad \text{By substitution}$$

$$3 = \frac{13,029}{A_3} \qquad \text{By substitution}$$

$$A_1 = 11,581 \qquad \text{By arithmetic}$$
$$A_2 = 10,134 \qquad \text{By arithmetic}$$
$$A_3 = 4,343 \qquad \text{By arithmetic}$$

The optimum advertising budgets for media 1, 2, and 3 are $11,581, $10,134, $4,343, respectively.

This allocation method assumes that the audiences of the selected media are mutually exclusive. This is often, but not always, true. Whenever multiple advertising vehicles are being considered, the marketer should ascertain whether he is buying redundant exposures. Redundant exposure is not bad per se. If the effect of advertising is truly cumulative, then redundant exposure is of some value, since it reinforces the original message. However, audience overlap should be taken into account in estimating the total number of prospects that will be reached by an advertising campaign.

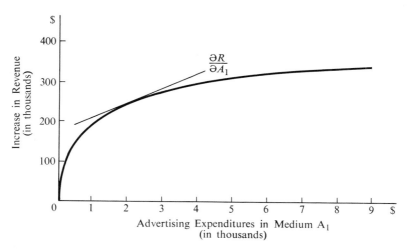

FIGURE 19.3

Relationship of revenue and advertising expenditure in medium 1

To illustrate, assume that an overlap in the audiences for media 1 and 2 in the previous example makes the additive function yield an inflated estimate of the total sales that will result from the simultaneous use of the three media. An adjustment in the revenue equation—in this case, the addition of the term 10,000 log A_1A_2—will correct for the assumed overlap of the audiences for media 1 and 2.[22] This changes the revenue equation to

$$R = 100,000 + 80,000 \log_{10} A_1 + 70,000 \log_{10} A_2 + 30,000 \log_{10} A_3$$
$$- 10,000 \log_{10} A_1 A_2$$

The optimum budget for each of the three media can be computed by setting the three partial derivatives equal to 3, the value of $\dfrac{1}{1 - \dfrac{V}{P}}$ and solving for A. The partial derivatives for the amended revenue function are

---

[22] In its most general form, the revenue equation for the three advertising media would be:

$$R = \alpha + \beta_1 f(A_1) + \beta_2 f(A_2) + \beta_3 f(A_3) + \gamma_1 f(A_1, A_2) + \gamma_2 f(A_1, A_3)$$
$$+ \gamma_3 f(A_2, A_3) + \gamma_4 f(A_1, A_2, A_3)$$

The exact form of the revenue equation would be determined by estimating the values of the coefficients α, β_1, β_2, β_3, γ_1, γ_2, γ_3, and γ_4, as well as the form of the function, f. In our example, we have assumed f to be a $\log_{10}$ form and γ_2, γ_3, and γ_4 to be zero (since only media 1 and 2 have overlapping audiences).

$$\frac{\partial R}{\partial A_1} = .4343(80,000)\left(\frac{1}{A_1}\right) - .4343(10,000)\left(\frac{1}{A_1}\right)$$ By rules of calculus[23]

$$\frac{\partial R}{\partial A_1} = \frac{34,744}{A_1} - \frac{4,343}{A_1}$$ By arithmetic

$$\frac{\partial R}{\partial A_1} = \frac{30,401}{A_1}$$ By arithmetic

$$\frac{\partial R}{\partial A_2} = .4343(70,000)\left(\frac{1}{A_2}\right) - .4343(10,000)\left(\frac{1}{A_2}\right)$$ By rules of calculus

$$\frac{\partial R}{\partial A_2} = \frac{30,401}{A_2} - \frac{4,343}{A_2}$$ By arithmetic

$$\frac{\partial R}{\partial A_2} = \frac{26,058}{A_2}$$ By arithmetic

$$\frac{\partial R}{\partial A_3} = \frac{13,029}{A_3}$$ By rules of calculus

To maximize profit, each of the partial derivatives is set equal to $\dfrac{1}{1-\dfrac{V}{P}} = 3$. Thus the optimum values for A_1, A_2, and A_3 are:

$$\frac{30,401}{A_1} = 3$$

$$A_1 = \frac{30,401}{3} = 10,134$$

$$\frac{26,058}{A_2} = 3$$

$$A_2 = \frac{26,058}{3} = 8,686$$

$$\frac{13,029}{A_3} = 3$$

$$A_3 = \frac{13,029}{3} = 4,343$$

[23] $\dfrac{d}{dx}\log_e u = \dfrac{1}{u}$. Since $u = A_1 A_2$, $\dfrac{\partial}{\partial A_1}(10,000\log_{10}A_1A_2) = .4343(10,000)\dfrac{\partial}{\partial A_1}(\log_e A_1 A_2)$, but $\dfrac{\partial}{\partial A_1}(\log_e A_1 A_2) = \dfrac{1}{A_1 A_2} \cdot A_2 = \dfrac{1}{A_1}$.

The new optimum advertising budget would be $21,163, with $10,134 allocated to medium 1, $8,686 allocated to medium 2, and $4,343 allocated to medium 3. The exposure overlap between media 1 and 2 thus results in a smaller optimum budget for these two media. The optimum budget for medium 3 remains the same.

Unfortunately, the total advertising budget is seldom optimized mathematically. Generally, it is set by one of the subjective criteria discussed earlier in the chapter. Thus, it is more realistic to view the media-allocation model as subject to a constraint, in the form of a budget limitation. This can be stated notationally as

$$\sum_{i=1}^{n} A_i \leq A_B$$

The aggregate advertising expenditure, ΣA_i, for all the media, 1 through n, must be equal to or less than the advertising budget, A_B.

King suggests a practical, two-step solution to the allocation problem when the total advertising budget is set arbitrarily.[24] First, the optimum budget is calculated for each medium as in the unconstrained model. If the total budget thus computed $(A_1 + A_2 + \ldots A_n)$ does not exceed the constraint, A_B, there is no reason not to use the optimum allocations and save the remainder of the money initially allocated to advertising. If this step yields values whose sum exceeds the budget constraint, then each medium should be allocated a portion of the budget as a function of the ratio of the budget constraint to the optimum budget. In mathematical notation,

$$A_{i_B} = \frac{A_i}{\Sigma A_i} \cdot B, \text{ where} \tag{19–13}$$

A_{i_B} = allocation of the constrained budget to medium A_i

A_i = optimum unconstrained budget, and

B = constrained budget

To illustrate this technique, we can use the original example from page 436. The optimum budget in this case was $26,058 ($A_1$ = $11,581, A_2 = $10,134, A_3 = $4,343). If we assume that the advertising budget is limited to $15,000, then the money should be allocated as follows:

$$A_{1_B} = \frac{A_1}{\Sigma A_i} \cdot B \qquad \text{Given}$$

$$A_{1_B} = \frac{11,581}{26,058} (15,000) \qquad \text{By arithmetic}$$

[24] King, op. cit., p. 379.

$$A_{1_B} = 6,666 \qquad\qquad \text{By arithmetic}$$

$$A_{2_B} = \frac{A_2}{\sum A_i} \cdot B \qquad\qquad \text{Given}$$

$$A_{2_B} = \frac{10,134}{26,058}(15,000) \qquad \text{By arithmetic}$$

$$A_{2_B} = 5,834 \qquad\qquad \text{By arithmetic}$$

$$A_{3_B} = \frac{A_3}{\sum A_i} \cdot B \qquad\qquad \text{Given}$$

$$A_{3_B} = \frac{4,343}{26,058}(15,000) \qquad \text{By arithmetic}$$

$$A_{3_B} = 2,500 \qquad\qquad \text{By arithmetic}$$

This allocation will make the partial derivative, $\partial R/\partial A$, the same for all three media. It was shown on page 437 that

$$\frac{\partial R}{\partial A_1} = \frac{34,744}{A_1}$$

$$\frac{\partial R}{\partial A_2} = \frac{30,401}{A_2}$$

$$\frac{\partial R}{\partial A_3} = \frac{13,029}{A_3}$$

Substituting the constrained-budget values for A_1, A_2, and A_3 yields

$$\frac{\partial R}{\partial A_1} = \frac{34,744}{6,666} = 5.2$$

$$\frac{\partial R}{\partial A_2} = \frac{30,401}{5,834} = 5.2$$

$$\frac{\partial R}{\partial A_3} = \frac{13,029}{2,500} = 5.2$$

Thus, the constrained budget has been allocated so that the marginal revenue produced by each medium is the same. However, it should be noted that the value of $\partial R/\partial A$ is 5.2 with the budget limitation, whereas it should be 3 in order to maximize profit. The firm could therefore increase its profits by increasing the total advertising budget. (This would be true whenever the constrained budget was less than the optimum budget.)

The quantification of the advertising decision has been the focus of considerable attention on the part of advocates of quantitative techniques in marketing. The elusiveness of answers in this area, as well as the vast number of variables, provides a challenging field for mathematicians, statisticians, and econometricians. Linear programming, game theory, and simulation, in addition to the classical tools of mathematics and statistics, are being used by both practitioners and academicians in an effort to make better advertising-allocation decisions.[25]

The models presented here have been samples of the more general methods for budgeting and allocating advertising resources. Techniques for data acquisition and the compilation of response functions, as well as the evaluation of advertising copy, media, and strategies, are explored in Part IX. For a further development of these subjects, the reader is directed to the supplementary readings at the end of Parts VIII and IX.

[25] See Willard I. Zangwill, "Media Selection by Decision Programming," *Journal of Advertising Research,* Vol. 5, No. 3 (September 1965), pp. 30–36; and Philip Kotler, "Toward an Explicit Model for Media Selection," *Journal of Advertising Research,* Vol. 4, No. 1 (March 1964), pp. 34–41.

CHAPTER 20

Personal Selling

FUNCTIONS AND CONTROL

Personal selling is analogous to advertising in many ways. Its purpose also is to increase sales, although salesmen may sometimes perform the yeoman function of processing sales orders. This latter task is more accurately considered part of the distribution process, especially when the order-processing function is clearly removed from the promotional functions, as is the case with a mail-order house (which solicits orders through advertising). For convenience, order processing is generally excluded from the discussion here, although it is recognized that a small portion of a salesman's energies is normally absorbed by this task.

Personal selling, like advertising, involves a characteristic that is difficult to measure quantitatively. This quality, called "salesmanship," is comparable to the creativity input in advertising. It is a mixture of both personality traits and learned skills. The learned skills needed by a salesman include proficiency in the use of sales psychology, a knowledge of the firm's goods and services, and an understanding of the personality and technical requirements of the customer. The latter two are especially important in the sale of complicated products such as machine tools, computers, and chemical plants.

One virtue of personal selling, from the managerial standpoint, is that it involves fewer choices and is more readily evaluated than advertising. The sales it produces can be measured directly.

A number of variables make up the personal-selling end of the promotional mix: the number of salesmen, the number and size of territories, the type of compensation, the procedures for recruiting, selecting, and training personnel, the type of performance standards, the expenses for which salesmen are reimbursed, and work assignments.

Marginal analysis and the rule of proportionality can be used to optimize both the total personal-selling budget and the distribution of authorized funds among the various elements of the personal-selling mix. As a practical matter, however, few personal-selling decisions are made in this way, and where they are, the decision is usually constrained by convention, inertia, vested interests, and long-term commitments. The majority of decisions made by sales executives involve only one or two endogenous variables and a small number of alternatives. This suggests the suboptimum approach— which in fact is quite useful—to the management of personal-selling resources.

SALES-FORCE SIZE

The obvious rule in deciding the size of the sales force is to add additional men as long as the net marginal revenue produced by the last man exceeds the marginal cost of employing him. Conversely, the sales force should be reduced whenever the net marginal revenue produced by one or more remaining men fails to exceed the marginal cost of retaining them. This method will work well in adjusting the size of the sales force when the sales department approaches its optimum size and experience has provided enough data so that the relationship between sales-force size and revenue can be estimated. Of course, short-term economic fluctuations or employment constraints (such as union contracts) must be taken into consideration. However, the method may not be appropriate in setting the size of the initial sales force, particularly when the revenue and cost functions have not been precisely determined.

The optimum number of salesmen can also be estimated on the basis of potential sales or the size of the market population. This method requires some knowledge of (1) the potential market by territory and (2) the productivity of salesmen working under the conditions imposed by the product, the market, and the promotional plan. The manpower requirement can then be obtained by dividing the productivity factor into the potential sales. For instance, if one salesman could be expected to produce an average of $150,000 in revenues per year and a territory had estimated potential sales of $3,000,000, a sales force of 20 men would be required to fully exploit the area.

This method makes several precarious assumptions. First, it posits a linear relationship between revenue and the number of salesmen. Second, if only the size of the market population is known, it assumes that a sales territory will yield sales in proportion to the size of its potential-buyer population. Empirical studies indicate that high-potential territories do not produce revenues in proportion to their sales potential.[1] That is, a territory with 6 percent of the total potential market usually does not produce three times the revenue

[1] Walter J. Semlow, "How Many Salesmen Do You Need?" *Harvard Business Review* (May–June 1959), pp. 126–32.

of a territory with only 2 percent of the total potential market, even if the sales force is distributed proportionally. Third, it implies some knowledge of the correlation between revenue and the number of salesmen—a function that is very difficult to specify without prior experience (which is usually lacking when new-product promotion decisions must be made).

Estimates of manpower requirements based on the size of the market population are calculated as follows: First, the potential customers are tallied and then divided into classes according to their size, sales potential, location, or industry, or some other appropriate basis. Second, an estimate is made of the call frequency necessary to service each potential customer in each classification. Third, an estimate is made of the number of calls a salesman can be expected to make on customers of a given class. Once these values are computed, the total manpower requirement can be estimated using the following formula:

$$M = \sum_{i=1}^{n} \frac{F_i P_i}{C_i}, \text{ where} \tag{20-1}$$

M = manpower requirement (sales-force size)

F = frequency of calls required for a given class of customer

P = number of prospective customers of a given class

C = number of calls one salesman can make on a given class of customers, and

i = class of customer

For example, assume that a manufacturer is introducing a line of paper products suitable for both home and commercial use. Four markets are identified: (1) grocery chains and wholesalers, (2) institutional buyers, (3) large industrial buyers, and (4) small industrial buyers. The number of annual calls necessary to service each prospect in these four classes is estimated to be 18, 12, 8, and 8, respectively. The number of prospects (identified through government and trade sources), excluding those whose sales potential appears too small to justify personal selling, is 40, 210, 60, and 200, respectively. The number of annual calls that a salesman can make for each class, allowing for sick leave, vacation, training, travel, turnover, and any other factors that distract from the time allotted to selling, is 800, 700, 600, and 1,000, respectively. Now

$$M = \sum_{i=1}^{n} \frac{F_i P_i}{C_i} \qquad \text{Given}$$

$$M = \frac{F_1 P_1}{C_1} + \frac{F_2 P_2}{C_2} + \frac{F_3 P_3}{C_3} + \frac{F_4 P_4}{C_4} \qquad \text{Restatement of preceding formula}$$

$$M = \frac{18(40)}{800} + \frac{12(210)}{700} + \frac{8(60)}{600} + \frac{8(200)}{1000} \qquad \text{By substitution}$$

$$M = .9 + 3.6 + .8 + 1.6 = 6.9 \qquad \text{By arithmetic}$$

Thus seven full-time salesmen—or their equivalent in part-time personnel—are required. Seldom will the calculated number of salesmen be an integer; thus some subjective decision as to whether it is better to be slightly over-staffed or understaffed must usually be made.

In using this method, the marketer must keep in mind that the equation does not allow for changes in the call frequency required to adequately service a customer as the market develops. Call frequencies must be adjusted to reflect changes in exogenous conditions such as the aggressiveness of competitors and the life-cycle position of the product. For example, a more intense personal-selling effort is indicated during the introductory phase of a product than during the maturity phase. Normally, the frequency of calls should be greater in the initial stages, or more time should be allowed for each call, which would reduce the value of the denominator. The net result of such an adjustment would be to increase the sales-manpower requirement during the introductory phase. An alternative would be to hold the sales force con-stant and concentrate on the most promising prospects, hoping that the other members of the market population will follow once the innovators and early adopters have accepted the item.

As product and market experience accumulate, the marketer may ad-just the values of the decision variables to reflect actual experience. For ex-ample, a shift in personal-selling resources may be in order should the adoption of the new product not conform to the predicted pattern. Often the redefinition of market classes and shifting of assignments—once market conditions have been clarified—will improve the personal-selling operation. In the example, prospective customers were classified by type. It may be more appropriate to use geographical, product (if the line is varied), or natural markets as a basis for the assignment of sales personnel. ("Natural markets" are customer groupings already established by the individual sales-men. They are an appropriate choice when the salesman-buyer relationship is important and the sales staff has already established a favorable relation-ship.)

TERRITORIES

If the sales force is reasonably large or covers a significant geographical area, it is useful to split the aggregate market into manageable units, normally called "territories." This may be done after an initial division of work on a nongeographical basis, such as industry or product, has been made. Or, the market may first be divided into territorial units and the units then redivided into subsets according to the composition of the market. Another approach is to divide the sales organization one way for administrative purposes and another way for line, or operational, purposes. For example, regional sales offices may be established to provide logistics support (office space, secretarial services, order-processing, and so on) while the salesmen themselves are divided by product or customer and cover two or more geographical regions. The most common method is to use political boundaries to define geographical territories.

Once the territories are defined, personal-selling resources—as well as other marketing resources—can be more easily allocated, monitored, and controlled. The basis for the allocation may be any variable that is an index, or proxy, of the market size and for which there is data. Many such variables have already been explored in the discussions of trading areas and resource allocation. Population statistics (general censuses, or censuses of age groups, retail stores, manufacturing firms, and so on) as well as statistics on retail sales, income, and family size are widely used to divide resources. Indices like the buying-power index are often helpful. Frequently used data sources are the Bureau of the Census, the Department of Commerce, local chambers of commerce, trade associations, *Sales Management* and other publications,[2] and private research firms.

As a practical matter, sales territories are usually selected with the aid of one of these variables to ensure uniformity. It seldom makes sense to load one manager with a territory having a market population, a sales potential, and a sales force several times the size of another, unless special considerations—seller-to-buyer distances, for example—warrant a lopsided arrangement. Uniformity of territories is particularly important when all or a portion of the salesmen's compensation is based on an incentive program that relates their income to the sales they produce. An imbalance in the definition and distribution of territories can introduce a bias into the earning potentials of the salesmen handling the territories that can have a shattering effect on morale, hence performance. If conditions dictate uneven territories, a compensating factor—a special allowance, bonus, or commission differential—should be introduced to equalize the earning potentials.

The nature of the firm, the product, and the market will determine the relevant variable for the division of territories and the subsequent allocation of personal-selling resources. Obviously, a manufacturer of machine tools would not use the same criteria as a firm selling supplemental health insurance for Medicare recipients. Thus the same method of division and allocation is not applicable to every territorial problem. The following techniques

---

[2] Special-interest magazines, trade publications, and newspapers often publish such data.

are useful in many of the more common situations and can often be adapted to more unique conditions.

Political Subdivision. Perhaps the simplest method of determining territories and allocating resources is to divide the market into convenient political units—such as states or counties—and then distribute the sales force in proportion to the number of potential customers in each unit. Where a unit does not have enough potential to justify at least one salesman, it can be combined with an adjoining unit or units. If the total sales force is too large to be supervised by one manager, it can be divided among the number of managers required for adequate supervision. This division would combine adjoining territories into managerial areas, each containing approximately the same number of salesmen. If branch offices were needed for logistics or managerial purposes, they could be established accordingly, with their exact location depending on the availability of communications and office facilities. Decisions regarding the location of branch offices are often made in conjunction with distribution decisions, thereby combining sales offices with warehouses and customer service centers (although the three functions would not necessarily occupy the same or adjacent buildings).

For example, assume that a hardware wholesale house, previously having done business exclusively in the city of Cleveland, Ohio, has been granted an important tool franchise covering the entire state. Its new prospects are primarily hardware stores and farm-equipment dealers (SIC 525), whose total sales in Ohio during the previous year were $296.6 million. This data is contained in the current *Census of Business,* which also reveals that tools of the type covered by the franchise accounted for 21.8 percent of hardware-store and farm-equipment dealers' sales. Thus hardware-store and farm-equipment dealers' sales would be a convenient and reliable basis for estimating the potential market for the wholesaler's new tool line. The state's 88 counties would be appropriate subdivisions for the establishment of sales territories.

By applying the tool brand's present national market share of 6.4 percent to the Ohio market of $64.7 million (21.8% of $296.6 million = $64.7 million), we can estimate a market potential of $4.14 million. This is exclusive of the effect of the increase in personal selling that will result from the addition of the Cleveland wholesaler to the manufacturer's distribution system (thereby increasing its national market share).

The distribution of this potential market of $4.14 million among the 88 counties is presumed to be proportional to each county's share of the total hardware-store and farm-equipment dealers' sales of $296.6 million. Unfortunately, the data source does not distribute this total by counties. However, it does distribute building-material and farm-equipment dealers' sales (SIC 52) by county, and these sales should be approximately proportional to the sales of SIC 525, hence be a good proxy for the distribution of hardware-store and farm-equipment dealers' sales. By posting the percentage of SIC 52 sales for each county and multiplying that value by the firm's total Ohio market potential ($4.14 million), we can estimate the SIC 525 sales for each county.

Experience in the Cleveland market has indicated that the wholesaler can expect annual sales of approximately $600,000 from a single salesman. Dividing this value into the total potential market shows that seven men are needed to cover the state. Aggregating adjoining counties until their total sales potential approximates $.6 million ($\frac{1}{7} \times$ $4.14 million) will enable the wholesaler to establish seven sales territories—each with an approximately equal sales potential. Table 20.1 and Figure 20.1 show the distribution of the potential

Table 20.1   Distribution of Ohio sales potential for a national brand of hardware tools

County	Percentage of Building-Material and Farm-Equipment Sales (SIC 52)	Market Potential for Firm's Brand of Tools*
Adams	.34%	$ 14,076
Allen	1.70	70,380
Ashland	.39	16,146
Ashtabula	1.12	46,368
Athens	.38	15,732
Auglaise	.46	19,044
.	.	.
.	.	.
.	.	.
Wyandot	1.62	67,068
Total	100.00%	$4,140,000

* Computed by multiplying column 2 times $4,140,000, which is the estimate of the total Ohio market potential.

SOURCE: Based on a case study in U. S. Department of Commerce, *Measuring Markets* (Washington, D. C.: U. S. Government Printing Office, 1966), pp. 60–63.

market among the 88 counties and the subsequent aggregation of these counties into the seven sales territories.[3]

In the foregoing example, the manufacturer used counties as the common denominator for defining and allocating territories among its distributors (some distributors will probably be granted territories that consist of two or

[3] This example is based on a case study in *Measuring Markets*, pp. 60–63.

● The main office of each territory

FIGURE 20.1
Ohio sales territories for a national brand of hardware tools

SOURCE: U. S. Department of Commerce, *Measuring Markets* (Washintgon, D. C.:
U. S. Government Printing Office, 1966), p. 62.

more sparsely populated states). The Ohio distributor in turn used counties
as its basic denominator, aggregating them into seven approximately equal
groups to form sales territories for the seven salesmen it believes are needed
to capture the potential market. The problem could have been approached

differently by aggregating the counties on the basis of the number of hard-ware stores and farm-equipment dealers in each. This data is available in *County Business Patterns.*[4] These prospects could then be classified as large or small on the basis of their number of employees, and the frequency of sales calls varied accordingly. The total manpower requirement, as well as the equivalent salesmen needed for each county and territory, could then be computed by Equation 20–1.

A more sophisticated method would be to use both sales potential and the market population to aggregate counties into territories that would be approximately equal with respect to both sales potential and the number of calls the salesmen would have to make. This could be done, in the example, by a trial-and-error method, whereby the counties were initially divided into territories according to the market population, and the counties adjacent to other territories traded back and forth to bring their sales potentials into approximate equality. A final adjustment might also be made in order to accommodate geographical barriers (probably nil for Ohio) and convenience in travel. It might even be necessary to modify the political boundaries and occasionally to reassign a town or cluster of buyers to an adjoining territory.

Geometric Subdivision.   Another method of defining territories is to start with a preconceived geometric shape. Shape is normally used in con-junction with one or more other criteria, for the marketer cannot simply select a shape and then use it like a cookie cutter to chop out sales territories. Obviously, a circular territory twenty miles in diameter and centered in New York City would have little in common with a territory of the same dimen-sions centered in Pleasant Plains, Arkansas.

Standard shapes do serve to define and optimize sales territories, espe-cially those assigned to individual salesmen. However, they must invariably be modified to adjust the individual territory for the realities of geography, road systems, transportation terminals, customer locations, and sales poten-tial. Three common forms, the circle, the cloverleaf, and the wedge, are shown in Figure 20.2.[5]

The *circle* places the salesman's headquarters in the center of his territory and allows him to make calls on customers with a minimum of backtracking. He travels outward in a spiral path, returning directly to the center after completing his last call. This configuration minimizes the dis-tance between his headquarters and his farthest customer. It also minimizes the average distance between the salesman and customers.

[4] Like the *Census of Business, County Business Patterns* is published by the U. S. De-partment of Commerce and is readily available from the U. S. Government Printing Office. Both publications are updated periodically.
[5] Similar forms are described by Philip Kotler in *Marketing Management: Analysis, Planning and Control* (New York: Prentice-Hall, 1967), p. 504.

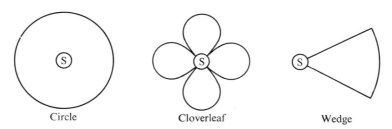

Circle   Cloverleaf   Wedge

FIGURE 20.2
Common forms of sales territories

The *cloverleaf* is a modification of the circle that is especially efficient when the salesman must return to his headquarters before completing a full cycle of calls. If the right size and number of leaves are selected, each leaf will represent a trip into the field. Like the circle, the cloverleaf places the salesman in the center and minimizes both the average distance between him and the customer and the distance to the farthest account. This is particularly important when the salesman must make a number of unexpected visits to customers.

The *wedge* is usually part of a larger, circular territory. The salesman's headquarters are at the edge of his territory, but at the center of the total, circular territory. This shape is frequently used in dividing large metropolitan areas among salesmen, especially when it is desirable for them all to share a common headquarters. It may also serve to divide a territory between metropolitan and rural areas. The obvious disadvantage of this shape is that it maximizes both the average and the maximum travel distances. This may be moderated if the salesman chooses to live midway between the center and the rim, perhaps in a suburban area, and is not required to visit the sales headquarters every day.

COMPENSATION

Salesmen may be paid a flat salary, work on a straight commission basis, or operate under some other arrangement involving a base salary plus commissions. Thus the direct labor costs to the firm of personal selling can run from entirely fixed to entirely variable. The nature of the firm, the product, the market, and the psychological makeup of the employee or agent will determine the appropriateness and efficiency of any given program. Which arrangement a salesman will prefer will depend on many factors, including his desire for security and his confidence in himself and the product.

The compensation plan serves to attract and maintain competent personnel and provides job motivation. It may also serve to direct the efforts of the sales force in the manner preferred by the company, particularly when the selection of prospects and the amount of time spent on different classes of customers is left primarily to the discretion of individual salesmen. The sales-commission method of compensation is typically used when sales personnel are spread over a large area and their daily activities cannot be closely supervised. For example, in order to ensure that its salesmen distribute their energies in accordance with the emphasis preferred by management, a firm may use a commission rate that varies with the type or size of a sale.

For example, a bonus or premium commission might be paid for new accounts. A salesman, especially one on straight commission, will generally concentrate his efforts where he perceives them as yielding the greatest personal gain. Missionary work is generally less rewarding than cultivating an established clientele, among whom sales are relatively certain. This may be a shortsighted view, but it is one that is often held. The firm, on the other hand, is interested in both short- and long-run profits, and the laborious missionary work that may be unrewarding and unpopular today is important to future revenues.

Salaries, commissions, and bonuses can be used singly or in combination to implement the firm's personal-selling strategy. Although no substitute for supervision, they serve as instruments of management. Salaries are useful when team selling is involved, as is typically the case with the marketing of complex goods and services. Sales of commercial aircraft and most government prime-contracting are illustrative. Salaries are also appropriate during training periods, for missionary salesmen, when sales are highly cyclic, and when close supervision is practical.

Commissions are useful when part-time salesmen are used, when supervision is impractical, when missionary work is not needed, and when a great deal of incentive is required to produce sales. Door-to-door and real-estate selling fit this description; hence salesmen doing this kind of work usually operate on a straight commission basis.

Bonuses, which are special payments for the achievement of a particular objective, are appropriate when the firm has specific selling tasks to perform or goals to achieve. Bonuses may be paid for either individual or group performance. Opening a new account, achieving a sales quota, or selling an obsolete, unpopular, or very profitable item is commonly encouraged by bonuses. A bonus may be money, or it may be a special award such as a trip, a car, a television set, or some other material prize.

The total compensation received by the sales force will reflect both the quantity of sales personnel and the prevailing salary structure for salesmen. Personal selling is an input in the production function and, like the other production inputs, should be purchased in the quantity that will optimize the production mix. In this respect the promotional mix—that is, the advertising and personal-selling combination—lends itself to the two-variable input analysis described earlier (page 124). The big difficulty with the personal-selling input, however, is that the labor market is imperfect. The marketing manager cannot order energetic salesmen with specific skills with the ease and precision that his counterpart in manufacturing can order raw materials.

Until actual performance data come in, the marketing manager can only guess at the marginal value of his sales force. When performance data become available, he can invoke the rule of proportionality to determine the optimum size of his sales department and the allocation of his compensation budget between salaries and each of his incentive programs.

RECRUITMENT AND SELECTION

Methods of recruiting salesmen vary so much between industries and firms that generalization is difficult. Obviously, the Woolworth Company faces a much different problem in finding sales clerks than IBM does in locating computer salesmen. Even within the same industry, the optimum approach to recruiting will vary considerably with the size of the firm. A company with a large sales staff might easily justify maintaining a team of professional recruiters, while a small competitor might find it far more economical to use an employment agency.

Employee referrals, other departments, other companies, employment agencies, colleges, advertising, walk-in applicants, and professional associations are the most common sources of job candidates. The present sales staff is often the best source of applicants, especially when the turnover of employees is low and morale is high.

The selection of candidates from the prospects provided by the recruiting programs usually involves a number of steps. First, the applicants are screened on the basis of appropriate selection criteria that eliminate candidates who do not meet the minimum requirements. Education, experience, age, and citizenship are common criteria. Information of this kind can be obtained informally, usually from a brief application form, a telephone conversation, or a short face-to-face interview. The objective of this preliminary screening is to reduce the candidates to a manageable number.

The surviving applicants are subjected to a more thorough inquiry, which may involve an in-depth exploration of their education, experience, and past performance. A detailed application form and a personal interview are useful here. For sales clerks and casual (part-time) help this may suffice, and the applicant can be accepted or rejected at this stage.

When compatibility, technical competence, or aptitude is important, or when an expensive company training program is involved, a third step is in order. This step involves the confirmation of the previous information and judgments and usually a precise evaluation of the candidate. Often, a psychological evaluation is made of the applicant, his references are checked, aptitude or proficiency tests are administered, and in-depth interviews are conducted by personnel specialists or the candidate's prospective supervisor. Finally, to obtain the caliber of person normally associated with professional sales, the firm will usually have to sell itself to the potential employee. This may mean plant visits, discussions with key executive personnel, or social gatherings involving the candidate and his wife and key personnel employed by the firm and their wives.

Tests. Testing is used extensively in the selection of sales personnel. The tests given fall into two broad categories—aptitude and skills. The first type attempts to measure the applicant's ability to learn and to adapt to the needs of the job and is concerned with intellectual, psychological, and social traits. The second measures specific skills or knowledge. The objective of both types of tests is to predict the candidate's probability of success on the job.

There are a variety of consulting firms and an inexhaustible supply of college professors and practicing psychologists that will happily design, adapt, or administer tests, for a varying range of fees. These tests may be either general or specialized, in order to conform to the needs of particular industries or firms. An example of tests tailored to special interests is the "Aptitude Index Battery" prepared by the Life Insurance Agency Management Association for insurance firms. It consists of a personal history section (90 items), a section on interests and attitudes (150 items), a trait-preference section (40 items), and a section measuring knowledge of insurance (30 items). Weights are assigned to each item, and a weighted score is computed for each section. These are aggregated to yield a composite score for the whole test. This score—called the "Aptitude Index"—is then used as a predictor of the applicant's success and as a device for ranking prospective salesmen.[6]

More general tests are also available. Examples are the "Otis Self-Administering Test of Mental Ability" and the "Army General Classification Test," which measure intelligence; the "Strong Vocational Interest Test" and the "Kuder Preference Record," which define areas of interest; and the "Minnesota Multiphasic Personality Inventory Test" and the "Bernreuter Personality Inventory Test," which reveal personality types and identify abnormalities. In addition, special subject tests such as the "Cox Mechanical Aptitude" and the "College Entrance Examination Board" tests in mathematics, English, language, physics, and so forth, all evaluate particular aptitudes and skills.

[6] D. Maynard Phelps and J. Howard Westing, *Marketing Management,* 3d ed. (Homewood, Ill.: Irwin, 1968), p. 653.

The validity of tests as predictors of performance depends not only on the tests themselves, but on how they are carried out and their relevance to the job. Whether a test actually measures those personal qualities that will determine the applicant's success will be influenced by the choice and design of the test; how it is administered, scored, and interpreted; and how performance standards are defined.

Not the least of the problems encountered in this area is the manipulation of the test scores by the applicant to conform to his perception of the profile or stereotype desired by the employer. Interest and personality tests are often susceptible to such manipulation. As *Fortune* editor William Whyte suggested in his classical exposition of life in the American business community:

The important thing to recognize is that you don't win with a good score: you avoid a bad one. . . . Your safety lies in getting a score somewhere between the 40th and 60th percentiles, which is to say, you should try to answer as if you were like everybody else is supposed to be. . . . When asked for word associations or comments about the world, give the most conventional, run-of-the-mill, pedestrian answer possible. To settle on the most beneficial answer to any question, repeat to yourself:

(a) I love my father and my mother, but my father a little bit more.
(b) I like things pretty well the way they are.
(c) I never worry much about anything.
(d) I don't care for books or music much.
(e) I love my wife and children.
(f) I don't let them get in the way of company work.[7]

Trained personnel are necessary to carry out employee-selection testing. Special skills, particularly a knowledge of statistics, are also needed in the validation of these tests (that is, in determining whether the tests actually measure what they purport to measure). The records of previous testers are most helpful in estimating the success probabilities associated with the range of test scores. Success itself must be defined. For instance, the Life Insurance Agency Management Association, which expends considerable effort validating its Aptitude Index rating, defines success as "one-year survival at a production level equal to or greater than the median production for one-year survivors in the agent's company."[8]

Once the success probabilities are estimated and performance standards defined, cut-off scores can be specified. In addition, the firm will know the

[7] William H. Whyte, Jr., *The Organization Man* (New York: Doubleday, 1956), pp. 449–50.
[8] Phelps and Westing, *op. cit.*, p. 653.

number of applicants it must hire to have enough qualified salesmen. For example, if a cut-off score is selected that yields a success probability of .7, then ten applicants must be hired for every seven fully qualified men the company needs on the job. Sometimes only a limited number of applicants can be recruited. In this case, a test-score probability combination must be selected that will yield the needed number of people. The following formula applies:

$$S = \sum_{i=1}^{n} P_i A_i, \text{ where} \tag{20-2}$$

S = number of salesmen needed

P_i = probability of success at test score i

A_i = number of applicants with test score i, and

i = test score, or range of test scores

If the sales manager knows the underlying distribution of test scores, he can compute the number of applicants that must be recruited to meet his staffing requirements. The relative success of a given group of people at almost anything—be it high-jumping, typing, or mathematical computation—can be approximated by the normal (Gaussian) curve, with values distributed symmetrically about the mean, μ. For example, if test scores are plotted on the X-axis and the number of applicants on the Y-axis, the points showing the number of applicants achieving a given score will plot as a bell-shaped curve, similar to Figure 20.3.

If the mean and standard deviation of the test scores are available (either from the agency that developed the test or from test data acquired by the

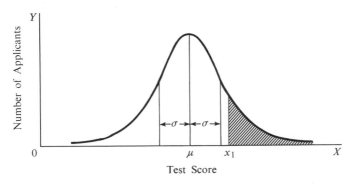

FIGURE 20.3
Normal distribution of test scores

firm), then each potential employee can be objectively rated. For example, assume that the firm uses a standardized test that has yielded normally distributed scores with a mean, μ, of 100 and standard deviation, σ, of 16. (These values are typical of I.Q. tests.) If an applicant had a test score, x_1, of 120, his ranking could be determined as follows:

$$z = \frac{x_1 - \mu}{\sigma}, \text{ where}$$

z = number of standard deviations between the mean and the applicant's score

x_1 = applicant's test score

μ = mean score for the test, and

σ = standard deviation for the test

Substituting the appropriate values, we have:

$$z = \frac{x_1 - \mu}{\sigma} = \frac{120 - 100}{16} = \frac{20}{16} = 1.25 \qquad \text{By substitution and arithmetic}$$

Probability of $z \geq 1.25 = .1056$ From Table I in Appendix II[9]

Thus the applicant would rank in the top 10.56 percent of the population.

The mean, μ, and standard deviation, σ, of test scores for a given class of applicants are usually provided with the tests. If not, they will have to be computed later from the test scores accumulated by the firm. The success probabilities of particular scores will vary among firms. However, the industry's experience can be used as a guide until the company accumulates enough employee data to compute its own values.

Another method is to give the tests to the present members of the staff to see how well they discriminate between marginal, satisfactory, and outstanding salesmen. If test scores have a high correlation with on-the-job performance, the tests are valid and the scores can be used to distinguish between different grades of applicants. However, there is one danger in this method. The bias introduced by the sample population, which presumably consists of competent employees, makes it uncertain that the test will identify the ill-qualified applicants. Only the actual testing of applicants will show this. Even then, the firm cannot be sure that it is not rejecting a disproportionate number of qualified people unless it is willing to hire, or can otherwise follow the history of, a sample of applicants with low scores.

[9] See p. 657. Appendix II contains a detailed explanation of normal distribution and the use of the z statistic.

TRAINING

Whether training is a rational expenditure of marketing resources depends on the availability of qualified salesmen and the complexity of both the product and the market. Even if the sales staff is already knowledgeable and skillful, the net marginal cost of training may still be exceeded by the net marginal revenues that result from the increased efficiency it induces.

If a training program can be tried on one segment of the sales staff, an "experimental group," and the resultant change in the output of the salesmen can be observed, net marginal revenue and marginal cost values can be computed. At that time, a decision to drop the program or extend it to the entire sales force can be made.

One subtlety that eludes many sales managers is the cost relationship between training, compensation, and recruitment. Training can be expensive, since often salaries must be paid to both instructors and trainees during the learning period—a period that qualified salesmen would be using to produce revenues. Hence, it may be cheaper to increase salaries or commissions in order to attract and maintain competent personnel. Ironically, many firms spend heavily on recruitment and training only to later lose these qualified people because of a noncompetitive compensation program. This is a wasteful allocation of promotional resources and may place the firm in the position of operating a training program for its competitors.

PERFORMANCE

On the surface, evaluating the sales force seems easy—one simply counts the sales. However, sales may also be the result of the other marketing variables, and personal selling may play a minor role. In many cases, a salesperson simply performs the clerical function of order-taking. Hence the evaluation of the aggregate influence of personal selling on revenue can require sophisticated analysis.

The appraisal of the performance of individual salesmen is less difficult. Personnel performance is measured relatively, and standards are usually easy to develop and refine in dealing with salesmen, especially those selling alone. The dollar volume of sales, unit sales, new accounts brought in, percentage increases in sales, and the number of calls made are the common criteria. Often the individual variables are weighted to adjust for differences between territories. For instance, one territory might include a disproportionate number of large accounts, another might be new and require considerable missionary work, and yet another might cover a vast geographical area and require an excessive amount of travel.

The quota is the most common standard for measuring individual performance. The base, or raw, quota is normally the salesman's share of the total potential market. This is derived by estimating the total market, as on page 449, and then adjusting the estimate for the expected market-saturation level and penetration rate. The salesman's quota is that portion of the total forecasted sales represented by the geographical territory, industry, or prospects assigned to him, adjusted for differences in territories. Achieving a quota may be considered a minimum, an average, or an outstanding performance, depending on the likelihood of its attainment. Frequently the quota serves as a threshold in an incentive-compensation program. If the quota is exceeded, a bonus is paid, a commission is paid in addition to the salary, or the commission rate is increased. Strangely, many firms reduce the incremental commission rate as the salesman's total volume becomes unusually large. If these firms were to take a marginal view of the upper increments of sales, they would see that revenues usually increase with a disproportionately small increase in the incremental costs of personal selling. This is because a large portion of the personal-selling cost—for example, supervisors' salaries and office space—often remains fixed in the short run. Thus the increase in net marginal revenue may well exceed the higher commission payments. On this basis, the last increments of sales should be generously rewarded. The compensation program should, if anything, stress the value of added sales, maintaining or increasing the commission rate as total individual sales increase.

Performance evaluation is a prerequisite to resource control in the area of personal selling. Once the standard is determined and actual performances can be compared against it, the sales manager can quickly identify where changes in personnel, assignments, or territories are indicated. The control techniques suggested in Part III are especially useful for this task.

SALESMEN'S EXPENSES

Prudence suggests that the costs incurred by sales personnel in the course of their work should be monitored and controlled. The accounting department will certainly take this view and will probably impose some restrictions, standards, and auditing procedures of its own. However, this seldom relieves the sales manager of responsibility in this area. Expense accounts are drawn against his budget, and, as they grow, the funds available for other promotional uses decrease.

In addition to the fixed rates and rule-of-thumb guidelines covering the more pedestrian aspects of expense accounts, such as mileage allowances, hotel costs, and meals (items for which a limit is usually specified by the accounting department), there are other bases for appraising expenses. One method is to compare output and expenses. As both sales and expenses should be indices of the salesman's level of activity, there should be a rough correlation between a person's output and his expenses. Normally, the two should increase together, at least over a period of time sufficient to average out the day-to-day variations. This is especially true if the relatively fixed costs of maintaining a man on the road—bills for meals, lodging, and transportation—are excluded.

If the sales manager plots individual output (sales) against individual expenses, he should get a series of points that move upward and to the right. Salesmen whose sales/expense points plot in the lower right portion of the diagram (low sales, high expenses) warrant scrutiny. Those in the upper left quadrant (high sales, low expenses) warrant commendation and may be able to contribute constructive suggestions with respect to cost control. Those in the lower left quadrant may be exerting insufficient effort to generate either costs or sales, and may need closer supervision. Those in the upper right quadrant are producing high sales as well as incurring high costs, suggesting that the sales manager should not be too critical of their large expense accounts.

WORK ASSIGNMENTS

The average salesman, unless he is a retail sales clerk, spends most of his time away from his immediate superior. This not only makes supervision difficult but also hampers the feedback of information on how the employee conducts himself, how he uses his time, and how he follows orders. This can be a serious problem, since sales personnel are not known for their proficiency in routing trips, scheduling calls, allocating time, or selecting prospects.

Solutions to this problem vary from abdication of responsibility by the sales manager to rigid control. Abdication is sometimes appropriate when salesmen are on straight commission, especially if they pay their own expenses. Door-to-door selling is usually handled in this manner; only the territory is specified by the sales manager. Rigid control is seldom attempted, since it is both costly and impractical. Besides, sales personnel, both salesmen and sales managers, traditionally are unreceptive to detailed directions and dislike paperwork.

However, the growing complexity of the marketplace has made the haphazard direction of personal selling no longer acceptable for many product classes. Even after territories are assigned and quotas established, salesmen often need direction in the allocation of their personal resources. They frequently need help in arraying prospects, arranging trips, scheduling calls, and distributing their time.

Ranking Prospects. Arraying, or ranking, prospects is usually the most important task in deciding where to assign salesmen, unless the sales potential of all the members of the market population is the same. This is seldom the case. The manner in which prospects are arrayed is normally of paramount importance, particularly when there are more prospects than can be contacted by the sales staff.

Several methods are commonly used to array potential customers. One system is to defer to the judgment of the individual salesmen. This is the easiest approach, but will seldom optimize the use of the sales force. Most salesmen are motivated primarily by their own interests, not those of the firm. As a result, they may tend to concentrate on established accounts or on those with which they have the most pleasant relationships. In addition, salesmen are plagued by the can't-see-the-forest-for-the-trees problem and have neither the time nor the data to thoroughly evaluate the market population. This is a job for management, supported by the marketing-research staff.

A better approach is to rank prospects using estimates of their actual or potential purchases. This method is extremely useful when the firm is entering a new territory or introducing a new product. Sometimes the potential demand can be computed precisely, as is the case with many institutional and industrial products such as hospital supplies, food, chemicals, and steel. Other times proxies must be used to estimate the potential demand. For example, the use of cardboard containers is a function of the industry and the size of the firm. Figures on the consumption of this product by various industries, as well as on the size of each firm in the industry in terms of its dollar volume of business and the number of employees, are readily available. Assuming that consumption is proportional to the size of the firm, employment or sales data can be used as a proxy for estimating the prospect's sales potential.

As experience or research provides additional information, it is possible to estimate the sales potential of each prospect with greater precision. In addition, success probabilities may be estimated that will allow computation of the expected value of the revenue that will result from the personal-selling effort which is directed toward a given prospect. Bayesian methods[10] or statistics on past sales may provide the probabilities for each of the prospects or classes of prospects. Thus, the expected value of revenue becomes the basis for ranking prospects. Expressed mathematically,

$$R_{E_i} = P_i S_i, \text{ where} \tag{20-3}$$

R_{E_i} = expected value of revenue (sales) to be derived from prospect i for a given level of personal selling

P_i = probability of making a sale to prospect i, and

S_i = sales potential of prospect i

---

[10] "Bayesian methods" are a group of statistical techniques used to make subjective estimates of probabilities when there is not enough data available to make objective estimates by classical statistical methods.

Different prospects will require different levels of sales effort to get the same results. This may be due to differences in buying habits, how well-entrenched the competition is, or the location of the customer. Hence it may be helpful to calculate the personal-selling cost incurred to produce a reasonable success probability. This cost is usually the product of the number of calls needed times the cost per call. This cost, C, would include both compensation for the salesman's time and the expenses associated with the sales call. For ranking purposes, a sales-efficiency index can be computed, using the ratio of the expected value of revenue to the personal-selling cost associated with the prospect:

$$I_{S_i} = \frac{R_{Ei}}{C_i}, \text{ where} \tag{20-4}$$

I_{S_i} = index of sales efficiency for prospect i

R_{S_i} = expected value of revenue (sales) from prospect i, and

C_i = cost of personal selling for prospect i

For example, assume that a prospect's consumption—hence its sales potential, S—of Product A is \$5,000 per year. The sales manager of a firm producing a brand of product A estimates that his salesman in that territory has a 50–50 chance of selling to this prospect. Four separate calls are normally needed to get an order or to confirm that the prospect is very unlikely to buy the brand. These calls will cost the firm \$80 apiece. The prospect would be evaluated as follows:

$R_{E_i} = P_i S_i$ Given

$R_{E_i} = .5(5,000)$ By substitution

$R_{E_i} = 2,500$ By arithmetic

$I_{S_i} = \dfrac{R_{Ei}}{C_i}$ Given

$I_{S_i} = \dfrac{2,500}{320}$ By substitution

$I_{S_i} = 7.82$ By arithmetic

If the index of sales efficiency, I_{s_i}, for a given prospect, i, is greater than the ratio between the net marginal revenue and the marginal selling cost required to assure coverage of all other marginal costs (that is, the production and distribution of the goods sold), then the prospect should be included, even if the sales force must be expanded. In other words, as long as I_{s_i} is larger than the net marginal revenue–marginal cost ratio, serving the ith customer will increase profit. However, if a constraint is imposed on the decision—for instance, if the number of salesmen or the personal-selling budget is limited—then the index should be used to rank prospects. The sales force would then be assigned to each prospect, starting with the first (who would have the highest I_{s_i}) and continuing down the list until the sales force was fully utilized.

Established Accounts vs. Unsold Prospects.   Another method of allocating personal-selling resources is to make an arbitrary or intuitive division of the salesmen's time between established accounts and unsold prospects. Sometimes this is necessary to force salesmen to devote adequate time to missionary work, the benefits of which are not immediate. The two classes of buyers can then be arrayed in their respective categories on the basis of one of the criteria described earlier. It is difficult to mix the rankings of the two groups, since a great deal may be known about an established account, and very little about an unsold one. Also, the probabilities of success are quite different for established customers and unsold prospects. Yet the latter should not be neglected unless their expected revenue is below the total marginal cost of selling to them.

Dividing the market population into these two categories and aggregating their respective expected revenues is also helpful in designing the advertising strategy. For example, when the established customers clearly outweigh the unsold prospects in importance, the advertising should stress brand loyalty. This condition would also indicate a need for product differentiation in order to discourage the present buyers from generalizing the product and thereby switching to a competitive brand. This strategy is especially relevant in markets where the dominant firm faces competition from lower-priced substitutes.

Routes, Schedules, and Time.   Questions of the routing and scheduling of salesmen's travel and the distribution of salesmen's time between prospects are best dealt with collectively once the market population has been evaluated and arrayed. Operations research, linear programming, and regression analysis can be used to handle more complex problems. However, common sense will often suffice to resolve many conflicts in routes, schedules, or time.

When appointments are required, the customers will often make the schedule decisions and a travel agent will take care of the routing. Hopefully, the amount of time spent traveling and waiting will not be excessive. In many cases, the salesman can use this non-selling time to plan new calls, prepare orders, and write reports. How a salesman distributes his time with respect to the number of calls he makes on various classes of prospects is a different matter. The quantity of calls made on a buyer is usually governed by the salesman. The number of appointments he requests and the number of uninvited visits he makes are up to him, or his boss. Some guidance in this area may help him to optimize his call frequency.

One possibility is to tally the number of calls that are made on each prospect to the point where a sale is consummated. By grouping the prospects by class, the average number of calls required for a sale, and their distribution, can be calculated. It is then easy to plot the success probability associated with a given number of calls. Where the improvement in the success probability resulting from an additional call is very small, no additional call should be made and the prospect should be labeled a "no sale."

Although personal selling lends itself to direct measures of sales effectiveness, a successful personal-selling program must take into account subjective factors, such as the characteristics of individual salesmen, as well as their objective performance ratings. The management of personal selling, like that of advertising, is simply another aspect of resource allocation. To fully utilize this promotional resource, the firm must allocate its sales force wisely and assures its efficient performance through skillful control and personal motivation.

Summary of Promotion Decisions

Promotion—advertising and personal selling—is used to shift the demand curve for a product by influencing buyer tastes. The prospect is led from ignorance through awareness, interest, and desire, and hopefully, across the decision threshold to the purchase point. Creativity and imagination are more important in promotion than in any other area of marketing, yet this instrument also lends itself to many of the techniques of optimization used in allocating resources and evaluating performance.

Promotion has only one goal—to increase or maintain sales. Unfortunately, the promotional mix is often so complex that the sales effect of a particular decision, especially advertising, cannot be measured directly. Hence the marketer must measure the degree of awareness, the interest, or the attitude of prospective customers as proxies of the instrument's ultimate effect on sales. This lack of precision is also reflected in the common methods of advertising budgeting, where a percentage-of-sales, spend-all-you-can, spend-nothing, task-alternative-cost, or competitive-parity approach or Peckham's formula is often substituted for analytic methods, especially when the latter require information that is beyond the reach of the decision-maker.

Given the constraints, especially budget constraints, imposed on this marketing function, suboptimization techniques are often appropriate, especially in media selection. Although the possible media-mix combinations number in the thousands, geographical, demographic, and institutional considerations, as well as promotional objectives, will generally reduce the number of appropriate mixes to a manageable few. Quantitative media-selection methods may then be invoked to determine the distribution of the advertising budget.

Personal selling, like advertising, is undertaken to increase or maintain sales. The sales staff may also perform the yeoman function of order-processing. Salesmanship—analogous to the creativity input in advertising—is a mixture of personality and learned skills. It is part of the personal-selling mix, which includes sales-force size, territories, compensation, recruitment and selection, training, performance, salesmen's expenses, and work assignments.

Marginal analysis and the rule of proportionality serve to optimize the total budget and distribute it in the right proportions among the various elements of the personal-selling mix. However, since budgetary and other constraints operate here too, the marketer must often make suboptimum decisions.

466

The size of the sales force may be determined by marginal analysis (which gives the ideal size), the sales potential of the market, or the customer population. Territories may be defined by geographical area, industry, or a combination of the two. The allocation of personal selling and other marketing resources among territories may be based on any variable that is an index or proxy of the market size. Common proxies are population (consumer, retailer, wholesaler, or industry), income, retail sales, and special indices such as the buying-power index.

Monetary compensation plans for personal selling range from a flat salary to commission only. Thus personal-selling costs may range from entirely fixed to entirely variable. A salesman's income may be fixed or volatile, depending on whether security or incentive is desired. Bonuses, premium commissions, and prizes are also used to tailor the compensation program to aid specific objectives of the firm, such as the capturing of new accounts and the achievement of sales goals.

Recruitment-and-selection practices vary considerably, depending on the technical requirements of the job and size of the firm. Referrals, other departments, other companies, employment agencies, colleges, advertising, walk-ins, and professional associations are common sources of applicants. Candidates may be subjected to single or multiple interviews, reference checks, and one or more tests. The tests range from general-intelligence tests to measures of aptitude, personality, and specific skills. Training may be given to reinforce the skills of qualified salesmen or to qualify unskilled personnel. The marginal increase in performance due to training, the availability of previously trained applicants, and cost are the determining factors.

Performance evaluation is essential to control. Sales is the obvious criterion for personal selling, but standards may have to be adjusted for differences in territories. In the short run, percentage increases in sales, the number of new accounts brought in, or the number of calls made may be more appropriate criteria. Salesman's expenses and work assignments also warrant monitoring and control. The extent to which this is necessary varies with the complexity of the market and the independence of the salesmen.

Questions and Problems

1. Cite and briefly describe an example of each of the following types of advertising strategies: (a) a campaign that departs from the norm, (b) a "me too" campaign, and (c) a campaign based solely on psychogenic appeals.
2. What role might advertising play in each of the following situations, and how might the advertising budget be determined? (a) The introduction of a new sports car, (b) the opening of a new regional market by a mail-

order house, (c) the sustaining of the market share of Avon cosmetics.

3. A new brand of gasoline is to be introduced into the West Coast market. The firm's advertising agency estimates that $2 million per year is being spent to advertise automobile fuels in the three western states by the established competitors. The firm has set its production capacity and is building service stations to handle 10 percent of the industry's sales in this market. How large a budget should the advertising director request to cover the first year in this market?

4. Assume that the variable cost and the optimum price of a convenience good are $1 and $2, respectively, and that the number of units that will be sold annually for a given advertising expenditure, A, equals $10,000 + 4,000 \ (\log_{10} A)$. What is the optimum yearly advertising allocation?

5. Sales of Product B have been running at a consistent, but disappointing, rate of 1,200 units per week in the Dallas SMSA, in spite of a continuous and expensive advertising outlay. Management decides it is uneconomical to continue its campaign and cancels its Dallas advertising. If experience indicates a sales-decay rate of .2, what sales might be forecast for the Dallas market ten weeks later?

6. A regional sales manager has been directed to submit a quarterly advertising budget for Product B, which sells for $100. Knowing that he will be allotted 500 units per week, that the market-saturation point is 600 units, that the sales-response constant is 30, and that the sales-decay constant is .3, how large do you think his budget should be?

7. Select four specific advertising media for each of the following products, and defend your choices: (a) Rolex watches, (b) Gerber's baby food, and (c) IBM 360 computers.

8. Suggest a proxy variable for estimating the effectiveness of each of the following advertisements: (a) a Cadillac ad in the *Wall Street Journal*, (b) an ad for this textbook in the *Journal of Marketing,* and (c) a spot commercial for Listerine toothpaste, to be shown simultaneously on three network television shows.

9. Three media have proven especially effective in promoting Product D. Regression analysis of their effect on revenue has revealed the following relationship between revenue, R, and expenditures, A_i, for each medium:

$$R = 1,000,000 + 8,000 \ (\log_{10} A_1) + 6,000 \ (\log_{10} A_2)$$
$$+ 2,000 \ (\log_{10} A_3)$$

Determine the optimum budget for each medium, assuming a variable cost of $2 and a price of $9.

10. a. Suggest a personal-selling program for each level in the distribution system for (a) *Life* magazine, (b) General Electric appliances, and (c) Cincinnati milling machines.

b. Outline a method for determining the sales-force size at each level in the distribution system for each firm.

c. How should each of the firms determine its sales territories for each level of its distribution system?

d. How should the sales personnel of each firm be compensated at each level of distribution?

11. Suggest a recruitment-and-selection program (including tests) for the sales department of each of the following companies: (a) New York Life Insurance Company (b) IBM, and (c) Encyclopedia Americana, Inc.

12. Experience has shown a firm that candidates for its sales position have an unacceptably low probability of success if they score lower than 80 points on a particular aptitude examination. The mean average of all candidates who have taken the examination in the past is 70, with a standard deviation of 10 points. On the average, how many men must be recruited to assure the firm 10 acceptable candidates for its sales training program?

13. The sales and expense data for ten salesmen for the past year are as follows:

		Sales	Expense
Salesman	1	$20,000	$ 6,000
"	2	50,000	10,000
"	3	45,000	9,000
"	4	60,000	20,000
"	5	40,000	15,000
"	6	25,000	5,000
"	7	30,000	8,000
"	8	5,000	5,000
"	9	8,000	6,000
"	10	10,000	2,500

Evaluate the expenses of salesmen number 2, 3, 5, and 9.

14. How would you rank the following prospects in order to assign a limited quantity of personal-selling resources? Prospect A spends $1 million annually to purchase products of the industry of which the firm is a part; B, C, and D spend $2 million, $.5 million, and $.8 million, respectively. The probability of capturing A's business is .3, while the chances of getting accounts B, C, and D are .1, .9, and .2, respectively.

15. The cost of making a competitive sales presentation to the firms in question 14 is $50,000. If the marginal cost of the goods, exclusive of personal selling, equals 80 percent of their price, which prospects should be selected for the sales presentation? (Assume no budget constraint.)

Supplementary Readings

BOOKS

ANTEBI, MICHAEL, *The Art of Creative Advertising* (New York: Reinhold, 1968).

BOGART, LEO, *Strategy in Advertising* (New York: Harcourt, Brace & World, 1967).

DAVIS, KENNETH R., and WEBSTER, FREDERICK E., JR., eds., *Readings in Sales Force Management* (New York: Ronald Press, 1968).

————, *Sales Force Management* (New York: Ronald Press, 1968).

MCMURRY, ROBERT N., and ARNOLD, JAMES S., *How to Build a Dynamic Sales Organization* (New York: McGraw-Hill, 1968).

SALES MANPOWER FOUNDATION, *Cost of Selling Survey of the Country's Fifteen Major Manufacturing Industries* (New York: Sales Executive Club of New York, 1968).

STANSFIELD, RICHARD H., *The Dartnell Advertising Manager's Handbook* (Chicago: Dartnell Corporation, 1969).

U. S. Department of Commerce, *Measuring Markets: A Guide to the Use of Federal and State Statistical Data* (Washington, D. C.: U. S. Government Printing Office, 1966).

WEINBERG, ROBERT S., "Developing an Advertising Planning Procedure: An Econometric Approach," in Association of National Advertisers, *How Much to Spend for Advertising* (New York: Association of National Advertisers, 1969), pp. 47–66.

ARTICLES

COTHAM, JAMES C., III, "Job Attitudes and Sales Performance of Major Appliance Salesmen," *Journal of Marketing Research,* Vol. 5, No. 4 (November 1968), pp. 370–75.

DIETZ, W. STEPHENS, "Ads Are Changing with Public Moods," *Advertising Age,* Vol. 40, No. 19 (May 12, 1969), p. 51.

————, "Which Way Do You Go in Today's Confusing Ad Scene?" *Advertising Age,* Vol. 40, No. 21 (May 26, 1969), p. 66.

GENSCH, D. H., "Computer Models in Advertising Media Selection," *Journal of Marketing Research,* Vol. 5, No. 4 (November 1968), pp. 414–24.

KUEHN, A. A., "How Advertising Performance Depends on Other Marketing Factors," *Journal of Advertising Research,* Vol. 2, No. 1 (March 1962), pp. 2–10.

LAVIDGE, ROBERT J., and STEINER, GARY A., "A Model for Predictive Measurements of Advertising Effectiveness," *Journal of Marketing,* Vol. 25, No. 6 (October 1961), pp. 59–62.

MONTGOMERY, D. B., and WEBSTER, F. E., JR., "Application of Operations Research to Personal Selling Strategy," *Journal of Marketing,* Vol. 32, No. 1 (January 1968), pp. 50–57.

PRAHALIS, C. P., "Personality Tests Are a Joke Because—," *Sales Management,* Vol. 102, No. 1 (January 1, 1969), pp. 35–37.

ROMAN, M. D., "Empathy, Key to Salesmanship," *Advanced Management Journal,* Vol. 33, No. 2 (April 1968), pp. 27–30.

SCHWARTZ, DAVID, "Measuring the Effectiveness of Your Company's Advertising," *Journal of Marketing,* Vol. 33, No. 2 (April 1969), pp. 20–25.

SEMLOW, WALTER J., "How Many Salesmen Do You Need?" *Harvard Business Review* (May–June 1959), pp. 126–32.

SIMON, J. L., "A Simple Model for Determining Advertising Appropriations," *Journal of Marketing Research,* Vol. 2, No. 3 (August 1965), pp. 285–92.

Part IX

MARKETING RESEARCH

Marketing research is defined by the American Marketing Association as "the systematic gathering, recording and analyzing of data about problems relating to the marketing of goods and services."[1] Marketing research was used as early as two millennia before the birth of Christ, when the merchants of Rhodes queried the travelers of the Aegean Sea about the markets and products of Athens and Corinth. Only in the twentieth century, however, and especially after World War II, has it become a significant variable in the marketing mix.

Marketing research has emerged as an important instrument of commerce for several reasons. First, important marketing decisions are frequently made by executives who are far removed from their markets and have little or no personal contact with their present or potential customers. Second, the technological revolution has vastly increased the number and complexity of marketing alternatives, especially with respect to the product variable. Third, the frequency and cost of failure have increased. Today, more than ever, the cost of a bad decision may be financial disaster. Many new products are extremely expensive to design, manufacture, and introduce and are not divisible into small increments that would permit the firm to enter the market gradually and withdraw quickly should the item fail to sell.

[1] Ralph S. Alexander, *Marketing Definitions* (Chicago: American Marketing Association, 1961), p. 16.

473

The proliferation of innovations, the rapid changes in consumer preferences, and the high mortality rate of new products have made systematic and analytical decision-making often imperative. Fourth, and perhaps most important, the marketer now has available the resources, equipment, and techniques for the acquisition, reduction, and rigorous analysis of market information.

Marketing research is not, except to the academician and consultant, an end in itself; it is justified only to the extent that it materially enhances the decision process. A marketing research program does not design, produce, distribute, or sell anything; it is valuable only because it increases the probability of success in the market for those who do perform these functions. Marketing research may use the inferential tools of statistics, probability theory, calculus, linear programming, econometrics, game theory, or the behavioral sciences. The end result may be a systematic description and classification of data or a hypothesis for future analysis and testing. It may be an equation or a system of equations (a mathematical model) that explains the relationship between variables. Or, it may be a verbal statement about the properties of a market or the behavioral pattern of a group of consumers.

Marketing research may affect the marketing decision at any stage. First, it may be needed to define the problem. For instance, if sales suddenly decline, the firm needs to know why before it can take action. Is it because the product is poor, because tastes have changed, or because a competitor has lowered his price? Or is it the result of a distribution or promotional problem? Second, research may be necessary to define alternative courses of action. If the problem is a drop in the price of competing goods, what strategies can be used to nullify the competitors' advantage? Third, research may be used to predict the consequences of alternative strategies by specifying the relationship between sales and the variables involved in each option. Finally, research may serve to test a decision in the marketplace. A typical strategy, such as a price cut, can be tried under controlled conditions in a limited test market before a final decision is made. Research cannot replace good executive judgment, but it is an important factor in effective decision-making when a complex of variables is involved.

CHAPTER 21

Types of Marketing Research

Marketing research can be divided into functional categories, according to the ends it serves, or into methodological categories, according to the techniques it employs. We shall examine the functional subdivisions first.

FUNCTIONAL CATEGORIES

There are three functional categories of marketing research: (1) descriptive research, (2) causal research, and (3) predictive research.

Descriptive research seeks to define its subject, which may be a market, an industry, a customer, a marketing channel, or anything else relevant to a particular decision. It attempts simply to state the "what" and "where" of things, without explaining "why." It may describe the size or geographical limits of a market, the number and size of competitors in an industry, the purchasing habits of a customer or class of customers, or the type of middlemen in a marketing channel. It may reveal the quantity of goods sold in a market, the prevailing prices, the amount of advertising used by competitors, or the order of consumer preferences. It will not explain why x number of units were sold, why y dollars is the prevailing price, what quantity of sales is due to advertising, or why one model outsells another. This is the task of causal research.

Descriptive research is usually a prerequisite to causal research. It provides the raw data for subsequent analytic work and may indicate the type of methodological research needed. When it performs this latter function, it is often called *exploratory research*.

Causal research is used to specify the relationships between variables. Sales (or revenue) is the most common dependent variable. The independent variables may include any endogenous or exogenous factor that influences sales. The endogenous variables (those that can be manipulated by the firm) are the product, price, promotion, and distribution instruments and their various elements. The exogenous variables (those generally outside the control of the firm) are ordinarily population, consumer income, consumer tastes, the prices of complementary and substitute products, and the marketing action of competitors.

To incorporate all the factors that in some way ultimately affect sales into a causal model would be a highly impractical and expensive task, if not impossible. A more practical approach is to confine the analysis to those variables that can be influenced by the firm. Most business decisions are suboptimum, involving only one or two variables and a small number of realistic alternatives. Thus, the number of factors that must be considered in the decision model is normally quite manageable.

Predictive research is used to forecast future values, particularly product demand. Knowledge of the aggregate demand function of the industry, the demand of a particular market segment, or the demand for the firm's brand is often critical to planning and the allocation of resources.

In order to predict the value of a dependent variable, the values of the independent variables must also be forecast, along with any changes in parameters that may occur with time. Some independent variables—such as adult populations and GNP—can be predicted with a reasonable degree of accuracy. Others—such as the consumption of a secondary or complementary good, consumers' leisure time, and tastes—can be very difficult to predict. Aside from instances where a simple mechanical extrapolation can be made, the prediction of future values places a heavy demand on both the technical skills and the imagination of the researcher. The development of the predictive model begins during the descriptive stage of marketing research and takes more definite form in the causal stage. Both stages are prerequisites to the design and application of a predictive model.

All decisions—whether they are made by individuals, firms, or governments—involve the following processes: (1) defining the problem, (2) describing the options (possible courses of action), (3) predicting the consequences of each option, (4) establishing criteria for judging the consequences, (5) ranking the alternatives according to how well they meet the criteria, and (6) selecting the most promising option.

This is precisely the approach we have used in the examples in this text. For instance, in the application of the risk model discussed on page 140, the problem was defined as the need to maximize the effect of the promotion variable. Three courses of action were described and their possible outcomes predicted; probabilities were then assigned to each. The expected value of profit was chosen as the relevant criterion, and the alternatives were arranged accordingly. The selection—that is, the final decision—was then obvious. In this example, the decision process was fairly simple. It is equally simple in the real world, *if* the model reaches a sufficient level of refinement. The difficulty, however, lies in obtaining the quantitative information that a sufficiently sophisticated model requires. The gathering, reduction, and analysis of the information needed to obtain values for the model can be an extremely difficult and costly task. In the example just discussed, the most difficult task— the stipulation of the outcomes and their probabilities—was neatly avoided by assuming hypothetical values. In the real world, values cannot simply be assumed. They must be estimated, using marketing research as a tool.

DESIGNING A RESEARCH PROGRAM

Research is useful when it makes the marketing decision process more precise, objective, and rational, and hence more efficient. These goals must be kept in mind in designing a research project, and the value of the project should be estimated before resources are spent on its execution.

In setting up a research project, the analyst—or project manager, if a team of researchers is needed—might take the following steps: (1) specify the research objectives, (2) estimate the value of the information to be acquired and analyzed, (3) specify the constraints (time and budget) involved in the program, (4) specify data sources and research methods, and (5) identify the optimum data sources and techniques. This process may be repeated several times if the problem is unique and if the initial research— which may be exploratory—brings to light unexpected opportunities or limitations. The complexity and formality of each step will depend on the magnitude of the marketing decision and the analyst's familiarity with the problem.

Executing a marketing research project is similar in principle to the managing of other projects within the firm. Human and material resources must be assigned, schedules prepared, controls established, and results evaluated. Ultimately, an analysis must be prepared and the results presented to the decision-maker. The project might terminate at that point or provide a guide for additional research.

The design of a research project depends largely on the availability of raw data. Marketing research can be divided into four methodological categories, according to how data is to be obtained. This is true whether the objective of a project is to describe a phenomenon, discover its cause, or predict its consequences.

METHODOLOGICAL CATEGORIES

The four methodological categories of marketing research are: (1) historical research, (2) survey research, (3) experimentation, and (4) motivation research. *Historical research* uses data that has already been recorded in some form. *Survey research* uses data specifically collected for the study, usually obtained by sampling in the marketplace. *Experimentation* uses data from observations made in the marketplace while selected marketing variables are manipulated. *Motivation research* uses the theories and techniques of the behavioral sciences to explain and predict consumer behavior. Each of these categories represents a fundamental method of marketing research. The four methods may be used independently, sequentially, or concurrently. Each has its own unique applications and limits, its own advocates and specialists, and its own cost function.

SCHOOLS OF MARKETING RESEARCH

There are several schools of marketing research, each with its own theorems, techniques, and orientation. The *statistical school* represents the traditional approach. It emphasizes statistics as a descriptive tool and statistical inference as a device for estimating and forecasting values and establishing causal relationships.

The *behavioral school* stresses the behavioral sciences, primarily psychology and sociology. Statistics are occasionally employed, chiefly to support behavioral studies. This approach to market analysis is frequently called "motivation research," or "MR" for short. Because it seeks to explain consumer behavior in terms that will allow the firm to manipulate or exploit this behavior, it is particularly applicable to problems of promotion, especially advertising and packaging. It also provides insight into aesthetic and symbolic aspects of product design. Motivation research became very popular in the early 1950's. Although still common, it has been displaced to some extent by quantitative methods.

The *quantitative school* uses mathematics and statistics to analyze data and quantify relationships between variables, often with the aid of a computer. Its basic tools are differential calculus, linear programming, game theory, probability theory, and econometrics. Its methods are especially applicable to causal and predictive research.

EVALUATING MARKETING RESEARCH

Research, except when it is performed by management-consulting firms, is not a marketable product. It generates cost, but never revenue—at least not directly. It is a means to an end, not an end in itself. When skillfully employed, research increases the probability of selecting the best course of action. It can indicate the probable consequences of the alternatives being considered, reveal new alternatives, and more clearly define the rewards of success and the penalties of failure.

The use of marketing research does not ensure that the marketer will always make the best decision; in fact, in some cases it may lead him to select a suboptimum—and possibly disastrous—alternative. However, research can improve marketing decisions if it is well designed and well executed. If the decision-maker understands and uses the information it provides, he will generally do a better job of selecting alternatives in the manipulation of his marketing instruments. An improvement in decision-making means a more efficient allocation of the firm's resources, hence an improvement in profit— the primary objective of the firm.

Value Analysis.   It is difficult to determine the precise value of a research project. The link between research and profit is seldom clear. The cost of research can usually be determined, but its contribution to cost reduction in the marketing program or to revenue improvement is frequently elusive. Even when the particular service performed by research can be defined—for example, the identification of the characteristics of customers in a given market or the distribution of color and size preferences in a given market population—its ultimate effect on profit may be impossible to specify. For one thing, it is difficult to know how much (if any) influence the marketing-research information has had on the decision process. Often it is ignored. Furthermore, even if it can be shown that marketing research has influenced a decision, we cannot always evaluate the correctness of the choice. Perhaps an alternative decision would have proven more profitable.

Nonetheless, the marketer needs to establish some basis for deciding whether to allocate a portion of his resources to marketing research. Fortunately, it is not always necessary to determine the precise value of a project before deciding to approve a budget for research. An approximation or a qualitative judgment is often adequate, especially when the information is essential or its benefit obvious. Sometimes the marketer will simply accept the need for research on the basis of faith or necessity, without demanding an exact accounting of its benefits. He may buy information because he feels it will improve his decision-making or yield new insights, or because it is essential to the operation of his business. For instance, he may hire an analyst to tally the inquiries about his firm's product received through different advertising media, thus gaining some insight into the productivity of each medium. Or he may join a trade association to get the names and addresses of the wholesalers and retailers in the distribution channel between his firm and its ultimate customers.

Quantitative Evaluation.   The marketer may also decide to use quantitative means (such as probability theory and statistical estimates of the outcomes of various alternatives) to determine the dollars-and-cents value of his marketing research. This method is not always precise, but it does provide a conceptual basis for the appraisal of research. And when adequate data are available, it can yield a very realistic approximation of the actual value of marketing-research information.

In any decision situation, management has two initial options with respect to research: (1) to use it or (2) not to use it. The gross value of the research is the difference between the expected value of the decision with the benefit of research and the expected value of the decision without the benefit of research. The net value is simply the gross value less the cost of the research project. The difficulty in making a quantitative value analysis rests in estimating the probability of each of the outcomes. There are two possibilities. First, the marketer can use Bayesian statistics, in which management estimates are used to establish the probabilities of the outcomes. Second, he can use classical statistics, in which probabilities are estimated using information from past experience. The latter method is useful only when the marketer has records of the results of similar decisions made in the past.

A simple example will illustrate the basic concept of value analysis for marketing research. Suppose that a marketing manager must decide whether to introduce a new product into a market that has a high mortality record (for example, the markets for prepared foods, drugs, toys, and cosmetics). Before he makes his decision, he may wish to authorize a research project—say, an experiment in a test market—that will provide information about how the product is likely to be received if it is introduced on a large scale. Before authorizing the research project, however, he would like to be certain that the value of the project is at least equal to its cost.

For instance, assume that accounting analysis has indicated that a new product's success will yield a profit of $100,000 and that its failure will cost $50,000. Previous new-product marketing programs have indicated that the success probability for a new product that has done well in a marketing research project is .8, while the success probability for new products that did not have such a project is only .4. Finally, the marketing staff estimates that there is a 40-percent chance that the new product will be introduced if a marketing research project is not performed and a 30-percent chance if it is performed. (These initial probabilities reflect the fact that a firm normally cannot introduce all new-product ideas.) The probability of a product being introduced is higher when no research is conducted because of the screening effect of marketing research. That is, marginal products that might be introduced if a marketing research project were not conducted will seldom be introduced if thoroughly evaluated.

After the marketer has established the probabilities for each of the outcomes that can result from the decision to conduct a research project, he can determine the expected value of conducting marketing research by computing the expected values of all possible outcomes. Figure 21.1 presents

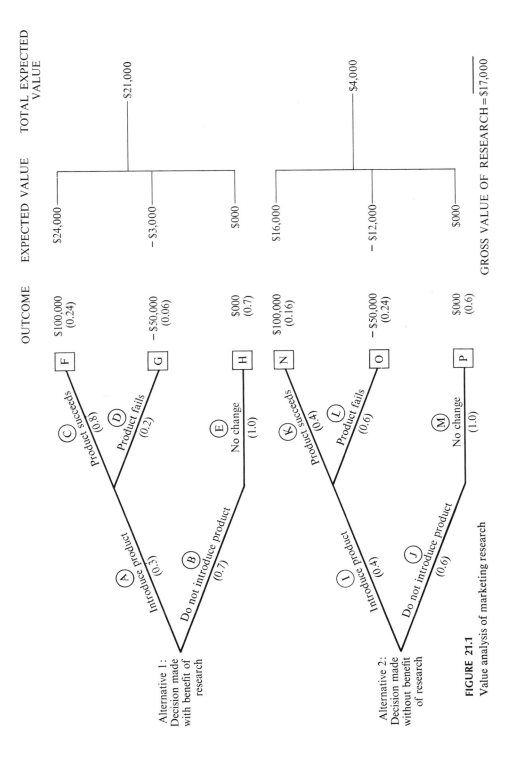

OUTCOME EXPECTED VALUE TOTAL EXPECTED VALUE

Alternative 1: Decision made with benefit of research

A Introduce product (0.3)
B Do not introduce product (0.7)

C Product succeeds (0.8)
D Product fails (0.2)
E No change (1.0)

F $100,000 (0.24) — $24,000
G — $50,000 (0.06) — — $3,000
H $000 (0.7) — $000

$21,000

Alternative 2: Decision made without benefit of research

I Introduce product (0.4)
J Do not introduce product (0.6)

K Product succeeds (0.4)
L Product fails (0.6)
M No change (1.0)

N $100,000 (0.16) — $16,000
O — $50,000 (0.24) — — $12,000
P $000 (0.6) — $000

$4,000

GROSS VALUE OF RESEARCH = $17,000

FIGURE 21.1
Value analysis of marketing research

the decision diagram. As shown in the figure, alternative 1 (decision made with research) has three possible outcomes: F, the product is introduced and is successful, yielding a profit of $100,000; G, the product is introduced and fails, yielding a loss of $50,000; and H, the product is not introduced, yielding a profit of zero. Alternative 2 (decision made without research) has the same possible outcomes, labeled N, O, and P.

Each event in the diagram has a probability (shown in parentheses) associated with it.[1] Some of these are conditional probabilities; that is, they are dependent on the occurrence of previous events. For instance, event C is dependent on event A; obviously, if the product is not introduced, it cannot succeed. Event A has a probability of .3; if event A occurs, event C has a probability of .8. Both events must occur if the outcome of $100,000 profit is to be realized. Hence the probability, P, of making a profit (outcome F) is equal to the probability of event A times the probability of event C; that is, $P(F) = P(A) \times P(C) = .3 \times .8 = .24$. Given the value of outcome F ($100,000) and its probability (.24), the marketer can determine the expected value of outcome F—in this case, $100,000 \times .24$, or $24,000. The same procedure can be used to determine the expected value of each of the other outcomes, as shown in Figure 21.1.

The total expected value of each alternative is equal to the sum of the expected values of its outcomes. Thus alternative 1 has a total expected value of $21,000, and alternative 2 has a total expected value of $4,000. Since the only difference between the two decision processes is the use of marketing research, the difference in their expected values ($21,000 − $4,000) can be attributed to the knowledge provided by the test-market experiment. Thus the gross value of the research is $17,000. The net value of the research, however, is equal to its gross value less its cost, so the marketer must determine the cost of the experiment before he can make a final judgment on its value. Many types of research, especially experimentation in a test market, can be expensive as well as time-consuming. Hence it is possible that the net value will be negative and the research uneconomical. But as long as the cost of the research is less than its gross value (in this case, $17,000), the project should be approved.

Qualitative Evaluation.   The financial benefit of a given piece of research is often so obscure that it cannot be quantified in terms of expected value. For instance, research may be necessary simply to define the problem or to clarify the firm's options. If a firm is planning to expand into another geographical market, a research project will probably be needed to determine the alternative distribution channels. If it is considering extending its product mix by diversifying into a new field through the acquisition of other firms,

[1] The success probabilities were derived through classical statistics, and the probabilities of introduction were derived through Bayesian analysis.

research may be needed to identify and evaluate potential subsidiaries. If it is displeased with the market performance of one of its product lines, research may be necessary simply to define the problem so that an appropriate research project can be designed to help solve it. Often the decision-maker must make a qualitative judgment of the value of such a study versus its cost.

Cost can often be estimated with a fair degree of precision. The exact cost of marketing research can be predicted if an outside consultant is hired on a fixed-price basis. Even when the contract is based on time and materials, total cost is usually predictable within an acceptable range and constrained by a maximum limit. Using consultants also has other advantages. They may be employed only for the term of the project and may therefore represent only variable costs to the firm. They offer the economies of specialization and unique skills. Their lack of involvement with the firm's working organization divorces them from the loyalties, politics, and biases that invariably emerge in a complex social group. Even large firms that have their own research staff will frequently employ consultants to handle overloads, to contribute special skills, or to perform research tasks that management wishes to keep secret.

Marketing research may be centralized under the direction of the firm's marketing manager, or it may be diffused throughout the company. The long-range-planning, engineering, marketing, and legal departments may each perform tasks that could legitimately be called marketing research. These tasks may include the determination of consumer preferences; the estimation or forecasting of demand; the measurement of the market population; the estimation of price elasticity; the specification of the relationship between sales and either advertising, personal selling, or the distribution channels; the evaluation of market performance; the analysis of competition; or the testing of the effectiveness of advertisements or advertising media.

In the following four chapters, we will use the methodological categories of marketing research—historical research, survey research, experimentation, and motivation research—as a framework for discussion. Finally, we will conclude our discussion of marketing research with a chapter on prediction and forecasting—the ultimate objective of every marketing research project.

CHAPTER 22

Historical Research

Historical research uses information that has been previously collected and recorded. This data may be classified as primary or secondary, depending on its source. *Primary data* are facts accumulated by the firm such as sales, cost, credit, and customer information. *Secondary data* are collected by organizations outside the firm, but are available to it. Examples are the income and population statistics provided by the federal government, economic information available from banks, and sales data on competing brands supplied by commercial services.

Historical data is often associated with descriptive research. However, it is frequently the basis for causal analysis and prediction. Some of the most sophisticated mathematical models have been constructed solely from historical data. Likely sources of historical data should be checked during the exploratory phase of a research project. They may offer information that will help define the problem, or lessen the need to gather data in the field. Gathering field data can be time-consuming. It is often far more expensive to obtain than historical data, even when the latter must be purchased from commercial services.

EXTERNAL DATA SOURCES

Recorded data is available from many sources, although the United States government is by far the largest single source. State and local governments, trade associations, commercial research firms, chambers of commerce, financial institutions, publishers, suppliers, customers, and the firm itself are additional sources of recorded data. Most of these organizations and groups supply data at virtually no cost.

Where should the marketing researcher start in his quest for data? While no master index of statistical data has yet been compiled, data-storage-

and-retrieval systems are being developed for many special-interest areas. For example, the several technology-dissemination centers that operate in conjunction with the National Aeronautics and Space Administration offer both literature-survey and information-retrieval services to marketers. The literature-survey service provides an annotated bibliography of publications that relate to the special interests of the client firm. Data-retrieval service is provided on request. When the subscriber has a particular problem, all relevant information is drawn out of the data bank, capsulated, and presented to the client. The system collects information from a variety of sources—current literature, NASA *Tech Briefs,* a number of federal agencies, and private sources.

A less exciting, though more common, approach is to search the prospective information sources manually. As in most research, the initial task is to decide which variables are relevant. For descriptive research, they may be industry or market statistics such as the number, names, and outputs of firms, consumption expenditures, or the locations of consumers. For a causal or predictive study, the variables might be statistics on population, income, prices, advertising expenditures, or product features. One of the limitations of historical data is that often only aggregate statistics are available, except for the information the firm has retained on its own activities. Data on competitors—or, for that matter, on suppliers or customers—is usually scarce except in regulated industries, such as the airlines, distilleries, and public utilities, or industries whose products must be registered, such as the automobile, aircraft, and recreational-vehicle industries.

Libraries, government agencies, trade associations, chambers of commerce, and the firm's own accounting, shipping, and marketing departments are likely data sources. Most libraries offer a number of indices of economic and business source material. The *Statistical Abstract of the United States, Monthly Catalog of U. S. Government Publications, Business Periodical Index, Wall Street Journal Index, New York Times Index, Index of Publications of Bureaus of Business and Economic Research,* and *Readers Guide to Periodical Literature* are all useful and easily obtainable. Two additional works of special interest to marketers are *Measuring Markets: A Guide to the Use of Federal and State Statistical Data* and *Marketing Information Guide.* These publications provide statistical data, qualitative information, and descriptions of methodology.

The most useful federal document is the *Statistical Abstract of the United States.* Others are the *Economic Almanac, Handbook of Economic Statistics, Census of Population, Current Population Reports, Census of Manufacturers, Census of Business, Census of Housing, Economic Report of the President, Survey of Current Business, Federal Reserve Bulletin, Economic Indicators, Business Cycle Developments, Statistics of Income,* and, of special interest, *Facts for Marketers.* These publications are usually available at larger general libraries or from small, specialized reference libraries.

State and local governments also collect and publish useful data, much of which is available at local libraries or directly from the responsible agencies. Retail sales data for various product classes, broken down by county, is usually available in states with sales taxes. A state without a general sales tax will still have data on regulated or registered product classes, such as alcoholic beverages, motor fuel, tobacco products, and highway vehicles.

Libraries normally keep copies of several commercially prepared reference works also. *Moody's* manuals are a family of books that cover industrial firms, the government, transportation companies, financial institutions, and public utilities. These manuals, which are updated annually, contain financial data such as gross sales figures, the names of the executive officers of listed corporations, and the locations of their major facilities, as well as a brief description of the organizations' history and functions. *Standard and Poor* publishes similar material, such as their *Trade and Securities Statistics,* which gives data by industry. *Fortune* magazine publishes directories identifying the largest U. S. and foreign corporations and reporting their sales, assets, net incomes, and rank. These directories are contained in the regular issues of the magazine (domestic industrial corporations, banks, insurance companies, merchandising companies, transportation companies, and public utilities are listed in the June issue; foreign firms are listed in the September issue) and are also published separately. The *Fortune Plant and Product Directory* lists the plants, products, and employee population of the 1,000 largest U. S. industrial firms, which produce well over half our domestic output.

These three sources, *Moody's, Standard and Poor,* and *Fortune,* are useful in analyzing an industry or a market in aggregate terms. They also serve to identify the larger competitors. However, they have several shortcomings. First, the data is seldom broken down by product line. Thus, because of the diversified product mixes of most large corporations, the sales figures are often useless. Second, the information is posted on an annual basis, which restricts its usefulness for short-run time-series analysis. Third, the indices contain data only on publicly held corporations. (Actually, this is seldom a real handicap since large, privately held firms are a rarity in most American industries.)

One commercially published periodical of special interest to marketing researchers is *Sales Management,* which compiles and publishes annually the buying power index and its companion indices described on pages 382–84. Complementing this is *Facts for Marketers,* a Department of Commerce publication that describes the 100 standard metropolitan statistical areas (SMSA's) in dimensions especially important for the definition and estimation of consumer-goods markets. Both documents are available in larger libraries.

Government agencies, particularly regulatory agencies such as the FAA, the FCC, the ICC, and the Maritime Commission, often provide a bonanza of data for the market analyst. Major government departments such as the Department of Commerce (the largest accumulator and publisher of economic and business data in the world), the Department of the Interior, and the Department of Labor all maintain some kind of statistical and research bureaus and are very obliging when queried for information. State and local agencies may also be helpful. Tax commissions, motor-vehicle departments, employment agencies, city manager's offices, and other organizations often give out specialized data that can be directly applied to a given research project or that are needed in designing a research program. For example, the census tract maps available from municipal and county governments are widely used in designing market surveys.

Trade associations frequently have considerable data available on particular industries and markets. For example, *Petroleum Facts and Figures,* published annually by the American Petroleum Institute, is an essential reference work for anyone analyzing the petroleum industry as a market for industrial goods and services or analyzing the petroleum market itself. The marketer can identify and locate trade associations that may be helpful in a particular study by reference to the *Directory of National Trade Associations.*

Chambers of commerce, as well as local, regional, and state development agencies, are potential sources of data on a particular geographical area. Although their information, especially their qualitative material, is often highly biased, it may still be useful to the analyst skillful in identifying the misuse of statistics.[1]

Banks, newspapers, and advertising agencies also offer considerable data on local markets, but their data generally are also published in order to attract business into an area or to sell their services. Suppliers will often provide elaborate market data that can be quite useful, even though it is usually selective.

Commercial data-gathering services provide marketing information on the consumption of selected products and the audiences of certain advertising media. This data is available *ad hoc* but on a recurring basis and can usually be purchased by geographical area and by product or medium class. Data may also be gathered specifically to meet the needs of the client firm. Such firms as Pulse, Inc.; the Opinion Research Corporation; National Family Opinion, Inc.; the Statistical Tabulating Corporation; Market Facts, Inc.; Time, Inc.; the Market Research Corporation of America; and the A. C. Nielsen Company specialize in providing market and media data to client firms. Economies of scale allow these commercial services to provide data on retail sales,

---

[1] See Darrell Huff, *How to Lie with Statistics* (New York: Norton, 1954), for a description of such techniques.

warehouse withdrawals, broadcast coverage, brand market shares, consumer buying patterns, and so on at a cost usually much lower than that which the client firm would incur by gathering such information itself. Most marketing research firms will also provide data-processing services and will assist the client in designing research projects.

INTERNAL DATA SOURCES

The marketer's own firm may have a wealth of useful information. Assuming that the marketing department has not previously arranged for a feedback of relevant data, the firm's accounting department is the likely place to start. Sales figures, advertising and personal-selling expenses, distribution costs, and price histories can provide the necessary inputs for regression analyses, particularly if the data have been collected in a manner that allows time-series or cross-sectional regression analysis. Regression analysis, which is dealt with in Chapter 26, is a fundamental tool of econometrics. Briefly, it allows the analyst to specify the relationship between variables. For example, if adequate data is given, it will reveal how sensitive sales are to changes in price, advertising, or personal-selling programs.

If the firm has a large number of credit accounts, as is usual in the case of large retailers such as department stores, it may have customer data—information on buying habits, income, occupation, family status, and so on—that the researcher can use in analyzing demand and drawing up a customer profile. This approach can be extremely useful in the preparation of a promotional strategy or the manipulation of the product variable (in deciding, for example, what class of goods should be offered).

APPLICATIONS OF HISTORICAL RESEARCH

Having accumulated the historical data on a problem, the researcher must turn to the task of data reduction and analysis. Presumably, the general relationship of the data to the marketing problem was determined before the information was obtained, since the problem dictates the type of data that is needed. However, the researcher may be only vaguely aware when the study is started of the kind of data that is both appropriate and available; thus his initial research may be simply exploratory. Even when sufficient resources are available for the gathering of survey or experimental data and its use for this purpose can be justified by the firm, a search for historical data is often prudent to preclude the duplication of this data by more expensive means. If the field of study is alien to the researcher, he may wish to first

Table 22.1 Public elementary and secondary schools: Enrollment, teachers, and schoolrooms
(States: Fall 1965)

[Fall enrollment data are not directly comparable with enrollment figures given for an entire school year in other tables. Except as noted, schools are classified by type of organization, rather than by grade-group; elementary includes kindergarten; secondary includes junior high schools]

| STATE | PUPILS ENROLLED (1,000) | | CLASSROOM TEACHERS | | | | INSTRUCTION ROOMS | | |
	Elementary	Secondary	Total Elementary	Total Secondary	Teaching under substandard credentials Elementary	Teaching under substandard credentials Secondary	Completed, 1964–65	Abandoned 1964–65	Available and in use, 1965–66
United States	26,416	15,728	967,635	748,650	51,632	30,116	65,200*	16,400*	1,595,150
New England	1,360	825	53,733	41,416	2,279	1,961	2,959	775	84,953
Maine	149	74	5,717	3,416	197	117	728	428	8,802
New Hampshire	83	46	3,239	2,290	147	97	306	44	5,209
Vermont	56	29	2,278	1,605	71	118	152	28	3,529
Massachusetts	616†	405	24,550	20,454	708	764	650	100	38,400
Rhode Island	89†	66†	3,374	3,256	256	165	255	54	5,957
Connecticut	368	207	14,575	10,395	900	700	868	121	23,056
. . .	.	.	.	.	.	.	.	.	.
. . .	.	.	.	.	.	.	.	.	.
Pacific	3,567	2,088	126,976	91,653	6,638	2,850	(NA)‡	1,030	212,866
Washington	402†	321†	15,656	14,196	450	50	410	350	28,940
Oregon	275	174	11,968	8,876	1,050	130	831	170	18,890
California	2,755	1,508	94,500	65,300	5,000	2,500	7,500	400	156,100
Alaska	42	18	1,554	1,127	1	2	116	9	2,339
Hawaii	94†	68†	3,298	2,154	137	168	(NA)‡	101	6,096

* Includes estimate for nonreporting states.
† Kindergarten through grade 6 for elementary and grades 7–12 for secondary.
‡ Not available.

SOURCE: *Statistical Abstract of the United States* (Washington, D. C.: U. S. Government Printing Office, 1966), p. 121.

Table 22.2   Estimated market for corrugated and solid fiber box by industry groups
(Phoenix, Arizona standard metropolitan statistical area, 1962)

SIC Major Group Code	Using Industry	Value of Box Shipments by End Use ($ 000) * 1	Employment by Industry Groups‡ 2	Consumption per Employee by Industry Groups (1÷2) (Dollars) 3	Maricopa County Employment by Industry Groups‡ 4	Maricopa County Estimated Share of the Market (3×4) ($ 000) 5
20	Food and kindred products	586,164	1,578,305	371	4,973	1,845
21	Tobacco	17,432	74,557	233	—	—
22	Textile-mill products	91,520	874,677	104	—	—
23	Apparel	34,865	1,252,443	27	1,974	53
24	Lumber and products (except furniture)	19,611	526,622	37	690	26
25	Furniture and fixtures	89,341	364,166	245	616	151
26	Paper and allied products	211,368	587,882	359	190	68
27	Printing, publishing, and allied industries	32,686	904,208	36	2,876	104
28	Chemicals and allied products	128,564	772,169	166	488	81
29	Petroleum refining and related industries	28,328	161,367	175	—	—
30	Rubber and miscellaneous plastic products	67,551	387,997	174	190	33

31	Leather and leather products	8,716	352,919	24	—	—
32	Stone, clay and glass products	226,621	548,058	413	1,612	666
33	Primary metal industries	19,611	1,168,110	16	2,889	46
34	Fabricated metal products	130,743	1,062,096	123	2,422	298
35	Machinery, except electrical	58,834	1,445,558	40	5,568	223
36	Electrical machinery, equipment and supplies	119,848	1,405,382	391	6,502	553
37	Transportation equipment	82,804	1,541,618	53	5,005	265
38	Professional, scientific instruments, etc	13,074	341,796	38	—	—
39	Miscellaneous manufacturing industries	200,473	369,071	543	376	204
90	Government	10,895	—	—	—	—
	Total	2,179,049†	—	—	—	4,616

* Based on data reported in Fibre Box Association, *Fibre Box Industry Statistics 1963.*

† U. S. Bureau of the Census, *1962 Annual Survey of Manufacturers: General Statistics for Industry Groups and Industries* (M62(AS)-1 Revised), Table 1—General Statistics for Industry Groups and Industries: 1962, 1961, and 1958, p. 10.

‡ U. S. Bureau of the Census, *County Business Patterns, First Quarter 1962,* Parts 1 and 9.

SOURCE: U. S. Department of Commerce, *Measuring Markets: A Guide to the Use of Federal and State Statistical Data* (Washington, D. C.: U. S. Government Printing Office, 1966), p. 51.

familiarize himself with the problems by a historical-data search. Following the completion of this phase, he will be in a much better position to define the problem and to specify what data must be obtained by other means.

In descriptive research, raw data is often adequate. For example, if a publisher needed a basis for the geographical allocation of his promotional and distributional resources for a line of elementary- and secondary-school textbooks, it might use the data in Table 22.1, from the *Statistical Abstract of the United States.*

Table 22.2 shows how historical data can be manipulated to serve a particular purpose. In order to determine the total market potential for corrugated and fiber boxes in the Phoenix SMSA, the firm used the national data contained in *Fibre Box Industry Statistics,* an annual publication of the Fibre Box Association. From this data, it was able to determine the consumption of fiber boxes by each of the SIC major code groups (column 1). Using the Bureau of the Census document *County Business Patterns,* which contains data on the number of employees in each SIC major-code-group industry (column 2), the firm was then able to compute the average consumption of fiber boxes per employee in each major SIC code industry (column 3). It could then estimate the market in the Phoenix area by multiplying the average consumption of fiber boxes per employee times the number of employees in each of the major SIC code industries in that area. (The latter data was also available from *County Business Patterns.*)

Another illustration of the use of historical data for descriptive research was given on page 448 in the discussion of personal selling. The objective in that case was to establish sales territories and quotas. Two federal documents, *County Business Patterns* and the *Census of Business,* provided store-population and retail sales data by county, and these data were used as a basis for establishing territories and sales quotas.

Historical data is also used in causal and predictive research. We shall examine these applications in Chapter 26, after we have learned more about some of the other methodological categories of marketing research.

CHAPTER 23

Survey Research

TYPES OF SURVEYS

Although all surveys are designed to obtain data, they can be divided into two distinct types. An *exploratory survey* is used if the marketer is uncertain of the nature of a problem. He may be aware of symptoms that something is wrong—sales are declining, the firm is unable to penetrate the market or is losing its market share, the firm's bid on a contract is turned down, and so on—but may be ignorant of the underlying cause. An exploratory survey is also appropriate if the marketer is interested in the size and character of a new market or the feasibility of introducing a new product. In some instances, enough information will emerge from an exploratory survey to make a decision possible without further research. The exploratory survey may reveal that a competitor has slashed prices, that the firm's product is not performing as represented, or that a prospective market is presently saturated. Given this sort of information, both the problem and the answer will be obvious. More likely, however, the exploratory survey will provide only enough new information to redefine, or more precisely define, the marketing problem. In this phase of the research project, the objective is to specify the relationships between the significant factors uncovered by the exploration so that predictions can be made, alternatives defined, and solutions recommended.

A *data-collection survey,* on the other hand, is usually undertaken to obtain quantitative answers to a specific set of questions for subsequent use in a research project. In this type of survey, the problem has already been well enough defined so that specific questions can be asked regarding it. Although most surveys include aspects of both types of surveys, the primary purpose of a survey—exploration of the problem area or collection of data on a defined problem—strongly influences its form.

Surveys are generally conducted by mail, by telephone, or by personal interviews. When a *mail survey* is used, a questionnaire is sent to selected respondents. This is the most common type of data-collection survey. However, it has several defects. First, certain classes of respondents, such as retired people, may be more inclined to answer a mail survey, thus introducing a bias into the results. Second, there is usually no way to determine the motives behind the answers. For instance, a brand preference given by a respondent may have significant psychogenic causes that could be discovered only through personal inquiry. Finally, there is generally no way to ascertain whether a respondent understood the question. Mail surveys do, however, have some advantages over telephone surveys and personal interviews. They are generally the least expensive type of data-collection survey. In addition, they prevent the interviewer from guiding the respondent's answer, intentionally or otherwise, and thus biasing the data. Finally, if the questionnaires are anonymous, the respondent may be less hesitant about giving truthful answers to psychologically loaded questions.

Telephone surveys or *personal interviews* are preferable for exploratory surveys. These techniques enable the interviewer to ensure that the questions are properly understood and (if he is skilled) to probe for the motives behind the respondents' answers. The latter advantage is significant in an exploratory survey, since at this point the marketer seldom knows the primary factors influencing the problem under study. In addition, an interview or telephone call is more open-ended and less structured than a mail inquiry—a useful characteristic for exploratory studies. Often, the interviewer's approach is to induce the respondent to discuss topics that relate to the marketing problem —such as his reasons for rejecting a product, preferring a particular brand, or shopping in a particular store—in the hope that the respondent will reveal a factor that has previously eluded the researchers.

The unit cost—that is, the cost per respondent—of telephone surveys is higher than that of mail surveys, and personal interviews are more costly than either. Hence the sample size must be reduced or the budget increased as the researcher progresses from mail survey to telephone survey to personal interview. The designer of the research project must weigh the advantages of telephone surveys and personal interviews (flexibility and in-depth inquiry) against those of mail surveys (economy and larger sample size). The objectives of the study and the availability of resources will largely determine the method he chooses.

POPULATION SURVEYS

Surveys can be further categorized as *population surveys* or *sample surveys.* A *population* is a set of elements with a given characteristic in common.[1] For example, a market population might be defined as all teenage girls, the

[1] The terms "population" and "universe" are often used interchangeably. To avoid confusion, we shall use the word "universe" here to refer only to the *total* set of ele-

inhabitants of a particular standard metropolitan statistical area, all domestic commercial-aircraft manufacturers, or the U. S. Post Office. The first market population cited would have millions of members, or "elements," the second would have hundreds of thousands of elements, the third would have only three, and the last would have only one. A population survey is a survey that gathers data from *each* element in a population. This provides a precise and statistically reliable description of the population with respect to the variable being measured—perhaps its color preferences, its purchasing habits, its material requirements, or its expectations regarding product performance.

Unfortunately, a population survey is normally outside the realm of fiscal and physical possibility. A shoe manufacturer can hardly ask every teenage girl what her favorite colors are, nor can a dairy contact every household in its market area to determine exactly how many prefer to have milk delivered, rather than purchasing it at a store. Although population surveys are practical for a number of industrial goods—Alcoa, for instance, could poll every airframe manufacturer on its aluminum needs—they are out of the question for most consumer goods.

SAMPLE SURVEYS

An alternative to surveying an entire population is to survey a sample of the population, and to infer the characteristics of the entire group from the information obtained from a few members. For example, the shoe manufacturer might send questionnaires to 1,000 teenage girls asking them what their favorite shoe color is. If half of the respondents said "black," the manufacturer might assume that 50 percent of its potential customers (the market population) preferred black shoes and design its product line accordingly. The dairy might send an interviewer to canvas a community. If he reported that 85 percent of the housewives queried preferred home delivery of their dairy products, the firm might allocate the bulk of its resources to promoting home-delivery service and design its distribution system accordingly.

However, these conclusions about the teenage girl and household populations could easily be erroneous if the two samples were not representative of the populations from which they were drawn. Chance may have led the shoe manufacturer to five hundred girls who preferred black, while possibly only 30 percent of the population as a whole would have chosen that color. The dairy survey could have been biased by the time of the visits if they were made during working hours, since this would exclude households where both husband and wife were employed from the sample. The purchasing

ments. Thus a universe may contain several populations. For example, a universe could be defined as "all residents of the United States" and as containing 50 populations (consisting of the residents of each of the fifty states). This distinction will become important when we discuss stratified sampling.

habits of these households might be considerably different from those where wives stayed at home.

Despite the likelihood of error, the marketer may have no other alternative than to rely on a sample survey. Population surveys are often an impractical alternative and historical data may not exist. Experimentation may be impossible or unacceptable for any of several reasons. While errors due to sampling cannot be eliminated, there are methods for minimizing the possibility of error and also for determining its magnitude. An essential tool is the use of random sampling.

RANDOM SAMPLES

A *random sample*—also called a "probability sample"—is one in which every element in the population has an equal, or "known," probability of being selected. For example, if the teenage-girl population in the United States is 30,000,000 and 1,000 questionnaires are to be mailed, each girl must have a probability of 1 in 30,000 of receiving a questionnaire for the sample to be random. Further, in order to retain its randomness, each questionnaire must have an equal probability of being returned. If this randomness, hence equality of probability, is retained, then meaningful statements can be made about the accuracy of the sample data with respect to the population it is supposed to represent. This property of randomness would be retained even if a survey of 2,500 teen-age girls were conducted by surveying 50 girls from each state. In this case, each of the 50 states would become a population and the total number of teenage girls in the United States a universe. If the selection of the 50 girls from each state were conducted in such a way as to satisfy the condition of randomness, then a random sample would result, even though the probability of any particular girl being selected would vary from state to state as a function of the population of the state.

In Chapter 7, we discussed the normal distribution and how a distribution could be specified in terms of two parameters—the arithmetic mean and the standard deviation. The arithmetic mean measures the location of the distribution, and the standard deviation measures the variation, or dispersion, of the distribution with respect to the mean. If a random sample were chosen from a particular population, we could hardly expect the arithmetic mean (average value) of the sample to be identical to the population mean, or the sample standard deviation to be identical to the population standard deviation. However, if different samples were repeatedly taken, we could expect half the sample means to be less than the population mean and half to be greater, and half the sample standard deviations to be less than the population standard deviation and half to be greater. As the size of the sample increased, we could expect the sample means and standard deviations to approach the population mean and standard deviation. These intuitive conclusions are quite correct. Furthermore, as the sample size increases, the distribution of the sample means will approach a normal distribution. This result, called the *central-limit theorem of statistics,* is an extremely powerful research tool because it holds true *regardless* of the shape of the distribution of the population.

Suppose, for example, that a dairy desires to estimate the total consumption of milk in a particular community. If it randomly samples a number of households to determine how much milk each household consumes, then the sample mean will be an unbiased estimate of the population mean. If this average value per household is then multiplied by the number of households, the firm will have an estimate of the total consumption of milk in the community. Stated mathematically,

$$\overline{X} = \frac{\sum_{i=1}^{n} X_i}{n}, \text{ where} \tag{23-1}$$

$\overline{X}$ = arithmetic mean of the sample

X_i = value of each observation, $i = 1$ through n, and

n = number of observations in the sample

and

$$P_E = N\overline{X}, \text{ where} \tag{23-2}$$

P_E = estimated population value, and

N = number of elements in the population

If the dairy queries 50 housewives, n, who altogether purchase 125 quarts of milk, ΣX_i, per day, then the average consumption, $\overline{X}$, is 2.5 quarts per household per day. If there are 2,000 households, N, in the community, the estimated consumption for the population, P_E, would be 5,000 quarts per day. However, this figure is merely a point estimate of the true consumption of milk in the community. If we repeated the experiment again, using 50 different housewives, it is quite unlikely that the same value would be obtained. If the sampling experiment were repeated a number of times, however, we would expect the sample values for the average milk consumption to be clustered about the population's average milk-consumption value. Such a clustering could be measured quantitatively by determining the standard deviation.

The standard deviation was defined in Chapter 7 as

$$\sigma = \sqrt{\frac{\sum_{i=1}^{N} (X_i - \mu)^2}{N}}, \text{ where} \tag{23-3}$$

N = number of elements in the population

X_i = value of a particular element in the population

μ = population mean, and

σ = population standard deviation

We can obtain an unbiased estimate of the population standard deviation by calculating the sample standard deviation as follows:

$$s = \sqrt{\frac{\sum_{i=1}^{n}(X_i - \overline{X})^2}{n - 1}} \cdot \sqrt{\frac{N - n}{N - 1}}, \text{ where} \tag{23-4}$$

s = sample standard deviation

X_i = value of a particular element in the sample

$\overline{X}$ = sample mean

n = number of elements in the sample, and

N = number of elements in the population

It should be noted that the population standard deviation is obtained by dividing by N, the number of elements in the population, and the sample standard deviation is obtained by dividing by $n - 1$ (to adjust for the number of degrees of freedom associated with the sample size[2]), where n is the number of elements in the sample.

The second element in the calculation of s, $\sqrt{\frac{N - n}{N - 1}}$, is known as the *finite sample correction factor*. Since in most sampling experiments the size of the population, N, is much larger than the size of the sample, n, the correction factor is usually excluded because of its closeness to unity. For instance, if a sample of 50 elements were taken from a population of 2,000, then

$$\sqrt{\frac{N - n}{N - 1}} = \sqrt{\frac{2,000 - 50}{2,000 - 1}} = \sqrt{\frac{1,950}{1,999}} = \sqrt{.975} = .988$$

In this case, only a small error (1.2 percent) would result if the finite sample correction factor were dropped from the formula for the sample standard deviation.

A small value for the sample standard deviation indicates that the values are clustered closely about the sample mean. Conversely, a large value indicates that the data are widely dispersed. If a sample is randomly selected,

[2] The interested student can consult an introductory statistics textbook for an explanation of degrees of freedom.

and the sample size, n, is greater than 30, then the sampling errors that cause the sample mean to differ from the true mean of the population will be normally distributed, due to the central-limit theorem. ("Normally distributed" implies that the sampling errors will follow a normal distribution, and therefor that the expected sampling error can be estimated.)[3]

SAMPLING ERRORS

The central-limit theorem tells us that the sample means will follow a normal distribution with a mean equal to μ (the population mean) and a standard deviation equal to $\sigma/\sqrt{n}$, where σ is the population standard deviation and n is the size of the sample. The sample mean, $\overline{X}$, is an unbiased estimate of μ, and the sample standard deviation, s, is an unbiased estimate of σ. Therefore, we can establish an interval about the sample mean in which we would expect the population mean to lie.

Since the normal distribution curve extends from ∞ to $-\infty$, we can be certain only that the population mean lies between these two extremes. Obviously, choosing a confidence interval (degree of certainty) of 100 percent would be meaningless. However, we can specify a meaningful confidence interval if we choose a confidence level of less than 100 percent. The confidence level chosen should be a function of the importance of the decision. If a mistake could mean financial disaster for the firm, a high confidence level (usually 95–99 percent) is appropriate. Of course, such a decision must be based on managerial judgment, not pure statistics.

Once we have chosen a confidence level, we can establish the degree of error of a sample estimate. Since we know from the central-limit theorem that the distribution of sample means will approach a normal distribution as the sample size increases, we can compute the maximum sampling error as follows:

$$E = z\frac{s}{\sqrt{n}}, \text{ where} \tag{23–5}$$

E = maximum difference between the sample mean and the population mean

s = sample standard deviation, calculated from Equation 23–4

n = size of the sample, and

z = appropriate z statistic for the confidence level selected

---

[3] See Appendix II, p. 657, for a full explanation of the properties of the normal distribution.

The z value merely measures the number of standard deviations that would enclose the percentage of the sample means equivalent to the chosen confidence level.[4] For example, a 99-percent confidence level has a z value of 2.58; a 95-percent confidence level has a z value of 1.96; and a 90-percent confidence level has a z value of 1.64.

Once the value of E is known, we can establish a *confidence interval*, $\overline{X} \pm E$, for the mean. To illustrate how these techniques are used, suppose that the dairy firm discussed earlier decided that it would be impractical to survey each of the 2,000 households in its territory, and elected instead to take a random sample of 50 households and use the results of the sample to estimate the total consumption of milk. Fifty households were randomly selected and were called upon by the interviewers. Follow-up visits were made to households that failed to respond to the initial call to eliminate any bias that might result from failure to contact working housewives. The daily milk consumption was then tabulated for each of the 50 households, and these values were used to calculate the average daily milk consumption, $\overline{X}$. In addition, the sum of the squares of the differences between actual consumption and average consumption was also determined, for use in further calculations. The data and associated calculations used by the firm are shown in Table 23.1.

The sample mean, $\overline{X}$, 2.5 quarts per day per household, is an unbiased estimate of the population's average consumption. A 95-percent confidence interval for the population's average consumption can be calculated as follows:

$$s = \sqrt{\frac{\sum (X_i - \overline{X})^2}{n - 1}}$$

Given as Equation 23–4 (without the correction factor)

$$s = \sqrt{\frac{39.7}{50 - 1}} = \sqrt{\frac{39.7}{49}}$$

By substitution (note that $\sum (X_i - \overline{X})^2$ was obtained from Table 23.1)

$$s = .81$$

By arithmetic

$$E = z \frac{s}{\sqrt{n}}$$

Given as Equation 23–5

$$E = 1.96 \cdot \frac{.9}{\sqrt{50}}$$

By substitution (note that $z = 1.96$ for a 95-percent confidence level)

$$E = .25$$

By arithmetic

---

[4] See Appendix II, p. 657, for a more detailed description of z values and their uses.

Table 23.1   Survey tabulation
                (Including calculations)

Household (i)	Daily Milk Consumption x_i	$x_i - \bar{x}$	$(x_i - \bar{x})^2$
1	3.0	.5	.25
2	0.0	−2.5	6.25
3	2.9	.4	.16
—	—	—	—
—	—	—	—
50	3.2	.7	.49
$n = 50$	$\sum X_i = 125.0$		$\sum(X_i - \bar{X})^2 = 39.7$

$$\bar{X} = \frac{\sum x_i}{n} \qquad \text{Given as Equation 23–1}$$

$$\bar{X} = \frac{125.0}{50} \qquad \text{By substitution}$$

$$\bar{X} = 2.5 \qquad \text{By arithmetic}$$

Thus from a relatively small sample of 50 households, the firm has established that the average daily milk consumption per household will be between 2.25 and 2.75 quarts (since $\bar{X} \pm E = 2.5 \pm .25$ at the 95-percent confidence level). It could obtain a higher confidence level, if necessary, simply by increasing the interval. A 99-percent confidence interval, for example, would be 2.17 to 2.83.

To go a step further, since total consumption, K, for the population will equal the average consumption (μ) times the size of the population ($K = \mu \cdot N$), the probable range of total consumption can be quickly computed for any given confidence level. In the example, at the 95-percent confidence level the dairy can say the total consumption of milk in the community studied is between 4,500 and 5,500 quarts per day (2,000 households times 2.25 quarts = 4,500, and 2,000 households times 2.75 quarts = 5,500).

If the firm's experience in comparable communities indicates that it can expect to capture 30 percent of the market, then it can be 95-percent confident that it will sell between 1,350 and 1,650 quarts per day (30% of 4,500 = 1,350, and 30% of 5,500 = 1,650), once it is established locally. A revenue range can be found by multiplying these values by price, which in this case is probably a linear function with respect to output. (Milk prices

are regulated in most states, and where they are not, the competitive structure of the industry discourages much manipulation.) The revenue range can
then be compared to the cost range to obtain the range of profit the firm can
anticipate in this prospective market.

SAMPLE SIZE

The size of a sample, *n,* is important because each observation costs both
time and money. It would be a waste of resources to take a larger sample
than is required to produce sufficiently accurate estimates. By using the
formula for calculating the sampling error, we can determine the required
sample size, and thus improve the efficiency of our sampling techniques.
If the standard deviation of the population can be estimated from experience,
then, once a confidence level has been chosen, the sample size required to
provide an acceptable error can easily be determined from the following
formula, which is obtained by manipulating Equation 23–5 to isolate *n*
on the left-hand side of the equation and substituting $\hat{\sigma}$, the estimate of the
population standard deviation, for *s:*

$$n = \left(\frac{z\hat{\sigma}}{E}\right)^2, \text{ where} \tag{23-6}$$

n = sample size

z = value of the z statistic that corresponds to the selected confidence
level

$\hat{\sigma}$ = estimate of the population standard deviation, and

E = acceptable estimation error

Although it appears that a number of a priori decisions must be made,
the problem is not usually too difficult. An estimate of the population standard deviation is often available from past studies made by the firm, trade
associations, or the government. If enough data is not available from past
studies, a fairly satisfactory estimate can be obtained by assuming that the
population standard deviation is one-sixth of the range of expected values,
since 99.7 percent of the area of a normal distribution is contained within
±3 standard deviations from the mean. For example, we might expect the
daily consumption of milk per household to range from 0 to 6 quarts. In this
case, we would estimate the standard deviation of milk consumption as
1 quart (one-sixth of the range, which is 6 quarts).

The acceptable error can normally be determined as a function of the
costs associated with an incorrect estimate. In the preceding problem, for

example, earlier surveys in other communities might have indicated an average σ, or s, of .8. Suppose that management wanted to be 99-percent sure that the population mean of the market under study would fall within .1 quart of the sample mean, $\bar{X}$. They would then be 99-percent confident that their estimate of the total potential market was off by no more than 200 quarts per day (since there are 2,000 households in the community). The required sample size, n, would be

$$n = \left(\frac{z\hat{\sigma}}{E}\right)^2 \qquad \text{Given as Equation 23-6}$$

$$n = \left[\frac{2.58(.8)}{.1}\right]^2 \qquad \text{By substitution}$$

$$n = (20.64)^2 \qquad \text{By arithmetic}$$

$$n = 426 \qquad \text{By arithmetic}$$

Thus a sample size of 426 is necessary if the survey is to perform within the limits of accuracy specified by management. However, if the firm was willing to tolerate a range of error equal to $\pm.2$ quarts—which would put its total market estimate within ± 400 quarts of the true value—the sample size could be reduced to 106. This would make the job of gathering the data considerably less expensive. Or, if management wished to keep the range of error within $\pm.1$ quart but was willing to operate at a 95-percent confidence level, a sample of only 250 households would be required.

ESTIMATING PROPORTIONS

In many cases, the objective of a survey is to estimate what proportion of a population prefers a particular alternative, rather than to find an average or an aggregate consumption figure. If there are more than two possible choices, the proportion, or percentage, of the total market preferring each one must be calculated separately. For example, if the shoe firm described earlier were to have surveyed five hundred teenage girls, their color preferences might have been tabulated as in Table 23.2.

If the conditions for random sampling have been fulfilled, then the sample data—and the resulting proportions and percentages—should be an unbiased estimate of the shoe-color preferences of teenage girls. In this case, the respondents were given six alternatives. Often, only two alternatives will exist—yes or no, black or white, like or don't like, and so forth.

Regardless of the number of alternatives, the factor being measured is always the *probability of occurrence*. The probability of an event's occurrence is the proportion of its occurrence in a given population. For example, if 30

Table 23.2   Color-preference responses

Shoe Color	Responses	Proportion of Total Responses	Percentage of Total Responses
Black	175	.35	35%
Brown	125	.25	25
White	75	.15	15
Red	40	.08	8
Blue	20	.04	4
All other colors	65	.13	13
Totals	500	1.00	100%

percent of the teenage-girl population prefers brown shoes, the probability that a randomly selected teenage girl will prefer brown shoes in .3. Stated in mathematical terms, if n equals the total population surveyed—that is, the number of observations, or trials (a trial being a single interview, questionnaire, or purchase) that are made—and x equals the number of occurrences of the event within that population, then the probability of the event is

$$P(x) = \frac{x}{n}, \text{ where} \tag{23-7}$$

x = number of occurrences of a particular event

$P(x)$ = probability of event x occurring, and

n = number of observations (trials)

For example, if the shoe company randomly samples 500 girls ($n = 500$) and finds that 25 prefer blue shoes ($x = 25$), then the probability of any girl in the population preferring blue shoes is .05 ($P = .05$). Five percent of the firm's prospective customers (for girls' shoes) prefer blue. This example may seem obvious, but it is useful because it illustrates how the researcher can apply probability theory both in designing surveys and in analyzing the resultant data.

The true probabilities of various alternatives (the number of the times that events will occur in a population) can be determined exactly only by a population survey—that is, a survey in which the number of sample observations, n, equals the number of elements in the universe, N. Research this extensive is usually impractical and often unnecessary, since the true distribution of preferences, hence the probability of occurrence of each event, can be estimated satisfactorily by a random sample.

Sometimes we are interested in only one event and all other outcomes are relevant only in that they represent the nonoccurrence of the desired event. For example, we may be interested only in the demand for green shoes; hence shoes of any other color would be categorized as "not green." In this case, our estimate of the proportion of teenage girls who prefer green shoes would be x_G/n, where x_G is the number of girls who preferred green shoes and n is the total number of girls surveyed. Again, this is only a point estimate, and thus, although it is unbiased, it is subject to error. The range of error for any proportion is a function of the sample size, n, the value of the proportion, x/n, and the desired confidence level. Calculating exact confidence intervals is difficult, but fortunately it is seldom necessary, since tables giving the confidence intervals for standard confidence levels can be found in most statistics books.[5] Where confidence intervals must be calculated, we can again use the central-limit theorem. We know the x/n is an unbiased estimate of $P(x)$. We can obtain an unbiased estimate of the standard deviation of $P(x)$ from the formula

$$S_{x/n} = \sqrt{\dfrac{\dfrac{x}{n}\left(1 - \dfrac{x}{n}\right)}{n}}, \text{ where} \qquad\qquad (23\text{--}8)$$

x = number of outcomes of a particular event, and

n = number of observations (trials)

The central-limit theorem states that as the sample size (n) approaches infinity, the distribution of responses will approach the normal distribution. If n is reasonably large and $P(x)$ is not too close to either 0 or 1, the distribution of the sample can be approximated by a normal distribution and the techniques developed previously for estimating the error associated with sampling techniques can be applied to the case of simple proportions.

Statistical theory provides a convenient rule of thumb for determining whether we can safely assume a normal distribution. If n is greater than 50 and $n(1 - x/n)$ exceeds 5, we can assume normality. Once this assumption is made, we can invoke the tools of inferential statistics to estimate various confidence intervals.

As an example, assume that in a random-sample survey of 400 teenage girls we find that 120 prefer red shoes. We would then estimate the true proportion of teenage girls in the population who prefer red shoes as:

$$P(x) = \frac{x}{n} = \frac{120}{400} = .30$$

[5] See Appendix II, pp. 670–71.

The standard deviation of x/n would be

$$S_{x/n} = \sqrt{\dfrac{\dfrac{x}{n}\left(1 - \dfrac{x}{n}\right)}{n}} \qquad \text{Given as Equation 23–8}$$

$$S_{x/n} = \sqrt{\dfrac{(.3)(.7)}{400}} \qquad \text{By substitution}$$

$$S_{x/n} = .023 \qquad \text{By arithmetic}$$

If x/n equals .3, then $n\left(1 - \dfrac{X}{n}\right) = 400(.7) = 280$. Since 280 is much larger than 5, we can safely consider the normal distribution an approximation of the actual distribution.

Since the effects of the sample size are already included in the standard deviation of x/n, the formula for calculating the error becomes

$$E = (z)(s_{x/n}), \text{ where} \qquad\qquad (23\text{–}9)$$

$E =$ maximum difference between the sample proportion and the population proportion

$z =$ appropriate value of the z statistic for the confidence level selected, and

$s_{x/n} =$ sample standard deviation, calculated from Equation 23–8

The 95-percent confidence interval for an estimate of .3 would then be

$$E = (z)(s_{x/n}) \qquad \text{Given as Equation 23–9}$$

$$E = 1.96(.023) \qquad z = 1.96 \text{ for 95-percent confidence level}$$

$$E = .045 \qquad\qquad \text{By arithmetic}$$

Thus, the 95-percent confidence interval is .255 to .345 ($.3 \pm .045$).

It is interesting to compare this result with that obtained by using Table 3a in Appendix II. The confidence interval shown in the table is also .255 to .345. There is no perceptible difference between the exact range and that calculated by approximate methods because of the large sample size and the nearness of x/n to .5. An analysis of Table 3a or Table 3b will reveal that as x/n approaches either 0 or 1, the confidence interval becomes smaller. This is evident from the formula for the standard deviation of the proportion:

$$S_{x/n} = \sqrt{\dfrac{\dfrac{x}{n}\left(1 - \dfrac{x}{n}\right)}{n}}$$

Clearly, $S_{x/n}$ will be maximum when $x/n = .5$ and will decrease as x/n approaches either 0 or 1. This fact is extremely important, since it allows us to develop a technique for choosing the optimum size of a survey.

Knowing that the standard deviation of the proportion is maximum when $x/n = .5$, we can use the following formula to find the sample size, n, that will yield a desired maximum estimation error, E, for a given confidence level.

$$n = .25 \left(\frac{z}{E}\right)^2, \text{ where} \tag{23-10}$$

$n =$ sample size

$z =$ value of the z statistic that corresponds to the desired confidence level, and

$E =$ maximum error acceptable in estimating the proportion

For example, suppose that we want to estimate the proportion of a potential market that reads a certain magazine and that we want to have a maximum estimation error of 5 percent at the 95-percent confidence level (that is, 95 times out of 100 the true proportion will be within $\pm.05$ of the estimated proportion). We can determine the required sample size by using Equation 23–10, where $z = 1.96$ and $E = .05$.

$$n = .25 \left(\frac{z}{E}\right)^2 \qquad \text{Given as Equation 23–10}$$

$$n = .25 \left(\frac{1.96}{.05}\right)^2 \qquad \text{By substitution}$$

$$n = 395 \qquad\qquad \text{By arithmetic}$$

Equation 23–10 was developed from the general error formula

$$E = (z)(S_{x/n}),$$

or

$$E = z \sqrt{\frac{\frac{x}{n}\left(1 - \frac{x}{n}\right)}{n}} \tag{23-11}$$

with x/n equal to .5. We used $x/n = .5$ since we had assumed no a priori information on the value of x/n. If we can establish a range in which we expect x/n to lie, we can reduce the size of the sample. Assume, for instance, that we can expect, based on past studies, that between 5 and 25 percent of the market reads the magazine. We then take the value of the a priori estimate closest to .5 and use this value in Equation 23–11. In this case, z and E are still 1.96 and .05, and $x/n = .25$. These values will result in a required sample size of 289, as follows:

$$n = \left(\frac{x}{n}\right)\left(1 - \frac{x}{n}\right)\left(\frac{z}{E}\right)^2$$ By rearranging Equation 23–11 to isolate n

$$n = (.25)(.75)\left(\frac{1.96}{.05}\right)^2$$ By substitution

$$n = 289$$ By arithmetic

Thus the required sample size is significantly reduced if we can establish a maximum range for the true proportion.

DESIGN CONSIDERATIONS

Once the optimum sample size has been established, the most important consideration is the *randomization of the sample*. This can be both difficult and expensive. The first task is to identify and locate every element in the population. Each element cannot have an equal chance of being selected if the sample-taker is unaware of some of the elements.

For instance, an advertiser may be interested in conducting a survey of the television viewing habits of households in the San Diego SMSA. The local telephone book seems like a convenient source of respondents. The researcher can easily make a random selection of as many names as are necessary. If telephone interviews, a mail questionnaire, or personal visits are in order, he can also pick up the phone numbers and addresses from the directory.

This survey design would not, however, provide a random sample of the San Diego SMSA population. It would yield a random sample of the households with listed telephone numbers, but this group may not be representative of the San Diego population as a whole. Households with low income levels would probably be excluded, as well as those who, because of their social position of affluence, have unlisted numbers. Inferences made from data gathered from the telephone directory and generalized to the San Diego population would clearly be biased, although using the biased method might be preferable to undertaking a more expensive truly random sample.

An alternative method would be to take tract maps of the population area, assign numbers to each recorded residence, and then make a random selection of a sample of those numbers, using a table of random numbers. However, identifying and numbering the residences can involve a great deal of work, hence cost.

Once the sample elements are selected, a mail, telephone, or personal-interview survey can be used. However, to retain the randomness of the sample, an effort must be made to ensure that the observations are not biased by the failure of a particular group to respond. Considerable follow-up work may be required to obtain responses from such subsets as working wives, illiterates, and shut-ins. When these elements are strewn about an area several hundred square miles in size, the follow-up procedure can be expensive.

CLUSTER SAMPLING

The geographical problem may be moderated by a technique called cluster sampling. In *cluster sampling,* the population is divided into small geographical groups, or "clusters." A random selection is made of a number of these groups, and a random sample—also known as a population sample—is made of the elements in each selected group. This method is commonly used in personal-interview surveys of populations spread over a large geographical area.

For instance, a department-store chain may want to obtain a profile of the shopping habits of households in the Boston SMSA, which covers over 100 square miles. Rather than have its interviewers crisscross all over the area, the firm could divide the area into city blocks and then take a random sample of the blocks. Interviewers would then be sent to the selected blocks, where they would interview either a number of households selected at random or every household on the block.

The efficiency of the survey with respect to the total population (in this case, that of the Boston SMSA) is a function of the homogeneity of the clusters with respect to one another.[6] Consequently, some judgment must be used in dividing the original population into clusters. If a geographical grouping is used, efficiency can often be increased by dividing the area into clusters having a nearly equal number of elements. As household density varies, it may be necessary to divide some blocks into two units, while grouping other blocks together as a unit. In the Boston SMSA, for example, the industrial and commercial sections would have few if any households per block, the suburbs would have several dozen, and the apartment areas and slums would have hundreds.

Cluster sampling does not necessarily provide more precision than unrestricted random sampling for a given confidence level and sample size. On the contrary, it may increase the sampling error if the clusters are not per-

[6] Efficiency, in this context, refers to the sample size required in order to yield the same amount of error, as measured by the confidence interval. If one sampling method requires fewer interviews than another sampling method yet has the same amount of error, it is more efficient.

fectly homogeneous. However, the cost savings can be considerable because of the mechanical problems in executing an unrestricted random sample.

STRATIFIED SAMPLING

In *stratified sampling,* the population is divided into subpopulations, called *strata,* that are internally homogeneous with respect to a particular characteristic, such as age, income, or ethnic origin. A proportional random (or population) sample is then drawn from each group. This data is aggregated, and appropriate statistical inferences are made about the whole population.

Stratification is useful because it prevents important subpopulations from being excluded, while still retaining the quality of randomness. Chance variation—commonly referred to as luck—will occasionally result in a distribution of the sample elements that does not reflect the distribution of the population. For example, high-income families, which constitute 2 percent of the population, may not receive any questionnaires or interviews in a particular survey. Conversely, in some cases, they may receive twice their share. This latter outcome is highly possible when personal, door-to-door interviews are used, since interviewers often prefer to do their sampling in upper-class neighborhoods.

If the population is stratified into homogeneous income brackets, or according to some other appropriate criterion, the aggregate sample can be distributed so as to increase efficiency. For example, suppose that in a particular area only 10 percent of the families had an annual income of $12,000 or more. If 1,000 families were randomly selected for interviews, we could expect approximately 100 of them to be in the $12,000-and-over income bracket and 900 to be in the under-$12,000 income bracket. The confidence interval for any data calculated for the under-$12,000 income group would be significantly less than that for the $12,000-and-over group. Any desired confidence interval could then be obtained more efficiently by stratifying families according to whether or not they had an income under $12,000 and then increasing the number of samples taken in the $12,000-and-over group and decreasing the number of samples in the under-$12,000 group.

The major disadvantage of stratified sampling is that the analyst must have some idea of the distribution within the strata in order to determine the optimum sample size. Stratification may be impossible if there is no historical data on the population elements. Often a preliminary survey is required to determine the proportions of the population in each of the strata. If this is the case, the primary purpose of the survey can often be achieved more cheaply by an unrestricted random sample.

NON-RANDOM SAMPLING

A non-random sample—also called a "judgment sample" or "non-probability sample"—is one that does not give every element in the population a known probability of being selected for observation. Its advantages over a random sample are its simplicity and lower cost. The disadvantage is that the techniques of statistical inference developed earlier in the chapter cannot be used for evaluating the results. Using non-random data, the analyst can describe the population in the same terms that he would use to describe random data. However, nothing rigorous can be said about the possible errors. One cannot legitimately invoke the statistical formulas to make quantitative statements about the confidence levels and errors associated with the survey results. Thus the reliability of the non-random samples is always questionable.

The classic example of the potential errors associated with non-random sampling was the *Literary Digest* poll of 1936, which predicted that Republican Alfred Landon would easily beat incumbent Democrat Franklin Roosevelt in the presidential election. The *Digest*'s survey showed that 56 percent of the respondents favored Landon and only 41 percent preferred Roosevelt, the rest being undecided. In fact, Roosevelt won with 60 percent of the votes, half again as many as the survey predicted. The error was so gross that it placed the hitherto respectable magazine in disrepute, and the magazine eventually ceased publication due to loss of circulation.

The error, of course, resulted from the failure of those conducting the poll to recognize the potential bias of a non-random sample. The *Digest*'s survey pretended to represent the American voting population, when in fact it represented only the elements of that population who were on the magazine's subscription list, who were listed as automobile owners, who had listed telephones, or who were previously registered voters. This subset of the national voting population was generally wealthier than the excluded elements, for in the depression days automobile ownership and private telephones were identified with the affluent elements, who tended to vote Republican. In spite of the gigantic size of the sample (2,350,176 people were polled), the results were in error by 50 percent.[7]

This does not mean that judgment samples should never be used. On the contrary, there are situations in which they are the optimum choice. For instance, randomness may be unimportant in taste-testing (used extensively by food and beverage manufacturers). What difference does it make if the respondents are not a representative selection of ethnic, political, economic,

[7] Richard D. Crisp, *Marketing Research* (New York: McGraw-Hill, 1957), p. 102.

geographical, or religious groups or do not have work habits or shopping patterns that reflect those of the market population?

In some cases, the researcher may be interested in biasing the survey toward particular elements of the population. For example, a survey of customer preference might well be slanted toward large purchasers. The U. S. Steel Corporation is far more interested in the needs and preferences of the "big-three" automobile manufacturers than it is in desires of the thousands of other buyers of sheet steel. This does not mean that small buyers should be ignored, only that the seller's decisions should be influenced more by its major customers. A survey that gave every customer in U. S. Steel's market an equal chance of being sampled would hardly serve the interest of the firm unless the observed values were weighted to correct for the size of the firm.

The survey can be a hazardous research tool; the market analyst who does not clearly understand its properties may draw erroneous conclusions that could lead to disastrous errors in his firm's marketing decisions. The strengths and deficiencies of survey research must be kept in mind during both the design and the data-analysis phases of a research project. When this is done, the survey can be a powerful and flexible tool of marketing research.

CHAPTER 24

Experimentation

Market experimentation is used to determine the relationship between a dependent variable (usually sales) and the independent variables that can be controlled or manipulated by various tactics. If really controlled experiments (experiments in which specific variables are changed and all other variables are held constant) could be performed, then market experimentation would be as straightforward as experimentation in chemistry or physics. Unfortunately, many market variables are difficult, if not impossible, to hold constant, and therefore their effect must be taken into account. Often competitors will intentionally attempt to invalidate market experimentation through short-run price changes, promotional activities, or special programs.

Market experimentation is most often used with consumer goods, and the marketing variables of greatest interest are usually those associated with promotion. Experimentation is most useful when it can be carried out on a small scale and when the change in marketing strategy would not precipitate an unacceptable response from the competition. For example, the price of a good might be varied for a short time to determine the elasticity of demand, a new package might be tried in a local market to test its effectiveness, the color of one of the firm's products might be varied to determine consumer preferences, or a new product might be introduced on a small scale to test consumer acceptance of an innovation in the product line. The effect of these actions on sales might be measured directly, or indirectly through the use of an appropriate proxy.

An experiment may be conducted throughout the producer's entire market or—as is more often the case—locally, in an isolated segment of the market. A localized test market has several advantages. The variables are easier to isolate and measure, control groups can be set up, costs can be kept down, and the firm can withdraw the new strategy with fewer complications if it fails.

For example, the Coca-Cola Company experimented with king-size bottles in several local areas before it added them to its product line nation-wide. The reaction to the larger-sized bottles in these local markets enabled the firm to estimate the demand for the product with considerably more pre-cision than would have been possible without experimental data. In addition, the costs of the experiment were relatively low. The company had only to purchase enough of the new bottles and modify enough of their bottling equipment to serve the local markets. Had the introduction of king-size Coca-Cola proven an unprofitable addition to the firm's product mix, the project could have been canceled without any significant damage to the firm's finan-cial position.

Television commercials are often selected in a similar manner. Two or three pilot commercials are prepared for showing in separate test markets. The changes in sales are recorded, adjustments are made for variations in exogenous variables between markets, and the figures for each area are compared. The most effective commercial is then selected for network viewing.

DEFINITIONS

A number of technical terms are widely used in experimental research litera-ture, and we shall define them at this point for subsequent usage.

The *experimental treatment* is the manipulation of the independent variables being tested. Examples are a price increase, a new package design, a new advertisement, and a change in a distribution system.

The *experimental effect* is the effect that the experimental treatment has on the dependent variable. For instance, the experimental effect of a reduc-tion in price might be an increase in sales.

Test units are the individuals, firms, or markets whose response to the experimental treatment is being studied. Examples are consumers, stores, distributors, and geographical markets.

Extraneous forces are all the variables, other than the experimental-treatment variables, that influence the dependent variable (the response of the test units). There are two types: (1) differences between test units, such as in geographical location or store size, and (2) uncontrollable variables, such as weather, local business conditions, or the action of local competitors. The differences in test units are normally determined by the experiment's de-sign; hence they are usually known and subject to some control. Uncontrol-lable variables are exogenous to the test but can influence the data. Frequently their effect can be minimized by using a selection of test units that will cancel out their aggregate effect.

Experimental error is the variation in the dependent variable not ac-counted for by the experimental treatment or by the effects of any extraneous forces that have been identified and measured. This unexplained variation in the response of the test units is caused by the inherent variability between even "perfectly" matched test units, the effects of unidentified exogenous forces, and non-constant errors in measurement. (A constant error in measurement, such as the persistent overstatement of income or an interviewer's preference for visiting upper-class neighborhoods, creates a statistical bias and is sometimes called a "systematic error." Experimental error is almost inevitable, but it can generally be limited by skillful design of the experiment.

EXPERIMENTAL DESIGN

Experimental designs vary from the simple and naive to the complex and sophisticated. As one moves from the first extreme to the second, the accuracy and precision of the experiments increase, but so do the costs. This will become apparent as we explore some of the basic experimental methods.

Naive experiments are based on the assumption that the extraneous forces affecting the test units will remain unchanged during the experimental treatment. Hence, any difference in values before and after the experimental treatment is assumed to be due to the treatment. Stated notationally,

$$E + U = Y_2 - Y_1, U = 0, \text{ where} \qquad (24\text{-}1)$$

E = effect of the experimental treatment

U = effect of a change in the extraneous forces (equals 0 by assumption)

Y_1 = value of the dependent variable before the treatment, and

Y_2 = value of the dependent variable after the treatment

To illustrate, assume that the manufacturer of a convenience good wants to test the effect of a new package on the sales of its product. Using a naive experimental design, the market analyst would probably select a test unit, say the Denver SMSA, measure the dependent variable (sales), introduce the new package, and again measure the dependent variable. Any difference in the variable would be attributed entirely to the new package.

If sales were 1,000 units per week immediately before the introduction of the new package ($Y_1 = 1,000$) and 960 units per week after its introduction ($Y_2 = 960$), the new package would be estimated to reduce sales by 40 units per week ($E = -40$), or 4 percent. The experimenter would have to conclude that the new package was inferior to the old one, and the manufacturer would be ill advised to adopt it unless it was so cheap that the company would make money by using it even with a 4-percent drop in sales.

This is a reasonable conclusion *if* one accepts the assumption that $U = 0$ (that there was no change in the extraneous forces between the observation of Y_1 and Y_2), or that, if there were changes, their effects were canceled out.

A naive experiment can be upgraded by including the effect of extraneous forces. For example, assume that in the previous illustration the experimenter was aware that his product had a cross elasticity with respect to the price of competing goods of .6. He would then be wise to observe the prices of competitors' products (an extraneous force) during the experiment also. Suppose, for example, that competitors reduced their prices by 10 percent immediately after the new package was introduced. Using the elasticity formula given on page 248 and the price of the competitor's product, we have:

$$\eta_{p_c} = \frac{\Delta Q}{Q} \div \frac{\Delta p_c}{p_c} \text{, where}$$

η_{p_c} = cross elasticity (elasticity of demand with respect to competitor's price

Q = quantity demanded

ΔQ = change in quantity demanded

p_c = competitor's price

Δp_c = change in competitor's price

The effect of the change in extraneous forces can be calculated as follows:

$$\eta_{p_c} = \frac{\Delta Q}{Q} \div \frac{\Delta p_c}{p_c} \qquad \text{Given as Equation (11–11)}$$

$$.6 = \frac{\Delta Q}{1,000} \div .10 \qquad \text{By substitution}$$

$$\Delta Q = 60 \qquad \text{By algebraic manipulation and arithmetic}$$

The price reduction would decrease sales of the experimenter's product by 60 units per week ($U = -60$). The effect of this on the decision variable, E, is significant, as is revealed by the following analysis, which uses Equation 24–1 but omits the assumption of the naive model that $U = 0$.

$$E + U = Y_2 - Y_1 \qquad \text{Given as Equation 24–1}$$

$$E + (-60) = 960 - 1,000 \qquad \text{By substitution}$$

$$E = 20 \qquad \text{By algebraic manipulation and arithmetic}$$

The effect of the experimental treatment—that is, the use of the new package—now appears clearly positive. Sales are up 2 percent over what they would have been without the new package. This suggests a marketing decision much different from that which was reached earlier on the basis of the naive experiment. The new package should be adopted, assuming that the increase in cost, if any, is justified by the resultant increase in sales.

The quality of the experiment just described was obviously improved by including the effect of an extraneous force. However, no general method was suggested for measuring the effect of such forces; in addition, the possibility of experimental error was ignored. We shall deal with each of these issues in turn.

CONTROL AND EXPERIMENTAL UNITS

It is frequently useful to divide test units into control and experimental subsets. A *control unit*—also called a "test-control unit"—is a test unit that is observed during the course of the experimental treatment but is not subjected to the treatment. Hence any variation in the value of the dependent variable associated with the control unit is *not* a result of the test treatment, and the control unit can be used to isolate the effect of changes in the extraneous forces, U.

An *experimental unit* is a test unit subjected to the experimental treatment. By pairing an experimental unit with a control unit, we can automatically adjust the experiment's results for the effect of extraneous forces. This is done by using a pair of simultaneous equations, one of which expresses the change in the dependent variable associated with the control unit, and one of which expresses the change associated with the experimental unit. The change in the dependent variable associated with the experimental unit, Y, is a result of E (the effect of the experimental treatment) and U (the effect of the extraneous forces). However, since the control unit is not subject to the experimental treatment, any change in the dependent variable associated with it, Y', must be due to a change in U. These statements can be made concurrently, and the resultant equation solved to yield Equation 24–2, which is very useful in marketing research. Thus,

$$E + U = Y_2 - Y_1 \qquad \text{Given as Equation 24–1}$$

$$U = Y_2' - Y_1', \text{ where} \qquad \text{Given}$$

U = effect of extraneous forces

Y_1' = value of dependent variable associated with the control unit, at the start of the experiment, and

Y_2' = value of dependent variable associated with the control unit, at the end of the experiment

By substituting $Y_2' - Y_1'$ for U in Equation 24–1, we have

$$E + (Y_2' - Y_1') = Y_2 - Y_1 \qquad \text{By substitution}$$
$$E = (Y_2 - Y_1) - (Y_2' - Y_1') \qquad \text{By algebraic}$$
$$\text{manipulation (24–2)}$$

If the researcher has properly matched his two test units, Equation 24–2 will yield an estimate of the effect of the experimental treatment, E, that excludes the effect of extraneous forces. The researcher need not identify and measure the effects of each of the extraneous forces, because these effects are aggregated and automatically eliminated by the inclusion of the control group in the experimental design.

The package-testing problem can again be used as an illustration. Suppose that the experimenter, feeling that other exogenous variables besides the competitors' prices may influence the results of his experiment, decides to employ a control unit. Two test units are selected, say two supermarkets that are nearly alike in terms of their exposure to extraneous forces. That is, each is subject to the same weather conditions, must meet the same competitive forces, and attracts the same type of customers. Ideally, each should do about the same volume of business and be subject to the same management policies during the course of the experiment, yet each should be sufficiently isolated so as not to significantly influence the sales of the other. One is specified as the control unit and the other as the experimental unit.

Observations of the dependent variable made at both units immediately prior to the experimental treatment (introduction of the new package) show daily sales of 105 and 90 units at the control and test units, respectively. A second set of observations, taken after the treatment, shows daily sales of 99 and 93 units, respectively. Using Equation 24–2, the reseacher concludes that the effect, E, of the new package on the dependent variable, sales, was to increase it by 9 units:

$$E = (Y_2 - Y_1) - (Y_2' - Y_1') \qquad \text{Given as Equation 24–2}$$
$$E = (93 - 90) - (99 - 105) \qquad \text{By substitution}$$
$$E = 3 - (-6) = 9 \qquad \text{By arithmetic}$$

Judging from the experience with the control unit, which did not have the benefit of the new package, the effect of the extraneous forces was to reduce sales of the firm's brand. To make a decision about packaging, it is not necesary to know what those forces were, but only their aggregate effect, so that it can be separated from the effect of the test package.

A difference in the volume of sales at the test unit and at the control unit can distort the results in this kind of experiment. In the example, this difference was slight, but it can be significant in actual experiments. For this reason, it may be better to compare relative values, which we can do by altering Equation 24–2 as follows:

$$E_\% = \left[\left(\frac{Y_2 - Y_1}{Y_1}\right) - \left(\frac{Y_2' - Y_1'}{Y_1'}\right)\right] \cdot 100, \text{ where} \qquad (24\text{–}3)$$

$E_\%$ = effect of the experimental treatment of the dependent variable, expressed as a percentage change, and

Y_1, Y_2, Y_1', Y_2' are defined as before

Substituting the values already given in the packaging problem, we have

$$E_\% = \left[\left(\frac{Y_2 - Y_1}{Y_1}\right) - \left(\frac{Y_2' - Y_1'}{Y_1'}\right)\right] \cdot 100 \qquad \text{Given as Equation 24–3}$$

$$E_\% = \left[\left(\frac{93 - 90}{90}\right) - \left(\frac{99 - 105}{105}\right)\right] \cdot 100 \qquad \text{By substitution}$$

$$E_\% = \left[\frac{3}{90} - \left(\frac{-6}{105}\right)\right] \cdot 100 = (.0333 + .0572) \cdot 100 = 9.05$$

Practically the same value would result if the effect, E, computed using Equation 24–2 were placed over the pre-test sales of the experimental unit $(9/90 = 10.00\%)$. However, had the test units not been so evenly matched, the results could have been quite different. For example, if the experimental unit had pre-treatment sales of 180 units and post-treatment sales of 186 units (twice the previous figures), Equation 24–2 would show the effect of the treatment as a 6.67-percent increase in sales:

$$E = (Y_2 - Y_1) - (Y_2' - Y_1') \qquad \text{Given as Equation 24–2}$$

$$E = (186 - 180) - (99 - 105) \qquad \text{By substitution}$$

$$E = 6 - (-6) = 12 \qquad \text{By arithmetic}$$

$$E_\% = \frac{12}{180} = 6.67\% \qquad \text{By substitution}$$

Again, however, the actual change is 9.05 percent, as Equation 24–3 proves:

$$E_\% = \left[\left(\frac{Y_2 - Y_1}{Y_1}\right) - \left(\frac{Y_2' - Y_1'}{Y_1'}\right)\right] \cdot 100 \qquad \text{Given as Equation 24–3}$$

$$E_\% = \left[\left(\frac{186 - 180}{180}\right) - \left(\frac{99 - 105}{105}\right)\right] \cdot 100 \qquad \text{By substitution}$$

$$E_\% = \left[\frac{6}{180} - \left(\frac{-6}{105}\right)\right] \cdot 100 \qquad \text{By arithmetic}$$

$$E_\% = (.0333 + .0572) \cdot 100 = 9.05\%$$

If it is not practical to pair test units with approximately even volumes, Equation 24–3 should be used. The experimenter will probably need to express the effect of the experimental treatment as a percentage anyway, in order to be able to generalize his results to the firm's total market.

EXPERIMENTAL ERROR

By using a control unit in the experiment, the researcher isolates the effect of the experimental treatment from the effect of extraneous forces. However, the results can still contain experimental errors. This problem can be dealt with by employing multiple test units that are selected *at random* from the universe of possible test units. Random selection causes the experimental error (which is likely to be different for each unit) to be randomly distributed among the test units. Such a random distribution enables the experimenter to use the tools of inferential statistics to estimate the range of experimental error. (In essence, the statistical techniques needed are similar to those used in the previous chapter, though a bit more complex.)

For example, if the firm's product were sold in 90 stores, 20 could be selected at random; 10 could then be used as control units (X_{Cj}) and 10 as experimental units (X_{Ei}). The distribution of the 20 units between the control and experimental categories should also be random.

For each of the 20 stores, the percentage change in sales can be calculated by dividing both sides of Equation 24–1 by the pre-experiment value of the variable (Y_1) and then multiplying by 100 to obtain a percentage:

$$E + U = Y_2 - Y_1 \qquad \text{Given as Equation 24–1}$$

$$\left(\frac{E + U}{Y_1}\right) \cdot 100 = \left(\frac{Y_2 - Y_1}{Y_1}\right) \cdot 100 \qquad \text{Division by } Y_1 \text{ and multiplication by 100 to obtain a percentage-change measure}$$

For the controlled stores $(E = 0)$, the change will be

$$\frac{U}{Y_1} \cdot 100 = \left(\frac{Y_2 - Y_1}{Y_1}\right) \cdot 100$$

Table 24.1 shows the data for each store derived by using these equations, and the average change in sales for each group. The difference between the average change in sales in the experimental stores $(X_E = 11.11\%)$ and the average change in sales in the controlled stores $(X_C = 2.23\%)$ can be attributed to the experimental effect (the new package). The effect of the new package is an increase in sales of 8.88 percent $(11.11\% - 2.23\%)$.

Table 24.1   Percentage change in sales for experimental and controlled stores

Store (i)	Experimental Stores % Change	Store (j)	Controlled Stores % Change
1	+13.7	1	+2.4
2	+ 7.0	2	+4.8
3	+ 9.8	3	−1.2
4	+14.6	4	+3.6
5	+ 6.2	5	+4.1
6	+13.8	6	+2.1
7	+ 5.4	7	+0.9
8	+18.6	8	−0.7
9	+15.3	9	+4.6
10	+ 6.7	10	+1.7

$$\sum_{i=1}^{10} X_{Ei} = 111.1 \qquad\qquad \sum_{j=1}^{10} X_{Cj} = 22.3$$

$$\overline{X}_E = \frac{\sum_{i=1}^{10} X_{Ei}}{10} = \frac{111.1}{10} = 11.11 \qquad \overline{X}_C = \frac{\sum_{j=1}^{10} X_{Cj}}{10} = \frac{223}{10} = 2.23$$

Before management uses this value in deciding whether to change over to the new package entirely, it should take into account the possible error. Thus the next task is to estimate the confidence interval for the experimental effect. Since the experimental effect is the difference between the two means $(X_E - X_C)$, we must first calculate the standard deviation of the difference between the two means. Once this is done, statistical methods can be used to find the confidence interval at the desired confidence level.

The formula for the standard deviation of the difference between X_E and X_C is[1]

$$s_{\overline{X}_E - \overline{X}_C} = \sqrt{\frac{\sum_{i=1}^{n_E} (X_{Ei} - \overline{X}_E)^2 + \sum_{j=1}^{n_C} (X_{Cj} - \overline{X}_C)^2}{n_E + n_C - 2}}, \text{ where} \qquad (24\text{-}4)$$

$s_{\overline{X}_E - \overline{X}_C}$ = standard deviation of the experimental effect

n_E = number of experimental stores

n_C = number of control stores

[1] The standard deviation of the difference between a pair of means is a pooled, or "combined," estimate of the standard deviation of the two means. Hence its formula is more complex than the formula for a simple standard deviation.

X_{Ei} = percentage change in sales for experimental store i

X_{Cj} = percentage change in sales for control store j

$\overline{X}_E$ = average percentage change in sales for the experimental stores, and

$\overline{X}_C$ = average percentage change in sales for the control stores

Substituting the values given in Table 24.1 for X_{Ei} and X_{Cj} gives us the values for $\sum_{i=1}^{n_E} (X_{Ei} - \overline{X}_E)^2$ and $\sum_{j=1}^{n_C} (X_{Cj} - \overline{X}_C)^2$ in Table 24.2.

Thus the standard deviation of $\overline{X}_E - \overline{X}_C$ is

$$s_{\overline{X}_E - \overline{X}_C} = \sqrt{\frac{194.549 + 40.041}{10 + 10 - 2}} \qquad \text{From Equation 24-4}$$

$$= \sqrt{\frac{234.59}{18}} = \sqrt{13.033} = 3.61 \qquad \text{By arithmetic}$$

The standard deviation, 3.61, is then multiplied by the z statistic for the desired confidence level. If management wishes a 95-percent confidence level, the value for $z_{.025}$ would be used.[2] The product of $z_{.025}$ and $s_{\overline{X}_E - \overline{X}_C}$ would be the maximum amount of error in either direction from the estimate

Table 24.2 Calculation of $\sum_{i=1}^{n_E} (X_{E_i} - \overline{X}_E)^2$ and $\sum_{i=1}^{n_E} (X_{Cj} - \overline{X}_C)^2$
for experimental and controlled stores

i	X_{Ei}	$X_{Ei} - \overline{X}_E$	$(X_{Ei} - \overline{X}_E)^2$	j	X_{Cj}	$X_{Cj} - \overline{X}_C$	$(X_{Cj} - \overline{X}_C)^2$
1	+13.7	+2.59	6.7081	1	+2.4	+0.17	.0289
2	+ 7.0	−4.11	16.8921	2	+4.8	+2.57	6.6049
3	+ 9.8	−1.31	1.7161	3	−1.2	−3.43	11.7649
4	+14.6	+3.49	12.1801	4	+3.6	+1.37	1.8769
5	+ 6.2	−4.91	24.1081	5	+4.1	+1.87	3.4969
6	+13.8	+2.69	7.2361	6	+2.1	−0.13	.0169
7	+ 5.4	−5.71	32.6041	7	+0.9	−1.33	1.7689
8	+18.6	+7.49	56.1001	8	−0.7	−2.93	8.5844
9	+15.3	+4.19	17.5561	9	+4.6	+2.37	5.6169
10	+ 6.7	−4.41	19.4481	10	+1.7	−0.53	.2809

$$\sum_{i=1}^{10} (X_{Ei} - \overline{X}_E)^2 = 194.5490 \qquad \sum_{j=1}^{10} (X_{Cj} - \overline{X}_C) = 40.0410$$

[2] See Appendix II, p. 668, for table of z statistics.

of the experimental effect $(\overline{X}_E - \overline{X}_C)$. Hence the range of possible error—that is, the confidence interval—can be expressed and calculated as follows:

$$(\overline{X}_C - \overline{X}_E) - (z_{.025})(s_{\overline{X}_C - \overline{X}_E}) \leq (\overline{X}_C - \overline{X}_E) \leq (\overline{X}_C - \overline{X}_E)$$
$$+ (z_{.025})(s_{\overline{X}_C - \overline{X}_E})$$

$8.88 - 1.96(3.61) \leq (\overline{X}_C - \overline{X}_E) \leq 8.88 + 1.96(3.61)$	By substitution
$8.88 - 7.08 \leq (\overline{X}_C - \overline{X}_E) \leq 8.88 + 7.08$	By arithmetic
$1.80 \leq (\overline{X}_C - \overline{X}_E) \leq 15.96$	By arithmetic[3]

Thus we can be 95-percent sure that the new package will increase sales by at least 1.80 percent and at most 15.96 percent.

FACTORIAL EXPERIMENTS

Factorial experiments[4] are experiments designed to reveal the effects of simultaneous changes in two or more variables. This makes the experiment more efficient and also gives the researcher the opportunity to detect interaction between independent variables.

Again, we need to first define the commonly used terms:

A *factor* is an independent variable manipulated or observed during an experiment. Examples are price, style, and color.

A *level* is the value at which a factor is examined. It may be quantitative (for example, $5, $6, or $7, if the factor is price) or qualitative (for example, red, gold, or white, if the factor is color).

A *treatment* is a set of levels (one for each factor) employed in a particular trial (observation). For example, a $5 price and a gold package could be a treatment, or a "treatment combination," as it is often called.

A *response* is the numerical result of a particular treatment. For instance, a sale of 340 units might be the response to the $5/gold-package treatment.

[3] Readers familiar with statistics will note that we have used the approximate, large-sample z-statistic test rather than the exact, small-sample t-statistic test. The exact 95-percent confidence interval, using the t-statistic test, is $1.30 \leq (\overline{X}_c - \overline{X}_E) \leq 16.46$. For an explanation of the use of both small-sample and large-sample statistics, see Appendix II, p. 660.

[4] One of the most lucid discussions of factorial design for either the marketer, the engineer, or the scientist is found in Owen L. Davis, ed., *The Design and Analysis of Industrial Experiments* (New York: Hafner, 1956), Chapter 7. The authors are indebted to this work throughout this section.

The *effect of a factor* is the change in response produced by a change in the level of that factor. For example, if the price factor has treatment levels of \$5 and \$6, while the color factor is held constant, and the responses at these levels are sales of 340 and 310 units, respectively, then the effect of the price factor is 30 units. If a factor has three or more treatment levels, its effect will have to be measured a bit differently—for example, by taking the average of the differences in responses at each treatment level.

The *main effect* is the average effect of a factor observed under all treatments. If the effect of a factor is the same at all levels, regardless of variations in the levels of other factors in the experiment, it is independent of the other factors. Its main effect is attributable entirely to changes in its level. If this is not the case, there is interaction between the factor and one or more of the other factors.

Interaction is the influence of one factor on the effect of another. For example, the effect of an increase in the size (level) of a soft-drink advertisement (first factor) may be to increase sales (response) by 4,000 units when the temperature (second factor) is 90° (level) but by only 1,500 units when the temperature is 70°.

The applications and virtues of factorial design are best explained by illustration. For example, suppose that a researcher wants to test the effect on sales of two factors, price and package color. The simplest experiment he can perform is to evaluate the effect of price at two levels, P_0 and P_1, and the effect of color at two levels, C_0 and C_1. Three treatments must therefore be conducted. The original price/color combination, P_0,C_0, is the first treatment. The response to that treatment would be $R(P_0,C_0)$. The effect of price can be tested by holding color constant and changing price, treatment P_1,C_0. Similarly, the effect of color can be tested by holding price constant and changing color, treatment P_0,C_1. The effect of the change in each factor can then be calculated by subtracting the response to each of the subsequent treatments from the first treatment:

$$\text{Effect of price} = R(P_1, C_0) - R(P_0, C_0)$$
$$\text{Effect of color} = R(P_0, C_1) - R(P_0, C_0)$$

Since there is no way to measure the effect of experimental errors, each treatment must be repeated at least twice if the effect of these errors is to be evaluated.[5] Thus at least six experiments are necessary.

In a factorial design, a fourth treatment, P_1,C_1, would be performed and its response, $R(P_1,C_1)$, also measured. If there is no interaction between

[5] Error and interactive effects can be identified only if the experiment is replicated (that is, if each treatment is repeated at least twice). The variance in response between identical treatments (error effects) and the level of treatments (main effects and interactive effects) can then be computed, using statistical techniques.

the effects of price and color, the four treatments will yield two measurements of the effect of price and two measurements of the effect of color:

$$\text{Effect of color} = R(P_1, C_1) - R(P_1, C_0)$$

and

$$R(P_0, C_1) - R(P_0, C_0)$$

$$\text{Effect of price} = R(P_1, C_0) - R(P_0, C_0)$$

and

$$R(P_1, C_1) - R(P_1, C_1)$$

Thus four experiments of a factorial design yield the same number of responses as six experiments of a non-factorial (one-factor-at-a-time) design if there is no interaction between the factors.

Matrices. Factorial designs can be conveniently shown in the form of a matrix. For the preceding example, the simple matrix in Table 24.3 is sufficient.

Table 24.3   Simple 2 × 2 factorial design

		Color		
		Gold (G)		*Red (R)*
Price	$5	$R(\$5,\text{G}) = 400$		$R(\$5,\text{R}) = 340$
	$6	$R(\$6,\text{G}) = 370$		$R(\$6,\text{R}) = 310$

The effect of the color factor can be seen by comparing response $R(\$5,\text{G})$ with response $R(\$5,\text{R})$; the change from gold to red reduced sales by 60 units. The effect of the price factor can be found by comparing response $R(\$5,\text{G})$ with response $R(\$6,\text{G})$; the increase in price from $5 to $6 reduced sales by 30 units.

Assuming that there is no interaction between the two factors, price and color, any difference in responses between pairs of observations must be the effect of either experimental error or exogenous forces. For example, the difference between $R(\$6,\text{G}) - R(\$5,\text{G})$ and $R(\$6,\text{R}) - R(\$5,\text{R})$ in the illustration is the experimental error in the observations of price. Since the difference in this case is zero, $(370 - 400) - (310 - 340) = 0$, we assume that there is no experimental error and that, if there are any exogenous forces at work, their effects cancel one another out. The experimental error in the observations of color is also zero, $(340 - 400) - (310 - 370) = 0$, which again suggests that we can discount any exogenous forces.

If the response to the fourth treatment was greater or less than 310, the difference in responses would not be zero and the researcher would be confronted with either an experimental error or the interaction of two factors. (This latter possibility would never be revealed by experimenting with only one factor at a time, hence this is another argument in favor of factorial design.) Suppose that the previous experiment had revealed the data in Table 24.4. A change in price now yields a different change in sales for each

Table 24.4   Factorial experiment revealing experimental error or interaction

		Color	
		Gold (G)	*Red (R)*
Price	$5	$R(\$5,G) = 400$	$R(\$5,R) = 340$
	$6	$R(\$6,G) = 370$	$R(\$6,R) = 300$

level of the color factor. $R(\$6,G) - R(\$5,G)$ now equals -30, while $R(\$6,R) - R(\$5,R)$ equals -40. The effect of color is also different at each level of price. $R(\$5,R) - R(\$5,G)$ now equals -60, and $R(\$6,R) - R(\$5,R)$ equals -70. If the experimenter is certain that the price and color factors do not interact, then either the discrepancy in the observations is due to experimental error or an unidentified exogenous variable is disturbing the observations.

Factorial designs can be multidimensional, with observations made on two or more factors at any number of levels. However, each additional level doubles the total number of treatments necessary. The total number of treatments necessary, T, hence the total number of cells in the matrix, can be expressed notationally as

$$T = \prod_{i=1}^{n} L_i, \text{ where} \tag{24-5}$$

T = total number of treatments (minimum)

$\prod$ = an operational symbol indicating that the following variables should be multiplied, [6] and

L_i = number of levels of each factor, 1 through n

___

[6] For example, $\prod_{i=1}^{4} x_i$ is equivalent to $x_1 \cdot x_2 \cdot x_3 \cdot x_4$. If $x_1 = 1$, $x_2 = 3$, $x_3 = 5$, and $x_4 = 6$, then $\prod_{i=1}^{4} x_i = 1 \cdot 3 \cdot 5 \cdot 6 = 90$.

For instance, if a market analyst wanted to measure the effect of color at 3 levels ($L_1 = 3$) and the effect of price at 4 levels ($L_2 = 4$), 12 treatments would be required. In the previous example, $L_1 = 2$ and $L_2 = 2$; hence only four treatments, $T = 2 \cdot 2 = 4$, would be needed. If 3 factors—say color, price, and size—were to be evaluated at 3, 4, and 2 levels, respectively, then 24 treatments would be necessary. Thus the minimum number of treatments increases rapidly with an increase in the number of factor levels. This makes the cost—and in some cases the impracticality—of an experiment increase sharply with increases in either the number of factors or the number of factor levels. However, the simultaneous manipulation[7] or observation of variables made possible by a factorial design makes the experiment much more efficient than it would be if the data were gathered by other means.

The effect of each factor in a multidimensional design can be estimated by taking the difference between the response (shown in the matrix cells) at different levels of the factor. If more than two levels are used and their differences are not equal, an average difference can be used. For instance, if price has three treatment levels (L_1, L_2, and L_3), the average of $R(L_3) - R(L_2)$ and $R(L_2) - R(L_1)$ could be considered to be the effect of the price factor. This would be appropriate if the distances between the levels were equal. ($5, $6, and $7, for example, are each $1 apart.)

If the price-treatment levels are equal distances apart and the differences in responses are not equal, three possibilities exist: first, the relationship between the dependent variable and the factor is nonlinear; second, there is interaction between factors; or, third, there is experimental error. Thus if the gross effect[8] of a factor is measured at several treatment levels and little or no variation exists, the differences in responses can be assumed to be primarily attributable to the changes in the factor. Hence the gross effect would be equal to the true main effect of the factor.

For example, suppose that a market analyst wants to determine the effects of two factors, price and advertising, at 3 and 2 treatment levels, respectively. His experimental design and the outcomes (responses) are indicated in Table 24.5. (For simplicity, the response notation, $R(P,A)$, has been dropped from the table.

The gross effect of the two levels of advertising, plans A and B, can be computed for each price level, P.

Gross effect at $P = 10: $R($10, B) - R($10, A) = 280 - 300 = -20$

Gross effect at $P = 12: $R($12, B) - R($12, A) = 260 - 240 = -20$

Gross effect at $P = 14: $R($14, B) - R($14, B) = 200 - 180 = -20$

[7] The experimenter cannot always manipulate the factors being evaluated. He can hardly, for example, change the weather or the price of competing goods.
[8] The gross effect is the effect of the factor plus any interactive effects and experimental errors.

Table 24.5   Experimental-treatment matrix

Advertising

		Plan A	*Plan B*
	$10	300	280
Price	$12	260	240
	$14	200	180

Since each observed effect is equal, there is no need to compute an average effect. The equality-of-factor effect at each level of price suggests that there is no interaction (that is, the effect of advertising is not influenced by price), there is no evidence of experimental error or unidentified exogenous variables influencing the observations. Advertising plan A will simply produce 20 more units of sales than plan B, at least when the price ranges from $10 through $14.

An examination of the responses to price reveals that a $2 increase in price reduces sales by 40 units between the $10 and $12 levels; $R(\$12,A) - R(\$10,A) = -40$ and $R(\$12,B) - R(10,B) = -40$. However, the same increase reduces sales by 60 units between the $12 and $14 levels; $R(\$14,A) - R(\$12,A) = -60$ and $R(\$14,B) - R(\$12,B) = -60$. This discrepancy may be due to a nonlinear demand function, experimental error, or the influence of an exogenous variable. The possibility of interaction between price and advertising can be rejected, since the effect of the price factor is the same between $12 and $14 regardless of the level of advertising. However, the other three possibilities should be given consideration.

Latin Squares.   If the researcher is confident there is no interaction between factors, he can drastically reduce the cost of a factorial experiment by using a special form of factorial experiment known as a Latin square. The assumption that there is no interaction between factors is not always as unreasonable as it may appear. Many empirical studies have indicated that interactive effects may not occur as frequently or have as great an effect as one might think.

In a conventional three-factor, three-level factorial design, 27 different combinations are possible; hence 27 different treatments would be required. If the three factors were A, B, and C and had levels A_1, A_2, A_3, B_1, B_2, B_3, C_1, C_2, and C_3, the 27 treatments would be

$$A_1B_1C_1 \qquad A_1B_1C_2 \qquad A_1B_1C_3$$
$$A_1B_2C_1 \qquad A_1B_2C_2 \qquad A_1B_2C_3$$
$$A_1B_3C_1 \qquad A_1B_3C_2 \qquad A_1B_3C_3$$
$$A_2B_1C_1 \qquad A_2B_1C_2 \qquad A_2B_1C_3$$
$$A_2B_2C_1 \qquad A_2B_2C_2 \qquad A_2B_2C_3$$
$$A_2B_3C_1 \qquad A_2B_3C_2 \qquad A_2B_3C_3$$
$$A_3B_1C_1 \qquad A_3B_1C_2 \qquad A_3B_1C_3$$
$$A_3B_2C_1 \qquad A_3B_2C_2 \qquad A_3B_2C_3$$
$$A_3B_3C_1 \qquad A_3B_3C_2 \qquad A_3B_3C_3$$

In a Latin-square design, only the following 9 treatments would be used:

$$A_1B_1C_1 \qquad A_2B_1C_2 \qquad A_3B_1C_3$$
$$A_1B_2C_2 \qquad A_2B_2C_3 \qquad A_3B_2C_1$$
$$A_1B_3C_3 \qquad A_2B_3C_1 \qquad A_3B_3C_2$$

Inspection reveals that the Latin-square design has three replicates of each individual treatment A_1, A_2, A_3, B_1, B_2, B_3, C_1, C_2, C_3 but no replicates of joint treatments, such as A_1B_1. In contrast, the general three-level, three-factorial design had three replicates of each of the joint treatments. The loss of replicates of joint treatments has no disadvantages if there is no interaction between factors; hence the Latin-square design is equally satisfactory for evaluating the effects of variations in A, B, or C.

To illustrate the applications of the Latin-square design, assume that a marketer wants to test three factors, price, advertising, and package color, each at three treatment levels. He makes the critical a priori assumption that the factors do not interact or that the interaction is so small that it can be ignored, which enables him to use the Latin-square method and reduce the total number of treatments needed from 27 to 9. However, if this critical assumption is erroneous—that is, if two or more factors do interact—the resultant data will be distorted and the researcher will be unaware of the distortion. What appears to be experimental error may be largely interaction, since Latin squares provide no means of identifying or measuring the latter.

The experiment can be structured as in Table 24.6, with the hypothetical responses (unit sales) shown in each cell.

The factors can be evaluated by aggregating and comparing the responses for each level of each factor. For instance, for advertising plan A_1, the aggregate sales are

$$\sum A_1 = R(\$3, A_1, C_1) + R(\$4, A_1, C_2) + R(\$5, A_1, C_3)$$
$$\sum A_1 = 750 + 820 + 850$$
$$\sum A_1 = 2{,}420$$

Table 24.6   Latin-square design for a three-factor experiment

Advertising Plan

		A_1	A_2	A_3
Price	\$3	$R(\$3,A_1,C_1)$ 750	$R(\$3,A_2,C_2)$ 875	$R(\$3,A_3,C_3)$ 900
	\$4	$R(\$4,A_1,C_2)$ 820	$R(\$4,A_2,C_3)$ 800	$R(\$4,A_3,C_1)$ 700
	\$5	$R(\$5,A_1,C_3)$ 850	$R(\$5,A_2,C_1)$ 650	$R(\$5,A_3,C_2)$ 810

Package Color
$C_1 = $ Red
$C_2 = $ Gold
$C_3 = $ White

For all levels and factors, the aggregate responses are

Advertising	Price	Color
$\sum A_1 = 2{,}420$	$\sum \$3 = 2{,}525$	$\sum C_1 = 2{,}100$ (Red)
$\sum A_2 = 2{,}325$	$\sum \$4 = 2{,}320$	$\sum C_2 = 2{,}550$ (Gold)
$\sum A_3 = 2{,}410$	$\sum \$5 = 2{,}310$	$\sum C_3 = 2{,}505$ (White)

If maximization of sales is the firm's goal (cost data is not provided in this particular problem), then advertising plan A_1, a price of \$3, and a gold package are the best choices.

It is important in using Latin squares to understand that the values of the responses contained within the square do not necessarily reveal the response to the best combination of factor levels. In the example, $R(\$3,A_3,C_3)$ —a price of \$3, advertising plan A_3, and a white package—brought the greatest response (900). However, the best combination as shown by comparing the aggregates of the factor levels is a price of \$3, advertising plan A_1, and a gold package. Unfortunately (and by chance), this treatment, $R(\$3,A_1,C_2)$, is not included in the design. Often this problem can be overcome, once the best treatment is identified, simply by executing an additional trial with the best treatment.

The major disadvantage of a Latin-square design is that the effect of a particular factor cannot be measured by computing the difference between cells. This is obvious in the example if we take the difference between any cell in the $3 row and the adjoining cell in the $4 row. Even where the effect of one factor can be nullified by staying within a given column, say advertising plan A_1, the effect of the changes in levels of the other factor—in this case, color—will influence the responses and prevent us from isolating the effect of the row factor, price. For instance, when price was raised from $4 to $5 with advertising plan A_1, sales increased 30 units. However, we cannot tell how much of that increase was caused by the simultaneous change in the color of the package from white to gold. More advanced statistical techniques are necessary to specify the effect of each factor on the dependent variable, and also the size and distribution of the experimental error.

However, as long as the assumption that there are no interactive effects is valid, a Latin-square design does allow the main effect of a treatment to be determined. For instance, in the previous example the main effect of advertising plan A_1 was 807 units $(2,420/3)$, while the main effects of advertising plans A_2 and A_3 were 775 units and 803 units, respectively. Thus a change from plan A_2 to A_1 could be expected to increase sales by 32 units.

VIRTUES, PROBLEMS, AND LIMITATIONS OF MARKET EXPERIMENTATION

Market experimentation is an excellent method of causal research. If an experiment is properly designed and executed, it will reveal the effect that a change in one or more marketing variables will have on sales in quantitative terms and within the maximum range of error associated with a desired confidence level. Since experiments can usually be conducted on a small scale, the effects of various manipulations can be determined before the decision is made to apply the changes to the firm's entire market. Since experimentation is normally done in the actual marketplace, the values analyzed are both real and current. Thus, in gathering data that will enable him to specify causal relationships, the experimenter is also obtaining information that may prove vital to the construction of a predictive model.

Unfortunately, practical problems often prevent experimentation or make its results considerably less reliable than the decision-maker would like them to be. For example, the experimenter may need one or more pairs of perfectly matched units to ensure that the effect of extraneous forces will be the same on each pair, or he may need a large number of dissimilar units in order to average out the effects of these forces when in fact his choice is limited to a small number of dissimilar units.

Another difficulty is contamination. One unit, usually the control unit, can be contaminated by another, usually an experimental unit. For instance, the experimental treatment may be a price cut. If the customers of the control unit (where the price is held constant) get word of the lower price at the experimental unit, they may shift their patronage to the latter. This would exaggerate the effect of the experimental treatment. The solution is to isolate the control units from the experimental units, but this can be extremely difficult, especially when the variable being manipulated is price or promotion.

The management of the test units may also prove troublesome. If the experimenter has no authority over the test units, the experimental treatment may be distorted. Lack of cooperation, rigidity of behavior, and undesired responses by test-unit personnel often cause problems. Where participation is voluntary—for example, when the test units are retail stores not belonging to the sponsor of the experiment—these difficulties can be severe. Often their resolution will depend on the persuasiveness and ingenuity of the experimenter. Salesmen may fail to cooperate, or may go to the other extreme and give an unusual amount of attention to the subject of the experiment. Sales personnel may be slow in adapting to the experimental treatment if it requires a disruption of their usual routine. A store manager may choose to exploit an experimental price by advertising it. Test units may record sales data inaccurately. Even the simple act of giving special attention to a group or its activities often leads to a change in the normal behavior pattern.

Time can also be a handicap. First, the design and execution of a market experiment may take many weeks. Decisions cannot always wait that long. Second, the duration of the experimental treatment is usually short, and the full effect of a particular manipulation may not be felt before the experiment is concluded. Thus, the results may understate the true effect of the treatment. Conversely, the effect of a change may wear off over time. This is especially true with new convenience goods, such as breakfast cereals, where novelty alone is often enough to induce sales.

The simple fact that variables are being experimentally manipulated can result in unrealistic conditions. For instance, when Coca-Cola introduced king-size bottles in a local market, sales were not the same in *that* market as they would have been had the firm introduced the product nationally. Transient consumers, who would have been exposed to the new product's promotion in their home towns had the change been general, were not aware of the item while visiting the test-market area. Local residents whose viewing and reading habits were confined to national media were much less sensitive to the company's promotional effort during the experiment, since advertising had to be confined to local media.

Test-unit mortality is often a problem when the researcher is dependent on consumers for time-series data and the experiment demands a long period of time. For example, take the case of a shoe manufacturer who introduces a new material into his product and then subscribes to a market-data service to measure its acceptance. The shoes may have to be worn for a year or two before the buyers can demonstrate their satisfaction or dissatisfaction by repeating their purchase or shifting to a brand using the old material. Obviously, a number of the buyers may die or leave the market area, thus reducing the sample size. If this is anticipated, the sample size chosen at the beginning of the experiment should be larger than necessary.

Lack of product divisibility also imposes limits on market experimentation. Often the technical properties of a product preclude the production of a small output for test purposes. With a commercial airliner, for example, the fixed cost is so high that the total cost of the few units required for test marketing would be prohibitive. Divisibility can also be a problem with respect to the promotional variable. Advertising in national media cannot always be purchased on a local basis. This increases both the cost and the possibility of contaminating the control units. However, recent technological advances in the publishing industry have made divisibility of national media considerably more practical. *Time, Life,* the *Wall Street Journal,* and many newspapers now offer regional editions.

Security can severely constrain market experimentation. The firm may fear to reveal new product variations or other marketing strategies to competitors, who might copy them or prepare retaliatory measures.

Finally, cost is always a limiting factor. Experimentation can be expensive and financially risky—although much less risky than a market-wide or permanent change in a marketing variable. The experimenter must compete both with other members of the marketing department and with other members of the firm as a whole for company resources.

Countless methods for circumventing, eliminating, or minimizing the effects of many of these problems can be found in the literature of applied marketing research. The *Journal of Marketing Research* is probably the best single source of information on these techniques. Most of them are designed to meet the needs of a particular experiment, but they can often be adapted to other research.

Like the other forms of marketing research, experimentation has its own limitations and advantages. It relies heavily on statistical data that can be easily biased if a project is poorly designed or executed; thus it shares many of the hazards associated with survey research. Unlike the survey, however, experimentation enables the researcher to manipulate key market variables that may generate useful data for predicting the success or failure of new ideas. For testing new promotional tactics and product designs, this information can be especially valuable. Finally, like surveys and motivation research, experimentation takes the study into the marketplace and actually involves the people who make the final judgment on the firm's product—namely, its customers, present or potential.

CHAPTER 25

Motivation Research

Motivation research, or "MR," uses the behavioral sciences, primarily psychology, to determine the "why" of product demand. Other forms of marketing research can describe or predict consumer behavior and explain the relationship between the way people act and marketing, economic, and social variables. Motivation research goes a step further, searching out the underlying causes of these relationships—the psychological determinants of demand. A marketer skilled in projective methods, the basic MR approach, can obtain extremely useful information about the root causes of buyer behavior that may mean the difference between success or failure in the marketplace. The nature of these causes was explored in Chapter 9. What motivation research offers is a methodology for identifying and analyzing the underlying determinants of demand with respect to a particular product class or brand. It is also appropriate, and often used, to analyze the behavior of voters and employees, although these applications are not of immediate concern here.

Motivation research promises much as an aid to both strategy design and decision-making, especially with respect to the promotion and product instruments. How useful it really is has been a subject of hot debate for two decades. MR first became common in the early 1950's and received considerable public attention after the publication of Vance Packard's best seller, *The Hidden Persuaders.*[1] It has since fallen into some disrepute, due in no small part to the Edsel fiasco. However, its success, its current level of usage, and the increasing sophistication of the sciences upon which it is based definitely warrant its inclusion in any general discussion of marketing research.

[1] (New York: McKay, 1957).

DEFICIENCIES OF CONVENTIONAL INQUIRY

Researchers have reason to believe that the answers to objective questions used in the more traditional research methods often fail to reveal either the respondent's true motives or the correct descriptive data. A number of years ago, for example, a brewery wanted to know what kind of people drank each of their two products, light and dark beer. The brews were physically different and labeled accordingly, the words "light" and "dark," respectively, having been incorporated into their trademarks. The firm sponsored a questionnaire survey that included the question "Do you drink 'light' or 'dark'?" with respect to the firm's products. The respondents who purchased the firm's brand indicated they preferred the "light" over the "dark" beverage by a ratio of 3 to 1. The sample was large enough to be a statistically valid representation of the firm's customer population. However, according to the company's sales records, the dark beer was favored over the light by a ratio of 9 to 1. Thus any conclusions about the differences between the light- and dark-beer drinkers, based on this sample data, would obviously be meaningless.

NESCAFÉ: A CLASSIC CASE

The Nescafé instant coffee study of Mason Haire[2] is a classic in the field of motivation research and provides a good deal of insight into this method of marketing research. A conventional survey—that is, one that used objective questions—had been made to determine attitudes toward Nescafé, a brand of instant coffee. The questions were, "Do you use instant coffee?" and (if not), "What do you dislike about it?" Most of the unfavorable responses were of the order "I don't like the flavor." In view of the simplicity and cliché-like quality of the responses, and because of the researcher's awareness of the psychological and sociological factors that tend to compromise answers to objective questions, this answer was suspected of being a convenient stereotype bearing little relation to the truth. In an effort to uncover the non-users' real reasons for rejecting Nescafé, the researcher tried a projective questionnaire that allowed the respondents to transfer their true feelings to a hypothetical third party, thus unwittingly revealing themselves to the interviewer.

A group of 100 housewives was given the following pair of shopping lists, which are identical except for the brand and type of coffee specified:

[2] Mason Haire, "Projective Techniques in Marketing Research," *Journal of Marketing,* Vol. 14, No. 5 (April 1950), pp. 649–56.

Shopping List I	*Shopping List II*
Pound and a half of hamburger	Pound and a half of hamburger
2 loaves of Wonder Bread	2 loaves of Wonder Bread
Bunch of carrots	Bunch of carrots
1 can Rumford's Baking Powder	1 can Rumford's Baking Powder
Nescafé Instant Coffee	1 lb. Maxwell House Coffee (Drip Grind)
2 cans Del Monte Peaches	2 cans Del Monte Peaches
5 lbs. potatoes	5 lbs. potatoes

Half the group was given List I and half was given List II. The participants were then asked to describe the kind of woman who had prepared their particular list.

An analysis of the responses showed a rather definite and revealing profile of the hypothetical Nescafé user, as opposed to the user of regular coffee. The predominant characteristics cited in the 100 responses were as follows:

1. 48 percent of the people described the woman who bought Nescafé as lazy; 4 percent described the woman who bought Maxwell House as lazy.
2. 48 percent of the people described the woman who bought Nescafé as failing to plan household purchases and schedules well; 12 percent described the woman who bought Maxwell House this way.
3. 4 percent described the Nescafé woman as thrifty; 16 percent described the Maxwell House woman as thrifty.
   12 percent described the Nescafé woman as spendthrift; 0 percent described the Maxwell House woman this way.
4. 16 percent described the Nescafé woman as not a good wife; 0 percent described the Maxwell House woman this way.
   4 percent described the Nescafé woman as a good wife; 16 percent described the Maxwell House woman as a good wife.[3]

The list that contained Nescafé clearly did violence to the accepted role of the housewife. As Haire pointed out, coffee-making is a ritual taken seriously by the homemaker. The rejection of instant coffee had little to do with its flavor, being rather the result of an implied threat to the user's self-image. The labor-saving property of Nescafé apparently detracted from the idealized role of wife and homemaker, and hence reduced the demand for the product. Additional surveys confirmed this analysis.

The Nescafé study also attempted to determine whether the psychological attitude toward the product actually affected its consumption. To obtain an answer, interviewers were provided with a list of women whose

---

[3] *Ibid.*, p. 652.

relevant characteristics appeared to be the same as those of the 100 respondents in the previous survey. These new women were confronted with
the original shopping lists and asked to describe the hypothetical shopper.
In addition, the interviewers, using the pretext that they wished to examine
the brands of food purchased, obtained permission to see the respondent's
pantry shelves and thereby determine which ones bought instant coffee. The
survey data revealed a high statistical correlation between possession of
instant coffee and attitude. Those who did not have instant coffee tended to
describe the hypothetical Nescafé user in the usual unflattering terms. Those
who had instant coffee perceived her in a much more favorable light.

Assuming that the Nescafé situation is not unique, the more traditional
methods of marketing research may be inadequate, and even misleading, in
many situations. This suggests the use of motivation research, perhaps in combination with the more conventional research methods, when a marketing
problem persists or sales are inexplicably low.

PROJECTIVE TECHNIQUES

Projective techniques are basic to motivation research. Essentially, they are
questionnaire or interviewing methods designed to penetrate the psychological barrier that exists between the respondent and the interviewer. This
barrier may be the result of social constraints or the suppression of subconscious desires. The respondent may be aware of his real motives but
refuse to reveal them because they are socially unacceptable or are contrary
to the image he is anxious to portray. For instance, a Dior dress or a Cadillac
may be purchased primarily as a status symbol, since many less expensive
brands offer essentially the same aesthetic and functional properties, but this
would seldom be the reason cited by the consumer. The respondent may
also be motivated by subconscious drives, and hence be unable to verbalize his
true motives, even when he is not inhibited by social constraints. For example, Freudian psychologists claim that a suppressed desire for oral gratification is the underlying cause of many pipe, cigar, and cigarette purchases.

Projective techniques attempt to penetrate such barriers by encouraging the respondent to transfer, or project, his feelings to a third person or
object. The type of projective technique used in any given study will depend
on the school of psychology to which its designer subscribes. A follower of
the Gestalt school sees the consumer as responding to rational drives but
being unwilling to verbalize many of them. A respondent may avoid flying
because he is afraid of planes, buy gaudy clothes to get attention, or go
bowling because it makes him feel like "one of the boys," but he is not
likely to say so when asked. Rather, he may claim that flying is too expensive, that the quality of workmanship and the material of the clothes is good,

or that bowling is good exercise. Motivation-research questions give the respondent an opportunity to reveal his true feelings by transferring them to a third object, thinking they will not be identified with him. In the Nescafé study, the third person was the hypothetical shopper.

The Gestaltist looks for rational reasons for behavior in analyzing responses. He attempts to define the predominant attitudes or perceptions that underlie the consumer's behavior and to relate them to biological drives or rational psychogenic needs. Where the attitudes or perceptions of buyers conflict with the goals of the firm, he may recommend promotional strategies to alter them or changes in the product to accommodate them, whichever are more feasible. Where the attitudes or perceptions of buyers favor the firm's products, the same instruments can be used to reinforce these attitudes.

The Freudian views this approach as superficial, arguing that the true explanation of consumer behavior with respect to a particular purchasing decision can be found only by a far more lengthy and complex inquiry. A Freudian analyst would search for a link between purchase behavior and suppressed desires, particularly sexual desires. Since the actors—in this case, the consumers—are themselves unaware of their true motives, the interviews and the analysis necessary to discover them are likely to be long and complex and to demand a high degree of professional skill. However, once the subconscious motives that determine the actors' behavior are identified and can be related to the properties of the product or promotional strategy under study, appropriate alteration can be made in the marketing mix.

The Freudian approach offers exciting possibilities for the marketing of nearly everything from soap to politicians. However, the costs of this type of analysis are high, and the results may be uncertain. Also, the validity of generalizing findings based on a small number of respondents (necessary because of the high cost per respondent) to the firm's market population as a whole is questionable. Nevertheless, the Freudian school is not without its successes. When instant cake mixes were first introduced, they met with limited acceptance. Exploratory research revealed no objectionable properties of the product; in fact, the cakes were considered very good. Price was not a factor, since an instant cake could be prepared at virtually the same cost as a regular cake. Promotion had been effective in educating the public, and most housewives were found to be aware of the new product. Finally, the mixes were available in most grocery stores. These conditions, combined with the labor-saving property of the product, indicated that sales should be much greater than they were.

A Freudian-oriented motivation-research project revealed that baking a cake is symbolically like having a baby. The procreative urge arising in the id is suppressed by the ego, and the resultant conflict between the id and the ego channels the reproductive drive into more socially acceptable channels —in this case, cake-baking. The superego which approves of motherhood but recognizes the need to limit the size of the family, reinforces this behavior pattern. The symbolic act, cake-baking, gratifies the drive while conforming to the psychological and sociological constraints. The instant cake mix compromised the symbolic act by reducing cake-making to a very simple and trivial job. The answer, according to the motivation researchers, was to remove the dehydrated egg from the mix, thereby allowing the woman to become reinvolved in the act of cake preparation through the task of adding and beating into the mix one or two raw eggs. The essential ease and simplicity of the product was preserved—thus appealing to the need to relax or avoid work—while the housewife was allowed to continue her symbolic role.

A Gestalt approach to the problem might have resulted in the same recommendation, but for slightly different reasons. The Gestalt analyst might have perceived the failure of the cake mix as analogous to the rejection of instant coffee in that it conflicted with the consumer's idea of the socially acceptable role of a wife and mother.

OBJECTIVE VERSUS PROJECTIVE TECHNIQUES

Objective questionnaires ask direct questions, the answers to which are interpreted at face value. They are the sort of thing the student is confronted with when he takes an examination—matching problems, fill-ins, multiple-choice questions, or essay questions. The questionnaires are administered by the usual survey techniques—mail, telephone, or personal interview. They are usually structured; that is, they contain specific, formal questions. However, they may be unstructured, so that the respondent can discuss the subject without any bounds being imposed. This latter method is sometimes suitable for exploratory research, when the analyst has yet to define the problem and is looking to a group of respondents to provide some clues and insights.

The following questions are typical of the objective method. Questions 1 through 4 are structured, while questions 5 and 6 are unstructured.

    1. Match the brands in Column 1 with the descriptive words in Column 2:

Brand	*Words*	
A. Chevrolet	1. Fast	_____
B. Ford	2. Reliable	_____
C. Chrysler	3. Conservative	_____
	4. Economical	_____
	5. Comfortable	_____
	6. Sporty	_____
	7. Cheap	_____

2. Your favorite brand of cigarettes is _____.
3. Your family's annual income is: ____Below $6,000; ____$6,000–$9,999; ____$10,000–$14,999; ____$15,000–$24,999; ____over $24,999.
4. What problems have you had with your present brand?
5. What are your views on life insurance?

Although objective questionnaires are the antithesis of the projective technique, they may be used during the exploratory phase of a motivation-research project to reveal problems—such as a general and distinct preference for another brand, or a prevalent demographic, social, or economic characteristic of the market population—that warrants investigation by projective methods.

Objective questions are especially useful when the subject has no emotional or psychogenic content. For example, one would expect that direct questioning would yield accurate data on the respondent's family size, occupation, length of vacation, and hobbies. Conversely, data on drinking habits, income, and magazine preferences can be very distorted when objective questionnaires are used, especially when the respondent has to identify himself. Whenever social norms or status are involved, answers tend to be distorted by the respondent's desire to conform to an idealized self-image. This is where projective techniques come into play.

Mechanical determinants of consumer behavior are physical conditions that constrain or channel the buyer's actions. For instance, if a man is driving through sparsely populated country and his car is almost out of gas, he will stop at the first gas station he comes to and purchase whatever brand of automotive fuel it sells. Projective techniques are obviously inappropriate to detect and evaluate mechanical determinants of sales. Objective questions may reveal them, although the buyer himself may be unaware of their influence. When such influences are suspected, a survey employing direct observation of consumers' behavior will generally provide the necessary information.

Error-choice tests consist of a statement, or series of statements, that has a scaled group of answers from which the respondent makes his choice. Hopefully the respondent is unaware of the normal answer, which usually rests toward the middle of the scale. His attitude or bias will be revealed by where he picks his response. For example, to determine if a respondent considers air travel expensive, the interviewer might confront him with this question: "The cost of the average one-way fare from Los Angeles to New York is (1) $100, (2) $110, (3) $150, or (4) $180." Answer 1 would imply that air travel is perceived as inexpensive (less costly than it actually is). Answer 4 would suggest that air travel is perceived as expensive (at least, more so than it actually is).

The advantages of the error-choice test, which straddles the line between projective and objective measurement, are simplicity of administration and analysis and the susceptibility of the data to statistical manipulation.

Word-association tests consist of a list of words—often 50 to 100—that the respondent is asked to match with words of his own choosing. This open-ended matching process is called "free association" and is intended to allow the respondent to reveal his inner feelings. By selecting an adequate and representative sample size, the researcher can determine the prevailing attitudes of the market population. Table 25.1 shows a typical word-association test.

Table 25.1 Word-association test

Word	Associated Word	Number of Seconds		
		1 2 3 4 5 6 7 8 9 10	Over 10	Blocked
Automobile	_____	_ _ _ _ _ _ _ _ _ __	_____	_____
House	_____	_ _ _ _ _ _ _ _ _ __	_____	_____
* Pullman	_____	_ _ _ _ _ _ _ _ _ __	_____	_____
Electric	_____	_ _ _ _ _ _ _ _ _ __	_____	_____
† Greyhound	_____	_ _ _ _ _ _ _ _ _ __	_____	_____
Grass	_____	_ _ _ _ _ _ _ _ _ __	_____	_____
Airplane	_____	_ _ _ _ _ _ _ _ _ __	_____	_____

* If association to Pullman is "train," ask for next word that comes to mind.
† If association to Greyhound is "bus," ask for next word that comes to mind.

SOURCE: From *Research Analysis for Marketing Decisions* by Chester R. Wasson. Copyright © 1965 by Meredith Corporation. Reprinted by permission of Appleton-Century-Crofts and the Chicago *Tribune*.

Word-association tests are often used to test the effect of brand names and words in advertising copy. These words, referred to as "stimulating" words, are mixed with a selection of "neutral" words that serve as padding and disguise the subject under study in order to avoid a bias in the answers. The reactions to each stimulating word are then tallied under categories such as "favorable," "unfavorable," or "indifferent," depending on the context of the subject under study. For example, the response "dangerous" might be classified as "favorable" if the stimulating word were being considered for a motion-picture title, but would hardly rate such a classification if the stimulating word were a candidate for the brand name of a cough medicine.

Word-association questionnaires, or tests, are normally administered personally. However, little skill is required on the part of the interviewer; he simply says the words and records the respondent's replies. Frequently he will time the responses. If the interviewee takes over twenty seconds to come up with a matching word, a mental block may be indicated. Analyzing the replies is a bit more difficult, and is normally done by a specialist.

There are a number of variations of this form of motivation research. Instead of recording only the first matching word, which is the usual method, the second, third, and fourth words to come to the respondent's mind may also be noted. Occasionally, free association is rejected in favor of a controlled test and the respondent is offered a list of matching words from which to select his choices. Another controlled-question approach is to ask the respondent to name a particular item within a general class defined by the question. For example, the interviewer might ask, "What brand of soap do you associate with soft skin?"

Sentence-completion tests are used to provoke a response that will be directed toward a specific subject, yet unconstrained. Examples are:

"Trading stamps are _____."
"I use Texaco gasoline because _____."
"I do not use Texaco gasoline because _____."
"Most people who do not fly do so because _____."
"An economical automobile is _____."

Where a projective approach is desired, the use of the first person in the sentences is normally avoided.

This kind of test is easy to administer, although a personal interview is usually necessary. The respondent is advised to state the first thought that comes to mind, and a time limit is placed on each question to encourage him to do so. The initial response is important, for it is often the only one that time will allow when consumers are confronted with a promotional message such as a radio or television commercial. Besides, a first impression may well determine whether the prospect will become interested enough to receive reinforcing messages or will reject the seller's proposition out of hand. This is especially important in non-personal selling, where there is no salesman to deal with the buyer's objections or confront him with alternative stimuli.

One disadvantage of sentence-completion tests is that they are more specific than word-association tests. This makes it more likely that the respondent will detect the true intent of the questionnaire and bias his answers accordingly. Also, sentence-completion tests, like word-association questionnaires, require skill in interpretation. Once past the tabulation stage, most MR data does not lend itself to mechanical analysis.

Story-completion tests are an expansion of the sentence-completion concept. The respondent is given the first part of a story and asked to complete it. For example, a housewife might be given a description of a woman about to enter a store to purchase a refrigerator. The details would be sketchy, including only such relevant information as family size and, possibly, income. The respondent would then complete the story, hopefully revealing thereby her own preferences, as well as other anxieties, motives, and attitudes pertinent to her purchase behavior.

Here again a personal interviewer of modest skill and a highly trained analyst are required. The answer possibilities are virtually endless, and the responses may be elaborate and complex. Although the answers may contain a great deal of information, the resultant data are not always amenable to classification, aggregation, and statistical manipulation. For these reasons, motivation-research methods are often useful in the exploratory phase of research, with objective and quantitative techniques being invoked after the problem is better defined. (Conversely, objective methods used in the exploratory phase may reveal problems that lend themselves to motivation research in the in-depth phase of the study.)

In *picture-frustration tests,* a picture is used rather than an incomplete verbal story, and the respondent is asked to describe the scene. The two basic types are the thematic apperception test and the cartoon.

The *thematic apperception test* is an ambiguous picture or series of pictures of a scene or scenes that involves people and some object associated with the good or service in question. The scenes are neutral in the sense that they do not reveal any suggestive facial expressions or motions. The respondent is asked to construct a story about the picture or describe some particular aspect of it. Sometimes balloons are drawn over the heads of the people in the pictures and the respondent is asked to write in an appropriate speech or dialogue. Or, the interviewer may ask such questions as, "What is the figure in the picture thinking?" Figure 25.1, is a typical thematic apperception test.

The second type of picture-frustration test is the cartoon. A *cartoon* consists of one or more frames depicting a situation into which the respondent can easily project himself and which is not ambiguous with respect to the relationship between the central figure or figures and the objects in the picture. Balloons above the figures, if they are used, are not left blank, but contain statements that clarify the relationship and sometimes the attitudes or beliefs of the characters.

The respondent is then asked to comment on the situation. He may be asked to identify with a character of his choice or be given a selection of captions and asked to pick the one that goes best with the cartoon. The captions, of course, are loaded statements designed to reveal the respondent's true attitude toward the relationships or objects depicted by the cartoon.

Like story-completion tests, picture-frustration tests are easy to admin-

FIGURE 25.1
Thematic apperception test

SOURCE: From *Research Analysis for Marketing Decisions* by Chester R. Wasson. Copyright © 1965 by Meredith Corporation. Reprinted by permission of Appleton-Century-Crofts and courtesy of the *Chicago Tribune*.

ister but harder to analyze. However, they may yield a wealth of information and expose problems that would have gone undetected had objective questionnaires been used.

Role-playing is a projective method whereby the respondent is given a set of conditions, or questions, and encouraged to project himself into the situation in much the same way an actor would play and interpret a particular character in a theatrical production. Either verbal or pictorial methods can be used. Open-end questions, story-completion tests, and picture-frustration tests are the most common techniques.

Role-playing gives the respondent a vehicle for expressing his true feelings and avoids the constraints of a highly structured interview. It is used frequently in exploratory research when the researcher is ignorant or uncertain of consumer attitudes or behavioral patterns with respect to his product.

In-depth interviews are exhaustive, unstructured, and often repeated personal interviews of respondents. Although used occasionally by researchers who subscribe to the Gestalt school, they are primarily identified with the Freudian school. In addition to being time-consuming and costly, they require an interviewer who is at least a highly trained technician, preferably a psychologist. The analysis of these interviews also usually requires a psychologist, and the results do not lend themselves to statistical manipulation. Furthermore, time and cost constraints normally limit the study to a small number of respondents, making it difficult for the researcher to generalize his conclusions to a market population.

Like the Rorschach inkblot test, the in-depth interview is primarily designed to reveal the abnormalities of individual patients. Since the marketer is interested in identifying the normal causes of human behavior so that he can generalize them to his whole market population, in-depth interviews are seldom a practical research tool except in exploratory research where the objective is to detect unknown causes of consumer behavior. In-depth interviews are most useful in defining a problem and suggesting hypotheses for examination by more conventional and rigorous methods.

Figure 25.2 summarizes the methods of acquiring behavioral data. Data on actual purchase behavior are gathered by conventional research methods, such as inquiry, observations, or examination of sales records. However, the method of motivation research used will depend on what the researcher feels is the probable explanation of the behavior. If the explanation is utilitarian, it can be revealed through an objective survey in which direct questions are asked. If the explanation is based on physical factors (for example, store location or brand availability), the consumer's state of consciousness is irrelevant, and information can be gathered through observation. The behavioral explanations provided by Gestalt instrumentalism and Freudian symbolism are more complex and must be explored through projective survey methods, using the sophisticated and largely subjective techniques of psychology.

LIMITATIONS AND VIRTUES OF MOTIVATION RESEARCH

The limitations of motivation research can be summarized as time, cost, and subjectivity. In addition, the results lend themselves poorly to statistical manipulation, and the validity of generalizing the findings—often drawn from very small samples (fewer than 30 respondents)—is open to question.

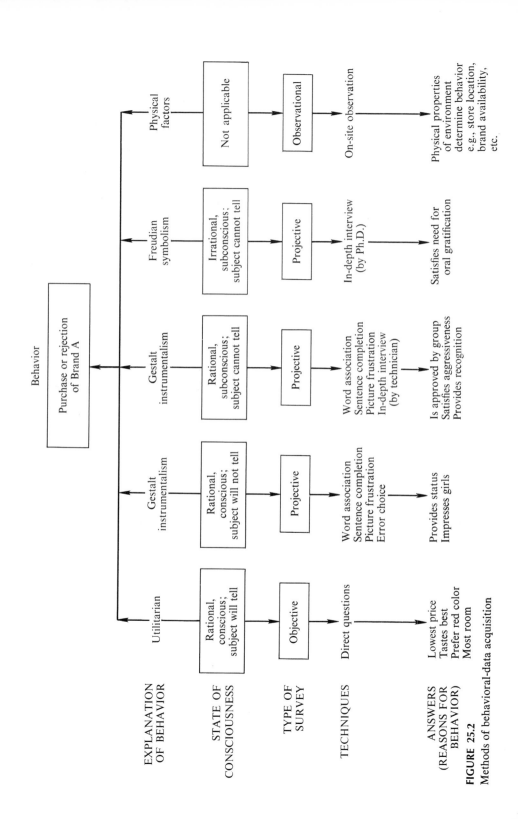

FIGURE 25.2
Methods of behavioral-data acquisition

The diagram is laid out in rows, read left to right:

EXPLANATION OF BEHAVIOR: Utilitarian | Gestalt instrumentalism | Gestalt instrumentalism | Freudian symbolism | Physical factors

STATE OF CONSCIOUSNESS:
- Rational, conscious; subject will tell
- Rational, conscious; subject will not tell
- Rational, subconscious; subject cannot tell
- Irrational, subconscious; subject cannot tell
- Not applicable

TYPE OF SURVEY:
- Objective
- Projective
- Projective
- Projective
- Observational

TECHNIQUES:
- Direct questions
- Word association / Sentence completion / Picture frustration / Error choice
- Word association / Sentence completion / Picture frustration / In-depth interview (by technician)
- In-depth interview (by Ph.D.)
- On-site observation

ANSWERS (REASONS FOR BEHAVIOR):
- Lowest price / Tastes best / Prefer red color / Most room
- Provides status / Impresses girls
- Is approved by group / Satisfies aggressiveness / Provides recognition
- Satisfies need for oral gratification
- Physical properties of environment determine behavior e.g., store location, brand availability, etc.

Behavior: Purchase or rejection of Brand A

Some critics would discard MR completely, preferring to rely on more conventional research techniques.

The more zealous advocates of MR minimize these limitations and argue that psychological traits are so universal that the revelations of a few well-chosen respondents can be generalized to an entire market population with a high degree of confidence. This line of reasoning rationalizes the small sample size inherent in MR and denies the need for statistical methods to establish the distribution of characteristics throughout the market population and to estimate experimental error. One simply accepts a psychological quality that prevails among the respondents as prevailing among the population from which they were drawn.

Perhaps a more reasoned approach is to recognize and accept the limitations of MR. Even with these limitations, it is often very useful in exploratory research projects. It can uncover factors that are significant determinants of consumer behavior and that strongly influence the firm's performance in the marketplace. These findings can be verified by conventional research methods stated in the form of hypotheses and tested by extensive sampling. The type of sampling necessary to confirm or deny the hypotheses can usually be accomplished without spending too much money, often by a mail questionnaire or a telephone survey. In this way, considerably more observations can be made, and a sample size that will yield an acceptably small error at the desired confidence level becomes practical.

The final argument for accepting motivation research as a research tool is that it offers the only methodology for exposing a rather large and at times influential body of consumer motivations. It is, despite its limitations, the best instrument for revealing the "why" of demand. Often it is the only way to detect a critical problem or to obtain meaningful and correct answers from a sample population. Thus it can be a powerful addition to the firm's marketing research methodology.

CHAPTER 26

Prediction and Forecasting

Prediction and forecasting are the ultimate tasks of marketing research. They are also the most difficult and precarious. Predictions and forecasts are really different subsets of predictive research, although the two terms are often used synonymously. *Prediction* is the estimation of the current value of a variable. For example, a firm may use present-sales, population, and income data from its current markets to derive an equation for predicting the potential sales in a new market. By substituting population and income data from the new market in the predictive equation, it could then estimate the sales potential for that market. For example, a predictive equation for sales in the Seattle SMSA might be:

$S = 10,000 + .005P + 1.5I$, where

S = annual dollar sales in the market

P = population in the market, and

I = average household income in the market

Forecasting is the estimation of the future value of a variable. For instance, the firm might determine a trend line relating past sales to time and then extrapolate that trend line into the future to obtain estimates of sales in future years.

If a predictive model relates the dependent variable (usually sales) to independent variables that can themselves be easily forecast, the model can also be used for forecasting. The researcher simply substitutes the values forecast for the independent variables in the equation. For example, by substituting the values forecast for population and income in 1980 in the predictive equation given above, he could obtain a sales forecast for that year. Suppose that the 1980 estimates of population and average household income for the Seattle SMSA were 5,000,000 and $9,000, respectively. The sales forecast for that year would then be

$$S_{1980} = 10,000 + .005(5,000,000) + 1.5(9,000)$$
$$S_{1980} = 10,000 + 25,000 + 13,500 = \$48,500$$

This is a workable approach, although a rather naive one, for it assumes that the relationship between the variables will be the same in 1980 as it was during the period from which the original data (used to determine the equation) was taken. An alteration in such things as consumer taste or the number of competitors could disrupt these relationships and make the forecasted value erroneous. However, if the researcher is sufficiently perceptive—or lucky—he can often correct for changes in variables that are exogenous to (not included in) the equation but that affect its structure.

The data necessary for a predictive model can be acquired through historical research, surveys, or experimentation. This information is then used to estimate the causal relationship between the dependent variable and the independent variables. This task is made easier when the independent variables can be accurately and inexpensively determined, such as population, disposable personal income, and retail sales. Ideally, they should be variables whose values are forecastable. Often, a lagged variable can be used.[1] For instance, the adult population can be accurately forecast twenty years in advance by lagging it against present child and adult populations and adjusting for mortality. The output of new cars as one of the determinants of the demand for replacement tires can be lagged three years. In other words, the demand, d, for replacement tires at time t is dependent on the consumption of new cars, C, at time $t - 3$, plus some other factors, x_i; expressed mathematically, $d_t = 4C_{t-3} + f(x_i)$.

Often a forecasting model will express the dependent variable, such as future demand, as a function of independent variables that must be computed. The computations may be made by manipulating historical or survey data. For instance, the future demand for shotgun shells might depend on the number of hunters and skeet shooters. These latter figures would have to be derived from survey information, which—if a sample survey were used—would then have to be generalized to the market population.

Most explanatory variables[2]—including two of the classical determi-

[1] A lagged variable is one whose value is measured at a different time than that of the other variables in an equation. For instance, a forecasting model for first-grade readers might be $d_t = .97B_{t-5}$, where d_t equals the demand for first-grade readers at year t and B_{t-5} equals total births in the year $t - 5$.
[2] The explanatory variables of an equation are the independent variables that actually determine the value of the dependent variable.

nants of demand, income and population—must be forecast if they are included in a forecasting model, except when they are lagged, in which case historical data can be employed up to the point where the time lag is no longer sufficient to put the lagged variable within the period of available data. Fortunately, both income and population can be forecast with a fair degree of precision, barring an economic crisis or an abrupt change in the birth rate during the period covered by the forecast.

In formulating a forecasting model, the researcher must find dependent variables whose future values can be estimated by one of the methods suggested above. These variables may be either determinants or proxies. *Determinants* are independent variables whose magnitudes determine the size of the dependent variable. *Proxies* are variables that do not influence the dependent variable but do vary in a constant relationship to one or more of the determinants. The advantage of proxy variables is that they can often be obtained more easily than values for the determinants themselves.

Time is often used as a proxy variable. The consumption of a commodity will often vary in a rather precise relationship with time. Actually, time per se may have nothing to do with the dependent variable; consumption just happens to be determined by a variable whose values change over time in a certain way. For instance, the demand for electricity is determined by a multitude of variables, ranging from the inventory of electrical appliances to the installation of air-conditioning systems and consumers' nocturnal habits. To identify each of these determinants and specify their effect on the consumption of electricity would be an extremely arduous task. Fortunately, their aggregate effect usually varies over time in a fairly consistent and mathematically describable manner. Hence the demand for electricity can be forecast using time as the dependent variable, even though it is not actually a determinant of demand.

It is practical to use the true determinants in an equation if they meet three requirements. First, they must be significant. That is, they must account for a reasonable proportion of the change in the dependent variable. Choosing trivial determinants simply adds to the equation's mathematical complexity without substantially illuminating the problem. Second, they must be sufficiently few in number to be mathematically manageable. Ideally, there should not be more than two or three explanatory variables. Third, their future values must be predictable with an acceptable degree of accuracy. Often, as in the case of electricity, this is impossible. Sometimes the task of identifying and evaluating the determinants and specifying their relationship to the dependent variable would simply put too much of a strain on the firm's resource capacity, and a proxy variable serves almost as well, at a fraction of the cost.

Regardless of the method used, the objective of forecasting remains the same—namely, to estimate the value of a variable, sometimes called the "criterion variable," at a future point or points in time. This does not necessarily mean that the variable will be a direct function of time. It may be completely independent, or it may be dependent on another variable, such as population, that is a function of time. If the criterion variable is both independent of time and uninfluenced by any variable that changes with time, it will remain constant with respect to time. If graphed, such a relationship would plot as a straight, horizontal line; the value for the criterion variable (plotted on the Y-axis) would be the same for each different value of time.

If the criterion variable depends on time or on a variable that changes with time, it is a "covariant" of time, and its relationship to time can be specified. The resultant function, or "growth curve," can take a variety of forms and can be generated in a number of ways. We shall examine some of the more common growth functions in the next section.

GROWTH FUNCTIONS

Growth functions are mathematical expressions that specify the relationship between a dependent variable—usually an industry or a firm's demand—and time. The type of growth curve appropriate to a particular product class or brand can generally be determined from prior experience or by economic analysis.

Causal Models. The one forecasting model that does not show the dependent variable as a function of time is the causal model. This type of model expresses the dependent variable as a function of one or more of its explanatory variables. Thus, if X, Y, and Z are explanatory variables that determine the value of demand for a product, d, at any time, t, the causal model in general form would be $d_t = f(X_t, Y_t, Z_t)$. If the values of X, Y, and Z are known or can be forecast for a specified time, t, then the causal model will reveal the value of d at that time.

A causal model of the demand for air cargo service will illustrate this point. By using historical data and regression analysis (to be discussed later in the chapter), one of the authors succeeded in establishing the following causal model of the demand for air cargo service:

$D_t = 1,694,276.0 + 208,488.9P_t + 2339.6G_t$, where

D_t = demand (in dollars) for air cargo service during year t

P_t = price of air cargo service during year t, measured in ton-miles per dollar, and

G_t = gross national product (in billions of dollars) for year t

This model uses two explanatory variables common to causal models —namely, price and gross national product. For convenience, the price, P, is expressed as the number of ton-miles received per dollar charged. Thus the total demand increases as the service gets cheaper—that is, as more ton-miles are provided for each dollar charged.

Once the causal model is specified, the future values of the independent variables must be estimated before a forecast can be made. Assuming that GNP will increase at an annual rate of 6 percent (which is typical of its growth during the past decade) and estimating a price of 8.33 ton-miles per dollar by 1980 (the latter figure being based on the rapidly improving technology in the aircraft industry) would yield a demand forecast of 3,953 million ton-miles for 1980. The quality of this estimate can be stipulated by regression techniques beyond the scope of this text.

Mechanical Extrapolation. In selecting or deriving a growth function, the researcher generally attempts to fit a curve to historical data or estimated values. This can be done graphically by plotting the dependent variable against time and drawing a line that best fits the points. This line, which represents the general *trend* of the data, is then extrapolated—that is, extended—into the future.

A straight line suggests a linear relationship between the dependent variable and time; a curved line suggests a nonlinear relationship. The graphs in Figure 26.1 show three different growth curves. The points represent historical data. The shapes of the curves are suggested by the data and, presumably, by the history of the industries. The broken segments represent the extrapolation, hence the forecast.

Curves can be constructed solely by visual means and the forecasted values read directly from the vertical axis. A more rigorous method is to

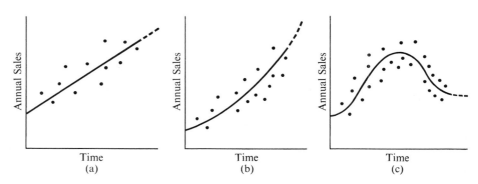

FIGURE 26.1
Examples of mechanical extrapolation

use mathematical techniques to develop an exact expression for the relationship between a dependent variable and time. These methods yield mathematical expressions for the growth functions and, in turn, can be easily graphed. Mathematical growth models are generally divided into two classes, linear and nonlinear. We shall examine the linear models first.

Linear Growth Models. Linear growth models are naive because they assume that what happens in the future will be exactly what happened in the past. They plot as a straight line—hence the adjective "linear." (Figure 26.1(a) is illustrative.) Their general mathematical form is

$Y_t = b$, where (26–1)

Y_t = value of the dependent variable (usually sales) at time t (note: Y_t is a constant; hence, $Y_{t-1} = Y_t = Y_{t+1} \cdots Y_{t+n}$), and

b = quantity of Y per unit of time, t (usually sales per week, month, or year)

This formula yields the value of Y for a specific time, t (for example, sales in 1967, revenue in May, or receipts for Monday). For a cumulative total value, such as cumulative sales through 1973, the following formula is used:

$$\sum_{t=1}^{n} Y_t = a + bn, \text{ where} \qquad (26\text{–}2)$$

$\sum_{t=1}^{n} Y_t$ = cumulative total value of Y through time period t

a = cumulative total value of Y prior to time period $t = 1$, also called the "intercept"[3] (note: $a = Y_{t-1} + Y_{t-2} + \cdots Y_{t-n}$)

b = quantity of Y per time period, t (usually sales per week, month, or year), and

n = number of time periods from $t = 0$ to $t = n$

To illustrate, assume an industry sold 2,000 units of product class S during the first full year of operation and 4,000, 6,000, and 8,000 units in subsequent years. This suggests a sales rate, b, of 2,000 units per year. If the first year is designated as $t = 1$, the second year as $t = 2$, and so on, and if the market analyst assumes that the rate of sales, b, will remain constant during the foreseeable future, then the general linear function can be stated in explicit form and applied as follows:

---

[3] Note that a is a fixed value—that is, a constant—throughout the range of t. It is called an intercept because it denotes the point where the curve intercepts the vertical axis. This is obvious, since if $t = 0$, then $Y = a$.

$$\sum_{t=1}^{n} Y_t = a + bn \qquad \text{Given as Equation 26-2}$$

$$\sum_{t=1}^{4} Y_t = 0 + 2,000(4) \qquad \text{By substitution}$$

$$\sum_{t=1}^{4} Y_t = 8,000 \qquad \text{By arithmetic}$$

Thus the cumulative total sales forecast through the fourth year ($t = 4$) would be 8,000 units. The sales in that year, as in all other years, would be 2,000 units ($Y_t = 2,000$). Linear models, though extremely naive, are occasionally useful, especially for short-run periods.

Nonlinear Growth Models.   A nonlinear, or curvilinear, growth model assumes that the absolute rate of total sales, or demand, will not remain constant but will change as a function of time. If the dependent variable (total sales or demand) is plotted against time, the resultant line will curve, since the slope (the rate of change of the function) is changing. Empirical studies indicate that these curves generally take one of the following mathematical forms: (1) logarithmic, (2) modified exponential-basic, and (3) modified exponential-Gompertz.

A *logarithmic function* is one step above a linear function. It is the simplest form of an exponential function—a family of curves so named because the independent variables are exponents or are raised to an exponential power. If the independent variable is time, then the dependent variable will increase by a fixed percentage each time period. For instance, if the dependent variable is sales and the time periods are expressed in years, then the logarithmic growth model assumes that annual sales will increase by a fixed percentage. Expressed mathematically,

$$Y_t = Y_1(1 + b)^{t-1}, \text{ where} \qquad (26\text{-}3)$$

$Y_t = $ sales in time period t

$Y_1 = $ increment of sales in time period $t = 1$ (usually defined as the first full period of operation)

$b = $ periodic rate of sales increase, and

$t = $ time (independent variable)

Cumulative total sales, or demand, is found by aggregating incremental sales. Thus cumulative sales for a four-year period would equal $Y_1 + Y_2 + Y_3 + Y_4 = \sum_{t=1}^{4} Y_t$.

For example, suppose that a product was introduced late in 1969 and that during the first full year of operation, 1970, 2,000 units were sold. A market analysis indicated that annual sales would increase at the same rate as GNP increased, or about 6 percent. Designating 1970, 1971, 1972, and 1973 as $t = 1$, $t = 2$, $t = 3$, and $t = 4$, respectively, the annual aggregate consumption (sales) can be forecast as follows:

$Y_t = Y_1(1 + b)^{t-1}$	Given as Equation 26–3
$Y_1 = 2,000(1 + .06)^{1-1}$	By substitution
$Y_1 = 2,000$	By arithmetic[4]
$Y_2 = 2,000(1 + .06)^{2-1}$	By substitution
$Y_2 = 2,120$	By arithmetic
$Y_3 = 2,000(1 + .06)^{3-1}$	By substitution
$Y_3 = 2,247$	By arithmetic
$Y_4 = 2,000(1 + .06)^{4-1}$	By substitution
$Y_4 = 2,382$	By arithmetic

Aggregate sales through the fourth year would thus be

$\sum_{t=1}^{4} Y_t = Y_1 + Y_2 + Y_3 + Y_4$	Given
$\sum_{t=1}^{4} Y_t = 2,000 + 2,120 + 2,247 + 2,382$	By substitution
$\sum_{t=1}^{4} Y_t = 11,774$	By arithmetic

Since the absolute value of Y_t (annual consumption) gets larger every year, by an increasing amount, both the cumulative total value, ΣY_t, and the incremental value, Y_t, will plot as logarithmic curves and continue to turn upward as they move to the right, as in Figure 26.2. Both values increase at an increasing rate.

This type of growth curve fits the empirical data on a number of product classes, such as electricity and household appliances. It also describes the growth of certain explanatory variables commonly used in causal models, particularly income and population. However, it is unrealistic to assume that the consumption of any good or service will increase at an increasing

[4] Students will recall that any value taken to the zero power equals 1; thus $x^0 = 1$, $(5)^0 = 1$, and $(3 + 2)^0 = 1$.

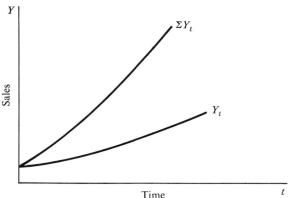

FIGURE 26.2
Logarithmic growth function

rate indefinitely. Sooner or later, an innovation becomes diffused throughout the market, fewer additional applications of a product can be found, optimum economies of scale are reached, marginal utility starts to drop, and annual sales, Y_t, stops increasing and may even begin to decline. When this happens, the growth curve becomes linear (Y_t is a constant) or begins to decline (Y_t decreases). This effect is observable graphically as an inflection point on the curve (see Figure 26.1(c), page 552, for an example). The logarithmic function, which may be appropriate during the early stages of a product's life cycle, does not provide for this effect. Hence, a different function is suggested if the analyst is attempting to forecast sales through the maturity stage of the product cycle. Modified exponential functions can be constructed to yield such a result.

Modified Exponential Functions—Basic Form. Modified exponential functions are adaptations of the basic logarithmic (i.e., exponential) function, $Y_t = ab^t$. The function is given certain properties that the analyst feels are appropriate to a particular application. These properties concern the direction of the curve, its limits, and its inflection points, if any. For example, the market analyst may conclude, from his experience with similar goods, that the consumption of a product is unlikely to increase at an increasing rate, as a simple, unmodified exponential function would indicate. Instead, he may feel that total cumulative sales will increase throughout the product's life cycle, but at a decreasing rate. This assumption—that a new product will be well received in the marketplace, but that the market will eventually become saturated and the demand for additional units, Y_t, will decrease as t increases, perhaps even falling to zero—has been proven valid for many product classes, such as commercial aircraft.

A modified exponential function has the form

$$\sum_{t=1}^{n} Y_t = K + ab^{n-1}, \text{ where} \tag{26-4}$$

$\sum_{t=1}^{n} Y_t$ = cumulative sales through time period n

Y_t = sales in time period t

K = asymptotic limit of cumulative sales $(K > 0)$

a and b are constants that define the form of the curve

t = time period, usually one year, and

n = total number of time periods

A graph of the function would be a curve similar to that in Figure 26.3.

The sales for a given time period, Y_t, can be computed by subtracting the cumulative total sales through time $t - 1$ from the cumulative total sales through time t. Expressed mathematically,

$$Y_t = \sum_{t=1}^{n} Y_t - \sum_{t=1}^{n-1} Y_t \tag{26-5}$$

Modified exponential functions are asymptotic; that is, total cumulative sales approaches, but never reaches, a limit. This limit, K, is usually defined as the maximum potential market—the demand, consumption, or sales that would occur if every potential buyer purchased the good or service.

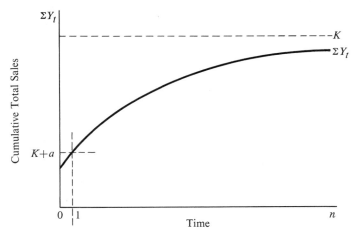

FIGURE 26.3
Modified exponential growth function

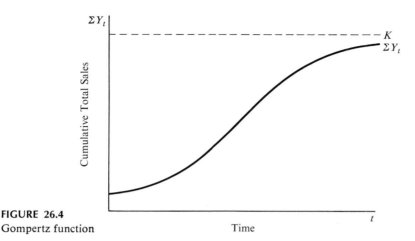

FIGURE 26.4
Gompertz function

The Gompertz Function. Innovation-diffusion research shows that if the level of market penetration is plotted against time, the result is an S-shaped curve like that in Figure 9–2 (page 212). The lower part of the curve corresponds to the unmodified exponential function described previously. The upper part corresponds to the basic form of the modified exponential function just described. Were we to combine in sequence the properties of both functions, the result would be an S-shaped growth curve like that in Figure 26.4. This type of curvilinear function is called a Gompertz curve, or function.

The Gompertz function most appropriate for market forecasting is

$$\sum_{t=1}^{n} Y_t = Ka^{b^{n-1}}, \text{ where} \tag{26-6}$$

$\sum_{t=1}^{n} Y_t$ = cumulative sales through time period n, and

K, a, and b are parameters,[5] with $K > 0$, $0 < a < 1$, and $0 < b < 1$

The sales for a specific time period, Y_t, can be computed by using Equation 26–5.

This form of the Gompertz function, when graphed, yields an S-shaped curve that conforms closely to the annual sales pattern of many products. This is evident if we plot the sales histories of a cross-section of products, as in Figure 26.5.

---

[5] Other Gompertz functions have the same general properties, but to be in the positive quadrant and move upward and to the right, a and b must be subject to the constraints indicated.

The K value, which is a constant, is the cumulative potential demand. Like all exponential functions, the Gompertz curve is asymptotic to a limit—in this case, K—as t increases. There are almost always some potential customers who refuse to adopt a product. Even if these non-adopters could be converted into late laggards, it is doubtful that the time and the marginal cost of the additional promotion, production, and price discounts would be justified by the marginal revenue from this final increment of sales. For example, as the market approaches saturation, large additional advertising expenditures produce very few additional sales.

A Gompertz function can be described mathematically in two ways, either in its natural form or in logarithmic form, as below:

$$\sum_{i=1}^{n} Y_t = Ka^{b^{n-1}}, \ 0 < a < 1, \ 0 < b < 1 \qquad (26\text{--}7)$$

or

$$\log \sum_{i=1}^{n} Y_t = \log K + (\log a)b^{n-1}, \ 0 < a < 1,$$
$$0 < b < 1, \text{ where} \qquad (26\text{--}8)$$

$$\sum_{i=1}^{n} Y_t = \text{cumulative value of the dependent variable (demand or sales) at time period } n$$

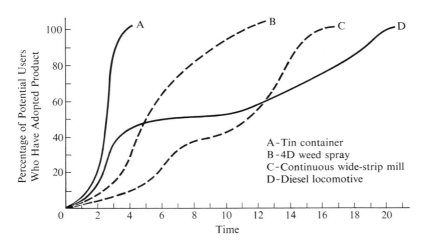

FIGURE 26.5
Market penetration over time

SOURCE: Adapted from Everett M. Rogers, *Diffusion of Innovations*, reprinted with permission of The Macmillan Company, © The Free Press of Glencoe, A Division of The Macmillan Company, 1962; and from Edwin Mansfield, "Technical Change and the Rate of Innovation," *Econometrica*, Vol. 29, No. 4 (October 1961), p. 743.

K = a constant and the asymptotic limit of the function (usually maximum potential cumulative demand, sales, etc.)

a and b are parameters that specify the shape of the curve, and

t = time period, usually one year

The logarithmic expression may appear more cumbersome, but it actually simplifies the mathematical manipulations.[6]

If the Gompertz curves appear to fit data that has already been accumulated, that data can be used to compute the parameters a, b, and K. The data—perhaps annual sales for each of the years $t = 1, 2, \ldots m$— is arrayed by consecutive years into three equal-sized groups. Obviously, if m is not divisible by three, a value of $n < m$ that is divisible by three becomes the data set. For example, if data existed for 23 consecutive years, only the data for the last 21 years would be used. Thus n would be 21, and each of the three groups would contain 7 observations. If we let

$$\sum\nolimits_1 \log Y_t = \sum_{i=1}^{n/3} (\log Y_t), \tag{26-9}$$

$$\sum\nolimits_2 \log Y_t = \sum_{i=(n/3)+1}^{2(n/3)} (\log Y_t), \text{ and} \tag{26-10}$$

$$\sum\nolimits_3 \log Y_t = \sum_{i=2(n/3)+1}^{n} (\log Y_t), \text{ where} \tag{26-11}$$

$\sum\nolimits_1 \log Y_t$ = summation of the logarithms of Y_t for the first third of the observations

$\sum\nolimits_2 \log Y_t$ = summation of the logarithms of Y_t for the second third of the observations, and

$\sum\nolimits_3 \log Y_t$ = summation of the logarithms of Y_t for the last third of the observations

then, in this example,

$$\sum\nolimits_1 = \log Y_1 + \log Y_2 + \log Y_3 + \log Y_4 + \log Y_5 \\ + \log Y_6 + \log Y_7$$

$$\sum\nolimits_2 = \log Y_8 + \log Y_9 + \log Y_{10} + \log Y_{11} + \log Y_{12} \\ + \log Y_{13} + \log Y_{14}$$

$$\sum\nolimits_3 = \log Y_{15} + \log Y_{16} + \log Y_{17} + \log Y_{18} + \log Y_{19} \\ + \log Y_{20} + \log Y_{21}$$

The values of the constants a, b, and K for the Gompertz curve that fits the data can then be found by solving the following equations:

[6] See Appendix II, p. 661, for a brief explanation of logarithms.

$$b^{n/3} = \frac{\Sigma_3 \log Y_t - \Sigma_2 \log Y_t}{\Sigma_2 \log Y_t - \Sigma_1 \log Y_t} \qquad (26\text{-}12)$$

$$\log a = (\Sigma_2 \log Y_t - \Sigma_1 \log Y_t) \cdot \frac{b-1}{(b^{n/3} - 1)^2} \qquad (26\text{-}13)$$

$$\log K = \frac{1}{n/3} \cdot \frac{\Sigma_1 \log Y_t - \Sigma_2 \log Y_t - (\Sigma_2 \log Y_t)^2}{\Sigma_1 \log Y_t - \Sigma_3 \log Y_t - 2\Sigma_2 \log Y_t} \qquad (26\text{-}14)$$

By simple arithmetic operations, the values for b, a, and K can be explicitly determined as:

$$b = \sqrt[n/3]{\frac{\Sigma_3 \log Y_t - \Sigma_2 \log Y_t}{\Sigma_2 \log Y_t - \Sigma_1 \log Y_t}}$$

$$a = \log^{-1}\left[(\Sigma_2 \log Y_t - \Sigma_1 \log Y_t) \cdot \frac{b-1}{(b^{n/3} - 1)^2}\right]$$

$$K = \log^{-1}\left[\frac{1}{n/3} \cdot \frac{\Sigma_1 \log Y_t - \Sigma_2 \log Y_t - (\Sigma_2 \log Y_t)^2}{\Sigma_1 \log Y_t - \Sigma_3 \log Y_t - 2\Sigma_2 \log Y_t}\right]$$

To illustrate the applications of the Gompertz function, let us assume that an analyst wants to forecast the sales of a particular model of microfilm reader to libraries. He has data on the annual sales of the device from its introduction in early 1948 through 1968. This data is presented in Table 26.1.

Using the equations just developed for Σ_1, Σ_2, and Σ_3, we can find the explicit form of the Gompertz function that will reflect sales of the microfilm unit. Table 26.2 shows these calculations.

Substituting these values in Equation 26–12 gives us a value for b, as follows:

$$b^{n/3} = \frac{\Sigma_3 \log Y - \Sigma_2 \log Y}{\Sigma_2 \log Y - \Sigma_1 \log Y} \qquad \text{Given as Equation 26–12}$$

$$b^7 = \frac{28.619963 - 25.282131}{25.282131 - 18.932023} \qquad \text{By substitution}$$

$$b^7 = \frac{3.337832}{6.350108} = .525634 \qquad \text{By arithmetic}$$

$$b = \sqrt[7]{.525634} = .912216 \qquad \text{By arithmetic (using table of logarithms)}[7]$$

[7] The seventh root can be calculated by finding the logarithm of .525364 in a table of logarithms, dividing the resulting logarithms by 7, and then finding its antilogarithm in the table. See Appendix II, p. 665, for an example of this method.

Table 26.1   Sales of microfilm readers to libraries

Year	Annual Sales (Y_t) (in units)	Cumulative Sales (ΣY_t) (in units)
1948	95	95
1949	125	220
1950	165	385
1951	210	595
1952	290	885
1953	305	1,190
1954	505	1,695
1955	500	2,195
1956	655	2,850
1957	585	3,435
1958	785	4,220
1959	760	4,980
1960	1,060	6,040
1961	975	7,015
1962	1,265	8,280
1963	1,355	9,635
1964	1,380	11,015
1965	1,505	12,520
1966	1,565	14,085
1967	1,550	15,635
1968	1,555	17,190

We then obtain a value for a from Equation 26–13:

$$\log a = (\Sigma_2 \log Y - \Sigma_1 \log Y) \cdot \frac{(b - 1)}{(b^{n/3} - 1)^2} \qquad \text{Given as Equation 26–13}$$

$$\log a = (25.282131 - 18.932023) \cdot \frac{.912216 - 1}{(.525634 - 1)^2} \qquad \text{By substitution}$$

$$\log a = (6.350108) \cdot \frac{-.087784}{(-.474366)^2} \qquad \text{By arithmetic}$$

$$\log a = -2.477248 \qquad \text{By arithmetic}$$

$$a = \log^{-1}(-2.477248) = .003332 \qquad \text{By arithmetic (using tables of logarithms)}$$

Table 26.2 Calculation of the explicit form of the Gompertz function

Year	t	Cumulative Sales (Y_t)	$\log Y_t$
1948	1	95	1.977748
1949	2	220	2.342452
1950	3	385	2.585493
1951	4	595	2.774552
1952	5	885	2.946980
1953	6	1,190	3.075586
1954	7	1,695	3.229210

$$\sum\nolimits_1 \log Y_t = \sum_{t=1}^{7} \log Y_t = 18.932023$$

Year	t	Cumulative Sales (Y_t)	$\log Y_t$
1955	8	2,195	3.341476
1956	9	2,850	3.454888
1957	10	3,435	3.535971
1958	11	4,220	3.625358
1959	12	4,980	3.697276
1960	13	6,040	3.781084
1961	14	7,015	3.846076

$$\sum\nolimits_2 \log Y_t = \sum_{t=8}^{14} \log Y_t = 25.282131$$

Year	t	Cumulative Sales (Y_t)	$\log Y_t$
1962	15	8,280	3.918080
1963	16	9,635	3.983902
1964	17	11,015	4.042035
1965	18	12,520	4.097656
1966	19	14,085	4.148809
1967	20	15,635	4.194151
1968	21	17,190	4.235329

$$\sum\nolimits_3 \log Y_t = \sum_{t=9}^{21} \log Y_t = 28.619963$$

Finally, Equation 26–14 gives us a value for K:

$$\log K = \left(\frac{1}{\frac{n}{3}}\right) \frac{(\sum_1 \log Y)(\sum_3 \log Y) - (\sum_2 \log Y)^2}{(\sum_1 \log Y + \sum_3 \log Y - 2\sum_2 \log Y)} \quad \begin{array}{l} \text{Given as} \\ \text{Equation 26–14} \end{array}$$

$$\log K = \left(\frac{1}{7}\right) \frac{(18.932023)(28.619963) - (25.282131)^2}{18.932023 + 28.619963 - 2(25.282131)} \quad \text{By substitution}$$

$$\log K = (0.142857)\left(\frac{541.833798 - 639.186148}{47.552986 - 50.564262}\right)$$ By arithmetic

$$\log K = (0.14287)\left(\frac{-97.352350}{-3.011276}\right)$$ By arithmetic

$$\log K = 4.616934$$ By arithmetic

$$K = 41,393.58$$ By arithmetic (using tables of logarithms)

Substituting the values for b, a, and K in Equation 26–7 gives us a Gompertz function of the following form:

$$\sum_{t=1}^{n} Y_t = (41,393.58)(.003332)^{.912216^{n-1}}$$

The saturation level of total cumulative sales is 41,394 units (the value of K). Figure 26.6 compares the actual cumulative sales of the microfilm unit (through 1968) and the cumulative sales predicted by the Gompertz function. Cumulative sales are also forecast through 1990.

An annual sales forecast can be obtained from the Gompertz function by using Equation 26–5,

$$Y_t = \sum_{t=1}^{n} Y_t - \sum_{t=1}^{n-1} Y_t$$

Figure 26.7 compares the actual annual sales and the annual sales predicted by the Gompertz function. Again, annual sales are forecast through 1990.

Often—as in the case of a brand new product—historical data is unavailable, and the method just developed for computing a, b, and K cannot be used. However, innovation-diffusion research findings suggest that the S-curve—hence the Gompertz function—is a reasonable approximation of the adoption of a new product by its potential consumers. Fortunately, there is a method of estimating such a curve, once the researcher has estimated the total potential demand, K, for the item. This can often be accomplished by analyzing the potential uses for the new product and then estimating the saturated demand for each use.

Having set K equal to the total potential demand (or sales, consumption, etc.), we must still select values for the parameters a and b. We can obtain a value for a by first estimating the demand (or sales) during the first year of the product's life cycle, $n = 1$. This results in the formula

$$a = \frac{Y_1}{K}, \text{ where}$$

$Y_1 = $ the first year's sales,

as follows:

$$\sum_{t=1}^{n} Y_t = Ka^{b^{n-1}}$$ Given as Equation 26–6

$$\sum_{t=1}^{1} Y_t = Ka^{b^{0}}$$ By substitution ($n = 1$)

By algebraic manipulation

$$Y_1 = Ka^1$$ (Note: $b^0 = 1$ by definition, and $\sum_{t=1}^{1} Y_t = Y_1$.)

$$a = \frac{Y_1}{K}$$ By algebraic manipulation (Note: By convention, the exponent 1 is not shown; hence $a^1 = a$.)

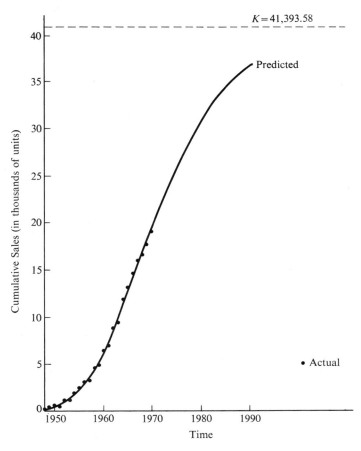

FIGURE 26.6
Cumulative sales

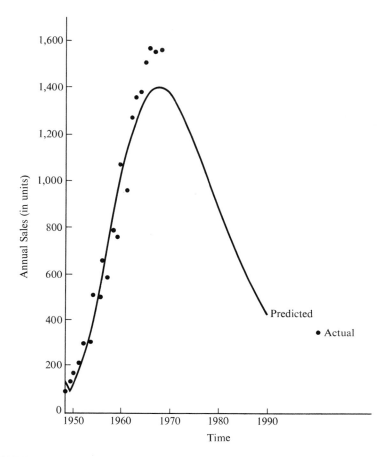

FIGURE 26.7
Annual sales

Having derived values for both *K* and *a,* we have only to select a value for *b*. Generally, the most practical way to do this is to estimate (1) the length of time between the introduction of the product and its maturity phase and (2) the percentage of the total potential market that will be penetrated by this time. The time span from introduction to maturity can be estimated by referring to the innovation-diffusion literature, which suggests time spans for many broad product classes, or by analyzing the firm or industry's experience, if any, with similar goods. The same sources will indicate the probable percentage of market penetration. This percentage, multiplied by the *K* value, will give us a value for $\sum_{t=1}^{n} Y_t$ at the time of maturity. The *b* parameter is now the only value still unknown. It is easily revealed by some simple mathematical manipulation and by converting the equation to the logarithmic form. The maturity period is designated as m; that is, $n = m$ at maturity.

$$\sum_{t=1}^{n} Y_t = Ka^{b^{n-1}} \qquad \text{Given as Equation 26–7}$$

$$\sum_{t=1}^{m} Y_t = Ka^{b^{m-1}} \qquad \text{By substitution}$$

$$\left(\frac{\sum_{t=1}^{m} Y_t}{K}\right) = a^{b^{m-1}} \qquad \text{By algebraic manipulation}$$

$$\log\left(\frac{\sum_{t=1}^{m} Y_t}{K}\right) = (\log a)b^{m-1} \qquad \text{By changing to logarithmic form}$$

$$b^{m-1} = \frac{\log\left(\frac{\sum_{t=1}^{m} Y_t}{K}\right)}{\log a} \qquad \text{By algebraic manipulation}$$

$$b = \left[\frac{\log\left(\frac{\sum_{t=1}^{m} Y_t}{K}\right)}{\log a}\right]^{\frac{1}{m-1}} \qquad \text{By algebraic manipulation} \tag{26–15}$$

Having derived a value for each parameter, K, a, and b, the analyst can substitute these values in Equation 26–15 and can solve for either Y_t or $\sum_{t=1}^{n} Y_t$ for any time period by using Equations 26–5 or 26–6.

REGRESSION ANALYSIS

The use of a growth model for forecasting is appropriate only when all variables, other than time, are assumed to be constant. If the other variables would logically vary, the explicit relationship between sales and the influential variables must be estimated by regression analysis. *Regression analysis* is a statistical method for estimating the explicit relationship between a dependent variable and one or more independent variables. *Econometrics* is the application of regression analysis to economics.

For instance, a firm's marketing manager might assume that the sales of a particular product is determined primarily by its advertising budget and its price. This is a logical supposition, but it is not sufficiently explicit to be useful in making advertising or pricing decisions. Besides, the manager could be wrong. The econometrician's response to this assumption would be to test it, by estimating the mathematical relationship between the product's sales, Y, and its advertising, X_1, and price, X_2. (We have deferred to the convention of econometrics in the selection of symbols in this section.) The first step would be to develop an equation expressing the estimated relationship between sales and the two independent variables—for example, $\hat{Y} = 5{,}200 + .35X_1 - 254X_2$. The second step would be to evaluate the equation. As the "∧" over the Y indicates, the equation is only an estimate of the relationship between the variables. Hence its dependability must be evaluated if management is to use it intelligently. It may be highly reliable and precise, or it may be so unreliable that the econometrician cannot be reasonably confident that the variables are actually related.

Linear regression analysis is by far the most common estimative technique. It is used to determine *linear* relationships between a dependent variable and one or more independent variables. In mathematical notation,

$$\hat{Y} = \hat{\alpha} + \hat{\beta}_1X_1 + \hat{\beta}_2X_2 + \cdots \hat{\beta}_iX_i, \text{ where} \qquad (26\text{--}16)$$

$\hat{Y}$ = estimated value of the dependent variable

$\hat{\alpha}$ = estimated value of the intercept

$\hat{\beta}_i$ = estimated value of the coefficient specifying the relationship between $\hat{Y}$ and X_i

X = independent variable, and

1, 2, ... i are subscripts identifying the variables

This method can be illustrated most easily by a simple, two-variable model. Suppose that a market analyst has recorded sales, Y, and advertising expenditures, X, for each of ten standard metropolitan statistical areas ($n = 1$ through 10). This data is presented in Table 26.3.

Graphing the observations for all ten areas yields a series of points, as in Figure 26.8. The analyst—now playing the role of econometrician—generates a line of best fit, $\hat{Y} = \alpha + \hat{\beta}X$, through the point scatter. This line is an estimate of the linear relationship, if any, between sales and advertising. The equation, which is simply a mathematical expression of the line, obviously does not account for every variation in sales. If it did, the line would go through every point; that is, the computed value of sales, $\hat{Y}$, would always equal the observed value, Y. The difference between $\hat{Y}$ and Y is the error, *e,* caused by the fact that some of the variables that influence sales—such as

Table 26.3 Sales and advertising data for ten standard metropolitan statistical areas

SMSA	Sales	Advertising Expenditure
1	$155,000	$18,000
2	121,000	10,000
3	219,000	29,000
4	120,000	16,000
5	231,000	41,000
6	225,000	37,000
7	168,000	22,000
8	195,000	24,000
9	219,000	33,000
10	120,000	20,000

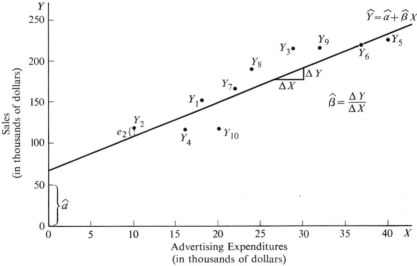

FIGURE 26.8
Linear estimate of relationship between sales and advertising
for a hypothetical product

price, consumer income, tastes, and the price of substitute products—are not
included in the equation. If the influence of any of these variables has been
significant during the period of observation, the equation will be of little
value. If, on the other hand, the influence of the other variables has been
negligible, the equation will be a useful statement of the relationship between
sales and advertising and can safely be employed in advertising decisions.

The fitting of the line—that is, the generation of the equation—is accomplished by using the *method of least squares,* a relatively simple statistical technique. By executing a series of arithmetic steps, the analyst can derive an equation of the form $\hat{Y} = \hat{\alpha} + \hat{\beta}X$ that minimizes the sum of the error terms squared ($\sum_{i=1}^{n} e^2_i = $ a minimum).

As an example of regression analysis, we will determine the unknown parameters $\hat{\alpha}$ and $\hat{\beta}$ in the two-variable equation $\hat{Y} = \hat{\alpha} + \hat{\beta}X$ for the data contained in Table 26.3. Normally, the unknown parameters are determined by the techniques of matrix algebra (usually through the use of a computer). However, in this simple case, where they are only two variables, the unknown parameters $\hat{\alpha}$ and $\hat{\beta}$ can be determined by solving the following two equations:

$$\hat{\alpha} = \frac{(\sum X^2)(\sum Y) - (\sum X)(\sum XY)}{n(\sum X^2) - (\sum X)^2} \qquad (26\text{--}17)$$

$$\hat{\beta} = \frac{n(\sum XY) - (\sum X)(\sum Y)}{n(\sum X^2) - (\sum X)^2} \qquad (26\text{--}18)$$

where all the summations are over the range 1 to n and where n is the total number of observations, or data points. Table 26.4 shows the calculations of the various summations. Y is the dependent variable (sales), and X is the independent variable (advertising expenditures). The total number of data points, n, is 10.

Table 26.4   Calculation of the explicit form of $\hat{Y} = \hat{\alpha} + \hat{\beta}X$

SMSA	Y	X	XY	X²
1	155	18	2,790	324
2	121	10	1,210	100
3	219	29	6,351	841
4	120	16	1,920	256
5	231	41	9,471	1,681
6	225	37	8,325	1,369
7	168	22	3,696	484
8	195	24	4,680	576
9	219	33	7,227	1,089
10	120	20	2,400	400
$n = 10$	$\Sigma Y = 1{,}773$	$\Sigma X = 250$	$\Sigma XY = 48{,}070$	$\Sigma X^2 = 7{,}120$

Substituting these values into equations 26–17 and 26–18 yields the values of $\hat{\alpha}$ and $\hat{\beta}$, as follows:

$$\hat{\alpha} = \frac{\sum X^2(\sum Y) - \sum X(\sum XY)}{n(\sum X^2) - (\sum X)^2}$$ Given as Equation 26–17

$$\hat{\alpha} = \frac{(7,120)(1,773) - (250)(48,070)}{(10)(7,120) - (250)(250)}$$ By substitution

$$\hat{\alpha} = \frac{12,623,760 - 12,017,500}{71,200 - 62,500}$$ By arithmetic

$$\hat{\alpha} = \frac{606,260}{8,700} = 69.685$$ By arithmetic

$$\hat{\beta} = \frac{n(\sum XY) - \sum X(\sum Y)}{n(\sum X^2) - (\sum X)^2}$$ Given as Equation 26–18

$$\hat{\beta} = \frac{(10)(48,070) - (250)(1,773)}{(10)(7,120) - (250)(250)}$$ By substitution

$$\hat{\beta} = \frac{480,700 - 443,250}{71,200 - 62,500}$$ By arithmetic

$$\hat{\beta} = \frac{37,450}{8,700} = 4.3045$$ By arithmetic

The resulting equation is $\hat{Y} = 69.685 + 4.3045X$, where $\hat{Y}$ represents estimated sales and X represents advertising expenditures, both in thousands of dollars.

If a third variable, X_2, is added, a linear equation of the form $\hat{Y} = \hat{\alpha} + \hat{\beta}_1 X_1 + \hat{\beta}_2 X_2$ will result. This can be shown graphically as a plane in three-dimensional space. More variables will expand the equation still further, but graphical methods of illustration must be abandoned at this point, since no techniques exist for indicating visually more than three dimensions. However, the mathematical properties of the equation remain the same.

Linear regression analysis allows one to fit a line—or its equivalent in an n-variable model—to any combination of variables. Thus an analyst could, if he wished, derive an equation estimating the relationship between Chevrolet sales and the water temperature in the Formosan Straits. The example is ridiculous, but it makes an important point: A regression equation must be evaluated before it can be accepted as valid. Often the relationship, if any, between variables is obscure and cannot be assumed or rejected without careful evaluation.

Three criteria are generally used to evaluate the equation. The first is its *economic significance*. Does the estimated relationship between Y and X make economic sense? The second is the *degree of explanation*. To what extent does the model explain the changes in the Y values? The third is the *precision of the parameters* (the $\hat{\beta}$'s). Is it highly probable that the true values of the β's will be close to the estimated values? In particular, how probable is it that a particular β could be zero, thus demonstrating no relationship between the dependent and independent variables?

The techniques for answering these questions, while not complicated, are outside the scope of this book. (Descriptions of them can be found in any econometrics text or in an advanced marketing research book.) They constitute a valuable package of tools for revealing explicit relationships between sales and marketing or economic variables, particularly since computers are readily available to handle the mathematical calculations.

TESTING AND REFINING MODELS

Forecasting models for new products are, at best, uncertain. Nevertheless, they can be very useful, especially when the alternative is to operate in the dark. Constructing a forecasting model will at least help to define the problem and reveal areas where further study is needed. It also reduces the research problem to manageable dimensions. Finally, it provides a basis for constructing a more realistic model once experience and data have begun to accumulate.

The accuracy of a sales forecast can be inferred initially by plotting actual sales against the forecast curve. After sufficient observations have been obtained, the parameters of the forecasting model can be recomputed. A change in the basic form of the model—say, from linear to nonlinear or from logarithmic to Gompertz—may even be in order.

After the initial market penetration, additional marketing insight can be gained through a *cross-sectional* or *time-series regression analysis*. In cross-sectional analysis, the total market is segmented into homogeneous subsets and an accelerated effort is made to reach saturation in several of those cells. Then sales are regressed against the supposed determinants of sales, and the coefficients revealed are estimations of the parameters appropriate to the demand model. If the market segments are not homogeneous—if they vary with respect to per capita income, family-cycle distribution, and so on—the parametric values might be adjusted through a time-series analysis to correct for these differences.

Risk is inherent in virtually all new ventures. Chance can be explicitly introduced into the model by assuming the original estimate to be the most probable, or mean, outcome, and then estimating a range of possible error. If the firm keeps a tally on its estimates of parametric values, especially the maximum potential market (K) and the time to product maturity (m), it might compute the distribution of the actual values about the estimates. An alternative is to examine the experience of the industry as a whole or to query the firm's management. Either managerial estimates might be tallied, and a mean and standard deviation computed to yield a measure of the error distribution about the estimated sales, or Bayesian analysis might be used.

Like the other methods of prediction and forecasting, linear regression analysis has its virtues and limitations. Its virtues include its ability to handle a large mass of data—assuming that a computer is available for manipulating the information—and its relative mathematical simplicity, as compared with the complexity of many nonlinear relationships. The Gompertz curve, for example, is not sophisticated but has a somewhat complex mathematical form. By using linear regression analysis, the analyst can invoke a number of powerful statistical tools that cannot always be adapted to nonlinear forms.

The most serious limitation of linear regression analysis is that in the real world few relationships are perfectly linear. However, many marketing relationships are sufficiently linear—at least within the range of values that concerns the decision-maker—to be approximated satisfactorily by linear models.

Summary of Marketing Research

Marketing research is the systematic search for information that will assist management in making marketing decisions. It is valuable to the firm, only to the extent that it improves the efficiency of its resource allocation. Thus the major criterion for evaluating marketing research is the net increase it induces in the expected value of the particular decision.

Types of marketing research can be divided into both functional and methodological categories; in practice, functions and techniques often overlap. The functional categories are (1) descriptive, (2) causal, and (3) predictive. These phases of marketing research are usually performed in that order, since the researcher must describe the problem before he can analyze causal relationships and, frequently, must know the cause of a market phenomenon before he can predict outcomes in new markets or forecast future values. In forecasting, however, the cause may sometimes be ignored and future values estimated as a function of time.

The methodological categories are (1) historical research, (2) survey research, (3) experimentation, and (4) motivation research. For the first method, historical research, the analyst uses data that have already been collected and recorded. This information may be found in the firm's own files or in records or publications prepared outside the firm. Libraries, government agencies, and trade associations are common sources of historical data. Historical research is usually the first method employed, for, in addition to being the cheapest and quickest way of collecting information, it is often a prerequisite for descriptive, causal, and predictive studies (and, in some cases, may make further studies unnecessary).

With survey research, the analyst goes directly into the marketplace to gather information first-hand, using the tools of inquiry and observation to collect data from a sample of the market population. Observation, telephone interviews, personal interviews, or questionnaires may be used to gather survey data. Each method has its limitations, and each can introduce its own, unique types of errors. Fortunately, there are statistical and managerial methods for detecting, analyzing, and reducing these errors. For instance, if the data are collected randomly, inferential statistics can be invoked to make an estimate of the range of error associated with the data.

Experimentation also takes the analyst into the marketplace, but in this case to manipulate variables as well as to collect data. This method is often used in causal research to estimate the relationship between a dependent variable (usually sales) and one or more independent variables that are manipulated by the researcher. Techniques range from the simple, naive experiment—which assumes that extraneous forces will remain unchanged throughout the experiment—to complex factorial experiments designed to reveal the influence of several factors that are manipulated simultaneously.

In motivation research, the analyst deals directly with members of the market population in an effort to explain the "why" of consumer behavior. This method relies primarily on the theories and techniques of psychology to determine a consumer's true motives or to reveal descriptive data that would elude the analyst if more conventional methods of research were used. The chief tools of MR are the projective questionnaire and the personal interview; both are designed to penetrate the respondent's psychological defenses and obtain subjective responses that might reveal new factors in the marketing problem. Unfortunately, the more sophisticated techniques of motivation research—such as the tools of Freudian psychoanalysis—have such a high cost per interview that the sample size must be very small. This limits the application of inferential statistics, hence reduces the researcher's ability to estimate the possible error. This difficulty in estimating error, as well as the subjective quality of the information obtained, make MR a rather limited research method.

Prediction and forecasting—the estimation of the current and future values of a variable, respectively—are the ultimate tasks of marketing research. Both methods employ causal models that relate the dependent variable (usually sales) to one or more explanatory variables for which values are available or can be forecast. An important tool of forecasting is the growth function, which relates the dependent variable to time. Mechanical extrapolation, simple linear growth models, and nonlinear growth models—such as the logarithmic function, the modified exponential function, and the Gompertz function—are the most common forms of growth curves associated with market forecasting. Regression analysis is another powerful tool of prediction and forecasting.

Each method of marketing research has its particular limitations. The descriptions and models developed through research are never exact replicas of the world they attempt to describe and explain. If intelligently applied, however, these methods can provide information of sufficient accuracy and usefulness to materially improve the quality of marketing decisions.

Questions and Problems

1. List some examples of information that marketing research might provide in the following decision situations: (1) Where should Macy's place its next department store? (2) What should be the price of a new Gen-

eral Electric steam iron? (3) Which of three recently prepared television commercials should be used for network showing?

2. Management must decide whether to use a new package for its breakfast cereal. Without the benefit of marketing research, the probability that the new package will be used is 50 percent. If the new package is used, the probability of success is 60 percent. If a marketing research project is conducted, the probability that the package will be introduced drops to 30 percent, since a market study will improve the firm's ability to identify inferior designs. However, management can be 90-percent certain that any design it chooses will succeed. A successful design (one that improves sales) will increase the firm's profit by $60,000; an unsuccessful one will lower its profit by $30,000. How much can the firm afford to spend on marketing research for this decision?

3. What sources might provide the following information? (1) The population of Atlanta, (2) the number of college students in California, (3) the size of a potential industrial customer.

4. A random-sample survey of twenty households provides the following data on the weekly consumption of fresh meat in a particular SMSA. The numbers represent the pounds of meat purchased by each household: 8, 6, 9, 12, 10, 16, 3, 9, 0, 11, 11, 8, 9, 20, 9, 11, 7, 12, 13, 6. The entire SMSA contains approximately 30,000 households. Estimate the total weekly meat consumption in the SMSA and the likely range of error at the 95-percent confidence level.

5. Given the data in question 4, what is the probability that a given household will purchase over 12 pounds of meat per week? Approximately what proportion of the market population buys meat in this quantity?

6. If the random sample in question 4 had consisted of 50 households and the same value of $\overline{X}$ and s had resulted, how would the answers to questions 4 and 5 have changed?

7. An experiment is conducted to determine the sales effectiveness of a promotional game that a firm plans to conduct in its retail stores. Five stores are used as experimental units and five as control units. The month before the game was used, the sales of the stores selected as control units were $10,000, $8,000, $11,500, $9,500, and $8,500. The sales of the stores selected for the experimental treatment were $9,000, $9,000, $10,500, $7,500, and $11,000. In the month the game was used in the experimental units, sales were $11,000, $8,000, $11,500, $9,000, and $9,000, respectively, for the control units and $13,000, $10,000, $13,000, $8,500, and $12,000, respectively, for the experimental units. Evaluate the effects of the promotional game, assuming that the firm desires to make decisions at a 95-percent confidence level.

8. Design a factorial experiment that will evaluate simultaneously the

effects of price, advertising, and display location on the sale of Pepsi-Cola.

9. Cite some examples of marketing information that might not be revealed correctly by objective questioning of respondents.
10. If a firm conducts an objective personal-interview survey to determine a population's drinking habits, the results will invariably understate the quantity of alcoholic beverages actually being consumed. Why? What type of inquiry might reveal the true consumption, and how might it be worded?
11. What are the most important shortcomings of motivation research?
12. A firm's sales during the last five years have been $18 million, $19 million, $20 million, $22 million, and $24 million, respectively. Forecast the sales for the present year and each of the next three years. Show the mathematical expression for your model and explain its underlying assumptions.
13. What types of growth curves might be appropriate for forecasting demand (hence sales) for each of the following? (1) Next year's Buick, (2) a new and highly innovative machine tool, (3) the total line of goods carried by an established chain of supermarkets.

Supplementary Readings

BOOKS

CARTER, C. F., and WILLIAMS, B. R., *Industry and Technical Progress* (New York: Oxford University Press, 1957).

CHU, KONG, *Principles of Econometrics* (Scranton, Pa.: International Textbook Co., 1968).

CROXTON, F. E., and COWDEN, D. J., *Applied General Statistics,* 2nd ed. (Englewood Cliffs, N. J.: Prentice-Hall, 1955).

DAVIES, OWEN L., *The Design and Analysis of Industrial Experiments* (New York: Hafner, 1956).

FERBER, ROBERT, and VERDOORN, P. J., *Research Methods in Business and Economics* (New York: Macmillan, 1967).

FURST, SIDNEY, and SHERMAN, MILTON, *Business Decisions That Changed Our Lives* (New York: Random House, 1964).

GREEN, PAUL E., and TULL, DONALD S., *Research for Marketing Decisions* (Englewood Cliffs, N. J.: Prentice-Hall, 1966).

ARTICLES

ADLER, LEE, "Time Lag in New Product Development," *Journal of Marketing,* Vol. 30, No. 1 (January 1966), pp. 17–21.

ALEXANDER, RALPH S., "The Marketing Manager's Dilemma," *Journal of Marketing,* Vol. 29, No. 2 (April 1965), pp. 18–21.

BARCLAY, WILLIAM D., "A Probability Model for Early Prediction of New Product Market Success," *Journal of Marketing,* Vol. 27, No. 1 (January 1963), pp. 63–68.

"Cutting It Finer," *Sales Management,* Vol. 102, No. 5 (March 1, 1969), pp. 27–28.

HAIRE, MASON, "Projective Techniques in Marketing Research," *Journal of Marketing,* Vol. 14 (April 1950), pp. 649–56.

KOTLER, PHILIP, "Marketing Mix Decisions for New Products," *Journal of Marketing Research,* Vol. 1, No. 1 (February 1964), pp. 43–49.

MUNN, HENRY L., "Brand Perception as Related to Age, Income, and Education," *Journal of Marketing,* Vol. 24, No. 3 (January 1960), pp. 29–34.

MYERS, J. H., and ALPERT, M. I., "Determinant Buying Attitudes: Meaning and Measurement," Part I, *Journal of Marketing,* Vol. 32, No. 4 (October 1968), pp. 13–20.

MYERS, J. H., and WARNER, W. G., "Semantic Properties of Selected Evaluation Adjectives," *Journal of Marketing Research,* Vol. 5, No. 4 (November 1968), pp. 409–12.

"Product Tryouts: Sales Tests in Selected Cities Help Trim Risks of National Marketings," *Wall Street Journal,* August 10, 1962, p. 1.

SANDELL, ROLF G., "Effects of Attitudinal and Situational Factors on Reported Choice Behavior," *Journal of Marketing Research,* Vol. 5, No. 4 (November 1968), pp. 405–08.

WENTZ, WALTER B., and EYRICH, GERALD I., "Product Forecasting Without Historical, Survey, or Experimental Data," *Proceedings of the American Marketing Association* (1968).

Part X

LAW AND MARKETING

The free-wheeling days of laissez-faire economics are over in the industrialized nations. They may never arrive in the underdeveloped countries, most of whom are attempting to industrialize under strict government supervision. The philosophy of "the public be damned," "the business of the nation is business," and "what's good for General Motors is good for the country" is no longer acceptable as a basis for public policy decisions.[1] Both federal and state governments are actively involved in the regulation of the marketplace and the firms that compete there.

Legislation, executive decrees, agency regulations, and court decisions control in some manner every major area of business activity. IBM must offer to sell as well as lease its computers; Swift & Company must grade its beef in conformity with federal standards; the Great Atlantic & Pacific Tea Company cannot collect brokerage fees even though it performs that function for its own stores; the Los Angeles Times may not purchase another newspaper in southern California; Sears, Roebuck and Company may not specify a particular sex in its want-ads for sales clerks, even for the lingerie department; and the Sheraton Hotel must get written permission from thirteen local agencies, including the Department of Health and Sanitation, to offer its Los Angeles customers the use of a heliport. Virtually every function of the firm must be performed within limits specified by public policy.

[1] Quotations are by J. P. Morgan, Calvin Coolidge, and Charles Wilson, respectively.

For the marketer, government intervention is both a blessing and a curse. Although it surrounds him with constraints and adds to his paperwork, it also provides him with considerable protection. It assures him exclusive use of his trademark and his proprietary innovations; it shields him from many predatory acts of competitors; it restricts unethical practices on the part of competitors, suppliers, and customers; it discreetly allows and occasionally protects monopolistic practices; it sometimes permits and enforces price-fixing; and it assures him access to most domestic marketplaces.

But government intervention also restricts the marketer's freedom of action. He is seldom allowed to hold 100 percent of a market. He cannot cooperate with his competitors except in agriculture, shipping, and, to a limited extent, a few other select industries. He cannot fully exploit the economic advantages of financial strength and market position. He cannot design labels or write advertising copy with complete freedom. In destroying competition, he must conform strictly to the rules of the game established by legislatures, courts, and administrative agencies. And his products must often be manufactured and sold in rigid conformance with the design, material, and performance specifications of regulatory agencies.

Although most of the body of public policy dealing with the business community impinges in some obvious or obscure way on the marketing function, in order to keep the discussion within reasonable bounds we shall examine here only those laws dealing directly with the five basic instruments of marketing. Laws directly affecting marketing generally fall into two broad categories: (1) laws dealing with restraint of trade and (2) laws dealing with deceptive practices. In addition, there are a few miscellaneous statutes that are pertinent but do not fit into either category.

The United States Constitution provides the basis for federal regulation of business by granting Congress the power "to regulate commerce with foreign nations, and among the several states, and with the Indian tribes" and "to promote the progress of science and useful arts, by securing for limited times to authors and inventors the exclusive right to their respective writings and discoveries."[2] The first statement has been broadly interpreted to cover almost every firm whose goods, services, or facilities cross state lines. The last statement is the foundation of patent, copyright, and trademark-registration laws.

[2] *United States Constitution,* Article I, Section 8, paragraphs 3 and 8.

The Bill of Rights further proclaims that "The powers not delegated to the United States by the Constitution, nor prohibited by it to the states, are reserved to the states respectively, or to the people."[3] This amendment and the various state constitutions legitimatize the regulation of commerce by state and local governments, provided that such regulation does not conflict with federally passed and upheld statutes.

[3] *United States Constitution,* Amendment X.

CHAPTER 27

Restraint-of-Trade Laws

HISTORY OF TRADE RESTRAINT

Competition has been part of the American political-economic tradition since the start of the Industrial Revolution. A laissez-faire economic system was acceptable when the size and number of enterprises made markets competitive. However, as technology and the entrepreneurial spirit combined to produce larger firms and fewer competitors, the competitiveness of the market diminished. Technology made it possible to attain economies of scale at higher and higher levels of output. Entrepreneurs sought growth and security, and bigness offered both.

As some firms grew, they began to enjoy competitive advantages that had nothing to do with economies of scale or managerial efficiency. They were so big that they could dominate suppliers and customers and destroy competitors almost at will. By the late nineteenth century, less than a dozen corporations virtually controlled the American economy. Each dominated a basic industry in which it operated much like a monopolist. The enormous size of these companies allowed them to engage freely in such practices as predatory pricing, collusion, tying agreements, exclusive dealing, discriminatory pricing, coercion, and bribery. The economic consequences of these policies were inferior products, high prices, and barriers to competition. Without the constraint of competition or government regulation, the surviving companies could exploit their monopolistic positions for their own benefit and to the detriment of the public.

The abuses became progressively more excessive until public outrage, along with the complaints of the victimized segment of the business community, precipitated federal action. The first government action came in 1890 when Congress passed the Sherman Antitrust Act. This statute specified the intent of Congress to prohibit monopolies and prevent the restraint of trade but was so vaguely worded that attempts to enforce it met with little success.

582

Ironically, the Sherman Act was most frequently used by big business, as an instrument for strike-breaking. The Sherman Antitrust Act was first successfully invoked against a union (the American Railway Union) in the Pullman strike of 1894.

President Theodore Roosevelt soon joined the crusade against big business as a self-proclaimed trust buster. The law was enthusiastically enforced during his administration, and this marked the beginning of the end for laissez-faire policies. A precedent had been set for the active participation of the executive branch in the control of business enterprises.

In 1914, President Woodrow Wilson signed the Clayton Act, which significantly reinforced the Sherman Act. Since that time there has been an almost uninterrupted flow of legislation regulating business and the relationship between competitors. Most of the laws have attempted to encourage competition. Some, however, have served to restrict it, primarily in areas where competition could adversely affect the American economic system.

The zeal of legislators in passing antitrust statutes has been matched by that of federal agencies, lawyers, and the courts in enforcing them. The number of cases successfully prosecuted far exceeds the number of those decided in favor of the defendants. The United States Supreme Court, under the leadership of Chief Justice Earl Warren, was especially unsympathetic toward individuals and firms accused of conduct in violation of one or more of the antitrust acts. As a result, the volume of such cases brought to the courts— to say nothing of those settled outside of court—increased drastically in the past two decades (see Table 27–1).

We shall discuss first the laws that encourage competition and then those that restrict it. Most of the latter were passed because of the adverse effects the restraint of trade laws had, or would have, on specific industries or foreign trade.

Table 27.1 Average annual volume of antitrust cases

Plaintiffs	1944–1949	1950–1969
Federal Trade Commission	100	600
Justice Department	36	78
Private firms or individuals	60	378
Total	196	1,056

SOURCE: Professor Jesse Markham of the American Bar Association's Commission for the Study of the FTC, in a lecture at the UCLA Institute of Contemporary Economics, July 11, 1969.

LAWS THAT ENCOURAGE COMPETITION

Sherman Antitrust Act (1890).   The Sherman Act was the first formal congressional response to the power of big business to injure both competition and the consumer through price-fixing, rigged outputs, and the division of markets by conspiratorial agreement. It sought to strengthen existing common-law statutes, which had proved inadequate to preserve competition.

The Sherman Act is a vaguely worded statute, containing only eight brief sections, the most important of which are the first two. Section 1 declares illegal "every contract, combination in the form of trust or otherwise, or conspiracy in restraint of trade or commerce among the several states, or with foreign nations." Section 2 prohibits "monopolies or attempts to monopolize."

The law proclaims that violators of the act, either persons, corporations, or associations, are guilty of a misdemeanor and are subject to criminal prosecution. The sanctions it prescribes are fines and imprisonment, proceedings for restraining orders and injunctions, and civil suits for triple damages.

The statute's history of enforcement is a curious one and demonstrates the amazing variations that can occur in the application of a law due to the different interpretations of courts. Labor unions were the first to feel the sting of the Sherman Act, and union leader Eugene V. Debs received the first jail sentence handed down under the act, in 1894.[1] Later the Standard Oil Company and the American Tobacco Company fell victims to the act. Their conviction resulted in the dismemberment of both firms and the subsequent formation of competing firms. It was out of these cases, which came before the Supreme Court in 1911, that arose the rule-of-reason dictum that only behavior which "unreasonably" restrained trade was illegal under the act.[2] This meant that each case had to be judged individually. Since there were no clear guidelines as to what constituted "unreasonableness" in the restraint of trade, this introduced an element of confusion into the law that has not been totally resolved even today.

Early in this century, Section 2 of the Act was used to break up monopolies, as in the oil and tobacco cases, while Section 1 was used to break up trusts (groups of firms conspiring to act like a monopoly). Although the act was occasionally invoked in price-fixing cases, it was not until the 1960's that this application became common. A precedent was set in 1961 when the government invoked Section 1 of the act to successfully prosecute several electrical-equipment manufacturers for price-fixing. Such prestigious corpo-

---

[1] Debs, President of the American Railway Union, disobeyed an injunction issued under the act and was subsequently jailed.

[2] *Standard Oil Co.* v. *United States,* 221 U. S. 1 (1911) and *United States American Tobacco Co.,* 221 U. S. 106 (1911).

rations as Westinghouse, General Electric, and McGraw-Edison were convicted of conspiring to fix prices in restraint of trade.[3] The convictions resulted in jail sentences for several executives and subsequent civil suits that involved payment of triple damages to victimized customers.

The establishment of identical prices by several competitors is not prima-facie evidence of criminal conspiracy or price-fixing under the act. On the contrary, it may be a sign of competition, especially when products are identical or nearly identical substitutes for one another. Hence, the marketer can set the price of a product equal to that of competing goods, if it is necessary to sustain his firm's competitive position and if he is not acting in collusion with one or more of his competitors.[4]

Although Section 2 of the Sherman Act outlaws monopolies and attempts to monopolize, the law fails to define these terms. The courts, to whom one must defer for the ultimate clarification of such matters, have been of little help. The rule-of-reason criterion has only confused the issue. A number of decisions have cited market share as the determining factor in establishing an illegal monopoly. However, the critical percentages have been so varied as to defy generalization. In a case against the Aluminum Company of America in 1945, the Supreme Court interpreted the defendant's 90-percent share of the aluminum-ingot market as an illegal monopoly.[5] On the other hand, the Court decreed in 1962 that a merger between the Brown and Kinney Shoe Companies would be unacceptable because the combined firms would have 5 percent of the market for women and children's shoes.[6] (The latter case was prosecuted under the Clayton Act, which is virtually an amendment to the Sherman Act.) The government for years has tolerated General Motors' majority share of the automobile market and U. S. Steel's near 50-percent share of the steel market.

To complicate matters further, the Court has allowed Sections 1 and 2 to be invoked simultaneously in support of the government's charge that firms are in collusive agreement to share a monopolistic portion of the market. For example, three manufacturers were convicted of violating the act when it was determined that they collectively held 65 percent of the coathanger market east of Colorado. The firms were fined and were forced to desist from certain practices that the Court perceived as unreasonable restraints of trade.[7]

---

[3] For a detailed account, see Richard Austin Smith, "The Incredible Electric Conspiracy," *Fortune,* Part I (April 1961), p. 132 and Part II (May 1961), p. 161.

[4] For a humorous and enlightening exposition of conspiratorial price-fixing, see "How to Conspire to Fix Prices," *Harvard Business Review* (March–April 1963), p. 95.

[5] *United States* v. *Aluminum Co. of America,* 148 F2d 416 (2nd Cir.) (1945).

[6] *Brown Shoe Co.* v. *United States,* 370 U. S. 294 (1962).

[7] *United States* v. *L. A. Young Spring and Wire Corp., Cleaners Hanger Co.,* and *W. A. Laidlaw Wire Co., CCH Trade Cases* (1950–51), paragraph 62, 908.

Clayton Act (1914).   The Clayton Act, which supplemented the Sherman Act, attempted to eliminate the latter's ambiguity and to make it more effective as a preventive, rather than a curative or punitive, measure. Thus, the Clayton Act cited a number of specific practices that constitute a violation of the antitrust law "where the effect may be substantially to lessen competition or [where they] tend to create a monopoly." While attempting to clarify public policy by specifying certain practices as illegal, the authors of the act confused the entire restraint-of-trade issue by leaving such words and phrases as "substantially to lessen," "tend to create," and "monopoly" undefined. Since these terms are not defined by the law, they must be defined by the Court within the context of the case under trial. Thus the legality of many business decisions is uncertain, and many cases arise in which the courts must decide if the decision-makers are acting within the law.

Four sections of the Clayton Act define specific illegal practices relevant to marketing. Section 2 prohibits discriminatory pricing among purchasers of products of a similar grade, quality and quantity. This provision was considerably strengthened, expanded, and complicated by the Robinson-Patman Act, passed in 1936. The marketing implications of that act will be discussed later in the chapter.

Section 3 prohibits tying agreements and exclusive dealing arrangements. A tying agreement requires a buyer or lessee to accept certain other goods or services, often undesired, in order to get goods that he does want. An exclusive dealing arrangement obligates a buyer or lessee not to use or deal in goods or services offered by a competitor of the seller or lessor. This would appear to outlaw many of the franchise dealerships common in the automobile and retail-gasoline markets. However, the qualifier "where the effect will be substantially to lessen competition or tend to create a monopoly" prevents most tying agreements and exclusive dealing arrangements from being illegal.

Section 7, known as the "antimerger section," prohibits firms from acquiring stock in other corporations when those corporations are competitors and the effect may be "substantially to lessen competition." This section has been substantially revised by the Celler-Kefauver Act of 1950. Section 7, as amended, is very pertinent in view of the widespread use of the conglomerate merger as an instrument of product diversification.

Section 8, which prohibits interlocking directorates when companies are in direct competition, was written to make collusion more difficult. However, exceptions are made for banks, common carriers, and firms capitalized at less than one million dollars. Banks and common carriers are regulated under other statutes, while firms capitalized at under one million dollars represent trivial cases in the eyes of the legislators.

The Clayton Act specifically exempts labor, agricultural, and horticultural organizations from antitrust laws in general. Thus labor unions and agricultural and horticultural marketing cooperatives can be formed, with the members acting in association to divide markets, fix prices, and engage in other activities that would be construed as flagrant and illegal restraints of trade in other sectors of the economy.

Federal Trade Commission Act (1914). The Federal Trade Commission (FTC) Act was passed as companion legislation to the Clayton Act. Its provisions affect both restraint of trade and deceptive practices. This act was passed in answer to the need for an agency to provide specialized information on the technical and economic issues connected with the government's antitrust activities. To this end, it authorized the establishment of the Federal Trade Commission, which was given the authority to investigate allegations of unfair and deceitful practices and to issue cease-and-desist orders to offending individuals and firms. Although the Department of Justice is solely responsible for direct enforcement of the Sherman Antitrust Act, the Federal Trade Commission can treat most violations of the Sherman Act as unfair methods of competition under Section 5 of the FTC Act. In addition, the agency has primary responsibility for enforcement of the FTC Act itself.

Originally, the act outlawed only unfair and deceptive practices injurious to competition (Section 5). The phrase "injurious to competition" reflected the fact that at the time the bill was passed, legislators were more concerned with the interests of businessmen than with those of consumers. The rule *caveat emptor*[8] was still valid in the thinking of most politicians. In 1938, however, the passage of the Wheeler-Lea Act by a New Deal Congress changed Section 5 to prohibit unfair and deceptive practices even without "injury to competition." Thus the Federal Trade Commission Act now stands as the most basic and general law dealing with the product variable.

Paradoxically, the generality of the FTC Act is one of its virtues. By not incorporating into the act a list of specific practices deemed illegal, Congress granted the Commission and the courts the authority to investigate and judge individual practices on the basis of their effect on trade, even before they are declared illegal. However, although the act endowed it with broad powers, the Commission did not always have the sympathy of the courts. Its early efforts to curtail false and misleading advertising were ill-received by the judiciary, especially before the "injurious to competition" provision was removed by the Wheeler-Lea Act.

The liberalization of the Supreme Court in the 1930's and the passage of subsequent legislation have broadened the interpretation of "unfair methods" with respect to the legality of business practices, particularly those associated with the marketing function. Two broad applications of the unfair-methods dictum are of interest to the marketer.

---

[8] "Let the buyer beware."

First, a practice may be deemed "unfair" if it is "against good morals." Thus a firm may be brought to court for fraudulent and deceptive acts that are injurious to either competitors or the public, such as misrepresentation of the quality or quantity of products, their superiority over other goods, their price, or their origin. Misrepresentations about the origin of a good arise primarily with regard to imports and their place of manufacture or, in the case of agricultural or horticultural products, where they were grown or processed. Thus a sweater advertised as "100% virgin wool" must be made of nothing but virgin wool. A can of coffee sold as a two-pound can must have at least that much coffee in it. A cigarette advertised as "lowest in nicotine" must have a lower nicotine content than any of its competitors. A store advertising a sewing machine for $29.95 must offer a sewing machine at that price. A transistor radio claimed to be of domestic manufacture cannot be made in Japan.

Misrepresenting the identity, character, or purpose of the firm also falls in this first category of unfair methods, as does the disparagement of competitors, commercial bribery, deceptive selling practices, pirating styles from a competitor, and conducting illegal lotteries. Thus it is against the law to represent a commercial firm as a charitable enterprise (common in door-to-door selling), make derogatory statements about a competitor or its products, bribe a customer's purchasing agent, sell a good as "an advertising device that will result in the eventual refund of the purchase price" (also common in door-to-door selling), copy a competitor's dress design, or give a customer a lottery ticket for buying the firm's good or service.

A second application of the unfair-methods dictum applies to "unfair methods" that restrain trade, are monopolistic, or are destructive of competition. Thus collusive agreements, illegal mergers, holding companies, interlocking directorates, and most other forms of cooperation that artificially restrain trade or place the collaborating firms in a monopolistic position are prohibited, as are interference with competitors, boycotts, and below-cost sales of the firm's products.

Many practices that violate the Sherman Antitrust Act also clearly violate the amended Federal Trade Commission Act. Thus practices that fall under the jurisdiction of the Justice Department may sometimes involve the Federal Trade Commission as well.

The committing of an act that is specifically cited in the antitrust laws is not always illegal. In most cases, the government or civil plaintiff must establish beyond a reasonable doubt that the act is injurious to competition or does violence to the public interest. For example, a firm may dispose of obsolete inventory at a price below cost if that is the only way it can sell the goods. This is considerably different than selling goods below cost in order to destroy financially weaker competitors.

Revenue Act (1916).   The 1916 Revenue Act is illustrative of a series of minor antitrust laws that have been passed to accommodate the peculiarities of particular industries or product classes. This act seeks to protect American industry in the domestic market from unfair competition from abroad. It prohibits the sale of imported goods at a price substantially less than their cost when the intent is to injure, destroy, or prevent the emergence of an American industry; to restrain trade; or to create a monopoly. This discourages "dumping" (selling surplus goods in a foreign market in order to avoid creating an excess supply and a resultant decline in price in the producer's home market).

Packers and Stockyard Act (1921).   The Packers and Stockyard Act is a "little Sherman Act" that deals exclusively with firms handling the storage, slaughter, and processing of livestock. It prohibits unfair, discriminatory, and deceptive practices, as well as price rigging and conspiracies in the allocation of market territories. Similar laws have been passed regarding other industries when the Sherman Act, as amended, proved inadequate or cumbersome with respect to the peculiarities of the industry.

Tariff Act (1930).   The 1930 Tariff Act, another "little Sherman Act," enforces the protection against unfair foreign competition. It is applicable only to imported goods and makes illegal any unfair methods of competition and acts whose effect or tendency is to destroy or substantially injure domestic industry, to restrain trade, or to create a monopoly. The act also includes provisions against deceptive practices that will be discussed later, in Chapter 29.

Federal Alcohol Administration Act (1935).   The Federal Alcohol Administration Act sought to curb certain abuses found in the alcoholic beverage industry following the repeal of prohibition. The act prohibits unfair and monopolistic practices, such as exclusive dealing agreements and interlocking boards of directors of competing firms. It also outlaws commercial bribery in the industry. This latter provision arose from the poor record of the Federal Trade Commission in prosecuting such offenses under the "unfair methods" provisions of the previous antitrust laws. A 1920 court decision had seriously hampered the FTC's ability to deal with commercial bribery (payments to the purchasing agents of a firm's customers to induce them to buy its goods or services).[9] The statute also prohibits deceptive practices.

---

[9] *New Jersey Asbestos Co.* v. *Federal Trade Commission,* 264 Fed. 509 (2nd Cir.) (1920).

Robinson-Patman Act (1936). The Robinson-Patman Act supplements the Clayton Act, which in turn supplements the Sherman Antitrust Act, by outlawing discriminatory pricing subject to certain defenses. It is concerned solely with the marketing function and is probably the most important single piece of legislation in the field. It primarily affects pricing decisions, but in so doing it has important implications for promotion and distribution.

This statute, which is sometimes referred to as the "Price Discrimination Chain Store Act," was a legislative reaction to certain alleged practices of the large chain stores during the depression. As large middlemen emerged in the early 1930's, they began exploiting their size in a manner perceived by Congress as having little to do with economies of scale or managerial expertise. Specifically, they extracted price concessions from their suppliers that gave them significant cost advantages over their smaller competitors. This practice became especially abusive in the retail grocery field. The classic example is the Great Atlantic & Pacific Tea Company, whose actions precipitated the Robinson-Patman Act.

A & P, which operated, and still operates, a large chain of retail grocery stores, was the *cause célèbre* for the foes of big business and the champions of the small retailer. A & P coerced many of its suppliers into giving it price concessions that had no relation to the economies of large purchases or the administrative and materials-handling efficiencies of the buyer. On the contrary, they apparently were solely the result of A & P's threats to take its accounts elsewhere. Such a move would have been disastrous for many of the suppliers, who were heavily dependent on sales to A & P.

In addition, the grocery chain owned a subsidiary brokerage house and demanded the same brokerage fees that were paid to independent brokers who performed a truly legitimate brokerage function. The excessive price discounts and the brokerage fees reduced A & P's cost function so much that it was able to offer the retail buyer prices considerably below those of its smaller competitors, particularly the independent stores. Many independent stores failed as their price-conscious customers flocked to the big chain stores. The future of the small businessman in the industry began to look dim, and the retail lobbyists responded with their usual vigor and effectiveness. In the campaign to save small business from the chain stores, their chief weapon was the Robinson-Patman Act.

Under previous legislation, it was often difficult to prove that the pricing policies of the big chain stores substantially lessened competition. For one thing, it was the buyers, not the sellers, who were forcing the discriminatory practices. Previously it had been the sellers, such as the oil companies and the railroads, that had initiated and benefited from discriminatory pricing policies. The antitrust laws had been written with this in mind and did not serve to curb the new abuses. The Robinson-Patman Act explicitly deals with unfair competitive practices that benefit the buyer and seeks to preserve competition between buying firms.

Section 1 of the act amends Section 2 of the Clayton Act, making it unlawful to

discriminate in price between different purchasers of commodities of like grade and quality . . . where the effect of such discrimination may be substantially to lessen competition or tend to create a monopoly in any line of commerce, or to injure, destroy, or prevent competition with any person who either grants or knowingly receives benefit of such discrimination or with customers of either of them.

Three key points should be noted. The first is that discriminatory pricing is not illegal per se. On the contrary, it must be demonstrated that the defendant's pricing policy *may* substantially lessen competition, *tend* to create a monopoly, *or* injure, destroy, or prevent competition. In addition, the law cites several forms of differential pricing that are considered legal. These include discounts that are a direct function of cost savings obtained by the seller in dealing with different buyers, such as the economies of scale associated with a large sale.

The second point worth noting is the addition of the phrase "or to injure, destroy, or prevent competition," which was absent from the original Clayton Act. Thus, the enforcement of Section 1 (Section 2 of the Clayton Act) is not dependent on the prosecution's ability to demonstrate a lessening of competition. "Injury" is much easier to substantiate. One does not need to prove that the industry as a whole has suffered; evidence that a single competitor has been damaged by the defendant's discriminatory pricing is sufficient. Although the act is not intended to protect firms which are so inefficient that they cannot compete economically, many authorities argue that the law is often invoked to serve that end. There is little question that the act, particularly the injury-to-competition dictum, has increased the number of cases on the Federal Trade Commission's docket, made many firms uncertain about the extent to which they may legally manipulate the price variable, and provided steady work for a large number of corporate lawyers.

Third, the explicit reference in Section 1 to the effect of a firm's pricing policy on its customers is critical. A firm that either grants *or knowingly receives the benefit of* illegal and discriminatory pricing violates the law. Thus, the marketer must consider not only the effect of his price policy on his competitors, but also the effect it will have on competition between his customers and *their* competitors. In addition, the customers' buyers are liable if they accept prices that they know give their firm an unfair advantage and are injurious to competition.

Section 1 of the Robinson-Patman Act also amends Section 2 of the Clayton Act to exempt price differentials "which make only due allowance for differences in the cost of manufacture, sale or delivery resulting from the differing methods or quantities in which such commodities are to such purchasers sold or delivered." However, the act empowers the Federal Trade Commission to "fix and establish quantity limits . . . where it finds that available purchasers in greater quantities are so few as to render differentials on account thereof unjustly discriminatory or promotive of monopoly."

This exemption provision is difficult to invoke because of the problems associated with cost analysis. The FTC has found it very easy to fault accounting systems and their allocations of costs. Besides, most of the complaints filed under the act have been against small firms, few of whom have the accounting knowledge or the financial resources to prepare a strong cost-defense. Thus the exemption provision has seldom served the interests of a defendant.

The Robinson-Patman Act allows discrimination in the selection of customers provided it does not result in restraint of trade. In addition, it allows price changes when market conditions, the condition of the goods, a distress (bankruptcy) sale under court order, or discontinuance of the business warrant them. For example, a firm may legally elect to sell a product to only one class of buyers, such as firms in a particular industry. Or price may be substantially lowered when demand deteriorates, merchandise becomes obsolete, goods are perishable and in danger of spoiling, or the seller is going out of business. The fact that the buyers of such goods may enjoy a short-run advantage as a result of the lower and unique price does not make the price change a violation of the law.

Section 1 authorizes the Federal Trade Commission to issue a termination order against the seller if proof is submitted that it has discriminated in "price, services, or facilities furnished." However, such a prima-facie case may be rebutted by the seller if it can show that its action was in direct response to an offer of a competitor and was performed in good faith to meet competition. Thus the burden of proof is on the seller, once it is established that a discriminatory price did exist.

The Robinson-Patman Act amends Section 2 of the Clayton Act to prohibit the payment of a "commission, brokerage fee, or other compensation" to a party subject to the direct or indirect control of a buyer or a customer of the buyer. Thus a firm, such as the A & P chain, that is large enough to act as its own broker and deal directly with growers, processors, or manufacturers cannot receive the usual brokerage fee. Such fees, which can be paid in a variety of forms, constitute a reduction in the buyer's cost (hence in the seller's price), giving it a more competitive cost function. The law presumes that this advantage will be exploited to the detriment of the buyer's smaller competitors, who must include the broker and his fee in their incoming distribution costs.

Although the act was written in response to buyer abuses, the wording generally takes the form of prohibitions on what the seller can do. This would have the effect of constraining the buyer only indirectly were it not for the last paragraph in Section 1, which states

that it shall be unlawful for any person engaged in commerce, in the course of such commerce, knowingly to induce or receive a discrimination in price which is prohibited by this section.

The phrase "induce or receive" clearly places the buyer in jeopardy if he knowingly accepts a discriminatory price.

Competition can be injured at three levels in the distribution channel, according to the provisions and interpretations of the Robinson-Patman Act. The primary level is *competition between sellers.* For example, Firm A may not offer a lower price in one local market, to the detriment of competing Firm B, unless it offers the same price in all its domestic markets. Thus, when an interstate bakery lowered its prices in one town but not in others, and as a result a local bakery was forced out of business, the court decided that the price-cutter's action was discriminatory and that it had violated the law.[10] Presumably, had the defendant cut its price in each of its markets it would not have lost the case. Nondiscriminatory price cuts that reflect economies of scale or managerial efficiency and are not made for purely predatory reasons are considered legitimate. The fact that competitors are injured does not in itself make an act illegal. On the contrary, most successful marketing decisions do some damage to competitors. An increase in the sales of one firm is usually gained at the expense of another firm, whose sales are reduced.

The secondary level of competition is *competition between buyers.* In fact, it was abuses at this level that prompted the passage of the act. Under the act's provisions, a firm may not offer a different price to two competing buyers, except as provided by the law. Thus a manufacturer cannot sell to two middlemen at different prices if the price differential gives the final buyers of one a marketing advantage over the final buyers of the other. An exception is made when the seller enjoys economies associated with methods of delivery or quantity of goods sold when it deals with the favored buyer. However, the price differential must be proportional (preferably identical) to the savings, and the burden of proof rests on the seller or the favored buyer. The effect of this latter provision is thought by many businessmen and economists to deny the efficient firm the benefits of its economies, thus defeating one objective of

[10] *Moore* v. *Mead's Fine Bread Co.,* 348 U. S. 115 (1954).

the free-enterprise system. This objective, which is common to most economic systems, is the optimum allocation of the society's resources. An optimum allocation does not occur when less efficient firms are artificially protected from more efficient ones.

The tertiary level of competition is *competition between customers of a buyer* who buys from a firm engaged in discriminatory pricing. If one or more such customers enjoy a marketing advantage over their competitors and that advantage can be traced to a discriminatory price twice removed from their level in the distribution system, the law has been broken. For example, a manufacturer of heels and soles for shoe companies was ordered to cease and desist its discriminatory pricing when the FTC found that the customers of the shoe companies were competing against one another and the discriminatory pricing policy of the heels-and-soles manufacturer was giving some of them a marketing advantage.[11] In short, a discriminatory price that may be legal on the primary level, because it is not injurious to competition among buyers, but that results eventually in a marketing disadvantage at the level of the buyer's customers, is a violation of the act.

A distribution network comprising an independent manufacturer, independent wholesalers, and independent retailers could easily be involved in this sort of violation. The complexity of the pricing decision under these conditions—where the ultimate effect of a pricing strategy, say one involving different segments of the wholesale market, may be ambiguous—encourages a streamlining of the distribution system. The fewer independent intermediaries there are between the producer and the ultimate consumer, the less uncertainty there is regarding the manipulation of price and its legal consequences. This has important implications for the distribution variable, especially when the firm must use discretionary pricing to combat competitive moves in a large number of local markets. Price flexibility is important in convenience goods, where product differentiation does not eliminate the need for price competition at the retail level. Consequently, a high degree of vertical integration is common with such product classes as automotive fuel.

The distribution decision is also affected by the prohibition of brokerage fees paid to non-independent brokers, even when that function is actually performed, and the restriction on functional allowances (allowances given for the performing of specific functions in the distribution channel). The efficiencies of organization that allow the elimination of a broker or other middleman cannot be rewarded with a brokerage fee or a special price. If the fee or the savings cannot be awarded to the efficient wholesaler or retailer, it can hardly be expected to reach the ultimate consumer.

Functional discounts—the rebates, allowances, or commissions paid to intermediaries—are treated much the same way and are disapproved if the

---

[11] *Holtite Manufacturing Co. and Cat's Paw Rubber Co.,* 50 FTC 379 (1953).

middleman is integrated downward. For example, a firm may serve as both a distributor and a retailer but may not exploit its combined discounts in competing against its fellow retailers. If a firm performs both functions, its supplier may be ordered to discontinue giving it the wholesaler's discount and to charge it the same price other retailers are charged. Both the FTC and the courts examine the real price of the good or service in determining whether the act has been violated. Thus, deductions from the quoted or billed price are made for discounts, services, promotional allowances, and facilities provided to a buyer.

Promotional allowances and services are dealt with explicitly by Section 2 of the Robinson-Patman Act. Such allowances and services must be offered "on proportionally equal terms" to all buyers. The prohibition against favoritism is absolute, and injury to competition need not be proven. Nor can the cost-savings argument be used as a defense. However, the provision of Section 2 allowing the in-good-faith meeting of competition is an acceptable defense, although the burden of proving both "good faith" and the competitor's offer rests with the defendant.

Two types of promotional allowances and services are common. First, the seller can offer a rebate based on a certain amount of promotional assistance to be provided by the buyer. Examples are the payments to buyers (or reductions in price) to cover all or part of the advertising or personal-selling expenses incurred by them in promoting the product. Second, the seller can provide free services to the buyer. For example, the seller may provide advertising that names the buyer, it may lend the buyer the use of display space or other facilities without charge, or it may provide assistance in personal selling. All such practices are illegal unless the seller offers them on a proportional basis to all buyers.

When it is either not economical or not physically possible to divide an allowance or service on a proportional basis, an equivalent service may be offered to conform with the law. For example, a cosmetics manufacturer may find it desirable to occasionally have its products demonstrated in large department stores by a trained beautician. This service cannot be divided into sufficiently small units to be offered proportionately to the drugstores that carry the firm's line. Hence, the drugstores would have to be offered an equivalent service on an appropriate scale—perhaps an advertising allowance or special on-site displays.

To support a charge of discrimination, several conditions must be present. First, the defendant must be engaged in interstate commerce. Most companies are so engaged, under the broad interpretations set down by the Supreme Court over the past thirty years. This specification is usually easy to prove.

Second, the times and locations of the sales must be comparable, and the products sold must be similar. An advertising allowance or a price discount offered for one month does not have to be offered again later. A women's ready-to-wear shop in Pasadena, California, is not in competition with one in Bangor, Maine; hence it cannot demand the same price concessions from a common supplier. A supplier does not have to offer the same price, discount, and services on each item in his product line. Thus, if stores C and D are in competition, but do not buy the same items from manufacturer A, they do not have to receive the same treatment. However, the items must be different. Merely changing the label is seldom adequate to differentiate a product in the eyes of the law. For example, a tire manufacturer was convicted of discriminatory practices under the act when independent tire dealers discovered that they were being charged more for the same tires sold under a different brand name to a chain store.

Third, the seller must be aware of the discriminatory nature of its pricing policy in order to be criminally liable. However, the FTC or the injured plaintiff would presumably have advised the seller of the alleged discrimination well before formal legal action was taken.

Fourth, a disproportionate discount, promotional allowance, or service must have been given or rendered. However, although the act states that a benefit must be offered on "proportionally equal terms," it fails to set any standards for determining whether one benefit is proportionally equal to another. The FTC publication *Guide for Allowances and Services* is helpful here. Among other things, it points out that reasonable and practical alternatives must be offered when the seller cannot divide a service into small enough units to satisfy all its customers on a proportional basis. The previous example of the cosmetics manufacturer is illustrative. The FTC also states that the seller must provide ample notice of its allowances, services, and alternatives. When the allowances are money payments for advertising placed by the buyer, the seller must see that the money is spent solely for that purpose. The customer too is liable under the act (Section 2) if it fails to spend the allowance as prescribed.

Section 3 of the Robinson-Patman Act outlaws the use of "unreasonably low prices" to destroy competition. It also prohibits price discrimination between different parts of the country and between competitors of a customer and the customer that tends to destroy competition. This section is a criminal statute, and its enforcement falls outside the jurisdiction of the Federal Trade Commission. Since the Supreme Court has decided that Section 3 technically is not an antitrust law, Section 3 cannot be used to support triple-damage claims in a civil suit.[12] Consequently, this provision of the act is seldom invoked. However, violations that come under Section 3 can usually be prosecuted under the Sherman Act or the Federal Trade Commission Act.

---

[12] *Nashville Milk Co.* v. *Carnation Co.,* 355 U. S. 373 (1958).

A casual review of the provisions and the wording of the Robinson-Patman Act should be sufficient to convince the marketer of the complexities involved in either complying with it or enforcing it. If not, a count of the court cases and cases on the FTC docket being prosecuted and investigated under the act should do so. In addition to being the most important piece of legislation dealing with the marketing function, it is the most complicated. The Robinson-Patman Act is also widely applied to small businesses, whose size of operation is insufficient to place them in jeopardy under other statutes.

Critics of the act have argued that its net effect is to reduce or eliminate price competition, which is the very essence of a market economy. The uncertainty that exists concerning judicial interpretations of the act tends to discourage the use of price manipulation as a competitive instrument. In many respects, the restraints on pricing serve to sustain inefficiencies and deny the ultimate consumer the benefit of lower prices.

Critics also cite the effect the act has on the distribution variable as an example of the economies discouraged by the law. For example, the limitation on brokerage fees clearly lessens the advantage to small retailers who might join together to form a buyer's cooperative that would eliminate the need to work through a broker. Yet the prohibition does not seem to have inhibited the formation of retailer cooperatives. Thus the full economic impact of the act has yet to be established.

Anti-Racketeering Act (1948). The Anti-Racketeering Act was written in response to a series of Senate hearings on organized crime that revealed the frequent use of criminal methods by certain individuals to influence legitimate business transactions. It outlaws the use of threats of physical violence, extortion, and robbery in the restraint of trade. These prohibitions clearly repeat those of state and local laws. However, they enable the federal government to also prosecute violators, providing their crimes involve interstate commerce. To date, the act has not been extensively invoked.

Antimerger Act (1950). The Antimerger Act, also known as the Celler-Kefauver Act, amends Section 7 of the Clayton Act to considerably broaden the prohibition against mergers that may substantially lessen competition or tend to create a monopoly. The acquisition of the assets or stock of another company was declared illegal under the Clayton Act only when the result might be to create a monopoly or lessen competition within an industry. The 1950 Act, which deals with acquisitions of firms not competing directly against the acquiring company, throws open the door to control of vertical and conglomerate mergers. The act also broadened the definition of "market" in the Clayton Act. In short, it rewrote the first part of Section 7 of that act to give the government a very broad instrument for controlling mergers that might otherwise prove injurious to competition. Specifically, it states

that no corporation engaged in commerce shall acquire, directly or indirectly, the whole or any part of the stock or other share capital and no corporation subject to the jurisdiction of the Federal Trade Commission shall acquire the whole or any part of the assets of another corporation engaged also in commerce, where in any line of commerce in any section of the country, the effect of such acquisition may be substantially to lessen competition or tend to create a monopoly.

The act is obviously important to many decisions involving the distribution or the product variable. For example, will the movement of a manufacturer toward its consumers (vertical integration) through the acquisition of a chain of retail outlets violate the law? Will a retailer's purchase of a manufacturing plant owned by one of its suppliers (also vertical integration) be attacked? Will the merger of a large toy manufacturer with the dominant firm in the bicycle industry be prohibited?

These questions can only be answered by pointing to specific cases and reviewing the guidelines promulgated by the federal enforcement agency, the Antitrust Division of the Department of Justice. This division, through its business-review procedure and published guidelines, often plays an important role in defining the firm's distribution and product-mix alternatives. If the firm chooses to ignore the guidelines, the Justice Department may take an active part in undoing the management's decisions.

Government standards for horizontal and vertical mergers are more precise than those for conglomerate mergers.[13] This is because the economic effects of conglomerates are less well understood. The conglomerate did not become an important instrument of growth and diversification until the 1960's.

Most conglomerates begin with the acquisition of a relatively small firm by a major corporation, with payment made in the form of cash or previously unissued shares of stock. There are a number of exceptions, however. For example, the North American Aviation Company and Rockwell Standard Company, both giant companies, merged to form North American Rockwell, Inc., with a new stock certificate replacing the old certificates of both firms. The Justice Department permitted this merger on the condition that

---

[13] Mergers between direct competitors—such as two shoe companies, two department stores, or two food wholesalers in the same markets—are horizontal. Mergers between firms at different levels in the distribution channel—such as a movie studio and a theater chain, or a steel company and an iron mine—are vertical. All other mergers—such as a food-processing company and a trailer manufacturer, or a television network and a baseball team—are conglomerate. The latter types are sometimes called diagonal mergers.

Rockwell divest itself of its interest in its Jet Commander aircraft. In the eyes of the enforcement agency, the retention of the Jet Commander combined with North American's Sabreliner would have given the new company an excessive share of the executive-jet market. (In this case the "excessive share" was less than 20 percent of the total market.) As a consequence, the tooling, production, and marketing rights of the Jet Commander were sold to an Israeli manufacturer. It now competes in the same markets as the Sabreliner, with the obvious exception of the Arab states.

The importance of the Antimerger Act to distribution and product decisions warrants a review of the guidelines set down by the enforcement agency. Although mergers may be challenged under the Sherman Act, the Justice Department normally invokes Section 7 of the Clayton Act, which was rewritten by the Antimerger Act. Thus, it is the Antimerger Act that is ordinarily used to stop mergers.

". . . The primary role of Section 7 enforcement is to preserve and promote market structures conducive to competition."[14] The structure of the market as it relates to the law is defined by (1) the number of substantial firms selling in the market, (2) the relative size of their respective market shares, and (3) the strength of barriers to the entry of new firms. Market share is clearly a key value in the merger decision.

Horizontal Mergers. With respect to horizontal mergers, the intention of the act is interpreted by the Justice Department as

(1) preventing elimination as an independent business entity of any company likely to have been a substantial competitive influence in a market; (2) preventing any company or small group of companies from obtaining a position of dominance in a market; (3) preventing significant increases in concentration in a market; and (4) preserving significant possibilities for eventual deconcentration in a concentrated market.[15]

In short, the act seeks to prevent markets from drifting away from the competitive model and, when possible, to encourage them to move in the direction of greater competition.

The marketer who envisions the enlargement of sales through the simple device of purchasing the assets of a competitor had best examine his alternatives, unless the firm's present and proposed market shares are insufficient to give the combination a position of dominance in one or more of its markets. Even an aggregate share of only 4 percent can mean trouble under the wrong circumstances, as the Brown Shoe Company discovered when it attempted to acquire the G. R. Kinney Company. Brown had 4 percent and

[14] U. S. Department of Justice, *Merger Guidelines* (Washington, D. C.: U. S. Government Printing Office, 1968), p. 2.
[15] *Ibid.*, pp. 7–8.

Kinney only .5 percent of the total domestic market for women and children's shoes, yet their merger was denied by the Supreme Court upon petition of the Justice Department, which invoked Section 7 of the Clayton Act, as amended by the Antimerger Act.[16] It was the first case to be tried under the amended section.

In rendering its decision in the Brown case, the Court made reference to the government's intent to protect small business—a point that should not be overlooked by the marketing managers of major firms. In its ruling on this case, the Supreme Court stated:

Congress was desirous of preventing the formation of further oligopolies with their attendant adverse effects upon local control of industry and upon small business. Where an industry was composed of numerous independent units, Congress appeared anxious to preserve this structure. . . . We cannot fail to recognize Congress' desire to promote competition through the protection of viable, small, locally-owned business.[17]

As Standard Oil and the Great Atlantic & Pacific Tea Company had discovered earlier, Brown learned that small business—like the family farm and motherhood—is still a sacred institution in this country and cannot be long abused without Congress, the courts, and numerous lobbyists arising on its behalf. Thus, the effect that marketing decisions can have on small as well as large competitors often establishes a constraint that prohibits the firm from making an optimum choice in terms of marginal revenue and marginal cost.

In its guidelines, the Justice Department has established market-share criteria for horizontal mergers. While they are not adhered to religiously, the standards serve as an indicator for both the department and the business community as to which proposed mergers will be subjected to close scrutiny and possible challenge. Higher percentages will be tolerated under some conditions, and lower percentages will not be tolerated under others (for example, when the department perceives a significant trend toward increased market concentration, evidenced perhaps by the rapid internal expansion of one or more competitors). Table 27.2 summarizes the department's criteria.

Vertical Mergers. Since the passage of the Antimerger Act, vertical mergers have been viewed with only slightly less anxiety than horizontal mergers. It matters little whether the acquisitions would move the firm backward into the supplying market or forward into the final-good market. If mergers can result in changes in the market structure that are likely to eventu-

[16] *Brown Shoe Co.* v. *United States,* 370 U. S. 294 (1962).
[17] *Ibid.,* as quoted by Marshall C. Howard, *Legal Aspects of Marketing* (New York: McGraw-Hill, 1964), p. 81.

Table 27.2   Maximum allowable market shares for horizontal mergers

Market Concentration	Acquiring Firm	Acquired Firm
HIGH		
Shares of the four largest firms	4%	4% or more
total 75% or more of the total	10%	2% or more
market	15% or more	1% or more
MODERATE		
Shares of the four largest firms	5%	5% or more
total less than 75% of the	10%	4% or more
total market	15%	3% or more
	20%	2% or more
	25% or more	1% or more

SOURCE: U. S. Department of Justice, *Merger Guidelines* (Washington, D. C.: U. S. Government Printing Office, 1968), p. 9.

ally have significant anticompetitive consequences, they are attacked. The government believes such consequences can be expected "whenever a particular vertical acquisition or series of acquisitions . . . tends significantly to raise barriers to entry . . . or to disadvantage existing nonintegrated or partly integrated firms . . . in ways unrelated to economic efficiency."[18]

The Justice Department's guidelines for all mergers, horizontal or vertical, are framed primarily in terms of ease of entry and market share. Ease of entry cannot be as easily or rigorously defined as market share, which can be quantified. Hence, market share is relied upon far more frequently as a measure of market competitiveness. However, the ease-of-entry argument is invoked, particularly with respect to vertical mergers, when the department perceives that

(1) a significant trend toward vertical integration by merger such that the trend, if unchallenged, would probably raise barriers to entry or impose a competitive disadvantage . . . (2) it does not clearly appear that the particular acquisition will result in significant economies of production or distribution unrelated to advertising or other promotional economies . . . and (3) the acquisition . . . is for the purpose of increasing the difficulty of potential competitors in entering the market of either the acquiring or acquired firm, or for the purpose of putting competitors of either the acquiring or acquired firm at an unwarranted disadvantage.[19]

[18] U. S. Department of Justice, *op. cit.*, p. 13.
[19] *Ibid.*, p. 19.

Market-share standards are more specific and are defined in terms of the market shares of the supplying and purchasing firms.[20] The department will challenge under the Antimerger Act

a merger or series of mergers between a supplying firm, accounting for approximately 10% or more of the sales in its market, and one or more purchasing firms, accounting in toto for approximately 6% or more of the total purchase in that market, unless it clearly appears that there are no significant barriers to entry into the business of the purchasing firm or firms.[21]

The primary thrust of the vertical merger clause is toward the supplying firm, for there is no more certain way to assure sales and exclude competition than to get control of one's customers. The possession of even a minority block of a purchasing firm's stock is adequate in the eyes of the Court to constitute a violation of the act. The du Pont case discussed below is illustrative.

E. I. du Pont de Nemours & Company had acquired a 23-percent interest in the General Motors Corporation. The Justice Department argued that du Pont was using its GM holdings not simply as an investment but as a device to make itself the principal supplier of GM's automotive paints and fabrics. Thus the markets for automotive paints and fabrics were considerably limited by du Pont's hold on General Motors. This limitation was not a result of economies of scale, price, or product quality, but of an artificial (hence anticompetitive) barrier. The Supreme Court upheld the government's position and ordered du Pont to divest itself of its General Motors stock.[22]

The government also looks at the purchasing firm's market to see if competition will be substantially reduced there. A significant supply advantage achieved through an upward vertical merger may give the purchasing firm a selling advantage also. Thus, the Justice Department will

challenge a merger or series of mergers between a supplying firm, accounting for approximately 20% or more of the sales in its market, and a purchasing firm or firms, accounting in toto for approximately 10% or more of the sales in the market in which it sells the product whose manufacture requires the supplying firm's product.[23]

---

[20] In any vertical merger, one firm will be above the other and will sell downward to its merger partner's level. This is the "supplying firm." The other firm will be below and will be buying from its merger partner's level. This is the "purchasing firm." The two firms may or may not be transacting business with each other.

[21] U. S. Department of Justice, *op. cit.,* p. 17.

[22] *United States* v. *E. I. du Pont de Nemours & Co. et al.,* 353 U. S. 586 (1957) and 366 U. S. 316 (1960).

[23] U. S. Department of Justice, *op. cit.,* p. 18.

The supplies alluded to by the department are part of the variable-cost term in the purchasing firm's cost function. Thus, they influence its ability to cut price or allocate material-cost savings to nonproduction activities such as promotion. If the firm owns or controls a supplier of its material input, it may exploit this relationship in its own market to the detriment of its competitors. If this vertical integration occurs as a result of internal expansion, there is little the federal authorities can do under the Antimerger Act. However, if it occurs or is about to occur as a result of a merger, the government can step in to dissolve or prevent the merger.

Conglomerate Mergers. Prior to the 1960's, neither the frequency nor the magnitude of conglomerate mergers was sufficient to draw the interest of either government or industry. Large conglomerates are thus a relatively recent phenomenon, whose economic effects are not yet certain. Nevertheless, some guidelines in this area have been set down, and the usefulness of the Antimerger Act in controlling conglomerates has been tested in the courts. The general test of whether a conglomerate is anticompetitive is market structure. The government will attack conglomerate mergers in order to "prevent changes in market structure that appear likely over the course of time to cause a substantial lessening of the competition . . . or to create a tendency toward monopoly."[24]

The Department of Justice has defined two categories of conglomerate mergers that it perceives as "having sufficiently identifiable anticompetitive effects" to warrant action. These are (1) "mergers involving potential entrants" and (2) "mergers creating a danger of reciprocal buying."[25]

If a firm is considered a potential entrant—this judgment being made on the basis of its technological capability, financial resources, and economic incentive—its merger with a firm already established in the market is open to challenge. The usual standard is the market share of the merger partner already in the market and the degree of market concentration.

A merger between a likely potential entrant and a firm currently in the market will be questioned if the latter (1) has 25 percent or more of the market, (2) is one of the two largest competitors and their combined shares equal 25 percent or more of the market, (3) is one of the four largest competitors and their combined shares equal 75 percent or more of the market, provided the merging firm's share amounts to 10 percent or more, or (4) is one of the eight largest firms and their combined shares equal 75 percent or more of the market, provided the merging firm's share is substantial or is growing rapidly.[26]

The Procter & Gamble case is illustrative of the problems confronting the interpretation of the law as it applies to conglomerate mergers. It was

[24] *Ibid.,* p. 20.
[25] *Ibid.,* p. 21.
[26] *Ibid.,* p. 22.

prosecuted by the Federal Trade Commission, which often involves itself in the enforcement of Section 7 of the Clayton Act as amended by the Antimerger Act.

Procter & Gamble had acquired Clorox Chemical Company, producers of a household bleach, as a means of expanding its product line. The firm had one other alternative—namely, to enter the bleach market on its own as a competitor to Clorox. It was well equipped to do so, having both the technical capabilities and the financial resources necessary. In addition, its marketing organization called on the same customers as Clorox.

The acquisition eliminated a potential competitor in a market that was already obviously far removed from the ideal of pure competition. Clorox was a well-entrenched oligopolist, with 49 percent of the household-bleach market. The financial and marketing resources of Procter & Gamble reinforced this oligopoly by imparting to Clorox the cost advantages of large-lot buying of supplies and advertising, as well as the know-how and cooperative marketing capabilities of the parent company. Procter & Gamble and Clorox would also be able to exploit each other's products by using them as loss leaders or tie-in items.

The FTC's complaint contended that the acquisition was significantly anticompetitive with respect to the acquired firm's market and constituted a violation of Section 7. As a result, Procter & Gamble was ordered to divest itself of the Clorox Company, which was then operating as a division of the parent company. However, after nearly nine years of litigation, a circuit court overruled the Federal Trade Commission and directed it to rescind its divestiture order. In doing so, the court held that the acquiring firm had simply added another item to its product mix and that Clorox's competitors had not been significantly damaged by the action. On the contrary, the competing firms' sales of household bleach increased after the merger. The court also observed that Procter & Gamble had not engaged in any predatory practices as a result of its favored position in the household-bleach market after the merger.[27]

A more recent decision in the Procter & Gamble case, which was appealed by the FTC, illustrates the uncertainty prevalent in merger decisions. Eleven years after the acquisition, the Supreme Court reversed the order of the circuit court, and Procter & Gamble had to divest itself of Clorox.[28] Thus the conglomerate merger remains a questionable instrument for the expansion of the firm's product mix—a point that should not be overlooked by the marketer contemplating his alternatives for the manipulation of the product variable.

As a result of the Supreme Court's decision, a suit for triple damages, involving several hundred million dollars, was filed against Procter & Gamble

[27] *Procter & Gamble Co.* v. *Federal Trade Commission,* 358 F2d 74 (6th Cir.) (1966).
[28] *Federal Trade Commission* v. *Procter & Gamble Co.,* 386 U. S. 568 (1967).

by the Purex Company.[29] (Purex is a major competitor in the household-bleach market.)

Mergers that create a danger of reciprocal buying (the second category of undesirable conglomerate mergers) are considered deserving of the Justice Department's attention when

(1) 15% or more of the total purchases in a market in which one of the merging firms' "the selling firm's" sales are accounted for by firms which also make substantial sales in markets where the other merging firm "the buying firm" is both a substantial buyer and a more substantial buyer than all or most of the competitors of the selling firm.

(2) [they are] undertaken for the purpose of facilitating creation of reciprocal buying arrangements.[30]

For example, the General Dynamics Corporation had acquired the Liquid Carbonic Corporation, which sold industrial gases, in 1957. At that time, General Dynamics was the nation's largest government contractor, doing over $2 billion in federal business annually. Nearly half this revenue went to suppliers, giving General Dynamics the ability to enforce reciprocal buying of the products of its Liquid Carbonic Division. The Justice Department took a dim view of this form of selling and filed three civil suits against the corporation demanding that it divest itself of the acquisition.[31] The government contended that the defendant had on several occasions coerced suppliers into buying industrial gases from Liquid Carbonic. However, the government also claimed that the mere existence of this coercive power, regardless of whether it was used, warranted the divestiture order—a position clearly in conflict with the Procter & Gamble decision. After several years of litigation, the case was decided in the government's favor, and General Dynamics was ordered to sell its Liquid Carbonic Division. The contrasting outcomes of the Procter & Gamble and General Dynamics cases underscore the uncertainty still associated with the enforcement of the Antimerger Act as it applies to conglomerates.

There are defenses that can be invoked, even when the standards laid down and successfully enforced by the Justice Department are violated. One defense is a historical record of the merger which shows that a noncompetitive advantage did not occur as a result of it. (The Procter & Gamble case is an example of this defense, in principle, although it did not specifically involve the department or its guidelines.) Such records are usually impossible to accumulate, however, because the Justice Department and the Federal Trade

[29] Under the amended Clayton Act, triple damages may be claimed in a civil suit filed by the injured party.

[30] U. S. Department of Justice, *op. cit.*, p. 24.

[31] *United States* v. *General Dynamics Corp.*, Civil Action 62C3686, November 8. 1962.

Commission normally move to stop undesirable mergers before they occur.

Another defense, the only one recognized in the department's guidelines, is the "failing company" defense. If the firm being acquired would otherwise be forced to go out of business, the acquisition will probably be approved.[32] The department's reasoning is that competition in the failing firm's market would be reduced more by the loss of a competitor than by the merger.

The automobile industry offers two examples of the failing-company defense. The government looked favorably upon the horizontal mergers of Studebaker with Packard and Nash with Hudson. All four corporations had significant portions of the passenger car market but were losing money on their automotive-product lines. By permitting the two mergers, in violation of its market-share standards, the Justice Department increased the probability that this portion of the industry would survive and continue to provide competition for the major oligopolists, General Motors, Ford, and Chrysler. Without the economies of scale that resulted from their mergers, the firms stood little chance of surviving in the automobile market.

Once merged, the companies immediately consolidated their product mixes and distribution systems. The Studebaker Company (Studebaker-Packard merger) discontinued the Packard motorcar, but later gave the remaining dealers the sales rights to the imported Mercedes-Benz line. The American Motors Company (Nash-Hudson merger) eliminated the Hudson line and a portion of the Nash line, rebranding the remaining product line "Rambler." Studebaker survived for several years, then had to shift its operations to Canada, abandoning the U. S. market. American Motors flourished and expanded its product line; its successful innovation, the compact car, influenced the entire industry's product mix. However, the competitive edge it enjoyed through its clever use of the product variable was soon overcome by its big competitors, which followed the American Motors success with small cars of their own.

The claim of economies is not, according to the Justice Department, an adequate defense of any type of merger. At first, this may seem inconsistent with the intent of the law, which is clearly to protect competition. The rationale behind the protection and enhancement of competition is that it is the best way to ensure the efficient allocation of economic resources, which is a goal of most societies, although many do not subscribe to the belief that competition, particularly in a free marketplace, is the way to achieve it. Given efficiency as an objective, one might assume that economies of scale are a good reason to approve a merger. This is not the case.

The Justice Department generally rejects the claim of economies of scale as a defense, on the following grounds. First, the department does not nor-

[32] U. S. Department of Justice, *op. cit.,* p. 11.

mally challenge mergers between firms too small to achieve significant economies of scale on their own. Second, where greater economies of scale are
possible, they can normally be realized through internal expansion. Third,
there are severe difficulties in accurately establishing both the existence and
magnitude of the economies claimed for a merger. Fourth, where opportunities exist for expansion into suppliers' or purchasers' markets (vertical
integration), but barriers prevent internal expansion, the department will not
normally challenge a merger.[33]

The economies-of-scale argument is a single-edged sword. Although the
firm may seldom use it as a defense, the government may use it in challenging
a merger. For instance, in dealing with vertical integration, the Justice Department states that it may challenge mergers if "it does not clearly appear
that the particular acquisition will result in significant economies of production or distribution unrelated to advertising or other promotional economies."[34] Needless to say, the burden of proof of such economies will rest on
the management of the acquiring firm.

It is interesting to note that economies related to the promotional variable are excluded as a defense, whereas economies of distribution are acceptable. There is some justification for the government's position from the
viewpoint of the nation's economy. Efficiencies in promotion, especially the
economies of large-scale advertising, are often used to reinforce the already
large market shares of oligopolists and to make market penetration extremely
difficult for potential entrants. There is little doubt that the federal policy is
to encourage market structures, hence industry structures, that approach the
competitive model and have price as the primary instrument of competition.

LAWS THAT RESTRAIN COMPETITION

For economic and political reasons, as well as for reasons of national security, Congress has passed laws that exempt certain industries—sometimes
under particular circumstances—from provisions of the restraint-of-trade
statutes. This has been done to redress the balance of bargaining power between two factions of an industry (the Fishermen's Collective Marketing
Act), to encourage economies of scale (the Defense Production Act), and
in response to political influence exerted by powerful special-interest groups
(the *Capper-Volstead Act*). These acts virtually encourage firms to engage
in activities that would result in criminal prosecution were they performed in
other industries. Thus they represent one of the major inconsistencies in the
government's treatment of different segments of the business community.

[33] *Ibid.,* pp. 12, 20.
[34] *Ibid.,* p. 19.

Webb-Pomerene Export Trade Act (1918). The Webb-Pomerene Export Trade Act is typical of several exemption statutes that exclude particular industries, agreements, associations, and practices from the antitrust laws. This act exempts agreements and associations formed solely for the purpose of engaging in export trade from the Sherman Act but requires the firms involved to file information regarding their activities with the Federal Trade Commission. The FTC is responsible for processing this information and ensuring that the exporters' operations are conducted in conformance with the Webb-Pomerene Act. Congress's concern for the protection of domestic firms against practices that restrain trade or commerce or tend to create monopolies obviously does not extend to foreign companies, a legitimate position in view of the nature of such foreign enterprises as the Japanese monopolies and the German cartels.

Merchant Marine Act (1920). The Merchant Marine Act was designed to bolster the weak American merchant fleet with subsidies and protections against foreign competition. An important provision of this act was the exemption of associations of marine-insurance companies from antitrust legislation.

Capper-Volstead Act (1922). The Capper-Volstead Act excludes producers of agricultural products from certain provisions of the antitrust laws. Specifically, it permits them to join together in associations for the purpose of processing and marketing their goods. Hence, farmers can openly and formally do things that would be considered flagrant violations of the Sherman Act, as amended, in almost any other industry. They can band together to confront their buyers with a single seller that can set price, control output, and engage in other practices associated with monopolies. Thus, an almost perfectly competitive industry can be handily turned into a virtual monopoly, with both the government's blessing and its assistance. This legalized collusion serves to sustain marginal producers, thwart competition, and force buyers to accept unnaturally high prices.

Cooperative Marketing Act (1926). The Cooperative Marketing Act supplements the Capper-Volstead Act by allowing agricultural producers to act collectively in the acquisition, interpretation, and dissemination of both crop and market information. This provides each participating farmer with the same supply and demand information, as well as data on the activities of his competitors. It makes collaboration on price and output considerably easier.

Agricultural Marketing Agreement Act (1933). The Agricultural Marketing Agreement Act is the third in a series of laws exempting agricultural producers from antitrust legislation. Having previously permitted farmers to form associations to process and market food and to gather, interpret, and disseminate crop and market information, Congress elected in 1933 to actively involve the government in the establishment and maintenance of monopolistic practices in agriculture. Specifically, this act exempts from the antitrust laws agreements between the Secretary of Agriculture and farmers, processors, or their associations regarding the growing, processing, and marketing of agricultural products. It allows both output and prices to be set artificially by producers and wholesalers. This leaves only the retailers as independent manipulators of price, responding to the competitive demands of a free market. Even the retailers' flexibility is limited in many markets, where the prices of certain food products, notably milk, are set by state or local laws.

Fishermen's Collective Marketing Act (1934). The Fishermen's Collective Marketing Act exempts fishermen and growers of aquatic products from certain provisions of the antitrust laws. Specifically, it legalizes collective action in the marketing of catches and harvests. Its purpose is to encourage more equal bargaining between the numerous small sellers and the relatively few buyers in the industry, particularly between the independent fishermen and the fish canneries. However, the act gives the government a means of constraining the parties by providing the Secretary of Interior authority to issue cease-and-desist orders at such times as he perceives prices as becoming "unduly enhanced."

Defense Production Act (1950). The Defense Production Act is the most recent of the exclusion laws. It allows the President to exempt voluntary agreements that contribute to the national defense from the antitrust laws. The act is particularly applicable to the armament industry, where individual purchases may exceed one billion dollars and collaboration between two or more competitors is often necessary to amass the engineering and production capacity necessary to successfully fulfill a contract.

The Defense Production Act and similar exclusion laws have broad economic and legal implications but do not have general application. While almost all firms are affected in some way by the laws that encourage competition, only those firms established in, or contemplating entry into, specific industries are affected by the laws that restrain competition.

CHAPTER 28

Deceptive-Practices, Special, and State Laws

DECEPTIVE-PRACTICES LAWS

In the preparation and passage of deceptive-practices legislation, Congress has recognized its responsibility to both business and the consumer. Although the early laws were written primarily to prevent deceptive practices that were injurious to competition, in recent years the bulk of proposed legislation has been aimed at protecting the consumer.

Federal Food and Drug Act (1906). The Federal Food and Drug Act is one of the first and most significant pieces of federal legislation dealing with the protection of the consumer. It prohibits adulterated or fraudulently represented foods and drugs to be manufactured, sold, or transported in interstate commerce. The act established precedents for intervention by the federal establishment in the firm's manipulation of both the product and promotional variables and set the pattern for later consumer-protection legislation. In 1938 the act was replaced by the Federal Food, Drug, and Cosmetic Act.

Meat Inspection Act (1906). The power of the pen, wielded in this case by a fiery young socialist, Upton Sinclair, was largely responsible for the passage of the Meat Inspection Act. His novel *The Jungle*[1] was a purposely ill-disguised description of the meat-processing industry, particularly the two "great beef barons," Swift and Armour. Sinclair's revelations were so repulsive that Congress reacted with restrictive legislation that gave the government authority to inspect and certify the processing of meat. The act was one of the first to deal with abuses in a specific industry.

[1] (New York: Doubleday, 1906).

Federal Trade Commission Act (1914).   In addition to reinforcing the government's position against restraint of trade and establishing the Federal Trade Commission (see p. 634), this act, as amended by the Wheeler-Lea Act in 1938, declares unlawful "unfair and deceptive acts or practices in commerce." Since 1938, deceptive promotion in virtually every form of advertising medium and personal selling has been held to come under the jurisdiction of the Federal Trade Commission and one or more of the several laws it is charged with enforcing.

Prior to the amendment of the act in 1938, the commission had little success in using it to protect the consumer. On the contrary, it served almost exclusively to protect business firms from the unfair methods of their competitors. The welfare of the consumer was served only incidentally, when the welfare of a business enterprise was at stake. Today, the unfair- and deceptive-practice provisions of the act are generally enforced by the Federal Trade Commission, which is also charged with the enforcement of similar acts dealing with deceptive practices in specific industries.

Packers and Stockyard Act (1921).   The Packers and Stockyard Act is concerned primarily with controlling anticompetitive activities, such as price manipulation and conspiracy to fix prices, in the meat-processing industry. However, it also outlaws deceptive practices, making illegal such things as the misrepresentation of canned and packaged meat products. For example, the inclusion of horse meat in such products must be clearly indicated on the label.

Perishable Agricultural Commodities Act (1930).   The Perishable Agricultural Commodities Act is another example of federal legislation written to deal with abuses in the marketing of a specific class of goods. It condemns, in general, the misrepresentation of perishable agricultural commodities through the use of misleading marks and labels. In particular, it outlaws deception in the counting and weighing of such products.

Tariff Act (1930).   In addition to making unfair methods of competition in the importation of foreign products unlawful, the Tariff Act of 1930 contains a number of requirements for the labeling of imported goods. Although intended primarily to protect domestic industry from foreign competition, it does serve consumer interests to the extent that it requires imported goods to be clearly identified by their country of origin. However, the use of imported raw materials and components—such as German steel and Japanese transistors—in domestically manufactured products is not covered by the act. Hence goods may be represented as being of domestic origin when in fact a considerable portion of their content is from foreign sources.

Federal Food, Drug, and Cosmetic Act (1938). The Federal Food, Drug, and Cosmetic Act supplanted the Federal Food and Drug Act, in force since 1906. The new act uses much of the same wording as its predecessor, but has considerably more force. Perhaps the most important change is the addition of "significant omissions" as a factor in the determination of misleading labels. The act gives the Food and Drug Administration control over the labeling of foods, drugs, cosmetics, and therapeutic devices. (The Federal Trade Commission, however, has jurisdiction over the *advertising* of such products, under the Wheeler-Lea Act.)

Full disclosure of all ingredients is required by the statute. Inadequate information can be attacked as readily as fraudulent statements. Labels, enclosures, and containers are all vulnerable to FDA action under the law. The act also empowers the FDA to promulgate regulations, as required, to serve the objectives of the law.

The enforcement of the law, and the regulations that it authorizes, are aided by provisions giving the Food and Drug Administration the power to issue injunctions and seize goods. The act provides criminal penalties, including fines and imprisonment, for companies and persons found guilty by a court of law of violating the act. Examples of such violations are labeling one food as being another; making, forming, or fitting a container so as to mislead the purchaser concerning the contents, labeling a package of food inaccurately with respect to the weight, size, or number of the contents; and failing to indicate the name and place of business of the manufacturer or distributor. Finally, the act gives the FDA the authority to take action against firms engaged in the interstate manufacturing, transporting, and marketing of adulterated foods, drugs, or cosmetics.

The law has been used by the FDA to prohibit the phrase "kosher style" on foods not conforming to Jewish dietary requirements; the use of brand names which imply that the content of a food is other than what it is; the labeling of canned fruits and vegetables as "Grade A," "Grade B," or "Grade C" when they do not conform to those grades as defined by the Department of Agriculture; the failure to identify artificially sweetened jams or jellies as imitation; and the representation of oils, shortenings, and oleomargarine containing unsaturated fats as helping to prevent heart attacks and reduce blood cholesterol. Excessive ullage in packaging is also frowned upon, as is the use of such deceptive phrases as "jumbo quart," "economy size," and "four servings" to describe a product's quantitative characteristics.[2]

The Federal Food, Drug, and Cosmetic Act deals specifically with colored oleomargarine, which is a close substitute for butter. Colored margarine may not be sold at retail except in packages containing one pound or less and clearly labeled "oleomargarine" or "margarine" in lettering at least

---

[2] Marshall C. Howard, *Legal Aspects of Marketing* (New York: McGraw-Hill, 1964), pp. 123–24.

as large as any other on the container. The separate contents of the package must be individually wrapped and contain the same identification in letters no smaller than 20-point type. The law even prohibits the serving of colored margarine in a public eating place unless the fact is noted on a conspicuously posted sign, on the menu, and on the margarine patties themselves.[3] It looks almost as if the dairy farmer's lobby had participated in the framing of the law—which, in fact, it did.

The act's restrictions and controls on drugs and cosmetics are similar to those for food. In fact, the drug provisions, particularly those dealing with prescription drugs, are even more rigorous and specific. As a result of amendments, the act now involves the Food and Drug Administration in the control of advertising for this product class. The ingredients of all prescription drugs, instructions for their use, and a description of the possible side-effects must be indicated in any advertisements for such products. Furthermore, the ads must be approved by the administration prior to their dissemination. New drugs must have the FDA's approval before being released to the market.

Wheeler-Lea Act (1938). The Wheeler-Lea Act amendments to the Federal Trade Commission Act extended its coverage into the area of consumer protection and made it easier for the FTC to stop anticompetitive practices. The 1938 act's most important contribution to these ends was the rewording of Section 5 of the FTC Act to read: "Unfair methods of competition on commerce, and unfair or deceptive acts or practices in commerce, are hereby declared unlawful." Previously, injury to competition had to be established before the FTC could take action.

The Wheeler-Lea Act also added to the FTC Act Sections 12, 13, 14, and 15, which specifically prohibit the use of deceptive advertising, "exclusive of labeling" (which is covered elsewhere), in the promotion of foods, drugs, cosmetics, and therapeutic devices. Section 15 states that "representations made or suggested by statement, word, design, sound, or any combination thereof" should be considered in judging whether advertising is misleading. Hence, an advertisement does not have to lie to be illegal. Material omissions, especially of facts relevant to the results of using the good or service, can be construed as unlawful under the act.

Labeling Acts for Specific Products. The peculiarities of certain product classes, the unique marketing practices associated with particular industries, and specific abuses in certain markets have precipitated special labeling legislation that provides specific standards and restrictions for the labeling of various products. Most of these acts are enforced by the Federal Trade Commission, which is empowered to promulgate appropriate regulations. These rules have the force of law, and, like the acts themselves, can be

[3] *Ibid.*, p. 125.

enforced through injunctions and criminal proceedings in the courts. Many practices that fall under the special acts could be controlled under the amended Section 5 of the Federal Trade Commission Act. However, enforcement is easier under the more explicit provisions of the special statutes.

The Wool Products Labeling Act (1939) states that the label on a wool product must clearly specify the kinds of material it contains and the percentages of each. It also requires that the manufacturer or distributor of the item be identified.

The Fur Products Labeling Act (1951) stipulates that the content of a fur product must be fully disclosed either on its label, on an attached tag, or stamped on the good. This act has been so meticulously enforced that in one instance the Federal Trade Commission denied permission to use the word "fur" in the phrase "artificial fur" on the label of a coat made entirely of synthetic material.

The Textile Fiber Products Identification Act (1958) deals with both the labeling and advertising of textile-fiber products in their finished form. A label, tag, or stamp must disclose each of the different types of fibers used in the good, the respective percentage of each it contains, their manufacturer or distributor, and their country of origin if they are imported. The same requirements apply to the advertisement of such products, except that the percentages may be omitted. Under its rule-making authority, the Federal Trade Commission has promulgated a list of generic names for synthetic fibers that must be used in the descriptive material on markings and in the advertisements for textiles employing such materials.

The Automobile Information Disclosure Act (1958) was passed following the revelation of abusive practices in the retail marketing of new automobiles. Prior to the act, the factory-recommended retail prices of new cars were frequently inflated by dealers to allow exorbitant cash discounts or trade-in allowances. This led buyers to believe that they were getting a bargain, when in fact they were paying either the regular price or a higher one. The complexity of models and the vast assortment of accessories made comparing prices difficult.

The Automobile Information Disclosure Act attempts to eliminate these deceptive practices by requiring the pre-ticketing of all new automobiles by the manufacturer and the display of these tickets by the retail dealers. It is because of the act that the manufacturer's recommended retail price for the basic automobile and each factory-installed accessory, as well as the federal tax and the retailer's service and delivery charges, are conspicuously shown on a window of all new cars. These windows must be rolled up at all times when the automobiles are displayed for retail sale. Since automobiles are not fair-traded, the posted price is not mandatory. On the contrary, it normally serves merely as a point of departure for the higgling that traditionally transpires between buyers and sellers in the domestic car market.

The Federal Hazardous Substance Labeling Act (*1960*) requires that appropriate labels be attached to all substances, or containers of substances, that are hazardous and tend to enter into household use, including all flammable, irritating, toxic, or corrosive goods. The act is enforced by the Food and Drug Administration, which is empowered to seize improperly labeled products and to seek court injunctions against their manufacturers and distributors.

The labels of hazardous products must state clearly the name of the substance, the name and location of the manufacturer or distributor, a description of the principal hazard, storage requirements, precautions, and first-aid instructions. In addition, the labels must conspicuously display a general warning such as "DANGER" or "CAUTION" and the statement "Keep out of the Reach of Children" or its equivalent.

The Federal Cigarette Labeling and Advertising Act (*1967*) resulted from the Surgeon General's report that smoking was a major contributor to lung cancer and other respiratory diseases. The law requires that cigarette packages contain the warning "Caution: Cigarette Smoking May Be Hazardous to Your Health."

Incidental Consumer-Protection Acts. In addition to the major laws of general interest and the cluster of specialized acts dealing with product labeling, there are a number of statutes that deal with special consumer problems or are associated in some way with consumer protection. Some of these statutes are major pieces of legislation in other fields, but contain provisions that are pertinent to marketing.

The Securities Exchange Act (*1933*) provides protections for the investor, such as the requirement that promoters make certain public disclosures regarding the purpose, capitalization, and principals behind a stock or debenture issue. The act placed constraints on the advertising of securities and established the Securities and Exchange Commission to regulate the market for publicly held securities. The SEC's regulatory powers pertain to the issuance, promotion, and distribution of securities. The determination of price is left to the "invisible hand" of the marketplace.

The Flammable Fabrics Act (*1953*) outlaws both the manufacture and sale of clothing or fabrics that will burn so easily and rapidly as to be dangerous to the wearer. The act, which is unique in that it is one of the few acts that outlaws outright the manufacture and sale of a product, was the result of a series of tragedies involving small children and Halloween costumes. It is enforced by the Federal Trade Commission, which is empowered to promulgate standards, to initiate injunction proceedings, and to file criminal complaints.

The Federal Aviation Act (*1958*) established the Federal Aviation Agency, now under the Department of Transportation (formerly the Civil

Aeronautics Agency under the Department of Commerce), and updated the government's regulatory powers over the aviation industry. The act deals with a broad spectrum of activities in the manufacturing, marketing, and operation of both commercial and private aircraft. Of particular interest to marketing decisions is the act's power to control airline tariffs, both passenger and freight, and prohibit unfair and deceptive practices such as the use of misleading advertising by air carriers.

SPECIAL LAWS

There are three laws, or groups of laws, that do not fit into either of the previous classes (restraint of trade and consumer protection), but which are important to marketing decisions. These are the patent, trademark, and fair-trade statutes.

Patent Laws.   The basic patent law is the United States Constitution, which gives Congress the authority to promote "the progress of science and useful arts by securing for limited times to authors and inventors the exclusive rights to their respective writings and discoveries."[4] This broad provision of the Constitution was supplemented by the passage of separate patent laws in 1790, 1836, and 1870.

In 1952 Congress clarified and consolidated the existing laws by the passage of the United States Patent Code,[5] which prescribes the conditions under which patents may be granted and the length of time for which they are valid (a maximum of 17 years). The code is administered by the U.S. Patent Office. Although the Commissioner of Patents is authorized to issue patents, their enforcement is left to the civil courts, which respond only to the petitions of patent-holders. A patent-holder may request an injunction to protect his patent or file suit for damages resulting from its violation. However, such suits have had only limited success, and the prospects for enforcing a patent through an infringement suit are rather dismal. The majority of such cases have been decided in favor of the defendant.

A patent gives an inventor or his consignee a legal monopoly. Patent monopolies can be extended to products, processes, or brand names. (The latter are covered by trademark statutes, which are a special application of patent law.) Primarily, they reward the inventor for the creativity, risk, and expenditures normally associated with innovation. Concurrently, society also benefits—so the theory goes—from patent monopolies, because they provide an incentive to those persons and firms able to allocate a portion of their

[4] *United States Constitution,* Article I, Section 8, paragraph 8.
[5] United States Code Annotated, Title 35.

resources to exploring the unknown to do so. In the long run, competition may be enhanced because of the encouragement of innovation. Besides, the life span of a patent is at most 17 years. Upon its expiration, the invention enters the public domain, and thus is available to all competitors. Although there has been a great deal of debate over the net economic benefit of patent monopolies, there is considerable empirical evidence to suggest that the private sector would assume little of the risk and cost of product research were firms not given an opportunity to exploit their successes under the protection of a patent.

Patent monopolies obviously conflict with the intent of the antitrust laws, which also have their roots in the federal Constitution. Although the wording of the Constitution that supports patent law is more explicit than the wording that supports antitrust legislation, the courts have not always decided in favor of the patent holder when a question of restraint of trade was involved. Prior to the twentieth century, patented products and processes were comparatively simple; business organizations, too, tended to be less complex. Thus the patent laws and the antitrust statutes seldom came into conflict. This is no longer the case.

As D. Maynard Phelps and J. Howard Westing point out,[6] there are three issues involved in defining the line between a legitimate patent monopoly and the gain of unlawful monopolistic advantage through the leverage provided by a patent. *First* is the fact that the patentable item may be only a part of a complex product or process, but such a necessary part that the patent holder can control the entire product or process. *Second* are the provisions of the Patent Code, which allow the patent holder to license other individuals or firms to use his patent. In issuing such a license, the licensor may stipulate conditions in addition to the fee or royalty to be paid by the licensee. The patent holder often specifies both the price that will be charged by the licensee and the markets in which the patented item will be sold. *Third* is the difference in rigor between the Patent Commission's evaluation of the validity of the patent application and the court's evaluation of the validity of the resultant patent. The commission and the courts may differ on the inventiveness of the design or, more specifically, on whether the invention is sufficiently original and unique to warrant the award and subsequent enforcement of a patent. The courts' standards have generally been higher than those of the commissions' patent examiners. Consequently, the majority of infringement suits have not stood up in court, and, presumably, there are many "unpatentable" items enjoying patent protection simply because nobody has chosen to test them in court.[7]

---

[6] D. Maynard Phelps and J. Howard Westing, *Marketing Management,* 3rd ed. (Homewood, Ill.: Richard D. Irwin, Inc., 1968), pp. 561–62.

[7] *Ibid.*

One might hope that court decisions would by now have clarified the relationship between patent laws and restraint-of-trade laws. There have certainly been enough opportunities for judicial pronouncements on the matter, with Congress and the regulatory agencies, on the one hand, consistently strengthening the antitrust controls, and the Patent Office generously issuing patent monopolies on the other. Of the hundreds of judicial decisions in this area, however, few have illuminated the issues or established meaningful precedents.

Phelps and Westing cite three cases in particular.[8] One is the General Electric case of 1926.[9] Here the Supreme Court decided that it was permissible for the patent holder to specify the price at which the licensee would sell the patented product, as long as the patent holder did not attempt to control the product's resale price. In effect, the licensed manufacturer can accept a license agreement granting the patent holder control of its price variable, but the control cannot be extended to the next level in the distribution channel. In this case, G.E. held the key patent on electric filament lamps. It leased its patent rights to the Westinghouse Corporation, with the stipulation that G.E. would set the price on Westinghouse's light bulbs. The license contract was upheld.

Previously, the Court had held that a patent does not give the holder the right to control a product made under a license or its price.[10] Decisions subsequent to the General Electric case have leaned toward the earlier finding, but without reversing the G.E. decision. Hence the doctrine set forth in the G.E. case is still in force, but has been narrowed to the point where it is not an entirely reliable guide to licensing and subsequent marketing decisions.

The Hartford-Empire Glass case of 1945 was another landmark decision.[11] Here the Supreme Court found it unlawful to unite individual patent monopolies in a pool to be used as an instrument for the restraint of trade. In this case, an association of glass-container manufacturers assigned their 600 patents to a pool. The pool then licensed member companies to use the patents, which were primarily for glass-making equipment. So strong was the power of the pool that the association was able to regulate the production of an unpatented product, the glass containers made on the patented machinery. This gave the association, acting as a monopolist through its pool, control of 94 percent of the production of glass containers made on feeders and forms, the most practical way to mass-produce glassware. This monopoly was construed by the Court as extending far beyond the legal monopolies awarded by the machinery patents. However, the Court made it clear that

[8] *Ibid.*, pp. 562–64.

[9] *United States* v. *General Electric Co.,* 272 U. S. 476 (1926).

[10] *United States* v. *A. Schrader's Son, Inc.,* 252 U. S. 85 (1920), as cited by Phelps and Westing, *op. cit.,* p. 562.

[11] *Hartford-Empire Co. et al.* v. *United States* 323 U. S. 386 (1945).

cross-licensing and division of royalties violate the antitrust laws only when they are used to effect a monopoly, fix prices, or impose an unreasonable restraint on trade in interstate commerce.[12]

The decision in the International Salt Company case of 1947[13] defined another limit to patent privileges. International Salt held patents on two machines used in industrial processes that required salt as one of the ingredients. It leased these machines to other firms, one of the conditions of the lease agreements being that the lessees buy all the salt and salt tablets used by the two machines from International Salt, thus shutting out other salt suppliers. The Court found the company's action to be an illegal restraint of trade and declared that a patent holder may not use its patent to restrict its customers from purchasing supplies from its competitors. In other words, a patent cannot be used as leverage to force competitors out of a market for unpatented goods.[14]

The marketer who happily bases his estimate of a product's demand function on a patent monopoly may be in for a surprise. His figures are certainly vulnerable if they depend on a patent claim that has not yet been tested in court. In many cases, competitors can duplicate an innovation while a patent application is being processed. The Patent Office receives over 100,000 applications a year and has on occasion been as much as two years behind because of inadequate staffing and the need to search files to ensure that a patent will not infringe on any previously issued patents. Worse still, the issuance of a patent results in public disclosure of the innovation, as copies of the patent are readily available from the Patent Office at a nominal charge. Hence any secrecy the inventor may have been able to maintain is immediately forfeited.

If the marketer is dealing with a fad item, its life expectancy may make a patent useless, for competitors will have exploited the market before they can be expelled through an injunction. The recourse offered by a damage suit may not compensate the firm for its time and trouble in seeking a patent, let alone recoup the lost profits. Here, the best protection may well be a policy of tight security combined with an inventory and marketing organization large enough to satisfy demand before the competition can get the item into production and enter the market in force.

A *copyright* is an extremely strong, easily enforceable form of patent, which provides "the exclusive, legally secured right to reproduce (as by writing or printing), publish, and sell the matter and form of a literary, musical, or artistic work."[15] Copyrights are initially granted for a period of

---

[12] Phelps and Westing, *op. cit.*, p. 563.

[13] *International Salt Co., Inc.* v. *United States,* 332 U. S. 392 (1947).

[14] Phelps and Westing, *op. cit.*, p. 563.

[15] *Webster's Third New International Dictionary* (Springfield, Mass.: Merriam, 1965), p. 504.

28 years and may be renewed once. Because copyrights are inexpensive and easy to obtain and infringement is easy to prove, they should be obtained whenever possible.

Trademark Laws.[16] Brands that are given legal protection are called "trademarks." They may not be used by anyone other than the trademark owner. Under common law, the criterion for ownership of a brand was priority in use. However, common-law rights were difficult to enforce. In order to protect trademark users and consumers from fraud, Congress passed legislation codifying the conditions under which brands could be legally protected in 1905, 1920, and again in 1947. The latest act, the *Lanham Trademark Act (1947)*, supplants the previous laws and provides comprehensive legislation for the qualification, registration, enforcement, and disqualification of trademarks, service marks, certification marks, and collective marks.[17]

Trademark law, like copyright law, is a special form of patent law. Like patent law, it gives the owner a legal monopoly—in this case, the exclusive use of a distinctive brand. However, because the trademark does not hinder the diffusion of new technology, it is not so vulnerable to attack as an instrument for restraining competition and economic growth. On the contrary, the ability to reliably identify a product with its manufacturer or distributor gives the consumer some basis for discriminating between similar goods and encourages producers and distributors who use trademarks to maintain a level of quality that will reflect favorably on their brands.

The Lanham Act provides for the registration of qualified trademarks —as well as service marks, certification marks, and collective marks—with the U. S. Patent Office. The process is simple and inexpensive, provided that the mark meets the qualifications stipulated in Section 2 of the act. Specifically,

1. A mark must be in actual use in commerce at the time registration is granted.
2. A mark must be capable of distinguishing the goods or services of the applicant . . . from the goods or services of others.

[16] The material in this section is adapted with permission from Phelps and Westing, *Marketing Management,* 3rd ed. (Homewood, Ill.: Richard D. Irwin, Inc.), pp. 160–63.
[17] "Service-marks" are marks "used in the sale or advertising of services to identify the services of one person and distinguish them from the services of others." "Certification-marks" are marks "used upon or in connection with the products or services of one or more persons other than the owner of the mark to certify regional or other origin, material, mode of manufacture, quality, accuracy or other characteristics of such goods or services, or that the work or labor on the goods or services was performed by members of a union or other organization." "Collective marks" are trademarks and service marks "used by the members of a cooperative, an association or other collective group of organization and [including] marks to indicate membership in a union, an association or other organization.

3. A mark must not consist of or comprise immoral, deceptive, or scandalous matter or matter which may disparage or falsely suggest a connection with persons, living or dead, institutions, beliefs, or national symbols, or bring them into contempt or disrepute.

4. A mark must not consist of or comprise the flag or coat-of-arms or other insignia of the United States or any state, municipal, or foreign government.

5. A mark must not consist of or comprise a name, portrait, or signature identifying a particular living individual except by his written consent, or of a deceased President of the United States during the life of his widow without her written consent.

6. A mark must not so resemble another mark in use as to be likely to cause confusion or mistake or to deceive purchasers. However, concurrent registration may be granted by the Commissioner of Patents or a court of appeals when both claimants have become entitled to use marks as a result of their concurrent lawful use thereof in commerce prior to any of the filing dates of the applications involved and such concurrent use is not likely to cause confusion or mistake or to deceive purchasers.

7. Secondary meaning marks cannot be registered unless substantially exclusive and continuous use for five years prior to the date of application for registration can be proved.[18]

The term "secondary meaning" in paragraph 7 warrants explanation. When a brand name has an accepted meaning other than that imparted by the product, the product meaning may be considered subordinate, or "secondary." Examples would be names that are descriptive of other things, are surnames, or are geographical locations. For instance, an automobile can be called a "Mustang" or a "New Yorker," but those names cannot be monopolized and protected under the law, except in accordance with Section 7.

Technical trademarks are marks that are original or are used in an unusual context, such as "Kleenex" or "Tide" (a detergent). This type of mark is the easiest to register and the least likely to be contested, since the primary meaning, when the word is used in conjunction with the product, is clearly that which is imparted by the product. Ownership is clearly established by the applicant, provided that he is the first to use it as a brand.

Descriptive and geographical names, as well as surnames, can be used as marks, but they are much more likely to be challenged, and thus more difficult to register, than technical trademarks. This is why some firms use misspelled words as brand names. The misspelled word becomes an original one and can qualify as a technical trademark. "Kool" cigarettes, "Kleanbore" ammunition, and "Duz" soap are examples. Nontechnical marks are not entirely excluded from registration, however. Witness, for example, "North American Van Lines," "National Distillers," and "Ford."

[18] Phelps and Westing, *op. cit.*, pp. 160–61.

Marks that meet the qualifications listed above are placed in the Principal Register of the Patent Office and are afforded all the privileges and protections stipulated in the Lanham Act. Those that fail to qualify for the Principal Register may be placed in the Supplemental Register, if they meet the first five requirements listed. The Supplemental Register was established to aid firms who sell their products abroad, but whose trademarks do not qualify for the Principal Register. Many foreign nations are far more liberal than the United States in granting trademark protection, and names and symbols unacceptable domestically are frequently registered abroad. First registration, not first use, is often the criterion for ownership. In some foreign nations, registration in the seller's own country is a prerequisite for registration. Placement of a mark in the Supplemental Register meets these requirements for U. S. producers. Supplemental registration may also help support a later claim for primary registration when a mark's secondary meaning becomes sufficiently old and distinctive to qualify under paragraph 7.

There are several advantages of having a trademark registered—provided it qualifies for the Principal Register. First, infringement cases are tried in federal courts, where the decisions handed down are more consistent than those of the 50 state judiciary systems. Second, registration is prima-facie evidence of ownership. In case of a dispute, the burden of proof rests with the plaintiff, not the holder of the registration. Third, the court may award triple damages to the trademark holder in the event of an infringement suit. This provision not only gives a potential monetary benefit to the trademark holder; it tends to deter firms that are contemplating infringement. Fourth, registration provides protection against infringement by imported goods. Marks recorded in the Principal Register are also listed with the U. S. Treasury Department, which stops the importation of goods it perceives as infringing on the listed marks. Fifth, registration meets the "constructive notice" requirement of the law. This is a legal technicality, but compliance with it prevents the use of a registered mark outside the territories presently served by the registrant. Marks recorded in the Supplemental Register enjoy none of these benefits.[19]

Concurrent registration is a unique feature of the Lanham Act, as it was not recognized by preceding laws. However, it was recognized under common law, a fact that led to considerable confusion, inconsistency, and inequity prior to the passage of the Lanham Act. The law now allows concurrent registration when the mark in question was honestly and independently used by two claimants prior to the filing dates of both applications. However, it must have been used in substantially different geographical markets.

[19] *Ibid.,* p. 162.

Concurrent registration has seldom been awarded. It is contrary to the interests of the consumer, who can be easily confused by the duplication of trademarks, and it is equally undesirable from the firm's point of view. Once a concurrent mark is granted, the holders of that mark are constrained from using it in the product or geographical market of the other registrant. This conflicts with the desire to expand of most commercial enterprises.

Trademarks are subject to cancellation or loss unless the mark can be qualified as "incontestable" under Sections 15 and 33 of the act. Phelps and Westing neatly summarize the conditions that must be met to qualify the mark as incontestable:

1. It must presently be in use and must have been in continuous use in commerce for at least five years subsequent to registration.
2. There must have been no final decision adverse to the registrant's claim of ownership or his right to keep the mark on the Register.
3. There must be no pending litigation involving the owner's rights in either the Patent Office or the Courts.
4. Within one year subsequent to the expiration of any such five-year period, the registrant must file an affidavit with the Commissioner of Patents setting forth that the above conditions exist.
5. The mark must not have become the generic name of an article.[20]

Although the registrant is assured the use of his mark once it has been qualified as incontestable under these rules, he has no guarantee of his monopoly. Exclusive use can be challenged at any time, and a concurrent mark can be registered to another individual or firm.

Under the provisions of the act, cancellation may be ordered by a federal court or may be requested of the Patent Office by the Federal Trade Commission. Grounds for trademark cancellation are fraud, abandonment, the inclusion of prohibited material in the brand name, misrepresentation of the source of the product by an assignee, violation of the registration process, or the common use of the mark as a descriptive name of a product whose patent has expired. A certification or collective mark can also be cancelled if one of the above violations is made, as well as if the registrant fails to control the use of the mark, uses a certification mark on its own goods, grants an assignee permission to use the mark for purposes other than those for which it was issued, or shows discrimination in refusing to certify goods or services that comply with the standards of the mark.

An interesting phenomenon is the evolution of trademarks into generic names. A truly unique trademark can be lost in this way if it is widely accepted. For example, "aspirin," "shredded wheat," and "frigidaire" were

---

[20] *Ibid.*, p. 163.

once trademarks, but became so integral a part of our speech that they were considered by the courts as generic names, and hence in the public domain. Sometimes such an evolution can be foreseen, and the brand name can be separated from the product name and successfully registered and protected. One device for doing this is to use conventional spelling for the product name but misspell the brand name, which then becomes both original and separate. An example is the trademark "Fiberglas," which Owens-Corning uses for its fiberglass. The latter term is now the generic name for the good.

Although the evolution of a brand name into a generic product name is a sure index of the successful diffusion and general acceptance of a good, the firm may want to take steps to preserve its identification with the product. Trademark registration is obviously the first step. In addition, the company may combine the firm's name with the product name, extensively advertise the brand to enforce its identification with the firm, take prompt legal action against firms using the brand in a generic sense, rigorously control the use of the mark by licensees, and develop one or two alternative brand names in case the original name does evolve into a generic term.[21]

Fair-Trade Laws. "Fair trade" is a virtuous-sounding misnomer that signifies vertical price-fixing. It is more accurately called "resale price maintenance," a phrase frequently encountered in marketing literature. It means that the suppliers of branded goods impose a fixed resale price on their customers. The practice is generally confined to retail pricing and is permissible only in those states that have passed enabling legislation. Federal laws have declared vertical price-fixing exempt from federal antitrust statutes when it is practiced in states that have fair-trade laws on their books. Once widespread, and practiced by such major firms as General Electric, Motorola, Olin-Mathieson, and Florsheim, resale price maintenance has declined in recent years due to unfavorable court decisions, enforcement problems, and the disenchantment of many suppliers and retailers who no longer see fair trade as a viable pricing strategy. However, it is still a marketing option in the majority of states and is used by a number of firms.

The Great Depression saw, along with the stock-market crash, the bank crisis, business failures, and the worst unemployment in the history of the nation, the collapse of retail prices. Along with labor, big business, farmers, and other special-interest groups, the retailers turned to the government for help, both in Washington and in the state capitols. Numerous schemes were hatched. All promised to aid the return to prosperity, but most served only to move the economy further from the competitive model by placing artificial constraints on the operation of the firm, especially in the marketplace. This was usually done in the name of free enterprise.

[21] *Ibid.,* p. 166.

California, the spawning ground for some of the most outlandish legislation ever proposed in this country, was the logical birthplace for fair-trade legislation. In 1931, California passed a Fair Trade Act.[22] Five years later, the statute was upheld by the United States Supreme Court.[23] The California act appeared so advantageous to retailers in other states that their lobbyists immediately submitted carbon copies to their state legislatures. They were generally successful, and most states soon had statutes on the books that were similar to, if not outright duplicates of, the California law. By 1963, forty states had enacted such legislation.

These state laws authorize a manufacturer or distributor to stipulate in a contract the resale price of a branded good. The prescribed price may be either a minimum or a fixed value. The result of such contracts is horizontal price-fixing on a functional level below that of the supplier, usually at the retail level. This allows the resellers to act as monopolists with respect to the sale of that particular brand. If the supplier has selected a resale price that reflects both the monopolistic demand function for the branded product and the aggregate cost function of its resellers—that is, if it has selected the optimum price—then the resellers' aggregate profit will be maximized. Of course, this says little about the distribution of that profit among the participating resellers. Such a pricing decision may or may not benefit the small independent retailer whom the fair-trade laws claim to protect.

The contract between the supplier and the reseller stipulates the terms of resale, the most important of which is price. In many instances, it is impractical to negotiate contracts with every reseller, since there may be thousands. To alleviate this problem, twenty-three states have included "nonsigner" clauses in their fair-trade statutes. This unique legal clause binds all resellers to the terms of a resale-price-maintenance contract signed by the supplier and any one reseller. Without such a clause, a manufacturer of a widely distributed good might have a hard time maintaining a minimum fixed price at the retail level. Price-cutting is almost sure to occur somewhere, and without the nonsigner provision it is extremely hard to stop.

In 1937, the *Miller-Tydings Act* was passed to exempt vertical price-fixing from federal antitrust laws. The previous year, the Supreme Court had upheld the constitutionality of fair-trade laws—including the nonsigner provision—but the decision had concerned only intrastate movement of goods.[24] The Miller-Tydings Act amended Section 1 of the Sherman Antitrust Act to specifically exempt vertical price-fixing of goods in interstate commerce.

Later, the Supreme Court decided that the Miller-Tydings Act did *not*

[22] California Business and Professions Code, Section 16900.
[23] *Old Dearborn Distributing Co. v. Seagram-Distillers Corp.,* 299 U. S. 183 (1936).
[24] *Ibid.*

apply to the nonsigner provision of the state fair-trade laws.[25] Congress responded immediately with the *McGuire-Keough Fair Trade Enabling Act* (*1952*), which amended the Federal Trade Commission Act to allow for enforcement of the nonsigner provision. This made the nonsigner clause legal in interstate commerce and placed the Federal Trade Commission in the role of enforcement agency. The law was tested in the federal courts one year later. A district court of appeals upheld it, and the Supreme Court refused to review the case.[26] This placed the nonsigner provision in an anomalous position. It cannot be found unlawful under federal antitrust legislation, but it can be declared unconstitutional by a state court. Thus it is still a vulnerable piece of legislation.

Attempts to enforce a fair-trade price often run into problems. One is the mail-order shipment of cut-price goods from a state with an ineffective fair-trade law (or no law at all) to a state with an effective statute. Since the buyers take title to the goods in the state from which the goods are shipped, there is no legal recourse to prevent price-cutting. This issue was decided in the courts when the General Electric Company, then a believer in resale price maintenance, tried to stop a mail-order house in New Jersey (which has no fair-trade law) from cutting the fair-trade prices on goods sold to residents of New York (which does have a fair-trade law).[27] General Electric lost the case and has since abandoned resale price maintenance.

A companion problem is the inability of the manufacturer to stop the advertising of cut-rate prices in a fair-trade state. When a consumer can conveniently order by mail from, or make visits to, a non-fair-trade state, such advertising can reduce local demand, thereby discouraging the handling and promotion of the fair-traded goods by the local merchants.

Another problem is the use of subterfuges to reduce the real price of the fair-traded items. This can be done at the retail level by offering trading stamps or exaggerated trade-in allowances or by selling heavily discounted or "free" companion goods.

The sheer mechanics of enforcement, however, are the major reason for the decline of fair-trade pricing. The burden of enforcement rests on the supplier, and monitoring hundreds or thousands of resellers is costly. In addition, the enforcement cannot be selective. The supplier must be consistent; hence it cannot single out one or two renegade customers to serve as examples, while tolerating price cuts by others.

Perhaps the most practical enforcement technique is simply to refuse to do business with a reseller who violates or allows violations of the stipulated price. Such a refusal is legal under the "Colgate doctrine," which allows

[25] *Schwegmann Bros. Super Markets et al.* v. *Calvert Distillers Corp.,* 341 U. S. 384 (1951).
[26] *Schwegmann Bros. Super Markets et al.* v. *Eli Lilly and Co.,* 205 F2d 788 (1953).
[27] *General Electric Co.* v. *Masters Mail Order Co.,* 244 F2d 681 (1957).

producers to refuse to sell to middlemen who will not cooperate in maintaining the resale price.[28] This tactic uses the fair-trade law only as a tool for discriminating against middlemen or retailers who refuse to comply with the fair-trade price.

Not only the legal context of fair-trade pricing but its viability as a pricing strategy is important to the marketer. Given the difficulty of enforcement and the inconsistency of state laws, it is doubtful in many cases whether fixed prices are worth pursuing. Even in those rare cases where enforcement is practical, the answer may be negative.

There are many arguments—most of which originated in the retailing community—for fair-trade prices. Possibly the most persuasive argument is that fair-trade pricing maintains the gross profit margin on unit sales. This maximizes the resellers' gross profit at any given level of output. As a result, he will tend to promote fair-traded items as opposed to flexibly priced items, where price competition may drive down the profit margin. Hence, both the producer and the reseller benefit. The smaller dealer has a better chance of survival because he cannot be undercut by large-volume competitors who enjoy quantity discounts and other economies of scale not available to the little store. This results in a larger number of outlets for the producer (which will presumably derive increased sales as a consequence).

From the producer's viewpoint, the case for fair-trade pricing often includes the argument that the firm will be protected from the use of its product as a loss leader. That this can be disastrous was demonstrated by the experience of the Ingersoll Company. Ingersoll was successfully marketing a watch which it advertised at $1 and which became well known. This made it a fine choice as a loss leader, for consumers quickly recognized it as a bargain. The widespread price-cutting that ensued caused many dealers to stop handling the brand. The cut price soon became common, and the effectiveness of the product as a loss leader was destroyed. In the meantime, the public had been conditioned to think of the cut price as the prevailing value of the watch. The result was a drastic decline in demand in both the loss leader and regular-price markets, and Ingersoll went out of business.

Part of the loss-leader argument is the contention that price-cutting can destroy a brand's image by portraying it as a cheap, hence a less desirable and prestigious, good. According to the advocates of fair-trade pricing, this image—or "good will"—has been purchased with costly promotion, especially advertising, and should be protected by maintaining an appropriate price.

The consumer is not entirely neglected in arguments for resale price maintenance. Supporters point out that a fixed price relieves the buyer of the chore of bargaining. In addition, it supposedly prevents deceptive pricing.

---

[28] *United States* v. *Colgate & Co.*, 250 U. S. 300 (1919).

This latter contention may be valid if the fair-trade price is both published and fixed. However, fair-trade prices are often variable, with the supplier setting only a minimum price.

The arguments on the negative side are more persuasive. The opponents of vertical price-fixing claim that it is not a viable long-run pricing strategy and that the only true beneficiaries of such a program are inefficient retailers, whom the economy could well do without.

Fair-trade pricing restricts the operation of the price mechanism, which is the heart of a competitive economy. Fixed prices, especially those providing a substantial markup over cost, encourage excess capacity, high prices, and inefficiency in marketing. If the enthusiasm for fair-trade laws that has been displayed by retailer associations and their lobbyists is indicative, a segment of the retailing community may benefit from the practice. However, it is questionable whether manufacturers enjoy any net advantage, and consumers are only victimized, not benefited, by it.

Antitrust legislation is probably adequate to take care of any unfair practices, such as predatory pricing, that fair trade is supposed to prevent. Claims that the brand image will be lost if fair-trade pricing is not employed are of doubtful validity, given the widespread discounting and use of loss leaders now associated with American retailing. A repetition of the Ingersoll experience in the 1970's is hard to visualize.

In making a price decision, the marketer must ask himself whether the more favorable treatment he may receive from retail outlets if he uses retail price maintenance is valuable enough to compensate for the loss of business that will occur because of competitive pricing by other companies. If he does not allow retailers to cut their prices on his brand to meet competition, he may discover that consumers are attracted to the lower-priced brands. The extent to which these brands will cut into his sales will depend on the degree to which he has differentiated his own product. If there are no satisfactory substitutes, competitors' prices are not significant. However, under those circumstances there will probably be little need to encourage retailers to promote his product, and there will be no need to protect their markups. On the other hand, if there are ready substitutes, his brand will be price-elastic, and a fixed resale price may prove disastrous, particularly in a volatile market. For example, what would happen to the sales of a fair-traded gasoline in the event of a price war?

The emergence and wide diffusion of the discount department store— a marketing phenomenon of the 1960's—has made retail price maintenance an even less viable pricing strategy. These stores now purchase billions of dollars worth of merchandise and are not enthusiastic about brands that they cannot price at their discretion—a fact that has not gone unobserved by the manufacturers of consumer durables. Even the small retailer today must engage in price competition with most product classes. His alternative is to offer better services, generous credit terms, plush surroundings, and possibly a private brand. However, even these alternatives may prove inadequate inducements if the shopper can travel a short distance and buy a similar item for twenty percent less at a discount house. In short, in view of the economic realities of recent years, coupled with the many problems of enforcement, the decline in the use of retail price maintenance is not surprising.

Consumer Credit Protection Act (1968). The Consumer Credit Protection Act, sometimes called the "Truth-in-Lending Law," was passed following the revelation of abusive practices (some of which involved organized crime) in the field of consumer credit and collection. The act has four major provisions called "titles." Title I requires creditors to disclose their annual rate of interest and all their costs associated with credit transactions. Title II outlaws extortionary credit transactions—that is, using violence or the threat of violence to collect loans. Title III restricts garnishments, establishing a limit of 25 percent of the debtor's disposable earnings. Finally, Title IV establishes a National Commission on Consumer Finance to "study and appraise the functioning and structure of the consumer finance industry." The commission also reports and makes recommendations to Congress.

The act is enforced by a number of federal agencies. The appropriate agency in any given case depends on the nature of the creditor's business. For example, a case involving a national bank comes under the jurisdiction of the Comptroller of the Currency. A federally chartered credit union is under the Bureau of Federal Credit Unions. Common carriers are under the National Transportation Safety Board or the Interstate Commerce Commission. Creditors not allocated to a particular agency fall under the jurisdiction of the Federal Trade Commission. Criminal penalties are provided.

The passage of the Consumer Credit Protection Act is one indication of the increasing concern over consumer welfare that Congress has displayed in recent years. Numerous consumer-protection bills have been placed in the congressional hopper, and it appears likely that many of them will be passed. The fact that federal courts have become considerably more sympathetic to the claims of plaintiffs in product-liability cases is further evidence of the trend toward more stringent consumer protection.

STATE LAWS

From the marketing viewpoint, the most important state laws are the fair-trade laws. There is a hodgepodge of other legislation that is of occasional interest. Little of it is consistent between states, and much of it goes unenforced. About the only way a marketer can be sure that he is conforming with state and local laws is to check with a trade association, the Chamber of Commerce, or the company lawyer—preferably the latter.

Over half the states have broadly worded antitrust provisions in their constitutions, but these are seldom invoked in view of the substantial quantity of federal legislation in this field. Most states also have specific restraint-of-trade legislation, but it, too, is seldom enforced for the same reason. Every state has some form of anti-price-discrimination law.

States have been active in the passage and enforcement of price controls, especially with respect to dairy products, alcoholic beverages, insurance, and certain personal services such as haircuts. They have passed considerable legislation controlling entry into such occupations as medicine, psychiatry, architecture, real-estate selling, barbering, law, and accounting. Most states have passed legislation prohibiting false and misleading advertising, but it is seldom vigorously enforced. Local units such as counties and municipalities have enacted ordinances prohibiting certain types of promotion such as "bait" and going-out-of-business advertising, and their enforcement record is probably superior to the states' in this area. Common criminal acts, such as extortion, coercion, and arson, that might be committed in order to further marketing objectives are covered by state and local laws and are enforced at those levels.

One of the most interesting species of legislation is the sales-below-cost or minimum-markup laws that supplement the fair-trade statutes. These acts are peculiar to the states, twenty-eight of which still carry them on their books. Like fair trade, sales-below-cost legislation is a product of the Great Depression and the resultant disenchantment with price as an instrument of competition, especially among small retailers.

Half these statutes specify a minimum markup for wholesalers, usually 2 percent of the purchase price. Nineteen of them stipulate a minimum markup for retailers of 4 to 12 percent (most specify 6 percent as a minimum). Where a percentage is not cited, the acts state that the markup must cover all costs. Since this statement is open to considerable interpretation, a number of minimum-markup acts explicitly define those elements that can be counted as costs. These include labor, executive salaries, rent, interest, depreciation, maintenance, credit losses, licenses, taxes, insurance, personal selling, and advertising. Goods sold to charities or relief agencies, sold in the liquidation of a business or under a court order, sold in a clearance or close-out sale, or sold as damaged, deteriorated, seasonal, or perishable stock are normally exempt.[29]

These acts do not make sales-below-cost illegal per se. They do declare unlawful the advertisement, offering, or selling of goods below cost when the intent or the effect is to injure competition. This is an important quali-

[29] Howard, *op. cit.*, p. 45.

fication, and its interpretation and application depend on the exact wording of the statute. For example, if the words "injurious to competitors" are used, a price that attracts business from one firm to another may be construed as unlawful even though the competitive quality of the market as a whole may be enhanced. Thus, the standards for distinguishing between a competitive price and an injurious price vary among the twenty-eight states that have such legislation. The laws in all but three of these states, however, do make provision for below-cost pricing if it is done in good faith to meet competition.

If one starts to examine zoning ordinances, health codes, or the myriad of other laws that may in some way impinge on a marketing decision, the lists of statutes and enforcement agencies becomes endless. Compounding the problem is the lack of consistency both between the states and between local units within the states. However, the marketer should be aware of the general legal restrictions and protections confronting him and rely on qualified specialists to guide him in particular situations.

CHAPTER 29

Enforcement Agencies

The Justice Department, working primarily through its Antitrust Division, has primary jurisdiction in the enforcement of the Sherman Antitrust Act, but shares enforcement power with the Federal Trade Commission. The chief distinguishing feature between the otherwise concurrent jurisdictions of the Department of Justice and the FTC is that the Department of Justice can attack only actual violations of the Sherman Act. Its powers are essentially punitive and corrective, not preventive. The FTC, on the other hand, operating under Section 5 of the Federal Trade Commission Act, can take formal action to stop potential violations of the Sherman Act. Sections 2, 3, 7, and 8 of the Clayton Act are also enforced by both the Justice Department and the FTC with the letter handling most of the Section 2 cases.

U. S. DEPARTMENT OF JUSTICE

Most of the Justice Department's cases have been in the area of price-fixing. The majority of them have been civil, not criminal, actions. The major reason for this is that a criminal conviction cannot directly alter the structure of the market or the industry that serves it, whereas a civil suit gives the department the opportunity to petition the court to issue a decree stopping a certain practice or altering the structure of the firm. The defendant may even be ordered to divest itself of a portion of its enterprise. Thus du Pont was directed to dispose of its General Motors stock, and General Dynamics was forced to sell its Liquid Carbonic Division.[1] A civil suit allows the government to deal directly with the problem itself, not simply its illegal consequences.

This is not to suggest that criminal proceedings are without merit except as retribution for unlawful acts. Fines may be imposed on and prison terms

[1] *United States* v. *E. I. du Pont de Nemours & Co. et al.,* 366 U. S. 316 (1961) and *United States* v. *General Dynamics Corp.,* Civil Action 62 C 3686, November 8, 1962.

handed out to the convicted defendant, which may be either a corporation and/or one or more of its executives. This serves as a deterrent to the duplication or repetition of the offense and exposes the firm to possible civil suits involving triple damage payments to the plaintiffs. An injured party may use a criminal conviction as prima-facie evidence in a civil suit against the offending firm.

The possibility of subsequent penalties and the threat of privately initiated civil actions that can result from a criminal action provide an incentive to the firm to opt for one of the two other alternatives that may be offered by the Justice Department. The company may be asked to sign a *consent decree* prepared by the department in which the firm agrees to make specified changes in its structure or practices. Such decrees must be approved by a federal district court, but, as a result, have the force of law. The courts will view violation of the decree as an act of contempt, for which appropriate criminal penalties may be imposed.

Another course, often encouraged by the department, is for the defendant to throw itself on the mercy of the court with a plea of *nolo contendere*.[2] The court may reject such a plea, but if it does not, it may proceed as if a conviction had been obtained. Legally speaking, however, neither the signing of a consent decree nor a pleading of *nolo contendere* is an admission of guilt; hence neither can be used as prima-facie evidence in a suit for civil damages.

The most powerful penalties that can be invoked by the Justice Department are divestiture, divorcement, or dissolution, the three D's of antitrust legislation. These are applied through a consent decree or through petitioning the court, if a civil conviction has been obtained or the court has accepted a plea of *nolo contendere*. Such severe penalties are a rarity, and have been used in only about 100 cases. The number of productive enterprises actually broken up is limited to about 30.[3]

Generally, the Justice Department's action is less drastic. Most cases are settled out of court by agreement between the department and the offending firms. The courts have also tended to avoid such severe penalties in civil cases. For example, IBM was merely ordered to offer its computers for sale as well as for lease.[4] The United Shoe Machinery Company was directed to sell as well as lease its machinery, shorten and modify its leases, and license its patents to its competitors.[5] The marketplace has often made such orders

2 "No contest."
3 Marshall C. Howard, *Legal Aspects of Marketing* (New York: McGraw-Hill, 1964), p. 17.
4 *United States* v. *International Business Machines Corp.,* Civil Action 72–344, January 21, 1952.
5 *United States* v. *United Shoe Machinery Corp.,* 110 F. Supp. 295 (1953) as cited in Howard, *op. cit.,* p. 17.

virtually meaningless. Few customers have elected to buy IBM's computers or United Shoe Machinery's machines, preferring the leases instead.

The department places considerable emphasis on preventive measures as opposed to corrective and punitive action. It publishes guidelines to assist firms in making decisions that will be in conformity with the law. In addition, it provides a business-review procedure that makes available statements of the department's stand on a particular proposed merger or acquisition. Today, it is extremely imprudent for a major firm to attempt a significant merger or acquisition without getting prior clearance from the Justice Department. The general conformity with this practice is the main reason that relatively few cases wind up in court.

FEDERAL TRADE COMMISSION

The Federal Trade Commission was established in 1914 by the Federal Trade Commission Act. It is charged with the enforcement of this act, which prohibits unfair and deceptive practices. In addition, it may deal with certain violations of the Sherman Act by treating them as "unfair methods" under Section 5 of the FTC Act.

Both the Federal Trade Commission and the Department of Justice have the authority to enforce Sections 2, 3, 7, and 8 of the Clayton Act. However, by tacit agreement, the commission usually enforces Section 2 (which prohibits discriminatory pricing), whereas both agencies are active in the enforcement of 3, 7 and 8. Section 2, as amended by the Robinson-Patman Act, is one of the nation's most complicated pieces of legislation and the one most critical to the marketing function.

Orders issued by the commission are subject to review by the federal courts if the defendants elect to appeal them. Congress established the FTC primarily as a fact-finding body, but also placed it on the same level of authority as the federal district courts and charged it with the administration and enforcement of the law. The Wheeler-Lea Act of 1938 allows it to take action against a broad range of practices, including those it deems unfair to the public, regardless of whether there is any injury to competition. Thus false and misleading advertising in the fields of food, drugs, cosmetics, and therapeutic devices, for example, will be challenged by the commission. It may bring suit in a federal court, or it may, on its own authority, issue cease-and-desist orders. Such orders normally become effective 60 days after issuance, unless appealed.

The FTC is also responsible for administering the Webb-Pomerene Act (1918), which exempts agreements and associations formed solely for the purpose of engaging in export trade from the provisions of the Sherman Act. The commission is charged with processing the papers that must be filed in conformance with the act. It also monitors the operations of the parties to these agreements and associations to ensure that they are conforming with the law.

The FTC enforces a series of other acts covering the labeling of certain product classes and branding. It may institute proceedings for the cancellation of registered trademarks that are fraudulent, deceptive, or scandalous and concerns itself with a wide variety of selling practices that are deemed destructive of competition. The commission also enforces the Consumer Credit Protection Act (1968) when such enforcement does not fall under the jurisdiction of a particular federal agency. For example, violations by banks (other than national banks) that are members of the Federal Reserve System are handled by the Federal Reserve Board.

The commission supplements its enforcement activities with a program of cooperation and assistance to industry groups[6] anxious to eliminate unfair practices within an industry or to clarify the law as it applies to a particular field. This joint government-industry effort generally takes the form of a series of conferences between agency personnel and representatives of the industry group to establish "trade practice rules" for the industry. *Trade practice rules* are tailored to a particular industry and deal primarily with the firms' conduct in the marketplace, providing them with a recommended code of ethics.

A set of trade practice rules is normally divided into two sections. Those of the first group are designed to clarify and interpret the laws administered by the FTC as they apply to a particular industry. Practices that are considered unfair, deceptive, or otherwise illegal and whose violation will probably result in formal action by the commission are listed. This section of the rules is usually prefaced by a statement indicating that "appropriate proceedings in the public interest will be taken by the Commission to prevent the use, by any person, partnership, corporation, or other organization subject to its jurisdiction, of such unlawful acts in commerce."

The second section deals with practices deemed to be sound and ethical within the context of the industry. Compliance with this group of rules is usually voluntary, and their violation seldom warrants action by the commission.

Conferences are organized and trade practice rules issued under the auspices of the Division of Trade Practice Conferences and Guides, part of the Bureau of Industry Guidance of the FTC. Participation in this sort of thing is voluntary. Conferences are not held nor are rules promulgated except upon petition by representatives of an industry group.

In its role as the businessman's helper, the FTC has issued a series of industry guides that deal with a variety of activities over which the commis-

[6] "Industry" is used here in its broadest sense and includes all types of business organizations.

sion has jurisdiction. These guides include booklets on pricing, guarantees, bait advertising, and other marketing devices, as well as on deceptive practices associated with particular products such as shoes, batteries, tires, and sleeping bags. Product-group guides deal primarily with deceptive practices in labeling and promotion. To aid the businessman, in this case the marketer, the FTC spells out recommended or accepted standards or methods for describing product characteristics such as size, weight, construction, and performance.

The commission is directed by a bipartisan group of five commissioners, only three of whom can be of the same political party. They are appointed by the President for seven-year terms.

The FTC functions as investigator, prosecutor, and judge. As an investigatory agency, it conducts investigations of businesses on its own initiative, at the request of the President, Congress, the Attorney General, and other government agencies, or in response to referrals from the courts. It also investigates complaints from private parties alleging violations of acts under its jurisdiction. These include the Federal Trade Commission Act, as amended by the Robinson-Patman Act; the Clayton Act; the Webb-Pomerene Export Trade Act; the Flammable Fabrics Act; and the Wool, Fur and Textile Fiber Products Labeling Acts.[7]

In its role as prosecutor and judge, the FTC promulgates rules and regulations as provided for by certain acts under its jurisdiction, files complaints, issues cease-and-desist orders, and levies fines of up to $5,000 for their violation. Although $5,000 may be a nominal penalty for a large corporation, it can be multiplied by the number of days the company fails to comply with the restraining order, each day of violation being considered a separate offense. The party involved can appeal the FTC's action in the federal courts, but this can be a lengthy, expensive and often losing proposition.

Like the Antitrust Division of the Justice Department, the Federal Trade Commission makes extensive use of the consent decree. Frequently, the commission will notify the defendant of its intention to issue a formal complaint, as well as the nature of the restraining order it is preparing. If the party involved and the FTC can reach an agreement, it is formally recognized by the signing of a consent decree, and all other proceedings are stopped. The consent decree stipulates what actions will be taken by the defendant to end the alleged violation and has the same legal standing as a court order, yet it is not technically an admission of guilt. Also, like the Justice Department, the commission allocates much of its resources to preventive measures—issuing guidelines, establishing trade practice rules, and giving its opinion on proposed business activities.

---

[7] Howard, *op. cit.,* p. 17.

FEDERAL FOOD AND DRUG ADMINISTRATION

The FDA, now part of the Department of Health, Education and Welfare, is primarily responsible for the enforcement of the Federal Food, Drug, and Cosmetic Act, as amended by the Food Additives Act. Its chief task is to enforce the law with respect to the *adulteration* and *labeling* of food, drugs, cosmetics, and therapeutic devices. The Federal Trade Commission, on the other hand, is responsible for preventing the false and misleading *advertising* of such goods. However, the FDA may attack advertising that takes the form of literature enclosed with the product, since such material qualifies as "labeling" under the Federal Food, Drug, and Cosmetic Act. The regulation of prescription-drug advertising also falls under the jurisdiction of the FDA, as does the labeling of hazardous substances.

Congress has given the FDA some powerful tools to use in its enforcement work. It can effectively amplify the statutes it administers by promulgating regulations. It can petition the federal district courts for a condemnation decree authorizing the seizure of the defendant's goods. It can request injunctions, and it can file criminal complaints and civil suits in the name of the federal government. Failure to comply with FDA regulations can mean fines, imprisonment, or both.

The FDA also administers the Federal Hazardous Substance Labeling Act. This work supplements the enforcement activities of the Federal Trade Commission under the more generally worded Section 5 of the FTC Act, which is a broad condemnation of "unfair and deceptive acts in commerce." The statute enforced by the FDA is far more explicit, and hence a good deal more effective, with respect to this special class of products. The Federal Hazardous Substance Labeling Act gives the FDA the same powers of injunction and seizures as the Federal Food, Drug, and Cosmetic Act.

OTHER ENFORCEMENT AGENCIES

There are several federal agencies, in addition to the three major ones discussed here, of whose activities a marketer should be aware. The *Federal Aviation Administration* and the *National Transportation Safety Board,* both divisions of the Department of Transportation, regulate the product, promotion, and price variables in the aviation industry. The *Internal Revenue Service* of the U. S. Treasury Department regulates the production of alcoholic beverages; the *Securities and Exchange Commission* controls the marketing of securities; and the *Treasury Department* polices the marking of imported goods.

The *Department of Agriculture* inspects, grades, and marks agricultural products. The *U. S. Post Office* regulates the use of the mails for both advertising and the shipment of certain classes of goods. The *Interstate Commerce Commission* sets tariffs for truckers, the railroads, and shipping companies using inland waterways when such firms are engaged in interstate commerce. The *Federal Communication Commission* issues broadcasting licenses. All of these agencies play an active role in the day-to-day operations of the industries under their jurisdiction.

Summary of Law and Marketing

Having examined each of the major pieces of legislation affecting the marketing function, and the federal agencies charged with their enforcement, we can now summarize them within the context of four of the five marketing variables—price, product, promotion, and distribution. Figure 1 shows significant laws affecting the marketing practices of two or more industries. Specialized acts dealing solely with a particular industry are listed in Table 1. Finally, Table 2 presents a chronological summary of federal marketing laws.

Table 1   Specialized acts relevant to marketing*

Exemption Acts

Webb-Pomerene Trade Act (p. 608)
Merchant Marine Act (p. 608)
Capper-Volstead Act (p. 608)
Cooperative Marketing Act (p. 608)
Agricultural Marketing Agreement Act
   (p. 608)
Fishermen's Collective Marketing Act
   (p. 609)
Defense Production Act (p. 609)

Labeling Acts

Tariff Act (p. 589)
Federal Food, Drug and Cosmetic Act
   (pp. 610 and 612)
Wood Products Labeling Act (p. 614)
Fur Products Labeling Act (p. 614)
Textile Fiber Products Identification Act
   (p. 614)
Automobile Information Disclosure Act
   (p. 614)

Federal Hazardous Substance Labeling
   Act (p. 615)
Federal Cigarette Labeling and Advertising Act (p. 615)

"Little Sherman Acts"

Packers and Stockyard Act (p. 589)
Tariff Act (pp. 589 and 611)
Federal Alcohol Administration Act
   (p. 589)

Miscellaneous Specialized Acts

Meat Inspection Act (p. 610)
Perishable Agricultural Commodities Act
   (p. 610)
Securities Exchange Act (p. 615)
Anti-Racketeering Act (p. 597)
U. S. Patent Code (p. 616)
Flammable Fabrics Act (p. 615)
Federal Aviation Act (p. 615)
Trademark Act (p. 620)
Consumer Credit Protection Act (p. 629)

* Page numbers indicate text discussion of act.

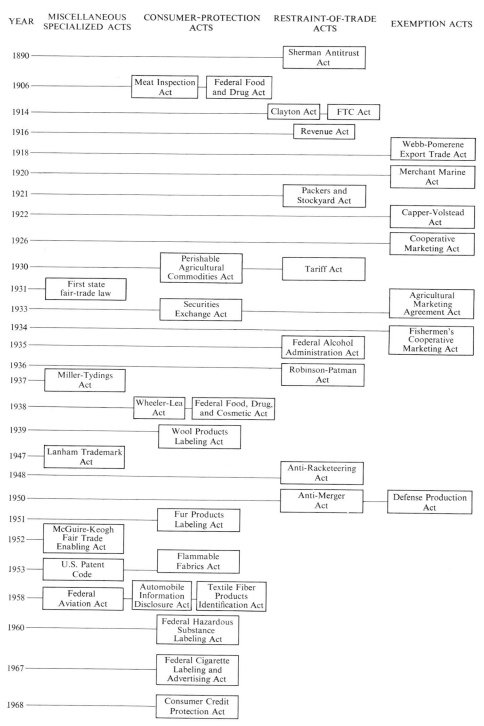

FIGURE 1 Chronology of marketing laws

Table 2 Federal laws applicable to specific marketing instruments

Law	Enforcement Agency	Marketing Instruments Affected
Sherman Antitrust Act (1890) Declares illegal contracts, combinations, and conspiracies in restraint of trade. Prohibits monopolies and attempts to monopolize.	Justice Department	Price: Effect is to discourage monopolistic pricing. Commonly used against price-fixing. Distribution: Effect is to prohibit allocation of markets through collusive agreement between competitors. Commonly invoked to limit or reduce a firm's market share, although the legal size of markets has not been specified in the general case.
Clayton Act (1914) Amends the Sherman Act to prohibit discriminatory pricing between purchasers of products of like grade, quality, and quantity when the effect may be to lessen competition. Exempts labor, agricultural, and horticultural organizations from the antitrust laws. Also prohibits tying agreements, exclusive dealing arrangements, acquisition of stock in a competing firm, and interlocking directorates when the effect is to substantially lessen competition.	Justice Department	Price: Effect is to tighten the Sherman Act with respect to monopolistic pricing policies, especially where price is used as an instrument to injure or destroy competition. Paradoxically, also protects monopolistic pricing by certain groups, such as agricultural marketing cooperatives. Product: Effect is to limit the use of mergers as an instrument for product diversification, when such diversification involves goods of the same general product class. Also restricts the offering of one product contingent on the purchase of another. Distribution: Effect is to constrain a firm's decisions with respect to distribution networks, vertical integration, and horizontal integration.

(Table 2 Continued)

Legislation	Agency	Effect on Marketing Mix
Federal Trade Commission Act (1914) — Establishes the Federal Trade Commission and outlaws unfair and deceptive practices injurious to competition. As interpreted by the courts, this now includes fraudulent and misleading advertising, particularly with respect to the quantity, quality, price, and place of origin of goods, as well as their superiority to other goods. Misrepresentation of the identity, character, or purpose of the firm is also interpreted as an unfair and deceptive practice. Lotteries tied to the product, the pirating of styles, and commercial bribery are outlawed, as is the sale of goods below cost when this would injure competition.	Federal Trade Commission	Price: Enables the Federal Trade Commission to take action against pricing violations that also fall under the Sherman Act, as amended, hence are under the jurisdiction of the Justice Department. Promotion: Effect is to force a degree of honesty in the preparation and use of advertising and personal selling and to restrict the use of lottery tickets as a promotional device. (They may not be offered contingent on the purchase of a product.) Product: Effect is to control product quality by forcing producers to offer goods that have all the properties publicized in their promotion. The law also discourages the exact copying of style innovations. Distribution: Effect has been to restrain, but not eliminate, the practice of giving monetary or material bribes to a customer's purchasing agent to induce him to buy the seller's products.
Revenue Act (1916) — Prohibits the sale of imported goods at a price below their market value or cost when the effect may be to injure, destroy, or prevent the emergence of American industry.	Treasury Department and Federal Trade Commission	Price: Effect is to protect domestic producers from "dumping" or predatory pricing by foreign producers.

Act	Description	Agency	Effect
Webb-Pomerene Export Trade Act (1918)	Exempts agreements and associations formed solely to engage in foreign trade from the antitrust laws.	Federal Trade Commission	Distribution: Effect is to allow the exporter to act as a monopolist in selling to foreign markets.
Tariff Act (1930)	Declares illegal unfair methods of competition and deceptive practices by foreign firms competing in the American market.	Treasury Department and Federal Trade Commission	Price: Effect is to protect domestic manufacturers from the restraint-of-trade activities of foreign competitors not adequately controlled by the amended Sherman Act.
State fair-trade laws (1931 to present)	Authorize vertical price-fixing. Most acts have a "nonsigner" clause that obligates all resellers to abide by the manufacturer or distributor's prescribed resale price once any single reseller has signed a resale price maintenance contract.	State commissions	Price: Effect is to allow manufacturers to stipulate either a fixed or minimum retail price for their goods. Recent court decisions have made enforcement difficult, and the use of this strategy has accordingly declined.

(Table 2 Continued)

Robinson-Patman Act (1936)	Justice Department and Federal Trade Commission	Price: Effect is to restrain the use of price as a competitive instrument. Both specific constraints and the uncertainty introduced by the act and court interpretation of it make the legality of many pricing strategies ambiguous. The fact that the seller is liable for the competitive effects of its price one and two levels removed makes price manipulation between customers and markets dangerous.

Amends the Clayton Act, which in turn amends the Sherman Act, to outlaw discriminatory pricing, subject to certain defenses, when the effect is to injure, destroy, or prevent competition. "Injury" is much easier to prove than "lessening of competition" under the Clayton Act. This act also holds liable the recipient of the benefit of discriminatory pricing. Price discounts that are a direct function of economies of scale are permitted, although limits may be imposed by the FTC. Discrimination is legal when it does not restrain trade. Price changes made to accommodate market conditions, depreciation of goods, or forced sale are also permitted. Use of "Unreasonably low prices" as an instrument to destroy competition is specifically outlawed.

Requires that promotional allowances and services be proportional to the quantity of goods purchased.

Prohibits the payment of brokerage fees and the granting of functional discounts when the broker or wholesale is not truly independent, even if a middleman function is performed.

Promotion: Effect is to constrain the promotional variable. If service cannot be divided to assure proportionality, an equivalent allowance or service must be offered to smaller buyers.

Distribution: Effect is to discourage vertical integration upward toward the source of supply, since the resultant efficiencies cannot always be rewarded by a more advantageous price. The rule of proportionality in granting promotional allowances and services encourages downward integration in the distribution channel.

Miller-Tydings Act (1937)	Justice Department	Price: Effect is to endorse state fair-trade laws.

Exempts vertical price-fixing from federal antitrust laws in states with fair-trade laws.

Act	Agency	Effect
Wheeler-Lea Act (1938) Amends the Federal Trade Commission Act to allow legal action when consumer interests are violated. Relieves firms of the requirement to prove injury to competition in the control of "unfair and deceptive acts." Makes material omissions and nonverbal misrepresentation in advertising illegal.	Federal Trade Commission	Promotion: Effect is to greatly increase the power of the FTC in the regulation of advertising. Product: Effect is to greatly increase government control over the sale of products that do not have the properties claimed for them.
Lanham Trademark Act (1947) Codifies the procedure and requirements for the registration of brand names. Also provides for disqualification of registered trademarks.	U. S. Patent Office and Federal Trade Commission	Promotion: Effect is to give exclusive use of a brand name to the holder of a registered mark.
Antimerger Act (1950) Amends the Clayton Act to broaden the prohibition against mergers resulting in the restraint of trade.	Justice Department	Product: Effect is to limit the use of mergers as an instrument for broadening the product line or mix. Horizontal mergers are most vulnerable to the law and conglomerate mergers the least. This law is invoked only when a major firm is involved. The Justice Department provides advice to prospective merger partners. Distribution: Effect is to limit the use of mergers or stock acquisitions to expand or control the distribution system. The act has been administered with discretion. Mergers have been prevented or dissolved infrequently and only when major corporations were involved. The act has also resulted in the Justice Department setting guidelines for mergers.

(Table 2 Continued)

McGuire-Keogh Fair Trade Enabling Act (1952) Amends the Federal Trade Commission Act to legalize the enforcement of the "nonsigner" clause and makes the FTC the enforcement agency for violations.	Federal Trade Commission	Price: Effect is to give state fair-trade laws further federal endorsement.
U. S. Patent Code (1953) Prescribes conditions under which patents may be granted.	U. S. Patent Commission	Product: Effect is to provide legal monopolies to patent holders for 17-year periods.
Consumer Credit Protection Act (1968) Requires disclosure of credit terms and charges, outlaws extortionary credit transactions, restricts garnishment, and establishes the National Commission on Consumer Finance.	Federal Trade Commission and other federal agencies	Price: Effect is to standardize methods of computing interest rates and force revaluation of the true cost of credit. Makes comparisons of competitors' credit charges much easier.

Questions and Problems

1. What is the Constitutional basis for both the federal and the state fair-trade laws?

2. A firm has captured 60 percent of the market for a certain product class. Its manufacturing and marketing production functions are such that its optimum price is below the direct unit costs of its competitors. What federal laws, if any, is it vulnerable to, and what might it use as a legal defense?

3. The General Motors Corporation could, if it chose, destroy part of its competition by engaging it in a predatory price war. This would be costly in the short run, but in the long run would give GM a monopoly in the automobile industry. Why is this an unacceptable marketing strategy for GM?

4. A major home-appliance manufacturer has an opportunity to acquire a major retail appliance chain that sells brands competitive with its product line. What laws and administrative regulations might apply here? What federal agency would probably become involved in the case?

5. Describe the differences between horizontal, vertical, and conglomerate mergers.

6. What laws apply to each of the three types of mergers, and under what circumstances?

7. A citrus grower is faced with a competitive (in the economist's sense of the word) market. Hence he cannot rationally manipulate the price variable. What might he do legally to alter this situation?

8. A drug manufacturer has chosen to add a line of home permanents to its line. What federal laws must it comply with, and how?

9. Which of the following would probably be acceptable and which unacceptable as trademarks for a new line of beer? (a) *New York,* (b) *John F. Kennedy,* (c) *High Life,* (d) *Best Brew,* (e) *Best Bru.* Why?

10. Once a trademark is granted, under what conditions may it be revoked, and by whom?

11. Discuss the difficulties in enforcing fair-trade prices for each of the following products: (a) a consumer durable sold through a small number of retailers in California, (b) a household appliance sold nationwide, and (c) an automobile.

12. Discuss briefly the roles of the U. S. Department of Justice, the Federal Trade Commission, and the courts in the formulation and enforcement of restraint-of-trade and deceptive-practices laws.

Supplementary Readings

BOOKS

GRETHER, E. T., *Marketing and Public Policy* (Englewood Cliffs, N. J.: Prentice-Hall, 1966).

HOWARD, MARSHALL C., *Legal Aspects of Marketing* (New York: McGraw-Hill, 1964).

PHELPS, D. MAYNARD, and WESTING, J. HOWARD, *Marketing Management* (Homewood, Ill.: Irwin, 1968).

STELZER, IRWIN M., *Selected Antitrust Cases: Landmark Decisions,* 3rd ed. (Homewood, Ill.: Irwin, 1966).

U. S. DEPARTMENT OF JUSTICE, *Merger Guidelines* (Washington, D. C.: U. S. Government Printing Office, 1968).

U. S. PATENT OFFICE, *Trade-Mark Rules of Practice of Patent Office,* rev. ed. (Washington, D. C.: U. S. Government Printing Office, 1963).

UNITED STATES TRADE-MARK ASSOCIATION, *Selection and Adoption of Trade-Marks* (New York: United States Trade-Mark Association, 1964).

ARTICLES

ASSAEL, HENRY, "The Political Role of Trade Associations in Distributive Conflict Resolution," *Journal of Marketing,* Vol. 32, No. 2 (April 1968), pp. 21–28.

BORK, ROBERT H., "Legislative Intent and the Policy of the Sherman Act," *Journal of Law and Economics,* Vol. 9 (October 1966), pp. 7–48.

BUGGIE, FREDERICK D., "Lawful Discrimination in Marketing," *Journal of Marketing,* Vol. 26, No. 2 (April 1962), pp. 1–8.

COHEN, DOROTHY, "The Federal Trade Commission and the Regulation of Advertising in the Consumer Interest," *Journal of Marketing,* Vol. 33, No. 1 (January 1969), pp. 40–44.

DAVIDSON, JOHN R., "FTC, Robinson-Patman, and Cooperative Promotional Activities," *Journal of Marketing,* Vol. 32, No. 1 (January 1968), pp. 14–17.

DIAMOND, SIDNEY A., "Protect Your Trademark with Proper Usage," *Journal of Marketing,* Vol. 26, No. 3 (July 1962), pp. 17–22.

FERRALL, VICTOR E., JR., "Quantity Discounts and Competition: Economic Rationality or Robinson-Patman," *Journal of Law and Economics,* Vol. 3 (October 1960), pp. 146–66.

KLAW, SPENCER, "The Soap Wars: A Strategic Analysis," *Fortune* (June 1963) p. 122.

LEVIN, HARVEY, "Economic Effects of Broadcast Licensing," *Journal of Political Economy,* Vol. 72, No. 2 (April 1964), pp. 151–62.

MCGEE, JOHN S., "Patent Exploitation: Some Economic and Legal Problems," *Journal of Law and Economics,* Vol. 9 (October 1966), pp. 135–62.

————, "Predatory Price Cutting: The Standard Oil (N. J.) Case," *Journal of Law and Economics,* Vol. 1 (October 1958), pp. 137–69.

MURPHY, DANIEL J., "The Federal Trade Commission of the 1960's," *Journal of Marketing,* Vol. 27, No. 2 (April 1963), pp. 1–5.

NARVER, JOHN C., "Some Observations on the Impact of Antitrust Merger Policy on Marketing," *Journal of Marketing,* Vol. 33, No. 1 (January 1969), pp. 24–32.

STIGLER, GEORGE J., "The Economic Effects of the Antitrust Laws," *Journal of Law and Economics,* Vol. 9 (October 1966), pp. 225–58.

WAYS, MAX, "Antitrust in an Era of Radical Change," *Fortune* (March 1966), p. 128.

Appendix I

DIFFERENTIAL CALCULUS

The rules of differential calculus needed to find the derivatives of commonly encountered functions were stated in Chapter 3 without proof. We shall now develop a general method for finding derivatives, illustrating it by proving several of the rules given earlier.

In Chapter 3 the derivative was defined as:

$$\frac{dy}{dx} = \lim_{\Delta x \to 0} \frac{\Delta y}{\Delta x}$$

This expression states that the ratio of an incremental change in y, dy, over an incremental change in x, dx, equals the limit of a finite change in y, Δy, over a finite change in x, Δx, as Δx approaches zero.

The difference quotient, $\Delta y / \Delta x$, can also be expressed as:

$$\frac{\Delta y}{\Delta x} = \frac{f(x_0 + h) - f(x_0)}{h}, \text{ where}$$

h represents Δx, the incremental change in x at the point x_0

Using this form of the difference quotient in the formula for the derivative, we now have

$$\frac{dy}{dx} = \lim_{h \to 0} \frac{f(x_0 + h) - f(x_0)}{h}$$

A derivative of $y = f(x)$ exists only if the limit as $h \rightarrow 0$ exists, and the value of that limit must be the same whether h is positive or negative. The latter requirement ensures that there can be only one value of the derivative, hence only one tangent to $y = f(x)$ at the point x_0. In other words, for the derivative at some value of x, such as x_0, to exist, $y = f(x)$ must be both continuous and smoothly varying at x_0. Figures 1a and 1b show two examples of functions for which the derivative does not exist at x_0. In Figure 1a, dy/dx does not exist at x_0 since $y = f(x)$ is not continuous at that point— that is, there is a break in the function. In Figure 1b, $y = f(x)$ does not vary smoothly at x_0; hence there are two possible values (T_2 and T_1) for the tangent to the curve at x_0.

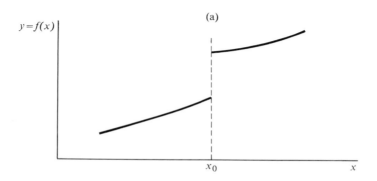

(a)

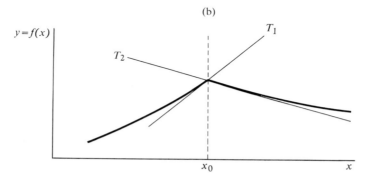

(b)

FIGURE 1
Functions for which the Derivative does not exist at x_0

In the following proofs it can easily be verified that the derivative exists for all values of x, since $y = f(x)$ fulfills both requirements.

RULE I   The derivative of a constant is zero.

$y = f(x) = k$ Given

$\dfrac{dy}{dx} = \lim\limits_{h \to 0} \dfrac{f(x_0 + h) - f(x_0)}{h}$ Definition of a derivative

$\dfrac{dy}{dx} = \lim\limits_{h \to 0} \dfrac{k - k}{h}$ By substitution, since $y = k$

$\dfrac{dy}{dx} = \lim\limits_{h \to 0} \dfrac{0}{x} = 0$ By arithmetic and the definition of a limit

RULE II   The derivative of an independent variable raised to the power one is one.

$y = f(x) = x$ Given

$\dfrac{dy}{dx} = \lim\limits_{h \to 0} \dfrac{f(x_0 + h) - f(x_0)}{h}$ Definition of a derivative

$\dfrac{dy}{dx} = \lim\limits_{h \to 0} \dfrac{(x_0 + h) - x_0}{h}$ By substitution, since $y = x$

$\dfrac{dy}{dx} = \lim\limits_{h \to 0} \dfrac{h}{h} = 1$ By arithmetic and the definition of a limit

RULE III   The derivative of an independent variable raised to a power is equal to the exponent times the variable raised to a power of one less than the original exponent.

$y = f(x) = x^n$ Given

$\dfrac{dy}{dx} = \lim\limits_{h \to 0} \dfrac{f(x_0 + h) - f(x_0)}{h}$ Definition of a derivative

$\dfrac{dy}{dx} = \lim\limits_{h \to 0} \dfrac{(x_0 + h)^n - x_0{}^n}{h}$ By substitution, since $y = x^n$

$$\dfrac{dy}{dx} = \lim\limits_{h \to 0} \dfrac{\left(x_0{}^n + nx_0{}^{n-1}h + \dfrac{n(n-1)}{2} x_0{}^{n-2}h^2 + \cdots + nx_0 h^{n-1} + h^n\right) - x_0{}^n}{h}$$

By expansion of $(x_0 + h)^n$

$$\dfrac{dy}{dx} = \lim\limits_{h \to 0} \dfrac{nx_0{}^{n-1}h + \dfrac{n(n-1)}{2} x_0{}^{n-2}h^2 + \cdots + nx_0 h^{n-1} + h^n}{h}$$

By arithmetic

$$\frac{dy}{dx} = \lim_{h \to 0} n x_0^{n-1} + \frac{n(n-1)}{2} x_0^{n-2} h + \cdots + n x_0 h^{n-2} + h^{n-1}$$

By algebraic manipulation

$$\frac{dy}{dx} = n x_0^{n-1}$$

By the definition of a limit

As an explicit example of Rule III, consider the function $y = x^3$:

$$\frac{dy}{dx} = \lim_{h \to 0} \frac{f(x_0 + h) - f(x_0)}{h}$$

Definition of a derivative

$$\frac{dy}{dx} = \lim_{h \to 0} \frac{(x_0 + h)^3 - x_0^3}{h}$$

By substitution, since $y = x^3$

$$\frac{dy}{dx} = \lim_{h \to 0} \frac{x_0^3 + 3x_0^2 h + 3x_0 h^2 + h^3 - x_0^3}{h}$$

By expansion of $(x_0 + h)^3$

$$\frac{dy}{dx} = \lim_{h \to 0} \frac{3x_0^2 h + 3x_0 h^2 + h^3}{h}$$

By algebraic manipulation

$$\frac{dy}{dx} = \lim_{h \to 0} 3x_0^2 + 3x_0 h + h^2$$

By algebraic manipulation

$$\frac{dy}{dx} = 3x_0^2$$

By the definition of a limit

The derivative of any other function can be found in a similar fashion.

Calculus can also be used to determine the minimum or maximum value of a function. The first derivative of a function is the slope of the function, and the slope must be zero at the minimum or maximum point. Therefore, if the first derivative of a function is set equal to zero, the value of the independent variable obtained by solving the resulting equation is the value of the independent variable that minimizes or maximizes the value of the function. The value obtained is a minimum if the second derivative (the derivative of the first derivative) is positive, and a maximum if the second derivative is negative. For example, consider the following functions:

$$y_1 = x^2 - 10x + 28$$
$$y_2 = -x^2 + 10x$$

Figures 2a and 2b are graphs of these two functions. Clearly, y_1 has a minimum value at $x = 5$ and y_2 has a maximum value at that point.

This can be readily determined using calculus.

$$y_1 = x^2 - 10x + 28 \qquad \text{Given}$$

$$\frac{dy_1}{dx} = 2x - 10$$ By taking the first derivative

$$2x - 10 = 0$$ By setting the first derivative equal to zero

$$x = 5$$ By algebraic manipulation

$$\frac{d^2y_1}{dx^2} = 2$$ By taking the second derivative (i.e., the derivative of $2x - 10$)

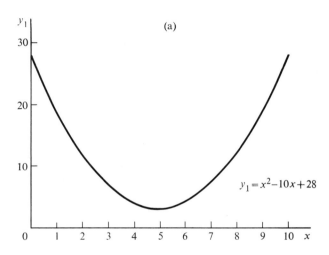

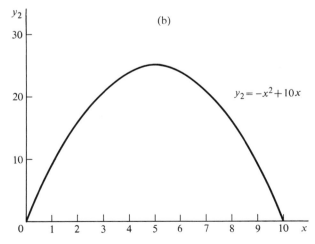

FIGURE 2
Minimum and maximum points

Thus, $y_1 = x^2 - 10x + 30$ has a minimum value at $x = 5$. We know this value is a minimum, since the second derivative is positive. The minimum value of the function (i.e., the minimum value of y_1) is 3, and is obtained simply by substituting $x = 5$ in the original equation.

In a similar fashion we can determine that y_2 has a maximum value of 25 at $x = 5$, since the value obtained by setting the first derivative equal to zero is again 5 and the second derivative of the function (-2) is negative.

The sign of the second derivative is determined by taking the value of the independent variable that maximizes or minimizes the function and substituting it in the second derivative. For example, suppose we are trying to find the maximum value of $y = x^3 - 12x + 30$.

$y = x^3 - 12x + 30$	Given
$\dfrac{dy}{dx} = 3x^2 - 12$	By taking the first derivative
$3x^2 - 12 = 0$	By setting the first derivative equal to zero
$x = \sqrt{4}$	By algebraic manipulation
$x = \pm 2$	By arithmetic

The second derivative ($d^2y/dx^2 = 6x$) is positive when $x = 2$ and negative when $x = -2$. Thus $y = x^3 - 12x + 30$ has a minimum value at $x = 2$ and a maximum value at $x = -2$. This can be verified by graphing the function.

In Chapter 3, we stated that profit would be maximized, or losses minimized, when marginal revenue equaled marginal cost. This can easily be verified using differential calculus.

$\pi = R - C$, where	Given as the profit function
$R = f(Q)$ and	
$C = g(Q)$	
$\dfrac{d\pi}{dQ} = \dfrac{dR}{dQ} - \dfrac{dC}{dQ} = 0$	By setting the first derivative of π equal to zero
$\dfrac{dR}{dQ} = \dfrac{dC}{dQ}$	By algebraic manipulation

By definition, dR/dQ is marginal revenue and dC/dQ is marginal cost, so marginal revenue must equal marginal cost for profit to be maximized or losses minimized.

Appendix II

USE OF TABLES

CUMULATIVE NORMAL DISTRIBUTION

The normal distribution is a bell-shaped curve that extends infinitely in either direction. Its importance stems from the central-limit theorem of statistics, which states that if the sample size is reasonably large, the distribution of sample arithmetic means will be normally distributed. The general shape of the normal distribution is shown in Figure 3.

The normal distribution depicts the probability, P, of obtaining particular values of z. Obviously, the total area under the curve must sum to 1, since the probabilities of achieving all possible values of z must sum to 1. The mathematical equation for the normal distribution is:

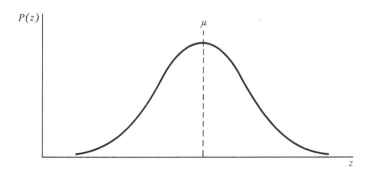

FIGURE 3
Normal distribution

$$P(z) = \frac{1}{\sqrt{2\pi}} e^{-z^2/2}, \text{ where}$$

$$z = \frac{X - \mu}{\sigma}$$

$$\mu = \text{the population mean} \left(\mu = \frac{\sum\limits_{i=1}^{n} X_i}{N} \right)$$

$$\sigma = \text{the population standard deviation} \left(\sigma = \sqrt{\frac{\sum\limits_{i=1}^{n} (X_i - \mu)^2}{N}} \right)$$

$X =$ a variable

$N =$ the number of elements in the population

$\pi =$ 3.1416, and

$e =$ 2.7183

In this equation the value of z, often referred to as the z *statistic*, represents the distance from the mean, μ, to a point, X, in terms of the standard deviation, σ. Thus a z value of 1.5 means that the value of X is 1.5 standard deviations from the mean.

Table 1 (p. 668) gives the area of the normal distribution contained between the mean and a point that is z standard deviations from the mean (the shaded area in the accompaying figure). The numbers that appear to the left of and above the table are the values of z, and the entries in the table are the areas of the normal curve that correspond to each value. For instance, the probability of a z value between 0 and 1.14 is .3729. This probability is obtained by reading the value for $z = 1.1$ in the column $z = .04$. In this example, we found the value of $P(0 \leq z \leq 1.14)$, where z was a positive number. Since the normal distribution is symmetrical, negative values of z can be treated as positive values in using the table. Thus, $P(-1.2 \leq z \leq 0)$ is equal to .3849, the value given in row 1.2, column .00. The following examples further illustrate the use of Table 1.

Example: A normal distribution has a mean, μ, of 5 and a standard deviation, σ, of 2. What is the probability that a single observation, X, will have a value between 4 and 8?

The probability that its value will be between 5 (μ) and 8 is:

$$z = \frac{X - \mu}{\sigma} = \frac{8 - 5}{2} = 1.5 \qquad \text{Conversion to } z \text{ statistic}$$

$$P(0 \leq z \leq 1.5) = .4332 \qquad \qquad \text{From Table 1}$$

The probability that its value will be between 4 and 5 (μ) is:

$$z = \frac{X - \mu}{\sigma} = \frac{4 - 5}{2} = -.5 \qquad \text{Conversion to } z \text{ statistic}$$

$$P(-.5 \leq z \leq 0) = .1915 \qquad \text{From Table 1}$$

Thus the probability that the observation will have a value between 4 and 8 is .4332 + .1915, or .6247.

Example: What z value should be used to establish a 92-percent confidence interval?

At the 92-percent confidence level, there is a probability of 8 percent that the true value will lie either above or below the confidence interval limits. Since the normal distribution is symmetrical, we need to find a value for z that contains 46 percent (.46) of the population. This value, shown on Table 1, is $z = 1.75$.

t DISTRIBUTIONS

If the population standard deviation is not known a priori, the sample standard deviation must be used as an estimate, thus making both the mean and the standard deviation variables. If it can be assumed that the population distribution is normal, (usually by appeal to the central-limit theorem), then the t distribution can be used as a basis for testing hypotheses and establishing confidence intervals.

The t distribution resembles the normal distribution in that it is also symmetrical and bell-shaped. However, its exact shape depends upon the degrees of freedom associated with the particular test. The number of degrees of freedom is a function of the particular statistical test being performed. For instance, in establishing a confidence interval for sample means, the number of degrees of freedom is $n - 1$, where n is the sample size. The t statistic is calculated in much the same way as the z statistic, except that the sample mean and standard deviation are substituted for the population mean and standard deviation. Thus,

$$t = \frac{X - \bar{X}}{s}, \text{ where}$$

$$\bar{X} = \text{the sample mean} \left(\bar{X} = \frac{\sum_{i=1}^{n} X_i}{n} \right)$$

$$s = \text{the sample standard deviation} \left(s = \sqrt{\frac{\sum_{i=1}^{n} (X_i - \bar{X})^2}{n - 1}} \right)$$

X = a variable, and

n = the number of elements in the sample

Table 2 (p. 669) tabulates the values of t as a function of the number of degrees of freedom and the proportion of the t distribution that is greater than the t value. For instance, if the t distribution has 11 degrees of freedom, then 10 percent $(t_{.1})$ of the distribution lies above the t value 1.363. The area tabulated in Table 2 is shown as the shaded area in the accompanying figure. The following examples illustrate the use of the table.

Example: In a sample of 20 observations, the sample mean, $\overline{X}$, is 10 and the sample standard deviation, s, is 2. What t value should be used to establish a 95-percent confidence interval for the mean?

In this example, the number of degrees of freedom is 19, or $n - 1$. To obtain the desired confidence interval, we need a value for $t_{.025}$ (since the probabilities of being above or below the confidence interval must be equal) with 19 degrees of freedom. This value, given in Table 2, is 2.093.

Example: A research project has been designed to test the hypothesis that the average sales of an item amount to 2,000 or more units per week. Over a ten-week period, sales averaged 1,800 units, with a standard deviation of 80 units. Past data indicate that the weekly demand for the product is normally distributed. Should this hypothesis be rejected at the 90-percent confidence level?

Since the hypothesis states that demand is 2,000 or more units per week, we have a single-sided test, i.e., we will reject the hypothesis if demand is significantly less than 2,000 units per week, but not if it is significantly more. The hypothesis should be rejected only if the calculated t value is negative and has an absolute value greater than the value in Table 2. Again, the appropriate number of degrees of freedom is $n - 1$, or 9. The value given in Table 2 is 1.383 ($t_{.1}$ with 9 degrees of freedom). Calculating the t value for the sample, we have

$$t = \frac{X - \overline{X}}{s} = \frac{1,800 - 2,000}{80} = \frac{-200}{80} = -2.5$$

Since the absolute value of the calculated t statistic is greater than the value in the table, the hypothesis should be rejected; that is, there is less than a 5-percent chance that the weekly demand is 2,000 or more units.

LARGE-SAMPLE AND SMALL-SAMPLE STATISTICS

The use of the normal distribution (z statistics) is often referred to as large-sample statistics, and the use of the t distribution (t statistics) is similarly referred to as small-sample statistics. As the number of degrees of freedom approaches infinity, the t distribution approaches the normal distribution. This can be verified by comparing the values in Table 2 for an infinite number of degrees of freedom with those in Table 1 for the normal distribution. In practice, therefore, large-sample statistics are usually used if the sample size is greater than 30, even if the population standard deviation is unknown. Only if the sample size is less than 30 are small-sample statistics used.

95- AND 99-PERCENT CONFIDENCE INTERVALS FOR PROPORTIONS

Tables 3a and 3b (pp. 670–71) show 95- and 99-percent confidence intervals for proportions with sample sizes from 10 to 250. The following examples illustrate the use of the two tables.

Example: A marketing research firm interviewed 250 housewives in an attempt to measure their responses to a new product. Of this group, 100 women liked the product. Based on this sample, what is the 95-percent confidence interval for the true proportion of housewives who would like the new product?

The sample proportion is $p = x/n = 100/250 = .4$. For this value of p and a sample size of 250, Table 3a yields a 95-percent confidence interval of .33 to .46. The 95-percent confidence interval, π, is therefore $.33 \leq \pi \leq .46$.

Example: In a sample of 18 items, 4 were found to be defective. What is the 99-percent confidence interval for the true proportion that is defective?

The sample proportion is $p = 4/18 = .222$. Both the sample proportion and the sample size must be interpolated from Table 3b to obtain the confidence interval, which is $.03 \leq \pi \leq .57$.

FOUR-PLACE LOGARITHMS

The following paragraphs present a brief description of logarithms, a mathematical tool whose use greatly simplifies many calculations. Students wishing to delve further into the subject may benefit by consulting a text that treats the subject more thoroughly.

The logarithm of a positive number is the exponent (or power) to which some base number must be raised in order to equal the positive number. For example, consider the positive number 100. If a base of 10 is used, then the logarithm of 100 is 2; i.e., $100 = 10^2$. The number 10 is the most commonly used base and may be assumed in this discussion unless another base is specifically indicated. Logarithms to other bases, particularly the Napierian number e (2.71828) and the binary number 2, are useful for certain problems.

A logarithm has two parts: a whole number, called a *characteristic,* and a set of digits to the right of the decimal point, called the *mantissa.* In the preceding example, the logarithm was an integer; the characteristic was 2 and the mantissa was 0000. Let us take a few more examples. Consider the numbers 31, 310, and 3,100. Clearly, the logarithm of 31, or log 31, as it is commonly abbreviated, must be greater than 1.0000 and less than 2.0000, since $10^1 = 10$ and $10^2 = 100$ and $10 < 31 < 100$. Thus, the characteristic of log 31 is 1. Similarly, the characteristic of log 310 is 2 ($10^2 < 310 < 10^3$), and the characteristic of log 3,100 is 3 ($10^3 < 3,100 < 10^4$). The mantissas of these three numbers are identical, and may be determined from Table 4 (pp. 672–73). This table is called a logarithmic table, but it is really a table of logarithmic mantissas, since the characteristic of the logarithm is a function of the placement of the decimal point. Combining the characteristic and mantissa (.4914) for each logarithm given above, we have:

log 31   = 1.4914

log 310   = 2.4914

log 3,100 = 3.4914

We can find the characteristic and mantissa for a number smaller than 10 in a similar fashion. For instance, consider the logarithm of 3.1. The mantissa is still 4914, but the characteristic is 0, since $10^0 = 1$ and $10^1 = 10$ and 3.1 lies between 1 and 10. Since $10^0 = 1$ and $10^{-1} = \frac{1}{10} = .1$ and $.1 < .31 < 1$, the value of log .31 is between -1 and 0. Thus the characteristic is -1 and the logarithm is -1.4914.

The characteristic for the logarithm of any other number can be found by similar reasoning, or the following rule can be applied:

Rule: To find the characteristic for the logarithm of any number, count the number of digits from the units digit (i.e., the digit immediately to the left of the decimal point) to and including the leading non-zero digit (i.e., the non-zero digit farthest to the left). If the leading non-zero digit lies to the left of the units digit, the characteristic will be positive and equal to the number of digits counted; if it lies to the right of the units digit, and hence to the right of the decimal point, the characteristic will be negative and equal to the number of digits counted. (The decimal point is not considered a digit when counting.) To show the application of this rule, suppose we place a small x above the counted digits:

$$\overset{xx}{\log .031} \qquad \text{characteristic} = -2$$

$$\overset{x}{\log .31} \qquad \text{characteristic} = -1$$

log 3.1	characteristic =	0
x		
log 31.	characteristic =	1
xx		
log 310.	characteristic =	2
$x\ xx$		
log 3,100.	characteristic =	3

If a number has more than three significant digits, the mantissa of the logarithm can be determined only by interpolation, since Table 4 contains only three significant digits (two in the column on the left and the third in the column heading). For example, the mantissa for the number 312 is 4942 and can be read directly from Table 4. If a number has four significant digits, say 3123, then the mantissa cannot be read directly from Table 4 but must be interpolated. Table 4 tells us only that log 312 = 4942 and log 313 = 4955. Fortunately, the differences between logarithms are small enough that linear interpolation is satisfactory for most applications.

The mantissa for log 3123 can be found by adding 3/10 of the difference between the mantissa for log 313 and the mantissa for log 312 to the mantissa for log 312:

$$
\begin{aligned}
\text{mantissa for log 3123} &= \text{mantissa for log 312} \\
&\quad + 3/10\ (\text{mantissa for log 313} \\
&\quad - \text{mantissa for log 312}) \\
&= 4942 + 3/10(4955 - 4942) \\
&= 4942 + 3/10(13) \\
&= 4942 + 4 = 4946
\end{aligned}
$$

The process of finding the mantissa for numbers having four significant digits can be greatly simplified by using a table of proportional parts such as that shown in Table 4. For instance, in order to estimate the mantissa of log 3123 we need only to read the proportional part in the column for 31 and the row for 3. The value in the proportional-part table that corresponds to a difference of 13 and a proportional part of 3 is 4. Thus, the mantissa for the logarithm of 3123 is 4942 + 4, or 4946.

If the logarithm is known and the number is not, the process above is reversed. In this case, we are looking for an *antilogarithm*. Suppose we want to find the number that has the logarithm 2.4924—the antilogarithm of 2.4924. The characteristic 2 tells us that the number will have two digits to the left of the units digit. A search of Table 4 tells us that the mantissa 4924 corresponds to a number between 310 and 311, since the mantissa for 310 is 4914 and that for 311 is 4928. Since no entry is identical to 4924, we must again interpolate to get an exact figure. The proportional-part entry for

10 (4924 − 4914) corresponds to a proportional part of 7. Since the number must contain two digits to the left of the units digit, the antilogarithm of 2.4924 is 310.7.

Logarithms are widely used in evaluating mathematical expressions that contain multiplication, division, or exponentiation because they have the following properties:

$$\log (A \cdot B) = \log A + \log B$$

$$\log \left(\frac{A}{B}\right) = \log A - \log B$$

$$\log (A^B) = B \log A$$

The use of logarithms reduces the calculations in these problems to simple addition, subtraction, or multiplication.

In the following examples, only the numerical calculation is shown. The problem of finding the logs of the numbers is left as a review exercise for the student.

Example: Evaluate $\dfrac{254.7 \times 8.435}{142.6}$.

$$\log \left(\frac{254.7 \times 8.435}{142.6}\right) = \log 254.7 + \log 8.435 - \log 142.6$$

$$\log 254.7 = 2.4060$$

$$\log 8.435 = .9261$$

$$\log 142.6 = 2.1541$$

$$\log \left(\frac{254.7 \times 8.435}{142.6}\right) = 1.1780$$

$$\log^{-1*} \left(\frac{254.7 \times 8.435}{142.6}\right) = \log^{-1}(1.1780) = 15.07$$

Example: Evaluate $\dfrac{2.547 \times 8.435}{142.6}$.

(Note that this problem is identical to the previous one except that 254.7 has been changed to 2.547 to demonstrate the antilogarithmic process when the logarithm is negative.)

---

* Log^{-1} is a notational device used to represent an antilogarithm.

$\log 2.547 = .4060$

$\log 8.435 = .9261$

$\log 142.6 = 2.1541$

$\log \left(\dfrac{2.547 \times 8.435}{142.6} \right) = -.8220$

Since there is a no direct way of finding the antilogarithm for a negative logarithm, we must first make the logarithm positive, by adding a positive integer to the characteristic and then subtracting the same number from the resulting logarithm. Any positive integer will do, as long as the final logarithm is positive. If we add the integer 5, then:

$\log 2.547 = 5.4060 - 5$

$\log 8.435 = .9261$

$\log 142.6 = 2.1541$ and

$\log \left(\dfrac{2.547 \times 8.435}{142.6} \right) = 4.1780 - 5$

We now have a positive logarithmic value but with a characteristic of -1 $(4 - 5)$. Thus,

$\log^{-1} (4.1780 - 5) = .1507$

Since the characteristic is -1, the first integer to the right of the units digit is placed to the right of the decimal point.

Example: Evaluate $15.7^{3.45}$.

$\log (15.7^{3.45}) = 3.45 \log 15.7$

$\log 15.7 = 1.1959$

$3.45 \log 15.7 = 3.45 \times 1.1959 = 4.1259$

$\log^{-1} (4.1259) = 13360.$

Example: Evaluate $e^{-.5}$.

$\log (e^{-.5}) = -.5(\log e)$	By the rules of logarithms
$\log (e^{-.5}) = -.5(.4343)$	By substitution
$\log (e^{-.5}) = -.21715$	By arithmetic

$$\log (e^{-.5}) = 4.78285 - 5 \qquad \text{By adding 5 to the characteristic}$$

$$e^{-.5} = \log^{-1}(4.7285 - 5) = .6064 \qquad \text{By taking antilogarithms}$$

Occasionally, it is convenient to be able to express logarithms to a base other than 10. Suppose we want to find the logarithm of 13.2 to the base e, where e is the Napierian number 2.71828; in this case, $\log_e 13.2$ is the exponent b such that $13.2 = e^b$, or 2.71828^b. Using Table 4, we can find $\log_{10} 13.2 = 1.1206$ and $\log_{10} e = \log_{10} 2.71828 = .4343$. $\text{Log}_e 13.2$ can then be found by applying the rule of logarithmic base conversion:

$$\log_a X = (\log_a b)(\log_b X) \qquad \text{The rule of logarithmic base conversion}$$

$$\log_{10} 13.2 = (\log_{10} e)(\log_e 13.2) \qquad \text{By substitution}$$

$$\log_e 13.2 = \frac{\log_{10} 13.2}{\log_{10} e} \qquad \text{By algebraic manipulation}$$

$$\log_e 13.2 = \frac{1.1206}{.4343} \qquad \text{By substitution } (\log_{10} 13.2 = 1.1206, \text{ and } \log_{10} e = .4343)$$

$$\log_e 13.2 = 2.5800 \qquad \text{By arithmetic}$$

This conversion process can be reduced to

$$\log_{10} N = .4343 \log_e N$$

$$\log_e N = 2.3026 \log_{10} N$$

The conversion factors, .4343 and 2.3026, are merely reciprocals.

In a similar fashion, logarithms to the base 2 can easily be found from a base-10 logarithmic table by the following conversion formulas:

$$\log_{10} N = .3010 \log_2 N$$

$$\log_2 N = 3.3222 \log_{10} N$$

These relationships, together with other commonly used logarithmic constants, are indicated at the bottom of Table 4 (pp. 672–73).

TABLES

Table 1 Cumulative normal distribution

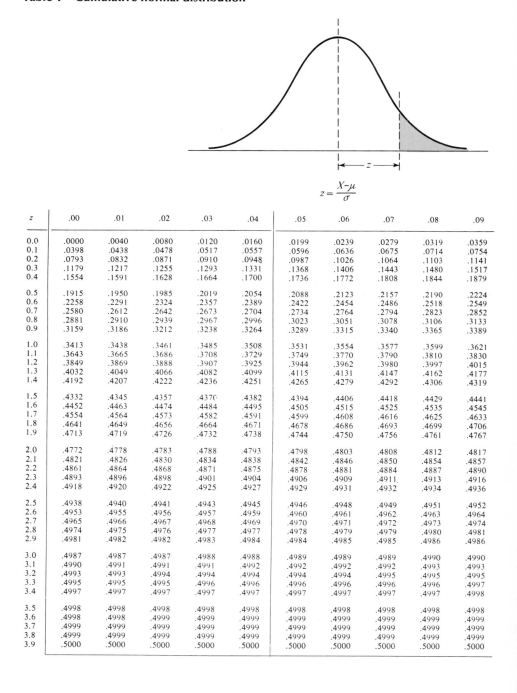

$$z = \frac{X-\mu}{\sigma}$$

z	.00	.01	.02	.03	.04	.05	.06	.07	.08	.09
0.0	.0000	.0040	.0080	.0120	.0160	.0199	.0239	.0279	.0319	.0359
0.1	.0398	.0438	.0478	.0517	.0557	.0596	.0636	.0675	.0714	.0754
0.2	.0793	.0832	.0871	.0910	.0948	.0987	.1026	.1064	.1103	.1141
0.3	.1179	.1217	.1255	.1293	.1331	.1368	.1406	.1443	.1480	.1517
0.4	.1554	.1591	.1628	.1664	.1700	.1736	.1772	.1808	.1844	.1879
0.5	.1915	.1950	.1985	.2019	.2054	.2088	.2123	.2157	.2190	.2224
0.6	.2258	.2291	.2324	.2357	.2389	.2422	.2454	.2486	.2518	.2549
0.7	.2580	.2612	.2642	.2673	.2704	.2734	.2764	.2794	.2823	.2852
0.8	.2881	.2910	.2939	.2967	.2996	.3023	.3051	.3078	.3106	.3133
0.9	.3159	.3186	.3212	.3238	.3264	.3289	.3315	.3340	.3365	.3389
1.0	.3413	.3438	.3461	.3485	.3508	.3531	.3554	.3577	.3599	.3621
1.1	.3643	.3665	.3686	.3708	.3729	.3749	.3770	.3790	.3810	.3830
1.2	.3849	.3869	.3888	.3907	.3925	.3944	.3962	.3980	.3997	.4015
1.3	.4032	.4049	.4066	.4082	.4099	.4115	.4131	.4147	.4162	.4177
1.4	.4192	.4207	.4222	.4236	.4251	.4265	.4279	.4292	.4306	.4319
1.5	.4332	.4345	.4357	.4370	.4382	.4394	.4406	.4418	.4429	.4441
1.6	.4452	.4463	.4474	.4484	.4495	.4505	.4515	.4525	.4535	.4545
1.7	.4554	.4564	.4573	.4582	.4591	.4599	.4608	.4616	.4625	.4633
1.8	.4641	.4649	.4656	.4664	.4671	.4678	.4686	.4693	.4699	.4706
1.9	.4713	.4719	.4726	.4732	.4738	.4744	.4750	.4756	.4761	.4767
2.0	.4772	.4778	.4783	.4788	.4793	.4798	.4803	.4808	.4812	.4817
2.1	.4821	.4826	.4830	.4834	.4838	.4842	.4846	.4850	.4854	.4857
2.2	.4861	.4864	.4868	.4871	.4875	.4878	.4881	.4884	.4887	.4890
2.3	.4893	.4896	.4898	.4901	.4904	.4906	.4909	.4911	.4913	.4916
2.4	.4918	.4920	.4922	.4925	.4927	.4929	.4931	.4932	.4934	.4936
2.5	.4938	.4940	.4941	.4943	.4945	.4946	.4948	.4949	.4951	.4952
2.6	.4953	.4955	.4956	.4957	.4959	.4960	.4961	.4962	.4963	.4964
2.7	.4965	.4966	.4967	.4968	.4969	.4970	.4971	.4972	.4973	.4974
2.8	.4974	.4975	.4976	.4977	.4977	.4978	.4979	.4979	.4980	.4981
2.9	.4981	.4982	.4982	.4983	.4984	.4984	.4985	.4985	.4986	.4986
3.0	.4987	.4987	.4987	.4988	.4988	.4989	.4989	.4989	.4990	.4990
3.1	.4990	.4991	.4991	.4991	.4992	.4992	.4992	.4992	.4993	.4993
3.2	.4993	.4993	.4994	.4994	.4994	.4994	.4994	.4995	.4995	.4995
3.3	.4995	.4995	.4995	.4996	.4996	.4996	.4996	.4996	.4996	.4997
3.4	.4997	.4997	.4997	.4997	.4997	.4997	.4997	.4997	.4997	.4998
3.5	.4998	.4998	.4998	.4998	.4998	.4998	.4998	.4998	.4998	.4998
3.6	.4998	.4998	.4999	.4999	.4999	.4999	.4999	.4999	.4999	.4999
3.7	.4999	.4999	.4999	.4999	.4999	.4999	.4999	.4999	.4999	.4999
3.8	.4999	.4999	.4999	.4999	.4999	.4999	.4999	.4999	.4999	.4999
3.9	.5000	.5000	.5000	.5000	.5000	.5000	.5000	.5000	.5000	.5000

SOURCE: *Outline of Theory and Problems of Statistics* by M. R. Spiegel. Copyright © 1961 by McGraw-Hill, Inc. Used by permission of McGraw-Hill Book Company.

Table 2   Values of the *t* distribution

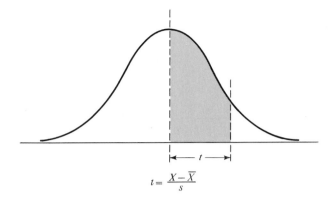

$$t = \frac{X - \bar{X}}{s}$$

Degrees of freedom *n*	Probability of a deviation greater than *t*					
	0.005	0.01	0.025	0.05	0.1	0.15
1	63.657	31.821	12.706	6.314	3.078	1.963
2	9.925	6.965	4.303	2.920	1.886	1.386
3	5.841	4.541	3.182	2.353	1.638	1.250
4	4.604	3.747	2.776	2.132	1.533	1.190
5	4.032	3.365	2.571	2.015	1.476	1.156
6	3.707	3.143	2.447	1.943	1.440	1.134
7	3.499	2.998	2.365	1.895	1.415	1.119
8	3.355	2.896	2.306	1.860	1.397	1.108
9	3.250	2.821	2.262	1.833	1.383	1.100
10	3.169	2.764	2.228	1.812	1.372	1.093
11	3.106	2.718	2.201	1.796	1.363	1.088
12	3.055	2.681	2.179	1.782	1.356	1.083
13	3.012	2.650	2.160	1.771	1.350	1.079
14	2.977	2.624	2.145	1.761	1.345	1.076
15	2.947	2.602	2.131	1.753	1.341	1.074
16	2.921	2.583	2.120	1.746	1.337	1.071
17	2.898	2.567	2.110	1.740	1.333	1.069
18	2.878	2.552	2.101	1.734	1.330	1.067
19	2.861	2.539	2.093	1.729	1.328	1.066
20	2.845	2.528	2.086	1.725	1.325	1.064
21	2.831	2.518	2.080	1.721	1.323	1.063
22	2.819	2.508	2.074	1.717	1.321	1.061
23	2.807	2.500	2.069	1.714	1.319	1.060
24	2.797	2.492	2.064	1.711	1.318	1.059
25	2.787	2.485	2.060	1.708	1.316	1.058
26	2.779	2.479	2.056	1.706	1.315	1.058
27	2.771	2.473	2.052	1.703	1.314	1.057
28	2.763	2.467	2.048	1.701	1.313	1.056
29	2.756	2.462	2.045	1.699	1.311	1.055
30	2.750	2.457	2.042	1.697	1.310	1.055
∞	2.576	2.326	1.960	1.645	1.282	1.036

SOURCE: J. E. Freund and F. J. Williams, *Elementary Business Statistics: The Modern Approach*, copyright © 1964. Reprinted by permission of Prentice-Hall, Inc. Table is taken from Table IV of Fisher: *Statistical Methods for Research Workers*, published by Oliver & Boyd Limited, Edinburgh, and used by permission of the author and publishers.

Table 3a   95-percent confidence intervals for proportions

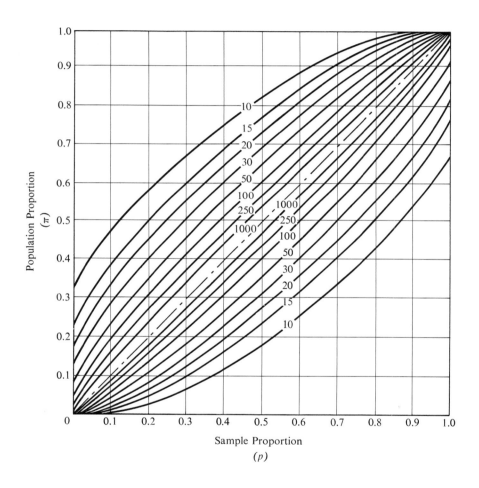

SOURCE: W. J. Dixon and F. J. Massey, *Introduction to Statistical Analysis* (New York: McGraw-Hill Book Company, 1969). Originally appeared in *Biometrika,* Vol. 26 (1934). Used with permission of McGraw-Hill Book Company and the Trustees of Biometrika.

Table 3b   99-percent confidence intervals for proportions

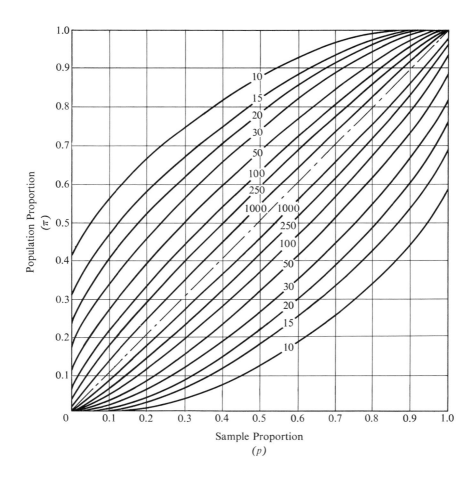

Sample Proportion
(*p*)

SOURCE: W. J. Dixon and F. J. Massey, *Introduction to Statistical Analysis* (New York: McGraw-Hill Book Company, 1969). Originally appeared in *Biometrika*, Vol. 26 (1934). Used with permission of McGraw-Hill Book Company and the Trustees of Biometrika.

Table 4 Four-place logarithms

N	0	1	2	3	4	5	6	7	8	9	1	2	3	4	5	6	7	8	9
														Proportional Parts					
10	0000	0043	0086	0128	0170	0212	0253	0294	0334	0374	4	8	12	17	21	25	29	33	37
11	0414	0453	0492	0531	0569	0607	0645	0682	0719	0755	4	8	11	15	19	23	26	30	34
12	0792	0828	0864	0899	0934	0969	1004	1038	1072	1106	3	7	10	14	17	21	24	28	31
13	1139	1173	1206	1239	1271	1303	1335	1367	1399	1430	3	6	10	13	16	19	23	26	29
14	1461	1492	1523	1553	1584	1614	1644	1673	1703	1732	3	6	9	12	15	18	21	24	27
15	1761	1790	1818	1847	1875	1903	1931	1959	1987	2014	3	6	8	11	14	17	20	22	25
16	2041	2068	2095	2122	2148	2175	2201	2227	2253	2279	3	5	8	11	13	16	18	21	24
17	2304	2330	2355	2380	2405	2430	2455	2480	2504	2529	2	5	7	10	12	15	17	20	22
18	2553	2577	2601	2625	2648	2672	2695	2718	2742	2765	2	5	7	9	12	14	16	19	21
19	2788	2810	2833	2856	2878	2900	2923	2945	2967	2989	2	4	7	9	11	13	16	18	20
20	3010	3032	3054	3075	3096	3118	3139	3160	3181	3201	2	4	6	8	11	13	15	17	19
21	3222	3243	3263	3284	3304	3324	3345	3365	3385	3404	2	4	6	8	10	12	14	16	18
22	3424	3444	3464	3483	3502	3522	3541	3560	3579	3598	2	4	6	8	10	12	14	15	17
23	3617	3636	3655	3674	3692	3711	3729	3747	3766	3784	2	4	6	7	9	11	13	15	17
24	3802	3820	3838	3856	3874	3892	3909	3927	3945	3962	2	4	5	7	9	11	12	14	16
25	3979	3997	4014	4031	4048	4065	4082	4099	4116	4133	2	3	5	7	9	10	12	14	15
26	4150	4166	4183	4200	4216	4232	4249	4265	4281	4298	2	3	5	7	8	10	11	13	15
27	4314	4330	4346	4362	4378	4393	4409	4425	4440	4456	2	3	5	6	8	9	11	13	14
28	4472	4487	4502	4518	4533	4548	4564	4579	4594	4609	2	3	5	6	8	9	11	12	14
29	4624	4639	4654	4669	4683	4698	4713	4728	4742	4757	1	3	4	6	7	9	10	12	13
30	4771	4786	4800	4814	4829	4843	4857	4871	4886	4900	1	3	4	6	7	9	10	11	13
31	4914	4928	4942	4955	4969	4983	4997	5011	5024	5038	1	3	4	6	7	8	10	11	12
32	5051	5065	5079	5092	5105	5119	5132	5145	5159	5172	1	3	4	5	7	8	9	11	12
33	5185	5198	5211	5224	5237	5250	5263	5276	5289	5302	1	3	4	5	6	8	9	10	12
34	5315	5328	5340	5353	5366	5378	5391	5403	5416	5428	1	3	4	5	6	8	9	10	11
35	5441	5453	5465	5478	5490	5502	5514	5527	5539	5551	1	2	4	5	6	7	9	10	11
36	5563	5575	5587	5599	5611	5623	5635	5647	5658	5670	1	2	4	5	6	7	8	10	11
37	5682	5694	5705	5717	5729	5740	5752	5763	5775	5786	1	2	3	5	6	7	8	9	10
38	5798	5809	5821	5832	5843	5855	5866	5877	5888	5899	1	2	3	5	6	7	8	9	10
39	5911	5922	5933	5944	5955	5966	5977	5988	5999	6010	1	2	3	4	5	7	8	9	10
40	6021	6031	6042	6053	6064	6075	6085	6096	6107	6117	1	2	3	4	5	6	8	9	10
41	6128	6138	6149	6160	6170	6180	6191	6201	6212	6222	1	2	3	4	5	6	7	8	9
42	6232	6243	6253	6263	6274	6284	6294	6304	6314	6325	1	2	3	4	5	6	7	8	9
43	6335	6345	6355	6365	6375	6385	6395	6405	6415	6425	1	2	3	4	5	6	7	8	9
44	6435	6444	6454	6464	6474	6484	6493	6503	6513	6522	1	2	3	4	5	6	7	8	9
45	6532	6542	6551	6561	6571	6580	6590	6599	6609	6618	1	2	3	4	5	6	7	8	9
46	6628	6637	6646	6656	6665	6675	6684	6693	6702	6712	1	2	3	4	5	6	7	7	8
47	6721	6730	6739	6749	6758	6767	6776	6785	6794	6803	1	2	3	4	5	5	6	7	8
48	6812	6821	6830	6839	6848	6857	6866	6875	6884	6893	1	2	3	4	4	5	6	7	8
49	6902	6911	6920	6928	6937	6946	6955	6964	6972	6981	1	2	3	4	4	5	6	7	8
50	6990	6998	7007	7016	7024	7033	7042	7050	7059	7067	1	2	3	3	4	5	6	7	8
51	7076	7084	7093	7101	7110	7118	7126	7135	7143	7152	1	2	3	3	4	5	6	7	8
52	7160	7168	7177	7185	7193	7202	7210	7218	7226	7235	1	2	2	3	4	5	6	7	7
53	7243	7251	7259	7267	7275	7284	7292	7300	7308	7316	1	2	2	3	4	5	6	6	7
54	7324	7332	7340	7348	7356	7364	7372	7380	7388	7396	1	2	2	3	4	5	6	6	7
N	0	1	2	3	4	5	6	7	8	9	1	2	3	4	5	6	7	8	9

$$\log_{10} 2 = 0.3010 = \frac{1}{\log_2 10}. \qquad \log_2 N = 3.3222 \log_{10} N. \qquad \log_{10} N = 0.3010 \log_2 N.$$

N	0	1	2	3	4	5	6	7	8	9	Proportional Parts								
											1	2	3	4	5	6	7	8	9
55	7404	7412	7419	7427	7435	7443	7451	7459	7466	7474	1	2	2	3	4	5	5	6	7
56	7482	7490	7497	7505	7513	7520	7528	7536	7543	7551	1	2	2	3	4	5	5	6	7
57	7559	7566	7574	7582	7589	7597	7604	7612	7619	7627	1	2	2	3	4	5	5	6	7
58	7634	7642	7649	7657	7664	7672	7679	7686	7694	7701	1	1	2	3	4	4	5	6	7
59	7709	7716	7723	7731	7738	7745	7752	7760	7767	7774	1	1	2	3	4	4	5	6	7
60	7782	7789	7796	7803	7810	7818	7825	7832	7839	7846	1	1	2	3	4	4	5	6	6
61	7853	7860	7868	7875	7882	7889	7896	7903	7910	7917	1	1	2	3	4	4	5	6	6
62	7924	7931	7938	7945	7952	7959	7966	7973	7980	7987	1	1	2	3	3	4	5	6	6
63	7993	8000	8007	8014	8021	8028	8035	8041	8048	8055	1	1	2	3	3	4	5	5	6
64	8062	8069	8075	8082	8089	8096	8102	8109	8116	8122	1	1	2	3	3	4	5	5	6
65	8129	8136	8142	8149	8156	8162	8169	8176	8182	8189	1	1	2	3	3	4	5	5	6
66	8195	8202	8209	8215	8222	8228	8235	8241	8248	8254	1	1	2	3	3	4	5	5	6
67	8261	8267	8274	8280	8287	8293	8299	8306	8312	8319	1	1	2	3	3	4	5	5	6
68	8325	8331	8338	8344	8351	8357	8363	8370	8376	8382	1	1	2	3	3	4	4	5	6
69	8388	8395	8401	8407	8414	8420	8426	8432	8439	8445	1	1	2	2	3	4	4	5	6
70	8451	8457	8463	8470	8476	8482	8488	8494	8500	8506	1	1	2	2	3	4	4	5	6
71	8513	8519	8525	8531	8537	8543	8549	8555	8561	8567	1	1	2	2	3	4	4	5	5
72	8573	8579	8585	8591	8597	8603	8609	8615	8621	8627	1	1	2	2	3	4	4	5	5
73	8633	8639	8645	8651	8657	8663	8669	8675	8681	8686	1	1	2	2	3	4	4	5	5
74	8692	8698	8704	8710	8716	8722	8727	8733	8739	8745	1	1	2	2	3	4	4	5	5
75	8751	8756	8762	8768	8774	8779	8785	8791	8797	8802	1	1	2	2	3	3	4	5	5
76	8808	8814	8820	8825	8831	8837	8842	8848	8854	8859	1	1	2	2	3	3	4	5	5
77	8865	8871	8876	8882	8887	8893	8899	8904	8910	8915	1	1	2	2	3	3	4	4	5
78	8921	8927	8932	8938	8943	8949	8954	8960	8965	8971	1	1	2	2	3	3	4	4	5
79	8976	8982	8987	8993	8998	9004	9009	9015	9020	9025	1	1	2	2	3	3	4	4	5
80	9031	9036	9042	9047	9053	9058	9063	9069	9074	9079	1	1	2	2	3	3	4	4	5
81	9085	9090	9096	9101	9106	9112	9117	9122	9128	9133	1	1	2	2	3	3	4	4	5
82	9138	9143	9149	9154	9159	9165	9170	9175	9180	9186	1	1	2	2	3	3	4	4	5
83	9191	9196	9201	9206	9212	9217	9222	9227	9232	9238	1	1	2	2	3	3	4	4	5
84	9243	9248	9253	9258	9263	9269	9274	9279	9284	9289	1	1	2	2	3	3	4	4	5
85	9294	9299	9304	9309	9315	9320	9325	9330	9335	9340	1	1	2	2	3	3	4	4	5
86	9345	9350	9355	9360	9365	9370	9375	9380	9385	9390	1	1	2	2	3	3	4	4	5
87	9395	9400	9405	9410	9415	9420	9425	9430	9435	9440	0	1	1	2	2	3	3	4	4
88	9445	9450	9455	9460	9465	9469	9474	9479	9484	9489	0	1	1	2	2	3	3	4	4
89	9494	9499	9504	9509	9513	9518	9523	9528	9533	9538	0	1	1	2	2	3	3	4	4
90	9542	9547	9552	9557	9562	9566	9571	9576	9581	9586	0	1	1	2	2	3	3	4	4
91	9590	9595	9600	9605	9609	9614	9619	9624	9628	9633	0	1	1	2	2	3	3	4	4
92	9638	9643	9647	9652	9657	9661	9666	9671	9675	9680	0	1	1	2	2	3	3	4	4
93	9685	9689	9694	9699	9703	9708	9713	9717	9722	9727	0	1	1	2	2	3	3	4	4
94	9731	9736	9741	9745	9750	9754	9759	9763	9768	9773	0	1	1	2	2	3	3	4	4
95	9777	9782	9786	9791	9795	9800	9805	9809	9814	9818	0	1	1	2	2	3	3	4	4
96	9823	9827	9832	9836	9841	9845	9850	9854	9859	9863	0	1	1	2	2	3	3	4	4
97	9868	9872	9877	9881	9886	9890	9894	9899	9903	9908	0	1	1	2	2	3	3	4	4
98	9912	9917	9921	9926	9930	9934	9939	9943	9948	9952	0	1	1	2	2	3	3	4	4
99	9956	9961	9965	9969	9974	9978	9983	9987	9991	9996	0	1	1	2	2	3	3	3	4
N	0	1	2	3	4	5	6	7	8	9	1	2	3	4	5	6	7	8	9

$$\log_{10} e = 0.4343 = \frac{1}{\log_e 10} \cdot \qquad \log_e N = 2.3026 \log_{10} N. \qquad \log_{10} N = 0.4343 \log_e N.$$

NAME INDEX

Page numbers in italics refer to tables and illustrations.

SUBJECT INDEX

Page numbers in italics refer to illustrations.

A & P (Great Atlantic & Pacific Tea Co.), 351, 579, 590, 600
Accounting periods, 88
Acquisitions, corporate, 319–20n.
Adopters of innovations, classification of, 212
Advertising, 410–42
    allowances, 259
    budgeting of, 413, 418, 421, 427
    communication, 435
    cooperative, 366
    deceptive practices in. *See* Law and marketing
    effects, hierarchy of, 412
    efficiency in, 424
    exposure, 435
    media selection in, 430, 435
    outlays for 1968, 23
    perception, 435
    revenue vs., *418*
    sales response in, 424, 435
    vehicle distribution and exposure in, 435
Agents, 366
Aggregation, market, 326
Agricultural Marketing Agreement Act, 608
Aluminum Co. of America, 585
American Motors Co., 310, 606
American Petroleum Institute, 487
American Railway Union, 583, 584n.
American Tobacco Co., 584
Antimergers, 586, 597
Antimerger Act, 597
Anti-Racketeering Act, 597
Antitrust cases, average annual volume of, 583
Antitrust Division of Department of Justice, 598, 606, 636
Anxiety products, 200, 201
"Aptitude Index Battery," 455
Arithmetic mean, 497
"Army General Classification Test," 455

Associate offices (of resident buyers), 369
Automobile Information Disclosure Act, 614
Average cost analysis, 84
Avon Co., 415

Bayesian methods, 462, 482n.
Behavioral school (of marketing research), 478
Behavioral sciences, 9
Behavioral sequence, 221
Behavioralism, 183
"Bernreuter Personality Inventory Test," 455
Bill of Rights, 581
Biological drives, 185
Booz Allen & Hamilton, Inc., 298
BPI (buying-power index), 382
Brands, 310
Break-even point, 102
Break-even quantity, 44
Brokers, 367
Brown Shoe Co., 585, 599
Brown Shoe Co. v. *United States,* 585n., 600n.
Bureau of Applied Social Research, 223
Bureau of Federal Credit Unions, 629
Bureau of Industry Guidance (of FTC), 635
Buying-power index, 382

Calculus. *See* Differential calculus
California fair-trade laws, 625, 625n.
Capital requirements, 111
Capper-Volstead Act, 607, 608
Cash discounts, 256
Cash flow, 111
Causal models, 551
Causal research, 475
Caveat emptor, 587
Celler-Kefauver Act, 586, 597
Census of Business, 448, 485, 492
Census data, sources for, 485

679